RUSSIAN FOREIGN POLICY

RUSSIAN FOREIGN POLICY

INTERESTS, VECTORS, AND SECTORS

Nikolas K. Gvosdev

U.S. Naval War College

Christopher Marsh

U.S. Army School of Advanced Military Studies

Los Angeles | London | New Delhi
Singapore | Washington DC

Los Angeles | London | New Delhi
Singapore | Washington DC

FOR INFORMATION:

CQ Press

An Imprint of SAGE Publications, Inc.

2455 Teller Road

Thousand Oaks, California 91320

E-mail: order@sagepub.com

SAGE Publications Ltd.

1 Oliver's Yard

55 City Road

London EC1Y 1SP

United Kingdom

SAGE Publications India Pvt. Ltd.

B 1/I 1 Mohan Cooperative Industrial Area

Mathura Road, New Delhi 110 044

India

SAGE Publications Asia-Pacific Pte. Ltd.

3 Church Street

#10–04 Samsung Hub

Singapore 049483

Printed in the United States of America

Library of Congress Cataloging-in-Publication Data

Gvosdev, Nikolas K., 1969–

Russian foreign policy : interests, vectors, and sectors / Nikolas K. Gvosdev, Christopher Marsh.

pages cm
Includes bibliographical references and index.

ISBN 978-1-4522-3484-7 (alk. paper)

1. Russia (Federation)—Foreign relations—21st century. I. Marsh, Christopher, 1969- II. Title.

JZ1616.G86 2014
324.47′009051—dc23   2013020368

This book is printed on acid-free paper.

Acquisitions Editor: Charisse Kiino

Associate Editor: Nancy Loh

Editorial Assistant: Lauren Johnson

Marketing Manager: Erica DeLuca

Permissions Editor: Jennifer Barron

Project Editor: Veronica Stapleton Hooper

Copy Editor: Kim Husband

Typesetter: C&M Digitals (P) Ltd.

Proofreader: Dennis W. Webb

Indexer: Kathleen Paparchontis

Cover Designer: Karine Hovsepian

13 14 15 16 17 10 9 8 7 6 5 4 3 2 1

CONTENTS

LIST OF TABLES, FIGURES, AND MAP

TABLES

FIGURES

MAP

Principal Vectors in Russian Foreign Policy

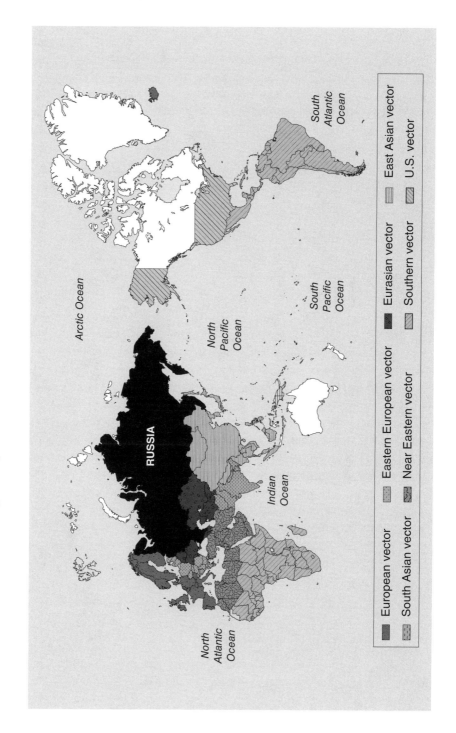

Legend:
- European vector
- Eastern European vector
- Eurasian vector
- East Asian vector
- South Asian vector
- Near Eastern vector
- Southern vector
- U.S. vector

On April 12, 2012, in his last address to the State Duma as Russia's prime minister, Vladimir Putin declared, "The post–Soviet period is over."[1]

It is in a similar vein that we wrote this book as a study of *Russian* foreign policy, not Russia's *post-Soviet* foreign policy. While it is undeniable that the legacy bequeathed by the USSR continues to have a powerful influence on contemporary Russia, Russian foreign policy today is not a continuation of Soviet policy. For one, the main problems that faced Soviet leaders—especially the ideological rivalry with the West and China—are no longer the ones that concern the Russian foreign policy establishment. Secondly, Moscow must deal with its former imperial possessions and Soviet siblings as independent states with their own foreign policy interests and strategies (which are often at odds with those of the Kremlin). Thirdly, and by no means finally, the contemporary international political, economic, and security environment is drastically different from that of the Soviet era—so much so, in fact, that even if the Soviet Union still existed, a contemporary Soviet foreign policy would scarcely resemble its predecessor in any way.

The Soviet Union itself has been relegated to the rubbish heap of history, but the dead hand of the Soviet past continues to exert an unhelpful influence over the way in which current Russian actions on the world stage are interpreted and understood. Even the casual slips of the tongue by many U.S. politicians and policymakers, who mistakenly refer to the Soviet Union instead of Russia, reflect the inability of some to escape the cognitive frame of the Cold War, or at least the temptation to want to define the present by the past. To continue to do so will result in missed opportunities at best or dangerous strategic miscalculations at worst. In writing this book, it is our hope that we can contribute in some way to the debate over the sources and conduct of Russian foreign policy that is placed within its proper historical context, one that recognizes the influence of the Soviet era while not ascribing every action taken by Moscow as having roots in that time period.

One way we seek to do this is by disaggregating Russian foreign policy into actors and avenues of approach, what we call the sectors and vectors of Russian foreign policy. During the Soviet period, outside analysts often interpreted Soviet actions through the lens of Communist ideology. Again, the Soviet period is over, and Communist ideology itself has no influence whatsoever on Russian strategic thinking. Russia today is a new entity, still significantly influenced by the actions of the Soviet regime but not tied to the ideology that directed its actions. To understand its foreign policy behavior more clearly, we must see Russia for what it is: a multinational state that has reemerged from the ashes of the USSR and is seeking to find its proper place in the international system. It is now more useful to examine the interests and preferences of different sectors of Russian society, each with its own ideas as to which vectors best accommodate their needs. How sectors and vectors intersect and are mediated through the policy process is the rationale behind this book.

NOTE

1. The quote was noted by Ezekiel Pfeifer and Ken Martinez, who were live-blogging the address. See *The Moscow* Times, no. 4863 (April 12, 2012), at http://www.themoscow times.com/news/article/archived-live-blog-putins-address-to-state-duma/456556.html.

ACKNOWLEDGMENTS

Nikolas Gvosdev would like to thank his colleagues at the U.S. Naval War College (especially those in the Europe-Russia Study Group) for their insights and support, beginning with the Provost, Ambassador Mary Ann Peters, and the chair of the National Security Affairs department, Dr. David Cooper, as well as Professors Tom Fedyszyn and Tom Nichols. He would like to thank *World Politics Review* and *The National Interest*, which gave us the opportunity to test-run many of the ideas subsequently contained in this book; the Dartmouth Dialogue for the chance to attend meetings with both U.S. and Russian experts and officials, as well as the Center for the National Interest, the Carnegie Endowment for International Peace, the Atlantic Council and the Carnegie Council for Ethics and International Affairs for invitations to seminars and events that provided unique insights into various aspects of Russian foreign policy. Many individuals provided ideas and comments that were used, including (but not limited to) Paul Saunders, Dimitri Simes, Matt Rojansky, Sam Charap, Fiona Hill, Angela Stent, Tom Graham, Ambassador Jim Collins, Ambassador Jack Matlock, Jeffrey Mankoff, Nick Petro, Andranik Migranyan, and Igor Yurgens.

Christopher Marsh would like to thank the leadership of the U.S. Army School of Advanced Military Studies (SAMS), including Dr. G. Scott Gorman and Mr. Richard Dixon, for their flexibility, assistance, and support throughout this project. He also thanks his many colleagues, especially those who have offered insights into his research and writing, including Dr. Robert Tomlinson, Dr. Jeffrey Kubiak, and Dr. Steve Lauer at SAMS and Dr. Lester Grau, Timothy Thomas, Matthew Stein, and Charles Bartles at the Army's Foreign Military Studies Office (FMSO). At the U.S. Air Force Special Operations School, Sue Alaniz, Stan Komitov, and Umid Khikmatov all provided encouragement and useful suggestions.

The authors would also like to thank the following reviewers, who provided useful feedback on the manuscript: Michael E. Aleprete Jr., Westminster College; Richard Farkas, DePaul University; Christopher Jones, University of Washington; Mikhail Rybalko, Texas Tech University; and Aron Tannenbaum, Clemson University.

Nikolas K. Gvosdev is a professor of national security affairs at the U.S. Naval War College. He was previously the editor of *The National Interest* and remains a senior editor there. He is also a weekly columnist for *World Politics Review.*

Christopher Marsh is a professor at the School of Advanced Military Studies, U.S. Army Command and General Staff College. He is the founding editor of *Special Operations Journal* (www.specopsjournal.org) and has previously held positions with the U.S. Air Force Special Operations School and the U.S. Army's Human Terrain System.

For Heidi and Adrian
—Nikolas Gvosdev

For Jeannette, Ashlyn, and Evan
—Christopher Marsh

Introduction

Lord Palmerston's adage that "great states have no permanent friends, only permanent interests" is as true in the 21st century as it was in the 19th. In a world with nearly 200 state actors, securing a nation's interests requires constantly managing foreign policy relationships with one's allies, protecting against one's adversaries, and seeking new opportunities to strengthen the former and weaken the latter. Moreover, the definitions of *friend* and *foe* are becoming much more fluid. Describing the world today as experiencing a "Palmerstonian moment," Richard Haass, president of the Council on Foreign Relations, notes that countries may not be clear adversaries or allies with the automaticity or predictability of either but instead may choose to cooperate on some issues and diverge on others.[1]

When analyzing another state's foreign affairs, therefore, it only makes sense to conceptualize of them not as a monolithic whole but as a collection of different policies with many disparate parts making up that whole. Working within a single foreign policy paradigm, state actors may switch alliances; their neighboring regimes may themselves shift their alliances or undergo domestic changes that prove unsettling (or inhospitable) to the maintenance of previous relationships (such as basing rights, use of airspace, or navigation and docking privileges). And the entire foreign policy paradigm itself of the nation under analysis may shift. This may be the result of domestic political change, as in the case of the collapse of the Soviet Union, or as a response to a larger global shift, as with the 9/11 attacks.

These considerations must be borne in mind when attempting to make sense of Russia's foreign policy. In order to understand Russian foreign policy, we must take account of Russia's foreign *policies*. The use of the plural is deliberate: It is our contention that there are in fact multiple, overlapping, and in some cases contradictory Russian foreign policies.

Popular culture has left us an enduring image of how the Kremlin formulates foreign policy: a small group of men seated around the table in Moscow—sometimes in a situation room equipped with the latest innovations in computer and telecommunications technology (as depicted in such films as *Shoes of the Fisherman* (1968) or in the 1983 James Bond thriller *Octopussy*)—discussing, planning, and crafting the best and most rational way to advance Mother Russia's interests (usually at the expense of the West). While this image lends itself to good cinema, it certainly is no basis for understanding the true dynamics of Russia's foreign policy. But this view—that Russian foreign policy is guided by a well-thought-out, coordinated plan developed by the leadership in the Kremlin that has balanced competing interests and imposed a single policy choice—is one that is often echoed in policy and academic circles.[2] Moreover, the Russian bureaucracy—whether tsarist, Soviet, or post-Soviet—is said to be structured in such a way so as to produce a unified, coordinated approach.[3]

Consistently, Western analysts have believed that Russian leaders possess "a carefully thought out hierarchy of objectives that balances strategic importance against timeliness."[4] In the 18th and 19th centuries, the "legend spread that Peter the Great had concocted a secret plan for global dominion that his successors were sworn to carry out," and in the 20th century, the belief that Vladimir Lenin and Josef Stalin had similarly developed a long-range plan for Soviet global domination took root.[5] This view has led to a tendency today to assume every action taken by Russian entities—both governmental and private—must be occurring in accordance with the directives of the leadership in executing some master foreign policy plan; that the leaders in the Kremlin "follow a 'master plan' . . . and that almost every major step in their foreign policy reflects such a long-range plan and even proceeds according to some secret timetable."[6] In recent years, this "master plan" narrative has been reinforced by a series of "Concepts"—documents that set down economic and national security strategies—that have been released by the Russian government detailing national security and foreign policy strategy. These include the latest revision of the *Foreign Policy Concept* (2008), the *Energy Strategy of Russia to 2020* (2003), the *Concept for the Social-Economic Development of Russia to 2020* (2007), the *National Security Strategy* (2009), and the updated *Military Doctrine* (2010).

This view, of a centralized Kremlin leadership able to effectively marshal all elements of national power in the service of a focused foreign policy agenda, postulates a high degree of state control even over nominally private actors (businesses, corporations, etc.) and assumes that the primary reason a Russian entity undertakes any sort of action is in support of the foreign policy plan as established by the Kremlin leadership.[7]

"Master plan" narratives to explain Russian foreign policy, however, largely disappeared during the 1990s because of the manifold weaknesses of the Russian state during the Boris Yeltsin administration (1991–1999). With an ailing president, a collapsed military, a dysfunctional bureaucracy, and a struggling economy, Russia was characterized as "Zaire with permafrost." A country characterized by "weak state syndrome" was in no position to have a central government be able to effectively coordinate Russian foreign policy.[8] Instead, the focus was on the contradictions generated by overlapping, multiple power centers. F. Stephen Larrabee and Theodore W. Karasik summed up the prevailing assessment of foreign and defense policy in the Yeltsin years as being "in a state of flux," defined by "institutional weaknesses that contributed to confusion and incoherence in foreign and security policies" and a "contest among rival factions" for power and influence.[9]

It was Vladimir Putin's first two terms in the presidency (2000–2008) that lent a new lease on life to the monolithic approach to Russian foreign policy. Certainly Putin's own calls for re-establishing a strong Russian state by creating a top-down system of power based on loyalty to the president (the so-called "power vertical") contributed to this. The assumption was that Putin and his team embodied a type of rational actor model—that they had a clearly identified Russian national interest in mind and that all the costs and benefits of various options (say, partnership with China or the United States) had been carefully weighed in order to make a choice.[10] In turn, the Kremlin would coordinate all aspects of national power to implement specific policy objectives set down by the leadership.[11] As one observer noted, "Putin and many of his close associates have a clear view of what they are about" and so were expected to translate this vision into clear policy directives.[12] The resurgence of Russian power during this time led to a resumption, certainly in the mass media, of the "master plan" narrative in Russian foreign policy.[13]

There have been many attempts by the Kremlin to coordinate Russian foreign policy, of course, but a great deal of incoherence still remains. To start with, as "authoritarian" as Russia may be today, it is not without numerous constraints on its policy directives. Not only does Russia continue to hold elections, which if not entirely free, generate great debates on the state of Russian democracy, but also, for every state-controlled media source, there are various other much freer sources. Through these media, Russian citizens debate the appropriateness of most every political issue, with the Kremlin quite often being the *moderate* voice in the conversation. Not only is Russia not monolithic, it is not a totalitarian state that can effectively stymie public debate. Public opinion matters, and there are a wide variety of different interest groups—industrial lobbies, regional leaders, different economic sectors, think tanks, nongovernmental organizations, and even religious organizations (especially the Russian Orthodox Church) that seek to influence the direction of the country's foreign policy.[14]

More importantly, there are deep divisions within the ruling elites over the direction the country should take. The "enduring interests" of the Russian state that are said to be the basis of Russian foreign policy[15] are nevertheless subject to interpretation and prioritization. The creation of an effective diarchy in Russia in 2008—when Dmitry Medvedev succeeded Vladimir Putin as president but Putin took the position of prime minister—has yoked together competing directions in foreign policy. As Tatyana Stanovaya argues: "[T]he presence of two leaders . . . the presence of two agendas, old and new; and the exacerbation of the debate within the elite about the country's development options—all of this makes an assessment of the Russian authorities' current policy difficult."[16] While the Russian political system vests an enormous degree of power and responsibility in the president, occupying the presidential chair is no guarantee that policy will be effectively coordinated, and at times it does appear that "no single person is really firmly in charge in the Kremlin."[17] While some assumed that Putin's return to the presidency in 2012 would once again ensure that the Russian government marches to the beat of one drummer, others note that the country's political and economic elite is more fragmented and less likely to be easily unified.[18] This is amplified because Putin himself moves back and forth between different perspectives.[19]

THE CHALLENGES FACING RUSSIA

Contemporary Russia is in a state of transition in terms of its role and position in the international community. Outsiders view it as a collapsed superpower, yet from Moscow, the view is more of a down-but-not-out regime in transition, holding the vast majority of weapons that once made it a superpower in the 20th century as well as significant energy reserves and technological knowledge that will help chart the path to its restoration in the 21st century. Russia is set on retaining its position as one of the world's great powers and is willing to make the sacrifices necessary to achieve that objective, including in its foreign policy strategy.

The world is a big place, and a country like Russia has no single foreign policy. There are priorities and national security agendas, but on the world stage, many bilateral relations can go to either friend or foe, even using the same foreign policy paradigm. Tsar Alexander III offered his version of Lord Palmerston's adage when he declared, "Russia had only two true friends in the world, its army and its navy." The notion of no permanent friends or enemies for Russia was aptly demonstrated during the 20th century, when both Germany and China were, at various points, Moscow's greatest ally and the main existential threat to Russia. Meanwhile, strategic protégé states, such as North Korea, Vietnam, and Cuba, have become little more than venues in which Russian leaders can continue to receive recognition as a great power, though not without significant financial cost.

For much of the 20th century, Moscow's foreign policy was constrained by the dictates of Marxist-Leninist ideology. Whether a state was friend or foe was determined (supposedly) by the nature of its regime. While Russia today no longer has an "ideological" foreign policy, Soviet-era relationships, particularly with former client states in what used to be termed the "Third World," still leave important legacies.

Today, the guiding focus is for post-Soviet Russia to "recover from its losses, become stronger and replenish its resources to regain its position, authority, influence and destiny"—the advice that Prince Alexander M. Gorchakov, foreign minister to Tsar Alexander II, proffered after Russia's disastrous defeat during the Crimean War. It is echoed in the 2008 *Foreign Policy Concept* of the Russian Federation, in which the principal objectives of the country's foreign policy are "to preserve and strengthen its sovereignty and territorial integrity, to achieve strong positions of authority in the world community that best meet the interests of the Russian Federation as one of influential centers in the modern world, and . . . to create favorable external conditions for the modernization of Russia."

No matter who sits in the Kremlin, there are several constraining factors in foreign policy that any Russian government—tsarist, communist, or post-Soviet—must deal with. Even with the reduction in its borders after the fall of the Soviet Union, the Russian Federation has no choice but to be involved in global affairs given its size and geographic position. Unlike other great powers such as Germany, China, or Brazil, whose national interests depend largely on securing one region of the world (Europe, East Asia, or Latin America) and who can choose when and where to act in other parts of the globe, Russia has concrete national interests in Europe, the Near and Middle East, Central and South Asia, and the Asia-Pacific region.[20]

Given that Russia controls more territory than any other state in the world, it is therefore the world's most "exposed" country in terms of the length of the borders it must defend. This largely accounts for its historical experience with invasion and occupation, from the Teutonic Knights (from the West) and the Mongols (from the East) during the 13th century to the German forces that invaded the Soviet Union on June 22, 1941. Russia is the only country in the world to share frontiers with the United States, Japan, Korea, China, and the European Union. Ensuring Russian security has been the country's leading priority. This includes the search for allies and the desire to create "buffer" zones that can protect the Russian homeland, even if they only slow an attack but not entirely prevent one.

The second factor is the fear of isolation. A constant worry of the Russian leadership from the 16th century onward has been that Russia can be isolated and bypassed, relegated to the periphery. Ensuring that Russia has direct and open access to the outside world—particularly to those countries that are Russia's major trading partners—is an important priority.

Russian strategists have generally tended to agree with the West's principal "geo-political" thinkers, such as Halford Mackinder (1860–1947), about the importance of the "facts of geography," especially the "natural pathways" that promote trade and development but also enable a country to project power. An overriding concern to Moscow has been the efforts of the "Midland Ocean" powers—the major states of the Euro-Atlantic alliance—to try and block the projection of Russian influence by forming a "tier of independent states between Germany and Russia," which would form "a broad wedge of independence, extending from the Adriatic and Black Seas to the Baltic. . . ." This "territorial buffer between Germany and Russia," wrote Mackinder, must have access to the ocean and must be supported by the "outer nations" (i.e., Britain and the United States).[21]

Unlike the Soviet Union, which had a number of formal (if, in some cases, unwilling) allies, contemporary Russia, in the description of Alexander Lukin, is "not a crucial and useful ally for anyone."[22]

The final factor is to establish a foreign policy that will promote internal development and modernization; the search is on for partners who can transfer skills to Russia and help it to modernize and to become partners in the development of its economy—for a stronger economy enables Russia to restore its status as one of the world's great powers. Russia needs to find partners that can assist its domestic development.

At present, there is broad agreement across the spectrum that Russia cannot afford the burdens of being a superpower and should not seek to regain this status that the Soviet Union was, in the long run, unable to afford.[23] At the same time, the greatest Russian fear is the emergence of a new global order in which the world's major economic powers—the European Union, China, Japan, and the United States—would be able to bypass Russia altogether. Russia's ability to remain in the first rank depends on its ability to be able to align with other powers in order to be able to contribute to the global agenda.[24]

Russia's elite still has a "will to *derzhava*"—a Nietzschean impulse to great power status—and policy over the last decade has been designed to restore what is seen as Russia's rightful place in the world. In other words, there is little appetite among Russian elites for the country to withdraw from world affairs into a more isolationist position.

But what does it mean when Russians say their country is and ought to be a great power? A 2006 poll conducted by the *St. Petersburg Times* noted that 55% of Russians define the country as a "great power" based on its energy resources and strategic location.[25] Many Russian foreign policy analysts have a two-tiered vision for Russia's position as a major power. This begins with a notion of Russia as the metropolitan power of the Eurasian space. This follows from the perception that a power is a great power first and foremost because it has the ability to create a regional bloc or to orient the economic and political lines of influence toward a central pole of attraction. Each great power, therefore, acts as the regional "node" for the global system. From this Eurasian platform, Russia is then seen as a natural candidate for inclusion in what commentators Sergei Karaganov and Vladislav Inozemtsev have described as a "global concert," perhaps consisting of the G-8 member-states, China, India, and several other regional powers, which would be in a position to "counter the growing chaos on the international stage through direct actions and push their policies through" for "expanding the zone of stability" around the world.[26] Russia could also maintain its leadership at the global stage by helping to coordinate other centers of power in the international system.[27]

In the popular view, this translates into some version of the Monroe Doctrine for Russia vis-à-vis its immediate region and in Russia having a consultative role on major international matters, without, however, having to make any large contribution of funds or personnel for "out of the Eurasian area" missions. This is also why questions of EU and NATO expansion remain such sensitive issues and why the Shanghai Cooperation Organization has assumed such an important role in reaffirming Russian predominance (as the "elder brother") in territories where China might otherwise have increased influence. There has been a shift in understanding what constitutes power away from military force toward economic factors, but for many Russians, tangible commodities, especially energy, are more important than intangibles—so the power to obtain, sell, transport, and withhold vital materials is seen as a new source of Russian power in the world. Sergei Kortunov sums up the Russian attitude: "Russia is a great power in terms of its political importance, intellectual might and influence on global affairs . . . it should claim an equitable role in the group of the world's top five countries, and not because it wants it. This is an objective and logical process, which cannot be disregarded."[28]

Yet these abstract attitudes shared among the business and government elites of post–Soviet Russia do not automatically lead to any sort of grand master plan or even to a well-coordinated foreign policy. There is no one prevailing set of interests or vision. Instead,

> Russia is run by a collective leadership—the Kremlin Corporation's board of directors, so to speak. . . . All key political decisions in Russia . . . are the result of deliberation and consensus among members . . . This inner sanctum, however, has always been fraught with bitter rivalries.[29]

Add to that the diverging economic interests of the country's major firms. An oil company like Rosneft sees its future in a close alignment with a Chinese market hungry for energy and supports greater economic interdependence with Beijing; Gazprom looks to consolidate its position as a pan–European energy provider in close alliance with German, French, and Italian companies. The managers of Russia's defense industry are anxious to expand markets for their products in India and Latin America, while the "modernizers" around Dmitry Medvedev look to renewed and expanded commercial relations with the United States.

So, if Russia is not a monolith, how then does one examine and understand Russian foreign policy? By considering Russian "foreign policy" not as a single coordinated thing but rather as a set of contrasting and competing "foreign policies." This highlights the multidimensionality of the foreign policy process, from policy formulation and implementation to management. Beyond the Foreign Ministry, actors include both the presidential and prime ministerial staffs, the Security Council, other ministries and agencies, the intelligence services, the state companies, the private sector, regional governments, and the nongovernmental sector. This reality of overlapping institutions led Konstantin Kosachev, then serving as the chairman of the Duma's Foreign Affairs Committee, to observe:

> Over the last fifteen years, the different departments of the Foreign Ministry have gotten used to the idea of conducting their "own" foreign policy. In light of the fact that the Russian Federation entities and major economic agents have their own interests abroad, the picture becomes even more variegated. As a result, in addition to the single foreign policy line there arises some "simple average" of sharply contrasting initiatives that exist in parallel with—and occasionally opposite to—the main policy vector set down by the President.[30]

Or, as political analyst Vyacheslav Nikonov once remarked, "Foreign policy has many towers. There's no single policy because each one [tower] has its own."[31] These "towers" can be understood as the different "sectors" of the Russian state and of the larger society—including the business community—that have interests in foreign policy. During the first two terms of his presidency, Putin brought a greater degree of order and coordination but did not succeed in imposing a monolithic approach.

Additionally, however, this approach also nicely encapsulates the important regional dimension of Russian foreign policy. Not only do state departments and organs have their own interests and objectives in various policy realms, these can often fluctuate substantially from region to region across the globe. For example, one can consider the "near abroad," a term referring to most of the successor states of the former Soviet Union. Even here, Moscow pursues various different strategies toward these states, ranging from approaching integration (Belarus) to preventing a slide toward Europe and NATO (Ukraine). Different departments, however, pursue their own objectives in these areas; for example, the Russian energy sector, which uses the price of oil as a foreign policy tool, rewards Belarus for its close ties to Moscow while using flow, price, and debt management as part of a "carrot-and-stick" strategy with Ukraine. And once one moves farther afield, Moscow's various strategies become even more complicated, and the decision calculus of its diplomatic interlocutors even more of a mystery.[32]

So this can produce what seems *in toto* to be an incoherent, confused foreign policy. Russia supports maintaining the territorial integrity of Serbia by not recognizing Kosovo and backing fully India's claims to Kashmir yet facilitates the independence of the separatist regions of Georgia. Russian sales of advanced weaponry to Venezuela complicate Moscow's efforts to improve relations with the United States. Russia proclaims its strategic partnership with China yet is actively aiding India's efforts to modernize its armed forces.

Trying to coordinate Russia's myriad foreign policies into an overarching foreign policy presents a real challenge to the Kremlin. It requires Russian leaders who can skillfully adjust the country's direction to take into account the shifting priorities of the Russian leadership as well as the changes in the global balance of power, especially in economics, that will give Russia the time it needs to recover its position. This includes being able to simultaneously engage the "old powers" of Europe with the rising powers of Asia; to accommodate the leadership position of the United States in the international system while seeking ways to enhance Russia's standing; and to retain the initiative in the Eurasian space. There is no one single "vector" for Russian foreign policy—one international orientation that defines its international position. Instead, Russia today is pursuing a policy of many vectors: It continues to engage the United States while working to restore its position as the dominant power in the Eurasian space and simultaneously reaching out to Europe and Asia. It seeks to join the Western world (on its own terms) while counterbalancing the influence of the Euro-Atlantic grouping of nations by forging stronger ties with emerging powers such as China, India, and Brazil. Different vectors, in turn, are embraced by different powerful interest groups within the Kremlin as well as outside of government.

The needs of different sectors can also drive contradictory foreign policy goals. For instance, the Russian defense industry is a major source of export revenue, both for specific companies as well as the Russian state, which benefits from its stock holdings and tax receipts.[33] In 2009, Russia exported some $8.5 billion in weapons and defense technologies. But the sale of arms to Venezuela, for instance, complicates Moscow's relations with the United States. China is a good "bulk" consumer of large amounts of basic Russian equipment, but China's own military development could eventually threaten Russia's ability to retain its Far Eastern territories. India's defense orders are the ones that have stimulated and supported the intensive investment in research and development needed to produce new sophisticated systems, but Russia continues to sell weapons to India's neighbors (and its major geostrategic rival, China).

When a vector joins with a sector, we can see the emergence of a foreign policy. For instance, the pro–China/Sinophile vector takes the position that the best way for the Kremlin to address the country's major foreign policy challenges (isolation, insecurity, economic development, and restoration of great power status) comes in forging a strong partnership with China. It rests on an emerging alliance between key members of the faction of the *siloviki*—those members of the government who come from the security services—and industries that view their prosperity as linked to China. As Andrei P. Tsygankov notes:

> Sinophiles push strengthening relations with China based on Russia's economic and security priorities. Although they want to defend Russia's sovereignty, they insist it would be better protected by closer economic and political ties with China rather than the West. This is driven by influential leaders in the defense ministry, foreign ministry and military-industrial complex. . . . In the area of economic relations, the pro-China position is often favored by energy producers and military enterprises seeking high-ticket defense contracts in Asia. . . . the chairman of Rosneft is Igor Sechin, who is a deputy prime minister and member of Prime Minister Vladimir Putin's inner circle. As the key negotiator, Sechin is now applying the model of a recently signed oil deal with China to other energy areas including electricity, natural gas and atomic energy.[34]

But this vector—calling for closer Russian engagement with China—will run up against other sources of opposition: regional leaders in the Far East who are concerned about empowering China, political and business lobbies that place a greater weight on ties with India, Korea, Japan, and Indonesia, and the competing imperatives of closer partnership with the United States and the European Union.

All of this leads to competing and sometimes conflicting foreign policy priorities which, in turn, affect Russia's bilateral relations with other states as well as its overall global posture. Exploring these foreign policies is the subject of this volume.

NOTES

1. Richard Haass, "The Palmerstonian Moment," *National Interest,* January/February 2008, at http://nationalinterest.org/article/the-palmerstonian-moment-1918.

2. See, for instance, the following description of the foreign policy pursed by Mikhail Gorbachev and Eduard Shevardnadze: "New thinking is a carefully thought out

construction that integrates domestic and foreign policy and carefully links policy in all regions of the globe." Deborah Nutter Miner, "Introduction," *Soviet Foreign Policy in Transition,* eds. Robert E. Kanet, Deborah Nutter Miner, and Tamara J. Resler (Cambridge, UK: Cambridge University Press, 1992), 2.

3. See, for instance, Leonard Schapiro's argument that in the late Soviet period, the International Department of the Central Committee of the Communist Party of the Soviet Union ensured that the actions of different organs were harmonized so as to produce a unified foreign policy approach. "The International Department of the CPSU: Key to Soviet policy," *International Journal* 32 (1976–1977): 41–55.

4. Michael McCgwire, *Military Objectives in Soviet Foreign Policy* (Washington, DC: The Brookings Institution, 1987), 126.

5. Karl E. Meyer and Shareen Blair Brysac, *Tournament of Shadows: The Great Game and the Race for Empire in Central Asia* (Washington, DC: Counterpoint, 1999), 117, 564.

6. Seweryn Bialer, "The Psychology of the U.S.–Soviet Relationship," *Political Psychology* 6, no. 2 (June 1985): 268.

7. See, for example, Janusz Bugajski, *Cold Peace: Russia's New Imperialism* (Washington, DC: Center for Strategic and International Studies, 2004), esp. 32–33.

8. See, for instance, William E. Odom, "Realism about Russia," in *Russia in the National Interest,* ed. Nikolas K. Gvosdev (New Brunswick, NJ: Transaction Press, 2004), 209–224.

9. F. Stephen Larrabee and Theodore W. Karasik, *Foreign and Security Policy Decisionmaking under Yeltsin* (Santa Monica, CA: RAND, 1997), vii, viii.

10. For more on the rational actor approach, see Richard Norton, "Policy Making and Process: A Guide to Case Analysis," *Case Studies in Policy Making,* eds. Hayat Alvi and Nikolas K. Gvosdev, 12th ed. (Newport, RI: Naval War College, 2010), 5.

11. See, for example, Kevin C. Smith, *Russia and European Energy Security: Divide and Dominate* (Washington, DC: Center for Strategic and International Studies, October 2008).

12. Harley Balzer, "The Putin Thesis and Russian Energy Policy," *Post-Soviet Affairs* 21, no. 3 (July/September 2005): 222.

13. See, for instance, Owen Matthews, "Why puppetmaster Putin is more dangerous than ever," *Daily Mail,* August 12, 2008, at http://www.dailymail.co.uk/news/article-1043684/Why-puppetmaster-Putin-dangerous-ever.html—ixzz0rcynBFUX; Michael Petrou, "Putin's master plan," *Maclean's,* August 13, 2008, at http://www.macleans.ca/world/global/article.jsp?content=20080813_118225_118225&page=1.

14. See, for instance, Michael McFaul's testimony before the House Committee on International Relations, May 12, 1999, for a discussion of the growing role of foreign policy lobbies in Russia. A copy is archived at http://www.carnegieendowment.org/publications/index.cfm?fa=view&id=424.

15. Donaldson and Nogee, 2009.

16. Tatyana Stanovaya, "Problema Nesoglasnikh: Yest' Li Konsensus?" *Politkom.ru,* June 7, 2010, at http://www.politcom.ru/print.php?id=10228.

17. Ian Bremmer, "Who's in Charge in the Kremlin?" *World Policy Journal* 22:4 (Winter 2005–2006).

18. Paul J. Saunders, "Protests, Putin and the Russian Elite," *National Interest,* January 5, 2012, at http://nationalinterest.org/commentary/protests-putin-the-russian-elite-6338.

19. See Clifford Gaddy and Fiona Hill, *Mr. Putin: Operative in the Kremlin* (Washington, DC: Brookings Institution Press, 2013).

20. A. I. Burkin, A. V. Vozzhenikov, and N. V. Sineok, *Natsional'naia Bezopasnost' Rossii* (Moscow: Izdatel'stvo RAGS, 2008), 192–93.

21. Francis P. Sempa, "Mackinder's World," *American Diplomacy* 1 (Winter 2000), at http://www.unc.edu/depts/diplomat/AD_Issues/14amdipl.html.

22. Alexander Lukin, "From a Post–Soviet to a Russian Foreign Policy," *Russia in Global Affairs,* 4 (October/December 2008), at http://eng.globalaffairs.ru/numbers/25/1239.html.

23. Sergei Markov, for instance, argues, "Russia was once a superpower, and that is a power that takes part in all conflicts around the world, and has influence around the world. Now Russia has moved away from that. Now it wants only to be a great regional power, one that defends regional interests and only sometimes interests in other regions as well." Quoted by Simon Shuster, "Why Obama's Reset With Russia Has Gone So Wrong: Full Interviews," *True/Slant,* March 19,2 010, at http://trueslant.com/simonshus ter/2010/03/19/why-obamas-reset-with-russia-has-gone-so-wrong-full-interviews/.

24. Yan Li, "Russia's Shadowboxing Wards off U.S. in 'New Cold War,'" *Washington Observer,* May 10, 2006, at http://washingtonobserver.org/en/document.cfm?documentid =48&charid=3.

25. Nikolas K. Gvosdev, "After the G-8: Putin, at least, got what we wanted," *International Herald Tribune,* July 18, 2006, at http://www.iht.com/articles/2006/07/17/ opinion/edgvosdev.php.

26. "Imperialism of the Fittest," *The National Interest,* Summer 2005.

27. Lukin, op. cit.

28. Sergei Kortunov, "Should Russia Claim Great Power Status?" *RIA Novosti,* September 25, 2006.

29. Brian Whitmore, "The Power Vertical: Medvedev vs. Sechin," *Radio Free Europe/ Radio Liberty,* February 24, 2009, at http://www.rferl.org/content/Medvedev_vs_Sechin/ 1498742.html.

30. Konstantin Kosachev, "Russian Foreign Policy Vertical," *Russia in Global Affairs,* August 10, 2004, at http://eng.globalaffairs.ru/numbers/8/578.html.

31. Quoted in Gregory Feifer, "Who Stands Behind Russia's Foreign Policy?" *St. Petersburg Times* 760, no. 26 (April 9, 2002), at http://www.sptimesrussia.com/index.php?action_id=2 &story_id=6929.

32. See, for instance, Ivan Krastev, "What Russia Wants," *Foreign Policy,* April 28, 2008, at http://www.foreignpolicy.com/articles/2008/04/10/what_russia_wants.

33. For a fuller picture, see Alexander Rybas, "Breakthrough into the Global Arms Market," *Russia in Global Affairs* 2 (April/June 2008), at http://eng.globalaffairs.ru/num bers/23/1198.html.

34. Andrei P. Tsygankov, "Eastern Promises," *Russia Now,* December 18, 2009, at http:// russianow.washingtonpost.com/2009/12/eastern-promises.php.

CHAPTER 1

The Historical Legacy for Contemporary Russian Foreign Policy

No other country in the world is a global power simply by virtue of geography.[1] The growth of Russia from an isolated, backward East Slavic principality into a continental Eurasian empire meant that Russian foreign policy had to engage with many of the world's principal centers of power. A Russian official trying to chart the country's foreign policy in the 18th century, for instance, would have to be concerned simultaneously about the position and actions of the Manchu Empire in China, the Persian and Ottoman Empires (and their respective vassals and subordinate allies), as well as all of the Great Powers in Europe, including Austria, Prussia, France, Britain, Holland, and Sweden.

This geographic reality laid the basis for a Russian tradition of a "multivector" foreign policy, with leaders, at different points, emphasizing the importance of relations with different parts of the world. For instance, during the 17th century, fully half of the departments of the *Posolskii Prikaz*—the Ambassadors' Office—of the Muscovite state dealt with Russia's neighbors to the south and east; in the next century, three out of the four departments of the College of International Affairs (the successor agency in the imperial government) covered different regions of Europe.[2]

Russian history thus bequeaths to the current government a variety of options in terms of how to frame the country's international orientation. To some extent, the choices open to Russia today are rooted in the legacies of past decisions. While a complete survey of Russian history is beyond the scope of this work,[3] we believe the most critical legacies from the pre–Soviet period to be the following:

- The selection of Orthodox Christianity by Grand Prince Vladimir of Kiev (988). When the ruler of Kievan Rus' selected a new state religion for his sprawling East Slavic domain, the choice for Orthodox Christianity—the faith of the Eastern Roman (Byzantine) Empire centered at Constantinople—instead of Islam or Roman Catholicism meant that Russia (along with Belarus and Ukraine) would be separate from the larger Islamic world (which stretched from Morocco to the Philippines), but also that Russia would not be a full member of the Romano-Germanic civilization that was to define an emerging Europe. For the most part, Russia would be left out of the historical ages that "made Europe," as historian John Lukacs observed—the high Middle Ages, the Renaissance, and the Enlightenment.[4]

- Alexander Nevsky's choice (1249). When the Mongol forces under Batu Khan ravaged the Russian lands beginning in 1237, they did not raid, devastate, and leave; instead, the principalities of Russia became the westernmost provinces of a vast Asian empire that was centered first in Karakorum, Mongolia, and then in Beijing. At the same time, the lands of northwestern Russia faced invasion from the West from the Swedes and the Teutonic Knights, a German Catholic crusading order bent on converting not only the pagan Balts but also the Orthodox Russians to their faith. Alexander Nevsky, prince first of the city-state of Novgorod but ultimately becoming the Grand Prince of all Russia, chose to resist the invaders from the West but to seek accommodation with the Mongols from the East. His choice—to reject the offers of the Pope in Rome and to submit to the Mongol khans—further deepened Russia's isolation from Europe but also forged links eastward across the vast Eurasian steppes.

- The Conquest of the Khanates of Kazan, Astrakhan, and Sibir (1552, 1556, 1582) under Ivan the Terrible. As the Mongol yoke receded, the principality of Moscow began the process of uniting the northern lands of Rus' into one state—but one that was still primarily defined as an Eastern European, Slavic, and Orthodox Christian realm. The conquest of the khanates of Kazan and Astrakhan added the entire watershed of the Volga River to Russia's control—and gave Russia access to the Caspian Sea. The emerging Russian Empire was no longer a small state at the eastern periphery of Europe but a Eurasian realm with significant numbers of non-Russian, non-Christian subjects. The conquest of Sibir started a process of Russian expansion and settlement across Siberia that was to reach the shores of the Pacific Ocean. Through this process of southward and eastward conquest, Russia acquired direct borders with the Ottoman Turkish, Persian, and Chinese empires.

- The Time of Troubles (1605–1612) reinforced the suspicion of the West that had been engendered by Nevsky's choice. As the Russian state collapsed, significant portions of its territory were occupied by Poland and Sweden, and Polish forces briefly captured Moscow itself. At the same time, these foreign interventions exposed the fundamental technological, military, and economic weaknesses of the Russian state vis-à-vis the more developed countries of Europe. How Russia could "catch up" while preserving its independence became a critical theme of Russian foreign policy objectives.

- The Treaty of Pereiaslav (1654). This agreement, reached between the Cossacks of Ukraine and the Russian tsar, saw the expansion of Russian power back to the heartland of the old Rus' state, Kiev. It marked the first stages of the disintegration of the Polish-Lithuanian commonwealth as the premier power of eastern Europe (culminating in the partitions of Poland during the 18th century) and the ability of Russia to project its power into central Europe. It also was to have lasting cultural impacts: Because Ukraine at this point was far more Westernized, the arrival in Russia of Ukrainian priests and scholars accelerated the process of Westernization in Russia itself.

- The Treaty of Nystad (1721). The gradual Westernization of Russia that had been promoted by Tsar Alexis (1645–1676) was overturned in favor of rapid (and sometimes forcible) change of Russian society and its institutions by his son, Peter, especially along German and Scandinavian models. Peter's desire to open a "window onto Europe" led to efforts to obtain ports on the Black and Baltic seas. The defeat of Sweden by a modernized Russian army and navy in the Great Northern War saw the cession of the Baltic states to the Russian Empire (adding another large non–Russian, non–Orthodox population), the creation of a new European-style capital, St. Petersburg, to replace Moscow, and Russia's emergence as one of Europe's great powers and a full member of the European state system. The Westernization of Russia continued under Peter's successors, especially Catherine the Great (reigned 1762–1796), who pushed Russia's frontiers westward and southward. Russia ceased to be on the periphery of Europe. Moreover, Russian armies ranged across Europe; both Berlin (1763) and Paris (1814) were to be occupied by Russian forces. This experience set down the precedent that no fundamental question of European security ought to be settled without Russian participation.

- Treaty of Küçük Kaynarca (1774). This agreement, which terminated a major conflict between the Russian and Ottoman Empires, is significant because it cleared the way for the establishment of Russian power in the Black Sea basin, guaranteed access for Russian merchant vessels into the eastern Mediterranean sea, and gave Russia the right to intercede on behalf of the Ottoman Empire's Eastern Christian populations in the Balkans and the Near East. This initiated Russia's modern-day vector toward the Middle East.

- The Capture of Tashkent (1865). The fall of this vital Central Asian city marked Russia's aggressive advance into Central Asia and its emergence on the doorstep of South Asia. When combined with the founding of the Pacific port city of Vladivostok (1859), on lands ceded to Russia from China as a result of the Treaty of Aigun, it marked the determination of Russia to establish itself as one of the premier powers of Asia.

Because of the simultaneous expansion and activity of Russia in different regions of the world, the Russian government could never focus on one area to the exclusion of others. And while popular versions of history depict tsarist Russia as an autocracy, with policy determined by an all-powerful tsar and implemented faithfully by his servants, the reality was quite different. Medieval Russia had a grand prince who in theory was styled an autocrat, but in reality "was essentially a referee among traditionally powerful boyar clans"—each pursuing different interests and objectives.[5] Muscovite Russia during the 16th and 17th centuries developed a more effective central governing administration grounded in what was termed the prikaz (department) system.[6] Prikazy were created, sometimes on an ad hoc basis, to deal with different aspects of the government's business.[7] As a problem or issue would arise, it would be assigned to a prikaz, but oftentimes different aspects of the same problem would be under the jurisdiction of different prikazy. Therefore, "bureaucratic growth was not linear; new prikazy would come into existence, be removed, and responsibilities shifted to other offices."[8] It also meant that policy might be the joint responsibility of several prikazy.[9] During the reign of Ivan IV ("the Terrible"), the Russian state was divided into two entities: the zemshchina and the oprichnina; some prikazy were in charge of affairs in both sections, others were established for one or the other, and when new administrative reforms were enacted, new prikazy might be set up to implement them[10]—all of this adding to the potential bureaucratic confusion.

The famous Russian historian V. O. Kliuchevksy, in assessing the *prikaz* system, concluded:

> As the needs and functions of the state increased in complexity, the number of departments mounted to about fifty. It is hard to discover any system in them. Rather they were a mass of big and small institutions, ministries, offices and temporary commissions, as we would call them now. The great number of departments and the haphazard assignment of the kind of affairs they dealt with made it difficult to control and direct their work. At times the government itself did not know to which of them some unusual case should be referred, and without further deliberation created a new department for the purpose.[11]

While there was an "Ambassadors' Office" (*posolskii prikaz*) that functioned as a Foreign Office in Muscovy, this department did not have sole and unchallenged responsibility for handling Russian foreign affairs during this period; instead, policy was divided among overlapping *prikazy,* including the "Secret Office." This was the department charged with handling the tsar's private affairs, which, among other things, comprised the monarch's charitable donations, his falcons, the salt and fishing industries, and diplomatic correspondence.[12] Responsibilities were shared out for policy among a series of different offices, usually connected to different leading families and factions within the tsar's court, and with no guarantees of coordination.[13] One *prikaz* might adopt a particular policy course and find that another would block implementation or be pursuing a contradictory course of action; until the tsar or a chief minister intervened, the result might be policy deadlock. In addition, 17th-century Russia experienced two periods of diarchy, when Patriarchs Filaret and Nikon were recognized alongside tsars Michael and Alexis as "great sovereigns," had their own staffs and bureaucracies alongside those of the tsar, and played leading roles in domestic and foreign policy.[14] The growth of *prikazy* during the 17th century led to greater policy confusion, although the overlapping mandates of different offices also enabled a rudimentary system of checks and balances to emerge.[15]

Peter the Great abolished both the patriarchate and the *prikazy* and attempted to rationalize the Russian bureaucracy, in part to create a more streamlined and efficient government that would attempt to more closely conform to his views on autocratic government.[16] But the *prikaz* model continued as different factions within the tsarist Russian bureaucracy continued to promote different foreign policies. Eugene Schuyler, an American diplomat posted to Russia in the 19th century, observed:

> Each minister being independent and responsible only to the Emperor, there . . . can be no united policy. The councils of ministers do not so much discuss questions of policy as questions of detail, the solution of which depends on two or three ministers jointly. . . . it is possible for a measure to be put into operation although it may be contrary to the ideas and desires of the Foreign Office.[17]

The lack of any overarching mechanism for coordinating Russian foreign policy was complicated by the development of different philosophical "schools" about where Russia belonged in the world. Two of the most famous were the 19th-century camps of the "Westernizers" (*zapadniki*) and the "Slavophiles." The Westernizers argued that Russia was part of Western civilization and that the goal of Russian foreign policy ought to be complete integration with Europe and that any divergence between Russia and other Western countries ought to be corrected in favor of prevailing Western models so as to bring Russia into harmony with the rest of the Western world. The Slavophiles tended to see Russia as separate from other European nations, a "Slavic-Byzantine" civilization that defined Eastern Europe in contrast to the "Romano-Germanic" one that defined the nations of the West. In foreign policy, they tended to support the establishment of a distinct Russian zone rather than complete and total integration into the West.[18] In the 21st century, their heirs are those who argue for Russia to pursue an "alliance" relationship with the United States and a U.S.-led European bloc (sometimes referred to in the contemporary discussions as the "Atlanticists") and those who see "European civilization" has having three branches, of which Russia-Eurasia is one, meaning that Russia should not subordinate its policies to "join" the West but instead structure relations between the United States, Europe, and Russia on the basis of equality.[19]

The Russian advance toward the Middle East, South Asia, and the Far East, however, engendered the rise of a different perspective, one that eventually coalesced around what become known as the Eurasian school. If the Westernizers saw Russia as Western and the Slavophiles viewed Russia as a distinct European civilization, the Eurasianists defined Russia as a primarily Asian actor. Prince Esper Ukhtomsky, who accompanied the future tsar Nicholas II on a grand tour of Asia in 1890–1891, wrote:

> The bonds that unite our part of Europe with Iran and Turan [a term indicating the Turkic peoples of Central Asia and Asia Minor], and through them with India and the Celestial Empire [China], are so ancient and lasting that, as yet, we ourselves, as a nation and a state, do not fully comprehend their full meaning and the duties they entail on us, both in our home and foreign policy.[20]

By the dawn of the 20th century, there was quite a robust foreign policy debate in the Russian Empire—and different perspectives were endorsed by different ministries. Should Russia concentrate on shoring up its position in Europe—and should this be done through an alliance with France or by reaching a new accommodation with a rising Germany? Should Russia extend and consolidate its hold on new territories in Central and East Asia? Was the time propitious for further advances southward at the expense of the Ottoman and Persian Empires? The ministers of War (Alexei Kuropatkin, served 1898–1904), Foreign Affairs (Vladimir Lamsdorff, served 1900–1906), and Finance (Sergei Witte, served 1892–1903) espoused radically different policies. The inability to commit to a single, overarching policy proved to be disastrous for the Russian Empire. Resources were overcommitted and bureaucratic politics on the *prikaz* model meant that Russia was not ready for the inevitable conflicts that would break out in Asia (the Russo-Japanese war, 1904–1905) and Europe (World War I, 1914–1918).[21]

Today, the Russian Foreign Ministry, in particular, attempts to examine the legacies of Russia's past foreign policies and in particular the work of diplomats such as Afanasii Ordin-Nashchokin (1605–1681), the advisors of Catherine the

Great, Prince Alexander Gorchakov (1798–1883), Alexander Izvolsky (1856–1919), and Sergei Sazonov (1861–1927) in shaping thinking about future foreign policy issues.[22]

THE SOVIET LEGACY

The Russian Empire was overthrown in 1917 by a group of revolutionary Marxists who proceeded to establish the world's first state ostensibly governed on the basis of "scientific socialism." Initially, Vladimir Lenin and his associates expected the imminent spread of revolution around the world in the wake of the devastation caused by the First World War. The new Soviet government proclaimed its desire for a "just and democratic peace" that would be without annexations, incorporations, or indemnities, in the words of the November 1917 decree on peace.[23] In so doing, the new regime expressed its desire to help spread the revolution throughout the world—not only in the advanced industrial nations of Europe but throughout the colonial world as well.

When the world revolution failed to materialize, the Soviet state was limited largely to the territories of the old Russian Empire. The proclamation of the Union of Soviet Socialist Republics in 1922—uniting Soviet Russia with other republics created on the territory of the old Russian Empire—was supposed to be a "decisive step toward uniting the workers of all countries into one World Socialist Soviet Republic," as the preamble to the new constitution stated. But the USSR was constantly torn between its ideological commitment to spreading the Soviet system throughout the world and the needs of safeguarding its national interests. The rapid (but, in human terms, costly) industrialization of the Soviet Union and the ultimate victory in the Second World War transformed the USSR from a regional power into an emerging superpower with global reach.

Under Josef Stalin, the USSR was guided by what Vladislav Zubok has labeled a "revolutionary-imperial paradigm," meaning that the Soviet state drew upon the geopolitical strategies of its tsarist predecessor but was also securing for itself the ability to spread the Soviet system around the world under Moscow's leading role.[24] Lenin's interpretation of Marxist thought had given preeminence to the "leading role" of a revolutionary party in accelerating the process by which a country might arrive at socialism; in terms of foreign policy, it meant that the Soviet Union was intended to play this role for the world as a whole. The legitimacy of the Soviet system, therefore, was connected with its ability to defend and spread the revolution. Stalin made this perfectly clear when he declared, "Whoever occupies a territory also imposes his own social system. Everyone imposes his own system as far as his army can reach. It cannot be otherwise."[25] This committed the Soviet state to a direct confrontation with the United States, leading to the Cold War. It also meant greater involvement in Asia, Africa, and Latin America, where the Russian state previously had few strategic interests. Stalin's successors—Nikita Khrushchev, Leonid Brezhnev, and even Mikhail Gorbachev at the beginning of his tenure—were all constrained by this paradigm (even if Khrushchev scaled back Stalin's emphasis on military means to spread the Soviet system when he acknowledged that the victory of Soviet-style socialism did not have to be achieved "through armed interference by the socialist countries in the internal affairs of capitalist countries").[26]

In particular, Brezhnev committed the Soviet state to changing the "correlation of forces" by diverting economic resources to achieving strategic parity with the United States and ultimate recognition in 1972 from Washington of its co-equal superpower status. But Moscow's global ambitions rested on a stagnating economic system that could only generate a fraction of the resources available to the United States. So the Soviet leadership, in contrast to the People's Republic of China, which successfully de-ideologized its foreign policy over time, remained committed to achieving ideological goals that drained the Soviet Union and helped to precipitate its demise. Moreover, the Soviet system was not immune to the bureaucratic divisions and rivalries that had plagued tsarist Russia. There were regular clashes over policy, especially between the Ministries of Foreign Affairs and Defense and between the Soviet government and the International Department of the Central Committee of the Communist Party.[27]

Brezhnev's immediate successors—Yuri Andropov and Konstantin Chernenko—because of their age and limited tenure as Soviet leaders, did not fundamentally alter the course and direction of Soviet foreign policy. Not until the elevation of a younger and more dynamic figure as General Secretary of the Communist Party of the Soviet Union—Mikhail Gorbachev—in 1985 would there be any dramatic change in Soviet foreign policy.

As Gorbachev continued in office, particularly after the 1987 Central Committee Plenum that marked the acceleration of his reform efforts, he attempted to break out of the Stalinist "revolutionary-imperial paradigm" in favor of his "new thinking"—a redefinition of the Soviet role in the world that de-emphasized confrontation in favor of cooperation with the United States to achieve security.[28] Gorbachev also endorsed the primacy of Europe as the principal vector for Moscow's foreign policy (the "common European home"), declaring in Prague in April 1987: "We assign an overriding significance to the European course of our foreign policy."

Gorbachev's most significant achievement, however, was, in the words of his former aide Anatoli Cherniaev, his "de-ideologization" of Soviet foreign policy, which "made possible such historic events as the unification of Germany, the democratization of Eastern Europe, and the creation of a new transatlantic

TABLE 1.1
Soviet Leaders, 1922–1991

Paramount Leader	Formal Position	Dynamics of His Tenure
Vladimir Lenin (1922–1924)	Chairman of the Council of People's Commissars of the USSR (1922–1924), effective head of the Communist Party (Bolsheviks).	Had served as Chairman of the Council of People's Commissars of the Russian Soviet Republic from 1918 until the creation of the USSR. From 1922, Josef Stalin served as General Secretary of the Party.
Josef Stalin (1924–1953) (NOTE: Stalin shared power within the Communist Party, first with Grigory Zinoviev and Lev Kamenev from 1924 until 1927 and then with Nikolai Bukharin until 1929.)	General Secretary of the Communist Party from 1922; became chairman of the government in 1941 and generalissimo of the Soviet Union.	Alexei Rykov served as Chairman of the Council of People's Commissars from 1924 until 1930; Vyacheslav Molotov succeeded him until 1941. While this was ostensibly the highest government post, Stalin's control of the Party made him paramount leader of the USSR.
Georgy Malenkov (1953–1955)	Chairman of the Council of Ministers.	Malenkov was seen initially as the strongest figure after Stalin's death, but he soon found himself sharing power with Nikita Khrushchev, who became General Secretary of the Communist Party.
Nikita Khrushchev (1953–1964)	General Secretary of the Communist Party; gradually became the paramount leader after pushing out rivals in 1955 and 1957; became Chairman of the Council of Ministers in 1958.	From 1955 until 1958, the Chairman of the Council of Ministers was Nikolai Bulganin. Khrushchev fired him in 1958 so as to be head of both the party and the government.
Leonid Brezhnev (1964–1982)	Succeeded Khrushchev as General Secretary after the former was ousted in 1964. In 1977, he became chairman of the Soviet parliament (Supreme Soviet) and as such was seen as the effective head of the government.	From 1964 until 1980, the Chairman of the Council of Ministers was Alexei Kosygin, who replaced Khrushchev and who initially shared power with Brezhnev but was gradually marginalized. He was replaced by Nikolai Tikhonov, who held this position until 1985.

(Continued)

(Continued)

Paramount Leader	Formal Position	Dynamics of His Tenure
Yuri Andropov (1982–1984)	Became both the General Secretary of the Communist Party and the chairman of the Supreme Soviet.	
Konstantin Chernenko (1984–1985)	Became both General Secretary and chairman of the Supreme Soviet.	
Mikhail Gorbachev (1985–1991)	Became General Secretary in 1985 and in 1988 became the chairman of the Supreme Soviet. In 1990, he created a new office, that of President of the USSR, and became the first president.	From 1985 until 1988, the head of state was technically Andrei Gromyko, who served as chairman of the Supreme Soviet; in 1988, Gorbachev took this position. With the creation of the presidency in 1990, Gorbachev attempted to transfer many of the powers traditionally held by the General Secretary of the CPSU to this office.

Source: Compiled by authors.

partnership."[29] De-ideologization rejected any idea of an eventual collapse of the Western system and was intended to release the Soviet system from committing most of its resources to preparing for a confrontation with the Western world, principally the United States. By the latter half of his tenure as General Secretary, Gorbachev had taken steps to end Soviet involvement in regional conflicts in Africa, Latin America, and Asia and set the stage for major improvements in previously chilly relationships with key powers, starting with the United States but also including China, Great Britain, France, and West Germany.

Gorbachev's efforts to reduce foreign tensions, however, could not rescue the Soviet system from its deep domestic crises, particularly the failure of the economy. The Soviet Union began to dissolve, in part because the leaders of the Russian Federation—the main core of the USSR—believed that the Soviet system had drained away the resources and vitality of Russia in the service of Communist ideology.[30] When the coup attempt launched by hardliners in August 1991 to prevent the signing of a new Union Treaty that would have replaced the Soviet Union with a far looser confederation failed, Russian president Boris Yeltsin took the step, with his Ukrainian and Belarusian colleagues, of formally dissolving the USSR in December 1991.

The collapse of the USSR in 1991 freed Russian foreign policy from any ideological constraints that had shackled Soviet policymakers, particularly the need to pursue foreign policies designed to shore up the domestic legitimacy of the Soviet system. However, as former Russian Foreign Minister Igor Ivanov has noted, one legacy of the Soviet past has been a "superpower mentality" by which Russia attempted to continue to "participate in any and all significant international developments, often incurring a greater domestic cost than the country could bear."[31] On the other hand, as Foreign Minister Sergei Lavrov has observed, Russia also inherited Soviet-era legacies in terms of relations with many nations in Africa, Asia, and Latin America—military relationships, economic ties, and so on—that continue to shape post–Soviet Russia's foreign policy.[32]

In the immediate aftermath of the Soviet collapse, the new Russian government had to try and formulate policies when "the country has yet to recognize itself as a state ... [and] does not have a sensible and formulated system of national interests on which foreign policy might be built," as Sergei Stankevich, who served as Boris Yeltsin's state counselor for policy issues, put it.[33] Initially, it appeared that the new Russian government was "keen to project an image to the West and the world at large that it was following a different policy than the one followed by the Soviet Union."[34] Over time, the Yeltsin administration attempted to determine which Soviet-era policies might still be beneficial for a post–Soviet Russia while also continuing Gorbachev's efforts at greater integration into the West.

Twice in the 20th century, Russian leaders attempted to reset their country's foreign policy, and both times—after the 1917 Bolshevik revolution and after the collapse of the Soviet Union in 1991—had to come to terms with Russia's historic legacies affecting their foreign policy choices. Boris Yeltsin summed up the challenge as follows:

> Russia's difficult transitional state does not allow us yet to discern its new or permanent character, nor does it allow us to obtain clear answers to the questions, "What are we turning away from? What do we wish to save?" and "Which elements do we wish to resurrect and which do we wish to create anew?"[35]

In the first two decades after the breakup of the Soviet Union, Russian foreign policy could very well be described as "post–Soviet": dealing with the consequences of the collapse and attempting to salvage the benefits of the Soviet state while charting a new direction. Today, this process is largely complete, and the formative period of Russia's post–Soviet foreign policy has come to an end.[36]

NOTES

1. As per the commentary of Alexei Pushkov. Cf. Nikolas K. Gvosdev, "After the G-8: Putin, at least, got what we wanted," International Herald Tribune, July 18, 2006, at http://www.iht.com/articles/2006/07/17/opinion/edgvosdev.php.

2. V. V. Pokhlebkin, *Vneshnaia Politika Rusi, Rossii I SSSR za 1000 let* (Moscow, Mezhdunarodnye Otnosheniia, 1992), 179–180.

3. We recommend, for a survey of Russian history, Nicholas V. Riasanovsky, *A History of Russia*, 6th edition (New York: Oxford University Press, 1999).

4. John Lukacs, Mark G. Malvasi, and Jeffrey O. Nelson, *Remembered Past: John Lukacs on History, Historians, and Historical Knowledge: A Reader* (Wilmington, DE: ISI Books, 2005), 434.

5. Paul Bushkovitch, *Religion and Society in Russia: The Sixteenth and Seventeenth Centuries* (New York: Oxford University Press, 1992), 33.

6. For a short overview of the *prikazy*, see the relevant entry in the *Slavianskaia Entsiklopediia: Kievskaia Rus'-Moskovskaia*, Volume II (Moscow: Olma-Press, 2002), 201–202.

7. George Vernadsky, *A History of Russia*, 5th revised edition (New Haven, CT: Yale University Press, 1961), 142–143; Walter G. Moss, *A History of Russia, Volume I, To 1917*, 2nd edition (London: Anthem Press, 2005), 174.

8. Matthew Paul Romaniello, *Absolutism and Empire: Governance on Russia's Early-Modern Frontier*, PhD Dissertation, Ohio State University, 2003, 47.

9. As was the case with military policy, before efforts were made to centralize the command structure. See Natalya Shepova, "Military Leader-Diplomat. Duke Vasily Golitsyn, Great Guardian of Russia's State Affairs," *Voennyi Diplomat* 5 (2004): 90.

10. See A. Zimin, "P. A. Sadikov's Studies in the History of the Oprichnina," *Voprosy Istorii* 12 (December 1950): 144–148, in *Current Digest of the Post-Soviet Press* 13, no. 3 (May 12, 1951), 7–9.

11. V. O. Kluichevsky, *A Course in Russian History: The Seventeenth Century*, ed. Alfred J. Rieber, trans. Natalie Duddington (Armonk, NY: M.E. Sharpe, Inc., 1994), 164.

12. Ibid., 165–66.

13. John P. LeDonne, *Absolutism and Ruling Class: The Formation of the Russian Political Order, 1700–1825* (New York: Oxford University Press, 1991), 64.

14. Vernadsky, 142.

15. Nicholas V. Riasanovsky, *A History of Russia*, 4th edition (New York: Oxford University Press, 1984), 191–92.

16. Moss, 238.

17. Eugene Schuyler, *Turkistan: Notes of a Journey in Russian Turkistan, Khokand, Bukhara, and Kuldja*, Volume II (New York: Scribner, Armstrong and Co., 1876), 263.

18. Nikolas K. Gvosdev, "Russia: European but not Western?" *Orbis* 51, no. 1 (Winter 2007), esp. 130–132; in turn, this sketch draws on the work of S. V. Utechin, *Russian Political Thought: A Concise History* (New York: Praeger, 1964).

19. Igor S. Ivanov, *The New Russian Diplomacy* (Washington, DC: The Nixon Center and Brookings Institution Press, 2002), 12; see also the transcript of Sergei Lavrov's remarks to

the Council on Foreign Relations in New York on September 24, 2008, at http://www.cfr
.org/publication/17384/conversation_with_sergey_lavrov.html.

20. Quoted in Karl E. Meyer and Shareen Blair Brysac, *Tournament of Shadows: The Great Game and the Race for Empire in Central Asia* (Washington, DC: Counterpoint, 1999), 243.

21. See especially William C. Fuller, *Strategy and Power in Russia, 1600–1914* (New York: The Free Press, 1992), esp. 328–393.

22. Ivanov, 26–32.

23. Cited in Victor S. Mamatey, *Soviet Russian Imperialism* (New York: Van Nostrand Reinhold Company, 1964), 113–115.

24. Vladislav M. Zubok, *A Failed Empire: The Soviet Union in the Cold War from Stalin to Gorbachev* (Chapel Hill, NC: University of North Carolina Press, 2009).

25. Milovan Djilas, *Conversations with Stalin*, trans. Michael B. Petrovich (New York: Harcourt, Brace and World, Inc., 1962), 114.

26. See Krushchev's report to the 20th Party Congress in February 1956, in *Current Soviet Policies II: The Documentary Record of the 20th Communist Party Congress and its Aftermath*, ed. Leo Gruliow (New York: Frederick A. Praeger, Inc., 1957), 37.

27. This was certainly the view of U.S. Secretary of State Kissinger (cf. Schapiro, 41), and the rivalry is attested to by Soviet defector Arkady N. Shevchenko; see his *Breaking with Moscow* (London: Grafton, 1986), esp. 310–311.

28. See, for instance, David Holloway, "Gorbachev's New Thinking," *Foreign Affairs* (America and the World 1988 edition) 68, no. 1 (Winter 1989): 66–81.

29. Anatoli Chernaiev, "Gorbachev's Foreign Policy: The Concept," in *Turning Points in Ending the Cold War*, ed. Kiron K. Skinner (Palo Alto, CA: Hoover Institution Press, 2007), 112.

30. "Yeltsin To Seek Russian Sovereignty as Part of New Soviet Union," *Associated Press*, May 30, 1990, at http://www.apnewsarchive.com/1990/Yeltsin-To-Seek-Russian-Sovereignty-as-Part-of-New-Soviet-Union/id-ed65a51284d1b351341d853a53dc4992.

31. Ivanov, 13–14.

32. See, for instance, Foreign Minister Lavrov's remarks to the Council on Foreign Relations, op. cit, on the importance of contemporary Russia building on these pre-existing ties and legacies as part of its return as a global power.

33. Sergei Stankevich, "Russia in Search of Itself," in *Russia in the National Interest*, ed. Nikolas K. Gvosdev (New Brunswick, NJ: Transaction Press, 2003), 19.

34. Jyotsna Bakshi, "Russian Policy towards South Asia," *Strategic Analysis* 23, no. 8 (November 1999): 1375.

35. Quoted in Ivanov, 11.

36. See the comments of former Foreign Minister Ivanov, who argues that this process of consolidation was coming to a close during the Putin administration. Ivanov, 8.

CHAPTER 2

Vectors and Sectors

The Russian Foreign Policy Mechanism

Foreign policy is not formed in an abstract vacuum. In any country—Russia included—governments must deal with a series of realities. There is rarely a clear-cut choice between "good" and "bad" options, but rather the need to choose between competing imperatives. Presidents and prime ministers may have impulses but must still exercise policy through other people—and it is "only by coaxing, prodding and compromise" that decisions are made and executed. Moreover, leaders rarely have a blank slate; "all problems and policies have already been worked by a thousand hands and the clay is mostly dry."[1] Despite the immense formal authorities given to the Russian president, his government is heir to the thousand-year legacy of the Russian state, discussed in the last chapter, which continues to have an impact on the country's possible vectors. In turn, the current structure of the foreign policy process affects how choices are made between different foreign policy options.

THE CONSTITUTIONAL
STRUCTURE: PRESIDENT AND PRIME MINISTER

The Russian Constitution of 1993 envisions a pyramidal foreign policy-making structure, centralized under the control of the president. The president represents the country in international relations (Article 80); supervises the conduct of the foreign policy of the Russian Federation and is the one who must sign all international treaties (Article 86); is the commander-in-chief of the armed forces (Article 87); and, as chief executive, appoints all ministers, ambassadors, and heads of agencies and sets down the foreign and national security strategies of the country (Article 83).

Boris Yeltsin, the first president of Russia, was initially very involved in the details of governing, but during his second term, ill health forced him to reluctantly turn over more authority to his prime minister. Vladimir Putin, who succeeded him, pursued what he referred to as a "vertical of power" to ensure that authority that had devolved both to others in the Russian government as well as to regional leaders was recentralized in the president's hands. From

TABLE 2.1

Presidents and Prime Ministers of Russia

President	Prime Minister (since the Soviet collapse), Acting and Confirmed
Boris Yeltsin (first term 1991–1996; second term 1996–1999)	Boris Yeltsin (1991–1992) Yegor Gaidar (1992) Viktor Chernomyrdin (1992–1998) Sergei Kirienko (1998) Viktor Chernomyrdin (1998) Evgeny Primakov (1998–1999) Sergei Stepashin (1999) Vladimir Putin (1999–2000)
Vladimir Putin (first term 2000–2004; second term 2004–2008)	Mikhail Kasyanov (2000–2004) Viktor Khristenko (2004) Mikhail Fradkov (2004–2007) Viktor Zubkov (2007–2008)
Dmitry Medvedev (one term, 2008–2012)	Vladimir Putin (2008–2012)
Vladimir Putin (third term, 2012–)	Dmitry Medvedev (2012–)

Source: Compiled by authors.

2008 until 2012, the third president of Russia, Dmitry Medvedev, governed in close coordination with Putin, who stepped down from the presidency to become prime minister. Having honored the constitutional prohibition against a person serving more than two consecutive terms in office, Putin returned to the presidential chair after the March 2012 elections.

The president is the "focal point" of the Russian government, but day-to-day control over policy is vested by the constitution in the hands of the chairman of the government (popularly referred to as the prime minister). Article 114 entrusts the prime minister with responsibility to "adopt measures to ensure the country's defense, state security and the implementation of the foreign policy of the Russian Federation." And while the president appoints ministers—including the foreign minister—it is the prime minister who is charged with presenting the chief executive with the nominations to fill government posts (Article 113). Under both the Yeltsin and Putin administrations, the prime minister was clearly subordinate to the president. Significantly, when former president Vladimir Putin became prime minister in 2008, he implicitly redefined the relationship, making the two positions more equal: "The president is the guarantor of the constitution and sets the main domestic and foreign policy guidelines. But the highest executive power in the land lies with the government . . ."[2]

Vladimir Putin was the first post–Soviet Russian prime minister to directly control the political party that held a majority of the seats in the Duma—United Russia—unlike previous prime ministers, who were completely dependent on presidential favor. Putin accepted the chairmanship of the party on April 15, 2008, noting that "a situation in which the head of the executive branch leads a party is a civilized and natural practice that is traditional for democratic states."[3] It also meant that while the president retained the constitutional right to dismiss the prime minister, the prime minister, in turn, controlled a supermajority in the Duma that could either impeach the president or change the constitution. This state of affairs was referred to as "the tandem"—a balancing of the presidency with the office of the prime minister. It also meant that some of the clear lines of authority between the two positions blurred. As Dimitri K. Simes and Paul Saunders observed,

> Medvedev summons ministers who report to Putin to issue public instruc-
> tions on the economy, while Putin often takes a visible role on security and
> foreign-policy issues, such as last year's war with Georgia, the decision to
> apply to the WTO as a customs union with Belarus and Kazakhstan
> (announced just days after Medvedev's advisers said Moscow would continue
> with its previous approach), and high-profile foreign trips, like a 2009 visit to
> Poland around the seventieth anniversary of the Molotov-Ribbentrop Pact
> and the German (and Soviet) invasion.[4]

But while the president and prime minister were now nearly co-equal, there was no guarantee that the 2008-to-2012 state of affairs would last and become the norm in Russian politics. Dmitry Medvedev's announcement at the United Russia party congress in September 2011 that he would not seek a second term as president and would nominate Vladimir Putin to return to the presidency, fol- lowed by Putin's declaration that he and Medvedev would preserve the tandem by switching positions after the March 2012 presidential elections, raised ques- tions as to how executive power will be wielded in the future.

In his third term, Putin has taken steps to restore the earlier pattern of presi- dential–prime ministerial relations, a dynamic characterized by the subordina- tion of the prime minister to the policy line set by the president. The clearest sign of this has been a series of decrees to take some of the powers Putin enjoyed as prime minister and to vest them in the presidency.[5] At the same time, the expan- sion of positions within the government and the continued need to maintain some degree of balance between competing factions may prevent the complete dismantling of the institutions created during the 2008-to-2012 period, meaning that future prime ministers may retain a greater degree of policy autonomy than their pre–Medvedev predecessors. The loss of United Russia's "supermajority" in the State Duma following the December 2011 elections also prevents any unilateral attempts to alter the Constitutional balance of power at will.

SEARCHING FOR A ROLE: THE LEGISLATURE

The legislature (the State Duma and the Federation Council) is not granted a major foreign policy role by the Constitution. The lower house, the State Duma, has the power to ratify or denounce treaties, while the upper house, the Federation Council, can review these actions (Article 106); the legislature also has the general "power of the purse" and ability to pass laws that could shape or affect policy. But the parliament does not have the power to appoint or dismiss individual ministers or ambassadors, nor can it set the overall direction of policy, powers the legislature enjoyed under the amended 1978 Soviet constitution that remained in force for the first 2 years of a post–Soviet Russia. In part fearing the strength of antireform elements in the legislature, Boris Yeltsin's constitutional commission deliberately limited the scope of authority given to the legislative branch.

The legislature does have some influence over the foreign policy process by its ability to hold hearings and to pass resolutions that, while they may not be binding on the executive branch, do signal the "vulnerability" of the executive branch "to the wider political environment," which may constrain the freedom of action enjoyed by the president.[6] For instance, in 1994, the Duma recommended revisions in the Partnership for Peace agreement signed with NATO that were incorporated by the Yeltsin administration in order to "to use the issue to bolster his attempts to build a wider coalition base."[7] At other times, the legislature may act in order to give the executive branch greater maneuvering room. For instance, at the end of 2012, to signal anger at the passage of legislation in the United States (the Magnitsky Act) that placed sanctions on Russian officials accused of human rights violations, the Duma enacted a ban on American citizens adopting Russian orphans. The legislature's actions allowed Putin to distance himself from having to make a direct response and so further jeopardize U.S.–Russia relations.[8]

The Duma was most influential in the latter half of the 1990s, when Yeltsin's health was failing and, in the midst of the 1998 financial crisis, he was forced to appoint Yevgeny Primakov as prime minister to appease powerful factions within the Duma. Because the Primakov cabinet explicitly relied on the support of a broad spectrum of political parties, including those of the Communist and nationalist opposition, the legislature found it could influence the policy process.[9] During the Putin administration, the character of the Duma changed, with the emergence of a strong, disciplined progovernment party (United Russia) and changes to the electoral law that eliminated single-mandate districts. This prevented independent (nonparty) candidates from running. In addition, the legislation raised the threshold a party needed to cross in order to gain seats, which effectively removed smaller pro-Western parties from the chamber. At the same time, the nature of the upper house changed as well; the Federation Council now serves as the representation for the regions, with delegates appointed by local governors (themselves now nominated by the Kremlin)—and Federation Council members (often styled as "senators" in imitation of the members of the upper house of the U.S. Congress) no longer serve fixed terms but are subject to recall at any point.

While the legislature, therefore, no longer takes a confrontational stance vis-à-vis the executive when it comes to foreign policy, both houses are still important because their members reflect a broad cross-section of national elites—business and commercial interests, regional powers, and different factions from within the federal system and the presidential administration.[10] The Duma, therefore, reflects the fragmentation of the leadership around multiple foreign policies. This allows individual members of the legislature to be able to mobilize support and resources for their own preferred policy outcomes.[11] More importantly, the parliamentary committees—particularly those dealing with foreign affairs, defense, and security and relations with the Commonwealth of Independent States—do scrutinize policies, offer policy options, and allow for some degree of elite debate over the direction of the country's foreign policies.[12] Finally, individual members of the legislature may be tapped to serve as experts and envoys; Mikhail Margelov, the chairman of the Federation Council's Foreign Affairs Committee, serves as the presidential special envoy for Africa and is sometimes employed as a troubleshooter for the Middle East.

Political parties represented in the Duma have espoused a variety of foreign policy positions. Liberal parties such as Yabloko or the former Union of Right Forces tended to support Russian integration with the West. In contrast, the Communist Party of the Russian Federation—the successor to the old Communist Party of the Soviet Union—took a consistently anti-American position and has had harsh criticism for post-Soviet Russian governments that pulled back from supporting traditionally pro-Soviet allies in Latin America, the Middle East, and Asia. The Liberal Democratic Party of Russia, led by the colorful demagogue Vladimir V. Zhirinovksy, espoused a jingoistic nationalism that called for the resurgence of a strong Russia capable of dominating the other states of the former Soviet Union and, in concert with other rising powers, act as a counterweight to the United States.

During the Putin administration, two new parties entered the political system. The first—United Russia—became the de facto "party of power," combining the pro-Putin Unity movement and the All-Russia/Fatherland bloc set up by former prime minister Yevgeny Primakov and then-Moscow mayor Yuri Luzhkov. This party, which had no clear ideology other than support for the stabilization of Russia under the guidance of Putin, has a number of "wings" within it, some attracting former pro-Western liberals from the Union of Right Forces, others encompassing those supporting closer Russian ties with China or other Eastern powers. The second was a nationalist-social democratic party, Just Russia. This party absorbed the nationalist Rodina (Motherland) party and provided an ideological home for those who were supportive of Putin but were less enthusiastic about free-market reforms.[13]

Under new rules promulgated for the 2007 elections, single-mandate districts were eliminated and parties were required to clear a 5% threshold in the general vote (now raised to 7%), meaning the only parties that are represented in the Duma are United Russia, the Communists, LDPR, and Just Russia. This pattern remained intact after the December 2011 Duma elections. However, due to growing dissatisfaction with the direction of the country under the Putin/Medvedev tandem and rising distrust of United Russia, increasingly viewed as the "party of crooks and thieves" (in the parlance of the blogger and activist Alexei Navalny), United Russia suffered losses in those elections, which were also marred by charges of fraud and ballot stuffing in favor of the ruling party. Other parties— the Communists, Just Russia, and the Liberal Democrats—increased their numbers of deputies in the legislature. New political reforms may make it easier for other parties and movements to contest elections in the future, which could create greater ideological diversity within the Russian parliament.

THE POSITION OF THE FOREIGN MINISTRY: ONE ACTOR AMONG MANY

In theory, all Russian foreign policy is supposed to be controlled and coordinated by the Foreign Ministry, per the November 1992 presidential decree that declared that the Foreign Ministry "will be entrusted with the formation of coordinating and monitoring" the work of all government agencies to "ensure a unified political line." The legal position of the Ministry was reiterated by the 1995 Statute of the Russian Foreign Ministry, which, on paper, subordinated all other agencies of the government to its supervision in all foreign policy matters. The foreign minister, in turn, was expected to ensure that the entire cadre of ministers, ambassadors, and other civil servants faithfully executed the policy directives of the president.

TABLE 2.2
Foreign Ministers of Russia

Foreign Minister	Years Served
Andrei Kozyrev	1990 for Russian Republic; continued as foreign minister of an independent Russia to 1996
Evgeny Primakov	1996–1998
Igor Ivanov	1998–2004
Sergei Lavrov	2004–

Source: Compiled by authors.

During the Yeltsin administration, the foreign minister was often a key figure in Russian domestic politics; Andrei Kozyrev was part of the team of "young reformers" who came into office with Yeltsin in 1991 (and who then took up a seat in the Duma), while Yevgeny Primakov, who served as foreign minister from 1996 until his appointment as prime minister in 1998, had a real base of support among nationalists and conservatives (and ultimately helped to create the Fatherland-All Russia bloc, which later merged with Vladimir Putin's Unity movement to create the United Russia party). In contrast, the tendency in the Putin era has been for the foreign minister to be a skilled practitioner of the diplomatic arts and to serve as an advisor on foreign policy rather than to be someone with a domestic political base who acts as an independent figure. Igor Ivanov (served 1998–2004) and Sergei Lavrov (in office since 2004) were both career diplomats and never emerged as political figures in their own right.

Foreign ministers serve a president, yet their own backgrounds, experiences, and preferences can help to shape policy. Kozyrev emphasized building strong relationships with the United States; Primakov, his successor, with extensive professional experience in the Middle East (and a former director of the foreign intelligence service), favored a more multipolar approach to policy that emphasized outreach to other rising powers, especially India and China, to counterbalance the United States, viewing Kozyrev's approach as cultivating too much of a Russian dependency on Washington. Ivanov, a former ambassador to Spain, put a great deal of effort into cementing Russia's ties to Europe. Lavrov's preference for maintaining good relations with all major global powers, his advocacy of a "multivector" policy, and his emphasis on the importance of forming interest-based coalitions with other countries has meant that he has been able to effectively navigate between competing foreign policy interests rather than being a partisan of one particular line or vector.[14] Lavrov, who started his service in Putin's second presidential term, was kept on as foreign minister during Dmitry Medvedev's administration and was reappointed to the position for the start of

Putin's third term, in part to ensure continuity in Russian foreign affairs. Lavrov is now the longest serving post–Soviet Russian foreign minister.

Despite the centralized ministry framework (at least on paper), however, foreign affairs in contemporary Russia remain parceled out among a number of different actors. The foreign minister occupies a potentially uneasy position in the cabinet, because although he is technically part of the government headed by the prime minister, he is directly nominated by the president, not by the prime minister—a state of affairs that has continued during the presidency of Dmitry Medvedev and the prime ministership of Vladimir Putin.[15] The foreign minister cannot be fired by the prime minister and is legally "insulated" from the prime minister and the rest of the cabinet by not being required to resign if the president asks for the dismissal of the government. So the foreign minister may end up caught between the president and prime minister if there are policy disputes. Moreover, the foreign minister does not fully control his own operation. He does not appoint his deputies; all the deputy foreign ministers are also directly appointed by the president.[16]

Moreover, in contrast to the very rigidly defined structure of the U.S. State Department, which has clearly demarcated assistant secretary positions based on geographic and functional criteria, the deputy foreign ministers are assigned different portfolios as individuals. For instance, in examining the current group of deputies (as of late 2012), two deputies, Andrei Denisov and Sergei Ryabakov, had no specific portfolio, but based on their background and experience, both were deeply involved in handling relations with key countries like the United States and China. Some of the deputies' responsibilities had clear areas of overlap; Alexander V. Grushko oversaw relations with European and Euro-Atlantic organizations (EU, NATO, etc.), but another deputy, Vladimir Titov, was in charge of relations with European countries. Mikhail Bogdanov handles Middle East and African affairs, while I. V. Morgulov is responsible for the countries of the Asia-Pacific region. Some of the deputies had a variety of responsibilities. Grigory Karasin was responsible both for relations with the countries of the Commonwealth of Independent States (CIS) and also for serving as liaison with the legislature; Gennady Gatilov oversees a variety of issues, including Russia's relations with multilateral organizations, issues of economic cooperation and human rights, and climate change.[17] But it is Bogdanov, in his capacity as the presidential "special envoy" for the Middle East, not Gatilov, who serves Russia's representative to the "Quartet," the Middle East peace process. As these individuals are replaced in the future, there is no guarantee that their successors will be tasked with overseeing the exact same set of issues.

Moreover, despite the language of presidential decrees, the foreign minister and his deputies do not control all aspects of Russian foreign policy. Other ministries and agencies, pursuing their own interests, have often impinged on foreign policy matters. Significantly, the Foreign Ministry was never granted the power to supervise Russia's foreign economic relations, which initially were the purview of a separate ministry altogether and have since largely come under the control of the prime minister and his deputies. Particularly during the 1990s, but continuing to the present day, economic imperatives have often overridden diplomatic necessities, so that the Russian government authorized continuing exports, particularly of nuclear technology and conventional weaponry, not to pursue foreign policy goals but to support the industrial base of a number of Russian regions. The Defense Ministry and the intelligence agencies, particularly in their efforts to maintain military bases or preserve networks of influence, have sometimes worked at cross-purposes with the Foreign Ministry as well.[18]

In addition, the existence of special envoys that report directly to the president, as well as specialized agencies of the Russian government entrusted with some responsibility for foreign affairs, complicates the position of the Foreign Minister as the first among equals in the Russian foreign policy system. For instance, in 2008, a separate organization—the Federal Agency for Commonwealth of Independent States Affairs, Compatriots Abroad and International Humanitarian Cooperation—was created; this agency controls 83 branch offices in 74 countries, including a series of Russian cultural centers.[19] A new ministry was also created in 2012 for overseeing the Russian Far East (and given to former presidential envoy to the Far Eastern District Viktor Ishayev); given the importance of the region's economic relations with China, Japan, and Korea, there is a potential for this new ministry to become a player in Russia's Asia vector.

Because Foreign Minister Andrei Kozyrev was unable to emerge as the sole coordinator of Russian foreign policy, president Boris Yeltsin created the Security Council in 1992 as an advisory and consultative body. While the Foreign Minister was represented on this body, he became one voice among several, and a new position—the secretary of the Security Council—was created, appointed by and directly reporting to the president. This person functions as a de facto national security advisor to the president[20] and, backed by his own staff, forms an alternate center for the formation of policy. Sometimes the secretary acts as a direct representative of the president, bypassing the foreign minister, especially in informal dealings with other heads of state.

Despite the legal position of the Foreign Ministry, it is the Security Council that has emerged to play a "coordinating role" in foreign policy—overseeing and harmonizing the work of different state organs and the nonstate sector. The Council, not the Ministry, reviews all foreign policy documents, and the Council and its Secretary are tasked with ensuring government bodies implement and execute state strategies, including those dealing with foreign policy.[21] Given this role, some assumed that the Secretary would play a role in foreign policy formulation akin to that of the U.S. national security advisor. In 2011, president Medvedev signed a decree further spelling out the powers and authorities of the Secretary, giving him responsibility for overseeing the national security infrastructure of the country and clearly designating him as someone who must play a role in formulating and implementing foreign policy. On paper, this move elevates the Secretary to a much more prominent position in the Russian government, but whether this translates into the Secretary becoming a more powerful actor within the Kremlin remains to be seen.[22]

But the secretary of the Security Council is not the automatic chief advisor to the Russian president on foreign policy either, and the degree of turnover in the position of its secretary has prevented any one person from using this post to decisively shape the parameters of Russian foreign policy. Moreover, the secretary is competing with others for the ear of the president; there is also a member of the presidential administration who serves as the advisor on foreign policy and international relations. Sometimes visiting national security advisors from other countries will meet with both the Security Council secretary and the presidential aide for foreign policy. For instance, when U.S. national security advisor Jim Jones visited Moscow in October 2009, he met both with the secretary of the Security Council, Nikolai Patrushev, and with the presidential advisor on foreign policy, Sergei Prikhodko.[23] To further muddy the waters, the prime minister has now acquired his own foreign policy and national security advisor—formally defined as a deputy chief of staff for foreign affairs.[24] In June 2010, when Ukrainian Prime Minister Mykola Azarov visited Russia for talks with Putin, the Russian prime minister was accompanied by his advisor, the former Russian ambassador to the United States, Yuri Ushakov.[25] When Putin

TABLE 2.3
Secretaries of the Security Council

Yuri Skokov (1992–1993)	Vladimir Putin (1999)
Eevgeny Shaposhnikov (1993)	Sergei Ivanov (1999–2001)
Oleg Lobov (1993–1996)	Vladimir Rushailo (2001–2004)
Aleksandr Lebed (1996)	Igor Ivanov (2004–2007)
Ivan Rybkin (1996–1998)	Valentin Sobolev (2007–2008)
Andrei Kokoshin (1998)	Nikolai Patrushev (2008–)
Nikolai Bordyuzha (1998–1999)	

Source: Compiled by authors.

returned to the presidency in 2012, Ushakov was transferred to the presidential administration to continue to serve as Putin's national security advisor, while Prikhodko joined now-prime minister Medvedev's staff with the rank of a deputy chief of staff.[26]

The role of the presidential and prime ministerial staffs—what Vytautas Sirijos Gira refers to as the "non-formal state government"—adds an additional level of complexity. These staffs have no constitutional role in the formation of policy, but their decisions and input can "establish the limits of power for the parliament and the government" in terms of the final adoption and execution of policy.[27] Indeed, the presidential staff has sometimes been viewed as a "parallel cabinet."[28] The more informal nature of the staff—in the sense that there are few clear geographic divisions of responsibility—means that members of the administration can be selected to fill foreign policy roles at will. For instance, during the first 2 years of the Obama and Medvedev administrations, the cochair of the U.S.-Russia working group on civil society and economic relations on the American side was the senior director for Russia at the National Security Council, Michael McFaul; his counterpart on the Russian side was Vladislav Surkov, the first deputy chief of staff of the presidential administration, rather than someone specifically designated as handling U.S. diplomacy. Presidential staffers often function as ministers without portfolio, being assigned a set of different responsibilities, rather than, as in the U.S. system, being handed specific geographic or functional responsibilities.

To bring order to the policymaking process during his presidency, Vladimir Putin instituted a series of regular meetings. On Mondays, he would convene a "governmental meeting" (sometimes referred to as a cabinet meeting) in the Kremlin, with the president, prime minister, the deputy prime minister, the head of the presidential administration (the chief of staff), and the foreign, defense, interior, and economic ministers attending every week (other ministers would attend if business specifically related to their areas was to be discussed). On Saturdays, he would assemble at his dacha (country house) those with especially responsible for national security issues to meet with the president—the prime minister, the heads of the various intelligence agencies, the secretary of the Security Council, and the foreign, defense, and interior ministers. Usually members of the presidential administration were also present at this meeting, including the presidential advisor on foreign policy. At both of these meetings, foreign policy would be discussed, and while the foreign minister was an integral part of both sets of meetings, he was in no position to set or dominate the agenda.[29]

The restructuring of the Russian government in 2008 created, in effect, a "dual-key" system that required both the prime minister and the president to be in significant agreement in order for policy to move forward.[30] The creation of seven deputy prime minister positions—all of them appointed by the prime minister—enabled the head of the government to exercise broad supervision over policy, even if the foreign and defense ministers remain appointed by the president. For instance, during the Putin cabinet (2008–2012), First Deputy Prime Minister Igor Shuvalov had broad responsibility for international policy and more specifically for international economic policy and pursuing Russia's integration with its immediate neighbors.[31] One feature of the 2012 "swap" has been for some of Putin's colleagues who served in the cabinet to move into positions in the presidential administration, while some of Medvedev's aides followed him into the government when he became prime minister.[32] Even if power in the Russian system increasingly gravitates back toward the president, the creation of new offices and positions has expanded the policymaking process.

THE REGIONAL GOVERNMENTS

The Russian Constitution gives to the federal government exclusive control over foreign policy (Article 71) but recognizes that the regions have a role to play in terms of foreign economic relations (Article 72). Given, as former Foreign Minister Igor Ivanov has observed, that "approximately half of the Federation's entities share land or marine borders with neighboring states,"[33] the regional governments are very interested in having some input in those foreign relations that directly impact their interests.

While power over foreign policy is vested in the central government, Russia's geographic, economic, and cultural diversity means that the regions all have an influence in determining which vectors become preeminent. For instance, while the federal center may stress the importance of Russia's ties with Europe, the growing economic and cultural links between the predominantly Muslim regions of the North Caucasus and the larger Arab and Islamic world ensures that the "southern vector" toward the Near East cannot be entirely neglected. In some cases, regional leaders (governors and presidents of the autonomous republics) carry out diplomatic activity on behalf of Russia.[34]

Sometimes international relations activity shifts from the Foreign Ministry and devolves to the regional level. The Orenburg region is an interesting case in point. This region, which has a more than 1,800-kilometer border with Kazakhstan, is responsible for generating some 10% of the trade between Russia and Kazakhstan, is the headquarters for a number of joint Russian-Kazakh firms, and has a large ethnic Kazakh minority. This region hosts the intergovernmental Russia–Kazakhstan forum to build on these existing ties.

Moreover, the regional governor set up an interagency working group, not under the Ministry of Foreign Affairs but under the Regional Development Ministry, to liaise with their Kazakhstani counterparts to pursue economic growth and the development of new projects.[35] Several Russian regions have been partnered with regions in China to help facilitate trade and development, among them the Far Eastern region (*Primorskii krai*) with Jilin province, the Altai region with Xinjiang, and the Amur region with Shanghai.[36] Sometimes regional governments will use their representatives in the Federation Council to act as envoys of their region abroad, especially to drum up foreign investment.[37]

THE STATE COMPANIES AND PRIVATE BUSINESS

During the Putin presidency, the core organizing principle of Russian foreign policy often seemed to be promoting economic development as the basis for state power.[38] The *Concept of the Long-Term Socio-Economic Development of the Russian Federation,* issued by the Ministry for Economic Development and Trade in September 2007, called for the "strengthening of Russia's position in the formation of the global energy infrastructure"; the renovation of Russia's high-technology industrial sectors, including in nuclear power, rocketry, and aerospace; and, finally, the "transformation of Russia into one of the world's leading financial centers . . . guaranteeing the leading position of Russia in the financial markets of the countries of the CIS, the Eurasian Economic Union, central and eastern Europe."

As a result, business plays a much greater role in Russian foreign policy these days. Russia now has what is often termed a "state capitalist" economic system, "in which the state dominates markets, primarily for political gain."[39] In some cases, the Russian government is the principal shareholder in a company—for instance, in the natural gas behemoth Gazprom; in other cases, companies are privately held (see Table 2.4). Nevertheless, the emergence of so-called "national champions" has forged a close relationship between business and the state. Sometime businesses are asked to undertake projects on behalf of the government; in other cases, businesses might ask the Russian state to use its diplomatic efforts to advance corporate interests.[40] So Russian governmental interest in using business as a means of advancing foreign policy goals "goes beyond the firms that it owns, and seems to affect the strategies of some privately owned companies too."[41] Business diplomacy matters to Russia because it is often through economic means that foreign policy objectives can be met—particularly in influencing other countries to align their policies with those of Russia.[42]

TABLE 2.4
Major Companies in Russia

Company	Main Business	Majority Shareholder(s)
ALROSA	Diamonds	Federal government and Sakha Republic
Bank VTB	Banking, investment	Federal government
Evraz	Steel	Private (Alexander Frolov, Alexander Abramov)
Gazprom	Energy	Federal government
LUKoil	Energy	Private (Vagit Alekperov)
Magnitogorsk Iron and Steel (MMK)	Steel	Private (Viktor Rashnikov)
Mechel	Mining and metals	Private (Igor Zyuzin)
Norilsk Nickel	Mining and metals	Private (Interros and RUSAL)
Novolipetsk Steel (NLMK)	Steel	Private (Vladimir Lisin)
Polyus Gold	Mining	Private (Suleiman Kerimov, ONEXIM)
Rosatom	Nuclear power	Federal government
Rosneft	Energy	Federal government
RUSAL	Metals	Private (Renova and Basic Element)
Russian Technologies	Holding company for major defense firms including Rosoboronexport, the state arms exporter	Federal government
Severstal	Steel and mining	Private (Alexander Mordashov)
UGMK	Metals	Private (Iskander Makhmudov)

Source: Compiled by authors.

Russia does not have the same "conflict of interest" statutes that bar serving officials in the United States government from sitting on corporate boards. Indeed, because the Russian state is a shareholder in companies, the government often sends officials or members of the presidential administrations to join companies or serve as officers. This tendency became very pronounced in the first term of the Putin administration, when key board appointments were distributed to key government officials and senior aides to the president. Indeed, Russia rejected the advice of the Organization for Economic Co-operation and Development (OECD), which advised against nominating public officials to sit on company boards.[43] Putin's then chief of staff, Dmitry Medvedev, became chairman of the board at Gazprom; deputy prime minister Aleksandr Zhukov became chair of Russian Railways (with presidential aide Igor Shuvalov also becoming a board member and another former deputy minister, Vladimir Yakunin, becoming CEO); presidential aide Viktor Ivanov became chairman of Aeroflot; Finance Minister Aleksei Kudrin took over the chairman's post at ALROSA; and other board positions were distributed to deputy ministers and other assistants. Former government officials may be transferred from government to run sensitive companies; former prime minister Sergei Kirienko went to head the Russian nuclear energy state company Rosatom, while former railways minister Vladimir Yakunin runs Russian Railways, which controls both passenger and freight service.

However, the presence of state officials on corporate boards "raises the question of whose interests are ultimately being served . . . influence flows in both directions, and it is unclear whether the board members will be loyal to the Kremlin or to the corporate interests they are charged with overseeing."[44] The financial imperative for a company to make profits and seek markets for its goods may often conflict with other foreign policy goals. It is a mistake to assume that Russian companies, particularly those that are state owned, are always being driven by the foreign policy imperatives laid down by the government.[45] Interrupting natural gas deliveries to Europe because the state gas company of Ukraine was unable to pay its bills or servicing contracts to build a nuclear power station in Iran might make excellent business sense—and provide jobs and income for Russia—but also produce diplomatic costs.[46] Further complicating matters, the state may sometimes subcontract some of its functions to state companies, "with all the conflicts of interest that such an arrangement entails."[47] In 2011, Medvedev took steps to try and separate political and business power by having ministers who chaired state companies or sat on corporate boards resign. Deputy Prime Minister Igor Sechin was required to resign from the board of directors of Rosneft. However, in 2012, when Sechin left the government, he was appointed to the board that oversees all of Russia's state energy holdings and reclaimed the chairmanship of Rosneft while remaining an advisor to Vladimir Putin. Sechin was also named to be the secretary of a presidential commission on energy, which supervises the energy industry in Russia.[48]

This tension is very clear when one sees that an industry of critical importance to the economic health of the country is the military–industrial complex. Some 20% of all manufacturing jobs in Russia are tied to the defense industry, and Russia is the world's second-largest exporter of weaponry (after the United States). Russia exported $13.2 billion in arms and weapons technologies in 2011, making this one of the country's most lucrative income streams. All Russia's arms exports are handled by Rosoboronexport; the revenues derived from weapons sales[49] have then been used to create a major holding company, Russian Technologies, to sustain Russian industrial and high-tech enterprises. Rosoboronexport, therefore, seeks to increase market share and sales of technology, following the advice of its director general, Sergei Chemezov, who has argued: "Our mineral deposits are finite. There are few remaining undiscovered gas and oil deposits in Russia. And they are non-renewable. But high tech, including for military use, can be refined without end, and its price is stable and predictable…"[50] But the imperative to increase sales may run up against the desire to preserve good relations with other states or secure Russia's own technological advantages in the defense sphere.

Beyond the state companies, Russia has a series of powerful financial-industrial conglomerates (see Table 2.5). While the power of the so-called "oligarchs" has diminished to some extent since the 1990s, private business figures still retain a great deal of influence and can bargain with the Kremlin in order to advance their corporate interests. In turn, the government may ask leading business figures to sponsor national projects. For instance, in 2010, Mikhail Prokhorov and his ONEXIM group invested more than $1.5 million to sponsor the Seliger Youth Festival on behalf of the Federal Youth Affairs Agency.[51] Prokhorov was also involved in attempts to create a new liberal/probusiness political party for the 2011 Duma elections. (Prokhorov also contested the 2012 presidential race as an independent candidate, polling a little under 8% of the vote.)

Business lobbying in contemporary Russia is often characterized as "elite exchange," meaning that "successful lobbyists gain influence by providing benefits to state officials."[52] Business interests are well represented in the political elite. A third of deputies to the State Duma are either senior figures in business or major stockholders in Russian companies, and the upper house, the Federation Council, is also understood to be a place for business to have its interests represented.[53] Private business in Russia has benefited from state action, such as legislation restricting foreign investment in "strategic sectors" or the use of Russia's financial surpluses to provide bailout funds to Russian businesses in the wake of the 2008–2009 global economic crisis.[54]

TABLE 2.5
Major Conglomerates, 2012

Name of Group	Key Sectors/Industries	Main Owners
Alfa Group	CTC Media, X5 Retail Group; Alfa Bank; Vimpelcom (telecom)	Mikhail Fridman, Pyotr Aven
Basic Element	RUSAL; EuroSibEnergo (power); GAZ group (automobiles); Glavstroi (construction); Ingosstrakh (insurance); Soyuz Bank	Oleg Deripaska
Interros	Norilsk Nickel; Prof-Media (media holdings); Rosbank (financial sector)	Vladimir Potanin
Metalloinvest	Owns a variety of mining and metal firms	Alisher Usmanov (who also chairs Gazprominvest and has significant media holdings and owns telecom giant MegaFon); Vasily Anisimov
ONEXIM Group	Polyus Gold, IFC-Bank, Soglassye Insurance Company, Renaissance Capital (investment firm)	Mikhail Prokhorov
Renova	RUSAL interests in regional energy producers, telecom services	Viktor Vekselberg
Sistema	Mobile TeleSystems; Moscow City Telephone Network; Moscow Bank for Reconstruction and Development; Bashneft Oil Company	Vladimir Yevtushenkov

Source: Compiled by authors.

The interests of the business community, therefore, can be critical drivers for foreign policy decisions. For instance, Russia's stated policies on nonproliferation matters and the promises made by the Foreign Ministry to Western governments, particularly the United States, about the export of sensitive technologies to the so-called "states of concern" repeatedly ran up against the vital interests of Russian enterprises. As a result: "Economic imperatives and sectional interests . . . impinged on traditional security considerations to a far greater degree than before, while understandings of security—including strategic security—were susceptible to increasingly diverse and self-interested interpretation."[55] Government agencies interested in promoting a particular "vector" in Russian foreign policy can easily form alliances with business interests in order to pursue a shared agenda. Alexei Arbatov concluded, "a poorly controlled conglomerate of agencies has merged with big business clans in order to develop their own financial/bureaucratic interests"[56]—and this development has fostered the competition and co-existence of multiple foreign policy vectors.

Companies may develop their own foreign policy vectors based on their commercial interests. Rosoboronexport, for instance, is a very strong supporter of close Russian ties with former Soviet republics in the Eurasian space. Esen Topoyev, an advisor to the firm, notes that the company's "preferred partners" are the states of "the Commonwealth of Independent States, which buy a large share of military products."[57] The Asia-Pacific region is where the bulk of the company's business is done, which makes the firm a supporter of a "balanced" foreign policy in the region, favoring neither China nor its opponents but seeking to preserve lucrative ties without having to choose sides. Preserving existing markets in Latin America, Africa, and the Middle East means that the company tends to support status quo regimes and is leery of endorsing Western-led efforts at regime change if it means a loss of markets for Russia. Finally, trying to develop a new security relationship with Europe that might open the door to Russian involvement in European defense procurement is a priority, since at present Rosoboronexport sales to Europe are minimal. Gazprom develops its own vectors for foreign policy—toward Europe, Asia, and the Middle East—based on markets for natural gas and the degree to which it can obtain a top price for its product, but also based on its existing infrastructure and deposits.

Any discussion of the business community would be incomplete without a survey of the energy sector. Russia is the world's largest non–OPEC producer of oil and second overall after Saudi Arabia, producing about 12% of the world's supply. It is the world's leader in natural gas, accounting for 22% of what the world consumes. In addition, much of the energy from other post–Soviet states, especially Kazakhstan and Turkmenistan, must cross Russian territory to reach global markets.[58] Russia also holds the world's second-largest coal reserves and has one of the world's most highly developed atomic energy industries; since 2007, the Russian government has consolidated various aspects of this industry under Rosatom's subsidiary Energoatom—combining the uranium-mining firm ARMZ, the uranium trader Tekhsnabexport, the nuclear fuel supplier TVEL, the nuclear power facilities constructor Atomenergomash, and the firm in charge of building nuclear plants outside of Russia, Atomstroiexport.

Natural gas production is concentrated in the hands of the state-controlled firm Gazprom, responsible for more than 90% of Russia's output; Novatek is the country's largest private natural gas producer. The oil sector in Russia is divided between private and public firms. Rosneft, the state-controlled company, acquired many of the assets of the formerly private YUKOS oil firm and in 2012 agreed to buy both of the private shareholders in the TNK-BP firm, Russia's third-largest oil company, which was a 50/50 partnership between a group of Russian private businesses and the international private oil company BP. Gazprom, via its oil subsidiary Gazprom-Neft, acquired the formerly private Sibneft firm. Private firms include LUKoil and Surgutneftegaz. The republic of Tatarstan holds a controlling interest in Tatneft.[59]

Russia is not only energy independent but is also a major supplier of energy to the rest of the world, exporting hydrocarbons to Europe and Asia and assisting a number of developing countries in building nuclear power plants or harnessing their own energy reserves. The revenues that the energy trade have accrued to the Russian state—from both its holdings in energy companies and taxes on exports (which brought in some $60 billion in 2009)—have fueled Russia's recovery from the Soviet collapse. Gazprom alone is responsible for generating 10% of Russia's current GDP. This has led many observers to conclude that "energy is the decisive driver of Russian foreign and domestic policy."[60] Yet there is no unified "energy team," because control of the major energy firms, particularly Gazprom and Rosneft, is divided among different political and business figures. Despite the belief in Western circles that the Russian government wields an "energy weapon," Steven Woehrel concluded in 2009, "It is not completely clear whether the pursuit of Russian foreign policy objectives is the primary explanation for the actions of its energy firms."[61] Moreover, different energy companies have their own competing "vectors" in terms of their major foreign partners, market partners, or areas of operation. Traditionally, Gazprom has been associated with the "modernizing" factions around Dmitry Medvedev and has looked to Europe as Russia's critical partner; Rosneft, associated with the "*siloviki*" (those associated with the security services) around the former deputy prime minister (and current Rosneft Chairman) Igor Sechin, has leaned towards stronger ties with Asia.[62] Other firms have concentrated on Russia's ties with its immediate neighbors in Eurasia or with the Middle East.

In addition, by distributing shares in major energy projects to a mix of foreign companies, the Russian government can balance competing foreign policy imperatives—as well as competing domestic interests—as an analysis of the Sakhalin-1 and Sakhalin-2 projects in the Russian Far East shows (see Table 2.7). Both of Russia's major firms, as well as different U.S., European, Japanese, and Indian firms, are stakeholders.

Business figures are also sometimes tapped to serve as official or unofficial foreign policy envoys. Sechin, although now only the Chairman of Rosneft, still

TABLE 2.6
Major Russian Energy Companies, 2012

Company	Private/State	Chairman	Key Foreign Partners/Areas of Operation
Gazprom	State controlled	Viktor Zubkov, a former deputy prime minister (former chairman was Dmitry Medvedev, now president of Russia)	Supplies Europe with 25% of its natural gas needs. Key partners include Total (France), E.ON Ruhrgas (Germany). BASF/Wintershall (Germany).
LUKoil	Private	Vagit Alekperov	Key partner: Conoco Phillips (U.S.). Areas of operation: CIS, Middle East, Latin America.
Novatek	Private	Alexander Natalenko	Total (France)
Rosneft[63]	State controlled	Igor Sechin, former deputy prime minister	BP (Britain), Petronas (Malaysia), China National Petroleum Company, Exxon-Mobil (U.S.).
Surgutneftegaz	Private	Vladimir Bogdanov	CIS and Eastern Europe

Source: Compiled by authors.

TABLE 2.7
Shareholders of Sakhalin-1 and Sakhalin-2

Sakhalin-1 Shareholders (Exxon Neftegas)	Sakhalin-2 Shareholders (Sakhalin Energy)
Exxon-Mobil (U.S.) 30%	Gazprom 50%
Sakhalin Oil and Gas Development Co. 30% (Japan)	Shell 27.5% (British/Dutch)
	Mitsui 12.5% (Japan)
ONGC Videsh (India) 20%	Mitsubishi 10% (Japan)
Rosneft 20%	

Sources: Exxon Neftegas Limited (http://www.sakhalin-1.com/Sakhalin/Russia-English/Upstream/about_consortium.aspx) and Shell Global (http://www.shell.com/global/aboutshell/major-projects-2/sakhalin/overview.html).

serves as the point man for Russia's relations with a number of states, notably Venezuela, and Miller, the Chairman of Gazprom, is also the special representative of the Russian president to gas-exporting countries.

THE NONGOVERNMENTAL ORGANIZATIONS

After the release of the 2000 Foreign Policy Concept, Foreign Minister Igor Ivanov noted that the ministry had solicited input not only from the government but also from "prominent social figures, diplomats and academics" in attempting to determine "what the role and place of our nation in the world should be."[64] Civil society—the nongovernmental sector—makes its voice heard in the foreign policy debate. Although there are concerns about freedom of the media in contemporary Russia and whether the state has undue influence over the press, foreign policy appears to be one area in which the Kremlin has not precluded a lively and, at times, rambunctious debate.[65]

Alongside the traditional network of academic institutes associated with the Academy of Sciences, the universities, and institutions of higher learning like the Moscow State Institute for International Relations (MGIMO), new think tanks on the American model have arisen. The most prominent of these has been the Council on Foreign and Defense Policy, set up in 1992. This organization brings together academics, journalists, business executives, and formal civil servants and positions itself as an advisory body to the government and the political elite. The Council was most influential in the Yeltsin administration, when it helped to push for the removal of Foreign Minister Andrei Kozyrev in 1996, but it still has the ability to bring its research and proposals to bear in subsequent administrations. While the Council's policy proposals may not be accepted by the government, it still helps to shape thinking.[66] Alongside the "first wave" of post–Soviet think tanks are newer institutions, such as the Institute for Contemporary Development (INSOR), which is close to president Dmitry Medvedev and his circle of advisors. Igor Yurgens, INSOR's chairman, explained the role of his institution (and by extension, other think tanks) as being

> to closely cooperate with the president's Administration and the Foreign Ministry of Russia, thus helping intellectually polish the priorities already set by the country's leadership and look into already needed yet still insufficiently studied areas and, "blank spots," as it were. This work should naturally result in concrete recommendations.[67]

Open lobbies are also beginning to take shape. For instance, the Armenian-Russian diaspora—numbering some 1.5 million people and organized into groups like the Union of Armenians in Russia—attempts to lobby for the "Armenian vector" in Russian foreign policy—pitted against a pro-Azerbaijan lobby, undertaken by some of the major energy firms such as LUKoil and Gazprom.[68]

The largest nongovernmental organization in Russia today remains the Russian Orthodox Church of the Moscow Patriarchate. The Church has become an important source of "soft power" for Russia in the world. It is a major advocate for the consolidation of political and economic ties between Russia and her immediate neighbors and for Eurasian integration. It works to promote Russian culture around the world. Intellectually, the Russian Orthodox Church has argued against the equation of Western values with universal norms, favoring instead a "dialogue of civilizations," and in that context has been important in Russia's outreach to the Islamic world.[69] The Church also calls for the development of a Russian–Slavic–Eurasian cultural space that would act as a brake against the influences of Western and specifically American culture and values, under the rubric of the "Russian World" (*Russkii Mir*).[70] Elements within the Russian Orthodox Church, along with sympathetic groups in both military circles and the business community, played a key role in shaping the "Russian Doctrine" project in 2007, which, in foreign policy terms, calls for Russia to organize and lead a bloc of "Eastern" (e.g. non–Western) countries to resist an American-led and -influenced process of globalization, in part calling for much closer political and economic relations with China, India, Iran, the Arab world, and the developing world.[71]

Sometimes the Church undertakes diplomatic activity on its own recognizance. For instance, an ongoing dialogue between the Russian and Georgian Orthodox Churches has attempted to repair the breach in Russian–Georgian relations. Patriarch Kirill I also undertook a mission to Syria in late 2011 as clashes between pro- and antigovernment forces accelerated in an effort to show support for the regime in Damascus and for the Orthodox Church in Syria. In an effort to help coordinate the efforts of church and state, the Russian Orthodox

Church has participated since 2003 in a joint working group on foreign policy with the Ministry of Foreign Affairs; Deputy Foreign Minister Grigory Karasin was appointed as the liaison between the ministry and the Church. Foreign Minister Sergei Lavrov expressed his hopes that the "collaboration between the Ministry of Foreign Affairs and the Russian Orthodox Church will continue to be fruitful and dynamic."[72] In turn, the late Patriarch Alexy II stressed that the Church "has a well developed relationship with the foreign policy agency of the Russian state."[73] As a result, the Church may lobby the Russian government for support of its interests overseas. For instance, during the 1990s, the Duma slapped economic sanctions on Estonia because the Estonian government would not register the local branch of the Russian Orthodox Church, and the Patriarchate lobbied for support to preserve its properties and standing in other former Soviet republics, including Ukraine, Latvia, and Moldova. Such interventions on behalf of the Moscow Patriarchate complicated the Kremlin's relations with other countries.[74] But this helps to show how Russian state interests can be subordinated to or affected by the lobbying efforts of nonstate actors.

What this brief survey illustrates is that many different actors in Russian foreign policy have their own particular visions of Russia's national interests. In commenting about foreign policy during the Putin administration, journalist Gregory Feifer concluded, "[N]o clear group influences foreign policy."[75] And all of these groups have input; as Nikolai Patrushev observed during a cabinet meeting when the National Security Strategy was unveiled in 2009, input for the document was solicited across the range of government, including both the prime ministerial and presidential administrations and from regional governments as well as nongovernment experts and representatives of the business community.[76] In addition, different actors beyond the foreign ministry—other government agencies and even nongovernmental actors—attempt to acquire their own capabilities for running their own foreign and defense policies.[77]

RUSSIAN NATIONAL SECURITY DECISION MAKING

In consolidated electoral democracies, there is a relatively transparent mechanism for how decisions are made and how competing (and contradictory) interests are balanced. In more closed political systems, how this occurs is much less clear.

The Russian system is often considered to be a hybrid between democratic and autocratic forms of governance (described as "managed pluralism"[78] or "soft authoritarianism"). In the present Russian system, the president is formally in charge and sits at the apex of the policymaking pyramid, but he is often a reconciler and balancer of diverging interests rather than being in a position to implement his autocratic will through the ranks of the bureaucracy. Ever since the

Yeltsin years, there have been a series of blocs, factions, or clans present in the executive branch, each representing distinct interests and having their own bases for power and authority,[79] with the president serving as the chief arbiter. After Putin stepped down in 2008, the situation was muddied by the emergence of two coequal power centers around the president (Dmitry Medvedev) and the prime minister (Vladimir Putin). This led analyst Kirill Rogov to argue that Russia of the Medvedev-Putin diarchy had in fact "at least three Governments"—each grouped around different political-economic factions (sometimes referred to as the Kremlin "clans") and with different institutional power bases.[80] At the center, the president and prime minister must find policy approaches that address the needs and concerns of these different blocs in order to avoid any sort of destructive rivalries that pull apart the entire governing structure. This is usually done by ensuring that the interests of the different factions are all accommodated to some extent.[81] However, this is rarely a transparent process. Interest groups are not organized in open political parties that jostle for influence among the electorate. Instead, post–Soviet Russian politics are defined by the competition and cooperation among various factions or "clans" for control of the executive branch.[82] These clans consist of leading government figures, presidential or prime ministerial aides, and businessmen. Russian policy making remains defined by its opaque nature. This leads observers to try and calculate shifts in the balance of power between the presidential and the prime ministerial teams, especially if there is the development of a consensus position that forms the basis for a foreign policy change.[83] The return of Putin to the presidency diminished but did not eliminate the blocs around Medvedev, and the balance of power between the factions remains important for trying to understand Russian foreign policy. Most decisions are still the result of compromises that are brokered between the interests of different clans.[84]

There are said to be up to 10 major Kremlin factions, grouped around different leaders and linked with competing financial-industrial groups, which in turn may coalesce into several larger coalitions.[85] These groups are not well defined but are fluid in their membership and goals; people are grouped together based on a disparate number of factors including ideology, shared business interests, and past professional associations. In the mid-1990s, U.S. diplomat Thomas Graham identified five major Kremlin factions: (1) the energy faction based around Gazprom and controlled by then-prime minister Viktor Chernomyrdin; (2) an alliance of emerging private oligarchs linked with Anatoly Chubais, who handled privatization for the Yeltsin administration; (3) security interests grouped around Alexander V. Korzhakov, a former KGB general who headed the presidential protective service; (4) the business and political interests headed by Yuri Luzhkov, the mayor of Moscow[86]; and (5) another faction, known as the

Family, emerged, consisting of president Yeltsin's relatives and their backers in government and business. During the Putin years, clans dissolved and reformed, as the new president fired senior government officials and cracked down on Yeltsin-era oligarchs (most notably Boris Berezovsky, Vladimir Gusinsky, and Mikhail Khodorkovsky) and turned to people whom he had served with in the KGB and the security services and in the St. Petersburg city administration (Putin was a vice mayor of the city from 1991–1996) to take over key positions.

By the end of the first Putin administration, the factions had stabilized (in a system a number of Russia experts called Kremlin, Inc.; see Table 2.8), and most observers concluded that there were two broad camps within the Russian establishment. One was composed of the security services group and its allies, now nicknamed the *siloviki* (from the word *sila*, for power, referring to their service in the "power" agencies like intelligence, internal security, or defense).[87] The others were the modernizers, often lawyers or economists, and their allies in the business

TABLE 2.8
Key Political-Economic Figures in the Kremlin, October 2007

Official	Government Position	Economic Position
Dmitry Medvedev	Deputy prime minister	Chairman of Gazprom
Igor Sechin	Deputy chief of the presidential administration	Chairman of Rosneft; chairman of United Shipbuilding
Sergei Ivanov	Deputy prime minister (and former defense minister)	Chairman of United Aircraft Corporation
Viktor Ivanov	Presidential aide	Chairman, Almaz-Antei (defense contractor); chairman, Aeroflot (national airlines)
Sergei Naryshkin	Deputy prime minister	Chairman, Channel One television network; deputy chairman, Rosneft
Vladimir Yakunin	Former railways minister	Chairman of Russian Railways, the second-largest company in Russia after Gazprom
Sergei Chemezov	Member of the State Military-Industrial Commission	General director of Rosoboronexport; chairman of AvtoVAZ (largest automobile manufacturer) and VSMPO-Avisma (a major global supplier of titanium)

Source: Compiled by authors.

community, sometimes referred to by outsiders as the *civiliki* (a play on the term for civil society) to contrast them with the *siloviki*, whose core was the St. Petersburg group.[88] Generally, these two coalitions are understood to be headed by Igor Sechin, a presidential aide and then a deputy prime minister, for the former, and then-deputy prime minister and then-president Dmitry Medvedev, with other factions leaning to one or the other or trying to remain neutral, but all attempting, as Russian political scientist Dmitry Oreshkin concluded, to "remain in the upper echelons" of government and business.[89]

The challenge has been to devise a governing system that, in Brian Whitmore's observation, "appeals to both the siloviki and civiliki factions of the elite."[90] In contrast to the Yeltsin administration, with its zero-sum struggles between groups, Putin's role, first as president, then as prime minister, has been, as Whitmore concludes, "to manage the personal, political, and commercial conflicts among its members, and preventing any one faction in the ruling elite from becoming too powerful."[91]

The 2008 presidential elections led to some reshuffling; in becoming president, Medvedev formally gave up the chairmanship of Gazprom, and Sechin moved into the cabinet as a deputy prime minister, but the overall balance of power was preserved. After the 2012 elections, many of those in the prime ministerial and presidential administrations swapped places to follow Putin or Medvedev in their new positions. The present "dual-key" system in place—with a series of overlapping presidential and prime ministerial appointments—means that a type of "checks and balances" has been set in place in the Kremlin. It ensures that there is a "continuous tension between competing clans and institutions."[92] Each of the factions has its people distributed through the bureaucracy and beyond—in the Duma, the media, and the business elite[93]—and this prevents any one individual or group associated with a particular foreign policy interest from imposing that choice on the Russian state to the detriment of others. On the other hand, this often leads to compromises that do not seem to result from a coherent policy approach. For instance, in June 2010, U.S. Secretary of Defense Robert Gates, in assessing Russia's foreign policy on Iran, labeled it "schizophrenic," pointing out that one part of the Russian foreign policy establishment was acting as if Iran's nuclear program were a threat, while other parts continued to pursue commercial deals in the oil and gas sector or looked for ways to wall off Russia's military-defense cooperation with Iran from the purview of international sanctions.[94] But this was an excellent example of how Russia has not a singular foreign policy but multiple foreign policies.[95]

Imposing order and a single line in foreign policy is difficult, because "for the sake of political stability, power must be divided among the elite groups with different preferences."[96] The tugs exerted on the policy process by competing clan interests make it very difficult for a central authority to impose a singular vision on Russian foreign policy. Policy documents such as the *Foreign Policy Concept* are drafted using general formulations, since, as Bobo Lo observed, "vagueness of definition was a means of accommodating a wide spectrum of opinion" within the government without committing the country to any one policy line.[97] Efforts in the past to try and create coordinating mechanisms have run into trouble, usually because the establishment of interagency mechanisms such as the Security Council has "generated further confusion" in the policy process, with a plethora of competing agencies and institutions claiming precedence.[98] In order to preserve some degree of coherence in Russia's relations with other key states, the government has sometimes tried to use a mechanism such as an intergovernmental commission, chaired by a senior member of the government, as a way to coordinate different sectors and produce some degree of policy coherence. (Governmental commissions will have as members ministers and deputy ministers; staff from the presidential and prime ministerial administrations; and representatives from state agencies. In addition, they may also have members drawn from the Duma, regional governments, the business community, and civil society.[99]) However, as Mikhail Tsypkin concludes, "Russia's domestic political situation has yet to achieve a degree of stability and continuity sufficient to provide the basis for a consistent, predictable and rational national security policy."[100] This led Dmitry Badovsky, the assistant director of the Institute of Social Systems, to make the following observations about the coherence of the policy process: "This state of affairs cannot help but affect the efficiency and consistency of the machinery of state. Sparks are flying with increased frequency in the relationships between the presidential administration, the White House [seat of the Russian government], the State Duma, the ministries, and among all sorts of interest groups."[101] As a result, the attempts by the Kremlin leadership to balance and reconcile competing Russian foreign policies will continue to produce "mixed signals" and a "zig-zag" approach.[102] It also opens up the prospect that there will be significant delays in making any final decisions on an issue, as well as the possibility of policy reversals.[103]

The Russian government is also plagued with difficulties in translating from strategy to action, which also complicates any analysis of its foreign policy. Nothing illustrates the *prikaz* nature of foreign policy more than the ability of competing government institutions to hold up, alter, or stall instructions that may conflict or damage the fundamental interests of the institution in question, as the following analysis of Russian decision making illustrates:

> Probably the most significant complaint made by President Dmitry Medvedev at a meeting devoted to the implementation of his instructions concerned the implementation of presidential directives by the government.

"The situation involving the implementation of instructions is rather complex," and "implementation discipline is poor" . . . [P]residential aide Konstantin Chuichenko, the head of the Chief Oversight Administration, cited the Energy Ministry, the Regional Development Ministry and the Defense Ministry as being at the bottom of the list in terms of implementing Kremlin instructions. . . . Oftentimes, delays and disagreements over the implementation of presidential instructions occur because the prime minister gets involved in dealing with the substance of a problem, or because there is "competition over issues" between branches of government and politicians. . . . Harmonizing "overlapping" instructions requires exceptional efforts on the part of the White House and Kremlin staffs. Since late 2009, this has concerned a whole range of issues, from the development of innovation to the reform of corporate law, given that the implementation of a substantial share of the instructions issued by both the president and the prime minister is supposed to be integrated into the government's "routine" procedures—for example, into the budgetary process. For their part, government agencies often regard "competition over issues" between the government and the president as a way to uphold their own positions in substantive disputes.[104]

The result, as Arbatov observed, is that policy is developed "on the basis of compromise between different groups."[105]

THE PRINCIPAL VECTORS

Any credible Russian foreign policy must match "its genuine strategic interests and the goals of economic and social development,"[106] but given Russia's global interests, there must be a set of priorities that define which areas of the world are most critical.

There have been two fundamental debates over Russian foreign policy since the collapse of the Soviet Union. The first is whether Russia's national interests are better served by pursuing closer ties and ultimate integration into a Euro-Atlantic world led by the United States or whether Russia ought to seek friends and partners to hedge and even constrain the exercise of U.S. power around the globe. The second is the extent to which Russia must promote the reintegration of the Eurasian space—and whether, in so doing, it must actively block the expansion of the political and economic influence of other major powers in this part of the world in order to secure Russian interests.[107]

In the first years following the disintegration of the Soviet Union, the Boris Yeltsin administration, in the analysis of Igor Ivanov, overwhelmingly concentrated its foreign policy efforts on "accelerated integration into the Euro-Atlantic structure" (and, some have argued, to the detriment of Russia's relations with other parts of the world[108]), which manifested itself in a "desire to join the ranks of the West as quickly as possible, even if to the detriment of Russia's real interests."[109] In 1992, Foreign Minister Andrei Kozyrev announced that the "developed countries of the West are Russia's natural allies"[110] and that Russian foreign policy would focus primarily on these nations, particularly the United States, France, the UK, and Germany. While not completely excluded, other areas of the world—the Eurasian space, the Far East, South Asia, the Middle East, and certainly Africa and Latin America—were part of the "second echelon" of Russian foreign policy interests.[111] By the early 2000s, however, Russian diplomacy focused on widening

> its circle of friends and partners in the world . . . The unique geopolitical position of our country—not to mention the realities of world politics and economics—dictate the necessity for Russia to cultivate cooperation equally with nations to our West, East, North and South.[112]

This leads us to the concept of vectors. With which powers should Russia most closely align in order to best advance its national interests?

The clash in the 1990s between Atlanticists and Eurasianists, the theory of multipolarity proposed by Foreign Minister (and then-Prime Minister) Yevgeny Primakov, the arguments in the Putin administration over whether to focus on a Western versus an Eastern vector,[113] the debate over being a Western status quo power or working with rising Southern and Eastern powers to shape a new global architecture[114]—all of these, in turn, have shaped the arguments for different vectors for Russian foreign policy.[115] Many would identify the principal vectors as follows:

- Commonwealth of Independent States/Eurasian: Russia's relations with her immediate neighbors, the other states of the former Soviet Union.

- Western/Atlantic: Russia's primary focus should be on relations with the United States and in joining the Western club of nations under U.S. leadership.

- European: Russia should focus on deepening its historic, economic, and security ties with the nations of Europe and, in turn, encourage the emergence of a Europe that is less tightly bound to the United States. Within this vector there can be preferences—for privileging relations with Germany, with France, with Italy, or with the states of Eastern Europe.

- China: Advocates of a close strategic partnership with Beijing argue this affords the best possibility to protect and enhance Russia's national interests.

A larger Asia-Pacific vector can either encompass the strategic partnership with China or be structured to provide some degree of balance to the relationship with Beijing.

- The Non-Western: If Russia will not be accepted as a full member of the Western world, its interests lie in helping to shape a coalition of rising non-Western powers in the Middle East, South Asia, Africa, and Latin America to counterbalance both the Euro-Atlantic West and an emerging China.

Those who advocate for a particular vector in foreign policy might do so for a variety of reasons, including ideological preferences, shared cultural or historical experiences, business opportunities, or security considerations. Different groups may coalesce around support for the same factor based on quite different motivations. For instance, support for pursuing closer integration with the Euro-Atlantic world initially came from intellectuals and political movements who, on the basis of their ideological predispositions, view Russia as part of the Western world. But the mainstay of support for this vector is no longer a group of pro-Western liberals in politics but powerful economic interest groups with tangible interests in pursuing better ties.[116] Support for closer ties between Iran and Russia (and resistance to applying greater sanctions against Tehran for its nuclear program) has come from a variety of interest groups, including the industries and companies that benefit from the business that is generated with Iran; those in the foreign policy and national security communities who view Iran as an "irritant" to the United States that limits Washington's ability to interfere in the Eurasian space or who see ties to Iran as a way to react to the expansion of NATO eastward; and even the Moscow Patriarchate, which has stressed the cultural and theological links between Orthodox Christianity and Islam and signaled its preference for dialogue over confrontation.[117]

Do the vectors drive the interests of the sectors, or is it the other way around? Some sectors embrace particular vectors out of necessity. The arms industry, for instance, often finds that its best customers are those countries—in Asia, the Middle East, and Latin America—that have poor relations with the United States or are seeking to acquire capabilities that reduce America's freedom of maneuver. Since the United States and the principal countries of Europe are not going to be major purchasers of Russian weaponry or investors in the country's military-industrial complex, it is not surprising that the arms industry would support the non-Western vectors and be hesitant to abandon potentially lucrative deals with countries like Iran or Venezuela in order for Russia to improve ties with the United States. Given the importance of the defense industry to the overall health of the Russian economy, it would be difficult for this sector to support abandoning a key customer unless there were other opportunities that could provide an alternative market.[118] Sometimes a vector may be embraced because of situational factors; the Russian Navy's interest in possible bases in Latin America surged after the 2008 Russian–Georgian war, after the United States deployed warships to the Black Sea. Some sectors are quite flexible and can shift their vectors; the growing demand for nonhydrocarbon-based energy solutions for electricity generation means that Russia's nuclear and hydroelectric industries find customers throughout the world and can more easily shift in response to the foreign policy demands of other sectors.

Established interests, as reflected in the various Kremlin clans, do have preferred vectors. For many of the *civiliki* groups, particularly those grouped around the natural gas monopoly Gazprom, which has close business and political ties to the key countries of Europe, "Germany and Continental Europe are considered as the natural partners and allies of Russia."[119] For some of the *siloviki*, beginning with former Deputy Prime Minister Igor Sechin and encompassing some of the natural resource firms and defense industries, "Russia is a natural partner for China."[120] Drawing on the work of Andrey Tsygankov[121] and Stephen White,[122] we can argue for the existence of several different foreign policy schools of thought:

- Liberals/Westernizers, the continuing heirs to the Atlanticist school, who argue for Russia's complete integration into the Euro-Atlantic world and the adoption of Euro-American norms of governance

- Pragmatic Westernizers, those who see Russia's future as linked to the West but want to negotiate Russia's entrance on its own terms

- Nationalists/Eurasians, who see Russia as the core of a distinct Eurasian civilization and economic space that ought to attain equidistance from the European, Middle Eastern, and Asian worlds

- Sinophiles, who see China's rise as a model for Russia to emulate and who argue for a Sino-Russian condominium in Eurasia

- Pragmatic Easternizers, who see Asia as the future for Russia but, like their Pragmatic Westernizer counterparts, want Russia to control the interaction, not simply be absorbed into China's orbit

- Penultimate Pragmatists, who have no particular predisposition to any given vector but support any and all directions which are seen as most beneficial to Russian interests

None of these schools are distinct, clear parties, although one can detect preferences within Russia's business community and political parties for different schools of thought. It also means that coalitions can form to prevent any one vector from becoming predominant. For instance, those proponents of a much closer relationship with China might find that both Liberal and Pragmatic Westernizers might ally to block measures and gain support from Eurasians concerned about the rise of China's influence in Central Asia and even from Pragmatic Easternizers who would be concerned about losing leverage vis-à-vis China. On the other hand, those who want a much closer relationship with the United States might find a similar situation—outright opposition from Sinophiles and Nationalists/Eurasians, as well as concerns expressed from the "pragmatic camps."[123]

At the same time, vectors need not be mutually exclusive; they can be combined and balanced as part of a larger foreign policy strategy. Indeed, the Putin administration championed what has been termed a "multidirectional balanced external strategy."[124] For instance, a Western-Eurasian vector would combine the pursuit of greater integration of the Eurasian space around Russia with forging a closer partnership with the United States as a strategy of creating a broad Euro-Atlantic coalition to balance against China and the Islamic world. Russia's efforts to develop the BRIC (Brazil-Russia-India-China) coalition reflect an attempt to forge a closer relationship with China but avoid strategic dependence on Beijing, as well as a desire to counter the continued economic and political dominance of the Euro-Atlantic bloc in world affairs. Nor, despite ideological affinities for one vector over another, are the various business and political factions prepared to ignore possible opportunities wherever they may arise. Even though Sechin has displayed a notable China "tilt" in how he has led Rosneft (securing long-term loans from the China Development Bank in return for guaranteeing oil deliveries to China and considering the inclusion of Chinese firms in the development of the Arctic), he has also pursued new strategic alliances with Western firms such as BP, Statoil, and Exxon-Mobil with the latter part of his effort to promote closer ties with the United States. In turn, Gazprom, although still committed to its traditional markets in Europe, is also looking at ways to increase its cooperation with the China National Petroleum Company to facilitate greater Russian supplies of natural gas to Asian markets.

Trying to balance competing vectors and sectors can be difficult. In recent years, the Kremlin has had to find ways to balance the "reset" with the United States while pursuing a strategic partnership with China and keeping a close tie with Europe but also diversifying Russia's options to encompass more of the non–Western world. Rarely does the Russian government ever want to completely close off a vector, so the balancing act is often a search for a compromise solution. For instance, to preserve relations with the United States and Western Europe, the Russian government instituted stronger export controls for so-called "dual-use" technologies, but, in order to continue to keep market share in other parts of the world, enforced such regulations in a lax fashion or found ways to generate loopholes to permit Russian industries to continue to sell their products.[125]

All of this produces considerable debate and discussion about Russian foreign policy both within and outside of government, as Foreign Minister Lavrov has indicated.[126] It also helps to explain why "Moscow's conduct of foreign affairs" has been "so uneven" and why "an elite consensus, no matter how rough, [has] failed to emerge."[127]

NOTES

1. David Brooks, "The Analytic Mode," *New York Times,* December 4, 2009, A35, at http://www.nytimes.com/2009/12/04/opinion/04brooks.html.

2. Quoted in Bridget Kendall, "Will Power Shift from the Kremlin?," *BBC News,* May 6, 2008, at http://news.bbc.co.uk/2/hi/europe/7273637.stm.

3. Quoted in "Putin to lead United Russia party," *BBC News,* April 15, 2008, at http://news.bbc.co.uk/2/hi/europe/7347124.stm.

4. Dimitri K. Simes and Paul J. Saunders, "The Kremlin Begs to Differ," *National Interest* (November/December 2009), at http://www.nationalinterest.org/Article.aspx?id=22344.

5. For instance, the president, not the prime minister, now appoints the heads of the major state companies. See "What the Papers Say," *Moscow Times,* August 23, 2012, at http://www.themoscowtimes.com/news/article/what-the-papers-say-aug-22-2012/466970.html.

6. Neil Malcolm and Alex Pravda, "Democratization and Russian foreign policy," *International Affairs* 72, no. 3 (1996): 539.

7. Ibid., 544.

8. See, for instance, "Putin: State Duma reaction to Magnitsky Law appropriate," *RAPSI,* December 20, 2012, at http://rapsinews.com/legislation_news/20121220/265852161.html.

9. Dimitri K. Simes, "Russia's Crisis, America's Complicity," *Russia in the National Interest,* ed. Nikolas K. Gvosdev (New Brunswick, NJ: Transaction Press, 2003), 198, 201.

10. See, for instance, Thomas F. Remington, "Majorities without Mandates: The Russian Federation Council since 2000," *Europe-Asia Studies* 55, no. 5 (2008): 667–691; Darrell Slider, "How United is United Russia? Regional Sources of Intra-party Conflict," *Journal of Communist Studies and Transition Politics* 26, no. 2 (June 2010): 257–275; Thomas F. Remington, "Patronage and Power: Russia's Dominant Party Regime," *Politische Vierteljahresschrift* 49, no. 2 (June 2008): 213–228.

11. Sarah Whitmore, "Parliamentary Oversight in Putin's Neo-patrimonial State: Watchdogs or Show-dogs?" *Europe-Asia Studies* 62, no. 6 (August 2010): 1008.

12. Stephen White, "Elite Opinion and Foreign Policy in Post–Communist Russia," *Perspectives on European Politics and Society* 8, no. 2 (2007): 148.

13. Vladimir Shveitser, "Power and Parties in Post-Soviet Russia," *Russia in Global Affairs,* 2, April-June 2009, at http://eng.globalaffairs.ru/number/n_13027; Leon Aron,

"The Duma Election," *AEI Russian Outlook,* Winter 2004, at http://www.aei.org/article/foreign-and-defense-policy/regional/europe/the-duma-election/.

14. Jeffrey Mankoff, "Russian Foreign Policy and the United States After Putin," *Problems of Post–Communism* 56, no. 4 (July/August 2008): esp. 46–47.

15. An addendum to decree 724 (issued May 12, 2008) reaffirms that the Minister of Foreign Affairs, along with the Defense Minister and the heads of the intelligence agencies, is to be appointed by the president, not the prime minister.

16. Robert H. Donaldson and Joseph L. Nogee, *The Foreign Policy of Russia: Changing Systems, Enduring Interests,* 2nd edition (Armonk, NY: M.E. Sharpe, 2009), 134–136.

17. Biographical sketches are available at the website of the Ministry of Foreign Affairs at http://www.mid.ru/bul_ns_en.nsf/kartaflat/en03.02.

18. Malcolm and Pravda, 545–46, 550.

19. "Working meeting with Konstantin Kosachev," website of the President of Russia, March 5, 2012, at http://eng.kremlin.ru/transcripts/3513.

20. The secretary of the Security Council is usually considered by other governments to be the equivalent of the U.S. national security advisor. In 2010, for instance, Nikolai Patrushev, the secretary of the Security Council, engaged with his counterparts, including India's national security advisor Shiv Shankar Menon and the Chinese equivalent of an NSA, Dai Binguuo. Cf. Siddharth Varadarajan, "BRIC, IBSA nations not keen on Iran sanctions," *The Hindu,* April 18, 2010, at http://www.hindu.com/2010/04/18/stories/2010041863681200.htm.

21. Keir Giles, "Russia's National Security Strategy to 2020," Russian Review Series of the NATO Defense College, June 2009, 4. These reviews are archived at http://www.ndc.nato.int/research/series.php?icode=9. See also the Decree of the President of the Russian Federation no. 537, May 12, 2009, archived at http://www.scrf.gov.ru/news/436.html.

22. Aleksandr Golts, "Tikhii Perevorot," *Ezhednevnii Zhurnal,* May 12, 2011, at http://www.ej.ru/?a=note&id=11018.

23. "Alexander Osipovich, "General James Jones assures Russia at nuclear talks," *Agence France Press,* October 29, 2009.

24. Brian Whitmore, "Russia: Medvedev, Putin Launch 'Two-Headed' Foreign Policy—But Who's Winning?" *Radio Free Europe/Radio Liberty,* June 6, 2008, at http://www.rferl.org/content/article/1144564.html.

25. "Azarov Leaves for Russia To Meet With Putin," *Ukrainian News Agency,* June 28, 2010, at http://un.ua/eng/article/272829.html.

26. Dan Peleschuk, "Putin's new team brings no changes?" *Russia Beyond the Headlines,* May 23, 2012, at http://rbth.ru/articles/2012/05/23/putins_new_team_brings_no_changes_15692.html.

27. Vytautas Sirijos Gira, "Who Will Determine Further Scenarios of Russia's Political and Economic Development?" *Lithuanian Foreign Policy Review* 21 (2008): 167.

28. Iulia Shevchenko, *The Central Government of Russia: From Gorbachev to Putin* (Aldershot, Hants: Ashgate Publishing Ltd, 2004), 176.

29. See Ol'ga Kryshtanovskaya and Stephen White, "Inside the Putin Court: A Research Note," *Europe-Asia Studies* 57, no. 7 (November 2005): esp. 1066–1069.

30. Whitmore, op. cit.

31. A breakdown of responsibilities is provided at the official site of the Russian government at http://www.government.ru/eng/gov/activity/.

32. "Russian Press—Behind the Headlines, May 16," *RIA Novosti,* May 16, 2012, at http://en.ria.ru/papers/20120516/173488353.html.

33. Igor S. Ivanov, *The New Russian Diplomacy* (Washington, DC: The Nixon Center and Brookings Institution Press, 2002), 151.

34. "Kadyrov Visits United Arab Emirates," *Moscow Times,* June 22, 2010, at http://www.themoscowtimes.com/news/article/kadyrov-visits-united-arab-emirates/408791.html.

35. See the interview with Orenburg Governor Alexey Chernyshev, Arnur Rakhymbekov, "Border does not separate us," KAZINFORM, September 1, 2009, at http://www.inform.kz/articleeng?select=ShowArticle&id=2194808.

36. Jeanne Lorraine Wilson, *Strategic Partners: Russian–Chinese Relations in the Post–Soviet Era* (Armonk, NY: M.E. Sharpe, 2004), 235.

37. For instance, on March 20, 2012, Vladimir Torpolov, a member of the Federation Council's Foreign Affairs Committee, and the representative of the Komi Republic (and the former chief executive of Komi from 2002 to 2010) visited the United States to promote investment in his region's timber and mining industries.

38. There is remarkable "message discipline" from the Russian government on this matter: that the conduct of foreign policy is subordinated to the need to ensure continued economic growth and development. This was the principal theme enunciated by outgoing president Vladimir Putin's spokesman Dmitry Peskov during his appearance at the Nixon Center on February 20, 2008 (transcript available via Federal News Service), and then reiterated by president-elect Dmitry Medvedev in his March 25, 2008, interview with the *Financial Times.*

39. Ian Bremmer, *The End of the Free Market: Who Wins the War between States and Corporations?* (New York: Portfolio, 2010), 43.

40. Ibid., 166.

41. Kalman Kalotay, "How to explain the foreign expansion of Russian firms," *Journal of Financial Transformation* 24 (2008): 58.

42. Andrei P. Tsygankov, "If Not By Tanks, then by Banks? The Role of Soft Power in Putin's Foreign Policy," *Europe-Asia Studies* 58, no. 7 (November 2006): 1083.

43. Alexander Filatov, Vladimir Tutkevich, and Dmitry Cherkaev, "Board of Directors at State-Owned Enterprises (SOE) in Russia," Organization for Economic Co-operation and Development, 2004, 8, at http://www.oecd.org/dataoecd/9/44/35175304.pdf.

44. Mankoff, 48.

45. Ian Bremmer, "Thinking Beyond States," *National Interest* 83 (Spring 2006): 66.

46. Mankoff, 48.

47. William Tompson, "Back to the Future? Thoughts on the Political Economy of Expanding State Ownership in Russia," *Les Chaiers Russie* (Ceri Sciences Po), 6 (2008): 12.

48. Ewa Paszyc, "The 'energy tandem': Putin and Sechin control the Russian energy sector," *EastWeek* 22 (298): June 20, 2012, at http://www.osw.waw.pl/en/publikacje/eastweek/2012-06-20/energy-tandem-putin-and-sechin-control-russian-energy-sector.

49. "Russia Sets Weapons Export Record," *Radio Free Europe/Radio Liberty*, February 16, 2012, at http://www.rferl.org/content/russia_arms_exports/24485949.html.

50. Quoted in Graham Stack, "ZAO KREMLIN: The Chemezov Code," *Business New Europe*, Septmber 5, 2007, at http://www.bne.eu/story565/rencap.swf.

51. "Russian billionaire Prokhorov to finance Kremlin's youth forum—newspaper," *RIA Novosti*, March 15, 2010, at http://en.rian.ru/russia/20100315/158199960.html.

52. Timothy Frye, "Capture or Exchange? Business Lobbying in Russia," *Europe-Asia Studies* 54, no. 7 (2002): 1021.

53. Sharon Werning Rivera and David W. Rivera, "The Russian Elite under Putin: Militocratic or Bourgeois?" *Post–Soviet Affairs* 22, no. 2 (2006): 130.

54. Andrew E. Kramer, "A $50 Billion Bailout in Russia Favors the Rich and Connected," *New York Times*, October 31, 2008, B4, at http://www.nytimes.com/2008/10/31/business/worldbusiness/31oligarch.html.

55. Bobo Lo, *Russian Foreign Policy in the Post–Soviet Era: Reality, Illusion and Mythmaking* (Houdmills, Basingstoke: Palgrave Macmillan, 2003), 131–132.

56. Alexei Arbatov, "Bureaucracy on the Rise," *Russia in Global Affairs* 2 (April-June 2007), at http://eng.globalaffairs.ru/number/n_8552.

57. "Aircraft Systems Account for Half of Rosoboronexport Sales," *Interfax-AVN*, May 2, 2012, at http://www.militarynews.ru/EMAIN.ASP.

58. Peter Rutland, "Russia as an Energy Superpower," *New Political Economy* 13, no. 2 (June 2008): at http://prutland.web.wesleyan.edu/Documents/Energy%20superpower.pdf.

59. For background on the majors, see, for instance, "LUKoil to lose the lead soon," *Russian Business Consulting*, January 11, 2007, at http://www.rbcnews.com/komment/komment.shtml?2007/01/11/31319500.

60. Comments of Vladimir Milov, at the roundtable event, "How Sustainable is Russia's Future as an Energy Superpower?" Carnegie Moscow Center, March 16, 2006, at http://www.carnegieendowment.org/events/index.cfm?fa=eventDetail&id=860.

61. Steven Woehrel, *Russian Energy Policy Toward Neighboring Countries*, Congressional Research Service Report RL34261 (September 2, 2009), 1.

62. Ian Bremmer, "Thinking Beyond States," *National Interest* 83 (Spring 2006): 66.

63. Rosneft completed its acquisition of the formerly private Russian oil company TNK-BP, which was jointly owned by BP and a Russian shareholder group, Alfa-Access-Renova, in 2013.

64. Ivanov, 9.

65. As Lavrov noted during his remarks at the Council on Foreign Relations, op. cit.

66. The Council's materials are available at its website at http://www.svop.ru/. For an analysis of the influence of various think tanks and institutes on Russian foreign policy, see Gregory Feifer, "Who Stands Behind Putin's Foreign Policy?" *St. Petersburg Times*, April 9, 2002, at http://www.sptimes.ru/index.php?action_id=2&story_id=6929.

67. "The Experts at INSOR Plan Russia's Modernization," *Diplomat* 9 (September 2008), at http://www.diplomatrus.com/article.php?id=1551&PHPSESSID=dd4548f38d6c0f.

68. Tony Halpin and John Hughes, "Living with Big Brother," *Armenia Now*, May 16, 2006, at http://www.armenianow.com/special_issues/moscow/6391/living_with_big_brother_armeniaru.

69. See, among others, Nikolas K. Gvosdev, "The New Party Card? Orthodoxy and the Search for Post-Soviet Russian Identity," *Problems of Post–Communism* 47, no. 6 (November/December 2000): 29–38; Nikolas K. Gvosdev, "Russia: European but not Western?" *Orbis* 51, no. 1 (Winter 2007): 135–37.

70. "Moscow promotes 'Russian world' as cultural alternative to McWest," *Russia Today*, November 3, 2009, at http://rt.com/usa/moscow-promotes-russian-world/.

71. The full text of the "Russian Doctrine" is available at the project's website at http://www.rusdoctrina.ru/page95507.html.

72. Transcript of Remarks by Russian Minister of Foreign Affairs Sergey Lavrov at the Foreign Ministry's Reception on the Occasion of Orthodox Easter, Moscow, April 22, 2009, at http://www.mid.ru/brp_4.nsf/0/3E6860616E4FA4F6C32575A2001CAFAC.

73. Patriarch Alexy, "The Russian Orthodox Church in the Modern World," *International Affairs* 2 (2009): 54.

74. An excellent case study on the Church's influence can be found in Katja Richters, "The Moscow Patriarchate in Estonia: Russian versus International Concerns," *Problems of Post–Communism* 55, no. 1 (January/February 2008): 3–11.

75. Feifer, op. cit.

76. See the transcript of the meeting with the Security Council, March 24, 2009, at http://archive.kremlin.ru/eng/speeches/2009/03/24/2056_type82913_214288.shtml.

77. Stephen J. Blank, "Civil-Military Relations and Russian Security," *Civil-Military Relations in Medvedev's Russia* (Carlisle, PA: Strategic Studies Institute, 2011), 11.

78. Nikolas K. Gvosdev, "Managed Pluralism and Political Parties in Russia," *Analysis of Current Events* 14, no. 3 (October 3, 2002): 15–17.

79. Shevchenko, 81.

80. Kirill Rogov, "For Friendship Between the White Houses," *Novaya Gazeta*, March 2, 2009. Archived at http://archive.premier.gov.ru/eng/premier/press/ru/2298/print/.

81. Mikhail Tsypkin, "Russian politics, policy-making and American missile defense," *International Affairs* 85, no. 4 (2009): 782; Sarah Whitmore, 1005.

82. Thomas Graham, then the first secretary of the U.S. Embassy in Moscow, called attention to the ongoing struggle for power and influence within the presidency as the defining motor of Russian politics in his November 23, 1995, essay, "Novyi Russkii Rezhim," that was published in *Nezavisimaia Gazeta*. For a discussion of the linkages between pluralism and the clans in contemporary, see, for example, Luke March, "Managing Opposition in a Hybrid Regime: Just Russia and Parastatal Opposition," *Slavic Review* 68, no. 3 (Fall 2009): 527.

83. See, for instance, Aleksei Mukhin, "Amerikantsy v' Kremle," *Argumenty Nedeli* 40 (October 14–20, 2010): 2.

84. For instance, in 2012, there were major disagreements over the plans of Igor Sechin to use his control over the state holding company Rosneftegaz to buy up assets; Prime Minister Medvedev wanted to use Rosneftegaz funds to close gaps in the Russian state budget. In the end, Sechin was cleared to purchase the TNK-BP oil company but had to give up some $1.6 billion in dividends to the Russian state budget and agreed not to purchase other assets. See Anna Arutunyan, "The Return of Sechin," *Moscow News*, October 15, 2012, at http://themoscownews.com/business/20121015/190364500.html.

85. Ian Bremmer and Samuel Charap, "The *Siloviki* in Putin's Russia: Who They Are and What They Want," *The Washington Quarterly* 30, no. 1 (Winter 2006-07): 85.

86. Graham's classifications are discussed in David Hoffman, *The Oligarchs: Wealth and Power in the New Russia* (Cambridge, MA: Perseus Books, 2002, 2003), 322-24.

87. Bremmer and Charap, 85-86.

88. Graham Stack, "Between Siloviki and Civiliki," *Russia Profile*, July 20, 2009, at http://russiaprofile.org/international/a1248108349.html.

89. Quoted in Brian Whitmore, "Medvedev vs. Sechin," *Radio Free Europe/Radio Liberty*, February 24, 2009, at http://www.rferl.org/content/Medvedev_vs_Sechin/1498742.html.

90. Brian Whitmore, "The Return of the Politburo," *Radio Free Europe/Radio Liberty*, March 7, 2011, at http://www.rferl.org/content/the_return_of_the_politburo/2330911.html.

91. Whitmore, "Medvedev vs. Sechin," op. cit.

92. Gira, 172.

93. Simon Saradzhyan and Nabi Abdullaev, "Russia: Looking Ahead," *ISN*, February 22, 2011, at http://www.isn.ethz.ch/isn/Current-Affairs/ISN-Insights/Detail?lng=en&id=1 27023&contextid734=127023&contextid735=127022&tabid=127022.

94. "Gates: Russia Policy Toward Iran 'Schizophrenic,'" *Agence France Press*, June 17, 2010. Archived at http://www.defensenews.com/story.php?i=4675078.

95. Nikolas K. Gvosdev, "Moscow's Foreign Policies," *National Interest*, July 30, 2010, at http://www.nationalinterest.org/Article.aspx?id=23750.

96. Gira, 166.

97. Lo, 127.

98. Lo, 37.

99. A list of some of the more important commissions and their members can be found on the website of the Russian government at http://government.ru/gov/agencies/.

100. Tsypkin, 799.

101. Dmitry Badovsky, "Peredacha Vlasti: Eshchye 307 dnei," *Vedimosti* 21, no. 2787 (February 8, 2011), at http://www.vedomosti.ru/newspaper/article/254555/esche_307_ dnej.

102. Vladimir Radyuhin, "The Russian-Iranian road map," *The Hindu*, July 26, 2010, at http://www.thehindu.com/opinion/lead/article535182.ece?homepage=true.

103. A phenomenon especially observed when economic interests are in play. Tompson, 11.

104. Dmitry Butrin, Pyotr Netreba, Irina Granik, and Oleg Sapozhkov, "Instructions Aren't Always Issued," *Kommersant*, March 17, 2010, cited in *Current Digest of the Post-Soviet Press* 62, no. 11 (March 15, 2010): 8-9.

105. Arbatov, op. cit.

106. Alexander Lukin, "From a Post-Soviet to a Russian Foreign Policy," *Russia in Global Affairs* 4 (October/December 2008), at http://eng.globalaffairs.ru/numbers/25/1239.html.

107. See, among other examples, Foreign Minister Lavrov's comments at the Council on Foreign Relations, op. cit.

108. Ibid. Lavrov notes that during the early 1990s, "we didn't even remember about relationships with our old friends."

109. Ivanov, 12.

110. Statement in *Izvestiia*, January 2, 1992.

111. Stankevich, 24.

112. Ivanov, 15.

113. Igor Torbakov, "Analysts Debate Pros and Cons of 'Eastern Vector' in Kremlin's Foreign Policy," *Eurasia Daily Monitor* 2, no. 137 (July 15, 2005), at http://www.jamestown.org/single/?no_cache=1&tx_ttnews%5Btt_news%5D=30660.

114. See Lukin, op. cit.

115. Lo, 94–97.

116. See, for instance, Michael McFaul, "A Precarious Peace: Domestic Politics in the Making of Russian Foreign Policy," *International Security* 22, no. 3 (Winter 1997/98): 22–24.

117. On business interests, see, for instance, "Gazprom Neft Seeks Expansion Into Cuba, Iran," *Moscow Times*, June 30, 2010, at http://themoscowtimes.com/business/article/gazprom-neft-seeks-expansion-into-cuba-iran/409348.html as well as Ralph E. Winnie, Jr., "Iran: Russia's strategic new client," *Russia Beyond the Headlines*, March 24, 2010, at http://rbth.ru/articles/2010/03/24/240310_iran.html; on the role of the Church in Iran policy, see Alexei Malashenko, "The Islam Factor in Russian Foreign Policy," *Russia in Global Affairs* 2 (July–September 2007), at http://eng.globalaffairs.ru/number/n_9133; on Iran as a "distraction" for the U.S. which benefits Russia, see the Council on Foreign and Defense Policy report, *Mir Vokrug Rossii: 2017—Kontury Nedalekosgo Budushchego* (Moscow: Izdatel'stvo "Kul'turnaia revoliutsiia," 2007), 103.

118. The arms export industry is attempting to reach the $10 billion level; cf. "Russia hopes to make $9.5 bln in 2011 arms sales," *RIA Novosti*, March 9, 2011, at http://en.rian.ru/mlitary_news/20110309/162920038.html.

119. Fyodor Lukyanov, "Germany is Russia's Natural Ally," *Looking Glass* 2 (2008): 34, at http://www.glasshouseforum.org/pdf/LG_02-08_russiagermany.pdf.

120. "Russia says to sign China gas deal by mid-2011," *Channel News Asia*, September 27, 2010, at http://www.channelnewsasia.com/stories/afp_asiapacific_business/view/1083596/1/.html.

121. Andrey Tsygankov, "What is China to Us? Westernizers and Sinophiles in Russian Foreign Policy," *Russie.Nei.Visions* 45 (December 2009): 1–22.

122. Stephen White, "Elite opinion and foreign policy in post-communist Russia," *Perspectives on European Politics and Society* 8, no. 2 (2007): 147–167.

123. A sense of these dynamics can be found in M. K. Bradrakumar's analysis of the "dual relationships" of Russia with China and the United States. "Russia resets with U.S., springs with China," *The Hindu*, October 11, 2010, at http://www.hindu.com/2010/10/11/stories/2010101155601000.htm.

124. Tatiana Zakaurtseva, "The Current Foreign Policy of Russia," *Eager Eyes Fixed on Eurasia*, Volume I, *Russia and Its Neighbors in Crisis* (Sapporo, Japan: Slavic Research Center-Hokkaido University, 2007), 91.

125. See Lo, 131–32.

126. See the transcript of Sergei Lavrov's remarks to the Council on Foreign Relations in New York on September 24, 2008, at http://www.cfr.org/publication/17384/conversation_with_sergey_lavrov.html.

127. Lo, 38.

CHAPTER 3

The United States

The Main Enemy or Strategic Partner?

For the last 60 years, the United States has been the main focus of both Soviet and Russian foreign policies. James Billington, the Librarian of Congress, noted that "the United States has been for a half century the . . . model that Russians first tried to 'overtake and surpass' in the late Cold War and, in some ways, emulate since then."[1]

Russia has always had a roller-coaster relationship with the United States. At the time of the Revolutionary War, King George III had initially approached Empress Catherine the Great to hire battle-tested Russian regiments to put down his rebelling colonists; when rebuffed by her, he procured the services of the Hessians instead. Catherine looked askance at any act of rebellion and so refused to recognize the new government; but because Russia's European partners France and Spain openly supported the Americans (as a way to damage their common enemy Great Britain), Russia indirectly supported American aspirations for independence. In February 1780, when Catherine announced the League of Armed Neutrality to defend European trade routes from British interference, the United States ended up as a clear beneficiary of Russia's willingness to force the British to respect the freedom of the seas.

For the next hundred years, the United States factored little in Russian foreign policy in its own right; Washington mattered only to the extent that the United States impacted the European balance of power. The United States posed an ideological challenge to the Russian state as a democratic republic that had thrown off its allegiance to a monarchy, and America's westward expansion eventually brought it into direct competition with a Russia that was trying to expand its own sphere along the Pacific coast of North America. However, the Russian government wanted to preserve good relations with the United States as a counterweight to the British. The 1824 treaty between Russia and the United States amicably settled outstanding territorial disputes between the two countries. U.S.–Russia relations warmed dramatically during the U.S. Civil War—the United States, worried about the possibility of the British and the French recognizing the independence of the Confederacy, welcomed Russian support of the Union; for its part, Russia, concerned that its fleets might be blockaded in the Baltic and Black Seas, sent contingents of its warships to U.S. ports. In the aftermath of these visits and the goodwill they generated, Russia sold its territory of Alaska to the United States after concluding that it was too far from Russia to be adequately defended in case of war with the British.[2]

The dynamic expansion of both Russia and the United States across the Eurasian and North American continents in the 19th century led a number of observers to conclude that these two countries would emerge as major powers in the 20th century. Alexis de Tocqueville, for instance, noted: "There are, at the present time, two great nations in the world which seem to tend toward the same end, although they started from different points. I allude to the Russians and the Americans. . . . Their starting points are different and their courses are not the same; yet each of them seems to be marked out by the will of heaven to sway the destinies of half the globe."[3] Meanwhile, Commodore Matthew Perry, who led the expedition that opened up Japan to foreign commerce in 1854, wondered, after observing the pattern of Russian and American expansion, whether the two countries would meet "in strife or in friendship" in the future.

Imperial Russia and the United States were uneasy allies during the First World War; while both were threatened by the rise of the German Empire, the nature of the tsarist autocracy nevertheless caused some concern in America. The overthrow of the tsar in February 1917 and the expectations that Russia might develop into a liberal democracy led President Woodrow Wilson to declare that "the great, generous Russian people have been added in all their naive majesty and might to the forces that are fighting for freedom in the world, for justice, and for peace." However, after the Communist takeover in November and the creation of the Soviet government, Wilson, along with other Western governments, saw the new regime as a threat. U.S. forces ended up deploying in northern Russia and in Siberia, ostensibly to protect supplies and strategic installations from falling into German hands, but also with a mandate to assist anti–Soviet Russian forces. While U.S. forces were withdrawn in 1920, the United States did not extend diplomatic recognition to the Soviet government until 1933.

The United States and the Soviet Union again found themselves allied during the Second World War—but this was an alliance based on a common foe, not on shared values. Nazi Germany's totalitarian system posed an equal threat both to the Soviet system and to Western democracy, and, as Josef Stalin himself recognized, it was "on this basis that the anti-fascist coalition of the Soviet Union, the United States of America, Great Britain and other . . . countries came into being and later played the decisive role in defeating the armed forces of the Axis Powers."[4]

Franklin Delano Roosevelt sought to preserve good relations with Moscow during the war and hoped that wartime cooperation could pave the way for an improved postwar relationship between the United States and the Soviet Union.

The Roosevelt administration accepted the premise that the USSR was entitled "to a Europe which is not hostile to her" and that governments in central and eastern Europe ought to be responsive to Soviet interests. In return, the United States assumed that governments friendly to Soviet interests need not be Communist but could remain democratic.[5] This understanding formed the basis for the compromises that FDR and Stalin reached at the Yalta summit in February 1945 on the disposition of Europe after the war. (British prime minister Winston Churchill had gone even further with his Percentages Agreement during his meetings with Stalin in October 1944 in an attempt to delineate Western and Soviet influence in specific countries.) The Declaration of Liberated Europe committed the Allied powers to "form interim governmental authorities broadly representative of all democratic elements in the population"—which the U.S. side understood to mean that, in the areas being liberated by Soviet forces, non-Communists would be included in coalition governments. Roosevelt also got Soviet support for the creation of the United Nations, an international collective-security organization he hoped would keep the peace and prevent any third world war from breaking out, in part by setting up the Security Council, on which the Soviet Union would have a permanent membership, and ensuring that the USSR (along with Britain, France, and China) would have the power to veto any proposed UN action.

Stalin's decision, however, to push for complete Soviet control in the countries that were occupied by the advancing Red Army was one of the major factors in bringing the wartime cooperation with the United States to a close. After World War II, the United States emerged as the strongest power in the world. The Soviet effort to expand its influence in both a war-devastated Europe as well as East Asia laid the basis for conflict between the two victor-powers. The Soviet position was that it was entitled to "special security arrangements" in Turkey, east-central Europe, and the Far East; Soviet foreign minister Vyacheslav Molotov later observed that "we had to introduce order" in these areas to consolidate Soviet gains.[6] Between 1945 and 1948, the "broad-based" coalitions in eastern Europe were replaced by Communist governments, which in American eyes represented a violation of the Yalta accords.[7]

But Stalin's clear desire to use Soviet military forces to extend the zone of Moscow's influence was matched by U.S. President Harry S. Truman's declaration, issued on March 14, 1947, that it would be "the policy of the United States to support free people who are resisting attempted subjugation by armed minorities or by outside pressures," in announcing U.S. aid to Turkey and Greece, designed to strengthen pro–Western governments against Communist pressure. But even without the ideological struggle, conflict between the United States and the Soviet Union might have been inevitable after World War II. Since the beginning of the

20th century, American strategic planners accepted the proviso that the security of the United States would be threatened if a single power were able to bring all or most of the industrial and economic power of Europe and/or East Asia and the immense natural resource endowments of the Eurasian plains under its control.[8] This reading of geopolitics provided strategic guidance in determining the U.S. response to the Soviet Union during the Cold War—especially Moscow's attempts to extend its influence and control into Europe and in other parts of East Asia and the Middle East. In 1950, the U.S. government, in a report prepared by the National Security Council (NSC-68), formally adopted the strategy of "containment" against the Soviet Union.[9]

Relations between Moscow and Washington became characterized by what was termed a "cold war": neither side engaged in open, direct hostilities—since the Soviet Union exploded its own atomic bombs in 1949, 4 years after the United States developed such weapons—but nevertheless engaged in a series of indirect conflicts and competition for influence. Both countries attempted to attract other countries under their respective banners, leading to the emergence of two major blocs in the international system.

LEGACY OF THE COLD WAR

The peculiar state of U.S.-Soviet relations, first described as the Cold War by American statesman Bernard Baruch in 1947, was to last until Moscow and Washington jointly announced the end of the Cold War at the Malta Summit in December 1989. On the one hand, the efforts of the Soviet Union to expand their influence, in part by backing revolutionary and anticolonial movements around the world, and those of the United States to contain and "roll back" Soviet influence, meant that both sides were poised for military conflict. On the other hand, the fact that both the United States and the USSR possessed nuclear weapons meant that any direct clash between the two could result in complete annihilation. Managing the Cold War's cycles of tension was essential for the survival of the world.

An initial period of Soviet expansion in the late 1940s was met by a U.S. strategy of containment (with some even holding out the prospect of "rolling back" Soviet influence in the 1950s)—with the United States prepared to commit its armed forces, as in Korea, to counter Soviet-backed governments and movements. Decolonization in the Third World offered new arenas for competition as newly independent states decided whether to affiliate with either the Soviet or Western blocs. However, the Cuban Missile Crisis of 1962—when the Soviet Union and the United States stood on the brink of nuclear war after Nikita Khrushchev authorized the deployment of Soviet nuclear weapons on the island of Cuba, 90 miles from U.S. shores—drove home the consequences of any miscalculation and helped to usher in a period of progress on arms control and confidence-building measures. By the early 1970s, relations were characterized by the term *détente*—a relaxation of tensions that permitted the signing of several critical arms-control treaties such as the ABM Treaty, which prohibited either side from deploying large-scale missile defense systems, and the SALT I (Strategic Arms Limitation Treaty) agreement, which limited both sides in the numbers of strategic weapons they could possess.

The perception that the United States was being outmaneuvered by the Soviet Union—heightened by the American withdrawal from Vietnam and the subsequent victory of Communist forces there—and by Soviet efforts to reach parity with the United States in military terms—led to a renewed period of confrontation. The Soviet invasion of Afghanistan in 1979 was the prelude to a new arms race between the two sides. However, the climate of relations changed during the second term of Ronald Reagan and the accession of Mikhail Gorbachev, with a belief that a new set of accommodations could be reached between the United States and the USSR.

Because of the global interests and reach of both the Soviet Union and the United States, few problems anywhere in the world were not affected by the Cold War. Civil wars and regional conflicts anywhere in the world soon had a Cold War dimension as one side or another would seek assistance from Washington or Moscow. In addition, the growing nuclear stockpiles of both countries raised the probability of accidents. The 1983 NATO exercise Able Archer, which simulated the steps the United States might take in the event of an actual conflict with the Soviet Union, was perceived by the leadership of the USSR as a prelude to an actual attack.[10] So it became a priority for both governments to try and reduce the chances of a misunderstanding leading to a nuclear exchange.

As a result, the relationship with the Soviet Union during this period was the top American foreign policy priority—and part of the way in which relations were managed was through direct talks between the leaders of both countries. Over time, a series of regular "summit meetings" (so called because the paramount leaders met directly) charted not only the bilateral agenda between the two countries—including efforts to reduce nuclear arms on both sides—but also provided an opportunity for U.S. and Soviet leaders to discuss a series of global issues. Sometimes, summit meetings would lead to major agreements between both sides; at other times, they were mainly an opportunity for Soviet and American leaders to take each other's measure or to reassure the international community that the diplomatic dialogue between the two superpowers was continuing.

During the Cold War period, managing the two countries' massive stockpiles of nuclear weapons was at the heart of the bilateral relationship, creating the

TABLE 3.1
Cold War Cycles

Crisis	Description	Result
Berlin Crisis (1948–1949)	Soviet blockade of Western sectors of Berlin	Soviets back down and restore access after Western powers successfully resupply Berlin by air.
Korean War (1950–1953)	Soviet-backed North Korean government invades South Korea.	United States and other countries intervene directly to defend South Korea; China (allied to the USSR at the time) intervenes on behalf of North Korea. All sides limit the fighting to the Korean peninsula. 1953 armistice preserves a Communist North and a non-Communist South.
Suez and Hungary (1956)	Britain, France, and Israel intervene against a pro-Soviet Egypt; Hungary attempts to break out of the Soviet bloc.	The British, French, and Israelis withdraw from Egypt; Soviet forces intervene in Hungary, depose the reform Communist government of Imre Nagy, and impose Janos Kadar; the United States tacitly recognizes a Soviet sphere of influence in Eastern Europe.
Berlin Crisis (1961)	Soviets demand withdrawal of Western forces from Berlin.	Western forces remain, but Soviet-backed East German government begins construction of barriers to prevent the free flow of people from Communist to non-Communist sectors (the Berlin Wall).
Cuban Missile Crisis (1962)	Soviets deploy offensive nuclear missiles in Cuba.	After the United States declares a "quarantine" of the island, the Soviets agree to withdraw the missiles while the United States promises not to engage in efforts to overthrow Cuba's Communist government; U.S. intermediate-range missiles in Turkey also withdrawn.
Vietnam War (1959–1975)	A Soviet-backed government in North Vietnam supports a Communist rebellion in South Vietnam.	The Soviet Union provides a great deal of aid and support for North Vietnam but does not directly intervene. At various points, intensified U.S. military activity leads to strained relations with Moscow. The collapse of the South Vietnamese government in 1975 unifies the country under a pro-Soviet Communist government.
Czechoslovakia (1968)	The Soviet Union intervenes in Czechoslovakia to depose a reform Communist government.	As with Hungary in 1956, the United States takes no action to oppose Soviet military intervention in what is perceived as the "Soviet sphere" in Europe.

Crisis	Description	Result
Arab–Israeli War (1973)	The Soviet Union threatens to intervene on behalf of its Arab clients against a U.S.-backed Israel to preserve a regional balance of power.	A series of agreements in 1973 and 1974 allows for all sides to disengage and end open fighting.
Angolan Intervention (1975–1977)	Cuba provides troops with Soviet assistance for Communist-backed forces.	A pro-Soviet government ends up in control of most of Angola; this represents a major step in Soviet ability to project influence beyond the Eurasian core; heralds a new wave of Soviet activity in Africa and Latin America.
Invasion of Afghanistan (1979–1989)	Soviet forces intervene to support a pro-Soviet faction in Afghanistan.	Seeing this as a Soviet push toward the Persian Gulf—a major source of energy for the West—the United States expands its military presence in the region. In addition, the United States secretly arms the anti-Soviet resistance and wears down Soviet forces, leading to their complete withdrawal by 1988; the pro-Moscow government falls in 1992. The United States and some other Western governments boycott the 1980 Moscow Olympics in protest; the Soviet Union and some of its allies do not attend the 1984 Olympics in Los Angeles.
Pershing Deployments in Europe (1982)	The United States deploys intermediate-range nuclear missiles in Europe.	Despite Soviet threats, the deployment proceeds—and provides the impetus for the negotiation of the 1987 INF Treaty, which eliminates an entire category of strategic weapons—the intermediate-range nuclear missile.
Grenada and Lebanon (1983)	U.S. interventions in Grenada and Lebanon	The U.S. invasion of Grenada toppled a pro-Soviet government and represented a willingness of the United States to use its military force to "roll back" Soviet gains in Latin America. The U.S. Marine deployment in Lebanon and the subsequent fighting between U.S.-backed and Syrian-backed factions in Lebanon raised the possibility of a direct U.S.–Soviet clash because of the presence of a Soviet military mission in Syria. Grenada ended up forming a pro-Western government; the United States withdrew from Lebanon in 1984.

Source: Compiled by authors.

TABLE 3.2
U.S.–Soviet Presidential-Level Summits, 1943–1991

Location	U.S./Soviet Leaders Present	Major Accomplishments
Tehran, Iran (November/December 1943)	Franklin Roosevelt and Josef Stalin (along with British Prime Minister Winston Churchill)	Strategy in prosecuting the Second World War
Yalta, Ukraine, USSR (February 1945)	Franklin Roosevelt and Josef Stalin (along with British Prime Minister Winston Churchill)	Political settlement for a postwar Europe, including the division of Germany
Potsdam, Germany (July/August 1945)	Harry S. Truman and Josef Stalin (along with British Prime Ministers Winston Churchill and Clement Atlee)	Adjusting aspects of the Yalta settlement and political settlement for postwar East Asia
Geneva, Switzerland (July 1955)	Dwight Eisenhower and Nikita Khrushchev (along with British Prime Minister Anthony Eden and French Prime Minister Edgar Faure)	Beginning of the arms-control process with attempts to reduce nuclear weapons; failed effort to consider German reunification
Camp David, Maryland, United States (September 1959)	Dwight Eisenhower and Nikita Khrushchev	First visit of a Soviet leader to the United States
Paris, France (May 1960)	Dwight Eisenhower and Nikita Khrushchev (along with French President Charles de Gaulle and British Prime Minister Harold Macmillan)	Summit considered a failure due to U.S. refusals to apologize for U-2 overflights over Soviet territory
Vienna, Austria (June 1961)	John F. Kennedy and Nikita Khrushchev	Inconclusive discussions over Berlin and Indochina
Glassboro, New Jersey, United States (June 1967)	Lyndon B. Johnson and Alexei Kosygin	Helped to decrease tensions and led to a modest improvement in U.S.–Soviet relations (the "spirit of Glassboro")

Location	U.S./Soviet Leaders Present	Major Accomplishments
Moscow, Russia, USSR (May 1972)	Richard Nixon and Leonid Brezhnev	Signing of the ABM (Anti-Ballistic Missile) and SALT (Strategic Arms Limitation Treaty) I Treaties; the ABM Treaty prohibited further research and development on ballistic missile defenses and limited both sides to one ABM site
Washington, DC, and San Clemente, California, United States (June 1973)	Richard Nixon and Leonid Brezhnev	Progress on European security and emigration issues
Moscow, Russia, USSR (June/July 1974)	Richard Nixon and Leonid Brezhnev	Partial ban on underground nuclear testing signed
Vladivostok, Russia, USSR (November 1974)	Gerald Ford and Leonid Brezhnev	Signing of Vladivostok Accord, which paves way for SALT II Treaty
Helsinki, Finland (July/August 1975)	Gerald Ford and Leonid Brezhnev	Held on the sidelines of the Conference on Security and Co-Operation in Europe and the signing of the Helsinki Accords
Vienna, Austria (June 1979)	Jimmy Carter and Leonid Brezhnev	Signing of SALT II
Geneva, Switzerland (November 1985)	Ronald Reagan and Mikhail Gorbachev	First direct contact between U.S. and Soviet leaders after heightened tensions of early 1980s
Reykjavik, Iceland (October 1986)	Ronald Reagan and Mikhail Gorbachev	Negotiations but no agreement on radical reductions in nuclear arms
Washington, DC, United States (December 1987)	Ronald Reagan and Mikhail Gorbachev	Signing of the INF Treaty, eliminating an entire class of strategic arms

(Continued)

(Continued)

Location	U.S./Soviet Leaders Present	Major Accomplishments
Moscow, Russia, USSR (May/June 1988)	Ronald Reagan and Mikhail Gorbachev	Progress on START and CFE negotiations; new efforts to resolve regional conflicts
Governors Island, New York, United States (December 1988)	Ronald Reagan and Mikhail Gorbachev	"Passing the baton" to incoming U.S. president George H. W. Bush
Malta (December 1989)	George H. W. Bush and Mikhail Gorbachev	End of the Cold War; discussion about changes in central and eastern Europe
Washington, DC, United States (May/June 1990)	George H. W. Bush and Mikhail Gorbachev	Chemical Weapons Accord signed
Helsinki, Finland (September 1990)	George H. W. Bush and Mikhail Gorbachev	Discussion of Iraqi invasion of Kuwait and possible responses
Paris, France (November 1990)	George H. W. Bush and Mikhail Gorbachev	Held on the sidelines of the conference that signed the Charter of Paris for a New Europe and the Conventional Forces in Europe Treaty
Moscow, Russia, USSR (July 1991)	George H. W. Bush and Mikhail Gorbachev	Signed the START I arms control treaty; both men had also met on the sidelines earlier that month at the G-7 summit in London
Madrid, Spain (October 1991)	George H. W. Bush and Mikhail Gorbachev	Held on the sidelines of the Madrid Middle East Peace Conference

Source: Compiled by authors.

legacy that it was via possession of such arms that "superpower" status was conferred. The need to pursue arms control created extensive expertise in the diplomatic services of both countries and provided the rationale for not only high-level summits but ongoing dialogues, usually in Geneva or Vienna, on a variety of technical issues. In addition, the regular series of summit meetings and their expansive agenda created an expectation that Washington should always consult with Moscow about global issues. The joint communiqué issued at the close of the 1972 Moscow summit enhanced the position of the Soviet Union as the peer of the United States and declared that a stable and constructive bilateral relationship between Washington and Moscow was a prerequisite "for maintaining world peace and for facilitating the relaxation of international tension."[11]

GORBACHEV: THE SEARCH FOR CONDOMINIUM

Because Mikhail Gorbachev's tenure as leader of the Soviet Union is now inextricably connected with the demise of the USSR, it is important to recall that Gorbachev's efforts to promote better relations with the United States—his so-called "New Thinking"—were not part of an effort to dismantle the Soviet Union. Instead, he hoped that an improved relationship with the West would diminish the need to divert a large portion of Soviet resources into the arms race and so permit a rehabilitation and revitalization of the Soviet Union itself. But Gorbachev still saw the USSR as a major global power and expected to forge a more cooperative relationship with Washington in order to share responsibility for world affairs.[12]

While an initial proposal for radical arms control proposed at the Reykjavik summit in 1986 went nowhere, both sides did agree to ban intermediate-range nuclear missiles in 1987. Gorbachev's desire to divert Soviet spending from the military toward the civilian economy also led him to announce reductions in other areas, among them major cuts in the size of Soviet conventional forces, during his speech to the United Nations in 1988.

Finally, after years of talks, the United States and the Soviet Union signed the Strategic Arms Reduction Treaty, or START I, on July 31, 1991. This accord limited both sides to 1,600 launchers and 6,000 nuclear warheads—representing major cuts in the atomic arsenals of both nations. Indeed, by the time the treaty's provisions were fully implemented (in 2001), more than 80% of the world's existing stock of nuclear weapons was removed from service. Moreover, the treaty provided for a comprehensive system of on-the-ground inspections and monitoring that would put Soviet and American observers in factories and installations.[13]

Beyond reductions, Gorbachev was also hoping that common ground could be found with the United States in international affairs. In a meeting during the

1988 Moscow summit with U.S. Secretary of State George Schultz, Gorbachev, after noting that both countries had interests around the world, declared, "Since we are present everywhere, we simply have to balance our interests. This kind of an approach would stimulate the search for decisions and solutions."[14] Between 1988 and 1990, the Soviet Union withdrew its forces from Afghanistan, terminated direct military aid to the Sandinistas in Nicaragua, and helped to broker settlements to conflicts in Angola, Mozambique, Namibia, and Cambodia. And after Iraq invaded Kuwait in 1990, the Soviet Union joined with the United States in supporting UN Security Council Resolution 678, which authorized an international coalition to use "all necessary means" to restore Kuwaiti sovereignty—the first time that the Security Council had given its blessing to armed action. All of this raised hopes about the world being on the verge of a "new world order"; Eduard Shevardnadze, who served as foreign minister for much of Gorbachev's tenure (1985-1990), argued that a good U.S.-Soviet relationship would be critical. Moscow and Washington could work together to promote a common agenda. "This general line of cooperation between our countries must be continued if we want to do the right thing for everyone on the planet," Shevardnadze maintained.[15]

At the 1988 summit at Governors Island, meeting with outgoing president Ronald Reagan and incoming president George H. W. Bush, Gorbachev stressed the "good prospects" for both countries to work together on a cooperative agenda that would promote peace.[16] For his part, Ronald Reagan later commented that, after the 1988 Governors Island summit, "Gorbachev sounded as if he saw us as partners making a better world."[17] In a follow-on meeting with Bush at Malta in 1989, Gorbachev signaled the end of the Cold War and declared, "We are at the beginning of a long road to a lasting, peaceful era."

Gorbachev's pursuit of better relations with the United States was grounded in his assumption that, in return for an end to Soviet expansionism as well as allowing Soviet-bloc countries the ability to choose their own political and economic systems, the United States would not seek to expand or extend its influence into formerly Soviet-controlled areas and would recognize the Soviet Union as a partner in international affairs. This guided the Soviet approach in the Two Plus Four negotiations, which produced the treaty in September 1990 that permitted the unification of West and East Germany.

Article 5 of that treaty, however, ended up becoming a major point of contention between the United States and post–Soviet Russia. That article prohibits the deployment of NATO forces and nuclear weapons in the territory of the former East Germany. The Russians have maintained that, alongside this formal commitment, they were given an informal pledge that the United States would not seek the expansion of NATO into the former Soviet zone and that the subsequent enlargement of the Western alliance since 1990 had violated that understanding.[18] Gorbachev himself has complained, "The Americans promised that NATO wouldn't move beyond the boundaries of Germany after the Cold War but now half of central and eastern Europe are members, so what happened to their promises? It shows they cannot be trusted."[19]

As the Soviet Union began to collapse in 1991, however, Gorbachev's vision of a U.S.–Soviet partnership became less tenable, because it soon became clear that Moscow could not be an equal partner with Washington. Gorbachev attended the London summit of the Group of Seven (G-7), the leading powers of the West, but Gorbachev's role was largely to solicit Western aid for a failing Soviet economy. The Soviet Union cosponsored the Madrid Conference in October, which was an attempt to broker a major Middle East peace settlement, but it was abundantly clear that the United States was the decisive player at these talks.

The George H. W. Bush administration continued to view Gorbachev as its primary interlocutor, but after the election of Boris Yeltsin as president of the Russian republic in July, there was growing pressure on the U.S. side to deal directly with Yeltsin and other directly elected leaders of the Soviet republics. Yet this debate became moot when the Soviet Union ceased to exist on December 25, 1991, and Russia was recognized as the successor state to the USSR.

THE YELTSIN ERA AND "TAINTED TRANSACTIONS"

As president, first of the Russian republic and then of an independent Russian state, Yeltsin made it clear he sought a completely different sort of relationship with the United States. Ronald Donaldson and Joseph Nogee have noted that while Gorbachev had tried to modify Soviet ideology, Yeltsin "jettisoned it completely."[20] In January 1992, the Russian president went so far to say that he saw the United States not merely as a partner of Russia but as an ally.[21] In a dramatic speech before the U.S. Congress in summer 1992, Yeltsin went much further than Gorbachev in what he was prepared to offer the United States. Russia ceased targeting the United States with its nuclear missiles, revealed the full dimensions of its biological weapons program (and stopped it), and terminated assistance to a number of anti–American regimes around the world. Invoking Woodrow Wilson, Yeltsin argued that "mutual, advantageous cooperation between Russia and the United States" would indeed help "make the world safe for democracy."[22]

Yeltsin had a particular vision for U.S.-Russia relations. Post–Soviet Russia would cease the arms race with the United States, especially the search for parity. While he frankly admitted that Russia could not afford to pursue superpower status, he at the same time wanted the United States to reward Moscow for ending the Cold War and allowing a "peace dividend" to revitalize the American economy. In announcing the termination of a number of Soviet-era programs that had threatened the United States, Yeltsin proclaimed, "We are departing from the ominous parity where each country was exerting every effort to stay in line, which had led to Russia having half its population living below the poverty line."[23]

Yeltsin also wanted the United States to recognize Russia as a great power and take its interests into account, but he also made the case that if Washington did not assist Russia's reforms, it ran the risk of alienating Russia and potentially restarting the Cold War. Yeltsin's early views were shaped by the Atlanticists within his entourage, who argued that Russia could rapidly join the major institutions of the Western world, led by the United States, and in so doing help to shape their agenda. They assumed that the United States would help underwrite the transition for Russia to become the "eighth member" of the Western world's set of seven major powers (as represented by the G-7).[24]

When Bill Clinton was elected president in November 1992, the Yeltsin team saw a possible partner to achieve this vision of the U.S.-Russia relationship. Clinton and Yeltsin quickly forged a strong personal relationship ("Bill and Boris"), and between 1993 and 1999 had 18 bilateral meetings, far more than any previous American or Russian leader. At their first meeting, in Vancouver in April 1993, Clinton and Yeltsin pledged to develop "a dynamic and effective United States–Russia partnership."

The Clinton administration looked at Russia as a nascent democratic state whose foreign policy would liberalize as its democratic transition progressed. One of the most familiar faces of post–World War II Soviet diplomacy for Americans, Andrei A. Gromyko (ambassador to the United States, ambassador to the United Nations, and ultimately Soviet Foreign Minister from 1957 until 1985), was known as "Mr. Nyet (No)" because his first reaction to U.S. diplomatic proposals was usually a negative.[25] But now there was an expectation that Russian foreign policy would converge with U.S. priorities as Russia's political institutions, business community, and defense establishment were reformulated along Western lines—and this, in turn, made Russian domestic affairs a concern of the United States, because this process would be derailed if the "wrong" people and parties came to power. This sentiment was expressed in the famous March 1993 memorandum prepared by Strobe Talbott, the special ambassador for the former Soviet states, for Clinton, "A Strategic Alliance with Russian Reform."[26] But it also created the impression that there should never be any substantive divergences between Russian and U.S. perspectives.

As a result, from Washington's perspective, there was no "natural" reason for Moscow to oppose American policy preferences in the world. If dissonance emerged in the bilateral relationship, the tendency was to assign blame to an ideology, to the personal venality of Russia's ruling elite, or its "democracy deficit" as explanations. The Clinton administration adopted the stance taken by George Kennan in his famous "Long Telegram," sent from the embassy in Moscow in 1946, that hostility to the United States "does not represent [the] natural outlook of [the] Russian people."[27]

The default assumption was that Russia and the United States ought to be friends and that past periods of unfriendliness between Moscow and Washington came about because of distortions of Russia's true national interests.[28] This led to a famous 1993 spat between foreign minister Andrei Kozyrev and Talbott in which Kozyrev raged, "Don't add insult to injury by also telling us that it's in our interests to obey your orders." Trying to bring Russian foreign policy into conformity with U.S. preferences was jokingly labeled "the spinach treatment" by Talbott's aide Victoria Nuland, who compared the process to trying to get children to eat healthy foods like spinach.[29]

Moreover, the rapid and sudden collapse in the Russian economy, combined with the incredible surge in the United States, now meant, as former foreign minister Igor Ivanov has acknowledged, that the United States "had pulled far ahead" of Russia during the 1990s, making it impossible to maintain even the pretense of superpower equality.[30] Washington no longer felt bound to consult with Russia on a variety of global issues or to make sure that Russia was a coconvener with the United States of international meetings, as had occurred during the Cold War.[31]

Moreover, the United States could insist on serving up the spinach because Russia was now a recipient of U.S. aid as it struggled to put its house in order. Under the provisions of the 1991 legislation sponsored by Senators Sam Nunn and Richard Lugar, Russia received U.S. funds to dismantle Soviet weapons and to ensure that scientists formerly employed by the Soviet nuclear program could continue to receive salaries, to prevent both Soviet technology and personnel from seeking patronage from other states. The 1992 Freedom Support Act committed the United States to assist Russia's transition to a free-market democracy. By continuing to appeal to the United States and other Western countries and Western-led global institutions such as the International Monetary Fund (IMF) for aid, assistance, and loans, Russia was no longer approaching the United States on a basis of equality but on one of dependency. In turn, U.S. officials assumed that they could intervene in Russia's domestic institutions to help shape reform along preferred American lines.[32]

The U.S.-led effort to advise Russia on economic and political reforms is one of the most controversial aspects in recent U.S.–Russia relations. Many Russians blamed Western advice for creating conditions that left Russia worse off economically, reinforced cultural predispositions toward corruption, and, by promoting a rapid sell-off of state enterprises, helped to engender the rise of a small group of ultra-rich oligarchs who took control of most of Russia's productive assets. Some even concluded "that the United States set out deliberately to destroy [the Russian] economy," as a way of "finishing off" America's erstwhile Cold War rival.[33] Russia, which also became the largest borrower from the IMF during the 1990s, found that its freedom to set its own economic policies was constrained by "conditionality"— the requirement to implement IMF directives in order to receive the funds. By the late 1990s, Russia was the single largest borrower from the IMF, racking up loans of nearly $20 billion. At the same time, the country's economy contracted by some 60%, and 60 million Russians were estimated to be living in poverty.[34]

Of this period, Andranik Migranyan has commented:

> Russian-American relations in the 1990s were tainted . . . The perception was widespread that all important decisions regarding personnel and key domestic and foreign matters were taken either directly in or with the approval of Washington. During this period, many Russians felt deeply humiliated due to their de facto loss of sovereignty at the time when the ex-superpower was undergoing an economic, social and psychological catastrophe. It found itself forced to negotiate all sorts of domestic and foreign policies with Washington just so it could receive the next transfer of IMF funds or political support for Yeltsin and the young reformers against the communist and great-power patriotic opposition. Since the 1990s, therefore, many Russians have harbored an aversion toward American meddling in Russian affairs—or otherwise put, toward American participation in managing Russian affairs either directly or through U.S. political and economic advisers.[35]

And even if the ideological conflict between Russia and the United States was over, their geopolitical and economic interests continued to clash during the Clinton years. The United States, concerned about the spread of advanced technologies to "states of concern," put a great deal of pressure on Russia to cancel contracts with countries ranging from China and India to Iran, Syria, and Angola and sought to curtail Russian arms exports. However, Washington did little to help Russian firms find new markets, particularly if it meant losing market share for U.S. companies. A July 1993 editorial in *Rossiiskaia Gazeta* declared: "The time has come to acknowledge that where arms exports are concerned, we and . . . the U.S. are not partners but competitors, both economically and politically."[36]

More troubling, as Igor Ivanov has noted, was the "U.S. attempt to force Russia out of territories" that historically were in the Russian sphere of influence in Eurasia and eastern Europe, particularly in the Balkans.[37] Russia also did not see eye to eye with the United States on the situations in Iraq and the former Yugoslavia, leading to tensions, particularly in the UN Security Council, where, after a few years of Moscow's acquiescence to America's perspective, the Russians "resurrected" their use of the veto to block U.S.-backed proposals.[38]

Until 1996, the Russian government was dominated by Atlanticists who tried to accommodate Washington's preferences, preferring to promote cooperation with the United States over supporting traditional friends of Moscow. But after the strong showing of nationalist forces in the 1993 and 1995 Duma elections, the mood in Moscow shifted. The appointment of Yevgeny Primakov as foreign minister in 1996 changed the tenor of U.S.–Russia relations. Although not hostile to the idea of partnership, Primakov nevertheless believed that "that U.S.–Russia relations were essentially and eternally a zero-sum game"[39] and openly sought to limit the influence of the United States by encouraging the rise of other powers such as China and India. Moreover, he was more inclined to support domestic Russian interests—including powerful lobbies in the defense and atomic energy industries—rather than Washington's preferences when considering proposals such as sanctioning Iran.

Yeltsin's earlier hopes for partnership with the United States were further weakened by a number of issues that began to dominate the U.S.–Russia bilateral agenda during the Clinton years and have remained constant irritants ever since. The United States has committed itself to preventing the emergence of any sort of Russian "sphere of influence" in the Eurasian space; to expanding Euro-Atlantic institutions such as NATO eastward to include the countries of the former Soviet space; to ensuring that there are multiple routes for energy and trade between Eurasia and the rest of the world, including routes that bypass Russia or are free from Russian influence; and to promoting liberal and free-market reforms in Russia and other former Soviet states, on the assumption that democratic states are more likely to be friendly to the United States and supportive of its international agenda.[40] In theory, there is nothing in this agenda that is explicitly anti-Russian, and if the United States committed to bring Russia into the institutions of the Euro-Atlantic world with a significant voice in shaping the agenda, including veto power over some decisions, then the points for conflict would be minimized.[41] But the Russian side has remained quite suspicious of U.S. intentions because the results of these policies appear to work against what Moscow views as its legitimate political, security, and economic interests. (Three of the major flash points for disagreements—the expansion of the NATO alliance, American opposition to Russian-led integration in the Eurasian space, and U.S. efforts to construct defenses against ballistic missiles—will be addressed in greater detail further later in this chapter.)

After the Russian financial crisis of 1998, which further devastated the economy and largely discredited American advice and counsel on how to reform Russia, the Russian government was far less inclined to follow America's lead. Matters came to a head in 1999 with the crisis over Kosovo. For Russia, facing its own separatist rebellion in Chechnya, the precedent of using military action against Yugoslavia for its campaign in Kosovo was problematic. The willingness of the United States to circumvent the UN Security Council and to deploy NATO in an operation in eastern Europe was quite troubling, despite the reassurances of U.S. National Security Advisor Samuel Berger that any NATO airstrikes against Serbia would not affect the U.S.-Russia relationship. When the operation began in March 1999, Primakov, now prime minister, was heading to Washington for talks with U.S. leaders; midway over the Atlantic, he ordered his plane turned around and returned to Moscow. At the time, as Dimitri Simes noted, "Moscow does have limited options in responding to whatever NATO does in Yugoslavia. But there will be a reaction sometime, somewhere—and perhaps on a matter of greater importance to America than events in Kosovo."[42] Moreover, a Russian-American clash was narrowly avoided when Russian peacekeepers arrived in Kosovo after the NATO air campaign and took control of the Pristina airport ahead of Western forces. The fallout from the Kosovo campaign—and the start of the second Chechen conflict later that year—also meant that emerging proposals for joint Russian–American action to neutralize a growing threat metastasizing in Afghanistan—the Taliban regime that was sheltering Osama bin Laden and his Al-Qaeda organization—ended up being stillborn.[43]

After Boris Yeltsin resigned the presidency on New Year's Eve 1999, his prime minister, Vladimir Putin, became acting president and then won the elections in March 2000. Upon taking office, Putin made it clear that he would reverse the situation of the 1990s by revitalizing Russian power so that it could defend its interests abroad. Putin showed little interest in continuing the "Boris and Bill" relationship with the Clinton administration. In the waning days of the Clinton presidency, the United States was eager to cement a series of final arrangements with Russia, especially an agreement that would clear the way for the United States to move forward on missile defense research. But Putin preferred a wait-and-see approach pending the outcome of the 2000 elections rather than reach any definitive agreements with a lame-duck president. The guiding assumption behind the Putin team's approach was that if Al Gore was elected, they could revisit the Clinton initiatives; but if George W. Bush entered the White House, there would be no guarantee he would be bound by any executive agreement crafted by his predecessor.[44]

PUTIN–BUSH AND OBAMA–MEDVEDEV: SOUL CONNECTIONS?

The George W. Bush administration took office in January 2001 extremely skeptical about Russia and eager to make a clear break with the policies of the Clinton administration. Indeed, one of the major attacks directed against Vice President Al Gore in 2000 was the "overpersonalization" of U.S.–Russia relations, both between Clinton and Yeltsin and between Gore and Russian prime minister Viktor Chernomyrdin. There was also a strong sense that the new Republican administration would work to contain Russia. One of the first steps the Bush team took was to dismantle the Clinton-era State Department configuration for diplomacy with Russia, effectively downgrading Moscow's importance.[45] For their part, key people within the Putin administration, beginning with the Russian president himself, were highly critical of what they perceived as the excessive deference of the Yeltsin presidency to U.S. preferences and interests. Putin made it clear that he would never consider himself to be a "tool" of the West.[46]

The June 2001 summit meeting in Ljubljana, Slovenia, between Bush and Putin was a turning point. The unexpected personal rapport between the two presidents and apparent similarities in their world views allowed for "a very good dialogue" that seemed to dissipate the problems that had been building up in the U.S.–Russia relationship.[47] This strengthened the position of the "pro-engagement" camp within the Bush administration, which argued that it would be possible to develop a better relationship with Russia, as opposed to the skeptics, who had predominated during the campaign and who argued that the differences between the two countries, especially in terms of values, could not easily be bridged.[48]

The Bush–Putin relationship was enhanced after the events of 9/11, when Putin was the first foreign leader to contact Bush and to offer Russian assistance in combating Al-Qaeda. Putin's willingness to override the recommendations of many of his senior military and foreign policy advisors to facilitate the deployment of American forces to Central Asia as a staging ground for Operation Enduring Freedom in Afghanistan also made a major impact on the Bush administration's tendency to view Russia more positively.[49] Both presidents believed that the strategic partnership that had eluded Clinton and Yeltsin now seemed to be achievable, based on common interests such as weapons nonproliferation, energy, and the global war on terror. For Putin, attempting to revitalize the Russian economy after the disastrous decade of the 1990s, cooperation, not confrontation, with the West was vital; he hoped that the United States would work to integrate Russia into the global economy and Western institutions. Bush wanted Russian cooperation in combating terrorism and nuclear nonproliferation. Both preached the virtues of an energy partnership—one that would give Russia guaranteed markets for its energy and help the United States reduce its dependence on Middle Eastern sources of supply. Initially, events seem to bear out an optimistic appraisal of the situation. As a sign of goodwill, and also reflecting the cash-strapped Kremlin treasury, Putin closed a Soviet-era intelligence installation in Cuba and registered only mild public protests against the U.S. decision to withdraw from the ABM Treaty at the end of 2001. Both countries cooperated in 2002 in a joint mission to remove enriched uranium from the Vinca reactor in Serbia to safekeeping in Russia, reducing the risk that it might fall into hostile hands. As a sign of the growing trust between both countries, Bush and Putin signed the Treaty of Moscow (Strategic Offensive Reductions Treaty) in May 2002, committing both sides to lowering their arsenal of operational nuclear warheads to between 1,700 and 2,200. Unlike earlier agreements, which contained elaborate and extensive verification mechanisms, the Moscow accords essentially operated on the honor system. At the time, National Security Advisor Condoleezza Rice declared that the agreement "codifies what President Bush and President Putin have decided independently are the levels needed to defend their countries . . . in a way that doesn't look like an agreement that you would make with an enemy like the Soviet Union, but rather more like a defense-planning guidance with the Russians."[50]

In addition, Bush and Putin initiated a "strategic energy dialogue" in June 2002, bringing together both government officials as well as representatives of energy companies, designed to give ballast to U.S.-Russia ties by allowing the United States to shift away from the Persian Gulf as a source of supply and to give Russia a greater stake in the U.S. energy market. One of the first proposals was for private Russian oil companies to build an export pipeline to the deep-water port of Murmansk to export oil directly to the United States via super-tanker. However, the dialogue stalled after the Russian government took action in September 2003 against the privately owned YUKOS oil company and arrested its owner, Mikhail Khodorkovsky (later sentenced to a long prison term in Siberia). Khodorkovsky was one of a group of powerful Russian businessmen collectively referred to as the oligarchs who, during the privatization campaign of the 1990s, had acquired many valuable Russian assets at low prices, in part due to their political connections. In addition, Khodorkovsky had cultivated important U.S. business and political leaders, including key members of Congress, and so his arrest became part of the fabric of U.S.-Russia relations.[51] While some of the reasons for Kremlin action against Khodorkovsky had to do with his domestic political activities, Khodorkovsky had also contemplated selling his firm to a U.S. company (Exxon Mobil), which would have given an American firm direct control over Russian energy reserves.[52]

The YUKOS affair was the start of a process that saw the Kremlin begin to scrutinize the terms of deals reached during the 1990s, leading to the revocation or modification of longstanding licenses that had been granted to Western companies to exploit Russian oil and gas fields.[53] Finally, the Duma passed a new subsoil law in 2008 which, in terms of energy, defined as strategic any field that contains more than 70 million tons of recoverable oil or 50 billion cubic meters of natural gas; such projects could only be developed by a majority-Russian partner and were not open to ownership by foreign interests.[54] The Bush administration's hope that American companies might be able to buy Russian energy assets evaporated. The energy dialogue also withered because the United States, concerned that Europe was becoming too dependent on Russian sources of energy, as well as the enormous leverage that energy supplies gave Russia over its neighbors, actively supported energy diversification efforts—finding both non-Russian Eurasian sources of supply for gas and oil and facilitating transport routes that bypassed Russian territory. The United States had played a lead role during the 1990s in engendering the Baku-Tbilisi-Ceyhan line, which, after beginning operations in 2005, shipped Caspian oil from Azerbaijan to a terminal in Turkey on the Mediterranean Sea, completely bypassing Russian territory. But the United States continued to promote other such projects during the Bush years as well. In particular, Washington strongly promoted the so-called NABUCCO pipeline designed to bypass Russia in bringing Central Asian gas to European markets and to give European states an alternative to Russia. The United States also tried to block Russian investment in other European energy projects. For instance, in April 2006, Secretary of State Condoleezza Rice, during her visits to Greece and Turkey, apparently lobbied both governments to block Gazprom participation in a Greece-Turkey gas pipeline "whether as a shareholder in the pipeline company or as a gas supplier." Russia, in turn, interpreted U.S. efforts as a way to limit Russian power, since so much of Russia's tax base comes from the export of energy.[55] By the middle part of the decade, therefore, the strategic energy dialogue was effectively at an end.

Without the incentives that growing business ties between the two countries might have provided to keep the relationship on an even keel, there was no mechanism to prevent inevitable disagreements from damaging hopes for a new partnership. Putin's economic policies plus rising energy prices enabled Russia to pay off its debts and thus removed what had been a key point of leverage that Washington had used to get Moscow to agree to U.S. preferences during the 1990s: the need for international loans to keep its economy afloat. Russia's willingness to challenge the United States—especially Putin's vocal opposition to the 2003 U.S. invasion of Iraq and Russia's decision, along with France and Germany, to block efforts to get the UN Security Council to authorize the use of force against Saddam Hussein—challenged the assumption that a post–Soviet Russia would defer to U.S. global leadership. It also undermined the positions put forward by the pro-engagement group in the Bush administration who argued that a viable U.S.-Russia partnership based on shared interests was possible, and it enabled the skeptics to argue that Russia would always be a rival to the United States. It meant that there was no consistent position on Russia to be found within the U.S. national security bureaucracy, and efforts to find, in Secretary of State Condoleezza Rice's words, a "balanced position" meant that U.S. policy was often the result of a compromise between engagers and skeptics that satisfied neither position and also did not produce a coherent U.S. approach.[56]

Russian opposition to U.S. policies, the arrest of Khodorkovsky, and the growing authoritarian bent of the Putin administration empowered the skeptics within the Bush administration as well as critics of Russia within the U.S. Congress, who argued that Russia's "democracy deficit" at home would make Moscow more hostile to U.S. interests abroad.[57] Michael McFaul, who became ambassador to Russia in 2012, argued in 2003 that some of the disagreements between Moscow and Washington would not have happened had a "fully consolidated democracy" been in place in Moscow, implying that a more democratic Russia would be a more pro–American state.[58] Congressional skepticism, in turn, impeded Bush's efforts to advance the U.S.-Russia relationship. Despite his personal assurances, Bush could not get the U.S. Congress to pass the legislation that would turn his promises into reality:

> After his first meeting with Putin, Bush promised that he would push to have Russia graduated from the Jackson-Vanik amendment, which was passed in 1974 to put trade restrictions on nonmarket (read Communist) economies that prohibited the free emigration of their citizens. This would create normal trading relations between the U.S. and Russia, a necessary precondition for Russia to be able to enter the World Trade Organization. He was unable to mobilize support to do this, however, because this remained a Congressional point of leverage over Russia.[59]

Similarly, at the 2006 G-8 summit in St. Petersburg, Bush pledged that he would work to secure a so-called 123 Agreement (named after the relevant section of the 1954 Atomic Energy act) that permits U.S. companies to work on nuclear projects with other countries and would clear the way for U.S.-Russia cooperation in the nuclear field. However, this requires Congressional approval. The deal was signed in May 2008 after prolonged negotiations but never made it past the U.S. Congress. Indeed, Senator Joe Biden frankly declared the 123 Agreement to be "dead" unless Russia did not "reverse course" on a number of issues that were at odds with American policy.[60]

At the same time, the influence of the Atlanticists within the Russian government had seriously waned since the days of the early Yeltsin administration, and the Putin government was less receptive to American criticism. When U.S. officials criticized Russia's domestic policies—particularly Putin's push for a greater centralization of power, limits on political and press freedoms, and some reversals of privatization, which went against the preferred American template for Russian reform—Russian officials denounced what they perceived as unwarranted interference in Russia's internal affairs. Putin himself has repeatedly denounced "direct or indirect foreign interference" in Russia's domestic policies and rejected "standards enforced on us from outside."[61] Furthermore, pro–American officials who served in the foreign policy apparatus in the beginning years of the Putin government, including Foreign Minister Igor Ivanov, left office and were replaced by those who were much more skeptical of U.S. intentions.[62]

In the first years of the Putin and Bush administrations, there was a sincere effort on both sides to try and promote a partnership; the skeptics in both Moscow and Washington had been temporarily sidelined in the aftermath of 9/11. The turning point appears to have occurred in 2004. In September of that year, Chechen separatists seized a school in Beslan in the North Caucasus. American criticisms of Russian actions, including the general scope of Russian counterinsurgency policies, as well as continued sympathy for the Chechen cause among some U.S. officials, convinced many in Moscow that the United States was not committed to helping Russia fight terrorism.[63] Later in the fall, the so-called Orange Revolution in Ukraine in 2004 (which will be discussed in greater detail in the chapter on the Eurasian space), which brought a pro–Western candidate (Viktor Yushchenko) to power after an attempt to install a more pro-Moscow figure was thwarted by wide-ranging protests, was interpreted as part of an overall U.S. effort to drive out Russian influence in the countries of the post-Soviet space altogether.[64] Given strong U.S. support for the Rose Revolution in Georgia in 2003, U.S. opposition to a Russian-supported plan (the memorandum penned by Dmitry Kozak, of the Russian presidential administration) for reuniting the separatist region of Transdnistria with Moldova and the subsequent U.S. support for a pro–Western authoritarian regime in Azerbaijan even against a nascent prodemocracy movement in 2005 reinforced Russian suspicions that the United States was not supporting democracy in the region per se but seeking to roll back Russian influence. These concerns were heightened when the United States formally supported the candidacies of post–Soviet states like Ukraine and Georgia to join NATO.[65] Initially, the Russian political elite interpreted partnership with the United States to mean the recognition of Russia as a "regional superpower" in Eurasia.[66] Now it seemed that Washington was working against Russia's security and economic interests in its own backyard. When Russia began to apply its political and economic leverage to secure its interests—for instance, by raising the price of natural gas shipped to Ukraine and then temporarily shutting off supplies (for instance, in January 2006) for nonpayment, this provoked a negative reaction in Washington. In turn, statements by Bush administration officials that it was U.S. policy to encourage the mergence "of independent, sovereign, pluralistic states that are territorially secure, free from external political domination and economically engaged with international markets"[67] was seen in Moscow as a signal that the United States would actively take measures to frustrate Russia's efforts to develop a common Eurasian market (then styled the Single Economic Space and now serving as the nucleus for a future Eurasian Union) on the grounds that this was an unacceptable manifestation of Russia's "imperial ambitions" and a plot to bring about a "reconstituted empire."[68]

Plans to expand NATO to encompass more former Soviet-bloc countries and even former Soviet republics—raising fears that the United States was planning to "encircle" Russia—and the U.S. proposal to deploy a missile defense system in Europe, ostensibly to protect against a threat from Iran (both of which will be discussed in greater detail below), further complicated matters. Putin's approach to the United States had been sold to key sectors in Russia as a way to generate concrete benefits through a closer partnership. When these initial hopes were not borne out by subsequent developments, the Russian government was less willing to accommodate U.S. policy priorities that damaged Russian interests. The Putin government gave the green light for Russian firms, including state companies, to expand their business contacts with states "of concern" to Washington—including Iran, Venezuela, and North Korea, among others. For instance, in December 2007, foreign minister Lavrov indicated that Russia would honor its contract with Iran to complete the nuclear reactor at Bushehr and to supply nuclear fuel for its operation and publicly challenged U.S. assertions that Iran was attempting to build a nuclear weapon.[69] Russia was also more likely to block U.S. initiatives in international institutions like the United Nations. As Alexey Pushkov, now the chairman of the Duma's Foreign Affairs committee, concluded, "Putin has not dropped the idea of partnership with the United States altogether, but he has definitely moved away from some of the more grandiose proposals in favor of a much more limited arrangement."[70] Bush and Putin met on the sidelines of the G-8 summit in Heiligendamm, Germany, in June 2007; Bush followed up this meeting with an invitation to his family's "compound" in Maine in July for the so-called Lobster Summit. But it was now clear that the personal friendship of the two presidents could not overcome these significant policy differences—no compromises were reached on the questions of NATO expansion, Kosovo independence, or missile defense. Bush's own room for maneuver was also circumscribed by the U.S. Congress, which in 2007 passed legislation (signed into law by the president) that made it U.S. policy to support the "timely admission" of "Georgia . . . and Ukraine" in NATO.[71]

U.S.–Russia relations deteriorated even further in 2008. The United States made a major diplomatic push to have NATO issue formal invitations to Georgia and Ukraine to begin the process of applying for membership, despite heated objections from Moscow. Washington also brushed aside Russia's concerns about Kosovo and formally recognized the province as a separate independent state instead of waiting for diplomatic negotiations between Serbia and the Kosovars to produce a settlement, which was Russia's preference. Finally, the George Bush administration signed agreements with Poland and the Czech Republic for deploying missile defense assets in those countries. Bush did attempt to bridge these growing gaps with Russia when he had his final summit meeting with Putin in Sochi in April, but no agreements were forthcoming; both presidents settled for a vaguely worded statement about the need for a "road map" for the future of U.S.–Russia relations.[72]

What brought matters to a head was the Georgia–Russia conflict in August 2008. There has been an increasing number of incidents along the cease-fire lines separating Georgia proper from the separatist regions of Abkhazia and South Ossetia, where Russian peacekeepers were deployed. Under the leadership of president Mikheil Saakashvili, Georgia had become one of the largest recipients of U.S. aid and, by becoming one of the largest contributors of forces to U.S.-led missions in Iraq and Afghanistan, had obtained a good deal of military training and equipment for his forces. With strong bipartisan support within the United States for Georgian membership in NATO, Saakashvili believed he would "have U.S. support in any clash with Russia. In August 2008, Georgian forces moved into South Ossetia. Russia responded by first pushing the Georgians out from the disputed territories, and then proceeded to cripple Georgia's military infrastructure by attacking Georgia proper, occupying territory, and destroying military equipment."[73]

The United States chose not to respond militarily to the Russian incursion, and after a EU-brokered cease-fire took effect, Russia took no further action against the Saakashvili government. However, the attack caused the United States and other NATO countries to suspend their military-to-military ties with Russia and effectively ended any chance of approving a civil nuclear deal between the two countries—a key part of Bush's energy partnership. The Georgia war and a further brief shut-off of natural gas supplies to Ukraine in January 2009 signaled that Russia was willing to risk good relations with the United States in order to protect its interests in Eurasia and eastern Europe.[74]

Russia emerged as an issue in the 2008 U.S. presidential elections between John McCain and Barack Obama, with both strongly condemning Russia for its attack on Georgia, but after the election, the president-elect and his emerging national security team (including incoming National Security Advisor Jim Jones, Secretary of State Hillary Clinton, and National Security Council Senior Director Michael McFaul, as well as Robert Gates, who was retained as secretary of defense) began to step back from some of the more damaging rhetoric. At the same time, some of the advisors around President Medvedev—including his national security advisor Sergei Prikhodko, Prikhodko's deputy Aleksandr Manzhosin, economic advisor Arkady Dvorkovich, and defense minister Anatoly Serdyukov—argued that a confrontational stance vis-à-vis the United States harmed core Russian interests, including the modernization of the economy.[75]

In February 2009, the Obama administration announced that it would pursue a "reset" in relations with Russia; the next month, Clinton traveled to Geneva to meet with Foreign Minister Lavrov; at those meetings, she presented him with a button that she thought was labeled with the word *reset* (in reality, the Russian word chosen, *peregruzka,* refers to overcharging for goods improperly weighed). Despite this inauspicious beginning, both sides seized upon the formulation of a reset as a way to put the problems in the U.S.-Russia relationship behind them.[76] Obama's interest in arms control and Medvedev's belief that Russia needed to address its "irritants" in its relationship with Washington paved the way for a productive summit meeting between the two presidents in July 2009. Personal factors also played a role: Both men were comparatively young, shared similar interests, and enjoyed each other's company (as was demonstrated on an impromptu visit the two leaders took to a hamburger restaurant in Arlington, Virginia, in June 2010). This camaraderie also fed into a narrative that Medvedev was more likely to move Russia in a liberal, "pro-American" direction.[77]

Obama's reset was also aided by factors that were not under America's control or direction. In February 2010, Viktor Yanukovych, whose last attempt to win the presidency of Ukraine in 2004 had triggered the Orange Revolution, won the elections to become president. Committed to a more balanced foreign policy for Ukraine between Russia and the West, he eschewed his predecessor's confrontational stance vis-à-vis Russia, stopped efforts for Ukraine to join NATO, and signed a new, long-term lease allowing the Russian Black Sea Fleet to remain in its base at Sevastopol. In April, the very public expressions of condolences by Russian officials in the aftermath of the tragic plane crash that killed Polish president Lech Kaczynski and other Polish officials on their way to the Katyn Memorial helped to create momentum for Russian-Polish reconciliation. The reset was also aided by the extensive diplomatic effort conducted by French President Nicolas Sarkozy and German Chancellor Angela Merkel designed to better integrate Russia in the overall discussion of European security matters as well as to accelerate the bonds of economic integration between key Western countries and Russia.[78]

The Obama and Medvedev administrations were able to make progress on a series of issues that had eluded Bush and Putin. The Russian government approved the use of the so-called Northern Distribution Network (NDN) to send nonlethal cargo to U.S. and NATO forces in Afghanistan, which began operations in February

2009.[79] However, by summer Moscow agreed to permit U.S. military forces and equipment to utilize the routes across Russia into Afghanistan, an important concession that aided the United States, especially after Pakistan closed its territory for transshipment purposes. In 2012, the Russian government expanded the scope of American usage of the NDN to include using Russian facilities to transport goods and personnel into and out of Afghanistan—giving the United States a secure route to withdraw its forces as the Western mission comes to an end.[80]

U.S.-Russia cooperation over Afghanistan was seen by many as a promising field for deepening the bilateral relationship. Obama's first Defense Secretary, Robert Gates, argued that the situation in Afghanistan offered "a number of areas" for closer U.S.-Russia interaction, including the very important role Russia has played in setting up the Northern Distribution Network, which is now the main supply line for U.S. and NATO forces, as well as for joint exercises to cope with terrorism and narcotics smuggling emanating from that country. In addition, the U.S. government has purchased Russian military equipment—including Mi-17 helicopters—to equip Afghan security forces—even at the cost of angering domestic U.S. manufacturers that were angling for these contracts.[81]

In 2010, the Russian government decided to support stronger economic sanctions against Iran, supporting a U.S. resolution at the United Nations, and cancelled existing contracts with Iran, notably for the sale of the advanced S-300 air defense system. The Russian government also agreed to sign a "new START" arms treaty to replace the original agreement, which had expired in 2009—and dropped its demands for linking nuclear arms reductions to the United States accepting any restraints on America's ability to deploy missile defenses.[82] In the agreement, which was signed on April 8, 2010, the Russians agreed to put their concerns about missile defense into the preamble, which the United States government noted is not legally binding. This compromise removed what had been the main holdup in talks prior to the expiration of the original START and allowed the Obama administration to claim progress in its goal to reduce nuclear weapons.[83] After signing the new treaty in Prague with Obama, Medvedev traveled to Washington for Obama's Nuclear Security Summit and signed further agreements with the United States that would transfer plutonium from weapons use to power generation.[84]

The Obama administration also moved ahead with the 123 civil nuclear agreement with Russia that Biden had declared to be dead back in 2008, strongly lobbying Congress to let the agreement go into force even despite continuing disagreements over Georgia as a way to demonstrate to key Russian commercial interests that interruption of lucrative ties with Iran could be compensated by new contracts with American firms in the nuclear power industry. To further avoid upsetting the reset, the administration also agreed not to sell advanced weapons to Georgia. In turn, Medvedev used these steps to persuade powerful interests in the defense and nuclear power industries that cooperation with the United States would be more profitable in the long run.[85] In keeping with this strategy, the Russian government also abstained from the vote on UN Security Council resolution 1973, which authorized the creation of a "no-fly zone" over Libya after the rebellion against Muammar Qaddafi broke out; Medvedev later signed a decree enforcing sanctions against the Qaddafi government.[86]

The reset also generated a major energy deal: a partnership agreement between the Russian state oil firm Rosneft and the U.S. company Exxon-Mobil, which created a joint venture for drilling for oil in the Russian Arctic and opened up some assets in the Gulf of Mexico to Rosneft. The deal, which was finalized in August 2011 and which gave a U.S. firm access to substantial Russian energy reserves, would not have been possible in the negative environment of U.S.-Russia relations prior to 2009, and it was seen by many analysts as proof that "the reset has had a positive effect on U.S.-Russia energy relations."[87]

Yet, despite these clear signs of improvement in U.S.-Russia relations, old problems reared their heads, primarily based around the same set of unresolved issues that had doomed the Bush–Putin efforts to forge a closer partnership.

The Obama administration did succeed in getting the 123 agreement through the Congress, but Congressional skeptics of the reset with Russia, particularly in the U.S. Senate, re-emerged when the new START agreement came up for ratification. The treaty, signed in April 2010, was ultimately ratified by a lame-duck session of the Senate in December 2010, but not until after significant opposition had been expressed by some members of Congress. To get the treaty passed, the Obama administration had to make firm commitments that it would continue with missile defense, even over Russian opposition. In addition, some of those who voted for the treaty noted that in other areas of the U.S.-Russia relationship, they would exercise greater scrutiny of Russia's record on human rights and democratization in deciding whether to advance cooperation.[88]

The second was how the United States and its NATO allies conducted the Libya campaign. Instead of focusing on creating "safe havens" for civilians, the mission soon shifted to aiding the forcible overthrow of Muammar Qaddafi by Libyan rebels. Russian officials took this as a sign that the U.S. was initiating a new wave of efforts at regime change but focused only on anti–American (and in some cases pro-Russian regimes), a charge that acquired salience when the United States chose not to support prodemocracy demonstrators in Bahrain, where the United States maintains military facilities.[89] The Russian government, as a result, throughout 2011 and 2012 decided to use its position in the United Nations to block a repeat of the Libya resolution in the case of Syria, leading to new tensions between Washington and Moscow.

The announcement in September 2011 that Putin would return to the presidency challenged one of the core assumptions of the reset: that it was designed to support and bolster a more liberal Medvedev.[90] The emergence of a protest movement in Russia over how the December Duma elections were conducted emboldened Congressional opponents of the reset, such as Senator John McCain, who warned Putin that the "Arab spring was coming to a neighborhood near you." This provoked a reaction from Putin, who in turn accused the United States of having assassinated Qaddafi and embarking on a new crusade to remake the world in America's image.[91] After Secretary of State Hillary Clinton described the Russian elections as neither free nor fair, Putin accused her of having helped to instigate protests to destabilize Russia; her remarks, Putin argued, "set the tone for some opposition activists, gave them a signal, they heard this signal and started active work."[92] Indeed, a constant theme since the December 2011 elections has been that foreign governments, usually understood to be led by the United States, are seeking to undermine the Russian political system, a point reiterated by Putin in his December 2012 annual address to the Duma.[93] By the beginning of 2013, the Russian government had placed new restrictions on the activities of groups receiving funding from American sources, following up on a ban enacted against the work of the U.S. Agency for International Development (AID) in Russia; the Foreign Ministry bluntly declared in September 2012 that "Russia's civil society has become fully mature and does not need 'external guidance.'"[94]

The Russian government also reacted badly to U.S. criticisms of its law enforcement and judicial systems after the death in November 2009 of Russian lawyer Sergei Magnitsky while being held in detention after he had uncovered compelling evidence of official corruption and malfeasance on the part of Russian law enforcement and government officials in defrauding his client, the Western investment fund Hermitage Capital. Criticisms grew in the wake of a Russian government crackdown on the political opposition and on perceived opponents of the Putin government, especially after the arrest, trial, and imprisonment of a punk-rock collective (Pussy Riot), which had staged an obscene anti–Putin "punk prayer" inside the Cathedral of Christ the Savior in Moscow in February 2012.[95] As the Obama administration pushed to graduate Russia from the requirements of the Jackson-Vanik legislation, many in Congress argued for a replacement set of "smart sanctions" that would target Russian officials accused of human rights violations. The Russian government denounced this legislation as unwarranted interference in Russia's domestic affairs. After the U.S. Congress granted Russia normal trading relations while passing the Magnitsky sanctions, at the end of 2012, Putin argued that this move "contaminates our relations" with the United States, although he also promised that the Russian response would be "measured."[96] To signal their displeasure, the Russian Duma responded by moving forward on legislation targeting U.S. officials that Moscow alleges have violated human rights, as well as banning adoptions of Russian orphans by U.S. citizens and putting limits on U.S.-funded nongovernmental organizations' activity in Russia.[97]

All of these developments have left "Russian-American relations . . . emotionally strained" and highlighted how the reset "failed to develop a new positive agenda for Russian-American relations."[98] At the start of 2013, however, there was a realization in both Washington and Moscow that further deterioration might jeopardize the positive gains of the last several years. Officials in both capitals have pledged that bilateral engagement will continue on a wide variety of issues. With normal trading relations finally established between the two countries, Putin has expressed guarded optimism that the relationship might acquire a "new quality" with the expansion of business and commercial ties.[99] When the new U.S. secretary of state, John Kerry, met with Lavrov in Berlin at the end of February 2013, both men described their talks as constructive, leading observers to speculate that the two could find ways to mediate the irritants in the bilateral relationship.[100] But this depends on whether both countries can navigate what appear to a series of enduring obstacles to closer relations.

SOME ENDURING OBSTACLES

A key tenet of the U.S. approach to Russia is what has been termed "selective partnership"—the idea that serious disagreements between Russia and the United States in some areas need not preclude effective cooperation in others. In 2009, speaking at the Munich Security Conference, U.S. Vice President Joe Biden declared,

> We will not agree with Russia on everything. . . . We will not recognize any nation having a sphere of influence. It will remain our view that sovereign states have the right to make their own decisions and choose their own alliances. But the United States and Russia can disagree and still work together where our interests coincide. And they coincide in many places.[101]

The problem, however, is that from the Russian side, "selective partnership" is understood to mean that Washington expects full Russian cooperation on a whole host of important matters to U.S. national security while being free to ignore Russian concerns that conflict with American preferences.[102]

Two of the most consistent and enduring issues that have frustrated a closer U.S.-Russia partnership have been U.S. plans to deploy antiballistic missile defenses and America's push to expand the North Atlantic Treaty Organization to encompass former Soviet-bloc states as well as former Soviet republics.[103]

As part of U.S. plans to prepare for the possibility that Iran would succeed in obtaining nuclear weapons, the George W. Bush administration had proposed setting up a theater ballistic missile defense system in Europe that would have included setting up a radar complex in the Czech Republic and deploying interceptors in Poland. This proposal raised hackles in Moscow because of fears that a U.S. antimissile system might be expanded one day to counteract the Russian nuclear deterrent. A secondary concern was that this would put American military personnel (even if in small numbers) in the heart of eastern Europe.

The Bush administration argued that the proposed system was designed to thwart an Iranian threat and was not structured to threaten Russia's own territory or capabilities. At the G-8 summit in Germany in 2007, Putin made a counterproposal: the creation of a joint U.S.–NATO–Russian system that would be controlled from the Gambala radar installation in Azerbaijan and use assets in Russia and other Black Sea countries to counter any possible Iranian threat.[104] Putin's offer was rejected in part because of concerns about a Russian veto over of the use of the system, but U.S. Defense Secretary Robert Gates, during his visit to Prague in October 2007 to negotiate U.S. access to facilities, tried to mollify Russian concerns by proposing that any U.S. system would not be activated "until there was concrete proof of the threat from Iran."[105] But such assurances did not mollify Moscow. In turn, the United States hardened its position by arguing that sovereign states like Poland and the Czech Republic were free to decide whether to host components of a missile defense system and implied that if Russia did not want to see the system activated, it could do more to prevent Iran from making progress on its nuclear and missile programs.

In September 2009, the Obama administration cancelled the Bush missile defense system for Europe. While this step was initially welcomed in Moscow— and criticized in the United States as an "abandonment" of Poland and the Czech Republic—the attitude of the Russian government soon shifted when it became clear that the Obama administration was not abandoning the idea of missile defense altogether but rather altering plans away from land-based sites in favor of using U.S. naval assets, with some components eventually being deployed in Europe.

The Russian military has been extremely troubled by this development. In February 2012, the then-chief of the general staff, General Nikolai Makarov, bluntly warned that the deployment of U.S. Aegis cruisers—the backbone of any proposed missile defense system—in either the Black Sea or other waters off of Russian territory "posed a threat" to Russia and would require the Russian armed forces to prepare appropriate countermeasures. He also warned that the

U.S. system would have the capability, by the end of the decade, "of shooting down strategic missiles over our territory."[106] Missile defense is also a problem for the Russian political elite, which remains unclear as to the ultimate purpose of the system.[107] Echoing Makarov, Deputy Prime Minister Dmitry Rogozin, Russia's former envoy to NATO, declared that if U.S. vessels that were part of a missile defense system appeared in the waters off Russia's coasts, it would provoke "the harshest reaction from Russia" and would imperil the U.S.-Russia reset.[108] In order to prevent new tensions, therefore, the Russian government has been insisting on a formal legal guarantee that any U.S. missile defense system would not be directed against Russia's own nuclear forces; for example, a treaty that would limit the number of interceptors that the United States might deploy in theater. But while the Obama administration has been willing to offer a nonbinding political guarantee about the intent of any system, key members of the Senate Foreign Relations Committee have made it clear that a "legal guarantee will not be necessary or possible, since that kind of a guarantee could never get through the Senate."[109] But the Russian side argues that other guarantees offered by U.S. administrations in the past have not constrained American actions and so do not carry much value.[110] Thus, the Russian government remains "deeply skeptical of America's long-term intentions," especially if Washington will not make Russia a partner in the operation and management of any missile defense system.[111]

Because the missile defense system was endorsed by NATO as a whole at its 2008 summit in Bucharest—a commitment reaffirmed by subsequent NATO summits, including the one held in Chicago in 2012—it ties into a larger problem: the vexed question of Russia's relationship to NATO and NATO's willingness to consider admitting new members from former Soviet-bloc allies and former Soviet republics. The alliance, created in 1949, initially was focused against the Soviet threat, although NATO itself regularly proclaimed, after the end of the Cold War, that it was not directed at any country anymore.

After the collapse of the Soviet Union, the Russian assumption was that NATO would disband, or, failing that, remain a military alliance comprising its existing members—an assumption buttressed by their understanding of what had been agreed upon at the time of German reunification.[112] The Russian government tended to view expansion of the alliance as an anti-Russian policy, an interpretation influenced by the fact that a number of states in central and eastern Europe sought NATO membership as a possible hedge against a resurgent Russia. However, while Moscow assumes that U.S. support for expansion is driven primarily by anti-Russian sentiment, the American interest in pushing for expansion has been driven by a number of factors. One is indeed the desire to fill the vacuum left by the collapse of the Warsaw Pact and to expand the strategic frontiers of the Euro-Atlantic world. But the willingness of aspirant countries (labeled New Europe by Secretary of Defense Donald Rumsfeld) to support U.S. interventions around the world and to supply forces to these missions was also an important factor in why Washington backed expansion of NATO. Given that a number of the former Soviet-bloc countries would not qualify for immediate membership in the European Union, expanding the alliance was also seen as a way to keep governments in central and eastern Europe committed to democratic reforms. This was an important reason a number of European countries backed U.S. expansion plans—in part to be able to draw out the accession process for former Soviet bloc countries to join the EU. Finally, domestic U.S. politics played a role, particularly given the expatriate Polish community in key swing states like Illinois as well as U.S. defense industries that saw additional markets for their products as new countries entered NATO, in terms of forming domestic coalitions in favor of NATO expansion.[113]

The creation of NATO's Partnership for Peace in January 1994 was designed, in part, to be a hedge on the question of expansion, with some concluding that the states of the former Soviet bloc and the former Soviet Union would never qualify for actual membership and with others hoping that the tangled question of Russia's position vis-à-vis the alliance could be resolved before the time came to admit new members. When it became clear that some eastern European states would meet the requirements for membership, the Clinton administration undertook a full-court diplomatic effort to get Russia to accept the inevitability that countries like Poland, Hungary, and the Czech Republic would enter the alliance—but also hoped that Russia could be mollified by giving it a role within NATO. The question was how to secure Russian cooperation with Western initiatives without giving Russia a share of actual decision-making authority.[114]

The compromise position was to give Russia a "voice but no veto" in the deliberations of the West. This was reflected in the negotiations that led to the Founding Act on Mutual Relations, Cooperation and Security between the North Atlantic Treaty Organization and the Russian Federation, signed on May 27, 1997. Washington hoped that, by giving Russia a formal association with NATO, the path could be cleared for enlarging the alliance by including former Soviet bloc states.[115]

The hallmark of the 1997 accord was the creation of a Permanent Joint Council (PJC) whereby Russia would sit down with the members of NATO. Yet, as Peter Trenin-Straussov concluded:

> The [two] sides...failed to agree on what the PJC would do and—as a result—they got a "disabled child." The council lacked a "home" and a permanent secretariat. It was also hugely asymmetrical in operation—Russia

was presented with a joint position of the NATO members, and could deal with NATO only *en bloc*. If the Russians made a bid, its NATO partners needed to go in retreat to discuss it and then present Russia with their joint reply. This was cumbersome, but "safe," from the NATO point of view. The Russians, for their part, soon discovered that dealing with individual NATO member states outside the PJC was more effective and satisfying. The PJC quickly turned itself into a talking shop for rather stale dialogue.[116]

A critical point of divergence was that Russia wanted this council to have a final power to veto NATO operations that occurred outside the territory of NATO members. The United States, for its part, was eager to classify a good deal of NATO's day-to-day operations as "internal" and not subject to the purview of the PJC. From the Russian perspective, the uselessness of the PJC was expressly demonstrated during the 1999 Kosovo campaign, during which Russia was unable to prevent the alliance from undertaking military action against Serbia.[117]

Partially at the initiative of British Prime Minister Tony Blair but with the full support of George W. Bush, the PJC was scrapped in 2002 in favor of the NATO-Russia Council. In contrast to the PJC, in which Russia met with the alliance only after the members had had their internal deliberations, in the NATO-Russia Council, Russia sat with the member-states at the beginning stages of any discussions before a set NATO position had been formulated. This new body allowed Russia to have a voice at the table and to have its views considered as part of the internal debate within NATO. Moscow expressed its hopes that this new structure would promote greater cooperation between Russia and the alliance and that, over time, the strategic interests of Russia and the West would align.[118]

But newer members of the NATO alliance, backed by the United States, were adamant that Moscow could never have a veto over NATO's actions. Nor would the United States agree to creating any new security architecture for Europe and Eurasia that would envision joint decision making between Russia and NATO. Most importantly, Moscow was not to be given any right to block the admission of new members.

When the second wave of NATO enlargement took place in 2004, bringing not only Balkan countries but also the three Baltic States into the alliance, the Russians expressed concern that the expansion of NATO to encompass these new members would complicate Moscow's relations with the alliance as a whole, as these states would bring their ongoing disputes with Russia into the framework of the NATO–Russia relationship.[119] More practically, NATO now had a presence directly on Russia's western frontiers, right on the doorstep of St. Petersburg, forcing the Russian military to maintain a defense perimeter within Russian territory itself, from St. Petersburg to Smolensk to Rostov, and producing a major sense of insecurity within the Russian military that previously had maintained defensive lines far to the west.[120]

All of this has led to a situation in which the Russia–NATO relationship has not been particularly fruitful. Major General Peter Williams, who headed the first NATO Military Liaison Mission in Moscow, made this assessment of the first 10 years of Russia's partnership with NATO: "Political will, structures and projects mean little without resources. . . . The resources committed for the execution of NATO-Russia Council policies and plans have been far below those suggested by the political rhetoric."[121]

In November 2007, Putin angrily lashed out against NATO for what he perceived as overly aggressive expansion, saying, "In violation of previous agreements, military resources of NATO members are being built up next to our borders . . . we cannot allow ourselves to remain indifferent to this obvious muscle-flexing."[122] Putin also suspended Russian obligations under the Conventional Forces in Europe Treaty (CFE), which limits the deployment of tanks, aircraft, and heavy conventional weapons in Europe. The Russian government made it clear that it believed it had the right to "redeploy heavy weaponry along its western and southern borders" but, as an olive branch to the United States and other Western states, made it clear that it "would do so only in response to any possible NATO redeployment."[123]

The Georgia crisis of 2008 led to a break in the official relationship between Russia and NATO. In early 2009, NATO ministers did propose a resumption of NATO–Russia contacts, including an offer to integrate the U.S.-led missile defense system with Russian components (without, however, giving Russia the ability to control the overall system). However, a NATO exercise with Georgia in May, plus the expulsion of Russian diplomats stationed at NATO headquarters in Brussels who were accused of spying that same month, led to a continued chill in relations between Russia and the alliance. Large-scale war games held in September 2009 in the Baltic region, the first since the collapse of the Soviet Union, also alarmed NATO members.[124]

But just as Obama sought to reset relations with Russia, so did NATO. The incoming secretary general, Anders Fogh Rasmussen, called for a "new beginning," downplaying the areas of disagreement and focusing on topics of common interest, including the campaign in Afghanistan and the fight against terrorism.[125] Indeed, despite much of the negativity in the Russia–NATO relationship, there have been some areas of fruitful cooperation. The Russian Navy holds regular exercises with the naval forces of NATO countries, both to further cooperation in the ongoing antipiracy mission off the coast of Somalia and to ensure safe navigation in the waters of the Arctic, which, as the ice recedes, is becoming a strategic waterway vital to Russian commercial and energy interests.[126]

Yet a final settlement of the contentious issues has not been reached. NATO expansion is currently off the table because the alliance is in no position to add new members at this point. But, as Charles Kupchan noted, the United States and other NATO members have not given up on the idea of welcoming new states like Ukraine and Georgia but instead have chosen "to put that eventual outcome on hold until it can occur under more auspicious geopolitical conditions."[127]

The question of NATO expansion highlights the continued undefined relationship of the so-called Eurasian space to Russia. Indeed, part of Russian strategy in recent years in trying to strengthen ties with the former Soviet republics—a process described in the chapter on the post–Soviet space—has been to ensure that the "more auspicious geopolitical conditions" that would permit a further round of eastward expansion for Euro-Atlantic institutions never materialize. Forming a Eurasian Union to act as a counterbalance to the West and China is now a priority in Russian politics. But while Russia sees the process of Eurasian integration "on the basis of new values, politics, and economy" as "the order of the day," in Putin's characterization, Secretary of State Clinton, in December 2012, described it as "a move to re-Sovietize the region" and promised that the United States would try "to figure out effective ways to slow down or prevent it."[128] Should the United States take active steps to try and block the Eurasian project from developing, it will generate a good deal of friction in the bilateral relationship.[129] The perception that Washington is prepared to block "even limited reintegration in the region" as part of a strategy of encouraging "geopolitical pluralism" in Eurasia (that is, preventing Russia from emerging as the dominant regional power) produces, in the characterization of Dmitry Ryurikov, a former Russian ambassador to Uzbekistan, "an objective conflict of interests and policies" between the United States and Russia that negatively impacts the overall bilateral relationship.[130] (Some of these dynamics will be discussed in greater detail in the chapter on the Eurasian space.)

If the preceding issues are the main obstacles as seen from Moscow's perspective, the United States continues to have issues with Russia. An ongoing irritant is the continued activity of Russian intelligence agencies within the United States, either to gain U.S. military secrets or to obtain useful economic intelligence.[131] In 2010, in the immediate aftermath of Medvedev's visit to the United States, a so-called ring of "sleeper spies" (Russian agents sent to live under long-term deep cover) charged with infiltrating American think tanks and companies was publicly rolled up by American law enforcement, with its members traded for Russians who had been imprisoned for spying for the United States.[132]

Beyond spying, a major concern in Washington is also how Russia operates within the key international multilateral institutions. A recurring complaint from Washington is about Moscow's obstructionist tendencies at the United

Nations or within other multilateral organizations such as the G-8 or the International Atomic Energy Agency (IAEA).[133]

Given Russia's dramatic decline from superpower status, participation in multilateral frameworks, such as the Six Party Talks on the denuclearization of the Korean peninsula or the Quartet for the Middle East Peace process are seen as "vital to Russian prestige"[134] and a recognition that Russia is still one of the influential countries of the current international system. This belief is reinforced by the fact that Russia, as the heir to the USSR, inherited its permanent membership in the United Nations Security Council, including the right of veto power. Initially, and under the influence of the Atlanticist position, the Russian government during the first Yeltsin term tended to defer to American preferences in these organizations. Former U.S. Secretary of State Madeleine Albright, who served as the U.S. ambassador to the United Nations during the first Clinton administration, observed that Russia was helpful in supporting U.S. positions on a number of issues that came before the global body.[135]

Yet given its weaknesses in political, economic, and military power vis-à-vis the United States, Russia tends to use its position in multilateral institutions like the UN to promote "negative diplomacy," using its ability to block action from going forward as a way to gain leverage and concessions, as well as more of a role in shaping outcomes that benefit its interests and those of its clients.[136] Stephen Sestanovich, the former U.S. ambassador at large for the states of the former Soviet Union during the second Clinton administration, observed, ""Russia cannot defend its authority in the UN Security Council . . . by supporting the United States, only by checking it."[137]

From the Russian perspective, acting as a spoiler at the United Nations, within the Organization for Security and Cooperation in Europe (OSCE), the Quartet, or other such institutions is important for preventing the United States from setting the rules and enforcing them on the rest of the world, in the formulation of former Russian foreign minister Igor Ivanov. To the extent that the norm now exists that no military action can take place without authorization from the UN Security Council, the requirement that the council operate on the basis of consensus requires that the United States and other Western powers give due consideration to Russian considerations.[138] In particular, Moscow has used its veto on a regular basis for the last decade to block resolutions that Russia interpreted as giving the United States a mandate for regime change by preventing action in places like Sudan and Burma (Myanmar).[139] Oftentimes the hope is that the threat of a Russian veto will cause the United States or another Western country to modify its proposal. Sometimes this has backfired; in 1999, after Russia threatened to veto any UN Security Council resolution to take action over Kosovo, the United States was "forced to take the issue out of the Security

Council and into a venue where the Russians effectively had zero leverage: NATO."[140] Similarly, in 2003, the United States went to war in Iraq without returning to the UN Security Council for an additional resolution. But in general, the United States, due to its desire for political legitimacy for its actions, does prefer the imprimatur of the United Nations or other global institutions, which gives Russia its ability to remain a key diplomatic player.

Yet Russian vetoes can also irritate Washington. After Russia used its veto power to block a resolution on Syria strongly supported by the United States in February 2012, U.S. Ambassador to the UN Susan Rice bluntly noted that the United States was "disgusted" with the Russian government and lambasted the Kremlin for "continue[ing] to prevent us" from taking action to end the civil war (and humanitarian crisis) in that country.[141] From the Russian perspective, however, Moscow's preference (in dealing with situations like Libya in 2011 and Syria from 2011 onward) is to work with existing regimes to create conditions for political transitions rather than to sanction and pressure those governments. Similarly, in dealing with regimes like Iran and North Korea, Russia prefers to emphasize the "carrot" of diplomacy in place of the "stick" of sanctions and the use of force.[142] Russia also does not perceive the same urgent level of threat from some of the so-called "rogue states" that the United States wants to sanction, coloring its perspective on U.S.-proposed resolutions submitted to the UN Security Council.[143]

Beyond the United Nations, Russia is a member of both the Group of Eight (G-8) and the Group of Twenty (G-20) fora and in fact holds the presidency of the G-20 in 2013 and will again chair the G-8 in 2014, as it did in 2006. This means that Moscow will set the agenda for these two important multilateral gatherings of the world's leading economic powers as well as having the ability to block items that conflict with its preferences.[144] However, given that the assessment of the international situation, particularly with regard to the global economy, is very different in Moscow than in Washington, there will be continuing challenges to try and find shared approaches.[145] Furthermore, Russia's membership in the G-8 has not been without controversy. A number of U.S. political figures, including key Congressional skeptics of Russia, have at various times called for Russia to be ejected from the G-8, arguing that its domestic and international policies have put it at odds with the general ethos of the group as a whole, composed of other North American, European, and East Asian industrial democracies.[146] There were criticisms of how Russia had conducted its presidency of the G-8 in 2006, with some arguing that Moscow had not done enough to focus on the economic problems facing the developed countries in advance of the global financial crisis of 2008 and with others complaining that Putin had used "his G8 presidency to reassert Russia's global role"[147] rather than to deepen coordination among the G-8 members. At the 2007 summit in Heiligendamm, a clear divide opened up on policy questions ranging from missile defense to the final status of Kosovo between Russia and most of the other members of the G-8, which again raised questions as to whether Russia's membership made the group function less effectively.[148]

In May 2012, Putin decided not to attend the G-8 summit in Camp David in the United States—the first meeting that a Russian president had not attended since Russia formally became a full member of the group in 1997—citing the need to focus on domestic issues and sending Prime Minister Medvedev instead. This reignited the debate in some U.S. political circles as to whether Russia belonged in the G-8, while some Russian analysts concluded that Putin's absence signaled that the G-8 process would occupy a lower priority in his foreign policy.[149] Putin subsequently attended the G-20 summit in Cabo San Lucas, Mexico, which suggested that he might prefer the G-20 format, which focuses largely on economic issues and contains his partners in the so-called BRICS format (Brazil-Russia-India-China-South Africa), in place of the G-8, where his views are in the minority when questions about democracy and humanitarian intervention are on the agenda.

The Russian approach in organizations such as the IAEA has also frustrated U.S. officials, who feel that Moscow is able to water down or alter final policy documents, which in turn makes it harder for the United States to achieve its preferred outcomes.[150] Especially problematic for Washington have been the times when Russia, as a member of more informal diplomatic coalitions created to find solutions to regional issues, has strongly diverged from the U.S. approach. For instance, in 2006, Putin, as a member of the Quartet for peace in the Middle East, invited leaders of the Palestinian group Hamas to Moscow for talks, even though the Americans and the Europeans refused to have any contact with that movement since it had not accepted Israel's right to exist nor renounced violence, a step that put Russia at odds with its Quartet partners and complicated the American strategy of using isolation to put pressure on Hamas.[151] In 2007, Russia made it clear to its partners in the so-called "Contact Group" for former Yugoslavia (the United States, Italy, Germany, France, and Britain) that it would oppose any plan for the independence of Kosovo from Serbia, again frustrating Washington's efforts to push for granting independence to the province under international monitoring.[152] All of this has reinforced strong sentiment within the U.S. government that Russia is uncooperative and unhelpful in working with the United States to find solutions for regional problems. From the Russian perspective, however, Moscow is under no obligation to rubber stamp decisions taken in Washington. In addition, the growing strategic partnership between Russia and China, which will be discussed in the next chapter, has resulted in

Moscow and Beijing coming together "to exchange views and coordinate actions on many international issues," which allows for Russia and China jointly to oppose U.S. preferences.[153]

INSTITUTIONALIZING THE RELATIONSHIP

The Russian–American relationship is still largely predicated upon the personal bond between the two presidents, but it seems unlikely that this is a sufficient foundation for a close and lasting partnership.[154] For instance, during her time in office, Secretary of State Condoleezza Rice often stressed the "excellent relationship" between Presidents Bush and Putin,[155] but this personal relationship was not translated into effective cooperation between the bureaucracies of the two countries. What has become clear over the last 20 years is that even with good personal ties between presidents, lower-ranking officials in both Russia and the United States have still found ways to preclude cooperation.[156]

In both countries, domestic politics have a major impact on the bilateral relationship. In the past, neither Russian nor American administrations have been willing to face down powerful domestic constituencies to make the case for improved relations. Russian officials often complain that domestic U.S. interest groups are able to influence the agenda to defend parochial interests or to play politics.[157] For their part, U.S. officials sometimes express frustration with the lack of a unified position on the part of the Russian government, the mixed signals sent by multiple camps within the Kremlin, and, echoing U.S. Defense Secretary Robert Gates, express puzzlement with a "schizophrenic" Russian government that seems unable to definitively express one coherent policy position.[158]

These problems can be attributed to the lack of a permanent framework that endures from administration to administration in managing relations between the two countries. In contrast to the well-established intergovernmental commissions that guide, oversee, and sustain the bilateral relationship between Russia and other major powers such as India, France, Germany, or China, the U.S.-Russia relationship has been characterized by a series of ad hoc, temporary arrangements—often originating in the personal relationship between presidents or their cabinet officers—that have not sunk permanent roots into the bureaucracies in either Washington or Moscow. Indeed, the lack of institutionalization has often meant that initiatives that top leaders may agree upon founder because of the lack of any structure that demands accountability for progress—a problem that became quite apparent during the second terms of both George W. Bush and Vladimir Putin. In turn, the fragility of any understanding reached between two presidents meant that there is no guarantee that any arrangement would last or endure when new people arrive in the White House or the Kremlin.[159]

During the Soviet period, there was no automatic series of regular summit meetings between the United States and the Soviet Union. During periods of détente, there might be ongoing contact, but when relations worsened, face-to-face meetings between Soviet and American leaders (as well as the lower-level encounters between U.S. and Soviet officials to prepare for high-level summits) stopped. This was particularly noticeable in the period between 1979 and 1985, when there was no direct contact between the American president and the Soviet premier.

After the 1986 Reykjavik summit, Secretary of State George Schultz and Foreign Minister Eduard Shevardnadze created a direct-level "ministerial dialogue" that would tie together U.S. cabinet departments and Soviet ministries. Four working groups—bilateral issues, arms control, regional issues, and human rights—were created, as well as functional sub-working groups to concentrate on issues such as health cooperation, energy, and trade.[160] This dialogue focused on winding down the Cold War and developing a new, more positive U.S.–Soviet relationship, but it did not survive the collapse of the Soviet Union.

In April 1993, at the Vancouver summit between Bill Clinton and Boris Yeltsin, both presidents agreed to create a new intergovernmental commission to develop a positive agenda for U.S.–Russia relations—the U.S.-Russian Joint Commission on Economic and Technological Cooperation—under cochairmanship of Vice President Al Gore and Prime Minister Viktor Chernomyrdin. The Gore-Chernomyrdin Commission, as it came to be called, created a series of working groups pairing high-level Russian and American officials. For instance, the energy working group twinned U.S. Energy Secretary Hazel O'Leary and Minister of Energy Yuri Shafranik. In order to pursue closer U.S.–Russia economic ties, the business development working group paired U.S. Commerce Secretary Ron Brown and Deputy Prime Minister and Minister for Foreign Economic Relations Oleg Davidov.[161]

But the Commission was not universally viewed as a positive development. Congressional Republicans attacked the Gore-Chernomyrdin relationship for covering up corruption in Russia and for compromises that did not bring the full weight of American disapproval for Russian activities that harmed U.S. interests, such as continued commercial relations with Iran.[162] In turn, many Russians, starting with Primakov, saw it as a tool for the United States to order Russia around, citing the same pressure that Congressional Republicans viewed as lax but that did cause the Russian government to restrict trade with Iran.[163] The Gore-Chernomyrdin Commission did permit some relationships to develop outside of the traditional channels of the State Department and the Foreign Ministry, but "it failed to build a lasting foundation for working-level U.S.–Russia cooperation independent of the personalities at the top."[164] The Commission did not survive the departures of Clinton and Yeltsin as national leaders.

After the 2002 Moscow summit between Bush and Putin, both leaders agreed to create a high-level working group to prepare the agenda for a U.S.-Russia strategic dialogue, cochaired by the U.S. national security advisor and the head of the Russian presidential administration. Yet a perennial weakness of this working group was its inability to task departments and ministries to act. Agencies frequently ignored deadlines without suffering any consequences, and the working group did not become the central driving force of the U.S.-Russia relationship.[165] The working group went the way of the Gore-Chernomyrdin Commission once Obama and Medvedev took over their respective presidencies.

During the July 2009 Moscow summit, Obama and Medvedev announced the creation of the U.S.-Russia Bilateral Presidential Commission (BPC) to become the central organizing point of the U.S.-Russia relationship. The two presidents became the cochairs of the dialogue, while the U.S. secretary of state and the Russian foreign minister became its cocoordinators. But each working group is then cochaired by ranking U.S. and Russian officials, broadening the dialogue beyond the two chief executives.[166]

At his press conference announcing the creation of the BPC on July 6, 2009, Obama declared:

> President Medvedev and I are creating a U.S.-Russian Bilateral Presidential Commission to serve as a new foundation for this cooperation. Too often, the United States and Russia only communicate on a narrow range of issues, or let old habits within our bureaucracy stand in the way of progress. And that's why this commission will include working groups on development and the economy; energy and the environment; nuclear energy and security; arms control and international security; defense, foreign policy and counterterrorism; preventing and handling emergencies; civil society; science and technology; space; health; education; and culture. And this work will be coordinated by Secretary [Hillary] Clinton and Minister [Sergei] Lavrov . . . [167]

The BPC is much larger than the Gore-Chernomyrdin commission, as it has 17 working groups. There is also much greater coordination to ensure that agenda items cannot be bottled up in the bureaucracy. The State Department and Foreign Ministry coordinate with officials from other relevant departments and ministries to report progress, while the White House staff and the Russian presidential administration set the overall priorities and shepherd the respective bureaucracies toward addressing the priorities of the two presidents.[168] What has been very important is that the work of the BPC has penetrated downward to tie into the mid-levels of the bureaucracy, especially through the creation of more specialized subgroups operating under the aegis of the principal BPC working groups. The Defense Relations working group, for instance, contains more specialized subgroups that deal with questions about military cooperation in Afghanistan, defense modernization, or the exchange of information.[169]

Another important difference between the BPC and previous efforts at a U.S.– Russia strategic dialogue has been to focus the BPC on delivering concrete achievements and to separate contentious diplomatic issues and sudden crises from the ongoing BPC agenda. Thus, the negotiations for a new strategic arms treaty and the conditions for Russia's accession to the World Trade Organization were not handled through the BPC but through separate teams of negotiators, meaning that problems that might arise in these delicate talks would not derail the work of the BPC.[170] This also has helped to isolate the BPC from the day-to-day ups and downs in the U.S.–Russia relationship, especially after heated comments were exchanged between the two sides during their respective elections in 2011 and 2012.

Senior U.S. and Russian officials acknowledge that the work of the BPC is uneven, with some commissions being more productive than others. However, they point to the increased connections between officials on both sides and the existence of new channels of communication between the U.S. and Russian governments.[171] The test is now whether the BPC is poised to develop into a permanent institution. When Medvedev stepped down as president in 2012, the BPC continued, with Putin becoming the new cochair. With Obama's re-election as U.S. president in November 2012, the risk that an incoming administration might abandon the BPC receded. But the challenge remains to move the BPC beyond "dialogue for the sake of dialogue" and instead focus it on being able to deliver concrete results if it is to become an effective institution for managing the U.S.–Russia relationship.[172]

THE BALANCE SHEET

Part of the problem in U.S.–Russia relations is that there remain very ambivalent attitudes on both sides about the prospects for cooperation.

Within the United States, views on Russia are divided. In one camp are the skeptics—those who believe that Russia is implacably opposed to U.S. interests and values. In the other are the partisans of a strong Russian–American partnership grounded in shared security and economic interests. But the majority of the U.S. policy establishment remains agnostic: open to improved relations with Russia, but not prepared to gamble that a wide-ranging partnership is possible or feasible and not willing to risk existing U.S. relationships or abandon long-standing U.S. positions in favor of making a major breakthrough with Russia.[173]

Within Russia, there is considerable debate over the direction of the "American vector." A modernizing faction, principally grouped around former President and now Prime Minister Medvedev, has looked favorably on the improvement of relations with the United States (in part as a counterweight to the rise of China).[174] Some parts of the business community, notably several of the leading private companies with considerable interests in the United States in the high-technology and mining fields, are strong proponents of closer ties with America.[175] But other factions within the Russian establishment still view the United States as an adversary or competitor, particularly those more committed to pursuing the strategic partnership with China. Segments of the military, the foreign policy establishment, and the intelligence services continue to view the United States as an antagonist, not as a potential partner. Significant portions of the energy and defense industries see Washington as hostile to their interests or are willing to do business in countries (such as Iran) with whom the United States has poor relations. Others in the Russian elite, while not opposed in principle to good relations with Washington, remained committed to the Primakovian vision of a multipolar world and so embrace policies that see Russia attempting to check U.S. influence.[176] Finally, there is reluctance to abandon other profitable vectors of Russian foreign policy in favor of concentrating on improving relations with Washington. All of these factors have helped to block the emergence of a strong pro-U.S. vector in Russian foreign policy.

At the beginning of 2013, a variety of irritants—ranging from Syria to missile defense to the Magnitsky Act to the prohibition on U.S. citizens adopting Russian children—had begun to erode the progress achieved by the reset of U.S.-Russia relations. A flurry of legislation adopted by both the U.S. Congress and the Russian Duma in the closing days of 2012 also demonstrated that "the destructive pendulum of tit-for-tat action in the U.S.-Russian relationship continues to swing unabated" and that "despite all the talk of reset and partnership, there are strong currents in both Washington and Moscow prepared to sweep in the opposite direction, to always assume the worst of the other side."[177] Once again, this highlights the difficulties in keeping U.S.-Russia relations on an even keel.

In contrast, as subsequent chapters will show, post-Soviet Russia has managed to develop and sustain productive relationships with other key global power centers.

NOTES

1. James H. Billington, "Orthodoxy and Democracy," in *Perspectives in Church-State Relations in Russia,* eds. Wallace L. Daniel, Peter L. Berger, and Christopher Marsh (Waco, TX: Institute of Church-State Studies, 2008), 20.

2. See, among other works, Albert A. Woldman, *Lincoln and the Russians* (New York: Collier Books, 1952).

3. Alexis de Tocqueville, *Democracy in America* (Oxford: Oxford University Press, 1947), 242, 243.

4. From Stalin's election speech of February 9, 1946. In J. Stalin, *Speeches Delivered at Meetings of Voters of the Stalin Electoral District* (Moscow: Foreign Languages Publishing House, 1950), 24.

5. W. L. White, *Report on the Russians* (New York: Harcourt, Brace and Company, 1945), 308, 36.

6. Vladislav Zubok and Constantine Pleshakov, *Inside the Kremlin's Cold War: From Stalin to Khrushchev* (Cambridge, MA: Harvard University Press, 1996), 98.

7. For instance, American president Ronald Reagan wrote in his autobiography *An American Life* (New York: Simon and Schuster, 1990), 305, that, as president, he sincerely wrote to the Soviet leadership and insisted that they honor their commitment to freedom in Eastern Europe as expressed in the Yalta agreement. He noted that "At Yalta, I reminded them, Stalin had promised Poland and all the countries of Eastern Europe the right of self-determination, but the Soviets had never granted it to any of them."

8. Even when the Cold War came to an end, preventing any one power from dominating the Eurasian land mass has remained a core U.S. national security objective. Former National Security Advisor Zbigniew Brzezinski summed up this view in his 1997 *Foreign Affairs* essay: "A power that dominated Eurasia would exercise decisive influence over two of the world's three most economically productive regions, Western Europe and East Asia. A glance at the map also suggests that a country dominant in Eurasia would almost automatically control the Middle East and Africa. . . . What happens with the distribution of power on the Eurasian landmass will be of decisive importance to America's global primacy and historical legacy." Zbigniew Brzezinski, "A Geostrategy for Eurasia," *Foreign Affairs* 76, no. 5 (September/October 1997), at http://www.foreignaffairs.com/articles/53392/zbigniew-brzezinski/a-geostrategy-for-eurasia.

9. NSC-68 observed: "Soviet efforts are now directed toward the domination of the Eurasian land mass. The United States, as the principal center of power in the non–Soviet world and the bulwark of opposition to Soviet expansion, is the principal enemy whose integrity and vitality must be subverted or destroyed by one means or another if the Kremlin is to achieve its fundamental design." Issued by the National Security Council, April 14, 1950. A copy can be found in the *Naval War College Review* 27 (May–June, 1975): 51–108.

10. Robert M. Gates, *From the Shadows: The Ultimate Insider's Story of Five Presidents and How They Won the Cold War* (New York: Simon and Schuster, 1996), 273.

11. The Joint Communique is archived by the *Washington Post* at http://www.washingtonpost.com/wp-srv/inatl/longterm/summit/archive/com1972-1.htm.

12. Dimitri K. Simes, "Gorbachev: A New Foreign Policy?" *Foreign Affairs* 65, no. 3 (1986), at http://www.foreignaffairs.com/articles/41714/dimitri-k-simes/gorbachev-a-new-foreign-policy; David Holloway, "Gorbachev's New Thinking," *Foreign Affairs* 67, no. 3 (1988), at http://www.foreignaffairs.com/articles/44001/david-holloway/gorbachevs-new-thinking.

13. A text of the START-I Treaty is archived by the U.S. State Department at http://www.state.gov/www/global/arms/starthtm/start/start1.html.

14. Record of Conversation between M. S. Gorbachev and the U.S. Secretary of State George Shultz, February 22, 1988. Archive of the Gorbachev Foundation (Moscow), Fond 1, opis 1. Translated by Anna Melyakova and archived at the National Security Archive at http://www.gwu.edu/~nsarchiv/NSAEBB/NSAEBB251/1.pdf.

15. "Relations between U.S. and U.S.S.R. central to 'new world order,'" Shevardnadze says," *Stanford News Service,* May 21, 1991, at http://news.stanford.edu/pr/91/910521Arc1363.html.

16. See the Memorandum of Conversation, "The President's Private Meeting with Gorbachev," December 7, 1988, contained in the National Security Archive at http://www.gwu.edu/~nsarchiv/NSAEBB/NSAEBB261/us08.pdf.

17. Quoted in Jack Matlock, *Reagan and Gorbachev: How the Cold War Ended* (New York: Random House, 2004), 304.

18. An assessment of the competing claims is provided by Uwe Klussmann, Matthias Schepp, and Klaus Wiegrefe, "NATO's Eastward Expansion: Did the West Break Its Promise to Moscow?" *Der Spiegel,* November 26, 2009, at http://www.spiegel.de/international/world/nato-s-eastward-expansion-did-the-west-break-its-promise-to-moscow-a-663315.html. The assertion of Western statesmen involved in the talks is that no formal pledge was given or required. Cf. Mark Kramer, "The Myth of a No-NATO Enlargement Pledge to Russia," *Washington Quarterly* 32, no. 2 (Spring 2009): 39–61.

19. Adrian Blomfield and Mike Smith, "Gorbachev: US could start new Cold War," *The Telegraph,* May 6, 2008, at http://www.telegraph.co.uk/news/worldnews/europe/russia/1933223/Gorbachev-US-could-start-new-Cold-War.html.

20. Robert H. Donaldson and Joseph L. Nogee, *The Foreign Policy of Russia: Changing Systems, Enduring Interests,* 2nd edition (Armonk, NY: M.E. Sharpe, 2009), 219.

21. See his remarks in *Rossiiskaia Gazeta,* February 3, 1992, in *Current Digest of the Post-Soviet Press* 45, no. 5 (1993): 11.

22. A transcript of the speech is archived at http://www.speeches-usa.com/Transcripts/047_yeltsin.html.

23. Donaldson/Nogee, 221.

24. Sergei Stankevich, "Russia in Search of Itself," *Russia in the National Interest,* ed. Nikolas K. Gvosdev (New Brunswick, NJ: Transaction Publishers, 2003), 20–21. Stankevich himself was a state counselor and policy advisor to Yeltsin during his first term of office.

25. See, for instance, "The Soviet 'Nyet' Man," *New York Times,* February 16, 1957, 2.

26. Strobe Talbott, *The Russia Hand: A Memoir of Presidential Diplomacy* (New York: Random House, 2002, 2003), 52–53. See also James M. Goldgeier and Michael McFaul, *Power and Purpose: U.S. Policy Toward Russia After the Cold War* (Washington, DC: The Brookings Institution, 2003), 89.

27. As quoted in George Kennan's original dispatch to the State Department, 861.00/2–2246: Telegram (February 22, 1946). A copy of the "Long Telegram" is archived at http://www.gwu.edu/~nsarchiv/coldwar/documents/episode-1/kennan.htm.

28. See Richard Pipes's essay, "Is Russia Still An Enemy?" *Foreign Affairs* 76, no. 5 (September/October 1997), as an example of this thinking.

29. Talbott, 76.

30. Igor S. Ivanov, *The New Russian Diplomacy* (Washington, DC: The Nixon Center and Brookings Institution Press, 2002), 110.

31. Cf. Talbott, 192–193, on the 1996 Sharm el-Sheikh conference.

32. Charles Flickner, "The Russian Aid Mess," in *Russia in the National Interest*, 188.

33. Janine Wedel, "Tainted Transactions: Harvard, the Chubais Clan and Russia's Ruin," in *Russia in the National Interest*, 115. For Wedel's assertions about a corrupted and flawed aid process and subsequent responses from some of the principals involved, cf. 115–146.

34. "Russia: The IMF's biggest failure," *BBC News*, September 23, 1999, at http://news.bbc.co.uk/2/hi/business/455673.stm.

35. Andranik Migranyan, "McFaul's Costly Mistake in Russia," *National Interest*, January 23, 2012, at http://nationalinterest.org/commentary/mcfauls-costly-mistake-russia-6395.

36. *Rossiiskaia Gazeta*, July 5, 1993, 5; quoted in Donaldson/Nogee, 225.

37. Ivanov, 112.

38. George J. Church, "Next, a Cold Peace," *Time*, December 19, 1994, at http://www.time.com/time/magazine/article/0,9171,982016,00.html#ixzz1kuFg3FSL.

39. Quoted in David Makovsky, "Defanging Iran Could Solidify U.S.-Russia Ties," *Los Angeles Times*, May 23, 2002, at http://articles.latimes.com/2002/may/23/opinion/oe-makovsky23.

40. See, for example, the testimony of Daniel Fried, Assistant Secretary of State for European and Eurasian Affairs, "U.S.-Russia Relations in the Aftermath of the Georgian War," the House Committee on Foreign Affairs, September 9, 2008; the testimony of Ivo Daalder, ambassador-designate to NATO, Senate Foreign Relations Committee, April 22, 2009.

41. See, for instance, Nikolas Gvosdev and Ray Takeyh, "Trans-Atlantic Putin," St. Petersburg Times, March 4, 2003, at http://www.sptimes.ru/index.php?action_id=2&story_id=9459&highlight=gladly%20at; Ian Bremmer and Nikolas Gvosdev, "NATO looks east: Why not really make Russia a partner?," *International Herald Tribune*, June 22, 2004, at http://www.nytimes.com/2004/06/22/opinion/22iht-edgvosdev_ed3_.html.

42. Dimitri Simes, "Russia's Crisis, America's Complicity," in *Russia in the National Interest*, 204.

43. See, for instance, Dov Zakheim and Paul Saunders, "Can Russia Help Us Withdraw from Afghanistan?" *New York Times*, December 2, 2011, A39, at http://www.nytimes.com/2011/12/02/opinion/can-russia-help-us-withdraw-from-afghanistan.html?_r=1.

44. Talbott, 386.

45. Talbott, 402–04.

46. Peter Rutland, "Putin's Path to Power," *Post-Soviet Affairs* 16, no. 4 (December 2000): 338.

47. Caroline Wyatt, "Bush and Putin: Best of Friends," *BBC News,* June 16, 2001, at http://news.bbc.co.uk/2/hi/1392791.stm.

48. Dana E. Struckman and Nikolas K. Gvosdev, "'Resetting' Relations between the U.S. and Russia," *Case Studies in Policy Making,* 12th ed., ed. Hayat Alvi and Nikolas Gvosdev (Newport, RI: U.S. Naval War College, 2010), 71.

49. See Talbott, 405–42, for an extended discussion of this process.

50. Quoted in James Lindsay and Ivo Daalder, "One-Day Wonder: The dangerous absurdity of the Bush-Putin arms treaty," *American Prospect,* August 2, 2002, archived at http://www.cfr.org/world/one-day-wonder-dangerous-absurdity-bush-putin-arms-treaty/ p6357.

51. Timothy L. O'Brien, "How Russian Oil Tycoon Courted Friends in U.S.," *New York Times,* November 3, 2003, at http://www.nytimes.com/2003/11/05/world/how-russian-oil-tycoon-courted-friends-in-us.html.

52. "Yukos boss cools on sale to Exxon," *BBC News,* November 12, 2003, at http://news.bbc.co.uk/2/hi/business/3264641.stm.

53. The most dramatic of these changes was when the Russian government, using environmental standards as a pretext, required the foreign partners in the Sakhalin-1 energy consortium to sell a majority stake to Gazprom to allow the Russian company to become the majority partner in the operation. See Abrahm Lustgarten, "Shell shake-down," *Fortune,* February 1, 2007, at http://money.cnn.com/magazines/fortune/fortune_archive/2007/02/05/8399125/index.htm.

54. See the legal brief prepared by Tobi Gati, "Russia's New Law on Foreign Investment in Strategic Sectors and the Role of State Corporations in the Russian Economy," released by Akin Gump, Strauss Hauer, and Feld, LLP, October 1, 2008, archived by the U.S.-Russia Business Council at http://www.akingump.com/en/news-publications/russia-s-new-law-on-foreign-investment-in-strategic-sectors-and-the-role-of-state.html.

55. Igor Torbakov, "Kremlin Tries to Convince Wary West that Strong Gazprom Is Good for It," *Eurasia Daily Monitor* 3:83, April 28, 2006, at http://www.jamestown.org/single/?no_cache=1&tx_ttnews%5Btt_news%5D=31634; see also Struckman and Gvosdev, 78.

56. Peter Baker, "Russia Relations Under Scrutiny," *Washington Post,* February 6, 2006, at http://www.washingtonpost.com/wp-dyn/content/article/2006/02/25/AR20060225 01399.html; Nina Hachigian, "From Russia—not with love, but with results," *WorldFocus,* July 7, 2009, at http://worldfocus.org/blog/2009/07/07/from-russia-not-with-love-but-with-results/6170/.

57. Statement of Chairman Lantos at Hearing, "Russia: Rebuilding the Iron Curtain," May 17, 2007, http://democrats.foreignaffairs.house.gov/press_display.asp?id=353.

58. McFaul's statement was made at a hearing, "Russia's Transition to Democracy and U.S.-Russia Relations: Unfinished Business," held before the Subcommittee on Europe of the House International Relations Committee on September 30, 2003, at http://com mdocs.house.gov/committees/intlrel/hfa89668.000/hfa89668_0f.htm.

59. Struckman and Gvosdev, 72–73.

60. Joseph Biden, "Russia Must Stand Down," *Financial Times*, August 12, 2008, at http://www.ft.com/cms/s/0/707f4ebe-686b-11dd-a4e5-0000779fd18c.html#axzz2HDyz B6wA.

61. "Vladimir Putin rejects foreign advice on democracy," *India Today*, December 14, 2012, at http://indiatoday.intoday.in/story/vladimir-putin-rejects-foreign-advice-on-democracy/1/237656.html.

62. See Alexei Veneditkov, "Igor Ivanov's Resignation Reinforces Kremlin Isolationism," *New Times*, 23, July 18, 2007, 14–16; also "Ivanov Resigns as Russian Security Council Secretary," *Press Trust of India*, July 9, 2007.

63. Putin himself told a group of visiting Western specialists at a 2004 meeting organized by the Valdai Discussion Club, including one of the authors, that he equated the call on the part of some U.S. officials for Russia to negotiate with Chechen separatists as akin to asking Osama bin Laden to visit the White House for talks with the U.S. government and expressed his frustration with apparent double standards between the U.S. prosecution of the global war on terror with its criticisms of Russia.

64. Comments of a former senior U.S. government official based on his interactions with Russian leaders. Such sentiments were fueled by comments of former senior U.S. officials such as former Secretary of State Madeleine Albright and former National Security Advisor Zbigniew Brzezinski, who argued that anything that would bring Ukraine into a closer relationship with Russia would threaten U.S. interests. Jean-Marie Chauvier, "Ukraine: A New Cold War," *Le Monde Diplomatique*, January 2005.

65. Alexey Pushkov, who is now the chairman of the Duma's Foreign Affairs committee, makes this argument; see his "Russia's Foreign Policy and its National Interests," in *Enduring Rivalry: American and Russian Perspectives on the Former Soviet Space*, ed. Paul Saunders (Washington, DC: Center for the National Interest, 2011), 27.

66. Nikolas K. Gvosdev, "Moscow Nights, Eurasian Dreams," in *Russia in the National Interest*, 256.

67. Testimony of James C. MacDougall, Deputy Assistant Secretary of Defense for Eurasia, before the House Committee on International Relations, Subcommittee on the Middle East and Central Asia, April 26, 2006.

68. Mikhail Gorbachev referenced these sentiments in his "A United Europe Needs an Integrated Russia," *The Financial Times*, April 30, 2004.

69. Jim Heintz, "Russia, Iran reach nuclear plant deal," *USA Today*, December 13, 2007, at http://usatoday30.usatoday.com/news/world/2007-12-13-2898307223_x.htm.

70. Alexey K. Pushkov, "Missed Connections," *The National Interest*, no. 89 (May/June 2007): 53.

71. Nikolas K. Gvosdev, "Obama's Russia Reset—Don't Forget about Congress," *New Atlanticist*, April 6, 2009, at http://www.acus.org/new_atlanticist/obamas-russia-reset-dont-forget-about-congress.

72. Susan Cornwell and Oleg Shchedrov, "Bush and Putin Fail to Resolve Missile Differences," *Reuters*, April 6, 2008, at http://www.reuters.com/article/idUSN04216524200 80406.

73. Struckman and Gvosdev, 80.

74. M. K. Bhadrakumar, "US-Russia Ties on a New Trajectory," *Asia Times,* April 4, 2009, at http://www.atimes.com/atimes/Central_Asia/KD04Ag01.html.

75. Aleksei Mukhin, "'Amerikantsi' v Kremle," *Argumenty Nedeli* 40, no. 130 (October 14, 2010), at http://argumenti.ru/politics/n259/80232/.

76. *U.S.–Russian Relations after the Reset: A Dialogue* (Washington, DC: The Nixon Center, 2010), 1–2.

77. Glenn Kessler and Michael D. Shear, "Presidents Obama and Medvedev bond at Ray's Hell Burger," *Washington Post,* June 25, 2010, at http://www.washingtonpost.com/wp-dyn/content/article/2010/06/24/AR2010062402479.html.

78. Nikolas K. Gvosdev, "The Reset Blooms," *National Interest,* October 28, 2010, at http://nationalinterest.org/commentary/the-reset-blooms-4309.

79. "Afghanistan: Northern Distribution Network Delivers," *Eurasianet.org,* March 17, 2009, at http://www.eurasianet.org/departments/news/articles/eav031809d.shtml.

80. "Russia broadens transit opportunities for NATO," *Russia Today,* June 29, 2012, at http://rt.com/politics/nato-transit-russia-afghanistan-059/.

81. "U.S. Secretary of Defense Robert Gates has given an interview to Interfax correspondent Peter Cheremushkin ahead of talks with Russian Defense Minister Anatoly Serdyukov due on September 15 in Washington," *Interfax,* September 14, 2010, at http://www.interfax.com/interview.asp?id=189125.

82. Paul Saunders, "Introduction," in *Enduring Rivalry,* op. cit., 1.

83. Gvosdev, "Reset Blooms," op. cit.

84. "Medvedev calls Washington nuclear summit 'a total success,'" *Russia Today,* April 14, 2010, at http://rt.com/usa/news/medvedev-hails-washington-summit/.

85. Gvosdev, "Reset Blooms," op. cit.

86. "Russian president signs decree backing U.N. resolution against Libya," *Xinhua,* August 12, 2011, at http://news.xinhuanet.com/english2010/world/2011–08/12/c_1310464 01.htm.

87. Darya Korsunskaya and Braden Reddall, "Exxon, Rosneft tie up in Russian Arctic, U.S.," *Reuters,* August 30, 2011, at http://www.reuters.com/article/2011/08/30/us-rosneft-exxon-idUSTRE77T20M20110830.

88. Stephen Sestanovich, "Why New START was Ratified," *Council on Foreign Relations First Take,* December 22, 2010, at http://www.cfr.org/proliferation/why-new-start-ratified/p23678.

89. Comments of senior Russian officials to a working group one of the authors is a member of.

90. Alexei Fenenko, "It is dangerous for Russia and the USA to ignore the looming conflicts," *RIA Novosti,* November 21, 2011, archived at http://valdaiclub.com/usa/35080.html.

91. Alex Spillius, "Vladimir Putin calls John McCain 'nuts' in outspoken attack," *Daily Telegraph,* December 15, 2011, at http://www.telegraph.co.uk/news/worldnews/europe/russia/8958294/Vladimir-Putin-calls-John-McCain-nuts-in-outspoken-attack.html.

92. "Putin accuses US of sparking election protests," *France 24,* December 8, 2011, at http://www.france24.com/en/20111208-vladimir-putin-blames-usa-election-protests-hillary-clinton-fraud-russia.

93. See, for instance, Putin's 2012 address to the Federal Assembly. "Putin, in Annual Address, Denounces Foreign Meddling," *Radio Free Europe/Radio Liberty*, December 12, 2012, at http://www.rferl.org/content/putin-annual-address-denounces-foreign-med dling/24796193.html.

94. Steve Gutterman and Nastassia Astrasheuskaya, "Russia says U.S. aid mission sought to sway elections," *Reuters*, September 19, 2012, at http://www.reuters.com/article/2012/09/19/us-usa-russia-aid-idUSBRE88I0EE20120919.

95. "Russia's Pussy Riot: Artists, Activists, or Extremists?" Panel discussion at the Center for the National Interest, Washington, DC, August 29, 2012, at http://www.cftni.org/8-29%20Summary.pdf.

96. "Putin calls adoption of Magnitsky Act unfriendly move," *Xinhua*, December 20, 2012, at http://news.xinhuanet.com/english/world/2012-12/20/c_132053532.htm.

97. "Duma Magnitsky Response Passes First Reading," *Radio Free Europe/Radio Liberty*, December 14, 2012, at http://www.rferl.org/content/duma-magnitsky-response /24798854.html; "Russian Parliament Gives Preliminary Approval to U.S. Adoption Ban," *Radio Free Europe/Radio Liberty*, December 19, 2012, at http://www.rferl.org/content/rus sia-us-adoption-ban/24802900.html.

98. Fenenko, op. cit.

99. Dan Steinbock, "The Russia-EU-US drama," *EU Observer*, December 18, 2012, at http://euobserver.com/opinion/118538.

100. Nikolas K. Gvosdev, "The Realist Prism: Can Kerry Salvage the Russia Reset?" *World Politics Review*, March 1, 2013, at http://www.worldpoliticsreview.com/articles/12756/the-realist-prism-can-kerry-salvage-the-russia-reset.

101. "Remarks by Vice President Biden at the 45th Munich Conference on Security Issues," Munich, Germany, February 7, 2009, at http://www.whitehouse.gov/the_press_office/RemarksbyVicePresidentBidenat45thMunichConferenceonSecurityPolicy/.

102. Nikolas Gvosdev and Dimitri Simes, "America Cannot Have It Both Ways with Russia," *Financial Times*, April 6, 2006, 19.

103. Thomas M. Nichols, "Improving Russia-U.S. Relations: The Next Steps." Policy Memo, International Security Program, Belfer Center for Science and International Affairs, Harvard Kennedy School, June 2009, at http://belfercenter.ksg.harvard.edu/publi cation/19135/improving_russiaus_relations.html?breadcrumb=%2Fexperts%2F1818%2Ft homas_m_nichols.

104. Peter Baker, "Putin Proposes Broader Cooperation on Missile Defense," *Washington Post*, July 3, 2007, at http://www.washingtonpost.com/wp-dyn/content/article/2007/07/02/AR2007070200131.html.

105. Nikolas Gvosdev, "What's Happening with Missile Defense," *National Interest*, October 23, 2007, at http://nationalinterest.org/commentary/rapid-reaction-whats-happen ing-with-missile-defense-1831.

106. Russia Warns U.S. Against Deploying Aegis Ships in Northern Seas, *Interfax*, February 14, 2012; Russia Preparing Countermeasures to U.S. Warships Near its Coast, *Interfax*, February 14, 2012, at http://english.ruvr.ru/2012/02/14/66033368.html.

107. "U.S.-Russia Relations After the Reset," 3.

108. "Moscow Fires Warning Shot Across Bow of US Naval-Based ABM," *Russia Today*, December 17, 2012, at http://rt.com/politics/russia-us-abm-moscow-rogozin-186/.

109. The quote is from Senator Jeanne Shaheen (D-NH), speaking at "The Future of U.S.-Russia Relations: Beyond 2012," Carnegie Endowment for International Peace conference, November 28, 2012, Washington, DC, at http://carnegieendowment.org/files/112812_REBeyond2012_keynote_transcript.pdf; see also the comments of Steven Pifer in "What Obama's Second Term Could Mean for U.S.-Russian Relations," *The Atlantic*, November 19, 2012, at http://www.theatlantic.com/international/archive/2012/11/what-obamas-second-term-could-mean-for-us-russian-relations/265426/.

110. Fenenko, op. cit.

111. Paul J. Saunders, *New Realities in U.S.–Russia Arms Control* (Washington, DC: Center for the National Interest, 2012), 18.

112. A great deal depends on the interpretation of then-U.S. Secretary of State James Baker's pledge in 1990 to Gorbachev about not expanding the NATO zone to the "east"—whether this refers only to East Germany or east Europe as a whole. For the most part, the Western assessment—backed up by the documents that so far have been declassified—is that Gorbachev was given no pledge about future NATO expansion to eastern Europe, in part because that question was not even discussed in 1990. Cf. Kramer, esp. 45.

113. See, for instance, former U.S. Secretary of Defense Donald Rumsfeld, "NATO Expansion Should Continue," *Wall Street Journal*, March 28, 2008, at http://online.wsj.com/article/SB120665952870370033.html. The various arguments for why the United States would want to expand NATO are covered in Barry Adams, "Examining Enlargement," *NATO Review* 1 (Spring 2004), at http://www.nato.int/docu/review/2004/issue1/english/book.html, and Marke R. Shelley and John P. Norris, "NATO Enlargement: The Case for Romania," *Proceedings* 123, no. 3:1 (March 1997): 129, at http://www.usni.org/magazines/proceedings/1997-03/nato-enlargement-case-romania.

114. Nikolas Gvosdev, "Parting with Illusions: Developing a Realistic Approach to Relations with Russia," *Cato Institute Policy Analysis* no. 611 (February 29, 2008): 5.

115. See the "Founding Act on Mutual Relations, Cooperation and Security between the North Atlantic Treaty Organization and the Russian Federation," signed May 27, 1997, archived at http://www.fas.org/man/nato/natodocs/founding_act.htm.

116. Peter Trenin-Straussov, "The NATO-Russia Permanent Joint Council in 1997–1999: Anatomy of a Failure," BITS Research Note 99.1, July 1999, at http://www.bits.de/public/researchnote/rn99-1.htm.

117. Stephen J. Cimbala, "Conclusion," in *Deterrence and Proliferation in the 21st Century* (Westport, CT: Praeger Publishers, 2001): 161–162.

118. See, for instance, Thomas M. Nichols, "Russia's Turn West: Sea Change or Opportunism?" *World Policy Journal*, Winter 2002/03, 13, at http://www.worldpolicy.newschool.edu/wpi/journal/articles/wpj02-4/nichols.pdf.

119. "Baltic States hinder Russia-NATO cooperation—Russian envoy," *RIA Novosti*, May 5, 2010, at http://en.rian.ru/world/20100505/158889222.html.

120. Cimbala, 161.

121. Peter Williams, "Partnership Has a Price," *St. Petersburg Times*, January 12, 2007, at http://www.sptimesrussia.com/index.php?action_id=2&story_id=20014.

122. Vladimir Isachenkov, "Putin Rips NATO 'Muscle-flexing,'" *Denver Post,* November 21, 2007, at http://www.denverpost.com/nationworld/ci_7519142.

123. Andrew E. Kramer and Thom Shanker, "Russia Suspends Arms Agreement Over U.S. Shield," *New York Times,* July 15, 2007, 1.

124. See, for instance, Marcel de Haas, *NATO–Russia Relations After the Georgia Conflict* (The Hague: Netherlands Institute of International Relations, 2009), at http://www.cling endael.nl/publications/2009/20090000_cscp_artikel_mhaas.pdf.

125. "NATO and Russia: A New Beginning," Speech by NATO Secretary General Anders Fogh Rasmussen at the Carnegie Endowment, Brussels, September 18, 2009, at http://www.nato.int/cps/en/natolive/opinions_57640.htm.

126. "Preparations for Northern Eagle Naval Maneuvers Underway in Murmansk," *Interfax-AVN,* May 22, 2012, at http://www.interfax.co.uk/russia-cis-general-news-bulle tins-in-english/preparations-for-northern-eagle-naval-maneuvers-underway-in-mur mansk/; "Russia, NATO Hold Naval Drills in Gulf of Aden," *Voice of Russia,* February 2, 2012, at http://english.ruvr.ru/2012/02/02/65144287.html.

127. Nikolas K. Gvosdev, Ted Galen Carpenter, Anatol Lieven, and Charles A. Kupchan, "Bucharest on My Mind: Experts React to the NATO Summit," *National Interest,* April 4, 2008, at http://nationalinterest.org/article/bucharest-on-my-mind-experts-react-to-the-nato-summit-2035?page=show.

128. "Clinton Calls Eurasian Integration an Effort to 'Re-Sovietize,'" *Radio Free Europe/Radio Liberty,* December 7, 2012, at http://www.rferl.org/content/clinton-calls-eur asian-integration-effort-to-resovietize/24791921.html/.

129. Nikolas K. Gvosdev, "The Realist Prism: U.S. Stance on Eurasian Union Threatens Russia Reset," *World Politics Review,* December 14, 2012, at http://www.worldpoliticsreview. com/articles/12569/the-realist-prism-u-s-stance-on-eurasian-union-threatens-russia-reset.

130. Dmitry Ryurikov, "Russia and the United States in the Former Soviet Union: Managing Rivalry or Business as Usual?" in *Enduring Rivalries: American and Russian Perspectives on the Former Soviet Space,* ed. Paul J. Saunders (Washington, DC: Center for the National Interest, 2011), 39, 40.

131. For instance, in 2012, U.S. law enforcement agencies broke up a ring headed by Aleksandr Fishenko, accusing his group of smuggling high-technology products to Russia that could be used to create advanced weapons systems. Cf. Robert Beckhusen, "Accused Spies Charged With Smuggling Semiconductors for Russian Military," *Wired,* October 4, 2012, at http://www.wired.com/dangerroom/2012/10/spies/.

132. Devlin Barrett, "Russian Spy Ring Aimed to Make Children Agents," *Wall Street Journal,* July 31, 2012, at http://online.wsj.com/article/SB10000872396390444097904577 537044185191340.html.

133. Howard La Franchi, "A cold-war chill? US-Russia relations falter over Libya and Syria," *Christian Science Monitor,* March 3, 2012, at http://www.csmonitor.com/USA/Foreign-Policy/2012/0303/A-cold-war-chill-US-Russia-relations-falter-over-Libya-and-Syria.

134. Donaldson/Nogee, 357.

135. P. J. Tobia, "Getting to 'No' Why Russia Loves the Veto," *PBS Newshour,* September 26, 2012, at http://www.pbs.org/newshour/rundown/2012/09/-un-security-council-get ting-to-no-why-russia-loves-the-veto.html.

136. Denis Corboy, William Courtney, and Kenneth Yalowtiz, "Russia's Veto Diplomacy," *New York Times,* August 14, 2012, at http://www.nytimes.com/2012/08/15/opinion/russias-veto-diplomacy.html.

137. Stephen Sestanovich, "Dual Frustration: America, Russia and the Persian Gulf," *Russia in the National Interest,* ed. Nikolas K. Gvosdev (New Brunswick, NJ: Transaction Press, 2004), 58.

138. Ivanov, 43, 47, 51.

139. Louis Charbonneau, "Russia U.N. veto on Syria aimed at crushing West's crusade," *Reuters,* February 8, 2012, at http://www.reuters.com/article/2012/02/08/us-un-russia-idUSTRE8170BK20120208.

140. Tobia, op. cit.

141. Cf. her February 2012 interview with the *Guardian* at http://www.guardian.co.uk/world/video/2012/feb/07/russia-china-syria-veto-us-video.

142. Comments of a senior Russian official to a working group one of the authors is a member of.

143. Saunders, "New Realities," 26.

144. Richard Gowan, "Multilateralism: Moscow Rules?" *ESharp,* August 2012, at http://esharp.eu/oped/richard-gowan/40-multilateralism-moscow-rules/.

145. Comments of a senior Russian official to a working group one of the authors is a member of.

146. See, for instance, "Kick Russia out of G8 says McCain," *Russia Today,* July 29, 2008, at http://rt.com/news/kick-russia-out-of-g8-says-mccain/.

147. John Kirton, "The Future G8 after St. Petersburg," *Russia in Foreign Affairs* 2 (April-June 2007), at http://eng.globalaffairs.ru/number/n_8542.

148. Judy Dempsey, "G-8 quandary: Dealing with Putin," *New York Times,* June 4, 2007, at http://www.nytimes.com/2007/06/04/world/europe/04iht-summit.4.5993622.html.

149. Anders Aslund, "Kick Russia Out of the G-8," *Foreign Policy,* May 15, 2012, at http://www.foreignpolicy.com/articles/2012/05/15/kick_russia_out_of_the_g_8?page=full; Vladimir Radyuhin, "From Russia, No Love," *The Hindu,* May 18, 2012, at http://www.thehindu.com/opinion/op-ed/article3429570.ece.

150. Steve Gutterman, "Russia opposes new Iran sanctions over IAEA report," *Reuters,* November 9, 2011, at http://www.reuters.com/article/2011/11/09/us-nuclear-iran-russia-idUSTRE7A857620111109.

151. "Putin ready for talks with Hamas," *BBC News,* February 6, 2006, at http://news.bbc.co.uk/2/hi/middle_east/4698240.stm.

152. "Contact Group Meets on Kosovo's Future as Tensions Rise," *Deutsche Welle,* July 25, 2007, at http://www.dw.de/contact-group-meets-on-kosovos-future-as-tensions-rise/a-2706414-1.

153. Qu Xing, "Why Has China Vetoed the Security Council Syria Resolution," *China US Focus,* February 29, 2012, at http://www.chinausfocus.com/foreign-policy/why-has-china-vetoed-the-security-council-syria-resolution/.

154. Paul J. Saunders, "The U.S.-Russia Relationship After the Iraq War," in *Russia in the National Interest,* 262.

155. Quoted in Peter Baker, "Bush, Putin Put Tensions aside for Moscow Meeting," *The Seattle Times,* May 9, 2005, at http://seattletimes.nwsource.com/html/nation world/2002268288_bush09.html.

156. Gvosdev, "Parting with Illusions," 15.

157. For instance, for the ways in which ratification of the new START treaty between the U.S. and Russia were affected by unrelated domestic political developments in the United States, see Bob Woodward, *The Price of Politics* (New York: Simon and Schuster, 2012), 63, 65; similar themes about domestic interests are raised in Angela Stent's keynote address and subsequent question-and-answer period, "The Current Status and Prospects for the U.S.-Russia Relationship," June 2, 2011, part of the Carnegie Council's program on *U.S. Global Engagement: A Two-Year Retrospective,* at http://www.carnegiecouncil.org/studio/multimedia/20110703/index.html#section-21852; see also Nikolas K. Gvosdev, "The Obama-Medvedev Summit," *National Interest,* June 25, 2010, at http://nationalinterest.org/commentary/the-obama-medvedev-summit-3576.

158. Comments of an Obama administration official to a working group one of the authors is a member of. Gates's public comment is cited in "Gates: Russia Policy Toward Iran 'Schizophrenic,'" *Agence France Press,* June 17, 2010, at http://www.defensenews.com/story.php?i=4675078.

159. Nikolas K. Gvosdev and Matthey Rojansky, "Keep the Reset Moving," *International Herald Tribune,* December 16, 2011, at http://www.nytimes.com/2011/12/16/opinion/keep-the-us-russia-reset-moving.html.

160. Matthew Rojansky, *Indispensable Institutions: The Obama-Medvedev Commission and Five Decades of U.S.-Russia Dialogue* (Washington, DC: Carnegie Endowment for International Peace, 2010), 10–12.

161. Rojansky, 10–11.

162. Lilia Shevtsova, *Lonely Power,* trans. Antonina W. Bouis (Washington, DC: Carnegie Endowment for International Peace, 2010), 35–37.

163. Talbott, 256.

164. Rojansky, 21.

165. Rojansky, 24–26.

166. For instance, the Innovation Working Group of the BPC is co-chaired by a State Department official in charge of business and commercial affairs and the Russian deputy minister for economic development.

167. The White House, Office of the Press Secretary, "Press Conference by President Obama and President Medvedev of Russia," news release, July 6, 2009, at http://www.whitehouse.gov/the-press-office/press-conference-president-obama-and-president-medvedev-russia.

168. Rojansky, 30, 32, 36–37.

169. Comments of an Obama administration official to a working group one of the authors is a member of.

170. Rojansky, 37.

171. Comments of both Russian and U.S. officials to a working group one of the authors is a member of.

172. See comments in the first panel of the conference, "The Future of U.S.-Russia Relations: Beyond 2012," Carnegie Endowment for International Peace conference, November 28, 2012, Washington, DC, at http://carnegieendowment.org/files/112812_REBeyond2012_Panel_1_transcript.pdf.

173. *U.S.-Russia Relations After the Reset,* 1–2.

174. See, for instance, the comments of Igor Yurgens, "Russia's Future," event at the Nixon Center, March 11, 2011, at http://cftni.org/indexec92.html?action=showpage&page=Yurgens-3-2010.

175. Gregory Karp, "Russian investment firm sees U.S. as land of business opportunity," *Chicago Tribune,* January 3, 2011, at http://articles.chicagotribune.com/2011-01-03/business/ct-biz-0104-digital-sky-20110103_1_groupon-digital-sky-technologies-russian-investment-firm.

176. See, for instance, the discussion on Russian elite preferences in Luke Harding, *Expelled: A Journalist's Descent into the Russian Mafia State* (New York: Palgrave Macmillan, 2012), 199–200.

177. Nikolas K. Gvosdev, "Washington and Moscow's Downward Spiral," *National Interest,* January 3, 2013, at http://nationalinterest.org/commentary/washington-moscows-downward-spiral-7926.

CHAPTER 4

The Bear and the Dragon

China and the East Asia Vector

f Russia has never fully seen itself as a part of Europe, neither has it considered itself fully Asian. In many ways, however, Russia is an Asian nation. Although its capital is in Europe, fully two-thirds of its territory rests beyond the Urals in Asia, while it has the longest coastline of any Asian country. Despite its vast territorial presence in Asia, little more than a quarter of Russia's population resides there, which complicates its position further. These complications include the vast distance between Russia's population in Siberia and the Far East and the country's political center, and the demographic disequilibrium along the Chinese border (the population of China's Heilongjiang Province, just across the Amur River from Russia, equals that of Russia's entire Asian population). These factors limit Russia's ability to engage Asia as an economic partner while simultaneously acting as something of an exposed flank from the military perspective.

Russia's first encounter with East Asia came as a result of the Mongol conquest of the Rus' lands (1237–1240). The Russian principalities became part of a large Eurasian empire headquartered first at Karakorum (in present-day Mongolia) and then at Beijing. Individual Russian princes, warriors, and merchants traveled eastward in the service of the Great Khan. Indeed, the Russian term for China (*Kitai*) is a reference to the nomadic tribe of the Khitan who ruled in northern China as the Liao Dynasty prior to the Mongol conquest and who were based in what is now modern Kyrgyzstan. Contacts were ruptured, however, after both the Chinese expelled the Mongols in 1368 and the Russians broke free of Mongol suzerainty in 1480.

The Russian conquest of Siberia, starting in the 16th century, led to new direct contacts between the two countries. Russia's eastward expansion was not simply an exploratory expedition; it was driven by the search for fur, an important trading commodity for Russia, and for the necessary resources to supply the colonists who would come to exploit the fur trade. In turn, this created interest in opening trade relations with the Chinese Empire. The Cossack Ivan Petlin is believed to have been the first Russian to visit Beijing, in 1618.

The areas that the Russians were entering, however, were considered to be vassal territories of the Manchu Emperors (Qing Dynasty) of China. The Turkic and Mongol indigenous peoples sent word to Beijing about the brutality of the

123

invading "barbarians," and, as subsequent Russian emissaries traveled to Beijing in the 1650s and 1660s, the Manchus began to gain a greater appreciation of the Russian threat to their northern boundaries. The result was China and Russia's first real encounter, as a small contingent of Manchu forces was sent to protect the pastoral tribes that lived in the Amur River basin from Cossack raids. The two armies came into contact in the spring of 1652 in Wuzhala (Achansk), just across the Sungari River north of Manchuria. The Russians, under Yerofei Khabarov (for whom the city of Khabarovsk is named), turned back the Chinese forces led by Haise.[1] Preoccupied with matters in Southern China, however, the Manchus were not able to focus on the Russian threat until after the conquest of Taiwan (1673). Subsequent clashes between Russians and Chinese came to a head in 1685, when the Kangxi Emperor ordered the Russian outposts to be cleared from the Amur River basin. Following this campaign, Beijing and Moscow moved to reach an agreement on their border, eventually concluding the Treaty of Nerchinsk in 1689, the first treaty between China and a European nation, which secured China's control of the Amur River basin for another two centuries. It was followed by the Treaty of Kiakhta (1727), which set the parameters for the Russia–China caravan trade.

The Manchus most certainly did not realize that Russia's advance was not simply a raid on their territory but was, rather, a forerunner to the colonization of the region. By the middle of the 19th century, the Russian Empire was expanding both in Central Asia and in the Far East. The Treaty of Kulja (1851) recognized Russian sovereignty over what is now Kazakhstan and provided for border trade with Xinjiang. A more significant agreement was the so-called "unequal treaties" of Aigun (1858) and Beijing (1860), in which the Chinese Empire was forced to give up some of its northern territories in the Amur River valley to Russia while simultaneously extending Russia's boundaries to the Korean peninsula. By these agreements, the Chinese also renounced any claims to Sakhalin Island—which the Russians, by the terms of the Treaty of Shimoda (1855), agreed to divide with the Japanese, an agreement that also marked the opening of diplomatic relations between Russia and Japan.

The movement of people and supplies across the region was greatly facilitated by the Trans-Siberian Railroad, with a rail link between Moscow and Vladivostok completed by 1898. The railway greatly facilitated Russian trade with Asia. It also helped to encourage the development of an Asian vector in Russian foreign policy. Beginning with figures like Count Nikolai Muraviev-Amursky, the governor general of Eastern Siberia, and espoused by senior officials like Finance Minister Sergei Witte and Prince Esper Ukhtomsky, an argument was put forward that Russia's future lay in its development as an Asian-Pacific power rather than trying to compete for dominance in Europe. Proponents of this policy of *Zheltorossiya*

(Yellow Russia) argued for Russia to take more territories from the crumbling Chinese Empire, beginning with Manchuria, and to extend protectorates over various East Asian regions, starting with the kingdom of Korea. Such policies, however, were bound to bring Russia into direct conflict with a Japan also bent on expanding its sphere of influence in East Asia. This resulted in the Russo-Japanese War (1904–1905), in which Russia's expansion in Asia was checked and signaled Japan's arrival as a modern power.

After the 1917 Revolution, the Soviet government saw the Chinese Nationalists as a possible ally in their struggle against the Western powers, and so Moscow renounced some of the concessions that had been extracted by the Russian Empire from China. Communist Parties also emerged in China and Japan. Yet the Soviets vacillated between their engagement of Asian governments and support for Communist movements. In turn, the Chinese Communist Party questioned whether the Soviets were acting on behalf of the revolution as a whole or were simply Russian imperialists in another form. Continued Soviet support for the Chinese Nationalist government (Guomindang)—even after it attempted to extirpate the Chinese Communists—led some Chinese Communists to question Soviet guidance.

Japan had supported the anti-Communist White movements during the Russian Civil War and occupied parts of the Russian Far East. During the late 1930s, after Japan had occupied large portions of eastern China, the Soviet Union and Japan skirmished along the borders of Manchuria and Mongolia. However, the two countries avoided an all-out war, and the USSR did not declare war on Japan until the final days of World War II, in August 1945. Once it did so, however, the Soviets rapidly occupied Manchuria and northern Korea (with southern Korea occupied by the United States) and seized a number of small islands (the Kuril Islands) to the north of the main Japanese islands. From this position of influence, they were able to provide a good deal of military support to the Chinese Communists as well as to the Korean Communists, enabling the former to defeat the Nationalists on the mainland and for the Korean Communists to set up a state in the Soviet occupation zone of Korea.

TRIANGULAR RELATIONS: OPPORTUNITIES AND CHALLENGES

Following the victory of the Communists in the Chinese civil war in 1949, Mao Zedong, Zhou Enlai, and other key leaders traveled to Moscow to meet with Josef Stalin and the Soviet leadership. They signed a Soviet-China Treaty of Friendship, Alliance and Mutual Assistance on February 14, 1950. This agreement immediately raised Western fears of an emerging Sino-Soviet bloc that would seek to spread Communism elsewhere throughout Asia. In April of that same year, reference to the Chinese Communist victory made it into the second sentence of NSC 68, the document that articulated America's Cold War strategy of containment. The fear of Communist expansion seemed further justified when Kim Il-Sung attempted to unify all of Korea under his government by sending his armed forces south across the 38th parallel to attack the pro–American government of Sygman Rhee, thus starting the Korean War. When U.S.-led forces had pushed the Communist armies to the borders of China itself, raising fears that America would press onward to depose the Communist government in Beijing, the Chinese intervened in Korea. The fighting ended in 1953 with Korea permanently divided between a Communist North and a non–Communist South.

Just as the Korean War was winding down, the battlefield shifted further south to Vietnam, where a Communist-led nationalist movement was fighting against the French. A 1954 agreement reached in Vienna between the United States, Britain, and France on the one hand and the Soviet Union and Communist China on the other provided for a division of Vietnam into a temporary Communist northern zone and a non–Communist southern one. But when it became clear that the Communists might come to power in national elections, the West made the choice to create a separate Vietnamese state in the south. In turn, the Communist north sponsored guerillas in the south (the National Liberation Front, or Viet Cong) to fight for reunification. The result was a proxy war, as the Soviets and Chinese supported their allies while the United States backed the south, ultimately becoming directly involved in efforts to suppress the Communist insurgency, leading to the Vietnam War.

Cracks soon appeared in the Sino-Soviet alliance. The Chinese felt that the Soviet Union was not doing enough to aid China's development, particularly in building up its military forces, and was proving too open to negotiating compromises with the United States. The leadership in Beijing had been increasingly questioning the wisdom of Soviet decisions and the appropriateness of the Soviet model for China ever since their 1950 visit to Moscow. By the 1960s, however, revolutionary leaders like Mao were even less inclined to defer to Soviets like Nikita Khrushchev who had not been involved in the 1917 Revolution. For their part, Soviet leaders were concerned about the radicalism of the Chinese leadership and its willingness to provoke the Americans, as occurred in the 1957 crisis over the islands of Quemoy and Matsu; they did not want the Chinese to drag the USSR into a war with the United States. In 1960, at a Romanian Communist party congress, the Chinese denounced the Soviets for their timidity and for the reforms initiated under Nikita Khrushchev, and the Soviets accused the Chinese of recklessness and "adventurism." The Soviets withdrew their technical specialists from China and sided with India in the latter's 1962 border skirmish with

China. Then in 1964, Mao declared that a counterrevolution had occurred in the USSR, and Beijing then broke relations with the Soviet Communist Party, indicating that the Chinese would no longer take Soviet policy guidance.

From this point forward, the Chinese considered the Soviet Union not as a Communist revolutionary state but simply as a modern iteration of the Russian imperial state with which they had been dealing for centuries. They soon began to advance claims to the territories that had been taken from China in the 19th century. Border disputes eventually led to armed clashes along the Amur in 1969. The friction between China and the Soviet Union along the Sino-Soviet border signaled to Washington that the communist world was not monolithic. Indeed, despite their seemingly common ideological commitments, relations between the two communist giants had deteriorated to the point of confrontation. In this environment, the Nixon administration began to make gestures toward China to improve their bilateral relations. Henry Kissinger observed that "the hostility between China and the Soviet Union served our purposes best if we maintained closer relations with each side than they did with each other."[2] It was by playing off the Russians and Chinese against each other that the United States got the Russians to the negotiating table, pushed through the Anti-Ballistic Missile (ABM) Treaty, and ushered in an era of détente with the USSR.

Meanwhile, the subsequent Chinese opening to the United States created the specter of the United States and China working together to contain the Soviet Union. Soviet premier Alexei Kosygin attempted to repair the damage in the relationship, but the Chinese moved ahead with strategic cooperation with the United States after the visit of U.S. President Richard Nixon in 1972 (which followed Kissinger's own "secret visit" to China in 1971). In 1979, the Soviet invasion of Afghanistan and the Chinese invasion of Vietnam, a Soviet ally, further complicated relations. In 1982, however, as China moved away from the radical days of the Cultural Revolution and the subsequent reactionary period, Soviet leader Leonid Brezhnev and Chinese leader Deng Xiaoping agreed to restart the Sino-Soviet dialogue. Following the 12th Congress of the Chinese Communist Party, held in September 1982, General Secretary Hu Yaobang made it clear that China "would never attach itself to any great power"—a statement that signaled that Beijing was not pursuing a closer alliance with the United States and helped to reassure the Soviets.[3]

After coming to power in 1985, Mikhail Gorbachev spoke about a new "Pacific community" that would promote peace and mutual security in the region.[4] In a landmark address delivered in Vladivostok in July 1986, Gorbachev called for creating a "comprehensive system" for regional security and signaled a willingness to compromise on long-held Soviet positions in disputes with neighbors. His speech was also accompanied by concrete steps to reduce the Soviet military presence on the Sino-Soviet border. In turn, Deng proclaimed that he had heard "new content in the political thinking" of the Soviet Union.[5]

However, the political reforms initiated in both countries during the 1980s actually complicated Sino-Soviet relations further rather than facilitating them. While both countries were attempting significant political, social, and economic reforms, their assessments of each other's reform efforts were quite negative.[6] The Soviets saw the Chinese as "neo-Maoist" and "right-revisionist," not truly moving away from the Cultural Revolution period. As the Russians proceeded with their reforms and launched *perestroika,* the Chinese model of reform was rejected because it was seen as being nothing more than a rejection of Marxism, not an embrace of market mechanisms and political liberalization.[7] For their part, the Chinese rejected the model pursued by Gorbachev for several reasons, most importantly because it was viewed as too ambitious and as a complete rejection of Marxism-Leninism, something the Chinese leadership was not yet ready to pursue (or considered too dangerous to attempt). In such an environment, Moscow and Beijing increasingly viewed each other with suspicion. In addition, the so-called "three barriers" (Soviet support for Vietnam's occupation of Cambodia, the Soviet presence in Mongolia, and major Soviet deployments along the Chinese border) also prevented a rapprochement between Moscow and Beijing.

THE DRAGON TURNS TO THE BEAR

Gorbachev visited China in May 1989 as circumstances began to change. Progress in the talks designed to resolve the Cambodia issue paved the way for a withdrawal of Vietnamese forces, while Gorbachev's desire to reduce military expenditures led to reductions in Soviet forces all along the Sino-Soviet border and in Mongolia. In addition, Gorbachev signaled a willingness to begin discussions on settling outstanding border disputes with China. The dismantling of the three barriers led to the first breakthroughs in the Moscow–Beijing relationship.[8] However, the Tiananmen incident of June 4th, 1989, changed the situation significantly, as Gorbachev was reluctant to condemn the crackdown by Chinese forces on the student protests in Beijing. Simultaneously, U.S.–China relations stalled in the aftermath of the June 4th incident, which was seen as a human rights atrocity. The United States immediately imposed an arms embargo against China in response, while the EU soon followed suit with its own embargo. With the rest of the world vociferously condemning the Chinese leadership, both Gorbachev (and, later, Boris Yeltsin) failed to condemn China for its actions and moved in to fill the void in Beijing's foreign relations, quickly becoming Beijing's largest arms supplier, with China eventually taking up to 40% of Russia's total arms exports.[9] In 1993, China signed a 5-year defense cooperation agreement with Russia, helping to cement this new critical economic relationship. Not surprisingly, therefore, Russia's defense industry was to become one of the key proponents of the China vector in Russian foreign policy.

However, just as China's relations with the outside world were at their lowest point in many years, Russia's successful emergence from the ashes of the USSR paved the way for improved relations with the West, particularly the United States. Moreover, the pronounced Atlanticist trend during the first Yeltsin administration meant that the American vector enjoyed pre-eminence in Moscow, particularly coupled with the expectation that a post–Soviet Russia would emerge as a major partner within an expanded Western alliance (expectations that have been discussed in the previous chapter on the U.S.-Russia relationship). Yeltsin did visit China in December 1992 to sign a nonaggression pact and to pursue commercial deals, but his initial focus was on promoting a new strategic partnership with Washington. As U.S.-Russia relations soured, however, China beckoned as an alternative. Subsequent visits by Yeltsin to China (April 1996 and November 1997) and by Chinese president Jiang Zemin to Russia (September 1994 and April 1997) saw Russian and Chinese leaders more prepared to discuss "constructive partnership" between the two states and a greater willingness to engage in shared action on the global stage. After Yevgeny Primakov became foreign minister of Russia in 1996, he encouraged Yeltsin to strive for a "Russo-Chinese strategic partnership" that could counterbalance the United States and check its tendencies towards unilateralism.[10]

By 1999, a new turn in the China–Russia relationship was evident. The NATO bombing of Serbia, a Russian ally, lead to a precipitous decline in U.S.-Russia relations, a development that coincided with Moscow's shift toward Beijing. One event that seemed to signal the impending sea change in Russia's relations with the United States and China was the pronouncement by Yeltsin during his visit to Beijing in the fall of 1999 that Russia was a nuclear power. This pronouncement was seemingly directed toward the United States, which had recently completed its military operations in the Balkans—where the United States could conduct military operations with impunity against Serbia, since it was not a nuclear power—and was becoming increasingly critical of Russia's renewed fighting in Chechnya. To Moscow, NATO intervention in the Balkans offered a clear analogy with Chechnya. Yeltsin's statement, therefore, was a warning to the West that Russia would not fall victim to the sort of intervention NATO had carried out in the Balkans. The rescinding of its no-first-use policy on nuclear weapons, codified in the 2000 National Security Concept of the Russian Federation (signed by Yeltsin in December 1999), provided a doctrinal basis for using nuclear weapons "in case of the need to repel an armed aggression when all other means of settling the crisis situation have been exhausted or proved ineffective." This move showed clearly that the heady days of the U.S.–Russia partnership were numbered.

China, for its part, also drew a negative analogy from the Kosovo intervention. This served not only to further stall the normalization of U.S.–China relations a full decade after the Tiananmen incident but also to nudge Russia and China closer together. As China scholar June Dreyer pointed out at the time, "the Chinese leadership discerned a dangerous precedent" in the NATO intervention in Kosovo "that could be used to oppose Beijing's designs on Taiwan and control of dissident ethnic minority areas."[11] Indeed, the criteria often cited as justification for Kosovo independence—the province's *de jure* status as an autonomous region within the Yugoslav Federation combined with the ethnic distinctiveness of the province—could easily be applied to regions of the People's Republic such as Tibet, Xinjiang, and Inner Mongolia. As Chinese commentator Yu Ligong observed, "It is very possible that the independence of Kosovo will be a precedent for territories pursuing independence around the world." From the Chinese point of view, if unchecked, America's Balkan intervention could establish a precedent that could later be used by the United States to intervene in the Taiwan Strait and similarly award Taiwan the status of a sovereign nation-state of which it has long dreamed.[12]

The events triggered a dramatic and seemingly persistent shift in the triangular relationship between Russia, China, and the United States. In the new millennium, Russia and China are being pushed together by America's hard- and soft-power preponderance, diplomatic language, and military posture worldwide. Both Russia and China feel threatened to some degree by the United States and are ill at ease, leading to voices in both countries calling for an alliance to balance against the United States. While there are certainly limits to this alliance, as Robert Legvold observes, "China [is] a natural soulmate on many critical foreign policy issues [which] renders Russia strong."[13] One area in which China and Russia have moved closer together, to the consternation of the United States, is to block U.S. and European calls for intervention at the United Nations. The threat of a double veto from China and Russia led the United States to circumvent the UN Security Council for authorization for the Kosovo war in 1999 and the Iraq War in 2003. In 2007, Beijing and Moscow cast a double veto to block a resolution that criticized the government of Burma (Myanmar), the first time this had happened since the days of the Cold War.[14] Since that time, Russia and China have cast double vetoes to block proposals for action against Zimbabwe and Syria and have used the threat of blocking action to force modification of other proposed resolutions, including those on Sudan. Moscow and Beijing have become the principal defenders of what is sometimes referred to as the "neo-Westphalian synthesis" in which state sovereignty is absolute, in contrast to American and European arguments that sovereignty is conditional on a government's respect for human rights.[15]

The fear of American encirclement also helped to drive the formation of a new regional organization. As China sought to demarcate its border with Russia and other former Soviet republics to prevent any future clashes as occurred between China and the USSR in 1969, Yeltsin, during his April 1996 visit to China, met in Shanghai with Jiang and the presidents of Kazakhstan, Kyrgyzstan, and Tajikistan to sign the Treaty on Deepening Military Trust in Border Regions. The signatories agreed to meet on an annual basis as a confidence-building exercise and in subsequent meetings expanded the scope of their discussions to discuss the rising Islamist threat to the region and greater cooperation in combating insurgencies. In 2001, Uzbekistan was invited to join and the six states agreed to formalize the relationship by creating the Shanghai Cooperation Organization (SCO), whose charter was promulgated in 2002 at a summit in St. Petersburg. The SCO was initially formed to address security issues in Central Asia; increasingly, however, it has been used by Moscow (and Beijing) as a way to reduce U.S. influence in the region.[16] In July 2005, wary of U.S. motives for long-term military presence in Central Asia, the SCO approved a Moscow-authored plan calling for withdrawal of U.S. and coalition military bases from Uzbekistan and Kyrgyzstan; later that year, Uzbekistan evicted American forces after the United States criticized the government's response to protests. At the same time, the SCO gave a negative reply to a tentative query as to whether the United States could be awarded observer status within the organization and thus participate in its summit meetings.[17]

While not a formal alliance, the SCO has given Russia and China the building blocks of a transnational organization that could serve as a counterbalance to the web of U.S.-led international organizations such as NATO or the G-8 or other Western groupings such as the European Union. Beyond the six full members, India, Pakistan, Afghanistan, Mongolia, and Iran are observers, while Turkey, Belarus, and Sri Lanka are "dialogue partners." This gives the SCO greater legitimacy in claiming for itself the role as the premier forum for discussing Eurasian security issues.[18] The SCO also strongly defends the principle of noninterference in the domestic affairs of its members and the right of each to choose its own particular path to social and economic development, making it attractive to many rising powers as an alternative to Western-led bodies.

The SCO has also been important as a way to regulate the competition between Russia and China for influence in Central Asia. China has proposed the eventual transformation of the SCO into a free-trade zone and suggested that an SCO development bank be created. But, so far, China has not used its extensive economic influence in the region to undermine Russian political leadership.

THE BEAR EMBRACES THE DRAGON

Since Russia and China first encountered each other in military and diplomatic spheres, their bilateral relations have ranged from enemy to comrade and every point in between, as the discussion above makes clear. Throughout the centuries of their interaction, no lasting pattern of bilateral relations between Moscow and Beijing has really ever emerged. Rather, their relations have always been based on the need for mutual coexistence, the necessity to protect one's rear flank, and the threat of other states in the international system and their ambitions on the Eurasian landmass. In his own assessment of this history, aired repeatedly on Russia's state-run English-language channel prior to the 2012 APEC summit, President Vladimir Putin acknowledged the ebb and flow of Sino-Russian relations, concluding that at present they are at an "unprecedented high level" and characterized by "a lot of mutual trust."[19]

Putin's comments must be understood against the backdrop of unprecedented levels of cooperation between Russia and China, including economic trade, natural resource exploitation, arms sales, military cooperation, the resolution of long-standing border disputes, and a multiyear program of cultural exchanges during his tenure as president and prime minister of Russia. In October 2004, the treaty setting forth the final demarcation of the Russia–China border was signed and ratified, bringing to a close any remaining disputes between the two powers.[20]

Though certainly the least strategic of the developments, programs such as the Year of Russia in China (2006), the Year of China in Russia (2007), and other similar programs—including a planned future "year of youth" exchange—set the stage for further strategic cooperation by facilitating high-level political leaders and diplomats to work together in noncontentious areas in which mutual praise was the message of the day. For example, while still first deputy prime minister, Putin tapped Dmitri Medvedev to serve as the chair of the organizing committee for the Year of China in Russia, while Chinese president Hu Jintao visited the Kremlin in 2005 and 2007 in connection with the "year of" programs. During his 2005 visit, Hu expressed admiration for Russia's contributions to world civilization, referring to China's "strategic partnership" with Russia every few sentences. Hu's speech also included praise for Russia's military achievements, and it was clearly designed to pay respect to the senior partner in the relationship. While China recognizes that Russia's power and stature have drastically declined, China—in its dealings with the Kremlin—showered praise upon Russia, feeding its desire for recognition of its status as a great power and former superpower.

During the Year of Russia in China in 2006, each month was filled with Russian cultural events throughout the PRC, including ice sculptures, traveling ballet troupes, and photo exhibits. The leading Russian news service, *RIA-Novosti*, even used the occasion to launch a Chinese-language website. Several academic and business conferences aimed at improving mutual understanding and promoting trade were also held. Of course, there were also high-level diplomatic meetings about strengthening mutual aid and collaboration.[21] These and other similar developments in the Sino-Russian relationship are more than simply cultural events or empty diplomatic maneuvers. For example, in accordance with the 2004 border treaty, Moscow and Beijing settled their long-standing border disputes after more than 40 years of heated debate over the ownership of islands in the Ussuri River separating the two countries. While the border was officially established in July 2007, the official transfer of about 375 sq. km. came with a low-key ceremony (and virtually no media coverage in Russia) in October 2008.

One of the most significant results of these exchanges has been their role in facilitating bilateral trade. By 2008, Sino-Russian bilateral trade had reached some $55 billion, although it subsequently began to fall in the wake of the global economic slowdown, especially as a result of the plunge in world prices for Russian oil, gas, and other raw materials.[22] It quickly rebounded, however, and today China has become Russia's largest trade partner, surpassing Germany, with 2012 bilateral trade hitting a record high of nearly $90 billion. This puts the two countries well on their way to reaching their bilateral trade targets of $100 billion

FIGURE 4.1
Russian–Chinese Bilateral Trade, 2007–2012 (in billions of U.S. dollars)

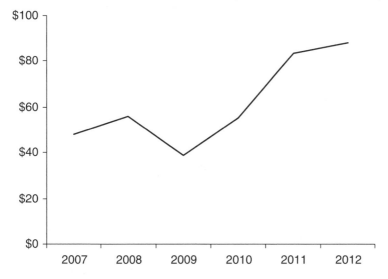

Source: Roskomstat.

in 2015 and $200 billion in 2020.[23] This trade is seriously imbalanced, however, with Russian exports to China consisting mostly of commodities, while Chinese exports to Russia consist mainly of consumer goods and high-value products. During their December 2012 meeting, however, China pledged its commitment to optimizing their trade structure. Both countries have also pledged to reduce their dependence on the U.S. dollar for bilateral trade and instead to increase usage of the Russian ruble and Chinese yuan.[24]

Energy cooperation is one of the most significant areas of Sino-Russian economic relations. In recent years, the two sides have made great achievements and maintained momentum in bilateral cooperation in such areas as crude oil, gas, nuclear energy, coal and electricity, and energy efficiency. The two countries established a China–Russia energy negotiation mechanism in 2008 and have since held nine official meetings and two additional working meetings designed to facilitate further bilateral energy cooperation. In 2009, for instance, the China Development Bank agreed to loan the state oil company Rosneft $15 billion and the pipeline operator Transneft $10 billion, financing that both companies desperately needed as a result of the 2008 global economic crisis; in return, the Russian side pledged to supply China with 15 million tons of oil per year for a two-decade period.[25] China received clear guarantees about a critical energy supply, and then-Deputy Prime Minister Igor Sechin, who brokered the arrangement, preferred to deal with Chinese banks rather than Western financial institutions that would have attempted to impose conditions or to seek shares as collateral. Not surprisingly, the China vector tends to be strongly supported by many of the so-called *siloviki* in Russia, who prefer that Russia's state companies deal with their Chinese counterparts.

This energy dialogue, however, has widened its scope far beyond oil and gas to cover nuclear energy, coal, and electricity, as well as encompassing measures meant to increase energy efficiency and promote renewable energy. The most recent was held in December 2012, scheduled to coincide with Premier Wen's visit to Russia at the same time. There Russia and China signed several deals, including one to construct an oil refinery plant in Tianjin. The two sides each agreed to give priority to the construction of the East natural gas pipeline.[26] Russia also agreed to build two additional reactors at the Chinese nuclear power plant Tianwan, marking Russia's further engagement in the project.

By beginning cooperation in these areas, Russian and Chinese leaders were able to develop relationships and modes of interaction on less contentious issues, with these relationships then facilitating cooperation in more contentious areas. Of course, the most controversial and sensitive area of cooperation is in the military and defense industries. Russia and China have organized a series of war games nearly every year since 2003, and the past few years have also seen the rapid institutionalization of cooperation through the Shanghai Cooperation Organization (SCO), an organization that Beijing refers to as NATO-East. The deepening of Sino-Russian military cooperation has provided some cause for worry. The 2005 war games simulated a coastal attack, apparently with Taiwan as a potential target. These actions can be seen as aggressive toward not only Taiwan but also the United States. According to a former member of Taiwan's National Security Council, a Russian envoy explained that Russia's actions, including its arms sales to China, were not directed against Taiwan. This Russian diplomat admitted that Russia was "playing the China card" against the United States. He indicated that Moscow felt that it had few other ways to respond to U.S. posturing against Russia, including NATO's eastward expansion, the stationing of troops in Russia's "near abroad," and U.S. intent to deploy a missile defense system in Europe.[27] Peace Mission 2007, held in Russia, marked the first time Chinese forces had entered Russian territory to conduct a joint exercise with the Russian military.[28] The 2012 exercises, proclaimed a success by Chinese Vice Admiral Ding Yiping and his Russian counterpart Rear Admiral Leonid Sukhanov, highlighted the growing capabilities of the Russian and Chinese navies to patrol the Pacific and to project military power offshore to control vital sea lanes of communication.[29] Continued Sino-Russian cooperation in the SCO is seen as important to both countries; Wang Lijiu, a senior researcher at the Chinese Institute of Contemporary International Relations, has commented that the "sooner the SCO becomes the alternative to NATO in the region, the better."[30] But how far will Russia go in cooperating with China in an area of such vital strategic importance as military and defense?

THE BEAR ARMS THE DRAGON

From Russian threats to launch a preemptive strike against deployed missile defense system sites in Eastern Europe to China's tugging of its Kuznetsov-class aircraft carrier into the sea lanes off Dalian—and declaring plans eventually to build as many as three aircraft carriers—these days there is no shortage of commentators on Russia–China relations and strategic cooperation. These range from those who see the issue as being of little importance and unlikely to go anywhere to those who see China as the single greatest threat to the United States and Russia's cooperation with the PRC as speeding up an inevitable clash between the two.

As a rising regional power that is quickly building up its military capability, China has concluded that its own interests are best served by a stronger Russia with a more independent foreign policy. Such a conclusion is not only offered by many Chinese commentators on the subject but is also apparent by its actions.

While it is premature to suggest that Beijing wishes to create a full-fledged alliance with Moscow against Washington, Beijing certainly would prefer that Russia be able to counter American influence. The 2001 Treaty of Good-Neighborly Friendship and Cooperation and the 2002 Treaty on Friendly Neighborly Relations were the first clear-cut concrete steps taken to define the emerging "strategic partnership" between Russia and China (though the term was first used as early as 1996). Although the treaties do not contain any sort of a mutual defense clause, with each side only pledging not to join an alliance that threatens the other party, these instruments were important signals to each other that they were prepared to bolster their security while balancing against the West.

The truly strategic interaction has been in the world of bilateral arms sales and joint military production. Following the Tiananmen imbroglio and the subsequent Western arms embargo on the sale of advanced military technologies to China, Russia stepped in to fill the void. From the early 1990s to the mid-2000s, China was one of the world's biggest arms importers and Russia's biggest defense customer.[31] The two countries first signed an agreement on military-technical cooperation back in December 1992, but following the 2001 and 2002 treaties, they formed a Russian–Chinese Commission on Military-Technical Cooperation. In November 2012, recently appointed Russian Defense Minister Sergei Shoigu made his first visit to China after taking over from Serdyukov to attend the 17th meeting of the Russian-Chinese Commission on Military-Technical Cooperation.

From the early 1990s to mid-2000s, China was one of the world's biggest arms importers and Russia's biggest defense customer. Estimates are that China was the destination for up to 40% of all weapons sold by Russia between 1992 and 2007. In 2004, it hit 57%, and in 2005, when Beijing took delivery of six Project 636M (Kilo Mod class) submarines and a Project 956EM (Sovremenny Mod class) destroyer, that proportion may well have been even higher.[32] A sharp decline then followed, partly due to the fact that such large procurements do not take place on an annual basis and partly due to the fact that China has already acquired much of the equipment that Russia is willing to sell Beijing. Current estimates are that Russian weapons sales to China still account for around 25 to 30% of its arms exports.

These sales stem from economic rather than strategic considerations. While they may appear on the outside to suggest the formation of an alliance— indeed, both sides seem to want to promote that appearance—in fact they are merely economic exchanges, although with strategic implications. As Richard Weitz argues, Russia and China are not really allies, but rather their relations hinge on what he calls "strategic parallelism," meaning that their interests are currently in alignment.[33] Russia needs to sell weapons to keep its military employees working (to help generate high-tech manufacturing employment), to generate revenue to use in defense research and development, and to generate seed funds for its next generation of military technology. So Russia must sell its weapons, and China is the biggest potential market out there. From the Chinese side, the deal makes sense for several reasons, the first being that as China began its big push in weapons procurement, Russia was the only major seller that was willing to sell to China (again due to the post–Tiananmen embargo). This also made sense because China had already fielded Soviet- and Russian-made weapons. Once they acquired even more Russian weapons in the 1990s, there were advantages to continuing to add Russian weapons to their arsenals, including benefits of interoperability and repair and replacement. The relationship worked quite well for China, as it allowed Beijing to acquire advanced conventional weapons that domestic firms could not yet manufacture. Thanks in large part to cooperation in military technology, China's defense industry today is capable of producing much more sophisticated weapons than it was only a short decade ago.

China's apparent reliance upon Russian weapons, however, should not be seen as dependence. China's defense planners are smart and realize the dangers and pitfalls of becoming overly reliant upon Russian weapons. Their answer has been to build capacity in specific sectors and slowly replace their importing of specific Russian weapons with domestic production and eventual export, sort of an "import-substitution industrialization" model of the defense sector. By first developing their domestic capacity, China is able to lay the industrial and technological foundation for the subsequent exporter phase. By successfully employing this strategy, within the next few years China will not only regain its status as a net exporter of weapons (indeed, it may have already done so), but it will actually become one of the world's leading arms exporters.

Russia is now becoming aware of this strategy, as China is beginning to encroach upon some of Russia's traditional market share in the global arms trade. The result is not only decreasing sales from Russia to China, but Russia also loses sales to other countries that are now buying Chinese-produced weapons. This leaves Russia bitter not only about China's illegal copying of Russia's military technology but also over the loss of sales of those weapons to third countries. Russia is faced with a dilemma: It can sit back and take the hit, or it can sell even more advanced weaponry to the Chinese to make up the sales shortfall (and risk that they will copy those designs, too, and then export them).[34] One factor weighing against the decision to transfer even more advanced military systems to Beijing is that Chinese engineers might learn enough from the technology to improve the quality of their indigenous production, helping them further capture traditional Russian arms markets.[35] Moscow has thus far been reluctant to sell such strategic weapons as long-range strategic bombers and ballistic missiles. This decision will mostly rest with Putin himself, since he has nearly omnipotent control over Russia's arms sales. Perhaps he is seeking to expand his country's economic cooperation with China to offset the eventual decline in arms sales, or perhaps he is prepared to sell more high-tech weapons systems to Beijing despite the strategic consequences to such a move.

As Richard Weitz points out, selling more "advanced weapons to China could undermine Russian interests in ways that, on balance, might exceed the benefits Moscow might accrue from the arms sales."[36] For one, regional players, such as Taiwan, the United States, and possibly Japan, could criticize such sales as having a destabilizing effect on the regional balance of power. Enhancing China's air and maritime power projection capabilities in this way, he argues, could lead to "military adventurism" by Beijing. And Moscow cannot simply ignore the long-term implications of China's growing military might, as China is developing a "more active and seemingly inevitable aggressive foreign policy."[37] Other Russian strategists fear that Beijing might one day present a "major threat" to Russia. They argue that, once the Taiwan issue is settled (either peacefully or through military conquest), Beijing would then be likely to redirect its future expansionist ambitions toward Central Asia or its own underpopulated Far East.[38] Would Russia engage in actions that lead to short-term economic gains but have huge long-term strategic costs?

Russia has done similar things in the past. As a way of circumventing the Treaty of Versailles, which forbade Germany from building or possessing armed aircraft, tanks, or armored vehicles, under the provisions of a 1921 commercial agreement (and later under the 1922 Treaty of Rapallo), Russia allowed Germany to build and test aircraft, armored vehicles, and weapons in Russia and to conduct joint armor and flight training, activities Germany was prohibited from conducting in its own country under the Treaty.[39] This is where Germany began to experiment with its combined arms tactics, which it would later use against the USSR itself during World War II. Likewise, during the Sino-Soviet border clashes of the late 1960s, the Chinese forces employed Soviet-supplied weapons against their former patrons. What are the chances that Russia's arms sales to China today will result in a similar outcome?

China, for its part, is also not pleased that Russia has expanded its weapons sales to countries that surround China. One of Russia's largest partners is India, with whom Russia has a highly developed strategic partnership (that will be discussed in greater detail in Chapter 9)—a country with which China has clashed militarily in the past. However, other countries with whom China has strained relations—including Malaysia, Indonesia, and Vietnam—have all increased their purchases from Russia as China's power grows.[40] Russia, for instance, is supplying Vietnam with Kilo submarines, part of Vietnam's desire to be able to defend its strategic interests in the South China Sea, where it has ongoing disputes over maritime claims with China.[41]

AN EMERGING STRATEGIC ALLIANCE?

During his latest visit to Beijing in June 2012, in his first foreign trip after reclaiming the Russian presidency (and, significantly, after Putin had declined President Barack Obama's invitation to visit Camp David as part of the G-8 summit), Putin and then-Chinese President Hu signed 11 agreements in the areas of energy, nuclear power and technology, tourism, journalism, investment, banking, industrial park management, and insurance. In a joint statement issued following their meeting, Putin and Hu emphasized the need to maintain "close high-level exchanges" and improve cooperation between their organs of government in order to better coordinate with each other over critical regional and global issues. In a similar vein, they pledged to build further confidence-building measures along the border regions and fight transnational crime and illegal immigration. They also restated their aims of expanding the value of their bilateral trade to $100 billion by 2015 and $200 billion before 2020, as well as promoting cultural, tourism, educational, and social exchanges.

In their joint statement, Putin and Hu explicitly referred to their cooperation in military spheres. The two sides pledged to deepen "cooperation at various levels and in all fields between the armed forces of the two countries, and carrying out joint military exercises aimed at improving coordinating capacity of the armed forces of the two countries and promoting regional peace, security, and stability." As Yu Bin pointed out, military–military relations are rarely raised in the annual Sino-Russian presidential joint statements, with only occasional reference to security issues or their common position on opposing missile defense.[42]

Such a statement seems quite in line with the increasingly frequent and high-level calls in China for establishing even greater formal security obligations between the two states. Recent discussion in China has led to the idea of forming a "quasi-alliance" with Moscow. PLA General Wang Haiyun of the China Foundation of International Studies in Beijing (and former PLA military attaché in Moscow) recently suggested that the "time is ripe" for a "united front" or quasi-alliance between Moscow and Beijing.[43] With Putin consolidating Russia's "near abroad" and "pivoting" toward the Asia-Pacific, Russia's strategic calculations "extensively coincide" with those of China and Beijing should take advantage of this opportunity to form an even stronger relationship with Moscow. During his visit to China in the summer of 2012, Putin had a chance to meet with the incoming president, Xi Jinping, with both agreeing that Russia–China strategic cooperation should continue and deepen.[44] In January 2013, the secretary of the Russian Security Council, Nikolai Patrushev, traveled to Beijing for the eighth round of the China-Russia Strategic Security Consultation with his counterpart State Councilor Dai Bingguo. Patrushev also met with Xi, who reiterated that "promoting relations with Russia is a priority for Chinese diplomacy" and pledged to continue the program outlined by Putin and Hu the previous year.[45] When Chinese foreign minister Yang Jiechi visited Moscow in February 2013, he consulted with the Russian government on joint positions that both China and Russia would defend in the United Nations on Syria, Iran, and North Korea and confirmed that Russia and China will hold two major military exercises in 2013—a combined antiterrorism drill (Peace Mission 2013) and a joint naval exercise in the Sea of Japan in June. Meanwhile Igor Sechin, the CEO of Rosneft, and Deputy Prime Minister Arkady Dvorkovich, who oversees the energy portfolio in Medvedev's cabinet, both visited Beijing to discuss expanding Russian energy supplies to China.[46] Signifying the importance that China places on its "strategic partnership" with Russia, Xi made Russia his first destination after formally being inaugurated as China's president in March 2013.

There are limits to such an alliance, however. Outside of the Kremlin and Zhongnanhai (the seat of the Chinese government), not all average Chinese and Russians are on board for such an alliance. Many in Russia are fearful of China and see their country as being overrun with Chinese. This is particularly true in the Russian Far East, where Chinese traders come across the border by the thousands every day, raising fears of a Chinese takeover of the region.[47] Even figures such as Prime Minister Medvedev have raised this scenario, warning in August 2012 that "the Far East . . . is located far away and, unfortunately, we don't have many people there and must protect it from the excessive expansion of people from neighboring countries."[48]

A 10-year analysis of Russian public opinion on China suggests that, although opinions fluctuate, consistently more than half of Russians say that China is a friendly nation (ranging from a low of 48% in 2006 to a high of 67% in 2002). This does not mean, however, that China is not seen as posing a threat to Russia. When asked if China's rise threatened Russia, 44% responded that it did. And of those who agreed that China was a friendly nation, 34% still believed that China's rise posed a threat to Russia.[49] In another survey from 2010, however, respondents were asked directly if China posed a threat to Russia. Only 13% responded affirmatively, while the largest response (32%) was that the threat was from the West, followed closely by the Muslim world (29%).[50]

Ideas of the "China threat" are increasingly popular in Russia, however. As early as 2000, Russian writers were coming out with warnings about the threat posed by China. Igor Malevich's *Vnimanie, Kitai!* aims primarily to inform readers from the former Soviet Union about China's dramatic rise to a position of influence in the world.[51] Malevich, a former Soviet astronaut, structures his work around the question of whether China represents Russia's future or its past, only to conclude that it is in some ways both. Most significantly, however, Malevich wants to warn his readers of the potential dangers of a successful and powerful China.[52]

Another example is a documentary by Russian investigative journalist Yelena Masyuk titled *The Character of Friendship,* which was aired on many stations throughout Russia despite an order from many local government agencies that it not be shown. The documentary "exposed" the dangers of China's rise and the double standards of China's "friendship" with Russia. In an interview with the Russian daily *Sobesednik,* Masyuk expressed a deep disagreement with the Putin administration and its policies toward China:

> I can't understand the position of Russia's Foreign Ministry, which doesn't react to the fact that China prints maps showing all regions between Vladivostok and the Urals as Chinese territory. We are keeping quiet on this score. Naturally enough, this won't yield any positive results because China, as well as any Asian country, respects force alone.[53]

Such sentiments are no longer limited to retired Soviet-era cosmonauts and xenophobic journalists. Increasingly, leading figures in the Russian military and defense industry are pointing to China as a threat looming just over the horizon. In addition to Barabanov and his colleagues at Moscow's Centre for Analysis of Strategies and Technologies discussed above, some figures within the military itself are beginning to speak out on the issue. In 2009, when questioned about the nature of threats Russia's armed forces are preparing to defend against, Lt. General Sergei Skokov, at the time chief of the ground forces general staff, responded that if "we talk about the east, then it could be a multi-million-man army with a traditional approach to conducting combat operations: straightforward, with large concentrations of personnel and firepower along individual operational directions." Leading Russian military expert Alexander Khramchikhin described the statement as "epochal" in an article in *Nezavisimoye Voyennoye Obozrenie.* Khramchikhin observed that, for "the first time since the early days of Gorbachev, a high-ranking national commander has de facto acknowledged officially that the People's Republic of China is our potential enemy."[54]

For their part, not all Chinese are great lovers of Russia. In Chinese cinema, literature, and the media, Russian men are often portrayed as mobsters and Russian women as prostitutes. Their history of interaction also does not help their case. The centuries of struggle between the two nations, discussed at the outset of this chapter, are fairly well known in China, and their more recent history has done little to suggest that such a past should be forgotten. It was precisely this history that was the subject of a recent editorial in the Chinese daily *Global Times*. The author pointed out that some Russia specialists in China are arguing that there is something to be "questioned" and "guarded against" deep in the Russians' psyche and that Russia is using China for its own strategic interests. The piece also highlighted what it called Russia's "strategic vacillation," its swaying back and forth between balancing against the West and engaging it. Nevertheless, Putin was seen a stable leader for Russia and the editorial suggested that China take advantage of the strategic opportunity to deepen Sino-Russian strategic relations during his period in power.[55]

For these reasons, many in Washington see the Russia–China tango as a show for the United States, arguing that mutual suspicions run so deep in Moscow and Beijing that any form of alliance is at best a remote possibility. It is ironic that throughout the 1960s, when evidence suggested to the United States that there was a rift between Russia and China, no one really believed it. For now, Russia and China are focusing on their mutual interests in securing their rear flanks and providing for stability in Central Asia. From the vantage points of both the Kremlin and Zhongnanhai, the greatest threat to peace and the international status quo seems to emanate from Washington. In such an international environment, Russia's and China's actions make good strategic sense.

But increasingly warm Sino-Russian relations could threaten the rest of the region. Russia's bilateral actions in Asia impact the regional balance; the choice of China as Russia's major strategic partner in Asia has implications for each other state in the region, both in terms of its relations with Moscow and with its relations with the United States. By equipping the world's largest army—almost 3 million soldiers—Russia is not only taking a strategic gamble with its own future but is helping shift the balance of power in Asia significantly in ways that potentially threaten China's neighbors and America's allies. Therefore, Russia's foreign policy does attempt to hedge against the possibility of a future downturn in Russia–China relations by reaching out to other Asian powers.

MENDING FENCES: RUSSIA–JAPAN RELATIONS

Although Japan and the USSR engaged each other in battle on the eve of World War II in a small border war near Mongolia-Manchuria, the two refrained from further direct military engagement and even concluded a neutrality pact in 1941. While Japan considered withdrawing from the pact after its Axis ally Germany invaded the USSR, it did not. After the Soviet defeat of Germany in May 1945, Stalin declared the pact null, however, and prepared to enter the war against Japan as requested by the Allies at the Yalta Conference. Stalin had his own reasons for entering the war in the Pacific, as he saw it as an opportunity to gain a strategic foothold in the region, something Moscow had long sought. Russia quickly mobilized forces from the European front to the Pacific and launched its attack between the dropping of the two atomic bombs over Japan. Soviet forces invaded Manchuria, followed by Sakhalin and the Kuril Islands. It swiftly defeated the Japanese Kwantung army in Manchuria and then moved on to liberate the northern half of the Korean peninsula.[56]

While the Soviet Union eventually withdrew from Manchuria and Korea (leaving these territories to its Communist allies), even to this day it has not relinquished control over the islands. Indeed, these territories were offered to the Soviet Union by the Allies in return for its participation in the war.[57] Japan, for its part, has never rescinded its claims on the islands and refuses to recognize this territorial concession, arguing that the islands in question are not the ones referred to in the Yalta Agreement. The result is that the two countries have still not concluded a permanent peace treaty following World War II.

While the issue of some remote and relatively uninhabited islands in the northern Pacific may seem irrelevant and like ancient history to outsiders, it is still a heated issue and consistently comes up in their bilateral relations. It is also one of the reasons Japan is not high on the list of countries, according to public opinion polls, with which Russia should orient itself. When asked what countries Russia should orient itself toward, Japan consistently comes up toward the bottom of the list (right there alongside the United States!). In 2012, only 18% selected Japan, and that number is down from 27% in 2001. By comparison, the corresponding rating for India and China was 34% in 2012.[58]

When the Soviet Union collapsed, Japan believed there was an opportunity to regain the territory by reaching an agreement with a post–Soviet Russia. However, while Yeltsin, prior to the disintegration of the USSR, had indicated possible interest in reaching a compromise with Japan, it became politically unfeasible for the president who had helped to dissolve the USSR to be seen "losing" Russian territory. When Japan pressed for negotiations, Yeltsin cancelled his scheduled September 1992 visit to Japan (but ultimately traveled to Tokyo the following October, in which he did acknowledge that there was a territorial dispute over the islands).[59] Over the years, the situation has grown increasingly tense. In 2006, a Japanese fisherman in the region was killed by a "stray bullet" fired by Russian forces, and in 2010, Russian border troops engaged two Japanese fishing boats near the islands. The Japanese apparently hoped that the resolution of the Sino-Russian border, in which Moscow essentially handed over the disputed territories to China, would be the same for the Kurils.[60] Apparently this is not what Moscow had in mind.

One reason the issue remains high and the tensions still run deep is the ongoing battle over history. Things really flared up in 2008 when newly issued

Japanese textbooks stated that Japan has sovereignty over the Russian-administered Southern Kuril Islands, sparking sharp criticism from Moscow. Russian bloggers even criticized Google for listing the islands as "disputed territories" on its maps. Dmitry Medvedev then took the opportunity afforded by a G-8 summit in Japan to meet with the Japanese prime minister to discuss the issue, but no real progress was made.[61] In turn, Medvedev's visit to the islands in November 2010 (the first by a Russian president) and then a follow-up visit in July 2012 sparked extremely negative reactions in Japan. Matters were not helped when the Russian General Staff announced plans to deploy new equipment and to modernize the air and naval defense systems on the islands and hinted that advanced Mistral helicopter carriers that Russia is purchasing from France might be deployed to protect the Kurils.[62]

The Kuril island dispute is the only real sticking point in what could otherwise be warm relations between the two countries. Ever since Gorbachev's 1986 Vladivostok speech, both sides have worked to improve their bilateral ties, especially in the economic area. For nearly two decades now, Japan has worked hard to develop Russia's automotive sector. Other sectors, including energy and natural gas, have also benefited from Japanese investment. Mitsui and Mitsubishi are both partners in the Sakhalin-2 energy project, with a number of Japanese power firms signed up as customers for the natural gas that is produced. Yet bilateral trade is still underdeveloped. Given Japan's need for energy, Russia would be the natural supplier, especially from its sources in Eastern Siberia. Yet in 2011, Russia was only ranked as Japan's fourth-largest supplier of coal, sixth for crude oil, and seventh for liquefied natural gas. After the 2011 earthquake and tsunami that struck Japan, Russia did agree to increase its supplies of gas, oil, and electricity to the island nation, and there is now a nuclear cooperation agreement between the two countries.[63] But Japanese firms have been reluctant to undertake major investments in Siberia, even when Russia has solicited Japanese participation as a way to develop alternatives to the China market. A number of ambitious projects, including an undersea gas pipeline to link Russia's Sakhalin Island and Japan, have withered on the vine.[64]

Shortly after his reelection in 2012, Putin declared that Moscow and Tokyo should strengthen economic cooperation between the two countries, giving priority to the auto industry and energy sector. Putin called for Russian–Japanese auto manufacturing projects and other joint projects to be implemented. Japan and Russia have been working closely in the energy sector, with Russian natural gas now providing 10% of Japan's consumption. Trade volume between Russia and Japan reached a record high in 2012—nearly $30 billion—but this is only a return to the pre–economic crisis level. As Putin himself pointed out, this figure is still relatively low compared to Russia's trade with its Asian partner, China. In a statement in 2012, Putin said that he is "sure the opportunities of both Russia and Japan make us think what can be and should be done to develop much rapid trade and economic relations." His counterpart at the time, Japanese Prime Minister Yoshihiko Noda, also stated that improved economic relations with Russia would be one of Japan's main priorities.[65]

The recent election of Shinzo Abe, head of Japan's Liberal-Democratic Party, as prime minister might offer the opportunity to resolve some of the long-standing conflicts. Shortly after his election, Abe spoke about intentions to solve the Kurils issue and sign a peace treaty with Russia. Putin responded favorably, saying that he acknowledges the peaceful signal sent by Tokyo. Given Abe's track record on security and foreign policy issues,[66] however, where he has historically taken a tough stand, as well as his strong nationalist views, it is hard to see how these long-standing issues can be resolved. However, both sides have decided to close no doors. Highlighting the importance of Japan as an economic counterbalance to China for Russia, Rosneft CEO Igor Sechin traveled to Japan in February 2013 to seek Japanese investment in helping Russia develop its Arctic energy reserves and build new distribution networks to supply East Asia with Russian energy. The hope is that Japan, which has increased its imports of natural gas after the 2011 Fukushima nuclear disaster, might be more inclined to assist Russia in this area.[67]

KOREA: UNPARALLELED RELATIONS

While Korea has a similar point of contention with Japan over island possession and the history of the region (the same Japanese schoolbooks that sparked sharp criticism from Russia also claimed that a group of islands owned by South Korea are part of Japan), fortunately Korea and Russia have no such disputes. Rather, the looming issue with regard to Korea is another festering issue from World War II: the division of the peninsula along the 38th parallel. Shortly after Soviet forces defeated the Japanese Kwantung army in Manchuria, they moved south to liberate Korea, quickly establishing a Moscow-friendly regime in the north. The decision to divide the peninsula in two was made quickly by Washington, based upon the exigency of needing Soviet forces to help liberate the peninsula from Japanese occupation, while also not wanting to deprive the United States of a toehold on the strategic land bridge.

The very powerful position the Soviet Union occupied in Korea at the end of World War II was significantly diminished by the effects of the Korean War and the subsequent Sino–Soviet split. As a border state directly threatened by UN forces in Korea, China became very involved, becoming the chief protector of the North Korean regime. While China would have liked to bring Korea back into the vassal-state status that it was under for centuries, neither regime on the peninsula was willing to allow itself to be so threatened, but each understood the importance, influence, and increasing power of the regime in Beijing.

Korea held an important place in Soviet Pacific strategy. Its proximity to the Sea of Okhotsk, a critical basing area for Soviet strategic missiles, and the importance of Northeast Asia as a staging ground for Soviet forces in Vietnam and the Indian Ocean region guaranteed that the region held a prominent place in Soviet military planning.[68] Moscow's military expansion in the region then altered the security policies of China, Japan, the United States, and South Korea, which in turn encouraged Pyongyang to seek even closer ties to Moscow. Another factor that contributed to this was the rapid expansion of the South Korean economy in the 1980s and subsequent military buildup. Advancements in the South contrasted sharply with the situation in the North, where they were still relying upon increasingly obsolete technology and the economy was backward. In the mid-1980s, in exchange for 50 MiG 23 fighter aircraft to Pyongyang and a drastic increase in Soviet-DPRK trade volume, Moscow secured overflight rights and porting rights for Soviet naval vessels, both commercial and military.[69] All this would soon change as new leadership emerged in the Kremlin.

Domestic regime change in both China and Russia in the 1980s provided an opportunity. As part of its "new thinking" in foreign policy, Moscow began promoting a policy of "peaceful unification" of the Korean peninsula. China's economic reforms didn't directly threaten Pyongyang and held the promise of improved relations with Seoul. Conversely, Gorbachev's *perestroika* held a similar promise for South Korea but threw the legitimacy of the North Korean regime directly into question. Though relations were improved in the early 1980s, with the arrival of the Soviet MiGs and the boost to bilateral trade, once the scope of Gorbachev's reforms began to become clear, Kim Il Sung had to respond. Kim feared the repercussions of a Korean-style *perestroika*. His fears proved realistic, as the regimes of Eastern Europe that did embrace Gorbachev's reforms (or fought them) all fell within 4 years. Gorbachev was patient with Kim and did not aggressively push reforms on Pyongyang the way it did in Eastern Europe. Perhaps this was because Korea was still important for Gorbachev, since he wanted to promote both the development of the Soviet Far East and increase the Soviet Union's role in the Asia-Pacific theater. Indeed, Moscow still has not, and has kept up ties today with both regimes, establishing relations with Seoul based upon an alignment of economic objectives and maintaining its long relationship with the regime in Pyongyang based upon its long-standing support of the regime.

By the late 1980s, Moscow began establishing ties with Seoul in the pursuit of economic cooperation. Moscow had already been doing business with South Korean companies like Samsung, Goldstar, and Daewoo, but at the time its trade with Pyongyang was greater than that with Seoul (unlike the Chinese, whose trade with the South was twice that as with the North already by 1987).[70] Since 1988, when the first trade agreement between Seoul and Moscow was concluded, South Korea has become one of the largest trading and investment partners of the Russian Far East, where the region's abundant natural resources—including oil, metals, timber, and fish—increasingly needed by Seoul. South Korea's trade and investment flows into the region continue to rise annually, and the region continues to enjoy a great potential for growth. By the mid-2000s, South Korea had become the third-largest trading partner of the Russian Far East (behind Japan and China). Recently, several Korean and Russian companies have established joint ventures for research and production, including in-home electrical equipment.[71] Overall, however, South Korea is still only a minor player in Russia's overall trade, ranking as Russia's 10th-largest trading partner. Its trade with Russia is inching closer to that of Japan, with a record $25 billion in 2011. Moscow hopes to expand its economic relations with Seoul through the large-scale export of Russian liquefied gas, oil, and electric power, as well as cooperation in the automobile and shipbuilding industries.

At the same time that it has been pursuing economic opportunities with Seoul, Moscow has sought to maintain ties with the North. Despite the abandonment of communism by Moscow and Pyongyang's persistent embrace, Russia has maintained warm cultural and diplomatic relations with its old client state. Moscow even opened the first-ever Russian Orthodox Church in North Korea in 2006, complete with priests supplied by the North Korean intelligence service. The idea apparently entered Kim's mind following his 2002 visit to Russia, where he observed an Orthodox service. A more significant recent gesture was the forgiveness of nearly $11 billion in Soviet-era debt. In September 2012, Moscow and Pyongyang signed a deal to write off nearly all of the country's Soviet-era debt, resolving an issue that had been on hold since the collapse of the USSR. The issue was moved forward in August 2011 following a meeting between then-President Medvedev and the late North Korean leader Kim Jong Il. At the meeting, Kim agreed to allow a pipeline project that would send Russian gas to South Korea via North Korea, in addition to securing other railway and electricity deals in the process.[72] Moscow was very pleased with this progress and is equally satisfied with cautious signals of reform and greater openness coming from North Korea's new leader, Kim Jong Un.

But the North Korean regime does not make it easy for Moscow. Russia has a common interest with the United States, the Republic of Korea, Japan, and even China in eliminating military threats in the region, and the main source of that threat is the military confrontation on the peninsula between the Pyongyang and Seoul regimes. The nuclear issue is what threatens the situation the most. Russia has thus taken a leading role in the six-party talks to get North Korea to halt its nuclear ambitions. Moscow, at least publicly, expresses consternation with Pyongyang each time it derails the process, as with its missile program. After its missile launch in spring 2012, Moscow spoke out against Pyongyang, saying that its pursuit of long-range missile capability violated the will of the international community as expressed in UN Security Council Resolution 1874. The same reaction came after the December 2012 missile launch. Moscow insists Pyongyang must cease launching ballistic missiles in violation of the UN resolution while simultaneously calling for restraint from the international community. After North Korea's 2013 nuclear test, Russia agreed to additional sanctions against the country in March but has also worked to limit the scope of international pressure. Moscow does not want to see the position of Pyongyang's hawks strengthened or an arms race provoked but would prefer to keep all diplomatic options on the table. To square its growing relationship with South Korea and its traditional support of North Korea, Russia sees the answer in joint economic projects as a means of promoting the normalization of inter-Korean relations. It is pushing for the linking of the Trans-Korean and Trans-Siberian railways, as well as the establishment of a unified energy system and the north-south gas pipeline—incidentally all projects that serve Moscow's interests. As Konstantin Vnukov, Russian ambassador to the Republic of Korea stated in May 2012, "the realization of such projects may provide not only considerable economic benefits for both Koreas, but also improve inter-Korean relations."[73]

VIETNAM: MOSCOW'S TOEHOLD IN SOUTHEAST ASIA

While the two-Koreas issue persists into the 21st century, the division of Vietnam was resolved shortly following the withdrawal of U.S. combat troops from South Vietnam in 1973. While the regime in Saigon attempted to hold out, it was ultimately unable to stave off pressure from the Communist north, and once Hanoi launched a full-scale offensive in 1975, it quickly fell and was incorporated into the newly established Socialist Republic of Vietnam. While the fall of South Vietnam meant the victory of communism, Vietnam was to prove no mere domino. Not only did no other regime in the region succumb to communism, but Vietnam's communist regime would quickly undergo dramatic economic and political reforms. Following harsh and radical economic and political policies in its first years of existence, Vietnam launched comprehensive reforms in 1986. *Doi moi* (renovation) was a reform initiative designed to carry out a managed transition from a planned economy to a "socialist-oriented market economy."[74] This was a full year ahead of Gorbachev's *perestroika*.

Again in contrast to Korea, this meant that Moscow and Hanoi were pursuing economic and political reforms more or less simultaneously. Despite this fact,

Moscow's interest in Vietnam was minimal in the late Soviet period, mostly concentrating on the value of Vietnam's Cam Rhan Bay for the Soviet navy. The first real progress in Russo-Vietnam relations was the establishment of a "strategic partnership" in 2001, significantly the first such relationship for Hanoi. Several other countries soon followed suit, including India, China, South Korea, and several European partners: Spain, UK, and Germany. Then in July 2012, shortly after reclaiming the Russian presidency, Putin met with Vietnamese president Truong Tan Sang in Sochi. Following their meeting, they issued a joint statement raising their relations to a "comprehensive strategic partnership." This is only the second such relationship for Vietnam, with China becoming a "comprehensive strategic partner" of Vietnam in 2009.

But no other country has engaged the Vietnam opportunity quite the same way Russia has, establishing economic and military ties that quickly made the two important partners. Vietnam is now Russia's fourth-largest arms buyer, just behind China, while Russia is Vietnam's leading source of arms. Civil trade and investment are also considerable, though modest. Bilateral trade reached $2 billion in 2011, but both Moscow and Hanoi hope to increase the volume of their trade to $5 billion in 2015 and $10 billion in 2020. The real story is in the oil and gas sector. Russia's cooperation with Vietnam in oil and gas dates back to 1981, when they formed the joint venture Vietsovpetro. The company has been active on Vietnam's continental shelf and has been Russia's most profitable enterprise. Vietnam and Russia also recently agreed to facilitate the operations of other joint ventures such as Rusvietpetro, Gazpromviet, and Vietgazprom to expand oil and gas exploration and exploitation activities in third countries. The two are also considering jointly developing offshore oil deposits in the South China Sea.

In an unprecedented move, Moscow also recently decided to admit Vietnamese partners into a major hydrocarbon deposit in the Yamalo-Nenets Autonomous Okrug in Siberia. This is a federal deposit, and Medvedev emphasized the significance of the agreement. "I can tell you frankly this decision was an exclusive one, considering our special relations with Vietnam," Medvedev said.[75]

A second area of energy cooperation is in the hydroelectric and nuclear power sector. Russia recently agreed to provide a soft loan worth $10.5 billion to Vietnam to build its first nuclear power plant. The Ninh Thuan Nuclear Power Plant will have two energy units with a capacity of 1.2 GW each, with an expected 2020 completion date. Discussions are also underway to build a second plant that would give Vietnam the capacity to produce 15 GW of nuclear power by 2030.

Of perhaps greatest significance have been developments in the defense industry. As mentioned above, Russia is Vietnam's largest provider of military weapons, equipment, and technology. Under a 2009 deal worth $3.2 billion, the largest deal in Russian exports of naval equipment, Moscow will sell Hanoi six Kilo-class diesel submarines, a submarine designed for antisubmarine warfare and anti-surface ship warfare, in addition to general reconnaissance and patrol missions. The submarines will be equipped with the Club-S cruise missile systems. Part of the deal are provisions for Russia to build a maintenance and service facility at Cam Ranh Bay, where it will also provide training for Vietnamese submariners.

Part of the 2009 submarine deal also included the purchase of 8 Su-30MK2 flanker-C multirole fighters, a deal worth $400 million. Vietnam is expected to order more Su-30 Sukhoi multirole jet fighters in the future. In the fall of 2012, Vietnam began expressing interest in acquiring the Russian Yak-130 combat trainers. These highly maneuverable aircraft have a combat payload of 3,000 kilograms.[76] Vietnam and Russia will coproduce antiship cruise missiles. Estimates are that Vietnam will consistently buy around $1 billion annually in arms from Russia in the years to come.

As with every other one of Moscow's relationships in Asia, it cannot be accurately grasped without understanding how a particular bilateral relationship is a response to/solicits responses from other actors in the region, indeed in the international system. In the case of Russo–Vietnam relations, that third actor is China. Russian military assistance improves Vietnam's defense capabilities and enables it to develop its own anti-access/area-denial capacity in the vicinity of the Nansha (Spratly) Islands. As Blank points out, Russia's arms sales and defense cooperation with Vietnam are "a direct rebuff to Beijing" and reaffirm Moscow's position that "it will not allow China to dominate Asia, deprive Russia of millions if not billions of dollars in energy revenues, or marginalize Russia in its quest for great power influence" in the region.[77] As Blank further observes, "It also is clear that the weapons that Moscow has already sold to Vietnam . . . represent a deterrent to the Chinese navy." These arms sales, Blank points out, "also underscore Russia's determination to prevent China from dominating the South China Sea and Southeast Asia" and marginalizing Russia's presence in the region. Arms sales to Vietnam, as well as to other regional powers like Indonesia, help to maintain the balance of power. Moscow is more determined than ever to play a major role in Asia, not just in Northeast Asia but in peninsular Southeast Asia as well, and Vietnam is a critical piece of Moscow's strategy in that regard.

SETTING ITS EYES ON ASIA

Putin used the opportunity afforded by the September 2012 APEC summit in Vladivostok to announce to Asia that Russia was serious about its engagement with its eastern neighbors. In the midst of global belt-tightening, Russia spared no expense in hosting the event on a scale incomparable to previous APEC summits, reportedly spending $20 billion. While Putin is clearly seeking to position Russia as a vital economic actor in Asia, promoting Russia as a land bridge between Asia and Europe, his ambitions in the region are not limited to the economic realm.

Some commentators are suggesting that Putin's third term as president will see a shift to the East, making the Asia-Pacific region its main foreign policy priority. Since his return to the presidency, Putin has repeatedly stressed the importance of the "eastern vector" for Russia's future development.[78] As one analyst pointed out, the first multilateral forum in which Putin participated was the June 2012 SCO summit in Beijing, and the first world leader with whom he met was Chinese president Hu Jintao. Meanwhile, Putin had snubbed the West by not attending the NATO summit in Chicago nor the G-8 summit at Camp David.

Putin's return also has led to speculation that he would pursue a broader Asian strategy, building on his inaugural efforts during his first two terms in office. Putin often became the first Russian leader to visit a number of states in the broader Asia-Pacific region that had been ignored by his predecessors' focus on Europe and the West—for instance, Indonesia and Australia in September 2007. Putin was invited to attend the first East Asia Summit (EAS) in Malaysia in 2005 after inaugurating the first summit meeting between Russia and the Association of South East Asian Nations (ASEAN), to which Russia had been an observer since 1996. In turn, some of the other regional states, beginning with Malaysia, have shown interest in cultivating ties with Russia to counterbalance Chinese and American influence. At the 2011 EAS meeting, Foreign Minister Lavrov has laid out a vision of greater economic connectivity between Southeast Asia and Russia's Far East.[79] However, Putin chose not to go to the 2012 EAS conclave in Cambodia, causing some to question whether Russia wanted to avoid being drawn into the increasingly heated territorial disputes between some of the Southeast Asian states and China and to having to publicly choose between its strategic partner in Beijing and the other regional powers.[80] How Russia will balance its competing interests in East Asia will become more important in the coming years.

For its part, the United States is also preparing to engage the Asia-Pacific region more actively. As outlined in the 2012 Strategic Guidance prepared by the Department of Defense, the United States "will of necessity rebalance toward the Asia-Pacific region." The Guidance pointed out that while the U.S. military would continue to contribute to security globally, it would seek to expand its "networks of cooperation with emerging partners throughout the Asia-Pacific to ensure collective capability and capacity for securing common interests." With both Russia and the United States simultaneously shifting their economic and security priorities toward Asia, the region is poised to become of the utmost strategic importance in the immediate future.

NOTES

1. Mark Mancall, *Russia and China: Their Diplomatic Relations to 1728* (Cambridge: Harvard University Press, 1971), 27.

2. Henry Kissinger, *White House Years* (New York: Little, Brown & Company, 1979), 712.

3. Joshua S. Goldstein and John R. Freeman, *Three Way Street: Strategic Reciprocity in World Politics* (Chicago, IL: University of Chicago Press, 1990), 122.

4. See the official statement in *Pravda,* April 24, 1986.

5. Goldstein and Freeman, 122–123. For excerpts of Gorbachev's address, "Excerpts from Gorbachev's Speech," *New York Times,* July 29, 1986, A6.

6. Gilbert Rozman, *A Mirror for Socialism: Soviet Criticisms of China* (Princeton: Princeton University Press, 1985); Gilbert Rozman, *The Chinese Debate about Soviet Socialism, 1978–1985* (Princeton: Princeton University Press, 1987).

7. Christopher Marsh, *Unparalleled Reforms: China's Rise, Russia's Fall, and the Interdependence of Transition* (Lanham, MD: Lexington Books, 2005), 31–32.

8. Dmitry Kosyrev, "Gorbachev and Deng changed the world 20 years ago," *RIA Novosti,* May 15, 2009, at http://en.rian.ru/analysis/20090515/155024227.html.

9. Mikhail Barabanov, Vasiliy Kashin, and Konstantin Makienko, *Shooting Star: China's Military Machine in the 21st Century* (Minneapolis, MN: East View, 2012), 51.

10. Iwashita Akhiro, "Primakov Redux? Russia and the 'Strategic Triangles' in Asia," *Slavic Research Center* 16, no. 1 (2007): 167, at http://src-h.slav.hokudai.ac.jp/coe21/publish /n016_1_ses/09_iwashita.pdf.

11. June Teufel Dreyer, *The PLA and the Kosovo Conflict* (Carlisle Barracks, PA: Strategic Studies Institute, U.S. Army War College, 2000).

12. Christopher Marsh and Nikolas Gvosdev, "China's Yugoslav Nightmare," *The National Interest,* No. 84 (Summer 2006): 102–108.

13. Robert Legvold, "US-Russian Relations: An American Perspective," *Russia in Global Affairs,* No. 4 (October–December 2006).

14. Colum Lynch, "Russia, China Veto Resolution on Burma," *Washington Post,* January 13, 2007, A13, at http://www.washingtonpost.com/wp-dyn/content/article/2007/01/12/ AR2007011201115.html.

15. On this, see Naazneen Barma, Ely Ratner, and Steven Weber, "A World Without the West," *National Interest* 90 (July/August 2007): 27.

16. Leila Saralayeva, "U.S. Warned About Central Asia," *The Washington Times,* 17 August 2007, 15, accessed August 17, 2007, at http://ebird.afis.mil/ebfiles/e20070817536921 .html.

17. Dilip Hiro, "Shanghai surprise," *The Guardian,* June 16, 2006, at http://www.guard ian.co.uk/commentisfree/2006/jun/16/shanghaisurprise.

18. Richard Weitz, "China-Russia's Anti-NATO?" *The Diplomat,* July 4, 2012, at http:// thediplomat.com/2012/07/04/is-the-shanghai-cooperation-org-stuck-in-neutral/?all=true.

19. "Vladivostok undergoes $25b makeover for APEC summit," *Straits Times* (September 6, 2012), accessed October 18, 2012, at http://www.straitstimes.com/breaking-news/ world/story/vladivostok-undergoes-25b-makeover-apec-summit-20120906.

20. A copy of the treaty can be found at http://russia.bestpravo.ru/fed2004/data03/ tex14451.htm.

21. A complete list of events related to "The Year of Russia" in China is maintained by the Russian Academy of Science's Institute of the Far East, "Programma Meropriyatii goda Rossii v Kitae," available at (now defunct).

22. Richard Weitz, "Chinese-Russian Relations the Best Ever?" *World Politics Review* (June 23, 2009). Available at http://www.worldpoliticsreview.com/articles/3961/global-insights-chinese-russian-relations-the-best-ever.

23. "Wen's trip promotes wide-ranging cooperation with Russia," *Xinhua,* December 7, 2012.

24. "China, Russia to Dump U.S. Dollar for Bilateral Trade," *International Business Times,* November 24, 2010, at http://www.ibtimes.com/china-russia-dump-us-dollar-bilat eral-trade-248234.

25. "China Makes 25mln Loan to Trans/Rosneft," *Oil and Gas Eurasia,* February 19, 2009, at http://www.oilandgaseurasia.com/news/china-makes-25mln-loan-transrosneft.

26. "China, Russia pledge to enhance energy cooperation," *Xinhua,* December 6, 2012.

27. Christopher Marsh, "Russia Plays the China Card," *The National Interest,* No. 92 (November–December 2007).

28. Nikolas K. Gvosdev, "Peace Mission 2007," *National Interest,* July 30, 2007, at http:// nationalinterest.org/commentary/inside-track-peace-mission-2007-1724.

29. "Russia to Send 4 Warships to Joint Drill with China," *RIA Novosti,* April 3, 2012, http://en.ria.ru/world/20120403/172583281.html; "China, Russia Conclude Joint Naval Drill," *Xinhua,* April 28, 2012, at http://english.peopledaily.com.cn/90786/7802712.html.

30. Quoted in Stephen Blank, "Shanghai Cooperation Organization: Russia, China Probing for Advantage," EurasiaNet, February 14, 2011, at http://www.eurasianet.org/ node/62893.

31. Barabanov et al., 51.

32. Ibid.

33. Richard Weitz, *China–Russia Security Relations: Strategic Parallelism without Partnership or Passion?* (Carlisle, PA: Strategic Studies Institute, U.S. Army War College, 2008), 25.

34. For an excellent overall assessment of the Russia–China arms trade, see Richard Rousseau, "The Tortuous Sino-Russian Arms Trade—Analysis," *Eurasia Review,* June 9, 2012, at http://www.eurasiareview.com/09062012-the-tortuous-sino-russian-arms-trade-analysis/.

35. Chzhan Ikhun, "Russko-Kitayskogo torgovlya po oruzhiya razvivaetsya," *Vremya Novostei,* May 27, 2003.

36. Richard Weitz, *China–Russia Security Relations: Strategic Parallelism without Partnership or Passion?* (Carlisle, PA: Strategic Studies Institute, U.S. Army War College, 2008), 30.

37. Barabanov et al., x.

38. Dmitri Trenin, "Russia's Threat Perception and Strategic Posture," in *Russian Security Strategy under Putin: U.S. and Russian Perspectives* (Carlisle, PA: Strategic Studies Institute, U.S. Army War College, 2007), 47.

39. Sergei Gorlov, *Sovershenno Sekretno: Moskva-Berlin 1920–1933: Voenno-politicheskie Otnosheniya mehdu SSSR i Germaniei* (Moscow: Institut Vseobshchei Istorii, Rossiiskaya Akademiya Nauk, 1999).

40. "Asian Nations Top Arms Buyers—China Seen as Threat," *Voice of America*, April 18, 2012, at http://blogs.voanews.com/breaking-news/2012/04/18/asian-nations-top-arms-buyers-china-seen-as-threat/.

41. Koh Swee Lean Collin, "Vietnam's New Kilo-class Submarines: Game-changer in Regional Naval Balance?" *RSIS Commentaries*, 162/2012 (August 28, 2012), 1–2, at http://www.rsis.edu.sg/publications/Perspective/RSIS1622012.pdf.

42. Yu Bin, "China-Russia Relations: Succession, SCO, and Summit Politics in Beijing," *Comparative Connections* (September 2012). January 11, 2013, at http://csis.org/node/39407.

43. Ibid.

44. "Putin Urges Military Alliance with China," Reuters, June 6, 2012, at http://www.reuters.com/article/2012/06/06/us-china-russia-military-idUSBRE8550BG20120606.

45. "Xi Jinping: China-Russia ties prioritized in Chinese diplomacy," *Global Times*, January 8, 2013, at http://www.globaltimes.cn/content/754519.shtml.

46. Irina Filatova, "Kremlin in Talks on LNG Exports to China," *Moscow Times* 5076 (February 25, 2013), at http://www.themoscowtimes.com/news/article/kremlin-in-talks-on-lng-exports-to-china/476061.html#ixzz2MuZRDXqT; "China-Russia Partnership to Combat Obama's 'Asia Pivot' Strategy: Duowei," *Want China Times*, March 7, 2013, at http://www.wantchinatimes.com/news-subclass-cnt.aspx?id=20130307000087&cid=1101&MainCatID=11.

47. See Mikhail Alexeev, "Economic Valuations and Interethnic Fears: Perceptions of Chinese Migration in the Russian Far East," *Journal of Peace Research* 40, no. 1 (January 2003): 89–106; Mikhail Alexeev, "Desecuritizing Sovereignty: Economic Interest and Responses to Political Challenges of Chinese Migration in the Russian Far East," in John D. Montgomery and Nathan Glazer, eds., *Sovereignty under Challenge: How Governments Respond* (New Brunswick, NJ: Transaction Publishers, 2002), 261–289; and Mikhail Alexeev, "Socioeconomic and Security Implications of Chinese Migration in the Russian Far East," *Post–Soviet Geography and Economics* 42, no. 2 (2001): 95–114.

48. Quoted in Simon Saradzhyan, "Russia needs to develop eastern provinces as China rises," *Russia and India Report*, March 7, 2013, at http://indrus.in/world/2013/03/07/russia_needs_to_develop_eastern_provinces_as_china_rises_22737.html.

49. Fond Obshchestvennoe Mnenie, "Rossiisko-kitaiskie otnosheniya i vizit V. Putina v Kitai," *Dominanti*, No. 43 (October 29, 2009). January 11, 2013, at bd.fom.ru/pdf/d43kitay.pdf.

50. From Levada Tsentr archive; question: "Ot kovo, na vash vzglad, prezhde vsego iskhodit vneshnyaya ugroza?" Available at http://www.levada.ru/archive/strana-i-mir/ot-kogo-na-vash-vzglyad-prezhde-vsego-iskhodit-vneshnyaya-ugrozav-ot-davshikh-p.

51. Igor Malevich, *Vnimanie, Kitai* (Minsk: Kharvest, 2000).

52. Ibid., see especially 79–81.

53. "Russian Journalist Warns about Chinese Threat," *Sobesednik,* June 16, 2004. *RIA Novosti, Digest of the Russian Press.* Transcript by Olga Saburova.

54. Simon Saradzhyan, "The Role of China in Russia's Military Thinking," *Russian Analytical Digest,* no. 78 (May 4, 2010): 5–7.

55. Yu, n.p.

56. David Glantz, "August Storm: The Soviet 1945 Strategic Offensive in Manchuria," *Leavenworth Papers,* no. 7 (Fort Leavenworth, KS: Combat Studies Institute, February 1983).

57. David Glantz and Jonathan House, *When Titans Clashed: How the Red Army Stopped Hitler* (Lawrence, KS: University Press of Kansas, 1995), 278.

58. From Levada Tsentr archive; question: "Vneshnyaya politika rossii otnoshenie k drugim stranam ... ?" Available at http://www.levada.ru/21-02-2012/vneshnyaya-politika-rossii-otnoshenie-k-drugim-stranam.

59. Robert H. Donaldson and Joseph L. Nogee, *The Foreign Policy of Russia: Changing Systems, Enduring Interests,* 4th edition (Armonk, NY: M.E. Sharpe, 2009), 286–289.

60. S. Vradii, "Rossiisko-Kitaiskoe Pogranichnoe Razmezhevanie: Vzgliad iz Yaponii," *Rossiya i ATP,* vol. 55, no. 1 (2007): 184–187.

61. "Japanese schoolbooks to claim Russia's Southern Kuril Islands," *Russia Today* (July 16, 2008).

62. "Russian Military Force in South Kurils to Be Strengthened, Upgraded in Coming Years—Makarov," Interfax, February 14, 2012, at http://www.interfax.co.uk/russia-cis-military-news-bulletins-in-english/russian-military-force-in-south-kurils-to-be-strengthened-upgraded-in-coming-years-makarov-2/; Denis Dyomkin, "Russia's Medvedev angers Japan with island visit," *Reuters,* July 3, 2012, at http://www.reuters.com/article/2012/07/03/us-russia-japan-islands-idUSBRE8620AV20120703.

63. Jeffrey W. Hornung, "Economic cooperation can strengthen Japan-Russia ties," *The Japan Times,* January 11, 2012, at http://valdaiclub.com/russia_in_foreign_media/37060.html.

64. Sergei Blagov, "Russia Sees Sakhalin-Japan Energy Projects as Bargaining Tool," *Eurasia Daily Monitor* 9, no. 222 (December 5, 2012), at http://www.jamestown.org/single/?no_cache=1&tx_ttnews%5Btt_news%5D=40200&tx_ttnews%5BbackPid%5D=7&cHash=e4e5c3bf34defe9f2cde0c86cbd73f44.

65. "Russia, Japan eye closer economic ties," *Xinhua* (July 29, 2012).

66. Boris Afonin, "Sindzo Abe: Novyi Prem'er-ministr Yaponii," *Rossiya i ATP,* vol. 55, no. 1 (2007): 115–120.

67. "Rosneft's Sechin to discuss offshore projects in Japan visit," *Reuters,* February 19, 2013, at http://uk.reuters.com/article/2013/02/19/rosneft-japan-idUKL6N0BJ0YL20130219.

68. Herbert Ellison, *The Soviet Union and Northeast Asia* (Lanham, MD: Asia Society/University Press of America, 1989), 43.

69. Ibid., 44.

70. Ibid., 48.

71. Konstantin Korenevsky, *Russia-Korea Trade and Investment Cooperation: Current Tendencies and Perspectives* (Unpublished research paper, Vladivostok, Russia: Department of World Economy, Far Eastern State Academy of Economics and Management. 2004).

72. Lukas Alpert, "Russia, North Korea Sign Debt Pact," *Wall Street Journal* (September 18, 2012).

73. Remarks by Ambassador Vnukov, The Asia Society Korea Center, May 15, 2012. January 11, 2013, at http://asiasociety.org/policy/strategic-challenges/ambassador-vnukov-russia-south-korea-united-joint-interest.

74. Geoffrey Murray, *Vietnam: Dawn of a New Market* (New York: St. Martin's Press, 1997), 24–25.

75. "Russia, Vietnam Mull Joint Oil Projects—Medvedev," *RIA-Novosti* (November 7, 2012). Available at http://en.rian.ru/business/20121107/177260501.html.

76. "Vietnam, Malaysia Eye Russian Yak-130 Trainer," *RIA-Novosti* (Nov. 14, 2012). Available at http://en.rian.ru/military_news/20121114/177459845.html.

77. Stephen Blank, "Russia's Ever Friendlier Ties to Vietnam—Are They a Signal to China?" *Jamestown Eurasia Daily Monitor,* vol. 9, no. 219 (November 30, 2012). Available at http://www.jamestown.org/single/?no_cache=1&tx_ttnews[tt_news]=40184&tx_ttnews[backPid]=13&cHash=80c3b5f214c7c628c19cb35d4aca1bdf.

78. "Rosneft's Sechin," op. cit.

79. Kavi Chongkittavorn, "Putin's Return Firms Russia's ASEAN Grip," *The Irrawaddy,* May 14, 2012, at http://www.irrawaddy.org/archives/4153.

80. Artyom Lukin and Sergei Sevastyanov, "Why did Russia snub the East Asia Summit?" *Russia and India Report,* November 27, 2012, at http://indrus.in/articles/2012/11/27/why_did_russia_snub_the_east_asia_summit_19355.html.

CHAPTER 5

The Eurasian Space

The *near abroad* is a term used by Moscow to refer to those countries, now independent states, that were once a part of the historic Russian Empire or that were union republics of the Soviet Union. Because of the close enduring cultural, political, and economic ties between post–Soviet Russia and these states, the Russian foreign policy establishment believes that Russia ought to pursue close relationships with the other states that also emerged from the USSR. Whether the intent of such behavior is benign or malevolent, however, is hard for anyone to determine, including some of the states themselves. As articulated by former foreign minister Igor Ivanov, the "former Soviet Union's geopolitical space" forms "a 'special interest zone' for Russia."[1] In August 2008, President Dmitry Medvedev formally announced that one pillar of Russian foreign policy would be to secure Moscow's "privileged interests" in "priority regions," starting with the countries that bordered Russia.[2] This assertion remains a controversial position given the desire of some of these countries to emerge more completely from under Russia's shadow.

Russia's engagement with the diversity of ethnic groups that span the Eurasian plain began in earnest in the 15th century, when the grand principality of Moscow under the rule of Ivan III (1462–1505) embraced the project of uniting all Orthodox Christian Eastern Slavic peoples under the scepter of Moscow. This process, referred to as the "gathering of the Russian lands," necessarily entailed pushing back against the remnants of the Mongol Empire to the south and east. Grand Prince Ivan also received emissaries from other rulers across the Eurasian plain, including one sent from King Alexander of Kakheti, a Georgian kingdom, in 1483. Under his grandson tsar Ivan IV ("the Terrible"), the first attempt was made to extend Russian territory to the Baltic coast. By conquering the khanates of Kazan, Astrakhan, and Siberia (1552, 1556, and 1580, respectively), a process of expansion was started that would eventually bring the tsarist banners to the shores of the Pacific Ocean and to the northern Middle East.

In 1654, the Cossacks in Ukraine signed the Treaty of Pereislavl, whereby they accepted the suzerainty of the Russian tsar; subsequent agreements with Poland (1667 and 1686) confirmed Russian possession of the eastern portions of what is now Ukraine and Belarus. The Treaty of Nystad (1721), which ended the Great Northern War with Sweden, confirmed the cession of the eastern Baltic seaboard to Russian control. The partitions of Poland (1772, 1793, and 1795) brought nearly all the Eastern Slavic peoples into the Russian Empire. A series of Russian victories over the Ottoman Empire in the 18th century opened up the path for Russia to colonize the northern Black Sea coast and allowed the Russians to project power across the formidable Caucasus mountain range, culminating in a union of the kingdom of Georgia with Russia in 1801 and control of the territory that today makes up Armenia and Azerbaijan by 1826.

Finally, starting in the middle of the 19th century, Russia began annexing territories in Central Asia in the wake of the decline of the Persian and Manchu (Chinese) Empires. By the dawn of the 20th century, the Russian Empire was a multiethnic Eurasian empire stretching from Poland to China in which ethnic Russians formed only a slight majority of the population.[3] The empire was a dynastic state in which a number of groups pledged loyalty directly to the Tsar and, in some cases, preserved significant internal autonomy, especially in several of the emirates of Central Asia. Yet by the end of the 19th century, under the rule of Alexander III and Nicholas II, the empire pursued policies of "Russification"— attempting to do away with national and ethnic distinctions in order to promote central control and a common identity—which in turn provoked growing unrest and discontent in non–Russian areas.[4] Vladimir Lenin described the Russian Empire as a "prison house of nations." Indeed, in the immediate aftermath of the October Revolution in 1917, which brought the Communists to power, Lenin and his associates, in the Decree on the Rights of the Peoples of Russia to Self-Determination (November 15, 1917), proclaimed the "equality and sovereignty of the peoples of Russia" and promised to respect "the right of self-determination of peoples even to the point of separating and forming independent states."[5]

In part, this decree reflected reality; as the Russian Empire collapsed, separatist movements began to proclaim new independent states. A Ukrainian People's Republic was proclaimed in January 1918; in February a Transcaucasian Federation comprising former Imperial territories south of the Caucasus mountains was created, which then split apart into separate republics for Armenia, Azerbaijan, and Georgia later that spring. A Belarusian People's Republic was declared in March 1918. Some of the Central Asian tributary rulers also attempted to reassert their independent status once the tsar was removed from his throne. The outbreak of the Russian Civil War between Communist (Bolshevik) forces, popularly referred to as the Reds, and non-Communist forces known as the Whites meant that by mid-1918, the new Soviet government controlled only a fraction of the territory of the former Russian Empire—roughly the same area that formed the Grand Principality of Moscow in the 15th century. Moreover, the Soviet government, as a price for peace with the German and Ottoman Empires, was required to recognize the independence of the former imperial borderlands in the Treaty of Brest-Litovsk (March 3, 1918). In less than a year, Moscow had seen the territories under its control diminish significantly.

When in opposition to the Russian Empire, revolutionary movements tended to support the right of non-Russian nationalities to complete self-determination. Once in power, however, the perspective of the new Soviet government changed. Josef Stalin, himself a Georgian, who served as the first Commissar of Nationalities, declared at the Third All-Russia Congress of Soviets in January 1918 that

> the principle of self-determination [is] the right to self-determination not of the bourgeoisie, but of the toiling masses of the given nation . . . The principle of self-determination must be means of fighting for socialism and must be subordinated to the principles of socialism.[6]

Lenin himself observed that while the Soviet government would recognize the non-Russian areas as independent states, it would also "stretch out a fraternal hand to the . . . workers and tell them that together with them we are going to fight against their bourgeoisie and ours."[7] As part of the Civil War struggle against non-Communist Russian forces, the Soviets also fought to establish Soviet governments in the newly independent states as well. For instance, a rival Provisional Soviet Republic was created in Ukraine in 1919, which eventually took control of most of the country. Soviet military pressure combined with coup attempts by local Communist forces ended the independence of Armenia and Azerbaijan in 1920. In other areas, Soviet power was established through the outright invasion of territory, as occurred in Central Asia and Georgia. Only the former Imperial holdings in Poland and Finland, along with the three Baltic states, remained independent after 1921. Moscow had recouped significant portions of its losses from 1918.

Between 1917 and 1922, Soviet Russia was, in theory, only "allied" to other republics, which technically remained independent and separate states.[8] However, these other countries were all governed by Communist Parties that were subordinated to the central control and discipline of the Russian-based party; this meant that the government in Moscow could and did impose a single set of policies.[9]

Stalin proposed his so-called "autonomization" plan, by which other republics would be incorporated into a Russian federation, creating a single, unitary country. In commenting on such plans, Lenin, in a letter to the Politburo in 1922, urged a different course, noting that, in dealing with the non-Russian Soviet republics, it was important "not to destroy their independence, but to establish a new echelon, a Federation of Republics with equal rights."[10]

The decision to create a Union of Soviet Socialist Republics, in which Russia would be simply a single constituent member, was an attempt at compromise.

On December 30, 1922, representatives of the Russian Soviet Federated Socialist Republic, the Ukrainian Soviet Republic, the Soviet Republic of Belorussia (Belarus), and the Transcaucasian Soviet Federated Socialist Republic concluded the Union Treaty that established the Union of Soviet Socialist Republics (USSR) as a united federation. On the one hand, it did create a single country, in essence reconstituting most of the old Russian Empire. On the other hand, as a nominal federation of states, it gave recognized borders and republican institutions to each union republic. The early Soviet policy of *korenizatsiia* (literally "indigenization")—focusing on developing "national elites" in each republic's government and bureaucracy[11]—combined with the detaching of territories from the Russian Soviet republic to create new, separate Union Republics in Central Asia—created very clear and distinctive republican identities.

THE DISINTEGRATION OF THE SOVIET UNION

For much of its existence, the Soviet Union was seen, as Stalin himself observed, "as a transitional form to a centralized republic."[12] Indeed, the October 1961 Communist Party Program adopted at the 22nd Party Congress asserted that "the borders between the union republics within the USSR are increasingly losing their former significance" as the peoples of the USSR "are all united into one family by common vital interests."[13] Yet the existence of republican governments and the provision, contained in each iteration of the Soviet Constitution, allowing for republics to secede from the Union (codified in Article 72 of the 1977 Constitution), kept open, if only as a theoretical possibility, that the republics might at some future date separate from each other. Indeed, the former chief analyst for the KGB, General Nikolai Leonov, has remarked that the federal structure of the USSR meant that "the Soviet Union resembled a chocolate bar. It was creased with furrowed lines of future division, as if for the convenience of its consumers."[14]

Yet no one expected that these paper authorities would ever be actually utilized by the republican governments. This began to change, however, when, as part of his campaign to dislodge conservative opposition to his reforms from within the middle and upper ranks of the Communist Party, Mikhail Gorbachev sought to draw nonparty elements into the political process, the so-called *neformaly* (informal organizations). Many of these groups were willing to discuss social and national questions beyond the limits previously established by the Soviet system.[15] This included the recovery of historical memory, in the non–Russian republics, in the efforts after the 1917 Revolution to create independent states. Gorbachev's democratization initiatives began to quickly backfire on his plans to hold the union together, as popular elections began to be held to republic-level legislatures

TABLE 5.1
Key Dates in the History of the Soviet Republics

Republic	Separation from Russian Empire	Creation of Soviet Republic	Separation from Soviet Union
Ukraine	Autonomy proclaimed 1917; full independence declared January 1918	Ukrainian Soviet Socialist Republic organized 1919; takes over most of Ukraine by 1921; Western Ukraine annexed from Poland 1939	Declared independence August 24, 1991
Belarus	Belarusian People's Republic proclaimed March 25, 1918	Soviet republic proclaimed 1919; merged with abortive Lithuanian Soviet republic; separate Soviet Republic of Byelorussia created 1920	Sovereignty declared July 27, 1990
Georgia	Transcaucasian Republic proclaimed February 24, 1918; Democratic Republic of Georgia declared May 26, 1918	Georgian Soviet Republic established February 5, 1921; from 1922 until 1936 part of the Transcaucasian Soviet Federated Socialist Republic (TSFSR)	Act of Restoring State Independence adopted April 9, 1991
Armenia	Part of the Transcaucasian Republic; separate Democratic Republic of Armenia declared May 28, 1918	Armenian Soviet Republic established December 1920; from 1922 until 1936 part of the TSFSR	Declared independence September 21, 1991
Azerbaijan	Part of the Transcaucasian Republic; separate Azerbaijan Democratic Republic proclaimed May 28, 1918	Azerbaijan Soviet Socialist Republic set up April 28, 1920; from 1922 until 1936 part of the TSFSR	Declared independence August 30, 1991
Kazakhstan	Alash Autonomy created December 13, 1917	Established as an autonomous republic within the Soviet Russian Republic on August 26, 1920; set up as a separate Union Republic December 5, 1936	Recognized dissolution of Soviet Union on December 16, 1991

(Continued)

Republic	Separation from Russian Empire	Creation of Soviet Republic	Separation from Soviet Union
Uzbekistan	Khanates of Khiva and Bokhara; other territories	Turkestan Autonomous Soviet Socialist Republic (within the Soviet Russian Republic) created April 30, 1918; Khorezm People's Republic declared April 1920; Bokharan People's Republic created October 8, 1920. Creation of unified Uzbekistan Soviet Socialist Republic October 27, 1924	Recognized dissolution of the Soviet Union on December 26, 1991
Kyrgyzstan		Part of Turkestan ASSR until 1924; autonomous republic within Soviet Russian Republic until 1936; set up as a separate Union Republic December 5, 1936	Declared independence on August 30, 1991
Turkmenistan		Part of Turkestan ASSR until 1924; separate republic created October 27, 1924	Declared independence October 27, 1991
Tajikistan		Separated from Uzbekistan Soviet Socialist Republic on December 5, 1929	Independence declared September 9, 1991
Moldova	Independent republic of Moldavia declared February 6, 1918; union with Romania April 9, 1918	Autonomous Moldavian Soviet Republic created in Ukraine in 1924; after Soviet occupation of Bessarabia in 1940, creation of a Moldavian Soviet Republic	Independence declared August 27, 1991

Source: Compiled by authors.

in the winter of 1990 (prior to Gorbachev's own "selection" as Soviet president in mid-March). Perhaps the most significant such republic elections were those in the Baltic republics, where the fall of the Berlin Wall and the collapse of communism in Eastern Europe had led these East Europeans—who had joined the Communist camp at roughly the same time as the satellite states of Eastern Europe and to whom Soviet rule was perhaps just as alien—to dream of their own independence. Nowhere were the calls for independence greater than in Lithuania, where several groups had begun to emerge from within civil society demanding reforms and greater freedom, the most important of which was the Lithuanian Movement for Restructuring (*Lietuvos Persitvarkymo Sajudis*), or simply *Sajudis* (the Movement).

Sajudis won nearly all of the seats it contested in the February 1990 elections to the Lithuanian parliament, and under the leadership of Vytautas Landsbergis, Lithuania quickly declared its independence. As the Lithuanian Supreme Council stated in its declaration of independence from the USSR, "The Lithuanian nation has an old and strong tradition of statehood that it has never renounced of its own free will; it therefore has the natural and inalienable right to reestablish independent Lithuania."[16] Estonia and Latvia quickly followed Lithuania's example, while Ukraine joined the list in July. Although perhaps too late, Gorbachev began to recognize the degree of discontent felt by many in the republics, and he began to propose a new form of union among the republics, one that would give greater autonomy and sovereignty to the republics while still preserving the union. In March of 1991, Gorbachev put the issue to the people in a national referendum, asking Soviet citizens their decision on preserving the Union. While more than 75% of those who took part expressed a desire to preserve the Union, Armenia, Georgia, Moldova, and the Baltic republics boycotted the vote, clearly expressing their opinion to be in charge of their own fate. And while the vast majority of Russia's citizens supported the referendum, the Russian Parliament declared its own sovereignty in June.

Perhaps of more immediate significance was the election of Boris Yeltsin as president of the Russian Republic at the same time. The creation of a Russian presidency and Yeltsin's election to the post put the Soviet Union in a precarious position. Although Gorbachev continued to search for solutions to the Soviet Union's many ills, the Russian presidency provided an alternative power structure, which Yeltsin used to continue his call for the sovereignty of Russia over the Soviet Union while encouraging the leaders of the other republics to "take all the sovereignty they could swallow." As if the situation were not perilous enough, a group of Communist hardliners staged an attempted coup d'état on August 19, 1991, on the eve of the signing of a new Union Treaty that would have led to a looser union among the Soviet Union's republics and perhaps pacified the nationalist aspirations of the secession-minded republics. Once the coup attempt had been put down by Yeltsin and other liberal forces, however, the torch seemed to pass to Yeltsin, the man who had stood up against the hardliners. Yeltsin himself began to swallow as much sovereignty as he could, taking over for Russia as many of the functions of the Soviet state as possible, including the Ministry of Foreign Affairs, the Ministry of Finance, and even the KGB. Meanwhile, Gorbachev stood by apparently unwilling or unable to do anything to prevent Yeltsin and the other republican leaders from dismantling the bankrupt and quickly disintegrating Soviet state, continuing in his attempt to hold the union together with a new union treaty. These hopes seemed to fade as well when on November 25, Gorbachev stood publicly humiliated as Yeltsin refused to sign the new treaty. Then, on December 7, the leaders of Ukraine and Belarus joined Yeltsin at the state dacha at Belovezh in Belarus to discuss the future of the Soviet Union, quickly declaring the founding of a Commonwealth of Independent States. The Belovezh Accords, signed the next day, proclaimed that the three founding republics of the USSR (Russia, Ukraine, and Belarus) were dismantling the Soviet Union. At a meeting at Almaty in Kazakhstan on December 21, the rest of the Soviet republics, with the exception of the Baltic States and Georgia, met to ratify the dissolution of the union and to join the Commonwealth of Independent States (CIS). The Baltic states of Lithuania, Latvia, and Estonia refused to join the CIS; because of their status as independent states between World Wars I and II and because many Western countries had not recognized their incorporation into the USSR, the Baltic nations refused to classify themselves as "post–Soviet" states. Georgia joined the CIS in 1993.

One reason the CIS was created was to try and preserve some of the connections that had been forged in the Soviet period. Moreover, with some 25 million people who considered themselves Russian now separated from the new Russian state and living in what were now considered to be other countries, there were hopes that the CIS might be able to diminish possible tensions if Russian-majority areas outside the borders of the Russian republic pressed for inclusion in the new Russian state. One of these flashpoints was the Crimean peninsula, once a part of the Russian Soviet republic but "transferred" to Ukraine in 1954 to commemorate the 300th anniversary of the Treaty of Pereislavl. With its large ethnic Russian population with little attachment to the notion of an independent Ukrainian state (in contrast to the Russians living in Eastern Ukraine), as well as its strategic importance given its location for the main bases of the Black Sea Fleet, it epitomized the potential Pandora's box of trying to sort through the internal borders of the Soviet state, and there was little confidence that opening up Soviet-era borders for revision would remain a peaceful process.

Despite its name, the 11 republics that formed the CIS had no intention of forming a true commonwealth with common institutions. Instead, by design, the CIS remained a loose association of states with the stated goal of trying to coordinate economic and foreign policy, as well as manage the "divorce" of the republics. The only function of any genuine significance at the time of its founding was a collective organ based in Minsk that controlled nuclear weapons (and which became irrelevant once the states other than Russia that had weapons at the time of the collapse—Ukraine, Belarus, and Kazakhstan—agreed to dismantle them or to send them back to Russia). In a final demonstration of unity, the republics of the Soviet Union also agreed to field one last "unified team" at the 1992 Olympic Games.

THE EURASIAN VISION

Many of those who formed Boris Yeltsin's first administration were proponents of a foreign policy school that was labeled Atlanticism because it proposed that Russia ought to pursue close and lasting integration with the nations of the Euro-Atlantic basin. A secondary component of Atlanticism was to reject the historical project of the Russian state—to unify the Eurasian steppes under one government—and to reorient Moscow away from Eurasia toward the West.

The Atlanticist school had a certain appeal to Russian politicians because of the assessment that Russia had nearly bankrupted itself trying to fund the USSR and that the other republics had not contributed to Russia's own development. A number of dissidents during the 1970s had lamented that the Russian core was being drained away in order to prop up an unsustainable Soviet Union, and famed author Aleksandr Solzhenitsyn had even penned a short monograph distributed to Soviet legislators on "How to Rebuild Russia" (a title that was a play on words with Mikhail Gorbachev's concept of *perestroika*), which advised Moscow to let go of large portions of the Soviet empire.[17] The Atlanticists assumed that once Russia was freed of the burden of supporting other Soviet republics, it could prosper and seek integration with the West.

But there were also strong currents in favor of the Eurasian vector. "Eurasianism" goes back almost a century in Russian history. Shortly after the Bolshevik Revolution of 1917, a group of Russian émigré intellectuals, including George Vernadsky, Nikolai Trubetskoi, and Peter Savitskii, began taking a new approach to the issue of Russia's identity. As discussed briefly in the introductory chapters, Russia's geographic location places it between Europe and Asia, and throughout its history it has interacted with each but never truly identified with either. In the wake of the Bolshevik seizure of power in Russia, Vernadsky and his colleagues began to suggest that the roots of Russia's problems rested with its failed attempt to join the West, something that was incompatible with Russian culture and historical experience. In fact, even the name Russia, derived from the ethnonym *Rus,'* was a misnomer, since it did not accurately reflect the diversity of the people who inhabited this vast land between Europe and Asia. Instead, they suggested it should be called Eurasia (*Evraziya*), a term that more closely identified their cultural world.

Rather than a dark period in its history, in a series of books and articles, Vernadsky argued that the Mongol conquest of Russia actually helped the eastward expansion of the Slavs by organizing the nomadic steppe. Vernadsky also argued that, rather then being wild nomads as previously portrayed, the Mongols must have been highly organized and brought with them military technology from China, thus helping the Russian state to develop organizationally and technologically. Additionally, the descendants of Mongols that assimilated with the population contributed to Moscow's advancements. The Eurasian-Russian people thus emerged from Mongol rule stronger. Though in many ways horrible, the Mongol conquest had made the Russian state stronger.[18]

Although he provides no concrete examples and this interpretation is certainly open to critique, the point is that Vernadsky was breaking with tradition by writing a history that did not glorify Russia's European-ness or demonize its Asian aspects. In so doing, he was breaking with Russia's Orientalist tradition and expressing a new interpretation of Eurasia that would have profound consequences.

One of those consequences relates to the issue of Russia's relationship to democracy. While the Bolshevik seizure of power was seen by many émigré writers as a derailment of Russia's inevitable path to democracy, the Eurasianists argued that Russians were naturally predisposed to authoritarian rule.[19] As such, they were incapable of participating in Western culture, including democratic government. Rather, they should turn and embrace their neighbors to the east and form an alliance with other societies that sought to thwart the West's attempt to dominate the world.

Beginning even before the collapse of the Soviet Union in December 1991, intellectuals began to look back to the idea of Eurasianism once again in search of answers in a period of increasing uncertainty about the region's future. One of the first publications to raise the idea again was an article in the Communist Party of the Soviet Union (CPSU) magazine *Kommunist.* In reflecting on their ideas, the author praised the Eurasianists and their proposals, commenting that they understood that "Eurasianism was a special form or type of culture, thinking and state policy ingrained from time immemorial in the space of the greatest Eurasian state—Russia." As he continued, the "Eurasianists thought of themselves as expressing a special worldview, orientated primarily on spatial categories. The creation of their political constructs was acquired, therefore, above all from geopolitical measurements." It is precisely this attribute, the author proposed, that gives the Eurasian worldview "special relevance to our time, when geopolitical and national-territorial problems are extremely acute, when the concepts of Western and Eastern civilization, European and Asian republics, 'the turn to the East,' are once more coming into common usage."[20]

This mantra was soon picked up by others, including rising political leader Sergei Stankevich (Yeltsin would soon appoint him an advisor on ethnic and political issues). Writing in the pages of *Nezavisimaya Gazeta* the following March, Stankevich proposed that Russia was at a crossroads and could either turn West or East. Turning West, which he labeled the Atlanticist approach, meant becoming European, joining the global economy, and "putting emphasis" on Germany and the United States as "the two dominant members of the Atlantic alliance.[21] While he conceded that there were rational and pragmatic reasons for choosing such a course, such as credit, aid, and advanced technology, Stankevich proposed another direction. Recognizing that "our state emerged and grew strong as a unique historical and cultural amalgam of Slav and Turkic, Orthodox and Muslim components," Stankevich wrote, Russia should not seek to join the West but rather should seek to foster closer relations with "second-echelon" states such as Brazil, India, and China (today, along with Russia, referred to as the BRIC), as well as Turkey, Argentina, and Southeast Asia. Additionally, he proposed that Russia should preserve and even strengthen its special relationship with the CIS, establishing permeable borders, closer economic ties, and a military alliance.

Many of these sentiments were echoes of an earlier article by Sergei Goncharov, a leading intellectual from the prestigious Institute of the Far East, who the previous month had argued that Russia's geopolitical reality dictates that Russian foreign policy must concentrate on China and the Islamic world. "Both these directions already play a principal role now," he observed, "directly influencing our side not only purely militarily, but also the internal stability in our state."[22] As another observer expressed in a very similar idea, having "recognized the independence of her neighbors in the West [i.e., Eastern Europe and the Baltics], the country has involuntarily retreated East. Accordingly, its stabilizing function is naturally converted from a predominantly European one into properly a Eurasian one."[23]

The Russian Orthodox Church also began to promote its own version of Eurasianism by insisting that even though the republics of the former USSR might be separate countries, they were nonetheless united in a common civilizational space that the Russian Orthodox Church had helped to define and shape. The Church promoted the idea of a single spiritual and cultural space on the territory of the former Soviet Union. During the 1990s, the Church was to fight very strongly against efforts to set up independent Orthodox administrations in

Ukraine, Belarus, Estonia, and Central Asia that would be separate from Moscow and to preserve a single united Moscow Patriarchate.[24]

BREAKING UP IS HARD TO DO

Despite the initial optimism that the CIS would become an effective international organization, it has, over the past two decades, failed to live up to that promise. Most Eurasian states—including Russia, Armenia, Azerbaijan, Belarus, Kazakhstan, Kyrgyzstan, Moldova, Tajikistan, and Uzbekistan—remain members. Ukraine is a participant but not an official member (since its parliament failed to ratify the accession agreement),[25] while Turkmenistan withdrew in 2005 and Georgia did the same in 2009, one year after the war in South Ossetia. While Moscow, and perhaps even its member states, had initially envisioned the CIS becoming a significant economic, political, and security institution in the post–Soviet space, the varying rates of political liberalization among the members made the institution tenuous from the start. Because different states within the CIS were fearful of Russian domination, it also never acquired permanent institutions. Leaders were quick to sign documents, but, as former Russian foreign minister Igor Ivanov noted, "many of them exist only on paper. Of the 164 documents adopted [between 1991 and 2000] . . . that were to ratify or implement intrastate procedures, only seven have gone into effect."[26] For the 2009 CIS summit, not only did Georgia not attend, the presidents of the Central Asian states of Turkmenistan, Uzbekistan, and Tajikistan also boycotted the meeting, further bringing into doubt the relevance of the CIS.[27]

The failure of the CIS to consolidate itself reflects the fact that, since the breakup of the Soviet Union, each state has been free to determine its own relations with the outside world, and to varying degrees they have chosen to maintain or completely sever ties with Moscow. One group of states—including Kazakhstan, Belarus, and Armenia—has placed a high priority on pursuing close relations with Russia, including closer economic integration. A second tendency—manifested most strongly by Georgia—is to strive for the complete minimization of Russian influence wherever possible. Finally, countries like Ukraine, Uzbekistan, or Azerbaijan continue to remain ambivalent about whether to deepen their connection with Russia or to reorient themselves away from Moscow.

Interaction among the members of the CIS is facilitated more by other organizations than by the CIS itself, including the Eurasian Economic Community (EurAsEC), Collective Security Treaty Organization (CSTO), and the Single Economic Space (SES). Indeed, Igor Ivanov, when serving as the secretary of the Russian Security Council, observed in 2007 that the CIS was playing a much smaller role in the Eurasian space and identified the Eurasian Economic Community as the leading organization for regional integration.[28]

EurAsEC was created in 2000 by Russia and Kazakhstan—whose president Nursultan Nazarbayev is a proponent of closer Eurasian integration—along with Belarus, Kyrgyzstan, and Tajikistan. Uzbekistan's membership is currently suspended, and Armenia, Moldova, and Ukraine are observers. The Eurasian Economic Community concentrates its efforts on economics, including the creation of a common market, standardization of border security regulations, and the establishment of a standardized currency exchange system, as well as social programs and economic development projects. The endstate is the creation of a Single Economic Space that would be the Eurasian equivalent of the European common market—a zone in which capital, goods, and labor would be able to move freely. Belarus, Russia, and Kazakhstan launched a customs union between themselves on January 1, 2010, to further the process of integration.

The Collective Security Treaty Organization was created in 2002 and serves as a mutual defense alliance among Russia, Belarus, Armenia, and the four Central Asian states except Turkmenistan (more on this below) and to institutionalize the 1992 mutual security treaty. All of these organizations—and, more recently, the Eurasian Union—are strongly supported by Russia as part of its strategy to retain and even expand the linkages among the post–Soviet states. Though this can be interpreted by outsiders as an attempt at regional dominance, it is one that relies upon soft power rather than attempting to exercise old-fashioned imperial control over the CIS states.[29]

While many Western commentators see such initiatives as nothing more than thinly veiled attempts by Moscow to dominate its neighbors, there are good reasons for all sides to maintain economic ties, promote their development, and seek to provide for their security. In the economic realm, the Soviet economy was so heavily based on economies of scale and specialization of labor that the entire Soviet space, including Eastern Europe, was economically linked together to a degree well beyond anything free markets could achieve. As Dmitry Ryurikov, the former Russian ambassador to Uzbekistan, has noted, "The Soviet Union had been . . . an enormous, multifaceted, and self-contained Eurasian industrial corporation that linked enterprises and entire regions for decades."[30] This made economic independence both a strategic concern of the post–Soviet states as well as often an objective beyond their reach. Even the Baltic states had a difficult time extricating themselves from the Soviet orbit despite their intense desire to do so.[31] To those states that did not want to pay such a huge price to remove themselves from reliance upon Moscow, there have been benefits to maintaining relations with the region's dominant economic power.

This does not mean that other former Soviet states are not attempting, even at high cost, to try and break the links with Moscow. In particular, America's entry into Eurasia complicated matters for Russia. In the immediate aftermath of the Soviet collapse, the United States could promise and deliver even modest amounts of aid and assistance to newly independent republics that was beyond Russia's capacity to provide, leading the "high hopes" among "CIS states . . . for American help."[32] In the aftermath of the 9/11 terrorist attacks on the U.S. homeland, the American military's need for bases in order to support the campaign in Afghanistan offered new opportunities for post-Soviet states to court Washington as an alternative to Moscow. Uzbekistan and Kyrgyzstan, where U.S. facilities were ultimately sited, reaped the benefits not only of rental income for the facilities but also of increased military assistance, economic aid, and even security partnerships, a situation that was not entirely to Russia's liking, even if it grudgingly recognized the security value to Russia of the U.S.-led mission in Afghanistan.[33]

Georgia has been the post-Soviet state that has most consistently worked to change the geopolitics of Eurasia, especially by trying to forge a close relationship with the United States. Georgian skepticism of Russia started with the first president, Zviad Gamsakhurdia, who refused to join the CIS after the collapse of the USSR. He was overthrown in a coup, and the former Soviet foreign minister (and former Communist party secretary of Georgia) Eduard Shevardnadze was brought back to head the State Council (in 1992) and ultimately to become president in 1995. Shevardnadze had difficult relations with Moscow and attempted to move Georgia closer to the United States, ultimately asking for U.S. military assistance to train the Georgian military.

He also helped to organize cooperative mechanisms between other Eurasian states seeking to resist Russian influence. In 1997, Shevardnadze, along with the leaders of Ukraine, Moldova, and Azerbaijan, began to meet regularly to try and develop common positions, as well as to promote greater economic and security cooperation that would enable them to break free of Russian influence. In 1999, Uzbekistan also began to take part. In 2001, this association was formalized as the so-called GUUAM forum. This organization did receive some support from the United States, which supported its efforts to increase its members' independence from Russia—while at the same time helping to complicate the U.S.-Russia relationship. In 2005, the foreign ministers of the GUUAM countries attempted to maintain a common front against Russia at a meeting of the CIS; fearing that Uzbekistan's ability to balance its relationships with Russia and the United States might be affected, President Islam Karimov withdrew from the organization, now called GUAM. The organization was subsequently reorganized as the GUAM Organization for Democracy and Economic Development, but its effectiveness has ebbed and flowed depending on how Ukraine–Russia, Moldova–Russia and Azerbaijan–Russia relations are faring.[34]

Shevardnadze, nevertheless, always sought some degree of balance in Georgia's relations with Moscow. In November 2003, however, he was overthrown in the first of what became known as the "colored revolutions" within the Eurasian space, the Rose Revolution, so named because of the roses carried by those protesting Shevardnadze's efforts to falsify election results. The former justice minister and one of the leaders of the opposition, Mikheil Saakashvili, became president.[35] He began to pursue even closer ties with the United States and promised to secure NATO membership for Georgia, and, as a result, soon clashed with Moscow. Georgia's efforts during this time were often complemented by Ukraine. Its first postindependence president, Leonid Kravchuk, was interested in carving out a very distinct identity and position for Ukraine that would clearly differentiate it from Russia, including resisting efforts to promote a common currency and joint armed forces. He also drove a hard bargain for giving up former Soviet nuclear components on Ukrainian soil and becoming a nuclear-free state by demanding a doubling of U.S. aid and commitments from Russia to sell energy at below-market rates. Kravchuk was defeated in the 1994 elections, and his successor Leonid Kuchma promised to pursue better relations with Russia, in part to appease the large Russian population in the eastern part of the country as well as powerful business interests that benefited from closer ties with Russia.

Kuchma settled the issue of the Soviet Black Sea Fleet and continued Russian use of the naval base at Sevastopol (with a lease that was to run to 2017) and tried to find ways to settle questions related to the transit of Russian natural gas across Ukraine. In turn, in a 1997 treaty, Russia affirmed the borders of Ukraine, thus renouncing any claims to Crimea. However, Kuchma's desire for a balanced foreign policy meant he kept open options for Ukraine to try and pursue membership in Western organizations such as NATO. Kuchma also backed the efforts of Shevardnadze to better integrate the non–Russian countries of the CIS in order to form a more effective counterweight to Russia. As in Georgia, however, Kuchma's efforts to control elections (and to deliver the presidency to a hand-picked successor, Viktor Yanukovych, who believed that Ukraine should align itself more closely with Russia), led to popular protests. Labeled the Orange Revolution after the color used by the opposition, these protests forced a rerunning of the 2004 presidential race that elected a pro–Western candidate, the former prime minister Viktor Yushchenko. Subsequent elections also boosted the position of Yuliya Tymoshenko, an ally of Yushchenko's who became prime minister and who lobbied for the United States and Europe to support Ukraine's efforts to break out of Russia's orbit as part of a strategy of containing Russia.[36] Yushchenko and Tymoshenko put NATO membership for Ukraine back on the agenda and raised questions that Russia thought had been settled—especially the status of the Russian squadrons of the Black Sea Fleet stationed in Sevastopol in the Crimea.[37]

Because the United States had offered moral support (as well as aid money) to the groups that had led the Rose and Orange Revolutions, Russia interpreted this as proof that it was now U.S. policy "to squeeze Russia out of its positions across the entire CIS territory, both overtly and covertly."[38] U.S. president George W. Bush's visit to Georgia in May 2005 (following his trip to Russia) raised hackles in Moscow, especially when Bush alluded to deeper ties between Georgia and the United States and discreetly encouraged a closer relationship with NATO.[39] When Saakashvili and Yushchenko decided to form the Community of Democratic Choice (CDC), a joint effort to promote democratic change across the former Soviet space, this was seen as a direct challenge to Russia's pre-eminent role in the region. Russia believed that the U.S. support for democracy was, in actuality, designed to target the pro–Russian regimes of Eurasia. After the Rose and Orange Revolutions, *Rossiiskaia Gazeta* editorialized that after Ukraine, so-called colored revolutions would be fomented "in Belarus, Moldova, Kazakhstan, Kyrgyzstan and possibly Armenia"—in other words, the regimes in Eurasia closest to Moscow.[40]

The Orange Revolution in Ukraine also heightened tensions with Russia over natural gas deliveries. Ukraine was still receiving gas at below-market prices and had accumulated significant debts to Russia; the Russians insisted on higher prices and payment of debts, arguing that they should no longer subsidize a Ukrainian government not receptive to Russian interests. Twice—in January 2006 and again in January 2009—Gazprom attempted to cut shipments to Ukraine, which in turn led to decreased supplies in the rest of Europe as Ukraine claimed it had a right to take some of the gas that was transiting its territory. While these cutoffs were short lived, these crises damaged the reputation of Russia as a reliable supplier to Europe and also created the impression that Moscow was deploying the "gas weapon" to pressure Ukraine.

Russia also employed economic pressure against Georgia, cutting off imports of Georgian products like wine, a traditional export to Russia, as well as placing more pressure on the large Georgian migrant community in Russia that was sending remittances back to their families in Georgia, which comprised some 25% of the country's GDP in 2005.[41] As will be discussed below, relations deteriorated to the point that both countries fought a short war in August 2008.

THE FROZEN CONFLICTS

For the most part, the breakup of the USSR happened peacefully, but several conflicts did erupt on the territory of the former Soviet Union. These outbreaks were used by Russia to further its claims to have special responsibility for peace and security in the Eurasian region. The most famous and the most protracted of the conflicts outside of Russia has been the Nagorno-Karabakh dispute between Armenia and Azerbaijan. Nagorno-Karabakh, a majority-Armenian region within Azerbaijan, sought to join the Armenian Soviet Republic in 1988 and, as the Soviet Union was disintegrating, proclaimed its complete independence from Azerbaijan in 1991. The Nagorno-Karabakh Armenians, with well-equipped forces and with unofficial aid from Russia, were able to take control of their own republic and also parts of Azerbaijan proper. This took place at a time when the first postindependence government of Azerbaijan under Abulfaz Elcibey was attempting to reorient Azerbaijan away from Russia, especially in creating new energy export routes that would bypass Russia altogether.[42] After Elcibey was overthrown by Heydar Aliev, the former Communist Party secretary for Azerbaijan, the situation stabilized and a cease-fire took effect in 1994. Because Russia has close defense ties to Armenia (as well as the presence of a large Armenian diaspora community) but has important economic interests with Azerbaijan (starting with the oil industry), the Russian government has not given its full support to either side but instead tries to work for a solution "acceptable to both sides."[43] Moreover, both Armenia and Azerbaijan did not want to have Russia as the sole mediator and so involved the United States, Turkey, France, and other outside powers in their dispute. In 1992, the so-called Minsk Group was convened by the Organization for Security and Cooperation in Europe, co-chaired by Russia, the United States, and France. It has brokered an ongoing (but as of yet fruitless) series of negotiations between Azerbaijan, Nagorno-Karabakh, and Armenia. However, it does guarantee that Russia must be part of any solution that emerges.

When civil war broke out in Tajikistan between the reform Communists and Islamists in 1992, the ex–Soviet forces stationed in that republic, now reorganized as the Russian army's 201st Motorized Rifle Division, obtained a mandate to act as peacekeepers and to secure the border between Tajikistan and Afghanistan. These forces, at times, also helped to defend the government against rebel attacks. Russian forces remained in Tajikistan after the 1997 agreements that ended the civil war, helping to provide stability for the elections and facilitating the return of refugees. The Russian government, in turn, cited its performance in Tajikistan to bolster its claims that it was capable of regulating conflicts within the Eurasian space without outside assistance or involvement.[44]

Two other former Soviet states faced secessionist conflicts that independence from the USSR exacerbated. In Moldova, the Slav regions across the Dniestr River were concerned that an independent Moldova might seek union with Romania. Transdnistria declared independence in 1990 and in 1992 fought the Moldovan government to take control of former Soviet weaponry, unofficially aided by the ex–Soviet forces that were stationed in the region.[45] The Georgian nationalism of Zviad Gamsakhurdia and his attempt to cancel the autonomy enjoyed by South Ossetia and Abkhazia within Georgia caused both regions to try and break away from Georgia in 1991 to 1992, and, in the case of Abkhazia, led to large-scale cleansing of ethnic Georgians in 1992 to 1993 in order to change the demographics of the territory.[46] In all of these areas, Russian military forces, acting under mandates from the CIS that were then ratified by the UN Security Council, stopped the fighting and, by serving as peacekeepers to separate the combatants, helped to create de facto separatist entities. Russia insisted that its forces were sufficient to serve as peacekeepers or to prevent further violence from breaking out and that the involvement of other, non–CIS countries or regional bodies, such as NATO, was not required. This claim was aided by the fact that other countries like the United States, France, or Germany were not willing to send troops to undertake peacekeeping duties, particularly to separate the Georgian forces from the separatists in South Ossetia and Abkhazia.[47]

While Moscow's initial preference would have been to support the territorial integrity of Moldova and Georgia, the pro-Russian separatist territories (Transdnistria, Abkhazia, South Ossetia) became useful points of pressure when both Georgia and Moldova attempted to distance themselves from Moscow. Another tool the Russian government utilized was to grant Russian passports to the residents of these separatist regions, thus giving Moscow the right to intervene to defend its citizens.[48] Finally, despite commitments Russia had made to Georgia and Moldova at a 1999 summit in Istanbul of the Organization for Security and Cooperation in Europe to withdraw its forces stationed in both countries, the peacekeeping mandates allowed Russia to exempt some of its personnel from this pledge.[49]

But Russia also had its own vulnerabilities—just as Georgia had its separatist movements, within Russia, the Caucasian republic of Chechnya sought complete independence, with two unsuccessful wars fought (1994–1996 and again in 1999) for a separate state. Even after a decisive conventional military campaign crushed the separatist government, it spawned an insurgency that is still continuing against the Moscow-backed government to this day (which has also spread conflict to the other North Caucasian republics of the Russian Federation like Dagestan). Moscow remains very sensitive to any indication that other Eurasian and East European states—among them Georgia, the Baltic States, and Poland—are supporting the pro-independence Chechens or otherwise interfering in this region. Russia has repeatedly charged that Chechen rebels found sanctuary and support within Georgian territory. Russia carried out strikes against Chechen camps in Georgia's Pankisi Gorge in 2002, and as a result Georgia then turned to the United States to provide training and equipment for its military so as to better secure its own territory.[50] In 2010, Georgia again raised Russia's ire by allowing residents of the North Caucasus—but no other part of Russia—to travel to Georgia without visas, and Saakashvili presented his vision of a "unified Caucasus" that implied a complete Russian withdrawal from the region.[51] Saakashivili's declaration that "there is no North and South Caucasus, there is one Caucasus, which belongs to Europe and will one day join the European family of free nations, following the Georgian path" was not well received in Moscow.[52]

Russia undertook a major diplomatic push to settle the Moldova–Transdnistria dispute during the first years of the Putin presidency. Putin's then-chief of staff Dmitry Kozak proposed an asymmetric federation for Moldova, with provisions for Transdnistrian independence should Moldova seek union with Romania. If adopted, the Kozak Memorandum would have demonstrated that Russia could provide workable solutions to protracted conflicts in the Eurasian space. There was also an underlying subtext that a reunified Moldova would have to be more accommodating to Russian interests, with a corresponding cessation of efforts to oppose Russia (as Moldova had done by joining the GUUAM grouping). The last-minute rejection of the Kozak plan by Moldovan president Vladimir Voronin in November 2003, which the Russians stressed occurred as a result of "strong pressure from the European Union and the United States" (which felt the deal compromised Moldovan sovereignty, in part because Moldova would have agreed to the presence of Russian troops on its soil), led many in the Russian government, beginning with Putin himself, to conclude that the United States would actively seek to frustrate Russian efforts at conflict resolution in the Eurasian space.[53] From the perspectives of some in the Moldovan and Georgian governments, however, the message of the Kozak Memorandum was that the price for reunification was for them to abandon their efforts to join Western institutions.

After Saakashvili came to power in Georgia as a result of elections following the 2003 Rose Revolution, the Russians initially hoped that they could make a deal with him on reunifying the separatist regions with Georgia in return for greater Russian influence.[54] Saakashvili, however, made it clear that he would pursue reunification on his own terms, not Moscow's, and that he would continue and even accelerate Georgia's pursuit of membership in NATO and the European Union. Saakashvili's confidence was boosted after he successfully removed a leading pro-Russian politician, Aslan Abashidze, from his position as head of the government of Adjaria, an autonomous region in southern Georgia, in 2004. On May 7, 2004, speaking at a rally in Adjaria, Saakashvili proclaimed, ""I'm sure that very soon we'll go together to Abkhazia and will get [Georgia] completely united."[55] In August 2004, there were clashes between Georgian forces and the South Ossetians, raising fears that Saakashvili would use force if negotiations did not succeed in bringing the separatist regions back under Georgian control. Under diplomatic pressure not to widen the conflict, the Georgians backed down. Russian concerns were raised, however, by the acceleration of U.S.–Georgia military relations under the Georgia Train and Equip (GTEP) program. While Washington stated that U.S. military aid to Georgia was designed to help Georgian forces deal with counterterrorism at home and to take part in U.S.-led missions elsewhere (such as Iraq and Afghanistan), Moscow (as well as the Abkhaz and South Ossetians) saw U.S. assistance as giving Saakashvili a more effective military force to use against the separatists.[56] In 2006, the Georgian government reaffirmed its control over the Kodori Gorge in Abkhazia and took action against a local militia leader; it then established an alternative government for Abkhazia based in this area. Efforts were also made to set up an alternative South Ossetian administration.

Military incidents along the cease-fire lines increased during this time, as did allegations that Russian aircraft were violating Georgian air space. In September 2006, South Ossetian forces fired on a helicopter carrying Georgia's defense minister, claiming it had entered their area of control. In March 2007, the Georgian-backed Abkhaz government's headquarters were attacked by aircraft that were alleged to have come from Russian territory, and in August 2007, Georgia claimed that Russian aircraft had entered Georgian territory and fired on a village near the Georgia–Abkhazia line. Subsequently, Georgian air defenses opened fire on an unknown (but presumed Russian) plane.

After the United States and many European countries recognized Kosovo's unilateral declaration of independence in February 2008, the Russian government announced it would reconsider its position on Abkhazia and South Ossetia. At the Bucharest NATO summit in April 2008, Georgia—despite intense lobbying from the United States—was not given a membership action plan (the first step for NATO membership), but the alliance did make a commitment that, at an unspecified future date, Georgia would be allowed to join. That same month, a Georgian drone flying over Abkhazian airspace was shot down by a Russian Air Force jet. Continued incidents in the spring and summer, especially explosions and small-scale exchanges of fire, heightened tensions. Russia announced that it would reinforce its peacekeeping forces in order to deal with these incidents and also deployed engineering units to engage in infrastructure repair in Abkhazia. The South Ossetian government also began to fortify its border with Georgia. In response to all of these developments, Georgia announced it would deploy additional troops to protect its sovereign territory from any further incursions. In July, Russia held a series of exercises, Caucasus Frontier 2008, which included drills for rapid reinforcement of Russian peacekeepers in South Ossetia and Abkhazia. At the same time, Georgia and the United States held a joint exercise, Immediate Response 2008.[57] Less than a month later, many of the Georgian and Russian units involved in these drills were engaged in combat with each other.

THE GEORGIA–RUSSIA WAR AND ITS AFTERMATH

In July 2008, U.S. Secretary of State Condoleezza Rice visited Georgia. She stressed the importance of peaceful resolution of the conflicts with Abkhazia and South Ossetia but reaffirmed American support for Georgia's inclusion in NATO and publicly backed the Georgian position. Many observers believe that Rice's visit might have left Saakashvili and his government with "the mistaken impression that in a one-on-one fight with Russia, Georgia would have more concrete American support."[58] At the beginning of August, regular exchanges of gunfire between Georgian and South Ossetian security forces began.

When and how major hostilities started is contested, but most international observers concluded that the Georgian government's decision to target Ossetian militia positions with artillery fire on the evening of August 7, 2008, was the proximate cause of the conflict.[59] On the morning of August 8, Operation Clear Field was launched to capture the South Ossetian capital Tskhinvali, which brought Georgian forces into direct conflict with the Russian peacekeeping units. The Russian government then ordered military units to cross the border into South Ossetia to reinforce the Russian and South Ossetian forces. On August 9, Russian units also entered Abkhazia and assisted the Abkhaz forces in taking the Kodori region. The Russian military, however, moved beyond defending the status quo and entered Georgia proper, occupying a good deal of Western Georgia, and striking targets all over the country (including in the capital Tbilisi) with a particular eye to destroying or neutralizing Georgia's military capabilities. As a result of the war,

> Georgia has entirely lost its air and naval forces and air-defense systems. Reportedly, Russian forces captured and destroyed a significant portion of the Georgian army's arsenals. The Russians seized up to 150 units of Georgian heavy weaponry, including 65 T-72 tanks (including 44 in operational condition), 15 BMP armored fighting vehicles, a few dozen armored personnel carriers, vehicles, guns and SAM systems.[60]

No Western power chose to intervene to defend Georgia, and Dmitry Medvedev announced a cessation of hostilities on August 12, although Russian forces continued to take action to "demilitarize" Georgia. French president Nicolas Sarkozy, acting on behalf of the European Union, mediated a six-point ceasefire plan, which went into effect on August 15th. Russia agreed to withdraw to its prewar positions, although Russian forces did not fully evacuate their posts in Georgia proper until October, and Georgia also agreed to keep its military back behind the lines as they existed prior to August 7. However, on August 25, 2008, citing the Kosovo precedent, Russia recognized Abkhazia and South Ossetia as fully independent states and declared that these areas were no longer Georgian territory. Subsequent agreements signed with both governments gave Russia the right to possess military bases in these territories, and Russia argued that it was no longer obligated to withdraw its forces as per the 1999 agreement reached in Istanbul.

The Georgia War showed the relative impotence of the structures that had been created to oppose Russian dominance in Eurasia. In particular, despite the CDC, Ukraine was unable and unwilling to prevent units of the Russian Black Sea Fleet based in Ukraine from being used against Georgia. In addition, one major impact of the Georgia–Russia clash was that it disabused many of the Eurasian states that had been flirting with the West of the notion that, in the event of a serious clash with Russia, they could count on American or European help. Former Ukrainian president Leonid Kuchma bluntly noted in 2010, "Is there anybody [who] thinks we really need to tilt against Russia and someone will take our side? I'm sure neither [the] EU nor the US won't lift a finger . . ."[61]

The war also stalled plans for further NATO expansion eastward and put Georgia's bid for membership into a deep freeze, even though the alliance has repeatedly insisted that Georgia's candidacy is still under consideration. As will be discussed in the chapter on Europe, a number of major European states, starting with Germany, did not wish to interrupt growing economic and political links with Russia over the question of Georgia's admission to the alliance.[62]

Georgia broke diplomatic relations with Russia after the conflict, but other consequences, such as the temporary interruption of relations between NATO and Russia, were short lived. And while Georgia, a member of the World Trade Organization, could have perpetually vetoed Russia's inclusion in that trade body, Tbilisi came under a good deal of pressure from both the United States and Europe not to block Russia's accession (which finally occurred in 2012).[63]

The outcome of the Georgia war also had an important impact on politics in Ukraine. Already, disillusionment with the paucity of Western aid and support had undercut the Yushchenko presidency and its promise that Ukraine would be quickly integrated into the West; the rupturing of some of the ties with Russia also contributed to an economic downturn in Ukraine. All of this aided the resurgence of Russophile parties. The Party of Regions led by Yanukovych became the largest party in the Ukrainian Rada (parliament) after the 2006 elections, and Yanukovych even replaced Tymoshenko as prime minister until she regained her parliamentary majority in 2007. But Tymoshenko began to change her position vis-à-vis Russia, deciding that a more pragmatic course of accommodating Russia's concerns made more sense given Ukraine's uncertain position between east and west. She forged a new working relationship with Putin and reached a new deal with Russia on natural gas deliveries to Ukraine in January 2009. Significantly, in November 2009, she met with Putin in Yalta, traded jokes about Saakashvili (who had just been in Ukraine for meetings with Yushchenko), and stressed the importance of a "true partnership" between Ukraine and Russia.[64] Despite Putin's declaration that Russia found it "comfortable for us to work with the Tymoshenko government," the Kremlin was still pleased when Tymoshenko was defeated by Yanukovych in the 2010 presidential elections. The "loser" of the Orange Revolution had succeeded in coming to power 6 years later.

Yanukovych has settled many of the main points of dispute between Ukraine and Russia. In April, in Kharkiv, Ukraine and Russia concluded a pact by which the Russian lease at Sevastopol was extended to 2042 in return for Ukraine receiving Russian natural gas at a discount. In June 2010, the Rada passed legislation that prohibits Ukraine from joining any military bloc, including NATO (although it does allow for cooperation with the alliance, or with the CSTO). However, Yanukovych has been far less willing to commit Ukraine to joining Russian-led organizations, preferring to position Ukraine as a neutral but European state.

Despite some hopes in Russian circles that the debacle of the conflict with Russia might lead to Saakashvili's overthrow, his government remained intact. But his handling of Russia and the perceived "loss" of the separatist territories did extract a political cost. The opposition Georgian Dream coalition won a majority in the October 2012 elections. While Prime Minister Bidzina Ivanishvili also supports Georgia becoming a member of NATO and the EU, he was highly critical of the Saakashvili approach and argued that with "correct diplomacy," it would be possible to improve the situation with Russia.[65] Ivanishvili, for instance, has been less willing to intervene in the affairs of Russia's North Caucasus republics, a particular bête noir of Moscow.[66] Ivanishvili's Special Representative Zurab Abashidze and Russia's Deputy Foreign Minister Grigory Karasin met on December 14, 2012, in Geneva to start a new direct diplomatic dialogue between Russia and Georgia. In January 2013, the Catholicos-Patriarch of the Georgian Orthodox Church, Ilia II, traveled to Moscow. While the main purpose of the visit was to meet with Russian Orthodox leaders, Ilia has also often served as an unofficial mediator between Georgia and Russia, and his presence in Russia has also been interpreted as a sign that Ivanishvili's government is looking to improve relations.[67]

THE TIES THAT BIND

Despite conflicts and the efforts of some governments to redraw the economic and political map of Eurasia, there are still many factors that push the countries of the region toward reintegration with Russia. One advantage relates to the social capital that existed throughout the Soviet Union. As a result of interacting with each other for so long, people who have grown up in the region have a certain way of doing business, a distinct business culture, if you will. While this culture has proven formidable to outsiders from both East and West attempting to break into post–Soviet markets, local citizens from across the region easily interact with each other. Research by a group of Rand analysts shows that due to factors such as "the ease of crossing borders, knowledge of Russian (still the lingua franca of the CIS), and family, academic, and professional ties from the times of the Soviet Union, Russian entrepreneurs find operating in the CIS easier than do many Western investors."[68] This latter point applies not only to Western investors but also to those of the Middle East, which are potentially more significant for Central Asia and the Caucasus, if they were to pull away from the post–Soviet orbit and gravitate closer to their ethno-religious kin. The analysts also found that "Russian investors, especially expatriates, have benefited extensively from their knowledge of local industrial and commercial assets, familiarity with the workings of local and national bureaucracies, and personal contacts with government and business elites."[69] These factors contribute significantly to maintaining economic linkages among the CIS and to keeping Russians at the top of the economic ladder.

This leads to a further set of questions regarding economic relations among the states of Eurasia. As these Rand analysts have shown, Russian investment is greatest in Belarus, Kazakhstan, Azerbaijan, Ukraine, Moldova, Armenia, and Georgia. Kazakhstan itself accounts for nearly one-half of Russian foreign direct investment (FDI) in the former Soviet Union, while Azerbaijan and Ukraine each account for another 20%.[70] When investments from Cyprus, the British Virgin Islands, and other offshore accounts are included, Russian investment is even higher, with Russia becoming the single largest investor in Ukraine[71] (see Table 5.2).

The story does not end with Russian investment; inter–CIS trade also indicates that there are strong economic linkages holding Eurasia together. As Table 5.3 shows, when one looks at the primary trade partners of the CIS states, Russia figures prominently to say the least. For Ukraine, Belarus, Moldova, Armenia, Uzbekistan, and Kyrgyzstan, Russia is the number-one source of both imports and exports. Russia also figures prominently in all of the other CIS states, as does Ukraine. The only new story in terms of CIS trade is the emergence of Turkey and China as important trading partners. Given the

TABLE 5.2
Foreign Direct Investment (FDI) in the Eurasian States, 1992–2003 (in millions of U.S. dollars)

Country	Total FDI	Russian (or suspected Russian) FDI	Russian FDI as Percent of Total
Armenia	$793	$227.6	28.7%
Azerbaijan	$8,639	$509.5	5.9%
Belarus	$1,897	$709.7	37.4%
Georgia	$1,336	$103.8	7.8%
Kazakhstan	$17,567	$1271.0	7.2%
Kyrgyzstan	$491	$46.0	9.4%
Moldova	$789	$167.7	21.3%
Tajikistan	$36	$0.4	1.1%
Turkmenistan	n.a.	$0.0	n.a.
Ukraine	$7,502	$1262.2	16.8%
Uzbekistan	n.a.	$2.0	n.a.
Total	**$39,051**	**$4,300.0**	**11.0%**

Sources: Crane et al., compiled by authors from Goskomstat Rossii, 2004; IMF, 2004; National Statistical Services of the Republic of Armenia, 2004; State Statistical Committee of Ukraine, 2004; State Statistical Committee of the Azerbaijan Republic, 2005; Ministry of Economic Development of Georgia, n.d.; National Bank of Moldova, n.d.; UNCTAD, n.d.

geographical distribution of these countries, however, it is very unlikely that a Turkey-centered Central Asia could emerge, for Armenia would be stuck in the midst of it, Iran would work against it, and China's luring markets and interests in Central Asia will help prevent it.

The story of China is a more complex one. In the post–Soviet period, and during its own period of *gaige kaifeng* (reform and opening), China has greatly increased its trade linkages with Central Asia and has become an important trade partner for many CIS states, especially Russia, Ukraine, Kazakhstan, Uzbekistan, and Kyrgyzstan. After recovering from the economic crisis of 1998, Russia and the CIS have tripled their foreign trade in agricultural and aquacultural products with China.[72] Following WTO accession, China's exports in the sectors to the CIS grew nearly 62% during the period 2001 to 2007, the greatest increase in Chinese exports in any world region.

TABLE 5.3
Inter–CIS Trade by Primary, Secondary, and Tertiary Partners

Country/Trade Type	First	Second	Third
Russia			
Export	Netherlands (10.8%)	Italy (8%)	Germany (7.8%)
Import	Germany (13.4%)	China (12.8%)	Japan (6.5%)
Ukraine			
Export	Russia (23.3%)	Turkey (7.9%)	Italy (5.8%)
Import	Russia (23.9%)	Germany (11.8%)	China (8.5%)
Belarus			
Export	Russia (36.5%)	Netherlands (17.8%)	UK (6.3%)
Import	Russia (59.9%)	Germany (7.6%)	Ukraine (5.4%)
Moldova			
Export	Russia (25.3%)	Romania (13%)	Italy (10%)
Import	Russia (20.5%)	Ukraine (15.8%)	Romania (15%)
Georgia			
Export	Turkey (13%)	US (11.2%)	Azerbaijan (6.3%)
Import	Turkey (14%)	Russia (12.3%)	Ukraine (8.5%)
Armenia			
Export	Russia (17.5%)	Germany (14.7%)	Netherlands (13.5%)
Import	Russia (15.1%)	Ukraine (7.7%)	Kazakhstan (7.4%)
Azerbaijan			
Export	Turkey (17.4%)	Italy (15.5%)	Russia (8.7%)
Import	Russia (17.6%)	Turkey (10.9%)	Germany (8.2%)
Kazakhstan			
Export	China (15.5%)	Germany (11.5%)	Russia (11.2%)
Import	Russia (35.4%)	China (22.1%)	Germany (8%)
Uzbekistan			
Export	Russia (22.4%)	Poland (10.4%)	Turkey (9.4%)
Import	Russia (30.1%)	China (13.3%)	South Korea (13%)
Turkmenistan			
Export	Ukraine (51.3%)	Iran (18.5%)	Turkey (5%)
Import	UAE (14.3%)	Russia (11.6%)	Turkey (10.3%)
Kyrgyzstan			
Import	Russia (40.5%)	China (14.7%)	Kazakhstan (12.9%)
Export	Russia (20.7%)	Switzerland (19.9%)	Kazakhstan (18%)
Tajikistan			
Import	Russia (32.1%)	Kazakhstan (13.1%)	China (10.8%)
Export	Netherlands (38.9%)	Turkey (32.5%)	Russia (6.6%)

Sources: Crane et al., compiled by authors from Goskomstat Rossii, 2004; IMF, 2004; National Statistical Services of the Republic of Armenia, 2004; State Statistical Committee of Ukraine, 2004; State Statistical Committee of the Azerbaijan Republic, 2005; Ministry of Economic Development of Georgia, n.d.; National Bank of Moldova, n.d.; UNCTAD, n.d.

While these figures are useful, another important part of the story that does not show up in such statistics is the "trickle-down" effect of Russian investment and economic activity in Eurasia, especially Central Asia. While Russia invests heavily in Kazakhstan, it is much less involved in the rest of Central Asia, but here Kazakhstan itself is the main investor in the region (and the number-two CIS investor in Eurasia). In this way, economic vitality and wealth is shared throughout the region, with its true source being Russia again. These patterns are also observable, to a lesser extent, with Moldova—vis-à-vis both Russia and Ukraine—and the Caucasus. In this way, Russia invests in Kiev, Almaty, and Yerevan, and then benefits trickle down into the smaller neighboring states and cities. Although Moscow/Russia does not directly link all of the CIS together, it is still very much the major player in the economic food chain.

SECURING EURASIA

Russia is also the dominant military power in the region, and while the Warsaw Pact disintegrated along with the Soviet state, the Kremlin still views the post-Soviet space as its sphere of influence and will not allow any state in the region to take actions that could threaten its national interests. Indeed, Russia maintains a series of bases throughout Eurasia. As previously noted, the main bases of the Black Sea Fleet remain in Ukraine, including the headquarters at Sevastopol. But other installations include the Volga radar station in Belarus, the Gyumir base in Armenia, the Gabala radar station in Azerbaijan, and the Kant airbase in Kyrgyzstan.[73] Moscow has consistently maintained that its primary interest is to ensure that no other Eurasian state can obstruct Russian engagement with the outside world and that no foreign troops are based anywhere in Eurasia without Russia's blessing (for example, to combat international terrorism). As a result, Moscow maintains that no Eurasian state should belong to a military bloc or alliance of which Russia is not also a member.

The CIS includes several military structures/security organizations: the CIS Air Defense Coordination Committee (members are Russia, Armenia, Belarus, Kazakhstan, Kyrgyzstan, Tajikistan, Uzbekistan, and Ukraine); the CIS Antiterrorist Center (with all CIS members except Turkmenistan); the CIS Military Cooperation Coordination Headquarters; and the Council of Commanders of Border Troops.[74] But Moscow's primary vehicle for securing Eurasia is the Collective Security Treaty Organization. The CSTO grew out of the framework of the CIS, and its history goes back to the May 1992 Treaty on Collective Security Treaty (CST), or Tashkent Treaty, which Moscow initiated as a "regional security structure within the CIS." The initial agreement was set to last for 5 years, but in 1999, all members except Uzbekistan renewed their participation (they subsequently rejoined the organization in June 2006). In 2002, the treaty association was renamed the CSTO, or Collective Security Treaty Organization, as a recognition of the organization's development from a treaty into a more institutionalized form. This was no mere name change, however, as the formation of the CSTO was designed to create a collective security architecture, including the formation of a rapid-reaction force, the establishment of a common air defense system, and the coordination of foreign, security, and defense policies.

The mission of the CSTO is the preservation of territorial integrity and cooperation and coordination with other multilateral institutions, including the UN, the Organization for Security and Cooperation in Europe (OSCE), the Shanghai Cooperation Organization (SCO), and NATO. The Kremlin has even spoken of the CSTO as a potential Eurasian partner for NATO. The charter of the CSTO is made up of 10 chapters that establish the organization's purposes, principles, and areas of activity. The Treaty on Collective Security, which contains 11 articles, directs the organization on the use of force in response to conflicts. Under Article 4, any military response will be done in accordance with Article 51 of the UN Charter and states that CSTO members will inform the UN Security Council of any action taken.[75] In 2011, the CSTO amended its mission by pledging to defend its members from internal "unconstitutional disturbances," an apparent response to possible uprisings in Tajikistan mirroring those of the Arab Spring.[76]

The CSTO allows member states to purchase weapons and equipment from the Russian defense industry at the same price paid by the Russian military.[77] Additionally, the CSTO has had some form of a collective force since 2001. At the CSTO (then CST) summit in Yerevan, Armenia, in May 2001, members created the Collective Rapid Deployment Force for the Central Asian Region (CRDF CAR), sometimes referred to as Collective Rapid Reaction Force (CRRF). This force is made up of around 4,500 soldiers, with Russia, Kazakhstan, Kyrgyzstan, and Tajikistan each contributing either a battalion and/or a special forces unit with the goal of averting external aggression and terrorism. Additionally, Russia contributes a variety of fighter and transport aircraft and helicopters that are deployed to the Kant Airbase outside Bishkek, Kyrgyzstan.[78] At a CSTO summit in 2008 and in February 2009, members discussed the need for a new, separate collective force. They then created the Collective Operational Reaction Force (CORF) in June 2009. All CSTO members contribute to the force, which can be deployed to deal with threats from conventional militaries and nonstate armed groups, as well as emergency or disaster situations and for peacekeeping operations. CORF is composed of units from each member state, and all units are based in their home nations except for annual joint exercises, except for Russian air units stationed at Kant airbase in Kyrgyzstan, which are tasked to provide air support to the reaction force.

Uzbekistan had always been unenthusiastic about the CSTO. It chose not to renew its participation in the Collective Security Treaty in 1999 and instead flirted with the United States and joined the GUUAM grouping of states. But it changed course after harsh protests from the West over the government's brutal crackdown on protesters in Andijan in May 2005. Uzbekistan withdrew from GUAM and decided to reaffiliate with the CSTO in 2006. In July 2012, Tashkent withdrew again, this time over the pace and scope of the CSTO's development and expansion. As Cooley pointed out, Tashkent has long been uncomfortable with Moscow's moves to deepen the organization's activities and shape it into a counter–NATO institution.[79] Tashkent has consistently refused to allow Moscow to base forces in Uzbekistan and thwarted its attempts to establish a CSTO base in southern Kyrgyzstan, near its border. Uzbekistan also objected to moves it perceived as giving the right to station foreign troops on a member state's territory.

Moscow responded to Tashkent's announcement with caution and patience, even expressing optimism that Uzbekistan might eventually rejoin the organization. The Kremlin has not been very keen on Uzbekistan's security cooperation with NATO, including recent negotiations to expand its role in cooperating with the International Security Assistance Force (ISAF) forces during the drawdown in Afghanistan (nor is Moscow pleased about the arrangement whereby U.S. military equipment used in Afghanistan is handed over to the Uzbek military).[80] In fact, to a certain extent, Uzbekistan's suspension of CSTO membership is regarded by Russia as a positive step. Tashkent has been seen by the Kremlin and other members as often holding the CSTO for ransom, as it often blocked proposals that would create deeper levels of security cooperation due to its own concerns over sovereignty.[81] Apparently other members, including Belarus, had been putting pressure on Tashkent to either get on board with the CSTO or simply leave. In December 2011, Belarusian President Alyaksandr Lukashenka even publicly suggested that Uzbekistan should accept changes in the CSTO or simply leave the organization altogether (a statement apparently made at the request of the Kremlin).[82] With Uzbekistan's membership in abeyance, the CSTO agreed that Russia should have the power to veto the creation of new military bases by non–CSTO states within the countries of the alliance—a step designed to prevent a repeat of the immediate post–9/11 situation, when the United States was able to open facilities in Uzbekistan and Kyrgyzstan.

A EURASIAN CONVERGENCE ZONE?

While initiatives in the economic and security realm seem to suggest that cooperation is continuing apace in the post–Soviet world, some are not so sure. There was some discussion a few years back inside the Beltway that what would emerge in the post–Soviet space would be several subregions, with connections between the CIS states diminishing in scope and importance despite Moscow's best efforts to establish a political-military pact that would serve as a counterweight to NATO and the EU. As we argued at the time, the facts didn't seem to suggest anything of the sort.[83] An assessment of recent trade patterns, in fact, shows that little has changed over the past 20 years in terms of each country's leading export and import partner other than the rapid rise of China as a partner in the region (particularly in Central Asia). Rather than the emergence of subregions, with webs of communication and exchange within them, what is emerging is a rim-hub system of microregions connecting with Moscow as a regional hub. Russia-based trade accounts for more than a quarter of a country's trade (on average) among the CIS, while Russia is the leading source of imports in all CIS countries but two (Turkmenistan and Georgia), making Russia the most significant trade partner to almost all CIS countries. While smaller regions, such as Central Asia and the Caucasus, engage in commercial exchange and cultural interaction, this takes place in the shadow of Russian commercial and cultural influence.

The question then becomes one of the future trajectory of Eurasia and the possibility that the region may yet still break down into several subregions. Now more than 15 years into the post–Soviet period, there is little evidence that this is occurring or will occur in the future. The Baltic region is the only one that, for numerous reasons, immediately drifted back toward Europe, of which it has always been a part to a greater or lesser degree. The same is not true for the rest of Eurasia, which has either been tied to Russia for much of history (Belarus, Ukraine, Moldova, and the Caucasus) or not tied to any world region until the modern era (Central Asia). If one were to look for trends that might signal such a change of trajectory, the first thing one would look for would be greater security cooperation with a nation outside Eurasia. The Shanghai Cooperation Organization (SCO) is the only organization that currently even comes close to playing such a role, and its purpose is more to bring China into the regional security dialogue *with* Russia and Central Asia rather than to displace Russia from involvement in the region.

The second indicator of a trend toward Eurasian disintegration would be greater economic integration and reliance upon an outside actor. Turkey and again China are the two that appear most prominently. Both have become important trading partners of CIS states over the past decade, particularly for Georgia, Azerbaijan, and Kazakhstan. But in neither case are we seeing greater economic cooperation with an outside actor at the expense of existing ties within the CIS. Russia itself is increasing its ties with Turkey. In the aftermath of the Russo-Georgian War, Russia has begun to place a newfound emphasis on economic cooperation with Turkey, as will be discussed in Chapter 8. The outside international actor with the greatest

MAP 5.1
The Possible Geopolitical Map of the World by 2025

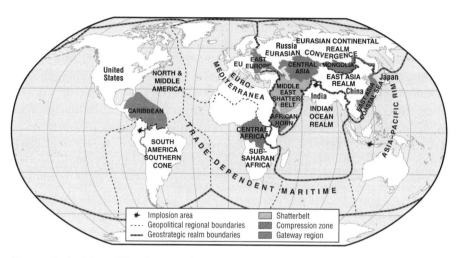

Source: Saul Cohen, "The Eurasian Convergence Zone: Gateway or Shatterbelt?" *Eurasian Geography & Economics* 46, 1 (2005), 1–22.

potential to shape the course of future events in the region is, of course, the United States. Cohen has lamented this fact, arguing that the penetration of the region "represents a serious threat to the stability of the world geopolitical system."[84] He is correct in highlighting the importance of this region, an arena "where five of the world's major geopolitical power centers—Maritime Europe, Russia, China, India, and Japan—converge . . ." Cohen also offers the useful conceptual frame of "shatterbelts" and "convergence zones" to view Eurasia and pinpoints the fault lines along which Eurasia would fracture if such a scenario were ever to occur. Cohen provides no real evidence, however, suggesting that such a scenario is likely or what factors would contribute to it. Indeed, U.S. involvement, including basing and joint military exercises, have significance, but they will do little to alter the trajectory along which Eurasia is evolving, for if the U.S. experience in Iraq and Afghanistan has taught us anything, it will be that we should be cautious about extending our reach and commitments into the region beyond their current levels. Unless the Obama administration changed its plan for a full withdrawal from Afghanistan by 2014, then we are likely to see a Russocentric, well-integrated Eurasia for the foreseeable future.

So, despite the predictions that the collapse of the Soviet Union would lead to the emergence of very distinct regions—a Central Asia tied to Turkey and

China, a Caucasus connected to Southern Europe, and a western periphery integrated into Europe—a Russian-led Eurasia still exists as a distinct entity in the early 21st century. Just as Mexico laments that it is "so far from God, so close to the United States," it is quite understandable that many of Russia's neighbors wish they could have a much greater degree of separation from Moscow, especially those forcibly incorporated into the Soviet Union after varying experiences of independence between the world wars.

Rather than witnessing the fragmentation of relations among the former Soviet states, what we are seeing is a surprising persistence of such linkages and the emergence of two new important players: China and Turkey. In other words, it is not the United States or Western Europe moving into the region to displace Russia but two other countries that also enjoy renewed friendly relations with Moscow. But barring fantasies about the complete disintegration of Russia as a state, Russia will continue to be a major factor in their deliberations. Contrary to predictions about the "end of Eurasia," a distinct global region will continue to exist for the foreseeable future between the European Union in one direction and a Chinese-dominated East Asia in the other, especially in terms of business.

THE EURASIAN UNION: USSR LITE?

In his last major address as Russia's prime minister before retaking the presidency, Vladimir Putin outlined five priorities for his third presidential term. His fifth task is to boost cooperation across the Eurasian space, enhancing Russia's global position by having it lead a new effort toward integrating the states of the former Soviet Union. Speaking before the Duma in April 2012, Putin said, "Creation of a common economic space is the most important event in post–Soviet space since the collapse of the Soviet Union." His vision was first announced the preceding fall, when he raised the idea of a Eurasian Union in an article in *Izvestiya*. As he explained, the Eurasian Union is to be an EU-like association among the post–Soviet states that would facilitate deeper economic integration among members and eventually pave the way for political integration. As an EU-like institution, the Eurasian Union would begin by working to lower trade barriers and harmonize regulations and currency policies. At later stages, political integration would be attempted. While it is modeled directly on the European Union, it is not designed to be competitor of the EU but rather a partner. As Putin explained, a Eurasian Union would be a natural partner for the EU and could eventually work with Brussels to ultimately create a joint economic space stretching from the Atlantic to the Pacific.[85]

Russia is already in a customs union with Kazakhstan and Belarus and is in the Eurasian Economic Community (EurAsEC), which includes Kyrgyzstan and

Tajikistan as well (with Belarus, Moldova, and Armenia as observers). These institutions, Putin suggests, could be used as the building blocks for constructing a closer political union between Russia and its neighbors. Russia has long sought to bring Ukraine into the common economic space, and Russia's entry into the World Trade Organization may help to remove some of the barriers that impeded Ukraine's participation. In addition, at the recent summit meeting of the Eurasian Economic Community in Moscow, the countries that make up the customs union, as well as the other Central Asian states that are members, committed to completing work on a proposed Eurasian Union treaty by 2015.

Throughout his time as president and prime minister, Putin has had a clear "Eurasian vision," seeing Russia as the metropolitan center of the region. With the eastward expansion of Euro-Atlantic institutions sputtering to a close and with China still primarily focused on South and East Asia, Moscow feels it has the window to begin consolidating a new Eurasia. Rather than have the territory of the former Soviet Union effectively "partitioned" into European and Asian "spheres of influence," Russia instead can reemerge as a leading global power by creating a new bloc of states that will balance the European Union in the West and a Chinese-led Asia in the East.

These aspirations, however, have always caused concern. Is Putin, who famously described the collapse of the Soviet Union as a geopolitical catastrophe, trying to put the USSR back together again? Putin himself declared in his Duma speech that the post–Soviet period is over. Given the rising demands of an increasingly restive Russian middle class, Putin has no desire to once again drain resources away trying to maintain a single, unified state. There is little interest in paying for education and health care expenses for Central Asians or Caucasians.

But Putin would like to see more of the old Soviet (and imperial-era) linkages restored, with trade, resources, and labor flowing between Russia and its neighbors. This would keep Moscow as the economic center of the area rather than seeing a Central Asia more tightly connected to South Asia and the western parts of the old Soviet Union pulled even more into the European orbit. A Russian-led regional economic order keeps the ruble as the regional currency and Russian as the de facto business language of the area, and it allows for more horizontal and vertical integration, especially between Russian, Kazakhstani, and Ukrainian firms.

There are sound economic and political reasons for deeper integration across the post–Soviet space, just as there are in other regions of the world, where organizations such as the EU, NAFTA, and ASEAN work to reduce barriers to trade and develop more prosperous societies. Why should the CIS remain on the sidelines? Relative isolation from global markets is responsible in no small part for the region's persistent underdevelopment.[86] Regional integration could help strengthen the weaker economies of the Union, in Central Asia in particular. For one, there is a pressing need to tackle the impediments to continental trade, including poor infrastructure, protectionism, and slow border crossings.[87] The Union will also allow member states to concentrate on areas in which they have comparative advantage, a move that would greatly reduce the costs of production (and something that is sorely needed, given the Soviet Union's heavy reliance upon economic specialization). The most significant benefit would be the creation of a huge single market with fewer barriers to the movement of goods and people. That would make it easier for migrant workers from Central Asia to move back and forth to Russia for work and to repatriate their earnings legally.[88]

But Russia-centered integration comes with a price. For one, by reorienting members' economies to focus on intra-union trade, a Eurasian Union would simultaneously dismantle barriers between members while erecting new barriers between member states and the outside world. It has not gone without comment that indeed this might be one of Moscow's goals, as it could limit the reach of foreign powers, whether of China in Central Asia or the EU in Ukraine.[89] But a Eurasian Union need not be designed in such a way. Central Asia holds the promise of developing into a transit region for overland continental transport: east–west from China to Europe and north–south from Russia to India. If the Eurasian Union can do what Putin promises—integrate the CIS *and* act as a bridge between Europe and Asia (which is clearly in Russia's economic interest)—then Eurasian economic cooperation holds the promise of developing into a chief driver of peace and prosperity on the Eurasian continent.[90] This, however, raises the question as to whether Russia can "pursue the functions of the Soviet Union—stability and integration within the Eurasian space—without adopting a neo-imperial policy?"[91] U.S. Secretary of State Hillary Clinton, in December 2012, expressed her concern that the Eurasian Union project is an effort to "re-Sovietize" Eurasia and committed the U.S. government to "figure out effective ways to slow down or prevent it." [92]

As Jeffrey Mankoff has argued, worries about some sort of "USSR lite" are probably overblown, and while the United States has reason to be concerned, it should withhold judgment for now. The best course of action at this point is to wait until Putin's intentions for the Eurasian Union and his other ambitions for the region become clearer, particularly with regard to the balance between economic, political, and security objectives and the extent to which Moscow pressures its neighbors into joining.[93] As he also rightly points out, it is more than just a little hypocritical for Washington to support regional integration in other parts of the world while opposing it in Eurasia. Of course, the United States has a legitimate and genuine interest in all post-Soviet states developing into stable and secure societies. As the United States draws down its forces and eventually withdraws from Afghanistan, it will be less ably positioned to influence the region and perhaps less interested in doing so as well. Nevertheless, it is in no one's interest for the region to break down into corruption and lawlessness, which would only fuel the already serious threats brought on by the drug trade and the rise of Islamist groups. Though Washington may fear a Moscow-led peace in the region, that is far better than a power vacuum.

EURASKEPTICISM

Just what kind of union will eventually emerge is unclear, however, and not all states in the region are optimistic about the prospects of Eurasian integration. Many Eurasian states are interested in closer economic relations with Russia and would be interested in the benefits Russia is prepared to offer—among them access to lower-cost energy and the ability to "export" their surplus labor force to Russia (both to decrease tension at home and to benefit from a steady stream of remittances). But Russia's neighbors are not so anxious to give up their sovereignty. While almost all post–Soviet states find the economic advantages of integration attractive, Russia's neighbors do not like compromising foreign-policy autonomy that increased dependence on Moscow could mean (indeed, in his *Izvestiya* article, Putin referred to the post–Soviet states as being in Moscow's "sphere of influence"[94]).

At first glance, the Eurasian Union appears to be an attempt to recreate the Soviet Union and seems to reflect Moscow's postimperial mindset, one that continues to see the newly independent states of Eurasia as within the Kremlin's sphere of influence rather than as sovereign nations free to make their own decisions about their relations with the outside world. While Moscow does promote regional integration, it appears to many as though it is doing so in an attempt to keep its new satellites within its orbit, strengthening the Kremlin's control and constraining the autonomy of its new subjects.

Kazakhstan, whose president Nursultan Nazarbayev first raised the idea of creating a "new Union based on the principle of confederation" back in 1992,[95] is probably the biggest supporter of the Eurasian Union project. The idea has evinced only a lukewarm response among the other CIS states. Belarus, despite its early enthusiasm for economic integration with Russia dating back to the 1990s, has raised concerns about how the Union might impinge upon domestic sovereignty. While president Alexander Lukashenko may continue to depend on Russia, that has not dimmed his enthusiasm for pushing for decision-making structures within any proposed Eurasian Union that would firmly defend national sovereignty (and he and other hesitant Eurasian leaders have plenty of ammunition provided by the Euroskeptics in the neighboring EU). At a 2012 summit, Lukashenko expressed his opposition to any Union-level decision making that could impose itself on the member states; decisions taken by any Eurasian Union ought to be ratified by the national parliaments, and national governments should have the ability to opt out of Union decisions.

Lukashenko's version of Euraskepticism is quietly shared by other CIS members. Kyrgyzstan and Tajikistan are likely to join, given Russia's importance as a market for their exports and source of investment. The jury is still out on Armenia, for although it lacks a border with other likely members, it is an ally of Moscow and has historically sought to stay on good terms with the Kremlin. These states may be prepared to make some concessions to Russia but not to sign away their hard-won independence.

Given Uzbekistan's position regarding other regional institutions, it is unlikely to join in the short term, and the same is probably true for Turkmenistan, which is seeking to limit its dependence on Russia. And then there is Ukraine. Kyiv rejected Moscow's invitation to join the Eurasian Union, arguing that it would block deeper integration with Europe—a process practically the entire Ukrainian political class believes should take priority over Russian-led integration projects.[96] But Putin is not one to take "no" for an answer. In his October 2011 *Izvestiya* article, he dismissed Ukraine's protestations that such a move would conflict with Kyiv's aspirations to eventually join the European Union. The EU is energetically pursuing deeper integration with Ukraine, seeking to entice Kyiv into a Deep and Comprehensive Free Trade Agreement (DCFTA) that would facilitate access to the European market. In an attempt to preempt the EU–Ukraine DCFTA, Moscow has repeatedly pressured Ukraine into joining the customs union and even engaged in retaliatory measures, including threats to take over Ukraine's oil and gas pipeline network as compensation for Kyiv's debts to Gazprom.[97] While declining membership in the Customs Union, it has indicated a willingness to accommodate Russia in strengthening its presence in the Ukrainian economy, where Moscow seeks greater involvement in Ukraine's energy infrastructure, probably hoping in exchange to get better prices for Russia's natural gas supplies.[98] Kyiv also renewed Moscow's lease on Crimean naval bases for its Black Sea Fleet.

Russia, for its part, does not want to become the Eurasian equivalent of Germany—the regional checkbook that underwrites the integration process and in turn pays the bills for the smaller states. Russia is also no longer willing to place its economic security in the hands of its Eurasian neighbors. If, during the 1990s, for instance, Ukraine retained a great deal of influence over Russia because of its geographic position as a critical transit country for Russian energy exports to reach Europe, Russia today has invested a great deal to create new, direct transit routes under the Baltic and Black Seas (Nord Stream, Blue Stream, and South Stream) to reduce that dependence. Indeed, part of the motivation for Yanukovych to sign his gas agreement with Russia in 2010 was "to forestall Russia's attempts to move away from using Ukraine as a prime transit route to Europe—which would mean, in the long term, a loss of income for Ukraine."[99]

PUTIN'S EURASIAN DREAM

Just as the Eurasian idea of the early 20th century raised concerns among Russians and outsiders alike, the same is true of Putin's Eurasian dream today. In the economic realm, Russia has expressed its continued interest in creating a single economic zone so that Russian capital and goods can move more efficiently across borders. While a Eurasian Union would facilitate the region's interaction with the world marketplace, it will also tie its member states more closely to Moscow's economic prowess. After all, this is no EU. Russia dominates the Eurasian landmass both economically and demographically. Russia's population of 140 million dwarfs that of the next-largest post–Soviet state, Ukraine, and it is still open to question whether or not its 46 million citizens will even join the Union. Additionally, Russia's GDP is approximately $1.4 trillion, more than 12 times that of Ukraine or Kazakhstan.[100] And while the EU emerged gradually over half a century as the result of policy initiatives launched by democratically elected governments, the Eurasian Union is very much Putin's brainchild, and he seeks to have the union in place by 2015.

Russia has no objection to other Eurasian states developing supplemental political and economic ties to other states, as long as Russian vital interests are respected. Within limits, Putin is attempting to create a Eurasian economic and political zone in which Moscow sets the overall agenda.

Assessing the political ramifications of the Eurasian Union project, Azamat Seimov points out, "The realization of the idea of Eurasian Union is the centerpiece of Putin's master plan to unite the efforts of the former Soviet republics to strengthen the Russian position in the geopolitical competition with the U.S., EU and China." Furthermore, Seimov suggests that the 2015 deadline for establishing the Union may be based upon Moscow's calculation that by that time, Washington will have withdrawn from Afghanistan and will be ready to turn its attention to Eurasia. He also speculates that by 2015, "the U.S. will have the ballistic missile defense sites ready for deployment in Central Europe."[101] If he is right, then Putin seems interested in presenting the world with a fait accompli: While Europe is consumed by its own economic troubles, while the United States remains bogged down in the Middle East, and while China focuses on its domestic transition, Russia will move ahead with setting the Eurasian Union in motion. Putin has done the easy part: He has signaled his intent to create a Eurasian

Union. Bringing it to fruition, however, may prove to be a far harder challenge than he expected. But it signals that the Eurasian vector has returned as a major component of post–Soviet Russian foreign policy.

NOTES

1. Igor Ivanov, *The New Russian Diplomacy* (Washington, DC: Brookings Institution Press, 2002), 84.

2. Paul Reynolds, "New Russian world order: the five principles," *BBC News,* September 1, 2008, at http://news.bbc.co.uk/2/hi/europe/7591610.stm.

3. See, for instance, the census data, particularly Table 6, of the 1897 Imperial census. *Pervaia Vseobshchaia Perepis' Naseleniia Rossiiskoi Imperii 1897 g.,* ed. N. A. Troitskii (St. Petersburg, 1905). A copy of the relevant tables can be found at http://demoscope.ru/weekly/ssp/rus_lan_97.php.

4. Nicholas V. Riasanovsky, *A History of Russia,* Fourth Edition (New York: Oxford University Press, 1963, 1984), 394–398.

5. Quoted in Victor S. Mamatey, *Soviet Russian Imperialism* (New York: Van Nostrand Reinhold Company, 1964), 117.

6. Quoted in Mamatey, 29.

7. Comments to the First All-Russia Congress of the Navy, November 22, 1917, quoted in Ariel Cohen, *Russian Imperialism: Development and Crisis* (Westport, CT: Praeger Publishers, 1996, 1998), 71.

8. For instance, the 1922 Treaty between the Russian Soviet Republic and Germany contained a supplement that applied its provisions to the Soviet republics that were allied with Russia, and, with the exception of the Soviet Ukrainian Republic, designated the Russian ambassador in Berlin as their representative. Cf. the relevant texts in "The Russo-German Treaty," *The American Journal of International Law* 20, no. 3 (July 1926): 120–121.

9. Mamatey, 30.

10. Quoted in Moshe Lewin, *Lenin's Last Struggle* (Ann Arbor: University of Michigan, 2005), 148.

11. See, for instance, George Liber, "Korenizatsiia: restructuring Soviet nationalities policy in the 1920s," *Ethnic and Racial Studies* 14, no. 1 (January 1991): 15–23.

12. Quoted in Grey Hodnett, "The Debate over Soviet Federalism," *Soviet Studies* 18, no. 4 (April 1967): 460.

13. Ibid, 461.

14. Quoted in Karl Meyer, *The Dust of Empires: The Race for Mastery in the Asian Heartland* (New York: Century Books, 2003, 2004), 48.

15. John B. Dunlop, *The Rise of Russia and the Fall of the Soviet Empire* (Princeton, NJ: Princeton University Press, 1993), 72–75.

16. V. Stanley Vardys and Judith Sedaitis, *Lithuania: The Rebel Nation* (Boulder, CO: Westview Press, 1997), 143.

17. Aleksandr I. Solzhenitsyn, *Rebuilding Russia*, trans. Alexis Klimoff (New York: Farrar Straus Giroux, 1991).

18. Charles Halperin, "George Vernadsky, Eurasianism, the Mongols, and Russia," *Slavic Review* 41, no. 3 (Autumn, 1982): 490–92.

19. Ibid., 487, 490–92.

20. I. Isaev, 'Evraziistvom: mif ili traditsiya?' *Kommunist* (1991), 12, 107.

21. Sergei Stankevich, "Derzhava v poiskakh sebya," *Nezavisimaya Gazeta* (March 28, 1992), 4.

22. Sergei Goncharov, 'Osobye interesy Rossii,' *Izvestiya* (February 25, 1992), 6.

23. A. Bogaturov, "The Eurasian Support of World Stability," *International Affairs* (Moscow), February 1993, 41.

24. Nikolas K. Gvosdev, "The New Party Card? Orthodoxy and the Search for Post-Soviet Russian Identity," *Problems of Post-Communism* 47, no. 6 (November/December 2000): 29–38.

25. In 2008, Ukrainian foreign minister Volodymyr Ohryzko reiterated that while Ukraine might take part in CIS projects, it was not a member of the organization. "Ukraine to analyze expediency of taking part in CIS projects," *UNIAN*, August 19, 2008, at http://www.unian.info/news/268085-ukraine-to-analyze-expediency-of-taking-part-in-cis-projects.html.

26. Ivanov, 83.

27. Bruce Pannier, "Russia Facing Resistance With Allies on CIS's Southern Flank," *Radio Free Europe/Radio Liberty*, October 9, 2009, at http://www.rferl.org/content/Russia_Facing_Resistance_With_Allies_On_CISs_Southern_Flank/1847880.html.

28. "Russia questions further existence of the CIS post-soviet organization," *InfoNIAC.com*, March 19, 2007, at http://www.infoniac.com/news/russia-nato.html.

29. Andrei Tsygankov, "Russia and the CIS in 2011: Uncertain Economic Recovery," *Asian Survey* 52, no. 1 (2012): 48.

30. Dmitry B. Ryurikov, "Russia and the United States in the Former Soviet Union: Managing Rivalry or Business as Usual?" *Enduring Rivalry: American and Russian Perspectives on the Former Soviet Space*, ed. Paul J. Saunders (Washington, DC: Center for the National Interest, 2011), 39.

31. Christopher Marsh, "Realigning Lithuanian Foreign Relations," *Journal of Baltic Studies* 29, mo. 2 (Summer 1998): 149–64.

32. Ryurikov, 41.

33. Alexander Cooley, "U.S. Bases and Democratization in Central Asia," *Orbis* 52, no. 1 (Winter 2008): 65–90.

34. For more on GUUAM, and particularly the U.S. role, cf. the State Department's report, FY 2007 U.S. Assistance to Eurasia, at http://www.state.gov/p/eur/rls/rpt/eur asiafy07/116185.htm, and Taras Kuzio, "GUAM as a Regional and Security Organisation," paper presented at the National Security and Foreign Policy of Azerbaijan conference, St. Michael's College, University of Toronto, March 28, 2008, at http://www.taraskuzio.net/conferences2_files/GUAM_Azerbaijan.pdf.

35. For more on the Rose Revolution and also on the U.S. role, see Lincoln Mitchell, *Uncertain Democracy: US Foreign Policy and Georgia's Rose Revolution* (Philadelphia: University of Pennsylvania Press, 2008).

36. See her essay, "Containing Russia," *Foreign Affairs* 86, no. 3 (May–June 2007): 69–82, at http://www.foreignaffairs.com/articles/62613/yuliya-tymoshenko/containing-russia.

37. Ryurikov, 44.

38. Ryurikov, 42.

39. The full text of President Bush's speech in Tbilisi on May 10, 2005, is available at BBC News at http://news.bbc.co.uk/2/hi/europe/4534267.stm.

40. *Rossiskaia Gazeta,* December 2, 2004. Quoted in Graeme P. Herd, "The 'Orange Revolution': Implications for Stability in the CIS," Conflict Studies Research Centre, January 2005, 3.

41. Nikolas K. Gvosdev, "Georgia on Our Mind," *National Review,* June 6, 2005, at http://www.nationalreview.com/articles/214613/georgia-our-mind/nikolas-k-gvosdev#.

42. Svante E. Cornell, *Azerbaijan Since Independence* (Armonk, NY: M.E. Sharpe, 2011), 312.

43. Ivanov, 90.

44. Vladimir Socor, "Warsaw Pact, CIS Peacekeeping, CSTO Operations: Moscow Develops 'Collective' Intervention Concept (Part Two)," *Eurasia Daily Monitor* 8, no. 170 (September 16, 2011), at http://www.jamestown.org/single/?no_cache=1&tx_ttnews%5Btt_news%5D=38414; Ivanov, 89.

45. Lyndon Allin and Matthew Rojansky, "Why Moldova Matters," *Carnegie Commentary,* August 31, 2010, at http://carnegieendowment.org/2010/08/31/why-moldova-matters/4782.

46. Tracey German, "Abkhazia and South Ossetia: Collision of Georgian and Russian Interests," *Russie.Nei.Visions,* 11 (June 2006), esp. 6–8.

47. Ivanov, 89; Socor, "Warsaw Pact," op. cit.

48. Inal Khashig, "Abkhaz Rush For Russian Passports," *Caucasus Reporting Service,* 135 (June 27, 2002), at http://iwpr.net/report-news/abkhaz-rush-russian-passports; see also German, 8, 9.

49. Wade Boese, "Russia, West Still Split Over Georgia, Moldova," *Arms Control Today,* January/February 2007, at http://www.armscontrol.org/print/2311.

50. Neil Arun, "Russia's reach unnerves Chechens," *BBC News,* January 16, 2008, at http://news.bbc.co.uk/2/hi/europe/7189024.stm. See also Jim Nichol, *Georgia's Pankisi Gorge: Russian Concerns and U.S. Interests,* Congressional Research Report, March 6, 2003.

51. Ghia Nodia, "What Is Georgia's Strategy In The North Caucasus?," *Radio Free Europe/Radio Liberty,* November 3, 2010, at http://www.rferl.org/content/What_Is_Georgias_Strategy_In_The_North_Caucasus/2208382.html.

52. Quoted in Valery Dutsev, "North Caucasian Activists See Relations with Georgia Under Threat," *North Caucasus Analysis* 13, no. 23 (November 27, 2012), at http://www.jamestown.org/single/?no_cache=1&tx_ttnews%5Btt_news%5D=40157.

53. Alexey K. Pushkov, "Russia's Foreign Policy and Its National Interests," *Enduring Rivalries,* 27; Ryurikov, 42–43.

54. German, 10.

55. Igor Torbakov, "Whither Saakashvili's reunification efforts in Georgia?," *Eurasianet.org*, May 17, 2004, archived at http://www.unhcr.org/refworld/topic,45a5199f2,4 5a519df2,46a484ef8,0,EURASIANET,,.html.

56. Nathan Hodge, "Did the U.S. Prep Georgia for War with Russia?" *Danger Room*, August 8, 2008, at http://www.wired.com/dangerroom/2008/08/did-us-military/.

57. "Georgia protests Russian military drills in North Caucasus," *RIA Novosti*, July 16, 2008, at http://en.rian.ru/world/20080716/114126411.html.

58. Helene Cooper and Thom Shanker, "After Mixed U.S. Messages, a War Erupted in Georgia," *New York Times*, August 13, 2008, at http://www.nytimes.com/2008/08/13/washington/13diplo.html?pagewanted=all.

59. For a full accounting of events leading up to the war, consult the report of the Independent International Fact-Finding Mission on the Conflict in Georgia, set up by the European Union under the direction of ambassador Heidi Tagliavini. The three volumes of their findings can be accessed at http://www.ceiig.ch/.

60. Mikhail Barabanov, "The August War between Russia and Georgia," *Moscow Defense Brief* 3, no. 13 (2008), at http://mdb.cast.ru/mdb/3-2008/item3/article1/.

61. "Ex-president Kuchma: Black Sea Fleet is in Crimea for ever," *Lenta.ru*, May 21, 2010, archived at http://rusnavy.com/news/othernavies/index.php?ELEMENT_ID=9626.

62. Judy Dempsey, "War in Georgia exposes NATO's fault lines," *New York Times*, September 3, 2008, at http://www.nytimes.com/2008/09/03/world/europe/03iht-letter.1.15864788.html?pagewanted=all.

63. "U.S. Official on Russia-Georgia WTO Talks," *Civil Georgia*, April 19, 2011, at http://www.civil.ge/eng/article.php?id=23360; John W. Miller and Giorgi Lomsadze, "EU Pushes Georgia to Let Russia Join WTO," *Wall Street Journal*, October 26, 2011, at http://online.wsj.com/article/SB10001424052970204644504576653302881291070.html.

64. Pavel Korduban, "Putin, Tymoshenko Agree on Gas and Deride Yushchenko, Saakashvili," *Eurasia Daily Monitor*, 6:220 (December 1, 2009), at http://www.jamestown.org/single/?no_cache=1&tx_ttnews%5Btt_news%5D=35785; Rachel Cooper, "Putin derides tie-chewing Georgian leader," *The Telegraph*, November 22, 2009, at http://www.telegraph.co.uk/expat/expatnews/6614585/Putin-derides-tie-chewing-Georgian-leader.html.

65. Joshua Kucera, "Ivanishvili On NATO, Russia And Georgia's Geopolitics," *Eurasianet.org*, October 3, 2012, at http://www.eurasianet.org/node/66000.

66. Dzutsev, op. cit.

67. "Georgian, Russian Diplomats Meet in Switzerland," *Civil Georgia*, December 15, 2012, at http://www.civil.ge/eng/article.php?id=25550; Giorgi Menabde, "Georgian Patriarch's Visit to Moscow: Is Georgia Leaning to the North?" *Eurasia Daily Monitor* 10, no. 5 (January 11, 2013), at http://www.jamestown.org/single/?no_cache=1&tx_ttnews%5Btt_news%5d=40294&tx_ttnews%5BbackPid%5d=7&cHash=2d9562f6e71801fd5d16bcf4f5936910.

68. Keith Crane, D. J. Peterson, and Olga Oliker, "Russian Investment in the Commonwealth of Independent States," *Eurasian Geography & Economics* 46, no. 6 (2005): 424.

69. Ibid.

70. Ibid., 411–17.

71. Ibid., 417.

72. Gregory Veeck, "China's Exports and Imports of Agricultural Products under the WTO," *Eurasian Geography & Economics* 49, no. 5 (2008): 569–585.

73. Sergei Markedonov, "Russia to stay the course in Eurasia," *Russia Beyond the Headlines*, March 13, 2012, at http://rbth.ru/articles/2012/03/13/russia_to_stay_the_course_in_eurasia_15053.html.

74. Matthew Stein, *Compendium of Central Asian Military and Security Activity* (Fort Leavenworth, KS: Foreign Military Studies Office, 2012), 4–5.

75. Ibid.

76. Andrei Tsygankov, "Russia and the CIS in 2011: Uncertain Economic Recovery," *Asian Survey* 52, no. 1 (2012): 50–1.

77. Stein, 2012, 4.

78. Ibid.

79. Alexander Cooley, "Global Insider: Fearing Russian Intentions, Uzbekistan Turns Back on CSTO," *World Politics Review* (July 11, 2012). Available at http://www.worldpoliticsreview.com/trend-lines/12151/global-insider-fearing-russian-intentions-uzbekistan-turns-back-on-csto.

80. Ibid.

81. Roger McDermott, "The Bear and the Bison Streamline the CSTO," *Eurasia Daily Monitor* 9, no. 132 (July 12, 2012), at http://www.jamestown.org/single/?no_cache=1&tx_ttnews%5Btt_news%5D=39619&tx_ttnews%5BbackPid%5D=587.

82. Ibid.

83. Christopher Marsh and Nikolas Gvosdev, "The Persistence of Eurasia," *Policy Innovations* (November 5, 2009). Available at http://www.policyinnovations.org/ideas/commentary/data/000152.

84. Saul Cohen, "The Eurasian Convergence Zone: Gateway or Shatterbelt?" *Eurasian Geography & Economics* 46, no. 1 (2005): 1–22.

85. Vladimir Putin, "Novyi integratsionnyi proekt dlya Evrazii—budushchee, kotoroe rozhdaetsya segodnya," *Izvestiya* (October 4, 2011), at http://izvestia.ru/news/502761.

86. Nicklas Norling and Niklas Swanström, "The Virtues and Potential Gains of Continental Trade in Eurasia," *Asian Survey* 47, no. 3 (2007): 351–73.

87. Ibid.

88. Jeffrey Mankoff, "What a Eurasian Union Means for Washington," *National Interest Online* (April 19, 2012). Available at http://nationalinterest.org/commentary/what-eurasian-union-means-washington-6821?page=show.

89. Ibid.

90. Norling and Swanström, 351–373.

91. David Kerr, "New Eurasianism: The Rise of Geopolitics in Russia's Foreign Policy," *Europe-Asia Studies* 47, no. 6 (Sep., 1995): 982.

92. Charles Clover, "Clinton vows to thwart new Soviet Union," *Financial Times*, December 6, 2012, at http://www.ft.com/cms/s/0/a5b15b14-3fcf-11e2-9f71-00144feabdc0.html#axzz2IUD80LJv.

93. Mankoff, op. cit.

94. Putin, "Novyi . . .," op. cit. at http://izvestia.ru/news/5027610.

95. John Dunlap, *The Rise of Russia and the Fall of the Soviet Empire* (Princeton, NJ: Princeton University Press, 1993), 293.

96. Mankoff, op. cit. .

97. Ibid.

98. Andrei Tsygankov, "Russia and the CIS in 2011: Uncertain Economic Recovery," *Asian Survey* 52, no. 1 (2012): 48.

99. Nikolas K. Gvosdev, "Courting Kiev," *National Interest,* February 15, 2010, at http://nationalinterest.org/article/courting-kiev-3375.

100. Mankoff, op. cit.

101. Azamat Seimov, "Will EurAsEC grow into Eurasian economic union?" *Registan. net,* April 4, 2012, at http://registan.net/index.php/2012/04/11/guest-post-will-eurasec-grow-into-eurasian-economic-union/.

CHAPTER 6

Eastern Europe

Comrades No More

"**E**astern Europe" has always been an amorphous concept.[1] Some trace its origins to the final division of the Roman Empire into western and eastern halves in 395 AD and the subsequent development of two distinctive forms of Christianity, one centered on the Pope in Rome and the other around the Patriarch of Constantinople. In a cultural sense, "Eastern Europe" has often been taken to designate those countries that were part of the Byzantine commonwealth of nations—including not only Russia and Ukraine but also Bulgaria, Serbia, Albania, Greece, and Romania.[2] In a geopolitical sense, the term has been used to designate "the lands between" that fell between the German and Russian spheres of influence.[3] The 19th-century political philosopher Nikolai Danilevsky (1822–1885) combined both definitions in his proposals for a Slavic Union that would unite Russia and much of what might be considered Eastern Europe, both on the basis of a shared Byzantine-Slavic heritage as well as geographic proximity.[4]

Given these fluctuating definitions, we define Eastern Europe to include the Baltic States, Poland, the Czech Republic and Slovakia, Hungary, Romania, Bulgaria, Albania, Greece, and the states of the former Yugoslavia. Most of these countries ended up under Soviet domination at the end of World War II and were collectively grouped together under the rubric of "the Soviet bloc," with the exception first of Greece, where the Communist attempt to take power was blocked, and then Yugoslavia and Albania, which, although they remained Communist, broke with Moscow.[5] These states were generally viewed as an intermediate zone between the Soviet Union itself and the rest of the outside world, separate countries in relationship to the USSR but not considered a part of Western Europe.[6] In the two decades since the collapse of the Soviet Union, the northern tier has generally been redefined as a part of Central Europe, while the southern set of countries is generally encompassed under the rubric of "the Balkans."[7]

Historically, Russia had particularly warm relations with the Balkans. The great medieval Slavic empires of Serbia and Bulgaria had enormous influence in shaping Russian culture by transmitting much of the civilization of the Greco-Roman world in a Slavonic idiom into Russia, particularly from the 13th to the 15th centuries. Also, many churchmen and scholars emigrated to the Russian lands, particularly after the Byzantine, Bulgarian, and Serbian empires fell under the control of the Ottoman Turks.[8] But the countries of northern Eastern Europe were traditional rivals of the Russian state. The Grand Duchy of Lithuania, especially from the 14th to the 16th century, was Moscow's main rival in its project of "gathering the Russian lands."[9] During this time, Lithuania was the largest country in Europe, controlling much of present-day Ukraine, Belarus, and Western Russia. The Lithuanian state checked both the "drive to the East" of the German princes and knightly orders as well as posing a formidable foe to the rising power of Muscovite Russia. After Lithuania's dynastic union with Poland (in 1386) and the unification of the two lands into the Polish-Lithuanian Commonwealth in 1569—in part due to Ivan the Terrible's attempts to take control of the Baltic coast—the Polish state became Russia's principal antagonist. At first, Poland had the upper hand, blunting Ivan's westward thrust and attempting, at the beginning of the 17th century, to install a Polish-backed pretender to the Russian throne, the so-called "False Dmitri." Polish forces ended up occupying Moscow and much of the country until they were expelled in 1612. In addition to the political rivalry between the two countries, a religious dimension was added, as the Polish kings believed they had a mission to spread Catholicism, while the Russian tsars saw themselves as defenders of Orthodoxy. In the popular mind, "the Poles" came to personify the main enemy of the emerging Russian state.[10] Eventually Russia began to erode the power of the Polish kingdom, in part by championing the rights of the Commonwealth's significant Orthodox minority. The Cossack rebellion in Ukraine that started in 1648 led to the breaking away of East Ukraine from Polish control and its union with Russia in 1654, marking the shift in the balance of power between Poland and Russia. Russia steadily expanded its territory westward until, in the three partitions of Poland (1772, 1793, and 1795), the Poland-Lithuanian Commonwealth ceased to exist as a separate state, with its territory divided among the Russian Empire, the Kingdom of Prussia, and the Hapsburg monarchy of Austria.[11]

After the defeat of Napoleon in 1815, Russian policy concentrated on preserving the imperial status quo in Eastern Europe, with the region effectively divided between Austria, Prussia (and, after 1870, a united Germany), and Russia. Two anti-Russian uprisings in Poland—in 1830 and in 1865—were put down. When the revolutions of 1848 threatened the Hapsburg monarchy, Emperor Nicholas I militarily intervened to crush the Hungarian revolution, turning the country back over to Austrian control in 1849, and "forever labeled the Russians in the minds of Hungarians as the oppressors and enemies of Hungarian freedom."[12] However, Russian support for the efforts of Greeks, Serbs, and Bulgarians to break free of a collapsing Ottoman Empire during the 19th century helped to build up pro-Russian sentiment in these countries.[13] Russophilia also increased among some of the Slavs of the Austrian Empire during this period, who saw the Russian Empire as sympathetic to their struggle for self-determination.[14]

The collapse of the Austrian, German, and Russian Empires after World War I created a collection of new states in the region. All were strongly anti–Communist in orientation, which placed them in direct opposition to the expansion of Soviet power and influence. A short-lived Soviet republic in Hungary was overthrown in 1919, and the war between a restored Poland and the Soviet state ended after the Miracle on the Vistula in 1920, when an invading Soviet army was defeated. French prime minister Georges Clemenceau called on the states of Eastern Europe to act as a *cordon sanitaire* to contain the Soviet Union, and Soviet diplomats routinely complained that countries like Poland, the Baltic States, Romania, Yugoslavia, and Czechoslovakia were working against Soviet interests.[15]

THE SECOND WORLD WAR AND THE CREATION OF THE SOVIET BLOC

By the mid-1930s, the Soviet Union's fear of encirclement—either at the hands of the Western Allies or by a rising Nazi Germany—made securing some sort of buffer zone in Eastern Europe imperative for Moscow's security. Adolf Hitler's willingness, in 1939, to concede some parts of Eastern Europe to Soviet control paved the way for the German-Soviet Non-Aggression Pact (sometimes referred to as the Molotov-Ribbentrop pact after the names of the two foreign ministers who conducted the negotiations) to be concluded, freeing up Germany for its war in the West. Per the secret annex of that treaty, the Soviet Union was permitted to occupy the Baltic States, eastern Poland, and parts of Romania.[16] However, Hitler's fateful decision in 1941 to reverse course and to invade the USSR, while it demonstrated the shortsightedness of trying to reach an agreement with Nazi Germany, nevertheless convinced the Soviet leadership that an even wider buffer zone between the Soviet Union and the West would be needed after the war. Its war aims from that point on always took that strategic objective into account.

In 1943, Joseph Stalin asked two leading Soviet diplomats, Ivan Maisky and former Foreign Minister Maxim Litvinov, to sketch out a postwar Soviet strategy. Maisky's report emphasized that the revision of Soviet borders accomplished as a result of the Nazi-Soviet Pact would have to remain intact and that the governments of many states in Europe, starting in Eastern Europe, should have significant Communist participation. Litvinov's report called for maximizing a "Soviet sphere of influence" that would include all the countries of Eastern Europe as well as Turkey and parts of Scandinavia.[17]

It was not immediately clear, however, how the Soviet Union would choose to exercise control over Eastern Europe. In 1944, the Baltic States were reabsorbed directly into the USSR, an incorporation the West never recognized but was unable to prevent from occurring in practice. However, in the treaties concluded between the USSR and Finland (1944, 1947, and 1948), a different paradigm was followed. Finland ceded some territory; accepted major limitations on its armed forces, as well as a prohibition on joining any anti-Soviet alliance; and agreed to pay reparations and to trade arrangements preferential to Soviet interests. In return, the Soviet Union agreed not to interfere in Finland's domestic affairs and "left her democratic institutions intact."[18] This state of affairs, in which a state was externally aligned with Soviet interests but in domestic arrangements remained non-Communist, was often described as "Finlandization." The Soviet Union also used this approach to normalize its relationship with Austria in 1955.

In most parts of Eastern Europe, however, the Soviets pressed for greater control. A Slovak partisan recalls meeting with a Soviet general who passed along instructions that the Communist Party should be "well organized" in every area liberated by Soviet forces, so that the Communists "would be able to run the political affairs of the section, either openly or behind the scenes."[19] In some countries, such as Poland or Hungary, the Soviet government had no confidence that democratic elections would bring to power governments that would be willing to cooperate with Moscow; in others, like Bulgaria or Czechoslovakia, there was an expectation that local Communists, with enough support from the Soviet military, could take power on their own. Throughout the region, the Soviets engaged in social engineering designed to bolster pro-Soviet forces and to eliminate or weaken anti-Soviet groups.[20] This occurred most dramatically with regard to the Baltic States, which were directly incorporated into the Soviet Union, and Poland, where much of the officer corps had been executed by the Soviet secret police at Katyn in 1940 and where the Soviet army let the Nazis crush a rebellion led by the Polish non-Communist Resistance in 1944.[21]

The Western Allies, at the February 1945 Yalta Conference, were prepared to recognize a "pre-eminent role" for the Soviet Union in Eastern Europe but insisted that non-Communists be part of coalition governments and that reasonably free elections be held in the region.[22] Initially, the Soviets focused on creating "popular fronts" between local Communists and non-Communist parties and did not insist on complete and total Sovietization. However, over time, Communist leaders, at the direction of Moscow, began to engage in what Hungarian Communist party secretary Matyas Rakosi referred to as "salami tactics": the gradual elimination of non-Communists from the governments of the region.[23] This process accelerated after the United States announced the creation of the Marshall Plan (aid for economic reconstruction of European countries) in 1947; Stalin and the Soviet leadership viewed this as a "large scale attempt by the United States to gain lasting and preeminent influence in Europe."[24]

By 1948, in every Eastern European country (and in the Soviet zone in Eastern Germany), the Communists were in full control, backed by Soviet military power. In addition, the Soviet Union backed the efforts of Greek Communists to seize control of that country. Former British Prime Minister Winston Churchill had ominously warned,

> From Stettin in the Baltic to Trieste in the Adriatic an iron curtain has descended across the Continent. Behind that line lie all the capitals of the ancient states of Central and Eastern Europe. Warsaw, Berlin, Prague, Vienna, Budapest, Belgrade, Bucharest and Sofia; all these famous cities and the populations around them lie in what I must call the Soviet sphere, and all are subject, in one form or another, not only to Soviet influence but to a very high and in some cases increasing measure of control from Moscow.[25]

The division of Europe into a Soviet (or Eastern) bloc and into the Western camp was now a fait accompli, and the countries of Eastern Europe were now rapidly Sovietized, acquiring the status of satellites—retaining the attributes of independent states but with both foreign and domestic policy being closely monitored and in some cases dictated by Moscow.[26]

The Soviet Union, however, suffered two setbacks. The Communists of Yugoslavia, led by Josip Broz Tito, had won power largely by their own efforts, not due to the prowess of the Soviet military (as did the Communists in Albania led by Enver Hoxha). In 1948, the Yugoslavs broke with the Soviets and refused to take Stalin's direction, carving out for themselves a precarious neutrality between East and West. In the following year, the Greek Communists, having lost the support of the Yugoslavs, suffered a final defeat on the battlefield, leaving Greece within the Western camp.

With the remaining Eastern European states, the Soviet Union took many steps to sever their traditional links to Western Europe and to bind them more closely to Moscow to prevent other states from following the Yugoslav path.[27] This began with major limitations on the ability of East Europeans to travel, culminating in such constructions as the Berlin Wall (erected in 1961) that inhibited freedom of movement. Each satellite state had its own bilateral treaty of friendship and mutual assistance with the Soviet Union, and in 1949 Stalin established the Council for Mutual Economic Assistance (CMEA), the Soviet response to the Marshall Plan.[28] The way in which trade links were reoriented toward the Soviet Union (and part of the reason that Yugoslavia broke away from the Soviet bloc) was by trying to create a closed-trade zone in which key raw materials and finished products from the satellites were redirected from world markets to the Soviet

Union, as well as through the use of nonmarket pricing and nonconvertible currencies (such as the Soviet transfer ruble) that made it difficult for the satellites to purchase goods from the West and instead created incentives to buy Soviet goods.[29] In turn, however, East European states became dependent on the Soviet Union for raw materials, especially energy.

In May 1955, in response to the creation of the North Atlantic Treaty Organization, the USSR and the rest of the Soviet Bloc signed a mutual defense treaty in Warsaw forming an integrated military alliance (usually referred to as the Warsaw Pact). Through this alliance, Soviet military forces could be dispatched to enable local Communist governments to retain power, and in many satellite countries, the Pact provided for the permanent stationing of Soviet troops. The creation of the Warsaw Pact enhanced Soviet prestige by creating a rival political-military-political bloc to the U.S.-led Western alliance, as well as showing that Soviet ideology could indeed be exported to other countries, enhancing the superpower status of the USSR.[30]

The Soviet bloc could only survive, however, because of Moscow's willingness to use force to hold it together when challenged. In 1953, riots in East Germany after the death of Stalin were put down by force. More serious challenges emerged in 1956 in Poland and Hungary after the Soviet leadership under Nikita Khrushchev announced a partial repudiation of Stalin and normalized relations with Yugoslavia. Skillful Communist leaders in Poland, led by Wladyslaw Gomulka, successfully navigated the minefield between appeasing the Soviets and responding to popular pressures for reform and were able to convince Moscow that a greater degree of freedom for Poland to run its own domestic affairs would not pose a threat to overall Soviet interests. In Hungary, however, the ousting of Communist party secretary Rakosi set in motion protests that local Communist leaders could not control. An initial Soviet military intervention in October 1956 ended with a cease-fire with the promise of reforms; but the new government under Imre Nagy crossed a number of Moscow's red lines, especially with its announcement that Hungary would withdraw from the Warsaw Pact. Khrushchev and his advisors, especially Defense Minister Georgy Zhukov (who as General Chief of Staff had lead the Red Army during World War II on its offensive to liberate Eastern Europe from German occupation), concluded that if Hungary broke away from the Soviet bloc, Moscow's entire position in Eastern Europe would collapse. On November 4, Soviet forces again intervened to remove Nagy from power and to create a new pro–Moscow government headed by party secretary Janos Kadar. While resistance continued for several weeks, the Soviet military succeeded in crushing the revolt, although some 200,000 Hungarians fled the country as refugees. Nagy himself was later executed as an example to other Eastern European leaders of their fate if they chose to defy the Soviet Union.[31]

The Soviet willingness to intervene in Eastern Europe was again tested in 1968, when reform Communists in Czechoslovakia led by Alexander Dubcek began implementing a series of reforms (the so-called Prague Spring) that caused concern in Moscow that Czechoslovakia might follow the Hungarian path. In August, Soviet forces entered Czechoslovakia to depose the government and to install a hardline Communist, Gustav Husak, to serve as leader. In November 1968, speaking to Polish workers, Soviet leader Leonid Brezhnev formally outlined the Soviet position: "The weakening of any of the links in the world system of socialism directly affects all the socialist countries, which cannot look indifferently upon this." Thus, other countries, especially the Soviet Union, had the right to intervene, "because Czechoslovakia's detachment from the socialist community, would have come into conflict with its own vital interests and would have been detrimental to the other socialist states."[32] This "Brezhnev doctrine" would be used, in 1979, to justify the Soviet intervention in Afghanistan, but it was primarily intended as a warning to other Eastern European Communist leaders that anything that threatened Soviet control of the region would be dealt with in summary fashion.

Brezhnev made it clear that the Soviet Union was not prepared to lose its bloc of client states in Eastern Europe, declaring, "For us, the results of the Second World War are inviolable, and we will defend them even at the cost of risking a new war."[33] After the invasion of Czechoslovakia, the Soviet Union focused on "normalization": not only to get the satellites to accept the inevitably of Soviet domination but also to convince West Europeans that the division of the continent was permanent (a process that will be discussed in greater detail in the next chapter). This culminated in the Helsinki Conference of 1975, which, in essence, ratified the status quo in Europe.

But trouble continued to simmer. In 1970, riots in Poland were deftly handled by the leadership, which again found a way to meet popular demands for change without provoking Soviet intervention (in part by using deadly force to disperse protestors), but the rise of the Solidarity trade union in 1980 created a new challenge to the system by threatening the Communist monopoly on power. In December 1981, in part to avoid triggering direct Soviet intervention, General Wojciech Jaruzelski created a military government, imposed martial law, and outlawed Solidarity.[34]

1989–1999: THE ATTEMPT TO PRESERVE EASTERN EUROPE

As Mikhail Gorbachev began to undertake his reforms in the USSR, many of the old, entrenched Communist leaders in Eastern Europe expressed opposition to his program. Gorbachev indicated that the satellite parties would have to do more to win popular support, secretly informing the party secretaries of the region in 1986 that he would not countenance further interventions like those the Soviet Union had undertaken in Hungary and Czechoslovakia to prop up their regimes.[35] In 1988, he abolished the special department within the Soviet Communist Party that had overseen the Communist parties of the Soviet bloc states and then announced that the East European parties would enjoy greater independence in how they ran their own affairs.[36] Gorbachev hoped that the satellites would pursue their own versions of his reforms; he believed that Eastern Europeans would voluntarily embrace a reformed version of Communism and maintain the integrity of the Soviet bloc.[37] Gorbachev also had strong economic motivations. While at the end of World War II, the Soviet bloc had generated some $14 billion in reparations and transfers to the Soviet Union (between 1945 and 1953), during the 1970s it was estimated that maintaining the Bloc was costing the Soviet Union some $4.63 billion on average per year in trade subsidies, mainly in the sale of energy at below-market rates, or 2% of the Soviet gross national product.[38]

Gorbachev attempted to engineer leadership transitions to replace entrenched figures throughout Eastern Europe. This included leaders such as Todor Zhivkov of Bulgaria (who had headed his country's Communist Party since 1954); Janos Kadar of Hungary (who had ruled since 1956); Nicolae Ceausescu of Romania (in power since 1965); and Erich Honecker of East Germany (a relative newcomer, ruling only since 1971). Gorbachev's hope and perhaps expectation was that East European versions of himself would come to power. However, his vision of a limited political opening was overtaken by events. In January 1989, the Polish government legalized the Solidarity trade union and promised partially free elections (which occurred in June), which brought a significant non–Communist presence into the government. In May, Hungary took the decision to dismantle its border fences, effectively opening the Iron Curtain.[39] By late August, East Germans began taking "picnics" along the newly opened Austrian border, crossing over to freedom in the West. When East Berlin caught on and prevented others from taking similar picnics, East German vacationers headed for Prague, where they made their way to the West German and American embassies and eventually to the West.

In October, as events began to accelerate, Soviet Foreign Ministry spokesman Gennady Gerasimov announced the Sinatra Doctrine—the states of Eastern Europe were free to "do it their way"—and Moscow would no longer intervene to prop up Communist regimes. Within weeks, the Berlin Wall was pulled down, followed quickly by student demonstrations in Prague in Wenceslas Square and culminating in the execution of Romanian Communist leader Nicolae Ceausescu on Christmas Day. By the end of the year, the Communist regimes of Eastern

Europe had fallen, and the winds of change were blowing east into the Soviet Union itself. As British Prime Minister Margaret Thatcher summarized the events, "What a fantastic year this has been for freedom! 1989 will be remembered for decades to come as the year when the people of half our continent began to throw off their chains."[40]

Initially, Gorbachev did not worry that these changes would doom the Soviet bloc. A Soviet Foreign Ministry analysis presented to him in February 1989 went so far as to claim that "It seems improbable that in the foreseeable future any of the allied countries will raise the question of leaving the Warsaw Pact."[41] The assumption was that these countries could be Finlandized, producing democratic regimes with full freedom to carry out domestic policies while coordinating their foreign policies to conform to Moscow's interests. Indeed, even as non-Communist governments came to power, particularly in Poland and Czechoslovakia, the fact that Germany had still not renounced claims to territory lost after World War II provided a rationale for a continuation of the Warsaw Pact—until Germany signed agreements (such as the 1990 Border Treaty with Poland) that accepted the postwar boundaries.[42] But Gorbachev had seriously "underestimated nationalistic tendencies" in Soviet-bloc countries and the strength of the desire to break out from Soviet control.[43] The Warsaw Pact was formally dissolved in 1991, and no Eastern European country permitted Soviet forces to continue to be stationed on its territory. Between 1992 and 1994, Russia withdrew all Soviet military formations from Poland, Hungary, Germany, and the Czech Republic.

If the Soviet bloc could not be saved, then Gorbachev's backup strategy, entrusted to Deputy Foreign Minister Yuli Kvitsinsky, was to preserve Eastern Europe as a zone of neutral states between NATO and the Soviet Union. As noted in the chapter on U.S.-Russia relations, Gorbachev believed that he had received informal guarantees that NATO would not expand eastward to take in new members. Gorbachev had told U.S. Secretary of State James Baker that "any extension of the zone of NATO would be unacceptable," and he also took notice of the position espoused by a number of the Eastern European dissidents who were now entering the new governments that the region should be demilitarized and function as a bridge between East and West.[44] To buttress this understanding, Kvitsinsky attempted to negotiate treaties to replace the Warsaw Pact in which Eastern European states pledged to remain neutral, but with no success.[45] There were also important economic linkages that Gorbachev hoped would keep Eastern Europe closely tied to Moscow. Nearly half of the region's industrial trade was within the Soviet bloc, and Eastern Europe depended on the USSR for cheap oil, natural gas, and other raw materials. In addition, much of the region's trade was conducted using the so-called "transfer ruble," which was not convertible into

Western currencies and could only be used in intrabloc trading.[46] Nor did Western Europe offer to open its own lucrative markets to the former Soviet-bloc states.

Had the Soviet Union remained intact, it might have continued to retain more economic influence, but its own disintegration helped to rupture important links with Eastern Europe, forcing them to adapt and to turn more to the West. The last meeting of CMEA in 1991 ended with a decision to disband the organization, especially since all countries had shifted to trade based on convertible currencies on the basis of market prices.[47]

Eastern Europe, however, interpreted demands for neutrality as a cloaked appeal for the retention of a Soviet (and then Russian) sphere of influence in the region. Moreover, the old Finlandization model itself seemed obsolete once the Soviet Union collapsed and both Finland and Austria eschewed their own nonaligned status and began the process of joining the European Union, with both countries joining in 1995.[48] In 1991, the leaders of Czechoslovakia, Poland, and Hungary, at their second summit meeting in Visegrad, Hungary (site of a 14th-century gathering of Kings Charles of Hungary, Casimir III of Poland, and John of Bohemia) agreed to form the Visegrad Group, with the intent to form a cooperative alliance to pursue integration with Europe and to join the NATO alliance.[49]

Initially, the Atlanticists who dominated the first Boris Yeltsin administration were optimistic that a post–Soviet Russia would be included in a pan–European security system and had high hopes that, with the dissolution of the Warsaw Pact, NATO might follow suit—or that Russia itself might be invited to join. Given the perception that Eastern Europe had also been a drain on the Soviet (and thus the Russian) economy, the loss of the satellites was initially seen as a net benefit, freeing up more Russian resources for sale on world markets to better-paying customers. These views were not shared by all within the Russian foreign policy establishment, but they were, at the beginning, shared by Yeltsin himself. On a visit to Poland in August 1993, he publicly waived any Russian objections to the Visegrad countries' attempts to secure membership in European institutions.[50] But as it became clear that Russia was not going to be quickly brought into Western organizations, Yeltsin's government resumed Kvitsinsky's efforts to push for neutral status for Eastern Europe.

After Yeltsin dissolved the Supreme Soviet in September 1993, he reversed his earlier position on NATO expansion, in part to cater to the armed forces whose loyalty he needed to secure in the face of the attempted rebellion by his vice president Aleksandr Rutskoi and members of the former parliament. The Russian military urged Yeltsin to do more to secure a defined Russian sphere of influence in the region.[51] In October, he sent a letter to U.S. President Bill Clinton arguing that expansion of NATO could only take place if Russia simultaneously became a member along with the states of Eastern Europe.[52] In December 1993, when Yeltsin visited NATO headquarters in Brussels, he formally reversed his earlier position taken in Poland and now insisted that the alliance not take in new members from Eastern Europe. In February 1994, he made it clear that "Russia is opposed to the expansion of NATO."[53] But Russian protests were ineffective. At a meeting of NATO defense ministers in Travemunde in October 1993, NATO Secretary General Manfred Woerner argued that the alliance needed to be able to offer countries seeking membership practical opportunities for cooperation. This led to the alliance announcing the Partnership for Peace (PfP) in January 1994 as a way for Eastern European states to take part in a formal, structured program of cooperation with NATO that could lay the path for eventual membership.[54] Russian efforts to stop this program or to secure a special status for Russia within NATO were rebuffed. Part of what drove the establishment of this program was the concern about the possibility for revanchism in Russia, especially after the December 1993 elections had seen major gains for the Communists and nationalist forces. The United States, in particular, saw the eventual incorporation of Eastern Europe into Euro-Atlantic institutions as a way to curb any resurgent Russian imperial impulses.[55] This also helped to drive the attitude of the EU toward further expansion. At the 1993 Copenhagen EU summit, in response to an appeal from the Visegrad countries, the Union agreed to offer membership to any Central or Eastern European state that met the criteria for admission.

At the 1997 Madrid summit, NATO formally invited Poland, the Czech Republic, and Hungary to join the alliance; these three states entered NATO as full members in 1999. This represented a clear defeat for Yeltsin's efforts to prevent the expansion of the Western alliance into the former Soviet bloc. In addition, at the 1997 Luxembourg summit of the European Union, the Commission recommended that Poland, the Czech Republic, Hungary, and Slovenia be invited to start the accession process (along with Cyprus).

The Russian Federation was in no position to exert pressure on Eastern Europeans to dissuade them from pursuing closer ties with the West, and in fact Russia needed these states. During the time of the Soviet bloc, the USSR had constructed a series of energy pipelines that ran to and through Eastern Europe such as the Druzhba oil network (in the 1960s) and the Trans-Siberian gas line (1982–1984). Russia could not reach its best customers in Western Europe without the active support of its former satellite states. Given the collapse of the Russian economy during the 1990s, Moscow was even more dependent on energy export revenue and so had little leverage to bring to bear against former Soviet-bloc states seeking to join NATO. Energy cutoffs to punish Eastern Europeans would risk Russia's lucrative contracts further west.[56] While trying to halt NATO expansion to encompass former Warsaw Pact members, the Yeltsin administration also struggled to prevent the Baltic States from slipping out of a de facto Russian sphere of influence.

THE BALTICS AND BEYOND: NATO'S REACH EAST

Sinatra's song was heard loud and clear in the Baltics. If the states of Eastern Europe, which had joined the Soviet bloc against the will of their peoples following World War II, were allowed to "do it their way" and chart a new course in their domestic affairs and foreign policy, then why should Latvia, Lithuania, and Estonia be treated any differently? Like the states of Eastern Europe, Communist rule had been brought to them not by indigenous Communist revolutions but by the Red Army that had "liberated" them from German occupation. Even before East Germany, Poland, Hungary, and Czechoslovakia had broken free from Moscow's control, the Baltics were launching their own drives for independence. While it took different forms in each of the Baltic states—the singing revolution in Estonia, an initial focus on environmental issues in Latvia, and poetry reading and a rock march in Lithuania—all eventually came to focus on their illegal incorporation into the Soviet Union as part of the secret protocol of the Molotov-Ribbentrop Pact that granted Moscow control of the Baltic region.

Lithuanians, Latvians, and Estonians used the occasion of the 50th anniversary of the Molotov-Ribbentrop Pact on August 23, 1989, to demonstrate against this historic injustice. Forming a human chain from Tallinn through Riga to Vilnius, more than 2 million people stood hand in hand to form the Baltic Way. While the event brought international attention to the issue, the world's attention was still focused on events in Eastern Europe, where things were quickly coming to a head. Less than 2 weeks after the fall of the Berlin Wall in November 1989, Lithuania's Supreme Soviet amended the constitution, making Lithuanian the official language and legalizing the Lithuanian flag and national anthem. They failed, however, to declare the supremacy of Lithuanian law over Soviet law, incensing *Sajudis* members who had expected nothing short of a declaration of independence. The leadership of *Sajudis* then declared Lithuania's moral independence:

No political requirements of the situation can restrain the free will of Lithuania. Its will is its highest law. Only Lithuania can decide and execute its laws. Until this principle becomes legal norm, only those laws will be respected in Lithuania which do not restrain Lithuanian independence. Disobedience to laws which violate our independence may incur juridical responsibility but they do not transgress against morality.[57]

Sajudis then took advantage of Gorbachev's moves toward democratization and prepared to seize power through the ballot box. As discussed in Chapter 4, in February 1990, *Sajudis* won 80% of the contested seats in the elections to the Lithuanian Supreme Soviet, and with Landsbergis as chairman, the Lithuanian Supreme Council quickly declared Lithuania's independence a month later, becoming the first of the Baltic states to formally declare its independence from the Soviet Union. For his part, Gorbachev realized that if Lithuania were to leave the union, other Soviet republics would soon follow suit. In an effort to keep the union from disintegrating, Moscow initiated an economic embargo against Lithuania, which it later lifted after Vilnius agreed to suspend its declaration of independence. On January 13, 1991, taking advantage of the West's engagement in the Persian Gulf, Soviet paratroopers were dropped into Vilnius and tanks rolled the streets, resulting in the death of 14 people. The August coup that summer illustrated to the world the extent of the Soviet Union's decay and its vulnerability to recidivist forces. Given the changed environment, all three Baltic states began to receive recognition of their independence, including from the Soviet Union itself in September 1991.

Having secured their independence from the USSR, Tallinn, Riga, and Vilnius each sought to distance themselves from Moscow and to join the West. To leaders in the Baltic republics, "joining the West" meant, first and foremost, joining Western economic and security organizations, primarily the EU and NATO. The Baltic states quickly expressed their position and were welcomed by the West, but the process would be a rather long and arduous one. According to the 1993 Copenhagen Criteria, the requirement for membership include that the candidate country "has achieved stability of institutions guaranteeing democracy, the rule of law, human rights, respect for and protection of minorities," as well as "the existence of a functioning market economy." Obviously, "stability" of these institutions isn't something that can be achieved overnight, and when the Baltic states first announced their intention to join the EU, they had only just begun their political and economic reforms. Before they could join the EU, therefore, they had to develop democratic institutions and lay the foundation for a market economy, including selling off state-owned enterprises. Simultaneously, they would have to remove themselves from economic reliance upon the Soviet Union, and later Russia and the CIS, with which it was heavily economically integrated. Each state quickly entered into a Free Trade Agreement with the EU in 1993 and then entered into EU Association Agreements the following year. This provided the framework for cooperation and facilitated the reorientation of their economies, which was an immediate concern after achieving independence. The Baltic States also benefited from considerable assistance rendered from the Scandinavian countries, which were eager to help the Balts succeed in their transition, as a way to help stabilize the entire Baltic basin.

Russia was not happy with the attempt of the Baltic States to leave the post–Soviet group of states. Because one of the Copenhagen criteria for inclusion in the EU was the protection of ethnic minorities, Moscow repeatedly raised the question of the status of the Russian-speaking population in the Baltic States, particularly in Estonia and Latvia, which had denied automatic citizenship to migrants and their descendants who had entered after the two countries had been forcibly incorporated into the USSR. Throughout the 1990s, the Russian government insisted that Euro-Atlantic institutions needed to "take action to ensure that the human rights situation of Russian-speaking populations in Latvia and Estonia fully conforms to accepted European standards."[58] Border claims were also raised. However, the Baltic States made a concerted effort to meet these concerns to the satisfaction of Western countries, if not of Russia.[59] Finally, in 1998, formal membership negotiations began, with the Baltic states being admitted to the EU in May 2004 along with other East European states of Hungary, Poland, Slovakia, Slovenia, and the Czech Republic (as well as Malta and Cyprus).

While the Russian government never welcomed the NATO expansion, Moscow clearly hoped that, having accepted Poland, the Czech Republic, and Hungary, the alliance would call a halt to further growth. The Baltic states, as well as other East European states, were anxious not to be left out and potentially exposed to a resurgent Russia. While Hungary, Poland, and the Czech Republic had a sizeable lead in joining NATO, participating early on in the Partnership for Peace program, the Baltics were eager to join as well. Despite being denied admission to NATO in the first round, they continued lobbying for their cause. Some even raised the issue that they were like high-risk applicants for insurance: Those who need insurance most are denied coverage.[60] Once the Visegrad states joined in 1999, however, NATO left open the possibility of further expansion. In May 2000, the Baltic states, along with Albania, Bulgaria, Croatia, Macedonia, Romania, Slovakia, and Slovenia, formed the Vilnius Group to lobby for their inclusion into Euro-Atlantic institutions. Several of these countries had sided with NATO during the Kosovo operation the preceding year and had helped to block Russia as it tried to exert influence in the former Yugoslavia.

George W. Bush's arrival in the White House initially spurred fears that NATO expansion might stall, as the policy of democratic enlargement had been a particular initiative of the Clinton administration. Moreover, there were concerns that admission of more members would unnecessarily antagonize Russia. One commentator even suggested it could trigger a security dilemma, as the extension of defense guarantees to an area such as the Baltics presents significant challenges to operational planners.[61] Indeed, he is correct, since planners on both sides have to plan for potential operations in the region. As they calculate how to defend and defeat each other, they will inevitably alter the security environment in terms of the size and type of forces, how they are arrayed, lines of communication, and so forth. As they improve their relative position, they simultaneously deteriorate their opponent's position. However, on his first official trip to Europe in June 2001, Bush gave a major speech in Warsaw in which he stated that "all of Europe's new democracies," from the Baltics to the Black Sea, should have an equal chance of joining Western institutions, even going so far as suggesting that failure to do any less would be the moral equivalent of the Yalta and Munich conferences, in which Eastern Europe was handed over to the Soviets. After Bush met with Putin the next day in Slovenia, Putin said that he would not let NATO enlargement undermine the potential for United States–Russia relations.[62]

The following year NATO held its summit in Prague—the first summit in a former Warsaw Pact state—and Estonia, Latvia, and Lithuania, along with Slovenia, Slovakia, Bulgaria, and Romania, were invited to join the Atlantic alliance. Formal admission came in March 2004, which then extended NATO's Article 5 security guarantees to a former Soviet republic.

BALTIC [IN]SECURITY

When the Baltic republics began the process of NATO ascension, they were hardly in a position to secure their borders. While Lithuania spent slightly more than 2% of its GDP on defense, still a paltry number for a state developing a military from scratch, Latvia spent less than 1%. Estonia was right in the middle, with little more than 1%.[63] Each republic had an army approximately the size of a U.S. brigade: 3,500 in Estonia, 3,600 in Latvia, and 5,250 in Lithuania. While there were also border guards that could be called on for defense, in no case did they even match the size of the armed forces.[64] Even combined, these forces do not provide much of a deterrent to the Russian army of approximately 2 million across the border.[65]

If the Baltic armies were not up to the task of defending their territory, their air forces were practically nonexistent. While Lithuania had no combat aircraft at all, Estonia had a single air defense battalion attached to its army, and Latvia's air force comprised four small planes and seven helicopters. In addition to border defense, this was more immediately problematic from the standpoint of exercising control of their sovereign airspace. In 1998, the United States gave a foreign military financing credit of $5.8 million to Estonia to set up and equip an Air Sovereignty Operations Center to service all three states. Immediately upon joining NATO, the Baltic Air Policing initiative began. Under this program, four fighters are based in Lithuania (provided on a rotating basis from NATO members) to support the air sovereignty of Latvia, Estonia, and Lithuania against any incursions into their airspace.

Despite these advances, the Baltics today remain incapable of successfully defending themselves against the one potential external threat: Russia. Since joining NATO, no Baltic country has tried to significantly increase the size of its standing army, with forces today remaining approximately where they were in the 1990s (with the slight exception of Lithuania, with a current force of 12,000). There have been significant structural changes, however, including dramatic shifts from conscription to all-volunteer forces. Estonia, which has kept its force level almost exactly where it was in the 1990s, has developed a huge reserve force of more than 200,000, with the defense minister stating that "it is possible to defeat an army, but not a nation."[66]

Of course, since joining NATO, the security of the Baltics is now guaranteed through Article 5 of the North Atlantic Treaty. The Baltic states are not security free riders, however, as they contribute to their own security and the security of the Baltic region as a whole, including sea lines of communication. Constrained by size and finances, there is of course no way that the Baltic states could build powerful armed forces that could deter foreign aggressors or match the contributions of the larger and richer members of the Alliance. Their contribution, rather, has come through the development of capabilities in specialized areas. Latvia, for instance, has been developing ordnance-disposal and minesweeping units. Estonia has also developed a minesweeping unit, while Lithuania has focused its efforts on a medical unit.[67]

The most critical specialized unit, however, is probably Estonia's development of a cyberarmy. Estonia has been at the forefront of cyberwarfare and defense, itself being the victim of a major cyberattack back in 2007. It is now becoming a model for how a country can defend itself against such attacks. At the center of the effort is a unit of computer scientists, programmers, and software engineers who comprise the Cyber Defense League, a volunteer force that, in the event of hostilities, would be mobilized and placed under a unified military command.[68] NATO has embraced Estonia's efforts in this area, establishing a cyberdefense center in Tallinn in 2012 to help train NATO forces as "cyberwarriors."

The issue that triggered the development of this cyberarmy was a 2007 cyberattack against Estonia, one of the world's most wired countries. The attack was traced back to Russia, and while no formal connection can be established to the Russian government, Estonia has concluded that it was conducted by "Russian government-inspired hackers" in retaliation for Tallinn's decision to move a Soviet-era statue from the center of the capital to a more modest location. The statue in question commemorated the Red Army's role in liberating the Soviet Union from German occupation, but to many of the local Russians in Estonia, it was seen as anti-Russian if not downright pro-Nazi.

Estonia's population is little more than 60% Estonian, with much of the remainder composed of ethnic Russians or Russian speakers, such as Poles, Ukrainians, Belarusians, or Jews whose first language is Russian and who lived in the country before the collapse of the USSR. The situation is similar in Latvia, where the Latvians comprise only slightly more than 55% of the total population. As mentioned above, these Russian speakers were not given automatic citizenship following the collapse of the Soviet Union (as compared to Lithuania, where their smaller minority of less than 20% was).

At the time of independence, nearly half of Latvia's population, two-fifths of Estonia's, and one-fifth of Lithuania's consisted of people whose first language was Russian. In the years following independence, they have had a difficult time assimilating into the post–Soviet societies. Some simply left, shifting the respective number of Latvians and Estonians up slightly from 52 to 56% and from 61 to 64%, respectively. By January 2001, only 113,764 individuals had acquired Estonian citizenship through naturalization, less than 30% of those who were not automatically granted Estonian citizenship in 1992.[69] This leaves almost 40% of Russian speakers stateless, while almost 20% took Russian citizenship instead.[70]

Moscow frequently and consistently speaks out on their behalf, often complaining that the Latvian and Estonian governments violate the human rights of these Russian speakers. Shortly after coming to power, Vladimir Putin raised the issue of making Russian an official language in the Baltic states.[71] While both Estonia and Latvia fund Russian-language schools, Russian speakers in both countries have embraced the idea of making Russian an official language. Latvia has gone the farthest, holding a national referendum on the issue in February of 2012. It failed miserably, with only around 25% of those who voted supporting the measure. In commenting on the referendum, Latvia's president called the vote "absurd."

Russia once again raised the issue of alleged violations of the Baltics' Russian-speaking communities with the UN in December 2012. During a round of talks on human rights in Brussels, Russia called on the EU to take steps to address human rights violations of the Russian-speaking population in the Baltic states, pointing to "the increasingly frequent manifestations of neo–Nazi sentiments, racial discriminations and xenophobia," in addition to "the excessive use of force in dispersing peaceful demonstrations."[72] In raising the issue, the Russian delegation accused the EU of using human rights issues as a means of foreign policy pressure on foreign governments and politicizing the issue of international human rights.

While human rights issues are a serious concern, the broader issue is with how the region's Russian speakers fit into the societies in which they live. While systematic discrimination is not condoned, unsanctioned forms of discrimination remain in daily life. In one recent case, two ethnic Russian soldiers in the Estonian Army alleged that they were forced to dig their own graves and were told "we will send you home in bodybags," and since they were armed, "it will look like defection."[73]

Tensions in Estonia and Latvia between Estonians and Latvians and their Russian-speaking neighbors can run high, and as the 2007 cyberattack illustrates, there is the potential for Russia to do more than just raise objections in Brussels. This has raised the idea of Russians in the Baltics as a "fifth column," a sleeper force of Russians that are loyal to Moscow, not to their country of residence. Some in Russia, unfortunately, promote this very idea. Anton Surikov, a well-respected researcher at Moscow's Russian Defense Research Institute, put the issue this way: "Your problem is that, when the Russian troops come in, instantly your society will divide between the two larger ethnic groups. Russians simply do not have anywhere to go other than to pick up a weapon and to fight against you."[74]

As conspiratorial as this sounds, there is evidence to suggest that there may be some truth to the idea. The fact is, some of the Russian speakers in the Baltics are former Soviet military or KGB personnel, and while some might not wish to return to active service for Moscow, there is always the chance that some might. As Clemens points out, even a small number of such people could agitate and mobilize other members of the Russian-speaking population, causing big trouble in these small nations.[75] Indeed, the process may already be underway. Clemens suggests that it may be exactly these sorts of people who are contributing to organized crime and corruption in the Baltics, including actions that resulted in serious bank failures. Again, as outlandish as this may sound, Russian criminals have confessed to fomenting ethnic tension in the Baltics, and Tallinn and Riga believe that Moscow is directing such operations.[76]

There are currently 7 million Russians in NATO. Actually, there is a total of around 7 million Russian *speakers* residing in NATO member states, either with or without local citizenship. That means there are more citizens in the EU who speak Russian than who speak Estonian, Latvian, or Lithuanian. While speaking Russian doesn't necessarily label one as a threat to domestic security, the point is clear: Do these people pose a security threat to their host nations and, by extension, to NATO itself? Writing back in 2003, Maibritt Lind of the Baltic Defence College Institute for Baltic Defence Studies considered this very issue, examining it from the perspective of the idea, physical base, and institutional expression of the Estonian state.[77] Her conclusion was that Estonia's Russian-speaking population can be considered a structural security threat, since the idea of the Estonian state is the preservation of the Estonian nation and culture. More surprisingly, Lind also concluded that even if Estonia changed its course and granted citizenship to all its residents and attempted to develop a multiethnic Estonian identity, such a course of action would ultimately fail because the East European and post–Soviet understanding of national identity is primordial and ethnic. Even with Estonian citizenship, she argued, Russian speakers would still be considered second-class citizens.[78]

While membership in the EU and NATO has increased the security of the Baltic states in many ways, it might have come at a cost. Now that NATO is at its doorstep, Moscow pays close attention to the situation of the Russian-speaking population there, and while being chastised by Moscow for their human rights record is not something that worries leaders in Tallinn, Riga, or Vilnius, there is no telling how far Russia would go if it felt that their rights were seriously being threatened—or if Moscow wanted to use the issue to justify its military and/or political objectives. As Blank observed more than 15 years ago: "Moscow's foreseeable pressures on the Baltic states are largely rhetorical, diplomatic, political, and economic to probe the limits of the possible and expand Russia's sphere of action." But, he concluded, "if Russia recovers and NATO and European integration stagnates, we can expect more pressure on the region."[79] While Blank may have seen Russia's powerful economic recovery on the horizon when he penned those words back in 1997, he certainly could not have predicted the euro crisis or Britain's recent proposal to renegotiate terms with the EU. Perhaps we shouldn't be too hasty in dismissing his prediction about Russia's pressure on the Baltics.

FROM TRAGEDY TO RECONCILIATION? DEVELOPMENTS IN RUSSIA–POLAND RELATIONS

While Russia–Baltic relations are tense, relations between Warsaw and Moscow have significantly improved over the past few years. It is perhaps ironic that this welcomed shift resulted from a tragic accident that itself occurred during a commemoration of one of the darkest pages in relations between the two countries. In April 2010, a plane carrying the president of Poland, Lech Kaczynski, and 94 other top Polish officials crashed in Smolensk, Russia, killing everyone on board. The delegation was there to commemorate the 70th anniversary of the Katyn massacre, a mass execution of Polish officers and members of the intelligentsia carried out by Soviet secret police during World War II. The episode has long been a thorn in Russia–Poland relations, and the April 2010 ceremony was an important step in healing what is considered a national tragedy by all in Poland. Due to poor weather conditions and pilot error, a second tragedy came to aggravate relations between the two nations, as suspicions run high in Poland that Russia was somehow once again to blame. Disagreements have even centered on the wording of the commemorative stone placed at the site of the crash.

But this tragedy may have a positive result as well. Since then, there has been a genuine outpouring of sympathy by Russia toward Poland, especially from Vladimir Putin himself. Putin has good reason to embrace Poland; the EU is Russia's largest trade partner, and many of those goods traverse Polish territory, including its energy exports. While bilateral trade remains limited (Poland imported a little more than $6 billion worth of goods last year, while Russia imported only $1.4 billion from Poland), both sides see the benefit of increasing their trade relations and improving their bilateral relations more generally. Polish foreign minister Radek Sikorski, who was once considered a neocon for his strong Atlanticist position, seems more recently to have determined that it is better to seek an accord with Russia than to aggravate it. For Moscow, Poland's influence in the EU makes it an attractive partner.

A significant step in improving relations between the two countries relates to the easing of border crossings. Russia and Poland share only a small border on the southern border of Russia's Kaliningrad exclave. Under a 2012 agreement, Kaliningrad's residents are now allowed to travel well into Poland without a visa, using a permit issued for 2 or 5 years instead.[80] The European Commission had to approve this border traffic agreement, since it permits Kaliningrad residents to travel 150 kilometers inside the EU, well beyond the 30-kilometer limit typical for this type of agreement. Russia had previously opposed any type of extension, fearing it would only further distance the exclave from Russia proper. This agreement suggests trust between the two is improving significantly.

Another significant story in Russia–Poland relations seems to be more symbolic gestures, such as the airing for the first time in Russia of a Polish film on the Katyn massacre. Other landmarks include the April 2012 visit of Patriarch Kirill, head of the Russian Orthodox Church, to Poland—the first ever visit of a Russian patriarch to the predominately Catholic country. During the visit, Kirill and Polish archbishop Jozef Michalik signed a joint declaration aimed at resolving the "painful pages of Polish and Russian history."[81]

But for all of the positive developments in Russia–Poland relations, it is certainly too soon to conclude that centuries-old animosities are put to rest. The biggest bone of contention in Warsaw's relations with Moscow is United States–Poland relations, in particular its role in U.S. missile defense plans for Eastern Europe. Only 24 hours after signing a landmark deal with Washington to site components of the U.S. missile shield in Poland, Moscow responded with bellicose language. General Anatoly Nogovitsyn warned that any new U.S. assets in Europe could come under Russian nuclear attack and that his forces would target "the allies of countries having nuclear weapons." In case this was not clear enough, Nogovitsyn told Russia's Interfax news agency that by "hosting these, Poland is making itself a target. This is 100% certain. It becomes a target for attack. Such targets are destroyed as a first priority."[82] This was no mere saber rattling from a rogue general. Russian president Dmitry Medvedev dismissed Washington's claim that the system is aimed as a deterrent against "rogue states" such as Iran as "a fairy tale." "The deployment of new missile defence facilities in Europe," he told reporters, "is aimed against the Russian Federation."[83]

This occurred, of course, in the midst of the Russia–Georgia War and before the warming of relations between Poland and Russia following the Smolensk tragedy. During a March 2011 visit to Washington, Sikorski reassured American audiences—including the U.S. State Department—that the thaw in Polish–Russian relations was legitimate and well on track. Later that year, however, Medvedev publicly stated that, if the United States moves forward in deploying missile defense sites in Poland and Romania, Russia would counter by deploying missiles in Kaliningrad aimed at those sites.[84] Moscow says if the system is truly aimed at countries other than Russia, then the system should be jointly run by NATO and Russia, a proposal the Atlantic Alliance rejects. Moscow is not backing down from the issue, and in May 2012, General Nikolai Makarov, Russia's most senior military commander, further warned that if NATO proceeds with its plans to deploy missile defense radar and interceptors in Poland and Romania, force will be used against it, adding that a "decision to use destructive force preemptively will be taken if the situation worsens."[85]

RUSSIAN IMPOTENCE IN THE BALKANS

Unlike Poland and the Baltics, which at certain points in their history had been part of the Russian empire, Moscow's grip on the Balkans had always been tenuous at best. It was not an area that Russia was going to give up easily, however, especially as it seemed that the West was quickly moving in. The Yeltsin administration tried to preserve some degree of influence in the Balkans, particularly through its support of Serbia during the Yugoslav wars of succession. Initially, Russia was not particularly involved in determining the fate of Yugoslavia. Gorbachev tended to support Western efforts to find a solution to head off the impending violence; in July 1991, Gorbachev joined with U.S. President George H. W. Bush at the Moscow summit in issuing a joint statement condemning the violence. Some of the hard-line elements within the Soviet government, however, were more eager to back the federal Yugoslav government's efforts to crush secession, seeing Yugoslavia's disintegration as a harbinger of what might happen in the USSR. In August 1991, Soviet Defense Minister Dmitry Yazov even agreed to send weapons to Yugoslavia. However, these plans were nullified in the aftermath of the failed coup attempt. In turn, when the Soviet Union itself collapsed, the Serbs did not find the successor Russian government in Moscow to be overly sympathetic, in part because Slobodan Milosevic, the president of Serbia, had supported the hardliners. Thus, given the marked Atlanticist tendencies of the first Yeltsin administration, it was not surprising that, after the Europeans had decided to recognize the independence of Slovenia and Croatia from Yugoslavia, Yeltsin followed suit in February 1992. Yeltsin also initially accepted the assessment that Milosevic, by supporting Serbian separatists in Bosnia and Croatia, was the main person responsible for the violence.[86] The Russian government supported United Nations Security Council Resolution 743, passed that same month, which authorized the deployment of a peacekeeping force to stop the fighting in Croatia and to pave the way for a political settlement. In addition, Russia agreed to dispatch Russian airborne units to take part in this peace-enforcement mission (UNPROFOR). As the Yeltsin administration had concluded, "Russian involvement was seen as necessary to enhance its standing as a major power committed to the establishment of peace and stability in post–Cold War Europe."[87] Participation in UNPROFOR seemed to validate the Atlanticist assumption that a close and productive partnership could develop between the West and post–Soviet Russia on European security issues. Russia also agreed in May 1992 to the imposition of economic sanctions against Yugoslavia[88] after the fighting began in Bosnia between that republic's Serb, Croat, and Muslim populations and supported the creation of a no-fly zone over Bosnia in October.

The Russians had hoped that they would play a substantive role in mapping out the parameters of a post-Yugoslav settlement but instead increasingly complained that they were being tasked to execute policies largely devised in Washington and other Western capitals. This divergence widened because Moscow began to see all parties in the Yugoslav wars as sharing some culpability for the fighting, in contrast to the tendency in the West to focus on the Serbs as bearing the lion's share of the responsibility for the conflict.[89] Problems also emerged when the Western countries wanted NATO to assume more of an active role in enforcing UN mandates, in contrast to the Russian preference for working through the UN or the Organization for Security and Cooperation in Europe (OSCE), two organizations of which Russia was not only a member but in which it could also exercise veto power.[90] Russian concerns were initially mollified by use of the so-called "dual key" system whereby NATO could only use force if authorized to do so by the United Nations, giving Russia some say over where and when the alliance could operate. Russia also helped to set up the Contact Group, made up of the permanent members of the Security Council (except for China) and other key European states like Italy and Germany as well as the European Union to try and coordinate policy.

Domestic factors also began to play a role. The Communist opposition condemned Western pressure directed against a former Communist state, while nationalists (as well as leading figures in the Orthodox Church) argued that Russia ought to do more to protect a Slavic Orthodox state. Yeltsin initially ignored a resolution passed by the legislature in 1992 calling for Russia to rescind its support for economic sanctions, but by 1993, growing public opposition to Yeltsin's policies began to have an impact. Russia abstained in April 1993 on a UN Security Council resolution tightening sanctions against Yugoslavia, and Russian diplomats like Vitaly Churkin, then serving as the

Russian president's special envoy for the former Yugoslavia, indicated that domestic pressure was having an impact on Russian policy, particularly in driving it toward a more pro-Serbian position.[91]

Matters came to a head in February 1994 after an explosion in a Sarajevo marketplace that many attributed to the Bosnian Serbs killed dozens of civilians. The United States led calls for using NATO air power to destroy Bosnian Serb artillery. Churkin, however, stepped in to negotiate a deal: The Bosnian Serbs would withdraw from their positions around Sarajevo in return for the deployment of 400 Russian troops into those areas to guarantee that Bosnian Muslim forces would not advance. Moscow believed that this would remove any need for NATO intervention.[92] However, NATO planes did intercept Serbian jets at the end of February, and NATO air strikes were launched against the Bosnian Serbs in the area of the town of Gorazde in April 1994. Although minor engagements, they "represented [NATO's] first military action since its creation in 1949."[93] NATO involvement in the conflict provoked anxieties among Russian military officers, who in turn accused the Atlanticist-leaning foreign minister Andrei Kozyrev of "exercising a supine policy over the former Yugoslavia in the face of Western initiatives and for too readily lending support to an essentially anti–Serbian policy contrary to traditional Russian/Soviet interests."[94] At the same time, the United States, itself frustrated by the deadlocks within the United Nations, was more inclined to take unilateral action on the basis of existing UN resolutions rather than to seek Russian approval. (A change in how the dual-key system operated also loosened the restrictions on NATO's use of force.)

In 1995, NATO began stepping up its use of air strikes, particularly in August and September when Operation Deliberate Force was launched against the Bosnian Serbs. The Bosnians and Croats were able, as a result of NATO airpower, to make significant gains against the Bosnian Serbs and the Serb separatists in Croatia. Russia was unable to stop the NATO air campaign, and Milosevic was forced to deal directly with the United States. The United States then took the lead in convening a conference in Dayton, Ohio, to hammer out a peace settlement for Bosnia, a process in which Russia played only a minimal role. While U.S. official rhetoric praised the Russian contribution, Moscow in fact had little influence over how the negotiations were conducted.[95] Instead of playing a coequal role in finding a solution, Russia found itself reduced to the role of being a "facilitator of Western policy."[96]

The United States wanted to avoid what it saw as the political limitations on previous UN missions in Yugoslavia and insisted that NATO lead the Implementation Force (IFOR) and subsequent Stabilization Force (SFOR) deployed to Bosnia. The Russians were placed in an unenviable position of having to potentially subordinate their forces to NATO command. Alexander Nikitin describes how this Gordian knot was unraveled:

> The structure and chain of command in IFOR and SFOR were problematic for Russia, since they were extremely NATO-centric. This was in contrast to the arrangements governing other UN-mandated operations in which Russia had a strong voice and the military side of the mission was subordinate to the political side. The solution that was eventually found involved the appointment at Supreme Headquarters Allied Powers, Europe (SHAPE) of a Russian general as a Special Deputy to NATO's highest-ranking officer, the Supreme Allied Commander, Europe (SACEUR), responsible for coordinating with SACEUR all matters concerning Russia's participation in IFOR and then SFOR.[97]

For some, the Bosnian mission showed how Russia and NATO could cooperate. But for many in the Russian national security establishment, it seemed that the only role for Russia in European security would be one subordinate to NATO and the United States.

The growing crisis in the Albanian-majority Serbian province of Kosovo, where a low-level insurgency (the Kosovo Liberation Army, formed in 1996) was fighting for the province's complete independence, was particularly problematic for Russia. Moscow was opposed to any action that might compromise the territorial integrity of Serbia. After all, the Russian Federation had its own internal separatist pressures, and one republic of the Federation, Chechnya, had already made one attempt to secede from Russia. A number of Russian politicians feared that Western policy toward Yugoslavia was a "dress rehearsal" for the eventual dismemberment of Russia as well.[98] As fighting escalated in Kosovo and international concern grew about a new war breaking out in the Yugoslav theater, Yeltsin brokered a deal with Milosevic in June 1998 to create the Kosovo Diplomatic Observer Mission and voted in favor of UN Security Council Resolution 1199 that September calling for both sides to negotiate. But as the fighting continued, NATO threatened to use force if the conflict was not halted. Russia was one of the countries that took part in the Rambouillet Conference designed to end the conflict between the ethnic Albanians of Kosovo and Yugoslavia. Yugoslavia finally accepted that Kosovo should enjoy "substantial autonomy" but rejected the demand to allow NATO forces to have unimpeded access to the entire country and expressed concern over the provision for an international review of Kosovo's status after 3 years that would determine the final disposition of the province, which both Belgrade and Moscow saw as tantamount to its full separation from Yugoslavia.[99] The Yugoslav and Russian delegations refused to sign the draft. On March 24, 1999, NATO forces began a massive air campaign against Yugoslavia that would last 11 weeks, involve 38,000 aircraft sorties, and expend approximately 12,000 tons of munitions.[100]

The United States deliberately bypassed the UN Security Council in order to avoid triggering a Russian veto of the campaign. After it was launched, Russia condemned the NATO operation as "an illegal military operation" and Prime Minister Yevgeny Primakov, who was en route to the United States for meetings with U.S. officials, ordered his plane to return to Moscow.[101] But Russia's impotence against NATO action was on full display as Moscow was unable to stop the air campaign. Despite Russian legislators' loud proclamations of support, proposals like those advanced by State Duma Chairman Gennady Seleznev, calling for Russia to provide "military aid . . . to Yugoslavia without fail and without delay," went nowhere.[102] Russia also declined Yugoslavia's request to set up a Slavic Union that would unite Yugoslavia, Belarus, and Russia, noting that Russia could not take on such obligations while Yugoslavia found itself in a military conflict. Former Prime Minister Viktor Chernomyrdin, tapped by Yeltsin to serve as his special envoy for the crisis, described NATO action as a "humiliation of my country." However, as the air campaign went on without the quick victory expected by the United States and other NATO countries, Chernomyrdin was able to play a leading role in opening talks between Milosevic and NATO, working closely with Finland's president Martti Ahtisaari to broker a settlement that permitted NATO to deploy peacekeepers into Kosovo. Milosevic accepted this deal, in part, because he became convinced that Russia would not be able to do anything to stop NATO.[103]

Russia attempted to reinsert itself as a relevant player by helping to sponsor UN Security Council Resolution 1244, which created an interim administration for Kosovo with an eye to giving the province "substantial autonomy" but without any reference to possible independence. Russia also agreed to take part in the NATO-led Kosovo Force (KFOR) in a deal reached between U.S. Defense Secretary William Cohen and Russian Defense Minister Igor Sergeyev.[104] Russian participation was seen as essential to help reassure the Serbian population of Kosovo that they would be protected. While Kosovo was to be divided into different sectors, each under the command of a different NATO nation (the United States, Germany, etc.), the Russians asked for but were not given their own sector, for fear that they would encourage Serb separatism in Kosovo. Instead, the Russians were to have "zones of responsibility" within the NATO sectors. The Russia–NATO partnership in Kosovo, however, was nearly scuttled right at the beginning, when 200 Russian peacekeepers stationed in Bosnia "dashed" to take control of the airport in Pristina, the capital of Kosovo, ahead of the arrival of NATO forces. U.S. General Wesley Clark, the Supreme Allied Commander-Europe and the top military officer in NATO, was prepared to use force to dislodge the Russian contingent, but the

British commander for KFOR, General Mike Jackson, reportedly told Clark, "I'm not going to start the Third World War for you."[105] The Russian forces did not inhibit NATO postconflict operations, and the issue was eventually settled.

The Kosovo war severely damaged Russian pretensions to still be a major player in East European affairs. Not only did NATO carry out an extended military campaign against Yugoslavia—something that could never have occurred during the Cold War—former Warsaw Pact satellites were now not only blocking Russian efforts to project its influence and power in the region, they were going over to the other side and expanding NATO's reach eastward, first to the Visegrad states in 1999, and then to the Vilnius group in 2004. In fact, the war in Kosovo probably sped up the process of further eastward expansion of NATO. Not only had several East European states sided with NATO during the Kosovo operation, some had even helped to block Russia as it tried to exert influence in the former Yugoslavia. During the air campaign, Hungary had blocked Russian convoys ostensibly traveling to resupply Russian peacekeeping forces in Bosnia in order to prevent any possible shipment of arms to Yugoslavia. At the end of the war, when Russian intentions in postwar Kosovo were still unclear, NATO requested that Hungary and Romania not allow Russian aircraft to overfly their territories.[106] Whether or not such cooperation convinced NATO of the value of eastward expansion, Russian behavior certainly convinced leaders in East European capitals that Moscow had not given up the ambition of exerting influence in the region. In the end, the Kosovo war drove home to Moscow that the "central reality in Europe" was now "the primacy of NATO." These developments also helped to further discredit the pro–Western, Atlanticist school of thought within the Russian foreign policy establishment, which was now blamed for having aided the forced retreat of Russia from its traditional bastions of regional and global influence.[107]

MOSCOW'S "RUBLE DIPLOMACY" AND RUSSIA'S RETURN TO EASTERN EUROPE

By the early 2000s, a major reorientation in Russian policy toward Eastern Europe was underway. Moscow's attempt to keep the West out of the former Warsaw Pact countries and even the Baltic States throughout the 1990s had failed miserably. After the whole Kosovo affair, Russia had no illusions to the contrary. As an editorial in *Izvestiya* from August 2000 opined, "Not a single country of eastern Europe, even the most Slavic, the most Eastern Orthodox one, will give up maintaining relations with the West for the sake of Russia."[108]

Having lost the battle to keep Eastern Europe in a Russian-led political and security union, the Putin administration realized that Russia needed a new approach to maintaining influence in the region, one focused on trade and economic cooperation and grounded in pragmatic considerations. The 2000 Foreign Policy concept stressed the importance of preserving and increasing economic ties with the region.[109] That policy would be accelerated with the appointment in March 2002 of Sergei Razov, as deputy foreign minister with oversight for policy toward central and southeastern Europe. Shortly after taking office, Razov, who had been Russia's ambassador to Poland during its accession to NATO, announced that a "new algorithm" for Russian ties with east-central Europe and the Balkans was being implemented.[110]

The recovery of the Russian economy from the collapse of the 1990s helped to rejuvenate some of the old commercial links between the region and Russia, and Russia also remained the primary supplier of Eastern Europe's energy needs. Even today, "the countries of Eastern and Central Europe . . . are from 70 to 99 percent dependent on gas and oil" imported from Russia.[111] The question was whether Russia might use its newfound economic clout to promote cooperation or as a tool for pressuring the states of the region—whether, instead of tanks, Russia could use its banks and other economic instruments to exert influence.[112] As Russian businesses, particularly energy companies, have found themselves flush with cash from Russia's economic boom of the past decade, opportunities have presented themselves as a number of Eastern European countries were prepared to sell off formerly state-owned assets or as Western investors reconsidered the value of their investments in the region. Eastern European states have thus had to weigh the possible consequences of having Russian firms return as key foreign investors, especially in strategic sectors of the economy.[113] These concerns were heightened because it became clear that Russian investment was not delinked from Moscow's political and strategic goals. After assessing the record, Stephen Blank concluded, "Evidence from the Czech Republic, Bulgaria, Hungary, Slovakia, Poland and the Baltic states is overwhelming and points to a strategic policy decision in Moscow" to use economic means to promote Russian state interests.[114]

Working from the assumption that "profitable accounts cement good friendships," Russia sought to envelop the region in a web of commercial ties that would engender pro-Moscow lobbies in Eastern European capitals and that would, in turn, help increase Russia's influence in the Euro-Atlantic community. Russian oil and gas companies began to buy up assets throughout the region, and Russian financial and telecommunications firms also expanded their holdings. As Russia re-emerged as a major foreign investor, it conveyed to the governments of the region that it was in their interests to create "appropriate conditions" that would facilitate Russian investment.[115] One of the largest Russian projects in the Balkans is the South Stream pipeline, designed to directly connect Russia to its natural gas consumers in Europe. This pipeline, which began construction in December 2012, will run through Bulgaria, Serbia, Hungary, Croatia, and Slovenia, ultimately reaching Italy and Austria (and from there being integrated into the larger European distribution grid). South Stream, which has extensive economic spillover effects in every country through which the line passes—from construction to gas storage to refining projects—has been seen as one of the most effective ways for Russia to promote its interests in the region.[116] Moreover, Russia got NATO and EU members to agree to develop the line even against clear opposition from the United States and some other European states that were concerned that South Stream would reinforce energy dependence on Russia. But Russian investment has proven to be a formidable tool to push for consideration of Russian interests. Once the expansion of NATO and the EU appeared to be a foregone conclusion, Russia hoped to gain greater influence in the deliberations in Brussels by relying on friendly intermediaries among its former satellite states. In 2002, Bulgarian Foreign Minister Solomon Passy noted that "Russia will be glad to have a friend like Bulgaria amidst NATO members," while its president Georgi Purvanov declared, "Bulgaria's European integration is not an alternative to our good relations with Russia. The new European security architecture cannot exclude or oppose Russia."[117]

Hungary is the best example of how Russian investment, and particularly the South Stream project, has helped to change the tenor of an Eastern European country's relations with Russia. At the end of the Cold War, there were still extremely negative feelings in Hungary toward Russia on account of the suppression of the Hungarian uprisings of 1848 to 1849 and 1956. Hungary was one of the Visegrad countries that sought rapid inclusion in NATO and the EU to escape any possibility of being reabsorbed into a Russian sphere of influence. Since 2002, however, Hungary had altered course to pursue a more balanced relationship with Moscow. When the Socialist Party (the former Communists) won elections that year, the new prime minister Peter Medgyessy called for re-establishing "close relations with Russia," noting that there were "big opportunities for economic relations" that would benefit Hungarian businesses.[118] His successor, Ferenc Gyurcsany, also a former Communist, put forward a vision of Hungary serving as GazProm's "energy hub" in Central Europe, committing Hungary to closer cooperation with Russia and breaking with the EU over support for an alternative line (Nabucco) that was supposed to reduce European dependence on Russian sources of supply.[119] In February 2008, he traveled to Russia to meet with Putin and to sign documents formally committing Hungary to take part in the Russian project, effectively sidelining the EU project.[120] What is most significant is that this closer Hungary–Russia relationship continued under the conservative Fidesz government headed by Viktor Orban, who as an opposition politician in 1989 had called for the immediate withdrawal of Soviet forces and who, when he had been prime minister in the 1990s, had worked hard to keep post–Soviet Russia out of Eastern Europe. Orban now sees opportunity in forging a more strategic relationship with Russia, and during a visit to Russia in 2009, he spoke of a "21st century partnership" between the two countries. This new openness to Russia occurred in part because of the ongoing economic crisis in the European Union, which was particularly damaging to Hungary, and Orban's growing belief that the EU's attempts to interfere in Hungary's domestic affairs are a bigger threat to Hungary's sovereignty than Russia.[121] Orban has not uncritically embraced Russia; he has taken steps to diversify some of Hungary's energy imports and to reassert control over Hungarian strategic enterprises, but his January 2013 visit to Russia helped to cement the new relationship. It also highlighted the growing institutionalization of the relationship, as Hungary was the first country of the region to create an intergovernmental commission with Russia to help manage bilateral relations.

Russia's renewed economic clout also helped to restore some of its geopolitical clout in the aftermath of the Kosovo setback. In contrast to the 1990s, when Russia tended to grudgingly accept Western solutions for the region, Moscow did not budge when the question of giving Kosovo full independence came onto the agenda. Russia made it clear that it would not countenance an independent Kosovo that did not come into existence as a result of a freely negotiated agreement with Serbia and has made clear it would deploy its veto at the UN and in other international organizations to prevent recognition of Kosovo after its unilateral declaration of independence in 2008. Russia demonstrated that it would no longer automatically accept Western direction for regional affairs.

In addition to closer economic relations, Russia regained its first foothold in Eastern Europe when, in 2011, Russia was permitted to set up a "humanitarian base" in the city of Nis, although the facility was to be used by Russia's Emergency Situations Ministry rather than the military.[122] Russia is also exploring using port facilities in Greece and Montenegro as supply points for a proposed naval task force that would be permanently deployed in the Mediterranean Sea for the first time since the Cold War.[123]

With more resources at its disposal, Russia also became more apt to resume interfering in Eastern European politics. One of the most dramatic cases was that of Lithuania's President Rolandas Paksas. Previously the country's prime minister (in 1999 and again in 2000–2001), he was elected in 2003 but impeached and removed from office in 2004 because of his national security advisor Remigijus Acas's alleged ties to Russian organized crime and because of an investigation into Paksas's largest campaign contributor, Yuri Borisov, a Russian business figure who ultimately received Lithuanian citizenship due to Paksas's assistance. It raised concerns that this was part of an effort to influence Lithuania's next round of privatization so that Russian interests could purchase formerly state-controlled gas, oil, and transportation enterprises.[124]

Russia has also shown more willingness to exercise economic pressure against Eastern European countries that are perceived as having taken hostile positions against Russian interests. If, during the 1990s, Russia's need to export energy to Western Europe required the active cooperation of Eastern European transit states—thus giving them leverage over Moscow—after 2000, Russia began to build up what was labeled as "bypass infrastructure" to allow Russia to directly reach key markets without having to use the traditional transit routes. When Baltic countries, for instance, refused to sell to Russian interests key portions of the energy transport infrastructure, Transneft, the Russian state company that controls the country's oil export pipelines, chose in 2003 to stop using the export terminals at the Latvian port of Ventspils to send Russian oil to markets overseas. It now sends oil that previously would have been routed to Ventspils to the new Baltic Pipeline System terminal at Primorsk, described as the "first example of bypass infrastructure built to reduce reliance on transit routes through neighboring countries."[125] The trunk line to Lithuania was also shut down in 2006.

The Baltic Pipeline System (BPS), which redirects oil shipments to new terminals in Russia, now allows Russia to send oil directly by tanker to Rotterdam. It has enabled Russia to begin reducing "oil export volumes through the overland Druzhba pipelines," which affects supplies not only to former Soviet republics like Ukraine and Belarus but also to Eastern European countries, especially Poland and the Czech Republic, which saw deliveries of Russian oil by these lines drop by 15% from 2010 to 2011. (Slovakia, which has maintained excellent relations with Russia, saw its oil deliveries increase during the same time by 15%.[126]) Similarly, the construction of the Nord Stream line under the waters of the Baltic Sea has created a direct natural gas line between Russia and Germany, "conspicuously avoiding the Baltic states and Poland," and was designed to reduce the leverage of the transit states against Russia. Alexandros Petersen concluded: "Russia's geopolitical message here is clear: It doesn't trust the new EU member states as transit countries or even as energy consumers and is willing to incur enormous costs to bypass them. The other message—or implied threat—is that Nord Stream will allow the Kremlin to cut off gas deliveries to Eastern Europe through current pipelines without reducing energy supplies to Germany" and by extension, to the rest of Western Europe.[127] Not surprisingly, Polish foreign minister Radek Sikorski blasted the Nord Stream project in 2006 as a new Molotov-Ribbentrop Pact, alluding to the 1939 agreement between the USSR and Nazi Germany to partition Poland. Poland and the Baltic States also warned that such projects would increase Russia's leverage on Europe and were critical of being left potentially vulnerable to supply disruptions by their European Union allies.[128]

The return of Russia as a key economic player in the region has therefore caused some Eastern European countries to reassess whether it makes sense to try to completely exclude Russia from the region. In 2007, Donald Tusk's Civic Platform party came to power in Poland, in part due to concerns that the Law and Justice party government under the leadership of prime minster Jaroslaw Kaczynski was too inflexible in managing relations with Russia. Tusk, in contrast, was interested in making business the main organizing principle of the Poland–Russia relationship.[129] Similarly, in 2012, the Czech prime minister, Petar Necas, questioned the policy of previous Czech governments to press Russia on various matters, including human rights, noting that such stances "had consequences for our exports."[130]

But Russia's attempts to use economic levers to influence Eastern European states sometimes backfired. A November 2005 Russian ban on imports of meat from Poland—ostensibly for health reasons but widely assumed to be a way to put pressure on the Polish government—led Warsaw to use its veto within the European Union to hold up trade negotiations with Russia. The Russian government erroneously assumed that other European states would put pressure on Poland to resolve the dispute in Moscow's favor, which did not occur. Only after Russia lifted the ban in December 2007 could negotiations move forward.[131]

The real limits of Russia's "ruble diplomacy" were on display after the United States announced its intention to deploy a limited ballistic missile defense system in Eastern Europe to deal with a potential threat from Iran, a proposal vigorously opposed by Russia, as discussed above. In part because of the perception that Russia remained a threat because of its use of economic factors like energy cutoffs to pressure Eastern European states, elites in some states in the region were eager to host elements of the system in order to gain further security guarantees from the United States, including the actual deployment of some U.S. forces and equipment. (Others, like Prime Minister Robert Fico of Slovakia, flatly ruled out taking any part in the system.) Despite Russian pressure, Poland opened negotiations in 2007 with the George W. Bush administration to host U.S. interceptors and signed a formal agreement with Washington in the immediate aftermath of the 2008 Russia–Georgia War, even after Medvedev threatened to deploy short-range missiles in the Russian exclave of Kaliningrad in response. The United States then agreed to station a Patriot Missile battery in Poland. The government of the Czech Republic also started talks to host a radar station to support the system, but public opinion was generally opposed, fearing to be drawn into a new clash with Russia, and the draft agreement was not ratified by the legislature.[132]

The Obama administration canceled this system in September 2009, citing technical difficulties, although it continued with the plan to send Patriot missiles to Poland. Initially interpreted as a betrayal of Eastern Europe in an effort to promote a U.S.-Russia reset, the administration has since announced a different missile defense plan, the European Phased Adaptive Approach. It would rely on ship-based systems (which would need port facilities in the region, particularly in the Black Sea) but eventually see some limited land components deployed in the region, in Romania in 2015 and in Poland in 2018, despite vociferous Russian objections as well as threats to target such installations in Eastern Europe.[133]

The countries of Eastern Europe may have hoped that they were done with their eastern neighbor after the collapse of the Soviet Union and that a post-Soviet Russia would turn inward. Russia has returned, however, seeking to regain some of its lost influence. However, Russia must now also accept that it can never regain a sphere of influence. With the 2009 round of NATO expansion, which brought Croatia and Albania into the alliance, and the 2013 round of EU expansion, which admitted Croatia, almost the entirety of the former Soviet bloc (with the exception of some of the former Yugoslav states) is now part of the Euro-Atlantic world. Within a two-decade period, Eastern Europe has completely repudiated its former position as Moscow's outer zone of influence. This has created two problems for Moscow. The first is that its former satellites now find themselves in a much stronger position vis-à-vis Russia, since they can leverage the economic, political, and military power of their allies in their dealings with Moscow. The second is that, "In Moscow's view, NATO, and the EU, have become more anti-Russian since the former Communist countries of Eastern Europe and the Baltic states joined both organizations."[134] This has complicated Russia's generally improving relationships with key Western European states, something that will be discussed in the next chapter.

NOTES

1. "Wrongly labeled," *The Economist,* January 7, 2010, at http://www.economist.com/node/15213108.

2. John Lukacs, "In Darkest Transylvania," *New Republic* 186, no. 5 (February 3, 1982): 15.

3. See, for instance, Oskar Halecki, *Borderlands of Western Civilization: A History of East Central Europe* (Safety Harbor, FL: Simon Publications, 2000), 11. See also Gale Stokes, "Eastern Europe's Defining Fault Lines," in *Eastern Europe: Politics, Culture and Society Since 1939,* ed. Sabrina Ramet (Bloomington, IN: Indiana University Press, 1998), 15.

4. Nikolai Danilevsky, *Rossia i Evropa,* 5th ed. (St. Petersburg, Russia: Panteleev Brothers, 1895), esp. 471–512.

5. The shared experience of Soviet domination helped to set apart this region of Europe from those states that were part of the USSR and those that remained non-Communist. Sabrina Ramet, "Introduction," in *Eastern Europe,* 2.

6. See, for instance, the perceptions of average Soviet citizens during the 1970s and 1980s about these countries, cf. David K. Willis, *Klass: How Russians Really Live* (New York: Avon Books, 1985), 73, 254–55; and Andrew Nagorski, *Reluctant Farewell* (New York: Holt, Rinehart and Winston, 1985), 151.

7. Robert D. Kaplan, *Balkan Ghosts: A Journey Through History* (New York: Picador, 1993, 1996, 2005), x.

8. See, for instance, James H. Billington, *The Icon and the Axe: An Interpretive History of Russian Culture* (New York: Vintage Books, 1966, 1970), 55–57.

9. Nicholas V. Riasanovsky, *Russian Identities: A Historical Survey* (New York: Oxford University Press, 2005), 35, 51.

10. Billington, 102–106.

11. Nicholas V. Riasanovsky and Mark D. Steinberg, *A History of Russia*, 8th edition. (New York: Oxford University Press, 2010), 264–267.

12. Andrew Felkay, *Out of Russian Orbit: Hungary Gravitates to the West* (Westport, CT: Greenwood Press, 1997), 1.

13. See, for instance, Biljana Vankovska and Haken Wiberg, *Between Past and Future: Civil-Military Relations in the Post-Communist Balkans* (London: I.B. Tauris, 2003), esp. 72; Kaplan, 207, 248.

14. See, for instance, Paul Vyšný, *Neo-Slavism and the Czechs: 1898–1914* (Cambridge, MA: Cambridge University Press, 1977).

15. See, for instance, Iu. M. Steklov's comments in *Izvestiia*, June 26, 1921, 1.

16. Victor S. Mamatey, *Soviet Russian Imperialism* (New York: Van Nostrand Reinhold, 1964), 48–52; the text of the Non-Aggression Pact and the secret additional protocol can be found at 130–132.

17. Vladislav Zubok and Constantine Pleshakov, *Inside the Kremlin's Cold War: From Stalin to Khrushchev* (Cambridge, MA: Harvard University Press, 1996), 28–30.

18. Mamatey, 85.

19. "Father George" (pseudonym of Stjepan Tomislav Poglajen] and Gretta Palmer),*God's Underground* (New York: Appleton-Century-Crofts, Inc., 1949), 58.

20. Mamatey, 82.

21. Tad Szulc, "Gorbachev, Jaruzelski Try Candor in Facing Bitter Soviet-Polish Past," *Los Angeles Times*, August 2, 1987, at http://articles.latimes.com/1987-08-02/opinion/op-663_1_soviet-union/2.

22. Zubok and Pleshakov, 32.

23. Mamatey, 84.

24. Zubok and Pleshakov, 50.

25. Modern History Sourcebook: Winston S. Churchill: "Iron Curtain Speech," March 5, 1946, at http://www.fordham.edu/halsall/mod/churchill-iron.asp.

26. Mamatey, 93.

27. Charles Gati, *The Bloc that Failed: Soviet–East European Relations in Transition* (Bloomington, IN: Indiana University Press, 1990), 3–4.

28. Mamatey, 85, 97.

29. This is discussed in greater detail in Vladimir Dedijer, *Tito* (New York: Simon and Schuster, 1952), esp. 268, 277–282.

30. Gati, 27.

31. An excellent summary of the developments in Hungary (and in Poland to a lesser extent) is found in John Gunther, *Inside Russia Today*, revised edition (New York: Harper and Row, 1962), 256–273.

32. Brezhnev's address was printed in *Pravda,* September 25, 1968, and is contained in L. S. Stavrianos, *The Epic of Man* (Englewood Cliffs, NJ: Prentice Hall, 1971), 465–466.

33. Quoted in Karen Dawisha, *Eastern Europe, Gorbachev and Reform,* 2nd edition (Cambridge, MA: Cambridge University Press, 1990), 9.

34. "Jaruzelski says martial law saved Poland," *Euronews,* October 2, 2008, at http://www.euronews.com/2008/10/02/jaruzelski-says-martial-law-saved-poland/.

35. Rodric Braithwaite, "Gorbachev was key in freeing eastern Europe," *Financial Times,* November 9, 2009, at http://www.ft.com/cms/s/0/c62f605e-ca41-11de-a3a3-00144feabdc0.html#axzz2I006wLmA.

36. Gati, 76, 164.

37. "From Brezhnev Doctrine to Sinatra Doctrine," *Demokratizatsiya* 13, no. 2 (Spring 2005): 292.

38. Dawisha, 111.

39. Gati, 167, 171.

40. Cited in Jeremy Bransten, "The East: Ten Years After 1989—The Revolutions That Brought Down Communism," *Radio Free Europe/Radio Liberty,* October 8, 1999.

41. "The Political Processes in the European Socialist Countries and the Proposals for Our Practical Steps Considering the Situation that Has Arisen in Them," Memorandum of the Soviet Ministry of Foreign Affairs, February 24, 1989.

42. Andrew Cottey, *East Central Europe after the Cold War* (Houndmills, Basingstoke: Macmillan Press, 1995), 14.

43. Comment of Gennady Gerasimov. Cf. "From Brezhnev Doctrine," 292.

44. Mary Elise Sarotte, "Enlarging NATO, Expanding Confusion," *New York Times,* November 29, 2009, at http://www.nytimes.com/2009/11/30/opinion/30sarotte.html?pagewanted=all&_r=0.

45. Paul Latawski, *The Security Road to Europe: The Visegrad Four* (London: Royal United Services Institute for Defence Studies, 1994), 83.

46. Andrei Kuznetsov, "The Economic Challenges of Post-Communist Marketization," in *Eastern Europe: Politics and Culture and Society Since 1939,* ed. Sabrina P. Ramet (Bloomington: Indiana University Press, 1998), 354; Gati, 114.

47. Robert Bideleux and Ian Jeffries, *A History of Eastern Europe: Crisis and Change* (Abingdon, Oxon: Routledge, 1998), 580–582.

48. Cottey, 17.

49. Latawski, 15.

50. Cottey, 145.

51. Roy Allison, "Military Factors in Foreign Policy," *Internal Factors in Russian Foreign Policy* (Oxford, UK: Oxford University Press, 1996), 261.

52. Roger Cohen, "Yeltsin Opposes Expansion Of NATO in Eastern Europe," *New York Times,* October 2, 1993, at http://www.nytimes.com/1993/10/02/world/yeltsin-opposes-expansion-of-nato-in-eastern-europe.html.

53. Latawski, 87.

54. Ibid., 71.

55. Ibid., 87–88.

56. Zeyno Baran, "EU Energy Security: Time to End Russian Leverage," *Washington Quarterly* 30, no. 4 (2007), 135.

57. Quoted in V. Stanley Vardys and Judith Sedaitis, *Lithuania: The Rebel Nation* (Boulder: Westview, 1997), 139–140.

58. Ivanov, 101.

59. Philip Gordon and James Steinberg, "NATO Enlargement: Moving Forward," *Brookings Policy Brief* 90 (December 2001), 5; Ivanov, 101.

60. Walter Clemens, "The Baltic Reborn: Challenges of Transition," *Demokratizatsiya* 6, no. 4 (Fall 1998): 724.

61. Stuart J. Kaufman, "NATO, Russia, and the Baltic States," PONARS Policy Memo No. 216 (January 25, 2002).

62. Gordon and Steinberg, 2.

63. Clemens, 722.

64. Clemens, 723.

65. Richard Starr, *The New Military in Russia: Ten Myths that Shape the Image* (Annapolis, MD: Naval Institute Press, 1996), 36.

66. European Defence Agency, http://www.eda.europa.eu/home.

67. F. Stephen Larrabee, "The Baltic States and NATO Membership," Testimony presented to the United States Senate Committee on Foreign Relations (Santa Monica, CA: Rand, April 2003), 2.

68. Tom Gjelten, "Volunteer Cyber Army Emerges In Estonia," *NPR's Morning Edition,* January 04, 2011. Available at http://www.npr.org/2011/01/04/132634099/in-estonia-volunteer-cyber-army-defends-nation.

69. Maibritt Lind, "Is the Russo-phone minority a Structural Security Threat to the Estonian State?" *Baltic Defence Review* 1, no. 9 (2003): 57.

70. Ibid.

71. RFE/RL Baltic States Report, 2001:16/10.

72. "Russia again raps Baltic states over Russian speakers' rights," *Interfax* (December 10, 2012). Available at http://www.interfax.com/newsinf.asp?id=381593.

73. "No trial as Estonian military accused of making Russian cadets dig own graves," *RT* (September 1, 2012). Available at http://rt.com/news/estonia-military-harassment-grave-131/.

74. Interview by Marko Mihkelson with Anton Surikov in Moscow, commenting on an institute report, in *Postimees,* 27 April 1996; translated by the Estonian Foreign Ministry. Quoted in Clemens, 721.

75. Clemens, 712.

76. Stephen Blank, *NATO Enlargement and the Baltic States: What Can the Great Powers Do?* (Carlisle Barracks, PA: U.S. Army War College Strategic Studies Institute, 1997), 12.

77. Lind, esp. 61–63.

78. Ibid., 61–62.

79. Blank, *NATO Enlargement and the Baltic States,* 19.

80. Judy Dempsey, "Why the Russian Patriarch's visit to Poland is important for Europe," Strategic Europe (August 16, 2012). Available at http://carnegieeurope.eu/strategiceurope/?fa=49122.

81. Ibid.

82. Damien McElroy, "Russian general says Poland a nuclear 'target,'" *Telegraph* (August 15, 2008). Available at http://www.telegraph.co.uk/news/worldnews/europe/geor gia/2564639/Russian-general-says-Poland-a-nuclear-target-as-Condoleezza-Rice-arrives-in-Georgia.html.

83. Harry de Quetteville and Andrew Pierce, "Russia threatens nuclear attack on Poland over US missile shield deal," *The Telegraph* (August 15, 2008). Available at http://www.telegraph.co.uk/news/worldnews/europe/russia/2566005/Russia-threatens-nuclear-attack-on-Poland-over-US-missile-shield-deal.html.

84. "Medvedev: Russia May Target Missile Defense Sites," *Associated Press* (November 23, 2011).

85. Bruno Waterfield, "Russia threatens NATO with military strikes over missile defence system," *The Telegraph* (May 3, 2012). Available at http://www.telegraph.co.uk/news/worldnews/europe/russia/9243954/Russia-threatens-Nato-with-military-strikes-over-missile-defence-system.html.

86. Mike Bowker, "The Wars in Yugoslavia: Russia and the International Community," *Europe–Asia Studies* 50, no. 7 (1998): 1247–48.

87. Jacob W. Kipp and Tarn Warren, "The Russian Separate Airborne Brigade–Peacekeeping in Bosnia-Herzegovina," *Regional Peacekeepers: The Paradox of Russian Peacekeeping,* eds. John Mackinlay and Peter Cross (Tokyo: United Nations University Press, 2003), 38.

88. Serbia, as part of its union with Montenegro, continued to use the name Yugoslavia to describe itself until 2003, when it became the State Union of Serbia and Montenegro.

89. Bowker, 1251.

90. Kipp and Warren, 38.

91. Alex Pravda, "The Public Politics of Foreign Policy," *Internal Factors,* 217–18.

92. "Bosnian Serbs Cheer Arrival of 400 Russian Peacekeepers," *Los Angeles Times,* February 21, 1994, at http://articles.latimes.com/1994-02-21/news/mn-25504_1_bos nian-serb-leader.

93. Bowker, 1252.

94. Allison, 260.

95. Scott Parrish, "Dayton at Midpoint: Russia's Marginal Role," *Transitions Online,* July 12, 1996, at http://www.tol.org/client/article/2784-dayton-at-midpoint-russias-mar ginal-role.html?print.

96. Semen Vasilievskii, "Bolshie poteri i malenkie dostizheniya," *Nezavisimaia Gazeta,* December 8, 1995, 5.

97. Alexander Nikitin, "Partners in Peacekeeping," *NATO Review,* Winter 2004, at http://www.nato.int/docu/review/2004/issue4/english/special.html.

98. Pravda, 215.

99. A copy of the text of the draft agreement can be found at http://www.state.gov/www/regions/eur/ksvo_rambouillet_text.html.

100. Daniel L. Byman and Matthew C. Waxman, "Kosovo and the Great Air Power Debate," *International Security* 24, no. 4 (Spring 2000): 5–38.

101. "Primakov Calls off Trip over Kosovo," *Moscow Times,* 1670 (March 24, 1999), at http://www.themoscowtimes.com/news/article/primakov-calls-off-trip-over-kosovo/279106.html; "Russia condemns NATO at UN," *BBC News,* March 25, 1999, at http://news.bbc.co.uk/2/hi/europe/303127.stm.

102. James Sherr and Steven Main, "Russian and Ukrainian Perception of Events in Yugoslavia," *Conflict Studies Research Center,* F64 (May 1999), 9.

103. See the PBS *Frontline* interview with Chernomyrdin, archived at http://www.pbs.org/wgbh/pages/frontline/shows/kosovo/interviews/chernomyrdin.html.

104. The Agreed Points on Russian Participation in KFOR was concluded in Helsinki on June 18, 1999, and is archived at http://www.nato.int/kosovo/docu/a990618a.htm.

105. "Confrontation over Pristina airport," *BBC News,* March 9, 2000, at http://news.bbc.co.uk/2/hi/europe/671495.stm.

106. Sherr and Main, 22; "Confrontation over Pristina airport," op. cit.

107. Sherr and Main, 3–4, 6, 16.

108. Nikolas K. Gvosdev, "Gas, Guns, and Oil: Russia's 'Ruble Diplomacy' in the Balkans." Available at http://www.wilsoncenter.org/publication/gas-guns-and-oil-russias-ruble-diplomacy-the-balkans.

109. Ivanov, 95.

110. "Russian Federation Deputy Foreign Minister Sergei Razov Answers a Question from Interfax News Agency about Russian Relations with the Central and Eastern European Countries," *Interfax,* April 3, 2002, archived at http://www.czech.mid.ru/press-rel/06042002_en.htm.

111. Keith C. Smith, *Russia–Europe Energy Relations: Implications for U.S. Policy* (Washington, DC: Center for Strategic and International Studies, February 2010), 6.

112. See, for instance, Andrei P. Tsygankov, "If Not by Tanks, Then by Banks? The Role of Soft Power in Putin's Foreign Policy," *Europe–Asia Studies* 58, no. 7 (November 2006): 1079–1099.

113. Tony Wesolowksy, "Russia Reconquers Eastern Europe Via Business," *Christian Science Monitor,* November 17, 2011, at http://www.csmonitor.com/World/Europe/2011/1117/Russia-reconquers-Eastern-Europe-via-business.

114. Stephen Blank, "Russian weapons and foreign rogues," *Asia Times,* March 26, 2003, at http://www.atimes.com/atimes/Middle_East/EC26Ak04.html.

115. Gvosdev, "Guns, Gas and Oil," op. cit.

116. Yelizaveta Isakova, "Russia to strengthen ties with Balkan states," *Voice of Russia,* April 19, 2011, at http://english.ruvr.ru/2011/04/19/49156407.html.

117. Gvosdev, "Guns, Gas and Oil," op. cit.

118. Stefan Bos, "New Hungarian Leader Wants Closer Relations with Russia," *World News Site,* April 22, 2002, at http://worldnewssite.com/News/2002/April/.html.

119. Judy Dempsey, "Hungary Chooses Gazprom over EU," *New York Times,* March 17, 2007, at http://www.nytimes.com/2007/03/12/world/europe/12iht-hungary.4885468.html?_r=1&.

120. "Hungary Signs Up to South Stream Plan," *St. Petersburg Times* 1352, no. 16 (February 29, 2008), at http://www.sptimes.ru/index.php?action_id=2&story_id=25199.

121. Dmitry Babich, "How Hungary's Viktor Orban reoriented his criticism from Russia to the EU," *Voice of Russia,* April 28, 2012, at http://english.ruvr.ru/2012_04_28/73248756/; "Orbán and the wind from the east," *Economist,* November 14, 2011, at http://www.economist.com/blogs/easternapproaches/2011/11/hungarys-politics.

122. Matthew Czekaj, "Does Russia Want a Toehold in the Balkans?" *Jamestown Foundation Blog,* November 30, 2011, at http://jamestownfoundation.blogspot.com/2011/11/does-russia-want-toehold-in-balkans.html.

123. "Russian Navy starts forming Mediterranean task force," *Russia and India Report,* March 12, 2013, at http://indrus.in/news/2013/03/12/russian_navy_starts_forming_mediterranean_task_force_22821.html.

124. Richard Krickus, "The Presidential Crisis in Lithuania: Its Roots and the Russian Factor," *Wilson Center European Studies* 292 (January 28, 2004), at http://www.wilsoncenter.org/publication/292-the-presidential-crisis-lithuania-its-roots-and-the-russian-factor.

125. John Lough, *Russia's Energy Diplomacy,* Chatham House Briefing Paper, REP RSP BP 2011/01 (May 2011), 8–9.

126. Vladimir Socor, "Russia Completing Baltic Pipeline System Construction, Reducing Druzhba Pipeline Flow," *European Dialogue,* March 2, 2012, at http://eurodialogue.org/Russia-Completing-Baltic-Pipeline-System-Construction-Reducing-Druzhba-Pipeline-Flow.

127. Alexandros Petersen, "The Molotov Ribbentrop Pipeline," *Wall Street Journal,* November 9, 2009, at http://online.wsj.com/article/SB10001424052748703567204574499150087261242.html.

128. "Nord Stream 'a waste of money,' says Poland," *EurActiv,* January 11, 2010, at http://www.euractiv.com/energy/nord-stream-waste-money-poland/article-188727.

129. "Visegrad countries and Russia," *Visegrad.info,* May 7, 2010, at http://www.visegrad.info/v4-eu-russia-relations/factsheet/visegrad-countries-and-russia.html.

130. "No more Mr Nice Guy," *Economist,* September 13, 2012, at http://www.economist.com/blogs/easternapproaches/2012/09/czech-realpolitik.

131. "Russia lifts embargo on Polish meat," *EurActiv,* December 21, 2007, at http://www.euractiv.com/trade/russia-lifts-embargo-polish-meat-news-219164.

132. "Under the New Missile Defense Plan There Are Still Options for Assurance," *CSIS,* September 18, 2009, at http://csis.org/blog/under-new-missile-defense-plan-there-are-still-options-assurance; "Visegrad countries and Russia," op. cit.

133. Tom Z. Collina, "The European Phased Adaptive Approach at a Glance," *Arms Control Association,* November 2012, at http://www.armscontrol.org/factsheets/Phasedadaptiveapproach; Andrew E. Kramer, "Russian General Makes Threat on Missile-Defense Sites," *New York Times,* May 3, 2012, at http://www.nytimes.com/2012/05/04/world/europe/russian-general-threatens-pre-emptive-attacks-on-missile-defense-sites.html?_r=1.

134. Judy Dempsey, "War in Georgia exposes NATO's fault lines," *New York Times,* September 3, 2008, at http://www.nytimes.com/2008/09/03/world/europe/03iht-letter.1.15864788.html?pagewanted=all.

CHAPTER 7

Europe

Russia's "Traditional Orientation"

Western and Central Europe have always had long-standing ties to Russia. Most historians accept the initial band of the "Rus'" were Vikings who settled among the East Slavs yet kept their close links with the Viking communities of Scandinavia and the trading centers of the Baltic Sea. The princes of Rus' intermarried with the nobility and royalty of Germany, France, and England; for instance, Gytha, the daughter of King Harold, the last Anglo-Saxon ruler of England, married Vladimir Monomakh (ruled 1113–1125), and her son, Mstislav, ruled in Novgorod and the north before becoming the ruler of a united Kievan state. During the Middle Ages, the city-state mercantile republic of Novgorod was connected to the medieval German trading network of the Hansa, while Italian craftsmen helped to design the cathedrals of Moscow's Kremlin. Yet the Rus' also clashed with the West. In the 13th century, Alexander Nevsky, prince of Novgorod, had to deal with both Swedish incursions as well as the threat of the German Teutonic knights, creating a narrative that has endured to the present day of European hostility to Russia (most notably in the 1938 Sergei Eistenstein film *Alexander Nevsky*).

As Russia emerged from the Mongol Yoke, and as the Byzantine Empire collapsed in the south, Western Europe became more important as a source of goods and technologies needed for the modernization of the Muscovite state. Italian artists and architects helped to design some of the cathedrals of the Moscow Kremlin, while Russian bishops attended the Council of Florence in 1439. Ivan III's second wife was an exiled Byzantine princess, Zoe-Sophia, who had lived in Rome. Under the rule of Ivan and Sophia's son Grand Prince Vassily III (ruled 1503–1533), the first "German suburb" (*Nemetskaia Sloboda*) was established near Moscow to provide a place for Western European merchants, craftsmen, and soldiers in the employ of the Russian state to reside. Vassily also received the famous embassy of the Holy Roman Emperor Maximilian; Maximilian's ambassador, Sigismund von Herberstein, produced the first major study of Russia, *Rerum Moscoviticarum Commentarii*. Vassily's son Tsar Ivan the Terrible attempted to take control of the Baltic coast to open direct links between Russia and the West and opened trade relations with England through the northern White Sea port of Arkhangelsk. A century before Peter the Great, Tsar Boris Godunov attempted to send young Russians to study in Western Europe.

But it was under Peter the Great that Russia fully reoriented itself to its "European vector." For the last 300 years, Europe has been the principal focus of Russian foreign policy. Peter and his successors made Russian entry into the European state system as a full member their top priority as well as starting the tradition for Russian monarchs to marry European royalty. One such German princess, Sophia of Anhalt-Zerbst, married Emperor Peter III, and, after her husband's deposition, ruled as Catherine the Great (1762–1796). Peter had no preconceived notions as to which Western European nations he wished to form alliances and trade relations with, although he had a preference for dealing with the Netherlands because of the important role of Dutch traders and engineers who were engaged in modernizing the Russian economy and military. At various points, Peter reached out to Britain, France, Austria, Denmark, and the Italian city-state of Venice as possible allies and partners. At the same time, Russia's participation in the Great Northern War (1700–1721) meant that Russian armies and fleets, for the first time, were operating in central Europe and the western Baltic region, beginning a pattern of Russian power projection into the heart of Europe that would see Russian armies occupy both Berlin (in 1763) and Paris (in 1814, foreshadowing the Soviet advance into the heart of Europe during the Second World War).

In the course of the 18th century, Russian statesmen attempted to determine what Russia's interests in Europe were. In a spring 1725 report to Emperor Peter, chancellor Andrei Osterman argued that Russia's principal strategic interests lay in the Baltic basin and that this area ought to be of prime importance to Russian policy. A. P. Betuzhev-Riumin, when serving as chancellor to Empress Elizabeth (1741–1758), argued for the development of alliances with Austria and Great Britain and saw France, Sweden, and Prussia as Russia's enemies in Europe. After his fall from power in 1758, his successor, M. L. Vorontsov, argued for keeping the alliance with Austria but preferred improving relations with France while being more hostile to Great Britain. During the first part of Emperor Catherine's reign, Nikita Panin proposed a "Northern Accord" that would ally Russia to Prussia and Denmark. These policy debates set in course the dynamics that have governed Russia's relationship to Europe ever since: Who is the favored partner and who is Russia's principal foe: France, Britain, or Germany?[1]

The zigzag nature of Russian relations with Europe continued when Russia found itself, at times, an opponent of Napoleonic France and its ally. These shifts also reflected changes in the balance of power in the Russian court, as different ministers and factions argued whether Russia's interests were best served by alliance with France or joining the coalitions against Napoleon with Austria, Prussia, and Britain.[2] After the defeat of Napoleon, Emperor Alexander I proposed the Holy Alliance (between Austria, Prussia, and Russia) as a way to ensure stability in Europe among the major powers; over time, it was expanded to include France and Great Britain and was intended to support the postwar settlements reached at the Congress of Vienna (1815) and subsequent pan-European Congresses. This system broke down, however, and during the Crimean War, Russia fought against Britain and France.

The unification of all the German principalities by Prussia and the proclamation of the German Empire (the Second Reich) in 1871 began to alter the geopolitical balance in Europe. The architect of German unification, Chancellor Otto von Bismarck, sought to preserve good relations with Russia, first by creating the *Dreikaiserbund* (Three Emperors' League) in 1873, which was an effort for Germany, Russia, and Austria-Hungary to maintain the European balance of power. This association dissolved in 1876, due in part to Austrian and Russian rivalries for influence in the Balkans, but was replaced by a Three Emperors' Alliance in 1881. This too foundered over Austro-Russia competition for influence, leading Bismarck to conclude a separate Reinsurance Treaty with Russia in 1887 that provided for a nonaggression pact between Germany and Russia. However, the new Kaiser Wilhelm II, in displacing Bismarck in 1890 from the chancellorship, decided not to uphold Bismarck's foreign policy legacy and let the treaty lapse in favor of cementing Germany's alliance with Austria, thus paving the way for the Russian-French alliance to follow.[3] Increasingly, "Russia viewed Germany both as a rival in east-central Europe and as a threat to the Russian heartland."[4] This rivalry ultimately led to the First World War.

In the aftermath of World War I and the Bolshevik Revolution, Vladimir Lenin and his cohorts initially expected that a wave of socialist revolutions would sweep through Europe, bringing to power friendly pro-Soviet regimes. Not only did this not occur, but tsarist Russia's allies—France and Great Britain—became Soviet Russia's enemies, supporting the anti-Communist (White) movements seeking to overthrow Lenin's government. France, in particular, also emerged as the Great Power patron to a group of east European states (such as Poland and the Baltic States). French assistance proved to be crucial in allowing Poland to repel the 1920 Soviet invasion, and French diplomacy worked to knit together an alliance in the region directed against both Germany and the Soviet (the so-called Little Entente).[5] As a result, the new Soviet state and the Weimar republic in Germany decided to find ways to cooperate, especially since both Soviet Russia and Germany were "losers" in the postwar order. The 1922 Treaty of Rapallo, the first major diplomatic agreement normalizing relations between a revolutionary Communist state and a Western capitalist country, paved the way for closer Russian-German ties, including Germany's ability to build and test military equipment inside Russia, far from prying Allied eyes, that the Treaty of Versailles had forbidden Germany to maintain.

When Adolf Hitler came to power in 1933, Soviet policy shifted several times. At first, the Soviet government aligned with France to counterbalance Nazi Germany, but then, in 1939, Josef Stalin reached out to sign a nonaggression pact with Hitler. Then, after Germany's attack on the USSR in 1941, he allied the Soviet Union with the three Western Allies (Britain, France, and the United States).

In the aftermath of World War II, the Soviet Union, guided by Stalin's dictum to the Yugoslav Communist Milovan Djilas that each great power would impose its social and political system "as far as its army can reach," created a bloc of pro-Soviet states in Central and Eastern Europe. Indeed, as Stalin told Djilas, "If now there is not a communist government in Paris, this is only because Russia has no army which can reach Paris." The division of Germany into zones controlled by each of the Allied powers (Britain, France, the Soviet Union, and the United States) was only supposed to be temporary. But when it became clear to Stalin that a unified Germany would not be particularly pro-Soviet, the USSR concentrated on transforming its sector into a German communist state (the German Democratic Republic, popularly referred to as East Germany), leading to a division of Germany that was to last until 1990.

So it was "the evolving perception of a Soviet threat to western Europe"[6] that forced an unprecedented degree of unity among the Western European states and also pushed them into a close alliance with the United States, leading to the creation (in 1949) of the North Atlantic Treaty Organization and of various economic arrangements that would culminate in the Treaty of Rome (1957), which led to the formation of the European Community (now the European Union). In turn, fear of the resurgent power of the Western bloc led the Soviets to take steps to isolate themselves and their east European satellites, most notably through the erection of the Berlin Wall in 1961, which separated the Soviet-controlled sector of the former German capital from the Western zones.

Post-Stalin Soviet leaders realized that they would need to weaken the transatlantic tie binding Western Europe to the United States (and Canada). In 1960, Nikita Khrushchev told Soviet officials, "We must work further at turning the United States against Europe, and Europe against the United States."[7] Soviet strategies fluctuated between relying on indigenous Communist parties in Western Europe, especially in France and Italy, to influence European governments to cultivating non–Communist leaders like French president Charles de Gaulle to take a more independent line vis-à-vis the United States. At times, Soviet leaders offered a settlement of the German question and the creation of a "neutral" united Germany as a way to create conditions for the United States to quit Europe.[8]

The Soviet Union was always concerned that a more unified Europe, in a strong alliance with the United States, would pose a major threat to its security.

Indeed, when de Gaulle, in 1964, offered his vision of a Europe united "from the Atlantic to the Urals," it initially caused a panic in Moscow. Since the USSR extended to the Pacific Ocean, was de Gaulle hinting at a breakup of the Soviet Union? Later de Gaulle privately clarified his remarks, commenting: "There will come a time when we will build Europe together with the Soviet Union." During his 1966 visit to Moscow, de Gaulle again reiterated the theme of the Soviet Union as an indispensable part of the European area.[9] De Gaulle's diplomacy was augmented by the launch, in 1969, of what was termed *Ostpolitik* ("Eastern Policy") by the West German government of Willy Brandt. As envisioned by Egon Bahr, Brandt's chief advisor on foreign policy, *Ostpolitik* was designed to reduce tensions in Europe by recognizing the permanence of the post–World War II settlement—including the existence of a de facto Soviet sphere of influence in Eastern Europe—and by offering the Soviet Union favorable trading concessions in order to foster stability.[10]

Brandt's government concluded the Treaty of Moscow with the Soviet Union, normalizing relations between the Soviet Union and West Germany in 1970; within this agreement, the West Germans recognized, for the first time, the post–World War II settlement in Europe. This treaty paved the way for a new Four Power agreement (between the four victor nations in World War II, Britain, France, the United States, and the USSR) in 1971, expanding connections between the divided city of Berlin and between East and West Germany, and ultimately the Basic Treaty of 1972 in which East and West Germany recognized each other as sovereign states. With these agreements in place, Brandt reached out to Leonid Brezhnev with a proposal for a general conference on European security. Bahr himself notes how this process, which started with talks on reducing armed forces in Europe, paved the way for the convening of the Conference on Security and Co-operation in Europe (CSCE) in 1973, which produced the Helsinki Final Act in 1975.[11] This declaration represented an acceptance by all states in Europe (with the exception of Albania) as well as the United States and Canada of the postwar settlement, including all border changes. The Soviet leadership also interpreted the Final Act as a belated recognition of the permanent division of Europe into a Western and a Soviet bloc.[12]

As the political situation on the continent stabilized, new economic linkages developed between Western Europe and the Soviet Union. By the 1970s, European companies began to export large amounts of high-technology goods to the USSR, even when confronted with strenuous American objections that such sales strengthened the Soviet Union's industrial base. The United States also unsuccessfully opposed the so-called "deal of the century"—the construction of a natural gas pipeline from Siberia to Western Europe. U.S. governments, particularly the Reagan administration, interpreted European economic interdependence with the Soviet Union as leading to a dependence on the USSR—and a weakening of the Western alliance.[13]

But, as Gordon Craig notes, this weaving together of Russian and European economic interests did not work "well on the political level,"[14] in part because competing security imperatives caused the Soviet military to pursue policies that undermined closer ties with Europe. In particular, the Soviet decision to deploy some 500 SS-20 intermediate-range nuclear missiles as a way to get around arms-control restrictions on ICBMs—and to be able to use such missiles against U.S. targets in Europe—led Western European governments to become much more supportive of U.S. proposals to deploy Pershing II intermediate-range missiles in Europe. An extensive Soviet-backed propaganda campaign to prevent the U.S. deployments between 1979 and 1983 failed.[15] Fear of a Soviet military threat to Europe helped to reinforce the security relationship with the United States.

So, by the late 1970s, the general polarities of the Europe–Russia relationship were set in place that have endured to the present day. On the one hand, there has been growing economic integration between Russia and Western Europe, especially in the field of energy; on the other hand, there is continued mistrust in the security arena, especially with the continued existence of NATO, still classed in Russian defense strategy as a threat to Russia.[16]

After coming to power in 1985, Mikhail Gorbachev promoted his concept of a Common European Home, one defined by reduced tensions and greater integration between the Soviet bloc and Western Europe. Speaking in Prague in 1987, he stressed the "overriding significance to the European course of our foreign policy" and called for "the acknowledgment of a certain integral whole" within the European continent. Two years later, in Strasbourg, Gorbachev proclaimed: "The philosophy of the 'Common European Home' concept rules out the probability of an armed clash and the very possibility of the use of force or threat of force—alliance against alliance, inside the alliances, wherever."[17]

By the end of the 1980s, the Soviet withdrawal from Eastern Europe offered the possibility that Western Europeans would "seek to reduce their political dependence on Washington, as tensions with the Soviets ease and as progress is made in rolling back the division of the continent."[18] The improvement in U.S.-Soviet relations also played a role. At the 1989 summit between Gorbachev and U.S. President George H. W. Bush in Malta, Gorbachev stressed that his proposal for a "Common European Home" was not intended, as Gorbachev's own spokesman has noted, "to decouple US security interests from Western Europe or to chase the Americans from the continent as has been the concealed, and even declared, goal of Soviet diplomacy" during previous years.[19] This cleared the way for the 1990 Paris Summit, which proclaimed an end to the Cold War in Europe. The Charter for a New Europe was also supposed to lay out the blueprint (in its

Guidelines for the Future) for the dismantling of the two competing blocs and for the creation of new, pan–European security institutions. Indeed, many Soviet officials assumed that the competing institutions of east and west—NATO and the Warsaw Pact; the European Community and the east European members of the CMEA—would merge together, giving Moscow an important role in the process of European integration.[20] These expectations were based, in part, on statements that had been made by Western leaders—starting with Winston Churchill's 1956 proclamation that "in a true unity of Europe Russia must play her part"—and continuing with proposals for a European Security Council and a European Confederation advanced by then-West German Foreign Minister Hans Dietrich Genscher and French President Francois Mitterrand.[21]

But the collapse of the Soviet Union radically changed the dynamic of Moscow's relations with Europe. The removal of any threat of a Soviet invasion of Western Europe and the return of Russia to its 17th-century borders—thus removing its ability to easily project power into Europe—eliminated the fear of a Russian threat to the peace and security of Western European states. It thus made these governments much more willing to work with Russia. At the same time, the consolidation of the European Union changed the balance of power with Russia. Today, it is the EU that "outweighs" a diminished Russia that emerged from the wreckage of the USSR.

RUSSIA AND THE EUROPEAN UNION SINCE THE SOVIET COLLAPSE

As the institutions that were to coalesce to form the European Community were being negotiated in the 1950s, the initial Soviet objective "had been to prevent or delay the formation of any politically or militarily united body in Western Europe."[22] Over time, however, the Soviet attitude changed; there was an expectation that a more integrated Western Europe would emerge as a separate actor in world affairs, diminishing its security ties to the United States, and that it would be possible for Moscow to chart a more productive relationship with a more assertive Europe.[23] In 1989, the Soviet Union concluded an agreement with the European Community that, according to its preamble, was designed "to establish direct contractual relations" between the EC and the USSR to promote economic cooperation.[24]

One day after Boris Yeltsin and the presidents of Ukraine and Belarus had agreed to dissolve the Soviet Union, the European Council meet in Maastricht, Holland, on December 9 through 10, 1991, to draw up the treaty that would create the European Union. Signed in 1992, the Treaty transformed the European Community into a closer economic and political confederation of its member-states. The power relationship between Moscow and Brussels, the capital of the Union, changed dramatically as a result. The Russian Federation inherited only some of the Soviet Union's territory, population, and economic infrastructure, while the Union has grown in several waves of expansion. Today, the EU encompasses a total population of more than 500 million that produces a gross domestic product (GDP) of some $17.5 billion per year; Russia has only 143 million and a much smaller economy, with a GDP of $1.8 billion—smaller even than the individual national GDP for Germany, France, or Italy.

The expectation that eastern and western institutions would merge also evaporated as the Soviet bloc dissolved and former Soviet satellites sought to join the surviving Western bodies like NATO and the EU, a process already discussed in the previous chapter. Instead of having a major role to play in European institutions, post–Soviet Russia now found herself on the outside, begging for admittance. In particular, the North Atlantic Treaty Organization did not disappear in the years following the dissolution of the Warsaw Pact but remained intact.

The stated position of the Russian government remains that Russia is a part of Europe. It is official policy to support the creation of political, economic, and security institutions bringing together the countries of Europe "from Lisbon to Vladivostok."[25] The European vector also enjoys broad popular support; some two-thirds of Russians agree with the proposition that "Russia is a natural part of Europe" and that Russia "will more closely be tied with that region of the world."[26]

Yet, in the two decades that followed the dissolution of the Soviet Union, Churchill's dictum that Russia would "play her part" in helping to forge a united Europe has not come to pass. In part, this is because of the legacies of the immediate post–Cold War period. The institutions created by the Soviet Union—the Warsaw Pact and the Council for Mutual Economic Assistance—collapsed, while those of the West—the North Atlantic Alliance (NATO) and the European Union (EU)—found new purposes following the Cold War and even began to admit former Soviet-bloc states as members. The only European organization that remained that the Soviet Union had been a member of was the Conference on Security and Cooperation in Europe, a byproduct of the 1975 Helsinki Accords; in 1994, it was transformed into the Organization for Security and Cooperation in Europe (OSCE). However, initial Russian proposals for NATO to disband and to be replaced by the OSCE never occurred, and, over time, the Russian view of the OSCE has changed. The Russians were quite critical that the OSCE had not been able to prevent the NATO intervention in Kosovo in 1999 and came to believe that OSCE institutions were complicit in the various "color revolutions" that swept the Eurasian space in the 2000s.[27] Today, the OSCE is no longer seen as an organization that contributes in any meaningful way to Russian security; it does not give Russia any real voice in European security affairs; and with its emphasis on monitoring countries for their compliance with human rights and free-election standards, the OSCE is now often seen as a "weak and ineffectual, but increasingly intrusive" organization.[28]

There are three principal approaches in Russian foreign policy toward the pan-European institutions. The first focuses on "remedial repair"—making no effort to change current institutions and instead concentrating efforts to make changes that will benefit Russian interests. The second, "partial reconstruction," attempts to create additional components that will allow Russia to have a voice within European institutions. The final approach, "fundamental transformation," seeks to create new European institutions altogether.[29] Russian policy toward European institutions has not consistently followed any one of these approaches, and government actions lurch between these three poles. This is due, in part, to differing evaluations of the European vector within different Russian foreign policy sectors. Liberalizing and modernizing segments of the Russian political and business elite have tended to strongly support closer integration with Europe; nationalists have preferred to hold Europe at arm's length; authoritarian modernizers, particularly those associated with the *siloviki* factions in the Kremlin, while not rejecting ties to Europe altogether, advocate for a closer partnership with China.[30]

Initially, in the immediate period following the collapse of the USSR, there were expectations that a post-Soviet Russia would immediately become a full member of Western European institutions.[31] The Yeltsin administration started the process by applying in May 1992 for membership in the Council of Europe, which, although separate from the European Union, also exists to promote greater integration among European states and is often the first step for states moving along the path to eventual membership in the EU. In 1996, Russia was accepted as a member, but when it joined, it took upon itself commitments to uphold standards found in various pan-European conventions, notably on human rights, and also accepted the jurisdiction of the European Court of Human Rights to hear complaints against Russia. Russia's membership in the Council has been problematic, creating tension between those who argue that Russia ought to be held to European standards in law and justice and those concerned about excluding a major European state from a pan-European institution.[32] For its part, Russia frequently complains that both the Court and the Parliamentary Assembly of the Council of Europe (PACE) attempt to interfere in matters that are the domestic affairs of Russia, notably the conduct of the antiseparatist campaigns in Chechnya or how Russia conducts elections. The chairman of the Russian Constitutional Court, Valerii Zorkin, has argued that Russia "should fight for the preservation of its sovereignty" and ought to take a "careful attitude" toward decisions of the Council in order to protect Russia "from inadequate, questionable decisions."[33]

Russia held up its ratification of Protocol Number 14 reforming the Court until it received guarantees that the Russian judge on the European Court would be able to review complaints brought against the Russian government.[34] Finally, in September 2012, the speaker of the Duma cancelled his scheduled appearance before PACE "in the face of the mounting criticism of Russia's domestic politics by other members of the assembly."[35]

The Russian experience with the Council of Europe has helped to diminish enthusiasm on all sides for rapid Russian integration into existing European institutions. The Russian side remains concerned about the loss of sovereignty and control that comes with membership in European organizations. Many European states, in turn, are worried that if granted membership, Russia would seek to undermine European institutions from within by weakening standards and enforcement mechanisms.

While Boris Yeltsin's government nurtured aspirations for joining the European Union, the EU was always reluctant to consider extending an invitation to Russia, based on its size and the problems in its economy. Instead, the EU proposed a Partnership and Cooperation Agreement (PCA) with Russia to Yeltsin at a summit in Corfu in 1994 (which ultimately went into force in 1997).[36]

Hopes for an improved relationship between the EU and Russia were raised during the tenure of Romano Prodi, a former prime minister of Italy, as president of the European Commission. A significant milestone was the 2002 decision of the EU to grant Russia "market economy status," which cleared away a number of trade barriers that had inhibited Russia's commerce with the countries of the Union. In announcing the decision at that year's EU–Russia summit, Prodi declared,

> I am happy to announce that we will grant Russia the status of a full market economy. What we promise we will keep. As Russia's principal trading partner it is right and proper that we be the first to recognise and reward the considerable efforts undertaken by this country in recent years by treating her as a fully fledged market economy.[37]

The Putin administration, however, took the question of Russian membership in the EU off the table. Instead, at the 2003 summit in St. Petersburg, the EU and Russia committed to working jointly to develop four "common spaces": the Common Economic Space (leading ultimately to freer movement of people, goods, and capital between the EU and Russia); the Common Space for External Security (envisioning Russia and the EU as a single security theater); the Common Space for Research and Education; and the Common Space for Freedom, Security, and Justice (permitting, in part, a closer alignment of legal and judicial norms). Prodi characterized this approach as "sharing everything with the Union but institutions."[38] In 2005, Russia and the EU adopted a series of "road maps" detailing the steps that would need to be taken to make the Common Spaces a reality. This process has led to an extensive institutionalization of the Russia–EU relationship. In any given year, there are a regular series of meetings convened under the aegis of the EU–Russia Permanent Partnership Council, which are held at the ministerial level, and the relevant Russian ministers and EU commissioners meet for each of the four Common Space working groups. All of this work culminates in the EU–Russia summits that are convened between the Russian president and the president of the European Commission.[39]

The Common Spaces approach was designed, in part, to square the circle that Russia is a part of Europe even if not a member of the European Union, by making Russia an associate of the European Union with some of the benefits that might accrue from full membership in the EU. At the 2007 EU–Russia Summit held in May in the Russian city of Samara, the president of the European Commission, Jose Manuel Barroso, declared that "Russia is a European country," while President Putin reaffirmed that the institutionalization of ties between the EU and Russia was for "coordinating our cooperation."[40]

In reality, however, the road map to achieving the Common Spaces has been difficult to follow. Trying to harmonize Russian rules and regulations with EU standards has threatened some of the benefits enjoyed by domestic Russian companies and makes them more vulnerable to competition from European firms. Russia is also not always interested in changing its laws to more closely harmonize with EU standards.[41] In the fields of security cooperation and foreign policy, the fallout of the Russian clash with Georgia in 2008, continuing acrimony over the U.S. plans for theater ballistic missile defense in Europe, and ongoing disagreements over international crises like Libya and Syria have impeded efforts for closer cooperation. The perceived "democracy deficit" in Russia and charges of human rights abuses levied against the Russian government have made it difficult for the EU to embrace Russia as a partner. For its part, the EU remains concerned about giving Russian energy firms even more access to the European market and has not been enthusiastic about extending the right to Russian citizens to travel visa free within the Union.

The EU–Russia dialogue is also complicated by the expansion of the EU itself, especially after the rounds of expansion in 2004 and 2007 brought many of the former Eastern European satellites of the Soviet Union into the EU, who have been more willing to question the value of EU-Russia cooperation and to place stringent requirements on Moscow. It also puts the Russian government in the uncomfortable position that countries Moscow formerly dominated now have the ability to block or thwart Russia's European interests. Given the ups and downs in Russia's relationships with Eastern Europe (discussed at length in the previous chapter), the expansion of the EU has further diminished Russian interests in working through the European Union as a whole.

In turn, Russia's effort to create a Eurasian Union also complicates its relationship with the EU; the customs union already concluded with Belarus and Kazakhstan has focused Moscow's attention on harmonizing its economic policies with its immediate neighbors at the expense of continuing with a process of closer integration with the EU. Each member of the existing customs union has already agreed that the proposed Eurasian Economic Commission will serve as its representative in regional and global trade talks.[42] It has also meant that EU negotiations with Russia must now take into account Russia's commitments with its other partners—which has complicated, for instance, EU efforts to isolate Belarus.[43] Finally, Putin himself has indicated that future EU–Russian discussions would "have to deal with the Eurasian Union commission along with Moscow," in effect shifting the discussion from the level of the EU with one country to that of the EU with a second regional organization.[44]

The original PCA was set to expire in 2007. But many of the tensions in the EU–Russia relationship, including the impact of the new Central-Eastern European members of the EU on the process, have complicated the efforts to conclude a new and more comprehensive PCA. Negotiations for a replacement agreement began in 2008 at the EU–Russia summit in Khanty-Mansiisk and have continued through 2012, but both sides are no nearer to concluding a new treaty. As a result, the original PCA must be annually renewed in order to provide a legal basis for Russia–EU relations.[45]

Although there is a regular dialogue between the Russian government and the EU—a biannual summit between the Russian president and the European Commission President and the European Council President—to discuss issues, in recent years, the summits have not achieved any major breakthroughs. Many of the details for accelerating the EU-Russia partnership are now bogged down at the technical level, leaving the relationship in a state of "optimistic stagnation."[46] Putin traveled to Brussels in December 2012 for his meetings with Jose Manuel Barroso (European Commission president) and European Council President Herman Van Rompuy, but there were no breakthroughs in resolving deadlock on issues ranging from visa-free travel to energy questions.[47]

Nowhere is the failure of Russia to fundamentally redefine its relationship with Europe more apparent than in the rise and fall of Dmitry Medvedev's initiative for a new European Security Treaty. In June 2008, Medvedev proposed that a new pan-European security treaty be developed, one that would erase the legacy of the Cold War and be based on the principle that "no nation or international organisation operating in the Euro-Atlantic region is entitled to strengthen its own security at the cost of other nations or organisations." In 2009, Medvedev dispatched a draft of the proposed treaty to other European leaders as well as to the EU and NATO for consideration. It contained some controversial points, including provisos that military alliances operating in the European and Eurasian areas would have to consult with all European security treaty members, as well as extending the principle that an attack on one European security treaty member would be considered as an attack on all—in effect, giving Russia a security guarantee.[48]

While individual European leaders expressed interest—the Italian, German, and Spanish foreign ministers and French President Nicolas Sarkozy acknowledged a willingness to discuss Medvedev's proposals[49]—ultimately, the process went nowhere. European leaders were particularly suspicious of Russia's intentions in proposing the draft. They saw the treaty as a way to constrain NATO's freedom of operation (including placing limits on the further expansion of the alliance) and perhaps even trying to commit European powers to come to Russia's assistance in the case that Russia faced problems with China over its Far Eastern provinces.[50]

In February 2010, Catherine Ashton, the High Representative for Foreign Affairs and Security Policy of the European Union, reiterated that European states would be interested in discussing Russian initiatives but would not concede the principle that every state in Europe has the right to determine what alliances and commitments it chooses to accept. At the NATO-Russia Council meeting in September 2010, no European state challenged the position articulated by the United States, that trying to negotiate a new pan-European security treaty among more than 50 nations—thus repeating the Helsinki process—would be too cumbersome and difficult.[51] Already largely a dead letter, Putin himself has dropped the pursuit of the treaty since returning to the presidency.[52]

More importantly, no European member-state of NATO has chosen to leave the alliance or block its plans in order to gain favor with Moscow. All members of the alliance approved U.S. plans for a ballistic missile shield for Europe, a proposal vehemently opposed by Moscow. While continuing to invite Russian participation in the project, no European state was willing to give Russia veto power to prevent deployment and activation of the system.[53] European states have not relaxed their vigilance for security threats that emanate from Russia. The alliance drew up contingency plans to cope with any possible Russian incursion against the Baltic states after the 2008 clash between Russia and Georgia, and individual European states continue to maintain a vigilant watch on Russian military activities.[54] In September 2012, for instance, Russian aircraft engaged in a training mission over international waters were nonetheless escorted by fighter aircraft from the German, Danish, and British air forces.[55]

On the whole, the Russian experience with Europe is that the bureaucracies of European institutions, starting with the European Commission, are more inclined to take what Moscow considers to be anti-Russian stands and policy positions. In October 2012, Foreign Minister Lavrov criticized what he termed a "politicized approach" on the part of European institutions in making progress toward implementing a visa-free regime between Russia and the countries of the European Union.[56] So the main thrust in Russia's policy toward Europe as a whole is now to ensure that pan–European institutions do not adopt policies that "are not actively looking to curb Russian influence in Europe."[57]

On the other hand, the EU is Russia's largest trading partner and main source for investment, so Russia is not free to simply disregard the EU's positions. More than half of Russia's foreign trade is with the European Union, and nearly three-quarters of its foreign investment originates from the states of the EU.[58] Europe remains Russia's largest trading partner, and Russia is Europe's third-largest trading partner. Moreover, Europe and Russia are locked into a mutually inter-dependent energy relationship. Eighty-eight percent of Russia's oil and 70% of its natural gas are exported to Europe, while Russia is Europe's main source for energy: 44.5% of Europe's natural gas consumption and 33.05% of its demand for oil is satisfied from Russia.[59]

FIGURE 7.1

EU Imports from and Exports to Russia, 2007–2011 (in billions of euros)

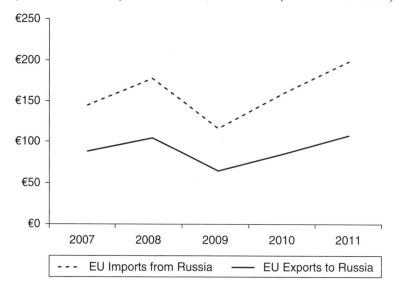

Source: Eurostat.

Given these realities, all of this creates the preference for Moscow to bypass the European center and to work directly with European countries on a bilateral basis—and to use these country-to-country relations to influence the EU as a whole.[60] The Russian government has identified its most important business and security relationships in Europe as Germany, France, Italy, and Britain.[61]

THE RUSSO–GERMAN RELATIONSHIP

Angela Stent describes the "interaction between Russia and Germany" as "one of the defining international relationships of the twentieth century."[62] The Russo-German relationship has often set the agenda for European international relations as a whole; the two powers, either by their cooperation or through their hostility, have, at several key points, reshaped the map of the continent.

After the Second World War, Germany was supposed to be temporarily partitioned by the victorious Allied powers, but Soviet concerns that a unified Germany might ally with the West and once again turn against the Soviet Union led to the permanent division of the country and the creation, in 1949, of an East German Communist regime (the German Democratic Republic, or GDR) closely linked to Moscow. East Germany soon emerged as a "valuable asset for [Soviet] domestic economic development" as well as a critical ally for asserting "Soviet hegemony over the Northern Tier in Eastern Europe and as a glacis from which to project Soviet influence westward."[63] The GDR soon became the Soviet Union's main trading partner, as well as serving as a center for high-precision industries for the entire Soviet bloc.[64] In part to preserve the East German state, which was menaced by a continuing outflow of population to the West, the Soviets authorized the construction of the Berlin Wall in 1961, which cut off the Western sectors of the city from East Germany and created a heavily fortified border that drastically cut down on the numbers of East Germans leaving—but also raised tensions by highlighting the division of Germany.

At the same time, the Soviet government continued to try and court West Germany, especially as a trading partner, through what Angela Stent and others have labeled *Westpolitik*—an effort to encourage West Germany to distance itself from the United States and embrace a closer relationship with the Soviet Union.[65] Westpolitik was a counterpart to the *Ostpolitik* pursued by the West German government, which had already been discussed earlier in this chapter.

In 1970, when the West German government signed the Treaty of Moscow, it delivered a Letter on German Unity to the Soviet government, pledging that West Germany would put the preservation of strategic stability in Europe over its desire for German reunification.[66] When the East German government opened the Berlin Wall in November 1989 and promised to liberalize travel requirements for

East Germans, momentum built up for unification. At first, Moscow resisted and argued for the continued division of Germany. West German foreign minister Hans-Dietrich Genscher gave a speech in the city of Tutzing in January 1990 that addressed many of the Soviet concerns, including a pledge that the eastern part of Germany would not be brought into NATO military structures, noting that "there will be no extension of NATO territory to the East, i.e. nearer the borders of the Soviet Union."[67] Gorbachev then gave his support for a diplomatic process, the Two Plus Four Talks (the two Germanies plus the four victors of World War II), to lay out the conditions that would permit German reunification. In turn, Genscher (acting on behalf of Chancellor Helmut Kohl) and the West German government pressed hard for the Western powers to extend the hand of friendship to Moscow. With a number of guarantees in place for Moscow's interests, Gorbachev signed off on German reunification, and the Treaty on the Final Settlement with Respect to Germany was signed in Moscow on September 12, 1990.[68]

The German government, in turn, made it clear that it would work to make sure that Moscow's interests were not neglected. Kohl concluded a 20-year Friendship Agreement with Gorbachev in November 1990 that pledged that neither country would go to war with the other—a significant concession given that the Soviet Union was still in existence and Germany was a member of NATO. Kohl was also the driving force behind the invitation extended to Gorbachev to attend the 1991 Group of Seven summit in London and to make his pitch for financial aid.[69] After the Soviet Union collapsed, Kohl continued to cultivate Boris Yeltsin, in part to make sure that post-Soviet Russia could continue to implement agreements calling for withdrawal of former Soviet forces from Germany. This also included generous amounts of financial aid to a cash-strapped Russian government. Kohl ended up forging a close political relationship with Yeltsin, giving him more explicit support than other Western leaders, including U.S. President Bill Clinton.[70]

Beyond the close political ties between the leaders, Germany had several other advantages in pursuing new relations with Russia. There was a cadre of ex–East Germans who had extensive work experience and personal contacts with people in post-Soviet Russia, thus helping to facilitate business and political connections. From the West German side, there was a reservoir of goodwill for Moscow's constructive role in the unification process. Both Germanies had been major trading partners with the Soviet Union, and those economic relationships—especially the trade of raw materials for advanced goods—continued to define the post-Soviet relationship between the two countries. Many Germans were comfortable assuming a role as an advocate for Russia to be part of the construction of a new Europe.[71] Finally, the German approach to cooperation with Russia—based on seeking a joint solution rather than imposing Western models (again, in contrast to the approach of the United States)—created more durable networks of trust.[72] Indeed, particularly as U.S. advice on Russia's political and economic transition began to be perceived more negatively in Russia during the 1990s, Russians preferred to emulate German models, which provided for a larger state role in society and the economy. German experts thus contributed to the revamping of Russia's commercial code and advised on how to strike a balance between continued privatization of the economy with the retention of some state ownership.[73]

The Kohl–Yeltsin relationship, sometimes termed by Germans as a *Männerfreundschaft* (a term connoting a very close friendship between two men, equivalent to the English slang term *bromance*)[74], was cemented at a summit meeting in December 1992. Kohl was anxious to have all former Soviet troops withdrawn from Germany before he had to face elections in 1994 and so was willing to offer 550 million deutschemarks more in aid for constructing housing for returning soldiers and to postpone collection of Soviet-era debts owed to Germany.[75] In 1993, defense ministers Volker Ruhe and Pavel Grachev signed a defense cooperation agreement in April 1993 providing for military cooperation between Russia and Germany.[76] This has expanded to include defense cooperation between Germany's defense industries and Russia; in 2011, Rheinmetall Defense, one of Germany's leading defense firms, signed a contract with the Russian Ministry of Defense to set up a state of the art troop training center.[77] And while U.S. President Bill Clinton was a supporter of expanding NATO to take in former Soviet satellite states and even ex–Soviet republics, Kohl, in contrast, "was always lukewarm about former Soviet republics joining NATO because he feared provoking negative reactions in Russia."[78]

Helmut Kohl's electoral defeat in 1998 and the replacement of his government by a so-called red-green coalition led by the Social Democratic Party (headed by Gerhard Schroeder) marked an important test as to whether the personally defined relationship between Kohl and Yeltsin would endure. Initially, the new chancellor, Schroeder, was very critical of the Kohl approach to lavishing Yeltsin's government with financial aid, promising that "there will be none of the so-called 'agreements with old friends.'"[79] However, Schroeder continued Germany's economic and defense cooperation with Russia and hailed the emergence of Vladimir Putin, first as prime minister, then as president, as a strong leader who would be able to put Russia back on the right track. There were powerful interests in Germany interested in maintaining a close relationship in Russia, from financial institutions eager to see debt repaid to industry growing more dependent on raw materials, particularly energy, from Russia as well as seeing in Russia a growing and dynamic market for German goods. Many of these interests were represented in an influential lobbying organization, the *Ostausschuss* (Committee on Eastern European Economic Relations), which has used its clout in German politics among all political parties to push for policies favorable to Russia.[80]

Whatever initial skepticism Schroeder may have had of Russia soon evaporated with the accession of Vladimir Putin, who had served in Germany as a member of the KGB and spoke fluent German—allowing for direct communication with the chancellor, who was not comfortable in speaking other languages. Putin, sometimes referred to as the "German in the Kremlin" for his attention to order and detail, soon forged a close personal relationship with Schroeder, who had adopted a Russian orphan.[81] But the improvement in Russia–Germany relations went beyond personal dynamics. Putin's emphasis on stability reassured nervous German creditors that Russia would in fact pay back its debts and that German investments in Russia would be secure.

The real cement of the Schroeder–Putin relationship has been energy. Schroeder identified Germany's economic security with unimpeded access to Russia's raw materials and, in turn, making Germany Russia's premier trading partner. He described Germany as the "motor" of Europe's engagement with Russia. Part of this relationship was to promote the construction of new energy pipelines that would directly link Russia to Germany so that Central and Eastern European states would have no influence on Germany's ability to receive Russian energy, culminating in the September 2005 signing of an agreement between Gazprom and the German energy firms BASF (via its subsidiary Wintershall) and E.ON for the construction of the North European Gas Pipeline (Nord Stream). Alexander Rahr, a leading German analyst of Russian affairs, argued that under Schroeder, "Germany's energy dialogue with Russia has turned into an energy alliance."[82] As a result, Germany was willing to downplay concerns about human rights inside of Russia and less likely to back other East European countries in their disputes with Russia. German officials compared their relationship with Russia with that of the United States and Saudi Arabia: an important energy supplier whose domestic failings are overlooked and whose foreign policy priorities are accommodated.[83]

During Schroder's tenure, the strategic partnership between both countries expanded. German exports to Russia nearly doubled, from €6.7 billion in 2000 to €14.9 billion in 2004. The intelligence services increased their cooperation in combating terrorism and organized crime. Schroeder and Putin also initiated a regular series of intergovernmental consultations and, in 2001, launched the Petersburg Dialogue, a yearly meeting that brings together both government officials and private individuals to discuss and assess the direction of Russia–Germany relations. Most importantly, Putin and Schroeder tended to see eye to eye on international issues, notably opposing the U.S. invasion of Iraq in 2003. Putin encouraged Schroeder to take a foreign policy line that was more independent of the United

States.[84] He also expressed his hope that future German chancellors would adhere to the Schroeder approach for dealing with Russia.

As the 2005 German elections neared, there were concerns that a successor to Schroeder might reverse the Russia-Germany entente, particularly because of Schroeder's close relationships with the Russians. Indeed, immediately after leaving office, he became the chairman of the company that was set up to operate the Nord Stream pipeline. Schroeder was replaced by Angela Merkel, a politician from eastern Germany who had briefly served in the last East German government in 1990 prior to reunification. Many expected that Merkel, who had no sentimental feelings toward the former Soviet Union, would end the chummy Schroeder–Putin relationship.[85] However, in her first government, which was a grand coalition between her Christian Democrats and Schroeder's Social Democrats, she appointed as her foreign minister Frank-Walter Steinmeier, who had been Schroeder's chief of staff. A policy paper leaked from the Foreign Ministry in the fall of 2005 described German policy as *Wandel durch Verflechtung* ("change through interdependence") that echoed Brandt's 1970s call for "change through rapprochement" (*Wandel durch Annaherung*).[86] In particular, Germany's large energy companies and industrial conglomerates, notably E.ON Ruhrgas and Wintershall, have consistently lobbied the government for continuity and stability in the Russia-Germany relationship.[87]

On her first visit to Russia, Merkel did meet with opposition figures, and she moved to repair the breach in relations that Schroeder had caused with the United States. Yet, as Angela Stent has observed, there was "much more continuity than change in German Ostpolitik" under Merkel.[88] Merkel took no steps to interrupt the further growth of Russia–Germany trade and, after taking office, scaled back campaign promises to cultivate closer ties with other Eurasian states. Merkel left intact the entire structure of Germany-Russia consultations and the system of regular biannual meetings between the German chancellor and Russian president. Merkel, a fluent Russian speaker, could also dialogue directly with Russian officials. But Merkel never developed the same close relationship with Putin that Schroeder enjoyed. Yet Merkel was also very concerned not to have Germany take on new security obligations by expanding NATO to encompass states neighboring Russia. Under her leadership, Germany played a major role in blocking U.S. preferences for extending membership action plans in NATO to states like Georgia and Ukraine at the 2008 summit in Bucharest.[89] Indeed, the chair of the foreign affairs committee of the Federation Council, Mikhail Margelov, has noted that Germany has been Russia's "biggest helper" in stopping the further expansion of NATO to encompass former Soviet states.[90]

When Dmitry Medvedev became president, moreover, Merkel found a Russian leader she was much more comfortable dealing with. Medvedev's advocacy for liberal economic and political reforms seemed to justify the German position that deep and sustained economic engagement with Russia might lead to ongoing political change.[91]

At her 2009 summit with Medvedev, Merkel agreed to the formation of a German–Russian energy agency, set aside €500 million more in credits to finance German exports to Russia, and inked deals for cooperation in transportation and atomic power. For someone who in opposition had been more skeptical of the relationship with Russia, Merkel now concluded that the relationship has "greatly intensified." Significantly, there was no lasting impact from the Russian incursion into Georgia on the acceleration of Russia–Germany relations.[92] Instead, Germany resumed its strategic partnership with Russia, despite the concerns of some of Germany's neighbors that their interests were being ignored by Berlin. In July 2010, at their regular bilateral summit meeting, Merkel had proposed to Medvedev the creation of a formal security forum between Russia and Europe at the level of foreign ministers,[93] continuing the traditional role of Germany serving as Russia's advocate in Europe. Most importantly, Merkel agreed to revive the three-way France-Germany-Russia summit meetings that had been a regular part of the interaction of Putin, Schroeder, and French President Chirac, meeting with Medvedev and French president Nicolas Sarkozy in Deauville, France, in October 2010. The purpose of this meeting was to have a friendly brainstorming session of the three European leaders, as strategic partners, prior to a NATO summit—drawing criticism that Russia could enjoy a "normal" security dialogue with two of Europe's leading powers even after the Russia–Georgia war.[94]

Despite intensive criticism of Schroeder for forging closer energy ties between Russia and Germany, Merkel did not fundamentally change the nature of the bargain he had forged, creating effective interdependence between the two countries. Medvedev and Merkel presided over the opening of the first line of Nord Stream in November 2011, while a second line began operation in October 2012. With the completion of this project, Germany (and other Russian gas customers in Western Europe) can now receive some 55 billion cubic meters of gas per year without any threat of interruption posed by Russian disputes with transit countries in Eastern Europe.[95] The German energy conglomerate Wintershall is also part of the consortium for the South Stream line, another Russian pipeline project (via the Black Sea) that is also designed to get Russian energy directly to European customers by bypassing Eastern European states with whom Russia has had difficulty in the past, starting with Ukraine. There has also been a process of integration between German and Russian firms, particularly via asset swaps that see German firms permitted to buy into sensitive Russian energy projects while offering opportunities for Russian companies to purchase stakes in European assets. One of the most significant examples has been the purchase by E.ON and Wintershall of equity stakes in the massive Yuzhno-Russkoye gas field in Russia. Negotiations on allowing German firms direct access began in 2004, and part of the deal was to allow corresponding purchases of stakes by Gazprom in both of these German firms' operations in Europe and elsewhere. Further assets swaps took place in 2012, with Wintershall transferring to Gazprom control over trading and storage facilities in Europe while gaining access to new natural gas fields within Russia. Rosneft, through its own investments in Germany, now controls some 20% of the oil-refining business in Germany.[96] Beyond energy, the Russia–Germany economic relationship encompasses the entire business spectrum, from cosmetics to construction to shipbuilding to finance.[97] As exports slow to other parts of Europe, the Russian market is now of even greater importance for the health of Germany's economy.[98] Some 6,000 German firms operate in Russia, having invested more than $30 billion into the Russian economy, while some 950 Russian companies are present in Germany.[99] These relationships not only help to buttress the national relationship but also help to create ties between specific German and Russian regions. The Russian state investment (via the FLC West fund) into the German shipbuilding industry in the Baltic Sea region is designed to produce new ships capable of navigating the Arctic and exploring and exploiting that region's oil and natural gas reserves.[100] Most Russian investment in Germany is focused in the areas of North Rhine/Westphalia, the Berlin region, Bavaria, and Hesse, which builds up regional constituencies that support stronger ties with Russia.[101] Meanwhile, the government of Tatarstan, for example, has invested in a fund designed to purchase German technology assets in order to help modernize the republic's infrastructure.[102] All of this activity is creating a web of interlocking business structures that acts as cement for the Russia–Germany relationship.

The return of Vladimir Putin to the presidency in 2012, however, has led to a slight chill in the Russia–Germany friendship, even though visiting Berlin was one of Putin's top priorities. Merkel's special envoy overseeing all aspects of the German relationship with Russia, Andreas Schockenhoff, began to be much more critical of Russia after Putin returned to the presidency in the summer and fall of 2012. In criticisms of various Putin policies, including a growing crackdown on activists and protestors, he noted that the Russian president was "harming his own objective of making Russia a modern, competitive country."[103] In turn, the Russian government ramped up its own criticisms of Schockenhoff and hinted that his approach might damage the bilateral relationship.

The Schockenhoff affair made public some of the divisions within German society over policy toward Russia. The Foreign Ministry has tended to want to tap down overt criticisms of Russia, as does the *Ostausschuss*. On the other hand, some

German politicians, from both the Christian Democrats and the Social Democrats, have been more critical of Russia's human rights record, while the *Mittelstand*—another business association representing small- and medium-sized enterprises investing in Russia—is more attuned to the problem of large-scale corruption within Russia.[104] Merkel traveled to Russia in November 2012 in the aftermath of a nonbinding resolution passed in the Bundestag asking her to raise human rights considerations, and her willingness to support a stronger EU outreach to Russian neighbors was also a sore point in discussions with Moscow.[105]

However, despite these setbacks, the Russia–Germany relationship is probably the single most important bilateral tie for Moscow, and Germany wants to retain its status as a priority economic associate, and despite increased criticisms, the November 2012 Russo-German summit has not changed that overall dynamic.[106] Putin calls Germany Russia's most important European partner, a sentiment that is echoed across the entire foreign policy establishment. Germany is "the preferred major foreign partner by almost all sections of the Russian elite" from Westernizers to nationalists.[107] In turn, within Germany, it is still the dominant position across the political spectrum, from the Social Democrats on the left to the Free Democrats on the right, that Russia is a "strategic partner" for Germany.[108] In 2011, Germany exported €27 billion to Russia while importing €25 billion worth of goods and services from Russia. Despite talk in both capitals about "diversification" to other countries, it is clear that Russia still needs German investment and technology, while Germany's dependence on Russian sources of energy is not expected to abate anytime soon.[109] Putin's scheduled visit to Germany in April 2013 to open the technology fair Hannover Messe and then to hold talks with his German counterpart reiterates why both sides continue to need each other.

THE RUSSIAN RELATIONSHIP WITH FRANCE

Historically, Russia has had a love-hate relationship with France. France's traditional allies in Eastern Europe—Poland and the Ottoman Empire—were longstanding opponents who stood in the way of the expansion of the Russian Empire. On the other hand, the Russian nobility copied French culture and, for a time, French was the language of the imperial court. In the 19th century, Russia clashed with France under the leadership of both Napoleon I (ruled 1799–1815) and his nephew Napoleon III (1852–1870). After the rise of a united Germany, a Franco-Russian entente was concluded in 1892 and formally ratified in 1894, setting the stage for World War I. After the Revolution, the French government initially took a strongly anti-Soviet stance, but, when faced again with the threat of a rising Nazi Germany, signed a Franco-Soviet Treaty of Mutual Assistance in 1935. Both countries ended up being allied again during the Second World War.

The Soviet Union had a complicated relationship with France. On the one hand, it had one of the largest Communist Parties in the Western world; immediately after World War II, the French Communists, having played a major role in the Resistance against Nazi Germany, entered the first postwar government organized by General Charles de Gaulle. As the Cold War began, however, the Communist Party was seen as taking its orders directly from the Soviet government; it was thus pushed out from government by not only the conservative parties but by the non–Communist socialist groups as well. The French Communists thus went into opposition, and France fully embraced the Western alliance, becoming a founding member of the North Atlantic Treaty Organization (NATO) alliance and pushing for closer economic integration among Western European states. But even in opposition, the French Communists still had a clear base of support within the French electorate, and they consistently supported any effort by France to reduce U.S. influence in Europe.[110]

Charles de Gaulle's outreach to the Soviet Union, particularly his 1966 visit to Moscow, was based in part on his vision of a future European order in which France and the Soviet Union would play the major roles (and with the United States playing a more secondary role on the continent).[111] De Gaulle's drive for an independent French approach to global security (including France's withdrawal from the unified command structure of the NATO alliance) meant that Paris would no longer automatically support U.S. positions vis-à-vis Moscow. De Gaulle's approach was followed by subsequent French presidents; between 1966 and 1986, 14 high-level meetings were held between the French and Soviet leaders in support of the special relationship between the two states.[112] And, as the Cold War was winding down in Europe, Mikhail Gorbachev, in meetings with the French president in November 1988 and July 1989, attempted to enlist Francois Mitterrand in a joint Franco–Soviet project for constructing new European institutions that would create a common political and security space from the Atlantic to the Urals. Mitterrand was also very concerned that a sudden collapse of Soviet power would reignite old conflicts and thus strongly backed both Gorbachev's reform efforts and the preservation of the Soviet bloc.[113] On New Year's Eve 1989, Mitterrand issued his call for a European Confederation and the development of an all-European process that would be able to oversee German reunification and the development of closer relations between the Soviet bloc and the European Community.

The breakup of the USSR ended these dreams, but Mitterrand nevertheless continued to reach out to a post-Soviet Russia as an important part of a French strategy to balance a newly reunited Germany. In February 1992, Boris Yeltsin traveled to France to sign a historic accord with Francois Mitterrand that reinstated the historic entente between the two countries, making it the first friendship pact concluded between a post–Soviet Russia and a Western state. More practically, the agreement committed Russia and France to joint consultations during times of crisis, provided for a yearly summit meeting between the French and Russian presidents, and extended some 3.5 billion francs in credits for Russia to purchase French goods and services. A separate barter deal swapping Russian oil for French industrial products, valued at 2.3 billion francs, was also concluded.[114] In addition, a regular series of high-level meetings, the Russian–French Commission on Bilateral Cooperation, was initiated, overseen by the two presidents and cochaired by the two prime ministers.

But Mitterrand never forged the same personal relationship with Yeltsin that he had enjoyed with Gorbachev. Moreover, French and Russian firms—particularly in the defense and atomic energy industries—were competitors for contracts throughout the world, inhibiting closer economic cooperation between the two countries. Yeltsin found more common ground with Mitterrand's successor as president, Jacques Chirac—so much so that in 1997, Yeltsin proposed that Chirac, Helmut Kohl of Germany, and he should meet as friends in a more informal setting, "without neckties," to discuss a whole range of issues, including NATO expansion and economic cooperation.[115] Thus begin a series of meetings between the Russian, German, and French leaders that enabled France, in particular, to be able to push back against U.S. proposals. At the same time, then-Foreign Minister Yevgeny Primakov's vision of a world system characterized by multipolarity resonated with Chirac's foreign minister Hubert Vedrine, who characterized the United States as a "hyperpower" and called for a group of powers of "world influence"—including countries like Russia, Germany, and India—to counteract American unilateralism.[116] One of the more fateful trilateral meetings—between Chirac, Gerhard Schroeder, and Vladimir Putin in February 2003—saw the three powers come out squarely against U.S. plans for an invasion of Iraq, scuttling any chance that the George W. Bush administration would be able to get a resolution authorizing military action through the UN Security Council. Chirac and Putin developed a good working relationship and also continued a tradition of regular Franco-Russian presidential meetings.[117]

Chirac and Putin also discovered a mutual interest in limiting the influence of the East European states within the European Union. Chirac saw the new members of the EU as more inclined to carry water for U.S. positions and to actively align themselves with Washington, notably on the Iraq war, threatening the traditional French predilection for the EU to serve as a counterweight to the United States. For his part, Putin welcomed French efforts to defend Russian interests within European institutions.

As with Merkel, there were initial expectations that Chirac's successor, the conservative Nicolas Sarkozy, would distance Paris from Russia and work to rebuild ties with the United States. After his election in April 2007, Sarkozy did promote closer Franco-American ties and increased the French role in NATO, but he also had a vision of France acting as a bridge between the West and Russia. He was leery of being drawn into "starting another Cold War"; when the Russia-Georgia conflict broke out in August 2008, Sarkozy focused his efforts on getting a cease-fire between both sides rather than pushing for outright Russian withdrawal. Sarkozy's willingness to engage with the Russians and to disagree with other Western powers that faulted Moscow for the conflict surprised many because of his skeptical comments about Russia during his presidential campaign. The Sarkozy plan saw the departure of Russian troops from Georgia proper but not from the separatist regions of Abkhazia or South Ossetia, which subsequently declared independence. Nevertheless, Sarkozy, during his visit to Russia in October, maintained that Russia had fulfilled all of its obligations under the plan and that Russia–France and Russia–EU relations should return to normal.[118]

In addition, Sarkozy, like Merkel, found it easier to push a more collaborative view of relations with Russia with Dmitry Medvedev in the presidency. Given Medvedev's clear orientation toward Europe and his more liberalizing attitudes, it was more politically feasible for Sarkozy to argue for deepening the France–Russia relationship.[119]

Part of the reason for Sarkozy's more accommodating stance toward Moscow was due to the flowering of France's economic relations with Russia. Between 2005 and 2012, the value of bilateral trade between France and Russia tripled to reach $30 billion.[120] Sarkozy facilitated this, in part, by positioning France as an alternative partner to Germany. Building on a program started under Chirac—to diversify France's export markets away from other EU nations toward other rising economies, including Russia—the major "industrial and infrastructure companies" that were key supporters of the Sarkozy administration saw their business with Russia expand.[121] In turn, Putin has praised this business "dynamic, developing closer ties between the main industries of our economy." He has consistently maintained that Russia regards "France and its business community as traditional and privileged partners that have proved their eagerness to cooperate with us in making modernisation initiatives a reality."[122]

The France–Russia economic relationship also gives a number of Russian regions direct stakes in the health of the Paris–Moscow connection. Renault has been a major investor in modernizing the massive Volga Auto Works in Togliatti and is now the second-largest shareholder in the company. Peugeot has built a car manufacturing plant in the region of Kaluga, outside of Moscow, while the Russian energy firm RusHydro and the French technology conglomerate Alstom have a joint venture in Bashkortostan to produce high-tech energy equipment.[123]

France is now one of the largest sources of foreign investment in Russia, having funneled some $10 billion into various projects inside Russia.[124]

Even though France traditionally has obtained most of its energy either from its own domestic nuclear program or from North African sources (particularly for natural gas), it has sought to diversify its own energy portfolio by reaching out to Russia. In 2007, the French energy giant Total was invited by Gazprom to be its strategic partner for the development of the Shtokman natural gas field in the Arctic. This started a process by which French firms entered into Russian energy projects. The Russians have welcomed the entry of French firms as a way to diversify their relations beyond the existing close partnership with German firms; in turn, French firms have opened up overseas projects to include Russian partners as well.[125] During Sarkozy's June 2010 visit to St. Petersburg, the French utility company GDF-Suez agreed to take a 10% stake in the Nord Stream pipeline project. In addition, its sister firm EDF decided to enter into the South Stream consortium. After these new contracts were signed, Sarkozy reiterated his position about engagement with Russia:

> I have the conviction that Europe and Russia must work together in a strategic way, very closely, in a relationship of confidence. The Cold War is over. The Wall is finished. Russia is a great power, we are neighbours, we are destined to be friends, we must come closer to each other.[126]

It also reinforced the earlier tendency, seen during the Chirac presidency, where France "has been reluctant at best to side with EU members overtly critical of Russia's policy such as Poland."[127]

This growing relationship of trust has meant that previously off-limits areas of cooperation have become accessible. Russian firms now act as suppliers to the Franco–German-led aerospace consortium EADS, which produces sensitive high-technology military products, among other things, and for a time the Russian state-owned investment bank VTB was a minority shareholder in this company. France and Russia now cooperate in rocket and missile technology for space launches, and France is now buying Soyuz launchers for its own space program. Most significantly, Sarkozy announced in December 2010 that France would sell four Mistral-class amphibious assault ships (also known as helicopter carriers) to the Russian navy—two to be built in France and two to be then built in Russian shipyards under license, which would help to modernize Russia's own shipbuilding industry. The Mistrals will greatly enhance Russia's power-projection capabilities, and as a result, the United States as well as some of Russia's neighbors has been concerned about Russia's acquisition of this platform from a NATO country.[128] In addition to the Mistral, France has been considering selling other advanced military technologies to Russia, including the Safran-Sagem package of avionics for fighters, in a package deal that would include both direct sales of equipment as well as licensing for joint production with Russian firms.[129]

The Sarkozy gamble has been that by treating Russia as a partner, Moscow might be more amenable to accommodating French (and European) national security interests. While many assert that Russia's decision to impose stricter sanctions on Iran in 2010 reflected a desire to improve relations with the United States, tightening sanctions on Tehran was also a priority of the Sarkozy administration—so the decision by Medvedev to change the Russian position also helped to bolster the France–Russia relationship.[130] In 2011, Russia abstained from the UN resolution that authorized the creation of a no-fly zone over Libya, which cleared the way for a NATO air campaign in which France played a leading role. In turn, Sarkozy pushed for ending the language of confrontation between Russia and the West and welcomed the resumption of the trilateral France–Germany–Russia consultations in 2010. At the Deauville summit, he discussed the creation of a European Security Council that would include Russia as a key participant.[131]

But can the close Russia–France relationship planted by Chirac and nurtured by Sarkozy survive changes in both Russia and France? Putin's return to the presidency, followed by Sarkozy's defeat by socialist Francois Hollande, raises the question as to whether the major gains in the France–Russia relationship were based largely on the personal relationship between Sarkozy and Medvedev. Hollande did stress, during his campaign, that relations with Russia would remain a priority under his administration, and the Russian government has signaled that cooperation between the two countries remains on track.[132] However, there are tensions. In recent years, Russia has called for the non–European countries of the BRICS (the Brazil-Russia-India-China-South Africa) forum to have more influence in international institutions, at the expense of the traditional leading role played by the Europeans, particularly the French. This, for a time, put Russia at odds with France over the nomination of former French finance minister Christine Lagarde to become the general director of the International Monetary Fund in 2011. The intensive French push to oust Libyan leader Muammar Gadhafi in 2011, followed by growing French calls for more robust intervention in Syria against the regime of Bashar al-Assad, a close Russian partner, has created tensions in the bilateral relationship.[133] There is also a more vocal human rights lobby in France that has been highly critical of domestic developments inside Russia. Yet both sides continue to express confidence that the growing economic and security ties between the two countries are sufficient to overcome these difficulties.[134] Finally, Russia's decision to grant citizenship to actor Gerard Depardieu, who became a "tax exile" to protest Hollande's policies of raising taxes on the wealthy, also helped to contribute to strains in the relationship. However, Prime Minister Medvedev, prior to his visit to France at the end of 2012, suggested that bilateral relations "have reached a level where they should not depend on who stands at the helm of our countries."[135]

Hollande visited Russia at the end of February 2013. During his meetings with Putin, he raised but did not press differences between France and Russia on the situation in Syria and on human rights. Instead, he stressed the importance of accelerating economic and business ties between the two nations, while Putin, for his part, reiterated that France was a "long-time privileged partner" of Russia.[136]

THE OVERLOOKED PARTNERSHIP: ITALY AND RUSSIA

The modern relationship between Italy and Russia has its roots in the creation of the Italian Communist Party in 1921. As in France, the *Partito Comunista Italiano* played a major role in the antifascist Resistance and after World War II emerged as one of the largest political forces in the country. Although Italy as a whole entered the NATO alliance and remained part of the West, the Italian Communists had considerable grassroots support and were able to have some impact on the bilateral relationship between Italy and the Soviet Union. Palmiro Togliatti, the Italian Communist leader, played a major role in the negotiations that led to the Italian firm FIAT setting up the AVTOVAZ automobile factory in the Volga town of Stavropol, which was renamed in his honor. The Italian state energy company Eni also turned to the Soviet Union as an alternate source for oil, signing its first contrast with the USSR in 1958, much to the irritation of the United States—because Eni's action broke the de facto embargo on Western countries purchasing Soviet oil and thus providing the USSR either with hard currency or with advanced technologies in exchange.[137]

Gorbachev forged good working relations with Italian Prime Minister Giulio Andreotti. During Gorbachev's November 1989 visit to Italy, prior to his summit meeting with U.S. President George H. W. Bush at Malta, he discussed Mediterranean security and signed contracts that permitted the expansion of Italian businesses in the Soviet Union.[138] In December 1991, as the Soviet Union was in the process of disintegration, Boris Yeltsin visited Rome to ensure that Italian credits and business activities would continue in a post–Soviet Russia. Some 80% of Italian investment in the Soviet Union was located within the territory of the Russian Federation, so as the Russian economy collapsed, the links with Italy became quite important.[139] By the mid-1990s, Italy was Russia's second-largest trading partner, after Germany.

A key figure in the Russia–Italy relationship has been Romano Prodi, who served as prime minister of Italy from 1996 to 1998, as president of the

European Commission from 1999 to 2004, and again as prime minister of Italy from 2006 to 2008. Prodi, like his German counterpart Gerhard Schroeder, believed that it was in Italy's—and Europe's—best interest to promote further and closer integration with Russia. In February 1998, Yeltsin returned to Italy to sign new deals with Prodi expanding the shipment of Russian oil and gas to Italy.[140] Italian diplomats also played a role in helping to set up multilateral diplomacy regarding the conflicts in the former Yugoslavia. The so-called Contact Group brought Italy and Russia together with Germany, France, Britain, and the United States and reflected the view, shared by the Italians, French, and Germans, that Russia ought to be part of any overall settlement of the Balkan wars.

As the president of the European Commission, Prodi argued for a closer EU–Russia partnership and also articulated his view that the expansion of European institutions eastward could not be open ended but should more or less be halted at the old Soviet borders, arguing in 2002 that the "integration of the Balkans into the European Union will complete the unification of the continent. . . . But we cannot go on enlarging forever."[141] At the EU–Russia summit in St. Petersburg in May 2003, Prodi was optimistic about the future of the Common Spaces between the EU and Russia as the basis for an effective partnership.[142] After returning as prime minister in 2006, Prodi pushed ahead with negotiations to build another pipeline network that would directly link Western European customers with their Russian supplier of natural gas, bypassing the transit countries, in this case Ukraine. The so-called South Stream pipeline was to be built on the floor of the Black Sea and connect Russia with Western Europe via Bulgaria, with extension lines running through Serbia and Greece. On June 23, 2007, the CEO of Eni, Paolo Scaroni, and the vice chairman of Gazprom, Aleksandr Medvedev, signed the initial memorandum of understanding that served as the foundation for the project. South Stream directly challenged an alternative pipeline project, the NABUCCO line, which was supposed to bring Central Asian gas to European markets, bypassing Russia altogether (which was the option preferred by the United States and some Eastern European countries that wanted to reduce Europe's energy dependence on Russia). Eni's endorsement of South Stream, however, helped to jump start the Russian-backed project, and Italy also lobbied various Balkan countries to agree to the pipeline project. In turn, Italian energy firms like Eni and Enel have been permitted to make large investments in Russian oil and gas projects inside of Russia, including minority stakes in Gazpromneft, the oil arm of Gazprom, and to acquire firms like Arctic Gas and Urengoil—smaller producers in the Russian North. Eni and Enel then forged a new strategic partnership to develop these assets with an eye to supplying the European market for energy.[143] Given the importance of Italy to Russian energy plans for Europe, Prodi, after stepping down as prime minister in 2008, was solicited by the Kremlin to head up the South Stream consortium, an offer he subsequently declined.

Prodi's predecessor and successor as prime minister, Silvio Berlusconi (who served from 1994 to 1995, from 2001 to 2006, and from 2008 to 2011) developed even closer ties with Russia, particularly a close personal friendship with Vladimir Putin that went beyond the rapport Putin shared with Schroeder. Even when out of office, Berlusconi has been a visitor to Putin's home or *dacha* (vacation home), including a skiing vacation with Putin to celebrate his return to the presidency in 2012.[144] Through Putin, Berlusconi also maintained a good relationship with Medvedev when the latter was president between 2008 and 2012. Berlusconi, a media magnate who is one of Italy's richest persons, was less troubled than other European leaders about the style of Putin's autocratic management of Russian politics, in part because it mimicked his own preference for focusing on results rather than on adherence to constitutional process. Some have also alleged that Berlusconi has personally profited from some of the Russia–Italy business deals. But Italy's tilt toward Russia is driven far beyond any personal relationship between the leaders and instead is driven by Italy's assessment that a close partnership with Russia advances Italy's position as the leading state of Southern Europe and as one of the major players in Europe as a whole.[145] Indeed, in June 2011, Italian Foreign Minister Franco Frattini described the Russia–Italy relationship as a "truly special strategic partnership."[146]

Much of the work of the partnership is coordinated through the Economic, Industrial and Financial Council cochaired by the Italian foreign minister and a Russian deputy prime minister that serves as the umbrella through which a number of projects are vetted. Many leading Italian firms are involved in critical projects in Russia or in advancing Russian interests elsewhere in Europe. For instance, the construction firm Saipem, a subsidiary of the energy giant Eni, has been one of the contractors that constructed the Nord Stream line between Russia and Germany.[147] Another project is the SuperJet 100, a joint venture between the Russian aircraft manufacturer Sukhoi and Alenia Aermacchi, an Italian aerospace company that is a subsidiary of the defense conglomerate Finmeccanica. This is seen as especially important to Russia's troubled aircraft industry, as the SuperJet is the only new Russian passenger aircraft to enter the commercial market in recent years.[148]

Beyond economics, there is now a growing security relationship between the two countries. The Italian army conducts joint exercises with the Russian military, with both training to cope with insurgencies. The first drills took place in fall 2011 in the North Caucasus and then were held in Italy in September 2012.[149] The Italian firm Iveco has set up a joint enterprise in Russia to manufacture its Lynx multipurpose armored vehicles, both for use in the Russian military and for export to other states, principally elsewhere in Eurasia. The S1000 project is a joint enterprise of the Italian shipbuilder Fincantieri and the Russian Central Design Bureau for Marine Engineering (Rubin) to build a small-scale diesel submarine that Rosoboronexport would market to rising powers like Indonesia and South Africa.[150]

Like Germany, Italy has served as a strong advocate for better EU–Russia relations. The Italians have also helped to build up support in other parts of Europe for the South Stream project by working to include other European stakeholders. The South Stream consortium is now a joint Russian–Italian–German–French enterprise, which helps to spread the costs but also ensures that the governments of these three major EU states remain supportive of the project.[151]

Even after Berlusconi resigned as prime minister (and was ultimately convicted in October 2012 of tax fraud), the overall direction of Italian policy toward Russia has remained unchanged. The technocratic prime minister who replaced him, Mario Monti, met with Putin in July 2012 to keep various Italian–Russian projects on track, including the construction of the South Stream line. Construction of this new line began on December 7, 2012, and is expected to become operational in 2015.[152] Monti's resignation as prime minister in December 2012 did not affect the general trajectory of Italy–Russia relations, which have moved beyond the personalities of individual leaders and are cemented in strong economic relations between the two countries.

THE BULLDOG AND THE BEAR: RUSSIA AND GREAT BRITAIN

Direct contacts between England and Muscovy started when Richard Chancellor arrived in 1553 via the White Sea near what would become the port of Archangel, creating a direct trading link between the two countries. Osip Nepay became the first ambassador from Russia to arrive at the Court of St. James in London in 1558. Indeed, a correspondence developed between Queen Elizabeth and Tsar Ivan the Terrible, who proposed marriage and also sought assurances that he might be received in England should he end up fleeing from Russia. Ivan's letters epitomized the conflicting attitudes that Russians would have about the British—a fascination with British life and culture but a sense that the British were guided in their policy decisions by the pursuit of wealth.[153] Russia and Britain have always had an uneasy interaction, oscillating between alliance and enmity. At times, the two countries have cooperated to defeat powers intent on establishing hegemony in Europe—against Napoleonic France or Germany during both World Wars. On the other hand, Britain was always worried about the expansion of Russian influence and, at various points, tried to block the rise of Russian power in both the Baltic and Mediterranean basins. Moreover, the two empires were rivals for influence in Central Asia, as the Russian empire expanded across Eurasia and the British consolidated their hold on India. For much of the 19th century, Britain and Russia engaged in a cold war throughout the region, what one British officer termed a "Great Game."[154] Compounding the diplomatic rivalry, a number of opponents of the Russian Empire, ranging from revolutionaries to representatives of minority nationalities, also found refuge in Britain, meaning that London's willingness to shelter the tsars' enemies created tension in the bilateral relations between the two countries.

After the Soviet Revolution, the British played a leading role in assisting the White anti-Communist forces during the Civil War, then reversed their position to sign a trade agreement with the Soviet Union in 1921. British attitudes to the Soviet state were divided, based on political allegiances; the Labour party tended to have a more favorable view of the USSR than either the Conservatives or the Liberals. In 1939, the British were unable to secure an alliance with Josef Stalin to oppose Hitler, but after Germany attacked the Soviet Union in 1941, the two countries became allies.

In 1944 at the Moscow Conference, British Prime Minister Winston Churchill (who had, as First Lord of the Admiralty during World War I, supported White forces after the revolution) attempted to reach a definitive settlement with Stalin regarding the interests of both powers in central Europe and the Balkans.[155] However, the belief that the Soviet Union would seek total control of the territories liberated by its armies and the perception that Moscow would try to expand its influence into Western Europe ensured that Britain retained its very close links with the United States, and during the Cold War, the United Kingdom was a firm partner with Washington to contain Soviet influence. In contrast to many of the continental European powers, who promoted détente with the USSR during the 1960s and 1970s, the British viewed themselves as the "Cassandra to the Western alliance" in warning about the continued Soviet threat, which earned Moscow's rebuke that London was "clinging to 'reactionary' Cold War attitudes."[156]

A key turning point occurred after British Prime Minister Margaret Thatcher began to explore the possibility of direct British engagement with the Soviet Union.[157] Hopeful that Thatcher might open up a new channel for discussions between the United States and the Soviet Union, Mikhail Gorbachev, in his capacity as a member of the Politburo, traveled to Britain in December 1984 to hold talks with the British leadership. After her meetings with Gorbachev, Thatcher signaled her belief, "We can do business together" and many believe that, due to Thatcher's influence on U.S. President Ronald Regan, she paved the way for the rapprochement between Gorbachev and Reagan.[158] From her earlier anti-Soviet position, by the late 1980s Thatcher also ended up believing that

Britain and the Soviet Union should work together as partners to ensure European security. In meeting Gorbachev in September 1989, she expressed concerns that turmoil in Central and Eastern Europe might lead to greater insecurity, especially if the postwar settlement was overturned by a united Germany.[159]

Initial British worries that the reunification of Germany and the disintegration of the USSR might lead to new wars in Europe, however, were set at ease by the diplomacy of Boris Yeltsin. He traveled to Britain in January 1992, 1 month after the Soviet collapse, to meet with Prime Minister John Major and to set the parameters for future Russia–Britain cooperation. A second visit later that year saw new agreements signed, and, in October 1994, Queen Elizabeth II paid a visit to Russia, the first by a British monarch. British firms, particularly consumer-goods firms like Cadbury's, moved in to set up production facilities in the Russian regions and to gain market share for British-branded products.[160] By 1997, when Tony Blair became prime minister, the United Kingdom was in second place (after Germany) in terms of foreign investment in Russia.[161]

Blair had a vision for a new partnership between Russia and the UK, based on the assumption that Russia was becoming integrated into the Western world, based on his assessment, "Our economic future is now bound up together."[162] He saw Vladimir Putin as a Westernizing reformer in the mold of Peter the Great, someone who could deliver on real change after the chaos of the Yeltsin years. Given the British experience in fighting terrorism emanating from Northern Ireland, as well as the fact that Chechen groups had kidnapped British citizens, Blair was also willing to give Putin the benefit of the doubt in how he handled the Chechen situation.[163] Blair made an unofficial visit to St. Petersburg in early 2000 to meet with Putin when he was acting president, and Putin made his first trip outside Russia after winning the election to the United Kingdom. Blair played a critical role in helping to redefine the dysfunctional NATO–Russia relationship, especially to give Russia more of stake in cooperating with Western institutions; at the end of a December 2001 summit meeting between him and Putin, he described the relationship as "exceptionally close."[164] Finally, Blair presided over the single largest foreign investment ever made in Russia, the $6.75 billion purchase by British Petroleum of a 50% stake in the Tyumen Oil Company (TNK). At a special June 2003 energy conference in London, where both Putin and Blair witnessed the signing of the deal, Blair praised the purchase, noting: "The things that bind us together in politics security and economics are very important. Together we can achieve our mutual goals of global stability, economic growth, and international development."[165]

But Russia–Britain relations rapidly deteriorated after this high point. Just as in the 19th century, Britain's generous asylum policies allowed a safe haven for critics and opponents of the Putin government, including Ahmed Zakayev, the foreign minister of the separatist Chechen government, and Boris Berezovsky, one of the famed "oligarchs" of the 1990s. Despite request for their extradition to Russia to face criminal charges, the British government refused to change its asylum policies, creating a major source of irritation for the bilateral relationship. Matters worsened in 2006. First, in January, the Russians claimed to have discovered a British spy ring operating in Moscow and televised footage of a "spy rock" (a hollowed-out container holding a receiver to pick up transmission downloaded from handheld computers); the Russian security services also accused the British of funneling money to antigovernment opposition groups.[166] Then, in November, a former Russian security agent, Alexander Litvinenko, who had received asylum in Britain (and is alleged to have begun working for British intelligence), and who was associated both with Berezovsky and Zakayev, was poisoned using a radioactive substance, polonium 210. An investigation into Litvinenko's death zeroed in on another former Russian agent, Andrei Lugovoy, as the prime suspect in the killing (although the British government did not accuse the Russian government itself of orchestrating the attack). The Russian government, however, citing British unwillingness to extradite Russians accused of crimes to Russia, argued that Russian law forbade Lugovoy's extradition to Britain to face charges; subsequently, he acquired parliamentary immunity after being elected to the Duma in December 2007. The Litvinenko affair severely damaged the Blair–Putin relationship; British–Russian intelligence cooperation was suspended, and diplomatic relations went into a deep freeze. Blair was reportedly incensed about the brazenness of the attack on Litvinenko and the use of a dangerous radioactive substance as the assassination weapon. At the G-8 summit in Heiligendamm, Germany, in June 2007—the last face-to-face encounter between Putin and Blair—the British prime minister took the Russian president to task for "steering his country into being a dictatorship and away from the Western democratic model he was supposed to be striving to follow."[167] As the Russia–Britain relationship deteriorated, the BP investment in TNK also came under pressure in 2008, as both the Russian state and BP's Russian partners used legal and bureaucratic pressure to change the terms of BP's involvement in the Russian oil sector.[168]

Despite the poor political relationship between the two countries, Britain and Russia remained key economic partners. Russia emerged as Britain's fastest growing export market, with export sales between 2001 and 2011 growing, on average, by 21% per year. Some 600 British companies are now operating in Russia, ranging from those involved in natural resource extraction to selling luxury goods. Russian companies, in turn, have tended to use British markets—especially the London Stock Exchange—to raise capital from international investors.[169] British company and tax laws make it easy for Russian businessmen to incorporate and raise funds. Russian elites also prize the ability to travel to, be educated in, and buy real estate in Britain, which offers a Western lifestyle and easy terms to obtain permanent residency. Hundreds of thousands of Russians now reside in Britain, to such an extent that parts of London are colloquially referred to as Londongrad.[170] The Russian government, therefore, is constrained in its ability to take harsh measures to retaliate against Britain because its business elites fear losing access to Britain.

The 2010 elections brought a Conservative-Liberal Democrat coalition to power in Britain, headed by David Cameron as prime minister. This offered an opportunity to move past the impasse in relations.[171] Cameron undertook his own "reset" in relations and traveled to Moscow with a number of leading British businessmen in September 2011. Acknowledging that there were "difficult questions"—beginning with the Lugovoy matter—Cameron nevertheless held talks with Medvedev designed to focus on bolstering the business relationship between the two countries.[172] Putin, in turn, visited Britain during the time of the London Olympics in 2012. On controversial issues, such as Lugovoy, the question of human rights in Russia, and differences over the crisis in Syria, the two leaders pledged to keep talking—but not to allow differences in these areas to negatively impact the economic relationship between the two countries.[173] Some of the negative currents in the bilateral business climate have been resolved; at the end of 2012, BP sold its investment in TNK to the state-owned Rosneft oil company, and, in turn, bought a minority stake in Rosneft itself, creating the basis for a new partnership between the British and Russian firms. Another sign of improved relations was the launch, in March 2013, of the first session of the Russia–UK strategic dialogue; Foreign Minister Lavrov and the new defense minister, Sergei Shoigu, traveled to London for talks with their British counterparts William Hague and Philip Hammond in a "two plus two" format.[174] This could work to better institutionalize the bilateral relationship.

Cameron and subsequent British prime ministers will have to carefully walk a tightrope between critiquing Russia's domestic and foreign policies and facilitating business ties.[175] That balance was challenged again in February 2013, when the British government decided to grant political asylum to a fugitive Russian banker, Andrei Borodin, the former head of the Bank of Moscow. While Borodin claimed to be the victim of a witch hunt organized by Dmitry Medvedev, the Russian government expressed irritation that any claim of political persecution was given greater weight than the criminal charges filed against Borodin for financial misconduct in how he ran the bank's affairs.[176]

OTHER RELATIONSHIPS

Britain's complicated relationship with Russia is echoed by other European countries, notably Sweden. During the 17th and 18th centuries, Sweden was Russia's main rival in Northern Europe, and although Sweden did not join the NATO alliance during the Cold War, preferring to retain its neutral status, it was not particularly friendly toward the Soviet Union, a feeling reciprocated by Moscow. Accusations that Soviet submarines regularly violated Sweden's territorial waters, particularly during the 1980s, contributed to a tense relationship. Russia–Sweden relations improved during the 1990s, in part because of the Atlanticist tilt of the Yeltsin administration, but Sweden took issue with a number of the policies of the Putin government—ranging from how the war in Chechnya was conducted to strong opposition to the Nord Stream pipeline. Sweden's traditionally close ties with the Baltic States also led Stockholm to be a strong advocate for the interests of Russia's immediate neighbors (such as Ukraine) within European institutions, and the Swedish government also continued to press forward on human rights concerns. Relations hit a major low after the Georgia–Russia conflict in 2008, given Sweden's diplomatic support for Tbilisi. In particular, the Russian government was incensed when Swedish Foreign Minister Carl Bildt compared Russia's actions in Georgia with those of Adolf Hitler's prior to World War II, as well as Bildt's attempts to keep the Georgia issue on the overall EU–Russia agenda.[177]

However, there was some improvement after Sweden (and neighboring Finland) finally gave its approval for the construction of the Nord Stream line to pass through its exclusive economic zones in the Baltic Sea in November 2009, clearing away the last obstacles for its construction.[178]

If political relations between Moscow and Stockholm are usually described as "frostily pragmatic," the economic relationship has expanded. Sweden is an important supplier of telecommunications products, chemicals, and automobiles for the Russian market, while Russia is an important oil supplier for Sweden. Swedish firms like Tele-2 and IKEA are major foreign investors in Russia.[179] Indeed, Sweden is the second-largest investor in Russia after Germany.[180] *The growing middle class in Russia makes it an important new export market for Swedish businesses. When Putin visited Sweden in April 2011, he and his counterpart Prime Minister Fredrik Reinfeldt created the Swedish-Russian Steering Commission—chaired by a Russian deputy prime minister and the Swedish minister for trade—to examine ways to facilitate the business relationship.*[181]

Like Sweden, other European countries, such as Switzerland or the Netherlands, are also important trading partners for Russia. Russia had historic links to both countries; Dutch merchants and shipwrights played an important role in the modernization efforts of Peter the Great, while Switzerland had given refuge to a number of Russian revolutionary figures, including Vladimir Lenin himself, before they returned to launch the 1917 October Revolution. Today, given the leading role of multinational corporations from Switzerland (such as pharmaceutical firms like Novartis or technology firms like Logitech) and the Netherlands (energy firms like Shell, technology firms like Philips, or Heineken), as well as both countries being financial safe havens and offshore zones (Switzerland due to its banking sector, the Netherlands via its Caribbean islands), both countries are the source of a good deal of investment into Russia (some of it Russian money reinvesting from the outside).[182] In addition, the Netherlands, given their extensive port facilities in Rotterdam and extensive European and global trading networks, often serve as re-exporters of Russian products to other markets. As a result, the Netherlands is usually in the top three in terms of destination for Russian exports.[183] However, the political relationships are not particularly strong. Switzerland's historic emphasis on neutrality and nonalignment means that the Swiss have not been particularly interested in Russian proposals for European security, and while the Dutch are major economic players in Russia, Moscow habitually ignores Dutch advice and criticism about its human rights records and its democracy deficit.

Because the European Union operates on the basis of consensus, with equal voting rights for all member-states, and given the efforts of countries like Sweden or the Netherlands to try and use the EU to pressure Russia, Russian foreign policy has adjusted to take into account the smaller, more peripheral European countries, whose friendship can be useful in helping to block what Moscow perceives as anti-Russian policies from being adopted by the EU as a whole. Some of these countries, like Spain, were particularly hostile to the Soviet Union during its existence. Spain did not enter into diplomatic relations with the USSR until after the death of the dictator Francisco Franco in 1977, in part because the Soviet Union had backed the Republican side during the Spanish Civil War of the 1930s. Today, even though Spain is not a major trading partner for Russia, the two countries now have similar views on a number of key international issues, most notably declining to recognize the emergence of an independent Kosovo separate from Serbia, since both Spain and Russia place a great deal of value on maintaining the territorial integrity of states. Having a NATO and EU member that was willing to break ranks with the United States and other major European countries on this issue has been very important to Russia's own diplomatic interests. Spain's insistence that NATO should focus more on security challenges arising from the south (the Middle East and Africa) has also meant that Madrid has not been a strong proponent of further NATO expansion to the east, another position that aligns with Russian interests.[184]

Russia's relations with Spain, as well as with a number of other smaller European states, are guided by the assessment that by cultivating every EU member, even those with little direct connection to Russia, it can be possible to "cut the ground" of those political forces in Europe that seek to exclude Russia from the European project.[185] Russia's newfound relationships with the states of

Southern Europe also help to promote a "southward trend" within NATO that reorients the focus of the alliance away from Russia and the Eurasian plain toward the Mediterranean basin.[186]

THE ARCTIC DIMENSION

"Russia is a northern country," then-Prime Minister Vladimir Putin declared at an Arctic forum in September 2010.[187] The melting of the Arctic ice has created a new dynamic in Russia's relationship with Europe. First, it opens up a new (and shorter) transport route between Europe and East Asia. The Northern Sea Route reduces the distance between the Far East and Asia by approximately 40% versus the traditional route through the Mediterranean, the Suez Canal, and the Indian Ocean (for a savings of nearly 3 weeks in transportation time). With the melting of the Arctic ice, the route is now navigable from late June to November.[188] Second, the opening of the Arctic makes accessible new sources of raw material, principally energy, which could meet the needs of the continent's economies. With some estimates of recoverable hydrocarbons in the Russian sectors of the Arctic reaching as high as 100 billion tons, the Russian government views this region as a special zone of national interest.[189] Much of the existing pipeline infrastructure would carry the oil and natural gas found in the Arctic to European customers, and part of the rationale behind the partnerships European energy firms like France's Total or Britain's BP have made with Russian state energy firms like Gazprom and Rosneft is to be able to tap into these undiscovered reserves.

Russia has authorized the use of the Arctic route for tankers carrying liquefied natural gas (LNG)—and this could be a way to send Arctic-produced natural gas to high-demand Asian markets as well as to Europe.[190] The Russian government is developing a network of 10 Arctic rescue centers, including at northern ports such as Murmansk, Arkhangelsk, Anadyr, and Provideniya, capable of carrying out search-and-rescue missions in the Arctic, and the system is expected to be operational by 2015.[191] The Russian shipping and transport industries see servicing cargo vessels and developing new ice-capable ships as growth markets for the future; firms like RIMCO—a shipping firm with Arctic-capable vessels—and the state-owned Sevmash shipyard, which builds icebreakers, are among the firms making up an Arctic lobby in the Russian government.[192] One of the most interesting business alliances is between the private natural gas producer Novatek and the Russian state atomic agency Rosatom to produce nuclear-powered icebreakers that would escort its LNG carriers transporting natural gas from its Yamal fields to its customers in China, Japan, South Korea, and Singapore.[193] Putin has committed the Russian government both to develop the resources of the Arctic and also to develop the Northern Sea Route, noting: "I want to stress the importance of the Northern Sea route as an international transport artery that will rival traditional trade lanes in service fees, security and quality."[194]

In 2007, to demonstrate its claims to territory under the waters of the Arctic Ocean that Russia maintains are part of its exclusive economic zone, including the so-called Lomonsov ridge (an underwater mountain range that Russia claims as part of its continental shelf) two mini-submarines (*Mir I* and *Mir II*) launched from a Russian icebreaker "planted" a Russian flag on the seabed at the North Pole. This symbolic act drew widespread criticism from other northern countries; Canada's foreign minister Peter MacKay lambasted the Russian action, noting, "This isn't the 15th Century. You can't go around the world and just plant flags and say 'We're claiming this territory.'"[195] The fear that Russia was attempting to dominate the Arctic led NATO's then-Secretary General Jaap de Hoop Scheffer to reaffirm that the Arctic was "a geographic region that has always been of great importance for the Alliance" and raised the "possibility of stepping up its focus in the region"[196]—remarks that were received with great concern in Moscow. Russia's strong preference is for all Arctic matters to be handled via the Arctic Council, to which all countries with territory abutting the Arctic are members (besides Russia, this includes Canada, Denmark, Finland, Iceland, Norway, Sweden, and the United States). Because this organization operates on the basis of consensus, no decision can be taken without Russia's consent. Russia's fear is that if NATO begins to play a formal role in Arctic security—given that five other Arctic Council states are alliance members and two, Sweden and Finland, cooperate with NATO and may eventually seek membership—it will be excluded from key decisions about regional security.[197] Russia has also reacted negatively to plans announced by the U.S. Navy to make the Arctic a new focus of attention and to improve NATO capabilities in this region.[198] Deputy Prime Minister Dmitry Rogozin has called for increased military deployments in the Arctic to counter a possible NATO presence.[199]

Part of the Russian strategy is to reach out to other Arctic nations to pursue common interests. Russia reached a settlement of its maritime boundary dispute with Norway, which was one of the main proponents of increasing the NATO presence in the Arctic. The agreement, signed in 2010 between Medvedev and Prime Minister Jens Stoltenberg, provided for an equal division of the zone in the Barents Sea lying between the Norwegian coast and Russia's Kola Peninsula, settling arguments over which country was entitled to exploit the fisheries and offshore hydrocarbon reserves.[200] After ratification of the treaty in 2011, both countries began to explore the possibility of joint development of the resources. The Russian willingness to accept a compromise was a clear concession on Moscow's part to abandon its claims to the entire territory, driven in part by its calculation that this would help to lower tensions—and so also reduce the argument that NATO was needed to provide security for its allies in the region.[201] Since then, the Russian and Norwegian militaries have expanded cooperation in the area of Arctic security. Russia and Norway now carry out a yearly naval exercise in the Arctic, the POMOR joint exercise. In April 2012, Russian Deputy Defense Minister Anatoly Antonov and Norwegian Defense Minister Espen Barth Eide discussed plans for more than 20 joint exercises that Russia and Norway would carry out in 2012 and 2013, as well for better coordination among their militaries in developing Arctic units.[202] Russian private oil company LUKoil—which has a strategic partnership with Norwegian companies North Energy and Det Norske and the Swedish company Lundin—and Russian state oil firm Rosneft, paired with Norway's state oil company Statoil, are now competing for the rights to explore and develop Norway's Arctic reserves.[203]

Russia has most successfully pursued its Arctic diplomacy with Canada. Canada and Russia share similar views about the Northern Sea Route and Canada's Northwest Passage being classed as "internal" waterways (e.g., passing through the national territories of Russia and Canada) rather than international waters.[204] A shared perspective on the Arctic, coupled with a growing economic relationship, has helped to foster closer ties between the two countries, which is coordinated via the Canada–Russia Intergovernmental Economic Commission, established in 1993—which in turn has a subgroup wholly devoted to Arctic issues.[205] Canada's willingness to be open to accommodation with Russia on Arctic issues is driven by the conclusion that increasing exports to the Russian market is critical for Canada's own economic health and a necessary diversification of Canada's economic relationships.[206] This spirit of cooperation also led Russia and Canada to take competing claims to the Lomonosov ridge to the United Nations for arbitration.[207]

Coordination between Moscow and Ottawa on Arctic issues has paid off. In 2009, Canada blocked the attempt to develop a NATO strategy for the Arctic,[208] and, the following year, Canadian Prime Minister Stephen Harper told de Hoop Scheffer's successor as NATO Secretary General, Anders Fogh Rasmussen, that "Canada has a good working relationship with Russia with respect to the Arctic, and a NATO presence could backfire by exacerbating tensions."[209]

At the 2010 Lisbon summit, NATO agreed to focus primarily on search-and-rescue and environmental missions rather than the ability to project military force into the Arctic.[210] Russia has also conducted joint exercises with NATO via the NATO-Russia Council focused on such missions as a way to promote greater transparency.[211] Russia's goal of having the Arctic Council serve as the primary forum for regional security was enhanced by the May 2011 agreement among all Arctic Council members setting up procedures for multilateral search and rescue missions—"the first legal instrument negotiated within the framework of the Arctic Council."[212] In April 2012, meeting under the aegis of the Arctic Council, seven respective chiefs of their country's general staffs, as well as the U.S. NORTHCOM commander, gathered to discuss joint operations among the member-states.[213] For the time being, therefore, Russia seems to have succeeded in preserving its freedom of action in this geostrategic region. Russia has no interest in sparking conflicts in the Arctic, "since this would impede upon its future trade and commercial interests by making the circumpolar north an unstable region."[214]

CONCLUDING THOUGHTS

In discussing Russia's European vector, Putin has noted,

> Russia sees itself as a natural integral part of the European family, both in spirit and its historical and cultural tradition . . . When I think about our relations from a long-term perspective, I do not see the fields which would be closed for equitable strategic partnership, based on common aspirations and values.[215]

Europe remains the most important set of countries for Russia, but Moscow is not prepared to beg for admittance to European institutions. It prefers to work with the EU and its members as an equal partner—and if such equivalence is not forthcoming, it is prepared to turn its attention to other parts of the world to compensate. Former Foreign Minister Igor Ivanov argues that "Russia and Europe must identify where their interests converge, and work to establish a mutually beneficial partnership in those areas." However, if this effort fails, Ivanov warns, there are those within the Russian elite who argue that "Russia . . . should form partnerships with more dynamic countries."[216] Russia's relationships with the rising powers of the global south and east will be examined in subsequent chapters.

NOTES

1. Summarized in Nikolas K. Gvosdev, *Imperial Policies and Perspectives Towards Georgia, 1763–1819* (Houndmills, Basingstoke: Macmillan Press, 2000), 10–13.

2. An excellent assessment as to the fluidity of Russian policy during the short reign of Emperor Paul (1796-1801) can be found in Hugh Ragsdale, "The Origins of Bonaparte's Russia Policy," *Slavic Review* 27, no. 1 (March 1968): 85–90.

3. One of the principal studies of the formation of the alliance is George F. Kennan, *The Fateful Alliance: France, Russia and the Coming of the First World War* (New York: Pantheon Books, 1984).

4. Angela Stent, *Russia and Germany Reborn: Unification, the Soviet Collapse, and the New Europe* (Princeton, NJ: Princeton University Press, 2000), 5.

5. For more on these developments, see Piotr S. Wandycz, *France and Her Eastern Allies 1919–1925* (Minneapolis: University of Minnesota Press, 1962).

6. Krzysztof Bobinski, "European unity: reality and myth," *Open Democracy*, March 21, 2007, at http://www.opendemocracy.net/democracy-europe_constitution/bobinski_rome_4456.jsp.

7. Quoted in Arkady N. Shevchenko, *Breaking with Moscow* (New York: Alfred A. Knopf, 1985), 103.

8. Vladislav Zubok and Constantine Pleshakov, *Inside the Kremlin's Cold War: From Stalin to Khrushchev* (Cambridge, MA: Harvard University Press, 1996), 159–160.

9. Yuri Dobinin, "About a 'Europe from the Atlantic to the Urals,'" *Russia in Global Affairs* 4 (October–December 2007), at http://eng.globalaffairs.ru/number/n_9784. Yuri Dubinin was a long-time Soviet foreign ministry official dealing with Western Europe.

10. Gordon A. Craig, "Did Ostpolitik Work?" *Foreign Affairs*, January/February 1994, at http://www.foreignaffairs.com/articles/49450/gordon-a-craig/did-ostpolitik-work?page=show.

11. Egon Bahr, "Germany's *Ostpolitik* and the Road to Helsinki," *OSCE Yearbook 2005* (Hamburg, Germany: Centre for OSCE Research, 2005), 24, at http://www.core-hamburg.de/documents/yearbook/english/05/Bahr-en.pdf.

12. Mike Bowker, "Brezhnev and Superpower Relations," in *Brezhnev Reconsidered*, eds. Edwin Bacon and Mark Sandle (Houndmills, Basingstoke: Palgrave Macmillan, 2002), 96–97.

13. James R. Kurth, "The United States and Western Europe in the Reagan Era," in *Crisis and Confrontation: Ronald Reagan's Foreign Policy*, ed. Morris H. Morley (Lanham, MD: Rowman and Littlefield, 1988), 62–64.

14. Craig, op. cit.

15. Raymond L. Garthoff, *Deterrence and the Revolution in Soviet Military Doctrine* (Washington, DC: Brookings Institution 1990), 72–74.

16. See, for instance, section II, paragraph 8 of the Russian Military Doctrine released February 5, 2010, at http://news.kremlin.ru/ref_notes/461.

17. "Excerpts from Speech by Gorbachev in France," *New York Times*, July 7, 1989, at https://www.nytimes.com/1989/07/07/world/excerpts-from-speech-by-gorbachev-in-france.html?pagewanted=2&src=pm.

18. Robert D. Hormats, "Redefining Europe and the Atlantic Link," *Foreign Affairs*, Fall 1989, at http://www.foreignaffairs.com/articles/44894/robert-d-hormats/redefining-europe-and-the-atlantic-link.

19. Andrej Grachev, "Towards a New EU-Russia Security Relationship? Another Chance for a United Europe," lecture delivered to the Cicero Foundation, Paris, April 12, 2002. The text is archived at http://www.cicerofoundation.org/lectures/grachev_apr02.html.

20. Ibid.

21. "Churchill the Provocative," *Time*, May 21, 1956, at http://www.time.com/time/magazine/article/0,9171,808488,00.html; Grachev, op. cit.

22. Goran Lysen, "The Joint Declaration by the EEC and the CMEA," 14 *N.C.J. Int'l L. & Com. Reg.* 369 (1989).

23. Robert M. Cutler, "Harmonizing EEC–CMEA Relations: Never the Twain Shall Meet?" *International Affairs* 63, no. 2 (Spring 1987): 262.

24. A copy of the treaty is available at http://trade.ec.europa.eu/doclib/docs/2008/july/tradoc_139580.pdf.

25. See, for instance, Putin's comment, as prime minister, in his op-ed of February 27, 2012. See also Michael Emerson, "A European view of Putin's foreign and security policy," *CEPS Commentary*, March 2, 2012, 1–2, at http://www.ceps.eu/book/european-view-putin's-foreign-and-security-policy.

26. M. K. Gorshkov, *Rossiia na rubezhe vekov* (Moscow: ROSSPEN, 2000), 406.

27. Dov Lynch, "The State of the OSCE," special issue of the *EU–Russia Centre Review* (Russia, the OSCE and European Security) 12 (November 2009): 5.

28. Dmitri Trenin, "Russia and Europe Still Need Each Other," *Strategic Europe*, November 16, 2012, at http://carnegieeurope.eu/strategiceurope/?fa=50046.

29. *U.S.–Russia Relations After the Reset: A Dialogue* (Washington, DC: The Nixon Center, 2010), 8, at http://www.cftni.org/FinalReset10.10.pdf. See also *Euro–Atlantic Security: One Vision, Three Paths*, a report of the EastWest Institute, issued June 23, 2009.

30. Nadezhda Arbatova, "Russia-EU Quandary 2007," *Russia in Global Affairs* 4, no. 2 (April–June 2006): 102.

31. See, for instance, Coral Bell, "Why Russia Should Join NATO: From Containment to Concert," *Russia in the National Interest*, ed. Nikolas K. Gvosdev (New Brunswick, NJ: Transaction Press, 2003), 33–47.

32. Jean-Pierre Massias, "Russia and the Council of Europe: Ten Years Wasted?," *Russie.Nei.Visions* no. 15 (January 2007), at www.ifri.org/downloads/ifri_CE_massias_ang_jan2007.pdf.

33. Valerii Zorkin, "Predel Ustupchivosti," *Rossiisakaia Gazeta*, October 29, 2010, at http://www.rg.ru/2010/10/29/zorkin.html.

34. Ellen Barry, "Russia Ends Opposition to Rights Court," *New York Times*, January 15, 2010, at http://www.nytimes.com/2010/01/16/world/europe/16russia.html?_r=2&ref=european_court_of_human_rights.

35. Trenin, op. cit.

36. "Yeltsin Says Russia Interested In EU," *Associated* Press, March 23, 1997; Timothy J. Colton, *Yeltsin: A Life* (New York: Basic Books, 2008), 269.

37. Press release of the European Union, "EU announces formal recognition of Russia as 'Market Economy' in major milestone on road to WTO membership," IP/02/775, May 29, 2002, at http://europa.eu/rapid/press-release_IP-02-775_en.htm?locale=en.

38. Romano Prodi, President of the European Commission, "A Wider Europe—A Proximity Policy as the key to stability," speech delivered at the Sixth ECSA-World Conference (Jean Monnet Project), "Peace, Security and Stability International Dialogue and the Role of the EU," Brussels, December 6, 2002, at http://europa.eu/rapid/press-release_SPEECH-02-619_en.htm.

39. This process is detailed in the report prepared by the European External Action Service, "EU-Russia Common Spaces: Progress Report 2010," March 2011, at http://eeas.europa.eu/russia/docs/commonspaces_prog_report_2010_en.pdf.

40. "Press Statement and Answers to Questions during the Joint Press Conference with President of the European Commission Jose Manuel Barroso and German Chancellor Angela Merkel Following the Russia-European Union Summit Meeting in Samara," May 18, 2007, www.delrus.ec.europa.eu/en/images/pText_pict/559/Transcript.doc.

41. For instance, in 2010, the Russian government signaled that, in opposition to previous indications, it was not willing to revise Russian legislation governing the chemical industry in order to align it with EU "REACH" legislation, which in turn would "create difficulties for EU chemical businesses exporting to Russia." Cf. the European External Action Service, "EU-Russia Common Spaces: Progress Report 2010," at http://eeas.europa.eu/russia/docs/commonspaces_prog_report_2010_en.pdf.

42. Olga Shumylo-Tapiola, *The Eurasian Customs Union: Friend or Foe of the EU?* Carnegie Endowment for International Peace paper, October 2012, at http://carnegieeurope.eu/publications/?fa=49548&lang=en.

43. "Trade within the Russia-Kazakhstan-Belarus customs union: early evidence," *EBRD blog*, July 10, 2012, at http://www.ebrdblog.com/wordpress/2012/07/trade-within-the-russia-kazakhstan-belarus-customs-union-early-evidence/; "Customs Union shows solidarity against Belarus sanctions plan," *Russia Today*, March 11, 2012, at http://rt.com/politics/union-belarus-sanctions-european-289/.

44. Nadia Alexandrova-Arbatova, "The EU-Russia partnership: a new context," *European Strategic Partnership Observatory* 5 (July 2012): 3, at http://www.fride.org/publication/1038/the-eu-russia-partnership:-a-new-context.

45. See, for instance, "Legal framework," information posted on the website of the Delegation of the European Union to Russia, at http://eeas.europa.eu/delegations/russia/eu_russia/political_relations/legal_framework/index_en.htm.

46. Timofei Bordachev, "Russia-EU summit: Optimistic stagnation," *Valdai Discussion Club*, December 21, 2012, at http://valdaiclub.com/europe/52901.html.

47. Nikolaus von Twickel, "EU-Russian Visa Regime Hot Topic at Summit," *Moscow Times*, December 23, 2012, at http://www.themoscowtimes.com/news/article/eu-russian-visa-regime-hot-topic-at-summit/473527.html.

48. "The draft of the European Security Treaty," posted November 29, 2009, at the website of the President of Russia, at http://eng.kremlin.ru/news/275.

49. Nikolas Gvosdev, "Sarkozy's Gamble," *The New Atlanticist*, November 5, 2008, at http://acus.org/new_atlanticist/sarkozys-gamble; Marcel H. Van Herpen, "Medvedev's Proposal for a Pan-European Security Pact," Cicero Foundation Working Paper WP-08-03 (October 2008), 7, at http://www.cicerofoundation.org/lectures/Marcel_H_Van_Herpen_Medvedevs_Proposal_for_a_Pan-European_Security_Pact.pdf.

50. Van Herpen, 1–3.

51. Richard Weitz, "The Rise and Fall of Medvedev's European Security Treaty," *On Wider Europe* (German Marshall Fund), May 2012, 4–5, at http://www.hudson.org/files/publications/1338307624Weitz_MedvedevsEST_May12.pdf.

52. Vladimir Frolov, "What's Good for Putin Is Bad for Foreign Policy," *Moscow Times,* July 29, 2012, at http://www.themoscowtimes.com/opinion/article/whats-good-for-putin-is-bad-for-foreign-policy/462796.html#ixzz24mfRK900.

53. "European missile defense shield up and running—NATO," *Russia Today,* May 21, 2012, at http://rt.com/news/nato-summit-missile-shield-739/.

54. Ulrike Demmer and Ralf Neukirch, "Fear of Russia: NATO Developed Secret Contingency Plans for Baltic States," *Der Spiegel,* July 12, 2010, at http://www.spiegel.de/international/europe/fear-of-russia-nato-developed-secret-contingency-plans-for-baltic-states-a-733361.html.

55. "Up to 10 Fighters From NATO Countries Escorted Pair of Tu-95 MS Strategic Aircraft Engaged in Aerial Patrol," *Interfax-AVN,* September 12, 2012.

56. Irina Filatova, "Lavrov Pushes Hard on Start of Visa-Free Regime with Europe," *Moscow Times,* October 9, 2012, at http://www.themoscowtimes.com/business/article/lavrov-pushes-hard-on-start-of-visa-free-regime-with-europe/469476.html#ixzz2AkUOrVeo.

57. "STRATFOR: Russia's Intensifying Diplomatic Courtship of Europe," *Warsaw Business Journal,* December 7, 2010, at http://www.wbj.pl/article-52398-stratfor-russias-intensifying-diplomatic-courtship-of-europe.html?typ=ise.

58. See the statistics provided by the European Commission at http://ec.europa.eu/trade/creating-opportunities/bilateral-relations/countries/russia/.

59. From statistics provided by the European Commission at http://ec.europa.eu/energy/international/bilateral_cooperation/russia/russia_en.htm.

60. Fyodor Lukyanov, "Flexibility offers Russian-British relations a new chance," *Russia Now* (supplement to the *Daily Telegraph*), July 10, 2012, at http://www.telegraph.co.uk/sponsored/russianow/opinion/9388538/russian-british-relations-new-chance.html.

61. Jason Corcoran and Maryam Nemazee, "Russian Investment Fund Seeking Germany, Italy, U.K. Targets," *Bloomberg,* January 26, 2012, at http://www.bloomberg.com/news/2012-01-26/russian-investment-fund-seeking-germany-italy-u-k-targets-1-.html.

62. Stent, *Reborn,* ix.

63. Melvin Croan, "The Development of the GDR Political Relationship with the USSR," in *GDR Foreign Policy,* eds. Hans-Adolf Jacobsen, Gert Leptin, and Ulrich Scheuer (Armonk, NY: M.E. Sharpe, 1982), 186.

64. Jochen Bethkenhagen, "The Development of the GDR Economic Relationship with the USSR," in *GDR Foreign Policy,* op. cit., 250, 254.

65. Stent, *Reborn,* 13.

66. Comment of Frank Elbe, a senior German Foreign Ministry official. See his lecture, "The Diplomatic Path to German Unity," delivered in Washington, DC, at the GHI German Unification Symposium, October 2, 2009, and reprinted in *Bulletin of the GHI* 46 (Spring 2010): 33, at http://www.ghi-dc.org/files/publications/bulletin/bu046/033.pdf.

67. Elbe, 36.

68. The comprehensive story of German reunification can be found in Philip Zelikow and Condoleezza Rice, *Germany Unified and Europe Transformed: A Study in Statecraft* (Cambridge, MA: Harvard University Press, 1995).

69. Stent, *Reborn,* 174.

70. Stent, *Reborn,* 159.

71. Germany was often described as "a defense lawyer for Russia in the construction of a new Europe," quoted in Robert H. Donaldson and Joseph L. Nogee, *The Foreign Policy of Russia: Changing Systems, Enduring Interests,* 2nd edition (Armonk, NY: M.E. Sharpe, 2009), 255.

72. Andreas Heinrich and Heiko Pleines, "Factors explaining the smooth co-operation between German and Russian gas companies," *Baltic Rim Economies* 1 (2010): 20, at http://www.tse.fi/FI/yksikot/erillislaitokset/pei/Documents/BRE2010/BRE%201-2010%20artik kelit/BRE_2_2010__20.pdf.

73. Stent, *Reborn,* 173.

74. Andrew Felkay, *Yeltsin's Russia and the West* (Westport, CT: Praeger Publishers, 2002), 191.

75. Randall Newnham, "The Role of Economic Aid in the German-Soviet Negotiations," *German Studies Review* 22, no. 3 (October 1999): 436.

76. Kristina Spohr Readman, *Germany and the Baltic Problem after the Cold War: The Development of a New Ostpolitik, 1989–2000* (London: Routledge, 2004), 116.

77. Vladimir Socor, "Made in Germany for Russia's Army," *Eurasia Daily Monitor* 8, no. 31 (February 14, 2011), at http://www.jamestown.org/single/?no_cache=1&tx_ttnews%5Btt_news%5D=37506&tx_ttnews%5BbackPid%5D=7&cHash=d8a6991209f09d8f ea696060eaf6f68d.

78. Alexander Rahr, "Germany and Russia: A Special Relationship," *The Washington Quarterly* 30, no. 2 (Spring 2007): 138.

79. Felkay, 191.

80. "German business circles want the visa regime with Russia to be lifted," *CeWeekly,* July 13, 2011, at http://www.osw.waw.pl/en/publikacje/ceweekly/2011-07-13/german-business-circles-want-visa-regime-russia-to-be-lifted.

81. See details on the relationship in Michael Thumann, "Russia And Germany, Schroeder And Putin—Cabinet Diplomacy 21th Century Style," prepared for the German Marshall Fund, at available at http://www.gmfus.org/doc/Thumann%20paper%20 Schroeder%20Putin.pdf.

82. Judy Dempsey, "Schröder and Putin cementing relationship," *New York Times,* September 8, 2005, at http://www.nytimes.com/2005/09/07/world/europe/07iht-ger many.html.

83. Comments of senior German officials to one of the authors.

84. "Germany's foreign policy more independent under Schroeder—Putin," *Russia Journal,* August 23, 2005, at http://russiajournal.com/node/19853.

85. Thumann, op. cit.

86. Samuel Charap (rapporteur), *Developing a More Comprehensive Russia Policy: Lessons Learned from the German and US Experiences,* report published by the Friedrich Ebert Stiftung, July 2012, 5, at http://library.fes.de/pdf-files/id/09214.pdf.

87. Gregory Feifer, "Too Special A Friendship: Is Germany Questioning Russia's Embrace?" *Radio Free Europe/Radio Liberty,* December 7, 2011, at http://www.rferl.org/con tent/germany_and_russia_too_special_a_relationship/24262486.html.

88. Angela Stent, "Berlin's Russia Challenge," *The National Interest* 88 (March/April 2007): 49.

89. Nikolas K. Gvosdev, Ted Galen Carpenter, Anatol Lieven, and Charles A. Kupchan, "Bucharest on My Mind: Experts React to the NATO Summit," *National Interest*, April 4, 2008, at http://nationalinterest.org/article/bucharest-on-my-mind-experts-react-to-the-nato-summit-2035?page=show.

90. Owen Matthews, "The New Ostpolitik," *Newsweek*, July 24, 2009, at http://www.newsweek.com/2009/07/24/the-new-ostpolitik.html.

91. Judy Dempsey, "Soft Power towards a Hardened Russia," *New York Times*, October 10, 2011, at http://www.nytimes.com/2011/10/11/world/europe/11iht-letter11.html?page wanted=all.

92. Benjamin Bidder, "Medvedev Charms Merkel at Munich Summit," *Der Spiegel*, July 17, 2009, at http://www.spiegel.de/international/germany/german-russian-relations-medvedev-charms-merkel-at-munich-summit-a-636653.html.

93. "Sarkozy Dreams of a European Security Council," *Der Spiegel*, October 18, 2010, at http://www.spiegel.de/international/europe/french-german-russian-summit-sarkozy-dreams-of-a-european-security-council-a-723664.html.

94. "Medvedev joins friendly talks in Deauville," *Euronews*, October 19, 2010, at http://www.euronews.com/2010/10/19/medvedev-joins-friendly-talks-in-deauville/.

95. Anatoly Medetsky, "Gazprom Launches 2nd Phase of $9.6Bln Pipeline," *The Moscow Times*, October 9, 2012, at http://www.themoscowtimes.com/business/article/gaz prom-launches-2nd-phase-of-96bln-pipeline/469455.html.

96. Ludwig Burger and Vera Eckert, "BASF, Gazprom agree on natural gas asset swap," *Reuters*, November 14, 2012, at http://www.reuters.com/article/2012/11/14/basf-gazprom-idUSL5E8ME10D20121114.

97. Alexander Jung, Matthias Schepp and Benjamin Triebe, "Moscow Investors Go on Shopping Spree for German Companies," *Der Spiegel*, April 1, 2008, at http://www.spiegel.de/international/business/the-russians-are-coming-moscow-investors-go-on-shopping-spree-for-german-companies-a-544714.html.

98. Matthews, op. cit.

99. "Russia praises German investments," *Voice of Russia*, July 6, 2012, at http://eng lish.ruvr.ru/2012_07_06/Russia-praises-German-investments/.

100. "German technologies for the Russian extraction and shipbuilding industries." *Eastweek* 33, no. 142 (October 16, 2008), at http://www.osw.waw.pl/en/publikacje/eastweek/2008-10-16/german-technologies-russian-extraction-and-shipbuilding-industries.

101. "A Close Working Relationship," a 2012 press release of Germany Trade and Investment, at http://www.gtai.de/GTAI/Navigation/EN/invest,did=600162.html.

102. Christoph Steitz, "Russian cleantech fund close to German investment," *Reuters*, November 21, 2012, archived at http://www.wermutham.com/news/article163.html.

103. Judy Dempsey, "Is Germany Getting Tough on Russia?" *Strategic Europe*, October 25, 2012, at http://carnegieeurope.eu/strategiceurope/?fa=49795.

104. Ibid.

105. Robert Coalson, "As Merkel Heads For Russia, Moscow Is In For A Schockenhoff," *Radio Free Europe/Radio Liberty,* November 16, 2012, at http://www.rferl.org/content/news-analysis-merkel-putin-schockenhoff/24768692.html.

106. "Merkel meets Putin in Kremlin for 'critical dialogue,'" *Agence France-Press,* November 14, 2012, archived at http://www.expatica.com/de/news/german-news/merkel-meets-putin-in-kremlin-for-critical-dialogue-_250186.html; see also Trenin, op. cit.

107. Andreas Umland, "Post-Soviet Russian Anti-Americanism and the Post-War German Experience," *Global Politician,* April 4, 2008, at http://www.globalpolitician.com/print.asp?id=4504.

108. V. Belov, "Russia-Germany: Partners for Modernization," *International Affairs* 5 (2010): 108.

109. Ralf Neukirch and Matthias Schepp, "German-Russian Relations Enter a New Ice Age," *Der Spiegel,* May 30, 2012, at http://www.spiegel.de/international/germany/german-and-russian-relations-are-at-an-impasse-a-835862.html.

110. See, for instance, the essay by Jean Kanapa, who was a member of the French Communist Politburo and responsible for foreign policy issues: "A "New Policy" of the French Communists?" *Foreign Affairs,* January 1977, at http://www.foreignaffairs.com/articles/27033/jean-kanapa/a-new-policy-of-the-french-communists.

111. Georges-Henri Soutou, "The Linkage Between European Integration and Détente," in *European Integration and the Cold War: Ostpolitik-Westpolitik, 1965–1973,* ed. N. Piers-Ludlow (New York: Routledge, 2007), 21–22.

112. Don Cook, "Gorbachev, Mitterrand End 17 Hours of Talks," *Los Angeles Times,* July 10, 1986, at http://articles.latimes.com/1986-07-10/news/mn-22485_1_soviet-space.

113. Andrei Grachev, "From the Common European Home to the European Confederation: Francois Mitterrand and Mikhail Gorbachev in Search of the Road to Greater Europe," *Europe and the End of the Cold War: A Reappraisal,* eds. Frederic Bozo, Marie-Pierre Rey, N. Piers Ludlow, and Leopoldo Nuti (Abingdon, Oxon, UK: Routledge, 2008), 214.

114. John Thor-Dahlberg, "Russia to Get New French Aid; Old Pact Revived," *Los Angeles Times,* February 8, 1992, at http://articles.latimes.com/1992-02-08/news/mn-1363_1_french.

115. Felkay, 169.

116. "To Paris, U.S. Looks Like a 'Hyperpower,'" *New York Times,* February 5, 1999, at http://www.nytimes.com/1999/02/05/news/05iht-france.t_0.html.

117. These meetings allowed both presidents to meet without an official agenda and to discuss collaboration in both commercial and diplomatic projects. Cf. "Chirac, Putin to meet in Paris to cement strong bilateral ties," *People's Daily* Online, November 5, 2003, at http://english.peopledaily.com.cn/200311/12/eng20031112_128116.shtml.

118. Nikolas Gvosdev, "Sarkozy's Gamble?" *New Atlanticist,* November 5, 2008, at http://acus.org/new_atlanticist/sarkozys-gamble.

119. Ariel Cohen, "Medvedev-Sarkozy Honeymoon: At What Price?" *The Foundry,* March 3, 2010, at http://blog.heritage.org/2010/03/03/medvedev-sarkozy-honeymoon-at-what-price/.

120. "Russia 'borrowed NGOs law from foreign legal practices'" (Interview of Dmitry Medvedev with the French media), *Russia Today,* November 26, 2012, at http://rt.com/politics/official-word/medvedev-interview-french-media-620/.

121. Louis Clerc, "Trade, trade, trade—Russia from a French Perspective in 2010," *Baltic Rim Economies* 5 (2010): 36, at http://www.tse.fi/FI/yksikot/erillislaitokset/pei/Documents/BRE2010/BRE%205%202010/BRE%205%202010_36.pdf.

122. See the remarks at "Prime Minister Vladimir Putin and French Prime Minister Francois Fillon chair the 15th meeting of the Russian-French Commission on Bilateral Cooperation," a summary posted by the government of the Russian Federation on December 9, 2010, at http://government.ru/eng/docs/13311/.

123. Ibid.

124. "Ties at the Top," *Partnership XXI* 1, no. 10 (2010): 7, at http://www.themoscow times.com/business/country_supplement/russia_france/2011/eng/article/ties-at-the-top/408513.html#no.

125. Pat Davis Szymchak, "Cooperation Offshore and Overseas, *Partnership XXI* 1, no. 10 (2010): 22, at http://www.themoscowtimes.com/business/country_supplement/russia_france/2010/eng/article/408534.html.

126. Douglas Herbert, "French firms seal Russian contracts during Sarkozy visit," *France 24,* June 19, 2010, at http://www.france24.com/en/20100619-saint-petersburg-economic-forum-russia-france-sarkozy-eu-cooperation-contracts.

127. Clerc, 36.

128. Cohen, op. cit.

129. Socor, op. cit.

130. Nikolas K. Gvosdev, "The Reset is Working," *National Interest,* June 21, 2010, at http://nationalinterest.org/commentary/the-reset-is-working-3605.

131. "Sarkozy Dreams of a European Security Council," *Der Spiegel,* October 18, 2010, at http://www.spiegel.de/international/europe/french-german-russian-summit-sarkozy-dreams-of-a-european-security-council-a-723664.html.

132. "Putin happy with Moscow-Paris relations," *Voice of Russia,* November 14, 2012, at http://english.ruvr.ru/2012_11_14/Putin-happy-with-Moscow-Paris-relations/; "Russian-French relations will remain strategic in character—Lavrov," *Voice of Russia,* May 7, 2012, at http://english.ruvr.ru/2012_05_07/74043127/.

133. "Russia called to mediate in Libya," May 26, 2011, at http://www.reuters.com/article/2011/05/26/us-g8-russia-libya-idUSTRE74P7H520110526; Gregory Viscusi and Ilya Arkhipov, "Hollande Clashes With Putin Over Ouster of Syria's Assad," *Bloomberg,* June 1, 2012, at http://www.bloomberg.com/news/2012-06-01/hollande-clashes-with-putin-over-ouster-of-syria-s-assad.html.

134. "Putin welcomes 'dear' Sarkozy back in Russia," *Agence France Press,* November 14, 2012, archived at http://www.expatica.com/fr/news/french-news/putin-welcomes-dear—sarkozy-back-in-russia_250237.html.

135. "Russia borrowed NGO law," op. cit.

136. Nikolaus von Twickel and Irina Filatova, "Hollande and Putin Warm Relations," *Moscow Times,* 5079 (February 28, 2013), at http://www.themoscowtimes.com/news/article/hollande-and-putin-warm-relations/476253.html.

137. Igor Veshny, "Lines of Mutually Beneficial Cooperation," *Oil of Russia* 1 (2010), at http://www.oilru.com/or/42/868/.

138. Clyde Haberman, "Clamor in the East; Gorbachev, Visiting Italy, Urges Talks on Naval Arms," *New York Times*, November 30, 1989, at http://www.nytimes.com/1989/11/30/world/clamor-in-the-east-gorbachev-visiting-italy-urges-talks-on-naval-arms.html?pagewanted=2&src=pm.

139. William D. Montalbano, "Yeltsin Visits Italy, Collects $1.3 Billion: Diplomacy: 'There is no more U.S.S.R. and no turning back,' he says as Rome frees up valuable credits," *Los Angeles Times*, December 20, 1991, at http://articles.latimes.com/1991-12-20/news/mn-620_1_yeltsin-visits-italy.

140. Donaldson/Nogee, 262.

141. Remarks of Romano Prodi, "A Wider Europe—A Proximity Policy As the Key to Stability." Speech delivered at "Peace, Security And Stability International Dialogue and the Role of the EU," Sixth ECSA-World Conference, Jean Monnet Project, Brussels, December 5, 2002.

142. Nikolas K. Gvosdev, "A Petersburg Tale of Three Summits," *National Interest*, May 28, 2003, at http://nationalinterest.org/article/a-petersburg-tale-of-three-summits-2353.

143. "Eni, Enel Gazprom sign Arctic Gas pact," *Scandinavian Oil and Gas Magazine*, October 31, 2008, at http://www.scandoil.com/moxie-bm2/news/spot_news/eni-enel-gazprom-sign-arctic-gas-pact.shtml; Vidya Ram, "Pipeline Diplomacy for Prodi, Putin," *Forbes*, November 22, 2007, at http://www.forbes.com/2007/11/22/putin-prodi-pipeline-face-markets-cx_vr_1122autofacescan02.html.

144. John Hutchinson, "Let's Toast My Victory," *Daily Mai*, March 8, 2012, at http://www.dailymail.co.uk/news/article-2112329/Vladimir-Putin-lets-Silvio-Berlusconi-hog-limelight-Italian-PM-joins-slopes.html.

145. Greg Caramenico, "Italy-Russia Energy Partnership Deeper Than Berlusconi," *World Politics Review*, January 27, 2011, at http://www.worldpoliticsreview.com/articles/7686/italy-russia-energy-partnership-deeper-than-berlusconi.

146. "Italy-Russia: Strategic partnership confirmed, says Frattini," press release of the Ministry of Foreign Affairs, June 24, 2011, at http://www.esteri.it/MAE/EN/Sala_Stampa/ArchivioNotizie/Approfondimenti/2011/06/20110624_itarus2.htm.

147. "STRATFOR: Russia's Intensifying Diplomatic Courtship of Europe," op. cit.

148. "Russian Sukhoi Superjet to be customised for Mexico," *BBC News*, October 8, 2012, at http://www.bbc.co.uk/news/world-europe-19871086.

149. "Russian-Italian drills start in Italy," *Voice of Russia*, September 10, 2012, at http://english.ruvr.ru/2012_09_10/Russian-Italian-drills-start-in-Italy/.

150. "Russia to manufacture Iveco armored vehicles under Iveco license," *RIA Novosti*, October 26, 2010, at http://en.rian.ru/business/20101026/161094748.html; "Media: Russian-Italian Submarine Project Gets Rolling," RusNavy.Com, October 23, 2012, at http://rusnavy.com/news/navy/index.php?ELEMENT_ID=16236.

151. The South Stream consortium to construct the pipeline is structured as follows: 15 percent Wintershall (Germany), 25 percent ENI (Italy), 10 percent EDF (France), Gazprom 50 percent (Russia). Andrea Bonzanni, "South Stream Revival and EU-Russian

Energy Relations," *World Politics Review,* April 5, 2011, at http://www.worldpoliticsreview .com/articles/8413/south-stream-revival-and-eu-russian-energy-relations.

152. "Work on Gas Line to Begin in December," *New York Times,* July 23, 2012, at http://www.nytimes.com/2012/07/23/business/energy-environment/russia-and-germany-to-start-gas-pipeline-in-december.html.

153. John Vincent, "Ivan the terribly rude," *The Telegraph,* January 2, 2004, at http:// www.telegraph.co.uk/news/worldnews/europe/russia/1450732/Ivan-the-terribly-rude .html.

154. The phrase, popularized by the author Rudyard Kipling, is said to have been coined by Arthur Connolly, an officer of the British East India Company. Peter Hopkirk, *The Great Game: The Struggle for Empire in Central Asia* (New York: Kodansha America, 1994), 1.

155. Albert Resis, "The Churchill-Stalin Secret 'Percentages' Agreement on the Balkans, Moscow, October 1944," *The American Historical Review* 83, no. 2 (April 1978): 368–387.

156. See the commentary in "Détente in Europe," in Series III of the Foreign and Commonwealth Office's *Documents on British Policy Overseas,* published in 2001 and archived at http://www.fco.gov.uk/en/about-us/our-history/historical-publications/docu ments-british-policy/detente-in-europe/.

157. Archie Brown, "The Change to Engagement in Britain's Cold War Policy: The Origins of the Thatcher-Gorbachev Relationship," *Journal of Cold War Studies* 10, no. 3 (Summer 2008): 3–47.

158. "Thatcher had a Definite Womanish Feeling towards Gorbachev," (interview with Leonid Zamyatin), *Kommersant,* May 4, 2005, at http://www.kommersant.com/p572821/ r_1/%E2%80%9CThatcher_had_a_Definite_Womanish_Feeling_towards_Gorbachev %E2%80%9D/.

159. Hasan Suroor, "How Margaret Thatcher pleaded with Gorbachev not to let the Berlin Wall fall," *The Hindu,* September 15, 2009, at http://www.thehindu.com/opinion/ columns/Hasan_Suroor/article20329.ece.

160. Micha Rinkus, "The Queens chocolate a hit in Russia," *BSR Russia,* June 1, 2008, at http://www.bsr-russia.com/en/country-reports/item/13-the-queens-chocolate-a-hit-in-russia.html.

161. Donaldson/Nogee, 206.

162. "Blair and Putin finish EU talks," *BBC News,* October 4, 2005, at http://news.bbc .co.uk/2/hi/europe/4306770.stm.

163. Andrew Jack, *Inside Putin's Russia: Can There Be Reform Without Democracy?* (New York: Oxford University Press, 2004), 274.

164. "'Constructive' Blair-Putin talks end," *BBC News,* December 22, 2001, at http:// news.bbc.co.uk/2/hi/uk_news/politics/1724685.stm.

165. "BP signs historic Russian deal," *BBC News,* June 23, 2003, at http://news.bbc .co.uk/2/hi/business/3021786.stm.

166. Alexandra Topping and Miriam Elder, "Britain admits 'fake rock' plot to spy on Russians," *The Guardian,* January 19, 2012, at http://www.guardian.co.uk/world/2012/ jan/19/fake-rock-plot-spy-russians.

167. Gary Gibbon, "Putin, Blair and the deep freeze that won't thaw," *Channel 4,* September 10, 2011, at http://blogs.channel4.com/gary-gibbon-on-politics/putin-blair-and-the-deep-freeze-that-wont-thaw/16304.

168. For more on this, see Gevork Papiryan, *BP in Russia: Settling the Joint Venture Dispute* (Cambridge, MA: Harvard Business School, 2008).

169. Tom Bawden, "Would you dare to trade with The Bear?" *The Independent,* August 3, 2012, at http://www.independent.co.uk/news/business/analysis-and-features/would-you-dare-to-trade-with-the-bear-8002181.html?printService=print.

170. Olga Dmitrieva and Yadviga Yuferova, "Why are Russians moving to Britain?" *The Telegraph/Rossiiskaia Gazeta,* April 27, 2011, at http://www.telegraph.co.uk/sponsored/russianow/society/8476412/Why-are-Russians-moving-to-Britain.html.

171. Fyodor Lukyanov, "Flexibility offers Russian-British relations a new chance," *The Telegraph/Rossiiskaia Gazeta,* July 10, 2012, at http://www.telegraph.co.uk/sponsored/russianow/opinion/9388538/russian-british-relations-new-chance.html.

172. Yevgeny Shestakov, "David Cameron's Moscow visit revives Russian-British relationship," *The Telegraph/Rossiiskaia Gazeta,* October 5, 2011, at http://www.telegraph.co.uk/sponsored/russianow/opinion/8808753/David-Cameron-Moscow-Russia-Britain.html.

173. "Putin, Cameron discuss energy and trade," *Voice of Russia,* August 2, 2011 , at http://english.ruvr.ru/2012_08_02/Putin-Cameron-discuss-energy-and-trade/.

174. "Russia and UK start dialogue in London," *Voice of Russia,* March 13, 2013, at http://english.ruvr.ru/2013_03_13/Russia-and-UK-start-dialogue-in-London/.

175. Bawden, op. cit.

176. Caroline Binham and Neil Buckley, "Russian Bank Chief Given UK Asylum," *Financial Times,* March 1, 2013, at http://www.ft.com/cms/s/0/bc88baa4-827c-11e2-8404-00144feabdc0.html#axzz2NfHEWAq5.

177. "Exclusive Interview with Swedish Foreign Minister Carl Bildt," *Tabula,* April 5, 2011, at http://en.tabula.ge/article-3625.html.

178. "Finland, Sweden Give Approval to Nord Stream," *Pipeline and Gas Journal* 237, no. 1 (January 2010), at http://pipelineandgasjournal.com/finland-sweden-give-approval-nord-stream.

179. Eva Hagstrom Frisell and Ingmar Oldberg, *"Cool Neighbors": Sweden's EU Presidency and Russia,* monograph in the Russie.Nei.Vision series issued by IFRI, no. 42 (July 2009), at www.ifri.org/downloads/ifrirussiaandswedenengjune09_1.pdf.

180. von Twickel and Filatova, "Hollande and Putin," op. cit.

181. "A Conversation With Sweden's Minister for Trade," *Partnership XXI* 2, no. 16 (2011): 10–11, at http://www.themoscowtimes.com/business/country_supplement/russia_sweden/2011/eng/article/435836.html; "Putin says prospects good for Sweden-Russia relations," *Xinhua,* April 28, 2011, at http://english.peopledaily.com.cn/90001/90777/90853/7364233.html.

182. See, for instance, the remarks of Federal Councillor Johann N. Schneider-Ammann, head of the Swiss Department of Economic Affairs, "Switzerland and Russia as economic partners: The role of innovation in economic success," delivered in Moscow on July 11, 2011, at http://www.evd.admin.ch/dokumentation/00379/00397/00399/index

.html?lang=en&msg-id=40061; "Prime minister of the Netherlands leads trade delegation to Russia," *Modern Russia,* October 31, 12011, at http://www.modernrussia.com/content/ prime-minister-netherlands-leads-trade-delegation-russia.

183. "China Becomes Russia's Top Trade Partner," *Xinhua,* September 26, 2012, at http://www.chinadaily.com.cn/business/2012-09/26/content_15784444.htm.

184. Alexander Gusev, "The relations between Russian Federation and Spain," *CIBOB International Yearbook 2010* (Barcelona, Spain: CIBOB [Barcelona Centre for International Affairs], 2010), 173–177.

185. See Sergey Karaganov, Andrzej Olechowski, and Horst Teltschik, "Hotel Europe: Guests and Permanent Partners," *Russia in Global Affairs,* October 23, 2011, at http://eng .globalaffairs.ru/pubcol/Hotel-Europe-Guests-and-Permanent-Partners-15367.

186. Daniel Larison, "The Consequences of the Libyan War for NATO," *The American Conservative,* April 6, 2011, at http://www.theamericanconservative.com/larison/the-conse quences-of-the-libyan-war-for-nato/.

187. Rimvydas Ragauskas, "Priorities of Russia's Arctic Policy," May 23, 2011, at http://eurodialogue.org/energy-security/Priorities-of%20Russia-Arctic-policy.

188. Ichiro Matsuo and Takashi Kida, "Northern Sea Route heats up between Europe, East Asia," *Asahi Shimbun,* August 21, 2012, at http://ajw.asahi.com/article/economy/busi ness/AJ201208210040.

189. John Kemp, "Russia's tantalising Arctic oil and gas deposits," *Reuters,* November 8, 2012, at http://www.reuters.com/article/2012/11/08/column-kemp-russia-oil-idUS L5E8M8HZ620121108.

190. Eric Yep, "Gas Tanker Takes Shortcut to Asia," *Wall Street Journal,* December 2, 2012, at http://online.wsj.com/article/SB10001424127887324020804578150563502056032.html.

191. Trude Pettersen, "Russia to have ten Arctic rescue centers by 2015," *Barents Observer,* November 18, 2011, at http://www.barentsobserver.com/en/topics/russia-have-ten-arctic-rescue-centers-2015.

192. Albina Kovalyova and Alissa de Carbonnel, "Arctic ice melt lifts hopes for Russian maritime trade," *Reuters,* January 27, 2012, at http://uk.reuters.com/article/2012/01/27/ uk-russia-arctic-idUKTRE80Q1DW20120127.

193. Steve Marshall, "Novatek pact to break Arctic ice," *Upstream,* November 12, 2012, at http://www.upstreamonline.com/live/article1269777.ece; Matsuo and Kida, op., cit.

194. Yang Jian, "The Arctic: New Shipping Routes and New Opportunities," *China Daily,* November 23, 2012, at http://www.siis.org.cn/en/zhuanti_view_en.aspx?id=10203.

195. "Russia plants flag under N Pole," *BBC News,* August 2, 2007, at http://news.bbc .co.uk/2/hi/europe/6927395.stm.

196. Speech by NATO Secretary General Jaap de Hoop Scheffer, "On security prospects in the High North," Reykjavik, Iceland, January 29, 2009, at http://www.nato.int/ docu/speech/2009/s090129a.html.

197. Marten Lindberg, "Is NATO Taking over the Arctic?" *ISN,* August 22, 2012, at http://isnblog.ethz.ch/international-relations/is-nato-taking-over-the-arctic.

198. Vyacheslav Apanasenko, "Razdor na prostorakh ledyanogo bezmolviia," *Voyenno-Promishlennyi Kur'er* 33, no. 450 (August 22, 2012), at http://vpk-news.ru/articles/9176.

199. Tom Fries, "News for April 1—April 7, 2012," *The Arctic This Week,* April 9, 2012, at http://www.thearcticinstitute.org/2012/04/arctic-news-weekly-update-april-9-2012.html.

200. Luke Harding, "Russia and Norway resolve Arctic border dispute," *The Guardian,* September 15, 2010, at http://www.guardian.co.uk/world/2010/sep/15/russia-norway-arctic-border-dispute.

201. Apanasenko, op. cit.

202. "Zamestiteli glav Minoborony RF I Norvegii obsudiat sotrudnichestvo," *RIA Novosti,* March 28, 2012, at http://ria.ru/defense_safety/20120328/607760177.html; Fries, op. cit.

203. Trude Pettersen, "Lukoil teams up with Norway and Sweden in Arctic oil bid," *Barents Observer,* September 7, 2012, at http://www.barentsobserver.com/en/energy/lukoil-teams-norway-and-sweden-arctic-oil-bid-07-09; Atle Staalesen, "Lukoil and Rosneft in new Norwegian licensing round," *Barents Observer,* December 7, 2012, at http://www.barentsobserver.com/en/energy/2012/12/lukoil-and-rosneft-new-norwegian-licensing-round-07-12.

204. Michael Byers, "Toward a Canada-Russia Axis in the Arctic," *Global Brief,* February 6, 2012, at http://globalbrief.ca/blog/2012/02/06/toward-a-canada-russia-axis-in-the-arctic/.

205. "Minister Fast Marks 70 Years of Canada-Russia Diplomatic Relations During Trade Mission," press release, Foreign Affairs and International Trade Canada, June 6, 2012, at http://www.international.gc.ca/media_commerce/comm/news-communiques/2012/06/06a.aspx?view=d.

206. "Closer Economic Ties with Russia Will Create Jobs and Opportunity for Canadians," press release, Foreign Affairs and International Trade Canada, June 2, 2011, at http://www.international.gc.ca/media_commerce/comm/news-communiques/2011/153.aspx?view=d.

207. Annika Bergman Rosamond, *Perspectives on Security in the Arctic Area* (Copenhagen, Denmark: Danish Institute for International Studies, 2011), 41–42.

208. Lindberg, op. cit.

209. Byers, op. cit.

210. Lindberg, op. cit.

211. Fries, op. cit.; see also comments at "The Future of U.S.-Russia Relations: Beyond 2012—Panel 2," Carnegie Endowment for International Peace conference, Washington, DC, November 28, 2012, 17–18, at http://carnegieendowment.org/files/112812_RE Beyond2012_Panel_2_transcript.pdf.

212. Byers, op. cit.

213. Fries, op. cit.

214. Bergman Rosamond, 42.

215. Quoted in Karaganov, Olechowski and Teltschik, op. cit.

216. Igor S. Ivanov, "Russia's European Prospects," *Project Syndicate,* November 23, 2012, at http://www.project-syndicate.org/print/basing-a-russian-european-partnership-on-human-capital-by-igor-ivanov.

CHAPTER 8

The Near-Eastern Vector

The Russian lands have always had close connections to the Arab and Islamic worlds. One of the first descriptions of the Rus' comes from Ahmad ibn Fadlan, who was an emissary of the Caliph of Baghdad who visited the areas that were to become Russia in the 10th century.[1] Prince Vladimir of Kiev seriously considered adopting Islam as the state religion of his realm before settling on Eastern Orthodox Christianity in 988. Nevertheless, even the choice of Orthodoxy meant that Russia would forge links with the Eastern Christian communities living in the Middle East. Moreover, the position of Kievan Rus' as the facilitator of the famous trade route "from the Varangians to the Greeks" meant that it served as a vast emporium linking the markets of Europe with those of the Byzantine Empire and the Islamic caliphates. Pilgrims began traveling to Palestine and Syria in the first decades after the conversion of the Rus,' and we have detailed accounts of the visits of Abbot Daniel of Kiev in 1106 to 1107 and Archbishop Antonii of Novgorod in 1200.[2] In the 17th century, the Orthodox Patriarchates of Antioch (by this point headquartered in Damascus, Syria), Alexandria, and Jerusalem also played an important role in sending clergy to visit and advise Russian leaders, continuing these ecclesiastical relations.[3]

The period of the Mongol Yoke and the collapse of the Byzantine Empire interrupted some of these links, but as Moscow began to consolidate its control over the northern Russian lands and to begin to take control of the major river routes (especially along the Volga), commercial ties with the Middle East revived, especially following the capture of the khanates of Kazan and Astrakhan in the 16th century.

Medieval Russia's interest in restoring the lucrative north–south trading routes that linked the Baltic and White Sea coasts with those of the Black and Caspian Seas also helped to re-engineer Russia's traditional vectors toward the Middle East.[4] In 1496, Sultan Bayezid II granted Muscovite merchants the right to travel to markets in the heartland of the Ottoman Empire, including in Bursa and Istanbul (Constantinople) itself.[5]

But the rising power of Moscow also threatened Ottoman interests in the Black Sea. The first direct clash between tsarist Russia and Ottoman Turkey occurred in 1569, when the grand vizier of the Ottoman Empire, Sokollu Mehmet Pasha, devised a plan to push back Russian power and to link the Don and Volga Rivers together with an Ottoman-controlled canal. The Turkish forces were defeated near Astrakhan and a treaty of peace reached in 1570 between both powers—but this clash presaged the Russo-Turkish wars of the next 350 years.

In their interests to find allies against the Ottoman Empire and to facilitate further trade and commerce, Russia turned to Persia (Iran), then under the control of the Safavid Dynasty. While no formal alliance was ever concluded, trade relations rapidly expanded, as Iranian merchants looked for ways to bypass Ottoman-controlled ports to reach European markets.[6] Over time, Russian interest in controlling this trade was to drive Russian expansion toward the northern Near East.

Peter the Great's initial efforts to break open a sea window to Russia for the outside world focused on the Black Sea, leading to the capture of the fortress of Azov in 1696. But Peter soon focused his attention on securing the Baltic coast for Russia. Under Catherine the Great, however, one of her chief ministers, Prince Gregory Potemkin, refocused Russian interest in the southward vector. Appointed governor general of New Russia—the territories acquired from the Ottoman Turks along the coast of the Black Sea (in today's Ukraine)—Potemkin was an advocate of reorienting Russian foreign policy away from the Baltic-European focus that had predominated since Peter's reign toward opportunities in the south. Catherine herself became enamored with what was termed "the Greek Project"—a restoration of the Byzantine Empire based at Constantinople, placed under the tutelage of her grandson Constantine and run as a vassal state of Russia.[7]

By the 19th century, Russian foreign policy had a clear Middle Eastern vector in place. Increasing Russian influence in the Ottoman and Persian Empires and securing Russia's economic links by unimpeded access to ports in the Mediterranean and Persian Gulfs became critical priorities. Count Nicholas Ignatieff, the long-serving Russian ambassador to the Ottoman Empire, was quite blunt when he noted:

> [Russia] must have a way out through the Straits as a direct or indirect guarantee of security for the commerce of the South and also for political and economic considerations. Russia cannot do otherwise than be master, either by assuming an exclusive influence over the sovereign and existing authorities at Constantinople or by annexing this place.[8]

Russian influence also began to spread in the Arab core of the Middle East with the formation of the Imperial Russian Palestinian Society. The cultivation and support of the Christian Arabs of Jordan and Syria, along with an endorsement of the emerging "Arab national cause," created a reservoir of goodwill among some Arabs for Russia that was to persist through to Soviet times.[9]

By the early 20th century, the Russian government appeared to have achieved many of its aims. The 1907 Anglo-Russian Agreement recognized an exclusive sphere of influence for Russia in northern Persia.[10] The 1915 Constantinople Agreement would have given Russia control over some of the core territories of the Ottoman Empire. The new Soviet government, however, repudiated these agreements after coming to power; the December 7, 1917, appeal to Muslims worldwide declared, "the secret treaties of the dethroned Tsar regarding the seizure of Constantinople . . . are null and void. . . . We declare that the treaty regarding the partition of Persia is null and void."[11] In 1921, the Communist Party, in a congress held in Baku, tried to call the masses of the Islamic world to a *jihad* against Western imperialism. But with few exceptions, communism had little appeal.

Agreements reached with Turkey and Persia in 1921 by the Soviet government gave up territories and rights acquired by the Imperial government. Instead, the Soviet government hoped to ally itself with nationalist leaders, particularly Turkey's Mustafa Kemal Ataturk and Persia's Reza Khan, who had overthrown the old monarchies and who were also fighting to secure their position against Western imperial interests in the Middle East. Indeed, Soviet foreign commissar Grigory Chicherin told the 14th Party Congress in December 1925 that support for these regimes, even though they were non–Communist, was necessary for "elemental security reasons."[12] While Turkey maintained a "neutralist" stance during the 1930s and the 1940s, it gradually moved into the Western camp and entered the North Atlantic Treaty Organization (NATO) in 1952. Turkey also helped to form a NATO-style alliance in the Middle East, CENTO (Central Treaty Organization), which lasted until 1979.

Initially, after World War II, the Soviet Union was a sponsor of the creation of the state of Israel in 1948. Soviet reasoning was that the Zionists tended to be socialists and many were of Eastern European origin; perhaps Israel might end up becoming a beachhead for Communism in the Middle East. Plus, at this time, most of the Arab monarchies were seen as being pro–British and pro–American.

Yet the USSR soon realized that Israel, even with a strongly socialist bent, was likely to end up in the Western camp. And a series of revolutions in the Arab world in the 1950s reawakened hopes for the spread of Soviet influence in the Middle East. After coming to power in a coup in 1952, Colonel Gamal Nasser of Egypt turned to the Soviet Union for economic and military aid. While he was not a Communist, Nasser's anti-imperialist ideology led to clashes with the Western powers, so the USSR saw an opportunity to gain a toehold in the region—but it also meant that the Soviet government increasingly backed Egypt against Israel. Revolutions in Syria and Iraq also brought Arab nationalist governments to power that turned to Moscow for aid and support.[13] In turn, Moscow increasingly identified with the Arab cause, even severing diplomatic relations with Israel after the 1967 Six-Day War and extending recognition to the Palestinians. Moscow accepted that there was "no realistic prospect of the emergence of a major Marxist-Leninist regime" and instead based its strategy "on alliance with . . . leading 'progressive' Arab powers."[14] This also led to efforts to promote a Soviet outreach to Islam. After 1964, Central Asia was opened up to delegations from the Islamic world, and a new Islamic academy was permitted to open in Tashkent in 1971.[15]

Nasser's successor, Anwar Sadat, reversed Nasser's course and in 1972 severed his links with the Soviet Union, expelling thousands of Soviet advisors and turning to the United States for support. But the Soviet Union continued to have strong allies in Syria and Iraq, and even Egypt still wanted the Soviet Union active in the Middle East to counterbalance Israel. After the 1973 Yom Kippur War, the United States had turned to the Soviet Union to help prevent a regional war from becoming a superpower clash; this helped to reinforce the USSR's perception of superpower equality with the United States.

The 1979 Islamic revolution in Iran created a unique situation: The government of Ayatollah Khomeini was both anti–Soviet and anti–American. The invasion of Afghanistan that same year helped to galvanize an Islamic reaction, and the United States worked closely with Saudi Arabia and Pakistan to fund anti–Soviet guerillas (the *mujahedeen*). But the United States quietly backed Iraq—a long-time Soviet ally that eventually racked up billions of dollars in debt to the USSR—after the start of the Iran-Iraq war in 1980—as a way to help keep Iran contained.

During the Soviet period, the Middle East was one of the top priorities of Soviet foreign policy, because, apart from Europe, it was seen as one of the major arenas of conflict between the superpowers.[16] As a result, Mikhail Gorbachev's "new thinking" in foreign policy extended to Soviet Middle East policy, particularly with an emphasis on superpower cooperation and coordination to solve regional problems. The run-up to the Gulf War allowed the USSR to play a role as possible mediator between Iraq and the coalition, and the Soviet Union worked closely with the United States to spearhead the passage of UN resolutions that authorized the use of force. After the Gulf War, the USSR become the cochair of the Madrid peace conference, which marked the first time that Israel and all the Arab countries gathered to begin to at least discuss some of the issues that had sparked regional conflicts.

The collapse of the USSR, however, altered the trajectory of Russian foreign policy. Although Russia continued to serve as honorary cochair of the Madrid process and is one of the members of the Quartet for the Middle East (along with the United States, the EU, and the UN), the Middle East peace process became dominated by the United States and determined largely by Washington. Russia found it had no major economic leverage and no longer had a network of client states that counterbalanced a U.S.-led group. Russia's inability to have the UN Security Council lift or modify sanctions on Iraq after the Gulf War also signaled to the region that Moscow could no longer provide an alternative to U.S. dominance.

The aims of Russian foreign policy in the region today are no longer driven by Cold War ideology, nor is Russia seeking to eject the United States from the area. Rather, the Russians have "returned" to the Middle East in the guise of offering themselves to both former allies and former foes as an alternate source for trade and technology. Russia also hopes to benefit from the recent difficulties faced by the United States in the region, especially in the aftermath of the 2003 invasion of Iraq. Part of this new diplomatic offensive has been to portray Russia itself as a Muslim country, given the status of Islam as a recognized traditional religion of Russia and the long-standing Islamic communities among some of the ethnic nationalities that make up the Russian Federation. In 2003, President Vladimir Putin attended the summit of the Organization of the Islamic Conference (OIC) in Malaysia and declared that Russia was a "Muslim power": 2 years later, in 2005, the OIC granted Russia observer status. In a December 12, 2005, address to the Chechen parliament, Putin declared: "Russia has always been the most faithful, reliable and consistent defender of the interests of the Islamic world."[17] Along with some elements in the Russian Orthodox Church, Putin has argued that Orthodox Christianity, in some ways, is closer to Islam than to Western Christianity.[18]

But this approach runs up against the interest of other sectors. Russia's "energy diplomacy," geared especially at creating new relationships with former adversaries like Turkey and Israel, runs up against the interests of the defense industry, which continues to sell arms and equipment to states like Syria and Iran. This irritates Israel but also complicates efforts to reach out to more moderate regimes in the region (and has proven to be an issue in improving Russia's relations with the United States as well).[19] The events of the Arab Spring of 2011 to 2012 have also had a major impact on Russia's relations with the region; the revolutionary ferment that brought down a number of long-established governments has exacted a toll on the Russian economy, particularly with the loss of a number of defense contracts estimated to be more than $10 billion in value.[20] Russia is thus less likely to back revolutionary changes and U.S. initiatives for the region if Russia sustains further losses.

RUSSIA–TURKEY: THE UNEXPECTED PARTNERSHIP

Russia and Turkey have had a dynamic and tumultuous relationship, usually marked by war and conflict but also by periods of close cooperation. Turkey sits across some of the key lines of communication for Russia, especially the sea lanes (the Dardanelles and Bosporus) that control access to southern Europe and the Middle East. The Soviet Union had hoped for good relations with Kemalist Turkey, but ties deteriorated as Turkey moved into the American camp after World War II. The Soviet Union attempted to woo Turkey with economic aid,[21] but the traditional distrust between Russia and Turkey was too difficult to overcome. As *Pravda* editorialized in 1960: "Turkish territory has been turned into a military base . . . used by the American militarists until very recently for provocations and aggressive acts against our country."[22] As a result, as Ihsan Bal, a leading Turkish security studies scholar, has noted, "the tension of the Cold War had . . . a strong effect on Russian and Turkish societies."[23] In the immediate aftermath of the dissolution of the USSR, in 1991, Russia felt that Turkey would work, for its own interests and on behalf of the West, to push back Russian influence in the Caucasus and Central Asia.[24]

In addition to the perceived rivalry for influence in Eurasia, the resurgence of Russia's traditional linkages with the Hellenic world—Greece as well as the Republic of Cyprus—seemed to presage a continuation of poor relations with Turkey, due to Ankara's own difficulties with Athens and Nicosia. Indeed, a major crisis erupted in 1997 when Cyprus sought to purchase the advanced Russian S-300 air defense missile system, which Turkey viewed as a threat. The crisis was resolved when Greece agreed to accept the system and deploy it on the island of Crete, but it further highlighted the poor relationship between Moscow and Ankara. Cyprus remains a close commercial partner of Russia, and because of the island's historic position as an offshore banking center, Cyprus is the third-largest source of foreign investment in the Russian economy.

Another source of tension between Ankara and Moscow was Chechnya. Given the historic links between Turkey and the Muslim regions of the Caucasus—and the ability of the descendants of those Caucasians who were exiled to Turkey after the tsarist empire took full control of that region in the 19th century to organize and express grievances as the Turkish political system liberalized in the 1990s—some Turkish citizens volunteered to fight with rebel groups against Russia, particularly after the outbreak of the First Chechen War in 1994. The sense that Turkey was not doing enough to dissuade its citizens from joining the *jihad* proved to be a major irritant in the bilateral relationship.[25] Because of all these tensions, relations between the Yeltsin administration and the government of Bülent Ecevit remained cool during the 1990s.[26]

After the Soviet Union collapsed, however, opportunities for Turkish businesses opened up in Russia, particularly in consumer goods and construction. The need to construct large amounts of housing for troops returning from Eastern Europe proved to be a godsend for Turkish construction firms, marking a new and promising area of economic interaction.[27] Russians were attracted to

Turkey not only as a tourist destination but also as a transit hub for the export of Russian energy. Over time, Turkey, which initially sought to promote energy transport routes that bypassed Russia (such as the Baku-Tbilisi Ceyhan Pipeline bringing crude oil from the Caspian to the Mediterranean[28]), changed course and has promoted itself as Russia's partner. A turning point proved to be the visit of Prime Minister Viktor Chernomyrdin in December 1997, as the Cyprus missile crisis was winding down, and the signing of the agreement providing for the construction of the Blue Stream pipeline. Instead of blocking Russia's access to outside markets, Turkey would now work to expand Russia's ability to send natural gas to European and Middle Eastern markets.[29] As the energy trade between the two countries picked up, as well as subsidiary business ventures created to construct pipelines and storage facilities, this created a "rapprochement driven by a vast expansion in Turkish-Russian trade."[30]

Today, Russia supplies more than 65% of Turkey's natural gas and, in turn, Turkey benefits from the re-export of Russian gas to other countries.[31] A critical part of Russo–Turkish energy integration has been the Blue Stream pipeline, which runs under the Black Sea, connecting Russia with Turkey. Completed in 2005, the pipeline joins Gazprom with the Turkish state oil and gas transport firm BOTAS. Now operating at its full capacity of 16 billion cubic meters per year, this pipeline helps not only to secure Turkey's own energy needs but also to strengthen its influence in Europe as a transit hub for energy. The value of this trade has made Russia one of Turkey's most important economic partners. This means that Gazprom is now one of the major supporters of Russia's newfound partnership with Turkey.[32]

Gazprom is not the only corporation with a major stake in the Russo–Turkish relationship. Both state and private companies have moved into the Turkish market. Oil companies like Tatneft and Bashneft found it more beneficial to deal with Tupras, the largest Turkish refiner, and even found it cost effective to route supplies to Turkey rather than to Europe.[33] Russia's Alfa Group owns 13.22% of Turkcell, a major cell phone and telecom provider. LUKoil has invested in an oil distribution network and storage facilities. Turkish commercial firms like Ramenka (the owner of Ramstores) and construction companies are major presences in Russia.[34]

By 2010, Russia, which 20 years previously had had a virtually nonexistent commercial relationship with Turkey, had become Turkey's largest trading partner, displacing Germany, and Turkey was Russia's fifth-largest trading partner (although the global economic crisis of 2008–2009 did have a negative impact on bilateral trade; see Figure 8.1). In addition, to strengthen integration, both countries are working to jointly manage port facilities on the Black Sea coast as well as other projects to tie together their economic infrastructure.[35] Visa-free travel between the two countries was inaugurated in April 2011.[36]

FIGURE 8.1
The Growth in Russian–Turkish Trade, 2005–2011 (in billions of U.S. dollars)

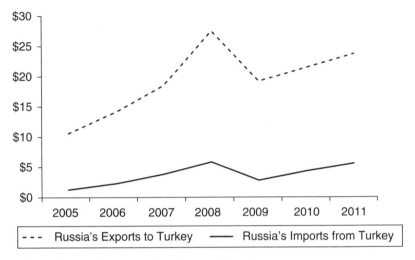

Source: State Customs Committee of the Russian Federation.

All of this has built up a powerful pro–Russian business lobby in Turkey, particularly among the rising new business elites associated with the AKP (Justice and Development) party, which came to power in 2002.[37] In turn, key business and political elites in Russia, starting with Gazprom, became invested in a much better relationship with Turkey, counterbalancing Russia's traditional affinities for Turkey's historic rival Greece (and Russia's long-standing ties to Cyprus).

Closer business ties helped to pave the way for better working relations among key government officials. In support of Russia's economic diplomacy, Vladimir Putin visited Turkey in 2004, the first Russian leader to arrive in the country for 32 years, and in his meetings with President Ahmet Necdet Sezer and Prime Minister Recep Tayyip Erdoğan stressed the importance of providing "moral support" to the businessmen of both countries.[38] During his August 2009 visit, Prime Minister Putin wooed Turkey's business and political elites with "grandiose vistas of a bilateral partnership on energy."[39] Gazprom also agreed to sell gas directly to private firms in Turkey.

Strengthened commercial ties, in turn, have laid the foundations for a closer relationship. As Bal concluded:

> The increasing number of trade relations paved the way for cooperation in other areas. Trade networks which were developed within the framework of this approach . . . have recently started to build up the most interesting side

of the changing relationship between Russia and Turkey from mistrust to confidence and from enmity to strategic partnership.[40]

In 2010, Russia was removed from the so-called Red Book, the principal national security strategy of Turkey, as one of the "external threats" to the country.[41]

Improved Russian–Turkish ties have also come about because of a shift in Turkish foreign policy, redefining Turkey as a rising Eurasian power, not simply an appendage of the West. In particular, Turkish Foreign Minister Ahmet Davutoğlu's "zero problems with neighbors" policy has focused on improving Ankara's ties with former enemies and foes and no longer taking on the role of America's surrogate in the region.[42] For Davutoğlu, historic enmity toward Russia does not serve Turkey's present-day interests. Turkey now views its relationship with Russia as grounded in close bilateral economic cooperation, strong trade ties, cooperation in energy projects, and a shared vision for stability in the greater Black Sea region.[43]

One of the areas in which this change is most notable is in the Eurasian space. After the collapse of the Soviet Union, Turkey, particularly the government under Prime Minister Tansu Ciller, saw an opportunity to extend a sphere of influence into the Caucasus and Central Asia and to push back Russian influence. The AKP government has continued efforts to build up Turkey's economic and political influence in Eurasia, but with a marked difference: Its program makes it clear that Turkey should not do this at the expense of Russia and so jeopardize Turkey's improving relations with Moscow.[44]

Turkey's shift in its orientation toward Russia became very clear in the aftermath of the 2008 Russo-Georgian conflict. Previously, one would have expected a Turkish government to strongly support the Georgians. Instead, Prime Minister Erdoğan tried to broker negotiations between Moscow and Tbilisi and called for a Caucasus stability pact that would take into account Russia's strategic interests in the region. Ankara's attempts to mediate "pleased the Russians but appeared to vex Western governments"[45] and sent a clear signal that Turkey was not going to automatically back and support a NATO/EU position that might put Ankara at odds with Russia. Instead, when the former foreign minister-turned-president of Turkey Abdullah Gul visited Moscow in February 2009, he promoted the acceleration of Russian–Turkish ties. And while Turkey has not recognized the separatist regions of Georgia as separate states, following the Russian line, it has not prevented the Turkish business community from pursuing economic links with them, particularly Abkhazia.[46] A growing sense in Turkey that regional problems in the area are best solved by Russia and Turkey working together and excluding outside powers (including the United States) from the process is also seen as more beneficial to Russia's own interests. The sense that the Euro-Atlantic community can no longer offer Turkey security guarantees given changed conditions in the Middle East is also fueling a search "to look for new ideas and its own unique contribution," as Guner Ozkan, a scholar at Ankara's International Strategic Research Organization, has concluded.[47] Turkey's increased turn toward a Eurasian orientation has manifested itself in efforts to secure Turkey observer status in the Shanghai Cooperation Organization.[48]

When President Medvedev visited Turkey in May 2010, he expressed satisfaction with the course of Russia's relations with Turkey, noting, "We can say with conviction that Russian-Turkish ties are reaching the level of full-scale strategic partnership."[49] The theme of a closer Russo-Turkish relationship was reiterated when Prime Minister Erdoğan traveled to Moscow in March 2011. This is certainly true when it comes to the energy partnership. Beyond the existing Blue Stream project, Russia may increase tanker shipments of oil to the Turkish port of Samsun for pipeline transportation to the terminal at Ceyhan on the Mediterranean.[50] Calik Energy and Rosneft are also announcing the start of a strategic partnership. Finally, at the beginning of 2012, Turkey agreed to allow Gazprom to route its South Stream pipeline, which will connect Russia to Southern Europe, through Turkey's territorial waters, "supplying the missing piece needed by Moscow to secure markets for its gas in Europe."[51]

Beyond hydrocarbons, Turkey is now turning to Russia to build up its nuclear power infrastructure, turning to Rosatom to construct and operate in Akkuyu-Mersin complex. In turn, Turkish companies like Park Teknik and the state electricity conglomerate EUAS will take shares in the project, and the electricity distributor TETAS will buy the electricity at a fixed price, guaranteeing a profitable return on Rosatom's investment. By the 2020s, this nuclear complex is expected to provide 5% of Turkey's overall electricity needs.[52]

Overseeing the day-to-day aspects of the Russo-Turkish energy partnership during the Medvedev years was Turkey's Minister of Energy and Natural Resources Taner Yildiz and Russia's Deputy Prime Minister Igor Sechin. In 2010, the two initiated a high-level collaborative working group, beginning a process of greater institutionalization of the relationship, with Yildiz and Sechin meeting again in Moscow in March 2011 to present to Erdoğan and Medvedev the roadmap for implementing the agreements the two leaders signed during Medvedev's 2010 visit to Turkey.[53]

Russia and Turkey have also expanded their governmental connection beyond the energy field. In January 2011, Davutoğlu and Russian Foreign Minister Sergei Lavrov chaired the first meeting of the Joint Strategic Planning Group to prepare the agenda for the intergovernmental High Level Cooperation Council, which is set to oversee all aspects of the Russo-Turkish partnership.[54] This sets up the agenda for a summit that will be held annually between the prime minister of Turkey and the president of Russia.

Beyond energy, multiple sectors in Russia support the Turkish vector. The Interior Ministry has forged close ties with Turkish police, and the Turkish government has taken steps to reassure Russians that there will be no sanctuary for terrorists in Turkey who act against Russian interest, a key concern given the ability during the 1990s for Caucasian separatists to find support within Turkey.[55] (In 1996, for instance, a group of Chechens and Turks hijacked a Black Sea ferry bound from Trabzon to Sochi and threatened to kill the Russian citizens on board unless offensive operations against Chechnya were ended; in 2001, hostages were seized at an Istanbul hotel, again to protest Russian military action in Chechnya.) Part of this shift has occurred because some of the Turkish *jihadis* who fought in Chechnya against the Russians joined forces with Al Qaeda and launched terrorist attacks inside of Turkey itself, a point of particular concern after the 2003 Istanbul bombings.[56] Finally, after decades of hostility based on Cold War divisions, the Russian and Turkish national security establishments find themselves in much greater agreement in terms of promoting stability in the greater Black Sea region.[57] Turkey successfully argued against putting the Black Sea Harmony naval initiative under the aegis of NATO and facilitated Russia's participation after 2006.[58] But Turkey remains sensitive to the protection of its sovereignty; the deaths of Chechen separatist leaders in the country in 2009 and again in 2011 raised concerns whether Russian special service agents were responsible and did cause some strain in the relationship.[59]

Russia's historically Turkic-Muslim regions have also factored into support for the Turkish vector. Turkish companies have invested in projects in Tatarstan and Bashkortostan.[60] The regional governments of Chechnya, the other Caucasian republics, and Tatarstan also regularly send delegations to Turkey and help to sustain the Turkish orientation in Russia's foreign policy.[61] When Prime Minister Erdoğan visited Russia in February 2009, he first went to Moscow to confer with President Medvedev and Prime Minister Putin, then traveled to Tatarstan, the largest of Russia's Turkic republics. In March 2011, he returned to hold additional talks with Tatarstan's president, Rustam Minnikhanov, especially on the expansion of trade—Tatarstan by itself accounts for some $1.3 billion in trade with Turkey.[62]

In December 2010, Sechin called Turkey "our strategic ally in this region [the Middle East]," reflecting the major shift that has taken place in the bilateral relationship.[63] The Turkish vector enjoys the overt support of most of the Russian foreign policy actors. The Turkish partnership is seen as a way to enhance Russia's energy links with core European markets by bypassing troublesome transit states in Eastern Europe, so it does not threaten Russia's interests in closer ties with Europe. It has the possibility of transforming a formidable rival for influence in the Caucasus and Central Asia into a partner. Finally, to the extent that a closer partnership with Russia gives Turkey the confidence to assume a more assertive role in regional and global affairs, it facilitates the emergence of the Primakovian multipolar system that helps to check U.S. influence.

In December 2011, Turkey cleared the way for Russia to begin constructing its South Stream gas pipeline through its territorial waters in the Black Sea, when Energy Minister Taner Yildiz traveled to Moscow to sign the agreement with Igor Sechin. This was a crucial development, because the pipeline, which Ukraine would not allow transit across its share of the Black Sea, needed Turkish approval. In return, Russia is likely to lower the price of its natural gas sold to Turkey and will cooperate on other energy projects that will reinforce Turkey's position as an energy hub.[64]

However, differences over how to approach the Syrian crisis, as well as Turkey's decision to host elements of a NATO ballistic missile defense system, could introduce renewed tension into the Russian–Turkish relationship. The main driver of the Russian–Turkish relationship is the energy industry, which has prevailing but not absolute influence in setting foreign policy. But even energy could become a source of tension, particularly by differing approaches to dealing with vast potential hydrocarbon reserves off the shores of Cyprus. While Turkey challenges the right of the Cypriot government based in Nicosia to move ahead with developing offshore fields, as long as the island remains divided (Turkey does not recognize the Nicosia administration and supports a separatist Turkish Republic in the northern part of the island), Russia has strongly supported Cyprus's rights, and Russian firms Gazprom and Novatek are eager to take part in developing Cyprus's offshore gas fields. After the Turkish government threatened Cyprus with the possibility of military action, Russia's foreign ministry in October 2011 issued a declaration affirming Cyprus's rights, and a Russian naval detachment visited Cyprus in a show of support.[65]

This is why some have concluded that because of such problems, "this partnership is declining" due to the "mounting tensions over the Kurdish issue, Middle East, missile defenses, Cyprus, and the Balkans. Furthermore, those difficulties will likely increase."[66] Other observers believe that any disruption would be short lived and that "once the Syrian question receives a resolution, Russian and Turkish relations will regain a positive dynamic."[67] And in commenting on the missile defense shield, Turkish Foreign Minister Ahmet Davutoğlu reiterated in January 2012 that Turkey does "not see any threat from any of our neighbors" and stressed the "strong political will on the Turkish side to cooperate with Russia," especially on energy issues.[68] While Russia's stance on Syria and these other issues might complicate its relationship with Ankara, Turkey, at the same time, must weight whether jeopardizing its growing partnership with Russia by putting its disagreements over Syria at the front and center of its bilateral relationship with

Moscow is worth the risk.[69] The October 2012 incident in which Turkish authorities forced a Syrian plane outbound from Moscow to land and confiscated military goods on board has tested those assumptions and whether Russia and Turkey
can find a way to separate and compartmentalize a very profitable energy partnership from geopolitical differences over Syria and other issues.[70] The Syrian crisis
and tensions over Cyprus signal that Russia and Turkey are still unsure how to
handle tensions that flare up in the bilateral relationship.[71]

Putin's rescheduled visit to Turkey in December 2012, however, showed that he
and Erdoğan could "agree to disagree" on issues like Syria or Cyprus without
wrecking the overall bilateral relationship. They signed a raft of new agreements
and pledged to boost bilateral trade to the level of $100 billion per year, an ambi-
tious goal. A "shared pragmatism" keeps the Russia–Turkey relationship on
track.[72] And just as the relationship between Ankara and Moscow has completely
changed over the course of the last two decades, in much the same way, another
formerly hostile Cold War relationship is undergoing a transformation of its own.

ISRAEL: "PRACTICALLY A RUSSIAN-SPEAKING COUNTRY"?

The Soviet Union severed diplomatic relations with Israel after the 1967 Six-Day
War, but Mikhail Gorbachev restored them as the Soviet Union was collapsing, in
October 1991. The relationship between Israel and a post–Soviet Russia found a
new footing in the 1990s. First, the arrival in Israel since the 1970s of more than
one million Russian-speaking/ex–Soviet citizens has created a Russian Jewish diaspora in Israel, which maintains many cultural and business ties with Russia.
Israeli–Russian economic ties are much more significant now, and a number of
leading Israeli conglomerates have strong business ties in Russia. Russian is the
third-most-spoken language in Israel, and when Israeli Prime Minister Benjamin
Netanyahu visited Moscow in 2010, Putin told him that Israel is Russia's "long-
term partner in the Middle East. We say again and again that there are over one
million Russian citizens living in your country. Israel is almost a Russian-speaking
country."[73] Second, the wars in Chechnya and Russian support for the Serbs in
their struggles in Bosnia and Kosovo weakened Russia's standing in the Islamic
world, decreasing the earlier Soviet tilt toward the Arab world, which in turn provided an opening to Israel, particularly to Israeli conservatives, who were eager to
explore the possibilities of greater cooperation with Russia.[74] These interests
found receptive audiences with some Russian leaders, notably Putin himself.

Prime Minister Ehud Barak visited Russia in August 1999, and just after his
resignation as president, Yeltsin traveled to Israel in January 2000 with a Russian
delegation. When Russia launched its campaign against Chechen separatism in
1999, a number of Israeli politicians—among them former Soviet dissident Natan

Scharansky—voiced support for Russia's military action. While not completely moving away from its previous support for the Palestinians, Russia became more sympathetic to Israeli positions. At the end of 2000, Russian Foreign Minister Igor Ivanov indicated that Russia would oppose the deployment of any international peacekeeping force to the Palestinian territories if Israel itself objected to such a move.[75] Russia has sometimes used its own influence in international organizations, including the United Nations, to block resolutions toward Israel that might set a negative precedent for Russia in how it deals with Chechnya, abstaining, for instance in a vote in the UN General Assembly in January 2004 that sought to involve the International Court of Justice in ruling on the legality of security measures taken by Israel against the Palestinians.[76] In October 2012, Russia again used its influence—this time at the United Nations Education, Scientific, and Cultural Organization (UNESCO)—to table a number of anti-Israel resolutions that had been put on the agenda.[77]

Israeli Prime Minister Ariel Sharon, who visited Russia twice, in 2001 and again in 2003, believed that joint security concerns would be the basis for a new Russia-Israeli relationship, as Israel's experience of dealing with Palestinian terrorism might have increasing significance for Russia's efforts to cope with Chechen terrorism.[78] To the extent that the United States expressed support for a Palestinian state, Sharon also wanted Israel to broaden its relationships and not remain totally dependent on Washington. Sharon's approach has been largely continued with Prime Minister Benjamin Netanyahu, as part of a strategy to provide Israel with additional options. Netanyahu has visited Russia nearly every year and maintains a regular pattern of contacts with Russian officials.[79] Netanyahu was also one of the first foreign leaders to congratulate Putin on his victory in the 2012 presidential election and to invite him to visit Israel. Putin's trip in June, the first international trip he took after his return to the presidency, made it the third Russian presidential visit to the country, after his visit in 2005 and Medvedev's in 2011.

Both sides have placed a great deal of emphasis on economics as the basis for the bilateral relationship. A number of Israeli businessmen, some who were born in Russia or other former Soviet republics, are actively engaged in investment projects in Russia.[80] Deputy Foreign Minister Saltanov called attention in 2010 to the vast potential of combining elements of the Russian and Israeli economies, especially in the fields of high technology and energy.[81] An Israel–Russia business council was created that year and held its first meeting in Moscow in March, which was addressed by Deputy Prime Minister Viktor Zubkov. Trade between Israel and Russia, which 20 years ago was practically nonexistent, has now passed the $2 billion mark.[82]

Israel's search for energy security also plays a role in strengthening relations. Russian proposals for shipping natural gas to Turkey and from there to Israel via the Ceyhan–Ashkelon route or for energy produced by Russian firms in North Africa to be sold to Israel, offering Russia new markets while giving Israel the option to obtain guaranteed supplies of energy not subject to disruption by the Arab world, were a key consideration after the 2012 cancellation of the Israel-Egypt natural gas contract.[83] With the discovery of large new gas fields in the Eastern Mediterranean, in the waters between Israel, Lebanon, and Cyprus, Russian energy firms have redoubled their efforts to help develop these new energy sources. In 2010, Gazprom attempted to buy a 50% stake in the Israeli firm Delek Energy, which holds the licenses to develop the Leviathan field; while this effort failed, Gazprom continues to lobby for inclusion in Israeli gas projects and has committed itself to purchase Israeli gas (for redistribution to Gazprom customers in southeastern Europe). In 2013, Gazprom announced that it had signed an agreement with Levant LNG Marketing to market natural gas from Israel's Tamar field, a deal that, if ratified by the Israeli government, would allow Gazprom to diversify its sources of supply for the European market.[84]

But significant roadblocks remain in pursuing a stronger Russian–Israeli partnership. Moscow's unwillingness to sever its ties with Syria and Iran makes it difficult to fully engage with Israel, given the bad relationships among all these countries. Syria and Iran both remain major purchasers of advanced Russian weaponry that has the capacity to threaten Israel, while Syria hosts Russia's only military base outside of former Soviet territory, which remains critical to Russia's ability to project power beyond the Black Sea. Israeli Prime Minister Netanyahu has never been able to convince the Russians to completely cut off both countries, although Russia did agree not to sell certain weapons systems to Iran that might be able to frustrate an Israeli raid on Iran's nuclear facilities.[85] At the same time, Israel's military cooperation with other former Soviet states, most notably Georgia, did complicate its relationship with Russia.

But the Netanyahu government continues to engage Russia. After the 2008 Russia-Georgia conflict, Israel, which between 2006 and 2008 had extended significant assistance to Tbilisi, halted ongoing defense arrangements. Israel has instead opted to pursue closer defense ties with Russia.[86] A military cooperation agreement was signed between Israel and Russia in 2010.[87] Given efforts to modernize Russia's own defense infrastructure and the growing cooperation between Israel and India—Russia's largest customer for weapons—this could pave the way for closer relations. Some have also speculated that Russia and Israel might cooperate in protecting oil and gas fields in the Eastern Mediterranean, which could further deepen security cooperation between the two nations.[88] During Putin's 2012 visit to Israel and Israeli President Shimon Peres's return visit to Moscow in November 2012, the Israelis did not convince Russia to break its ties with Iran but did ask Russia to use its influence to encourage Iran to renounce its nuclear program and signaled that they would not allow disagreements with Russia over Iran to block other areas of cooperation.[89]

Russia's efforts to forge a new relationship with a traditionally pro-U.S. nation are echoed in Moscow's outreach toward yet another Cold War antagonist, Saudi Arabia.

RUSSIA–SAUDI ARABIA: THE START OF A RAPPROCHEMENT?

One of the most profound transformations of the post–Cold War period has been the relationship between Moscow and Riyadh. During the Soviet period, the Saudis eschewed formal diplomatic relations with a state that espoused "an alien ideology that fostered instability and revolutionary change."[90] Saudi Arabia aligned itself with the United States against the Soviet bloc, and Riyadh viewed the USSR as a destabilizing force bent on radicalizing the Middle East and overthrowing the traditional regimes of the region. The Saudis worked hard to blunt Moscow's influence among the Arabs and used their oil wealth to support rebels against pro-Soviet regimes in Africa and other parts of the world.[91] Saudi Arabia's oil weapon also proved very damaging to a Soviet state that itself depended, as Ahmad Zaki Yamani (the country's famed oil minister from 1962 to 1985) reminded a Saudi audience, on oil exports for more than 50% of its hard currency earnings.[92] During the 1980s, whether as a deliberate act to weaken the Soviet Union or simply in pursuit of their own economic goals, the Saudi decision "to ramp up oil production in 1985 drove down global oil prices, causing significant harm to a Soviet economy already in recession."[93]

By the early 1990s, however, the view of the Saudis and the other Gulf Arab emirates of the Soviet Union was changing. Moscow normalized its relationship with the Gulf states, and Saudi Arabia, Oman, and other Gulf emirates extended a $2 billion loan to the USSR in 1990 to 1991 to help stabilize the Soviet economy.[94]

Since the end of the Cold War, there has been a major shift in Russia's relations with Saudi Arabia. The Saudi government has no fears that post–Soviet Russia wants to overthrow the monarchy or change Saudi society—but ever since the George W. Bush administration enunciated the "freedom doctrine" and the Hosni Mubarak regime was overthrown in Egypt in February 2011, there are real concerns about U.S. efforts to promote democratization and human rights. So, in contrast to the 1980s, when the Saudis could engage in economic warfare on the West's behalf, Saudi Arabia now needs to have a guaranteed "floor" in global oil prices in order to guarantee the income needed to sustain the Saudi welfare state, which is an important part of maintaining internal stability. The Saudi government is well aware that regimes in Tunisia and Egypt, which collapsed in 2011 due to sustained popular unrest, were unable to meet the economic needs of the citizens. Rather than working against countries like Russia to bring down the price of oil, the Saudis have needed to reach some sort of accommodation with other oil producers to stabilize the market.[95] This has fit well with Russia's own plans, and so over the past several years the Kremlin has focused its effort to "control global prices of oil in conjunction with Saudi Arabia basically, and natural gas prices with Qatar."[96]

During the Yeltsin years, however, there were irritants in the relationship between Riyadh and Moscow. The Saudis were dismayed by closer Russian ties with Israel and Russia's willingness to expand its oil production, undercutting Saudi efforts to regulate global oil markets. Russia, for its part, accused Saudi Arabia of support for Chechen separatists and turning a blind eye to the work of Saudi charities in supporting anti-Russian movements in the Caucasus. When then-Prime Minister Putin launched a second military campaign to retake control of Chechnya in 1999, the Saudi government accused the Russians of committing an "inhumane act against the Muslim people of Chechnya."[97]

The 9/11 attacks, however, changed the dynamic of the relationship. Because of U.S. pressure, the Saudi government began to crack down on charities that supplied money to jihadist groups; this had a secondary effect of cutting down the flow of funds to radical groups in the Caucasus. But in addition, concerns that the United States might turn against the Saudi government caused the kingdom to reach out to Russia as part of a "hedging strategy"[98] designed to decrease Riyadh's dependence on the United States.

In September 2003, Crown Prince Abdullah (who is now the king) became the highest-ranking Saudi official to travel to Moscow. In his summit meetings with Putin, the groundwork for a rapprochement was laid. The Russian side backpedaled its previous criticisms of Riyadh, while the Saudi government declared that Chechnya was an "internal affair" of Russia.[99] The Russian government also enlisted regional leaders of traditionally Sunni Muslim regions of Russia to act as intermediaries with the Saudis. Akhmad Kadyrov, the former chief mufti of Chechnya (and former supporter of independence) who aligned himself with the Russian federal government in 1999 and subsequently was elected president of Chechnya in 2003, met with Abdullah in Moscow and subsequently traveled to Saudi Arabia in early 2004 to further promote improved Russia–Saudi ties.[100] Russian companies—including LUKoil and the energy infrastructure firm Stroitransgaz—made their first inroads into Saudi Arabia's lucrative energy sector.

Putin's visit to Saudi Arabia in February 2007—the first ever by a Russian leader to the kingdom—was the high point of this Saudi-Russian rapprochement. Putin noted that for 60 years, there had been no relations at all between the two countries, but now they were finding ways to strengthen the "bilateral format of relations,"[101] particularly to ensure that two of the world's leading producers of energy did not find themselves pitted against each other.[102] In turn, Saudi Arabia, looking to diversify its international relationships as Riyadh began to be concerned about its overall relationship with the United States, pursued a more overt "Russia vector" in the subsequent months, with the Saudi foreign and defense ministers making trips to consult with the Russian leadership in Moscow and with the head of the Saudi national security council even signing a landmark defense cooperation agreement with Russia in July 2008.[103]

The Saudis have wanted to make sure that they have access to Russia as an alternate source of advanced technology if the United States is not willing to supply items to the kingdom, particularly for its nuclear program.[104] While the United States remains the main source of weaponry for Saudi Arabia, Russia has made slight inroads, providing arms that they cannot procure from the United States.[105] But Riyadh is also footing the bill for other states in the region, such as Yemen, to purchase Russian weapons; close Saudi allies like Bahrain have also turned to Russia to discuss sales of arms as traditional sources of supply in the West have hesitated to continue to provide weapons in the aftermath of the Arab Spring.[106] But the promise of major Saudi purchases from Russia has not materialized. Saudi Arabia has not emerged as a partner of Russia, but, as Deputy Foreign Minister Saltanov noted, the two countries "share common approaches" on a variety of issues, especially on the need to stabilize global energy markets.[107]

There also remain some major irritants in the relationship. Saudi Arabia looks askance at close Russian ties with Iran and Syria. Iran poses a challenge to Saudi interests in the Gulf, and Syria's close relationship with Iran (and the fact that the majority Sunni population of Syria has traditionally been kept out of power) has long troubled the Saudi leadership. There has been vague talk that, in return for Russian support for preferred Saudi outcomes in the region, Riyadh would be prepared to compensate Moscow for the loss of its markets and contracts by offering replacement deals for weapons and energy projects. But no such quid pro quo had emerged.[108] Continued Russian trade with both countries and the Russian veto of a UN Security Council resolution in February 2012 calling on Bashar al-Assad to step down have complicated the bilateral relationship. Moreover, after Medvedev called King Abdullah to discuss the Syrian issue after the Security Council vote, the Saudi monarch responded that there was no point in trying to find a common approach. Abdullah complained to Medvedev, "The Russian friends should have coordinated with the Arabs before Russia used its right to veto in the Security Council. Now any dialogue about what happened is pointless." In addition, the fallout from Moscow's defense of Syria has meant that Russia's newfound commercial and diplomatic relationships with Saudi Arabia and other Gulf Arab states may be threatened.[109] However, in an effort to stabilize the relationship between Riyadh and Moscow—and to repair some of the damage the Syrian crisis has caused—Foreign Minister Sergei Lavrov traveled to Saudi Arabia in November 2012 and met with the Saudis and other Gulf Arab leaders, allowing for at least a better understanding of each side's perspective on Syria.[110] Even though Russian-Saudi relations may never return to the nadir of the Cold War, it is unlikely that the dream of a new partnership between Moscow and Riyadh will be realized anytime soon.

TRADITIONAL ARAB PARTNERS

While exploring the possibility of new friendships, Moscow has not completely neglected its ties to former Soviet allies in the region, but these relationships have also undergone changes over the last 20 years.

During the Cold War, several North African states established close ties with the Soviet Union. The Soviet Union had strongly supported the Algerian independence movement in its uprising against the French, recognizing the provisional government *de facto* in 1960. Algeria turned to the Soviet Union for military and developmental aid and became a major customer for the Soviet arms industry, purchasing some $11 billion worth of military equipment between 1962 and 1989.[111] Algeria hosted one of the few visits of a major Soviet leader to the Third World—President Nikolai Podgorny, who traveled to Algeria in 1969. Algeria's neighbor, Libya, also moved into the pro-Soviet camp of nations. Muammar Gaddafi, the revolutionary who overthrew the pro-Western King Idris of Libya in 1969, also turned to the Soviet Union for aid and assistance. After the Soviet-Egyptian alliance was ruptured by Anwar Sadat's turn to the West, Libya under Gaddafi became an important replacement in maintaining Moscow's ability to project air and naval power in the Mediterranean basin.[112]

Just as Russian foreign policy was initially dominated after the fall of the Soviet Union by a pro-Western approach, the Soviet Union's former North African clients also attempted to improve their relations with the West. Algeria, for instance, joined NATO's Mediterranean Dialogue Program.[113] While Libya remained under sanctions throughout the 1990s, due to its support for terrorism and its attempts to produce weapons of mass destruction, Gaddafi reached a settlement in 2003 that saw him give up his WMD program, renounce his support for terrorist movements, and pay compensation to victims of past terrorist acts, such as the 1988 bombing of an American airliner over Lockerbie, Scotland. This cleared the way for Western firms to return to Libya, undercutting Russian interests. The Putin administration attempted to use business diplomacy as a means to reviving these past relationships, in part by offering cooperation on energy projects and continued access to Russian technology, particularly military equipment.

Because Western countries were concerned by Algeria's human rights record, Moscow was able to find a new opening for re-engaging with Algeria. Some deals were signed, but there were also problems. In 2007, Algeria rejected MiG-29 jets supplied by Russia, complaining about the inferior quality of components, and instead chose to purchase Rafaele jets produced by France.[114] And North African natural gas offered European customers an alternative to Russian supplies. In February 2006, Algerian Energy Minister Chakib Khelil proposed a new natural gas route to Italy that in turn could feed North African natural gas into the European market, "countries in Eastern Europe, such as Poland, which are looking for alternatives to supplies from Russia."[115]

Putin visited Algeria in March 2006, the first Russian leader since Podgorny to do so. During his visit, a Russian–Algerian intergovernmental commission on Trade, Economic, Scientific and Technical Cooperation was set up. This helped to align the business relationship with the bilateral political dialogue, and both countries realized that excessive competition would harm both countries' natural gas export markets. In particular, the state energy firms Gazprom, Rosneft, and Stroytransgaz (the firm that constructs pipelines) have been active. Algeria also succeeded in paying off a large portion of its Soviet-era debt to Moscow, which helped to improve the bilateral climate. Dmitry Medvedev did a follow-up visit in October 2010 to further push for increased commercial relations, not only in the energy sphere but also in telecommunications.[116] Today, Algeria and Russia see more value in cooperating than competing.[117] Algeria continues to be a major customer of Russian weaponry—signing a deal with Rosoboronexport in 2011 to supply frigates to the Algerian navy on top of an earlier deal to provide submarines and turning to Russian firms to modernize other ships in its navy—but Algeria also has options to diversify its suppliers with a 2012 contract with the German firm Thyssen Krupp for ships and helicopters.[118] Algeria has moved away from its earlier Cold War-era dependence on Moscow and now has a much more balanced relationship between Russia and the West.

Libya–Russia relations began to warm up after December 2007, in part because Gaddafi was concerned about becoming too dependent on the West. Putin visited Libya in April 2008 and agreed to write off most of Libya's old Soviet-era debt in return for Russian firms being given new lucrative opportunities in Libya itself. New contracts were signed, and Libya's state energy company agreed, in principle, to have Gazprom build new networks for transporting Libya's natural gas output to Europe, thus helping to neutralize the threat that Libya's reserves might pose for Gazprom's dominance of the European market by putting them under Russian supervision. Gaddafi also agreed to make new purchases of Russian weaponry. Putin's visit was followed by a second set of negotiations when Libyan Prime Minister Al-Baghdadi Ali al-Mahmudi traveled to Moscow in July 2008.[119]

However, Libya continued to focus most of its attention on attracting Western firms to Libya and did not restore any sort of preferential relationship with Russia. Gaddafi's erratic style of governance did not make him a predictable or reliable partner for Russia, and while all sorts of lucrative deals were being proposed, few had been executed, other than continuing purchases of weapons. When the rebellion began against Gaddafi in early 2011, the Russians chose to abstain when UN Security Council Resolution 1973 (authorizing countries to patrol a no-fly zone) came up for a vote, in part because concerted arguments were made that it was not worth defending Gaddafi—who had not particularly favored Russian interests—and also risking damaging Russia's relationships with France and the United States.[120] While Putin was highly critical of how NATO enforced that resolution and argued that the West overstepped its authority by pursuing regime change in Libya, Russia took no steps to protect Gaddafi.

However, because Russia chose not to actively support the rebels and was the main supplier of weaponry to the Qaddafi regime, the interim National Transitional Council initially signaled that Russian firms might lose their business interests in a post-Qaddafi Libya. But in November 2011, Prime Minister Abdel-Rahim al-Keeb indicated that the new government would honor legally binding contracts concluded with Russian companies,[121] which include Gazprom, Gazpromneft, and Tatneft. At the end of December 2011, Mikhail Margelov, the chairman of the foreign affairs committee of the Federation Council and Russia's special envoy for Africa, arrived for talks in Libya with proposals for continued Russian involvement in Libya,[122] but it does appear that Russian influence is set to dramatically decline in a post–Gaddafi Libya.

Whether Russia can make inroads in its relationship with a post–Arab Spring Egypt also remains to be seen. Relations between Cairo and Moscow soured after the expulsion of Soviet advisors by Anwar Sadat in 1972 and as Egypt moved firmly into the American camp under Sadat and his successor, Hosni Mubarak. During the Putin administration, modest progress was made in strengthening ties between Russia and Egypt. Mubarak, in part due to perceived pressure from the United States to engage in reforms, was willing to expand ties with Russia, including cooperation in the natural gas sphere and proposals for Russia to develop Egypt's civilian nuclear power infrastructure and to increase purchases of Russian grain. Egypt also became a popular destination for Russian tourists. Putin visited Egypt in 2005 and Mubarak traveled to Russia in 2006.[123] But Russia was not particularly invested in the Mubarak regime, and at the end of

December 2011, Foreign Minister Lavrov signaled that Russia would continue its efforts to build stronger ties with Egypt.[124]

Initially, the Kingdom of Iraq was a major anti–Soviet actor in the Middle East; Iraq was a founding member of the Central Treaty Organization (the Baghdad Pact) created in 1955 to check Soviet influence in the region. After the monarchy was overthrown in 1958, Iraq withdrew from this treaty, and subsequent revolutionary governments in Baghdad turned to the USSR for support. During the 1980s, Iraq (ruled by Saddam Hussein since 1979) became the largest recipient of Soviet military aid outside of the Soviet bloc, as part of a Soviet strategy to contain a revolutionary Iran.[125] But the Soviet Union did not attempt to shield Iraq from international pressure after Hussein's invasion of Kuwait in 1990 and supported American proposals to use "all necessary means" (in the language of UN Security Council Resolution 987) to expel Iraq from Kuwait.

Russia's relationship with Iraq during the 1990s was characterized by Russian efforts to "graduate" Iraq from international sanctions placed on Saddam Hussein after his invasion of Kuwait in 1990, in part to help bolster Russia's profile in the region. At various points, the Russian government attempted to mediate between Baghdad and the West as well as trying to resolve outstanding disputes. Russia did achieve some successes, notably in 1994 when it helped to convince Hussein to formally recognize Kuwait as a separate state. In turn, bolstered by Russian diplomatic support, Saddam Hussein bestowed some 30% of Iraq's oil vouchers (contracts allowing for Iraqi oil to be sold under the UN Oil for Food program, which provided a mechanism for Iraq to sell some of its oil to raise funds for humanitarian supplies) to Russian entities, including the government of Russia, the Russian presidential administration, the Russian Communist Party, the Russian Orthodox Church, and companies like LUKoil, Gazprom, Sibneft, and Rosneft. Russian companies like LUKoil also were awarded contracts to develop Iraqi energy assets once UN sanctions would be lifted.[126]

Russia did not support the U.S. invasion of Iraq in 2003, and initially, post-Saddam governments in Iraq were not particularly friendly to Moscow. However, Russia has regained some influence. In 2005 and again in 2008, Russia forgave much of Iraq's prewar debt, much of it incurred by Saddam Hussein during the Iran–Iraq war. As with other pro-U.S. governments in the region, Iraq, particularly under Prime Minister Nouri al-Maliki, has sought to balance ties with Washington by exploring options with other powers. LUKoil's right to develop the West Qurna field was reaffirmed, and the Iraqi government has started a process to review other Saddam-era contracts reached with Russia. This has cleared the way for a resumption of closer Russia–Iraq economic ties.[127] The Syrian crisis and a growing chill in U.S.–Iraq relations (in part due to domestic developments inside Iraq) have also helped to bring Moscow and

Baghdad closer again. Maliki visited Moscow in October 2012, meeting with both Putin and Medvedev, and signed new deals to purchase some $4.2 billion in Russian weaponry.[128]

MOSCOW'S TRADITIONAL ALLY SYRIA

Even as Russia has reached out to former Cold War foes in the Middle East, it has not neglected relations with Syria, its traditional ally from the Soviet period. The Soviet Union provided a great deal of aid to Damascus; the Syrian Ministry of the Economy concluded that the USSR was "responsible for 90 industrial facilities and pieces of infrastructure, one-third of Syria's electrical power capability, one-third of its oil-producing facilities and a threefold expansion of land under irrigation—aided in part by assistance with building the massive Euphrates dam."[129] Beginning in the 1950s, Syria turned to the Soviet bloc for arms, and future President Hafez al-Assad was trained by the Soviets as a MiG fighter pilot.[130] After Anwar Sadat broke with the Soviet Union and aligned himself with the United States, Syria became Moscow's most important Arab ally. Since 1971, Moscow has leased port facilities in Tartus (which now consist of Russia's only military base outside the territory of the former Soviet Union), allowing the Russian Black Sea Fleet to deploy in the Eastern Mediterranean.[131] The formal relationship between the two countries was detailed in a 1980 Treaty of Friendship and Cooperation.

After the collapse of the Soviet Union in 1991, Russian–Syrian relations deteriorated, in part because of Syria's inability to repay much of its estimated $12 billion debt to Moscow.[132] The Yeltsin years also were characterized by the new Russian opening to Israel, which further complicated relations.

Russian–Syrian relations began to improve for a variety of reasons during the Putin administration. The U.S. invasion of Iraq in 2003 led the Syrians to re-evaluate the importance of upgrading ties with a resurgent Russia, particularly as Syria itself felt threatened by the U.S. presence in Iraq. An agreement was soon reached whereby most of the Soviet-era debt was forgiven in return for Syria agreeing to new arms purchases from Russia. To the extent that there was a serious prospect for a Syria–Israel peace dialogue, Russia saw an opportunity to possibly broker a deal between the two countries. Finally, the Syrian government agreed that Russia could upgrade its port facilities in Tartus.[133] After the Orange Revolution in Ukraine in 2004, concerns that Russia might lose some of the ports used by the Black Sea Fleet raised the importance of retaining the Tartus base, a concern reinforced by the 2008 clash with Georgia and the fear of "NATO encirclement" in the Black Sea.[134]

The perceived support of Israel for Georgia in its conflicts with Russia also led to a reappraisal of Moscow's ties with Syria. Once Damascus signaled it was interested in again purchasing large quantities of Russian weaponry, Syria became a major customer of the Russian arms industry. To assuage Israel, the Russian foreign ministry stressed that "provisions in the contract specifically bar Damascus from transferring these weapons to a third party."[135] However, Russian-produced arms were found in Hezbollah's possession in Lebanon after the 2006 clash with Israel, leading to questions about how effectively the Russian government was supervising the ultimate disposition of the weapons it was selling to Damascus. However, the immense value of the arms trade to the Russian economy—with some estimates concluding that the total value of Syrian contracts with the Russian defense industry tops $4 billion[136]—means that Russia has little incentive to cut Syria off. In addition, because of long-standing U.S. sanctions against Syria, coupled with more recent European sanctions, Russian firms have enjoyed "preferential access" to the Syrian economy.[137]

When protests began against the Syrian government in 2011, Russia was one of the strongest backers of the Assad regime, backing its right to use force if necessary to prevent and then put down an uprising. Part of this is based on an assessment that a post–Assad government would not be as friendly to Russia and would probably cancel many of the ongoing projects between the two countries, including "the construction and export of two diesel-electric submarines, the modernization of the S-125 Neva anti-aircraft systems, the supply of fifty MIG-29 fighters and seventy-five IAK-30 training airplanes."[138] However, the ongoing violence in the country forced the oil firm Tatneft to suspend its operations in the country, and other firms may re-evaluate whether staying in the country makes commercial sense.

The Russian military and the defense industry are major supporters of the Syrian vector—and after Russia compromised with the United States to permit stronger sanctions on Iran in 2010 and abstained on the Libyan intervention in 2011, they signaled that losing Syria as well was a clear red line. In January 2012, the Admiral Kuznetsov carrier battle group made a visit to Syria, docking in Tartus, in what was seen as a sign of continued Russian support for the Assad government. It also underscored how the port at Tartus is critical if Russia is to be able to continue to project any military power within the Eastern Mediterranean.[139] The Russian Orthodox Church has also come out in support of Russia's stance on Syria, in part because of concerns over the possible fate of Syria's Orthodox Christian community should Assad's regime be overthrown.[140] The proregime orientation, therefore, has had a good deal of support from within the state administration, the Foreign Ministry, the military, some within the business community, and within civil society as well.[141] Moreover, this tilt toward the Assad government is sustained even when it is clear that it is causing damage with Russia's new relationship with Turkey—suggesting that the energy interests that have pushed the Russo–Turkish relationship forward cannot completely overrule the pro–Syrian groups within the Russian national security establishment. Russia has also been willing to cause friction in its relationships with the United States and key countries in Western Europe over its continued support for the Assad regime, including continuing to do business with Syria, to send weapons, and to use its veto at the UN Security Council to block authorization of any coercive measures against the government in Damascus.[142]

While Syria is often described as Russia's closest ally in the Arab world, it is Iran that, over the last 20 years, has become Russia's most valuable Middle Eastern relationship.

THE TRANSFORMATION OF RUSSIAN–IRANIAN RELATIONS

Both the Shah's regime and the Islamic Republic of Iran, in its first years, were strongly anti–Soviet. However, in the waning days of the USSR, the apparent erosion of Soviet ideology—especially its emphasis on atheism—opened up the possibility of a new rapprochement between Tehran and Moscow. In January 1989, Khomeini sent a personal letter to Gorbachev, calling on him to study Islam as an alternative to Marxism-Leninism, and dispatched three personal emissaries to the Kremlin.[143] Foreign Minister Eduard Shevardnadze then visited Tehran, and in June 1989, President Hashemi Rafsanjani traveled to the Soviet Union and agreed to purchase some $6 billion in weaponry—an important step because Iran could not buy weapons from the United States, its traditional supplier.[144] Two years later, Iran received permission (as well as the necessary technical assistance) to assemble T-72S tanks and BMP-2 infantry fighting vehicles.[145]

After the collapse of the Soviet Union, the Middle East assumed a much lower priority in Russian foreign policy, with the ascendancy of the Euro-Atlantic vector. Moreover, Foreign Minister Kozyrev focused on improving Russia's relations with the Gulf Arab states, which had prickly relations with Tehran.[146] The United States also applied a great deal of pressure to stop Russian contacts with Iran. Iran threatened the American strategic position in the Middle East; moreover, the United States was concerned that Iran was seeking to master the technological steps that would be needed to construct and deploy nuclear weapons. So, in 1995, a secret agreement reached between U.S. Vice President Al Gore and Prime Minister Viktor Chernomyrdin allowed Russia to complete its initial arms transactions with Tehran but to ban further sales.[147] U.S. pressure also caused Russia to abandon an agreement that would have allowed Iran to assemble MiG-29 fighters.[148]

But interest in Iran revived as it became clear Tehran could become a major consumer of Russian technology, particularly weapons—and that Iran's oil revenues meant it could pay in hard cash.[149] In addition, both Iran and Russia conducted their relations on the basis of pragmatism. Initially, there were fears in Moscow that the Islamic Republic might try to extend its influence in Central Asia and the Muslim regions of Russia itself. But Rafsanjani decided that backing revolutionary movements that had little chance of bringing pro-Iranian regimes to power but could turn Russia into an enemy were of little value to an Iran that was still being threatened by the United States.[150] An Iran weakened by the 8 years of the Iran–Iraq war needed to rebuild its military and its infrastructure, and Russia was seen as the best partner to assist in this process. As Ray Takeyh concluded:

> Far from instigating fundamentalist uprisings, Iran even sought to mediate conflicts between various Islamist movements and the new governments. Tehran developed good relations with Christian Armenia and sought to settle its dispute over Nagorno-Karabakh with Muslim Azerbaijan. In a similar vein, Iran constructively addressed the civil war in Tajikistan between the Islamist opposition and the Russian-backed government. The Islamic Republic realized that its influence in Central Asia, the viability of its economic prospects in the region and its ties to Russia mandated advancing stability along its northern frontier. In both the Chechen wars, Iran did not support the claims of Muslim Chechens, not only to avoid antagonizing Russia, but also from its own concern for the cause of territorial integrity. As a multi-ethnic country, Iran has always been alarmed about the impact of separatist movements on its national cohesion.[151]

A major breakthrough occurred in 1995 when, after several years of negotiations, the state nuclear construction agency Atomstroyexport signed a contract with Iran for completion of the Bushehr nuclear reactor, which had been left unfinished by German contractors. In 1996, Iran's Foreign Minister Ali Akbar Velayati declared that relations between Iran and Russia had "never been this good in the past five hundred years."[152]

The Russian defense industry ended up becoming a major booster of the Iranian vector. In 2000, the Russian government voided the secret agreement reached between Gore and Chernomyrdin. Russia has been a major supplier of conventional weapons to the Islamic Republic, selling T-72 battle tanks, Su-24 strike aircraft, MiG-29 fighters, Kilo-class diesel submarines, and various missile and air defense systems.[153] In addition, the Russian government, which initially delayed the implementation of a 1995 agreement to install a 1,000-megawatt nuclear power plant at Bushehr—again responding to American pressure—removed restrictions and allowed hundreds of Russian technicians to put the project back on schedule.[154] The contract was revised in 1998, but there were further delays, in part because of funding and equipment shortages.

Some of this commercial contact with Iran occurred in spite of, rather than in accordance with, Kremlin wishes. During the Yeltsin period, key figures in the nuclear power and defense industries had the habit of making deals with Iran without consulting higher authorities. In part, this allowed the Russian government plausible deniability when the United States complained that assurances given to Washington through the Gore–Chernomyrdin commission were being violated. When Putin began implementing his "vertical of power," however, he brought these various actors under closer control. This reduced Iran's ability to contract directly with Russian suppliers without the supervision of the Kremlin.

Rafsanjani's successor as president, Mohammad Khatami, continued his predecessor's policy of engagement with Russia. He met Putin in September 2000 in New York at the United Nations and then traveled to Moscow in March 2001. In August 2002, Iran and Russia concluded a long-term agreement to develop economic, industrial, and scientific cooperation.[155]

The Russian–Iranian relationship is directly affected by the trajectory of the U.S.-Russia relationship. When relations with Washington improve, Moscow has less incentive to pursue its ties with Tehran.[156] Conversely, when difficulties emerge between the two countries, Russia becomes less interested in supporting the U.S. agenda vis-à-vis Iran.

Russian foreign policy walks a careful line when it comes to Iran. Russia does not want Iran to have actual nuclear weapons capability, nor does it want to defend Iran in such a way as to complicate its relations with the United States. On the other hand, Iran has proven very useful in helping to tamp down Islamic radicalism in the North Caucasus and Central Asia, and it has been a lucrative commercial partner for Russia's nuclear and weapons industries. There is also a realpolitik recognition that a United States that is preoccupied with Iran is less likely to interfere with Russian priorities in other parts of the world—most notably the Eurasian space. At the same time, an Iran that remains at odds with the West is unlikely to emerge as a serious competitor to Russia for selling energy, particularly natural gas, to Russia's core markets in Europe.[157]

Putin vacillated on support for Iran's development of a civilian nuclear infrastructure, but when Hasan Rowhani, Iran's negotiator with the international community on these issues, announced in Moscow in November 2003 that Iran would voluntarily suspend its activities aimed at enriching uranium (a key step to developing an atomic bomb) and would sign an additional protocol allowing for snap inspections of its facilities by the International Atomic Energy Agency (IAEA), Putin praised Iran for its "self-restraint" and concluded, "I do not see any obstacle to our cooperation with Iran in the nuclear sphere."[158] A new and revised contract was signed in 2006 that cleared away remaining difficulties with finishing Bushehr. In 2010 a joint venture was created between the Russian state atomic energy company Rosatom and the Atomic Energy Agency of Iran to oper- ate the plant and for Russian to supply the nuclear fuel (and remove spent fuel back to Russia).[159]

At the same time, however, when Iran has engaged in deceptive actions—hiding sites and equipment from international scrutiny, or engaging in research activities that could pave the way for the development of nuclear weapons—the Russian government has shown its willingness to side with the West.[160] The election of Mahmoud Ahmadinejad to the presidency of Iran in 2005 also raised concerns that the younger hardliners grouped around him might seek to return to Iran's earlier hostility to Russia.[161] Meanwhile, the IAEA Board of Governors concluded in September that Iran had not complied with all of its obligations. Russia there- fore joined with other permanent and rotating members of the UN Security Council to pass resolution 1696 in July 2006, which called attention to these viola- tions and encouraged all states to prohibit the transfer to Iran of materials that could be used as part of a weapons program. Iran was also called upon to open up its program or face sanctions. Vitaly Churkin, representing Russia at the UN, clarified that the point of the resolution was to allow Iran to "clarify outstanding issues and restore trust in its nuclear programme."[162] To the extent that Iran has not fully opened up its nuclear program to international inspection, Russia has been willing to support further sanctions in the UN Security Council, voting in favor of Resolutions 1737 (2006), 1747 (2007), and 1929 (2010), which imposed further penalties on Iran for its noncompliance.

The Ahmadinejad administration, however, showed that it was willing to con- tinue the policy of engaging Russia, and continued to provide assistance to Russia against Chechen separatists and in deflecting criticism of Russia for its Chechen policies within the Organization of the Islamic Conference (OIC).[163] Ahmadinejad had a face-to-face meeting with Putin at the 2006 Shanghai Cooperation Organization summit, which helped to smooth over some differ- ences,[164] and in October 2007, Putin became the first Russian leader since Josef Stalin to visit Iran.

The Russian defense industry has the most equities in the relationship with Iran. In November 2005, Russia signed a contract with Iran to deliver Tor-M1 surface-to-air missiles to Tehran. But the Tor-M1 system would not be able to enhance Iran's air defenses against a possible American or Israeli strike unless combined with other, more advanced missile systems. In December 2007, Iran's Defense Minister Mostafa Mohammad Najjar announced that Iran had finalized a contract to purchase the S-300 system, a longer-range missile system considered to be one of the world's most advanced and capable anti-aircraft defenses.

Iran has tried to foster economic cooperation with Russia and with India via the North–South corridor that would link Russia, particularly its Caspian regions, to overland access to the Indian Ocean basin, while in return allowing Iran to send goods into the Russian network for eventual distribution in European markets. However, these efforts have been hampered by sanctions and overall doubt about the feasibility of making expensive infrastructure investments in Iran. As a result, the overall balance of Russian–Iranian trade remains low, approximately $2 billion per year (see Figure 8.2).[165] Many Russian firms are leery of doing business with Iran because of international sanctions and the growing risk that their more profitable interests in the United States and Europe might be jeopardized. As a result, only 0.2% of Russia's companies are "involved in Iran."[166]

So Russia's relationship with Iran is often examined in light of Russia's relationships with other key powers. Andrei Terekhov has concluded: "Moscow tries to balance its interests . . . it does not wish to help Iranians [against the United States] but does not wish to fight against them too."[167] Sergei Luzyanin, director of the Oriental Research Foundation, has noted that "Russian-Iranian cooperation is strictly meted out in doses."[168] In September 2002, then-Iranian Defense Minister Ali Shamkhani corroborated Luzyanin's analysis, complaining that

FIGURE 8.2
Balance of Russian–Iranian Trade, 2008–2010 (in billions of U.S. dollars)

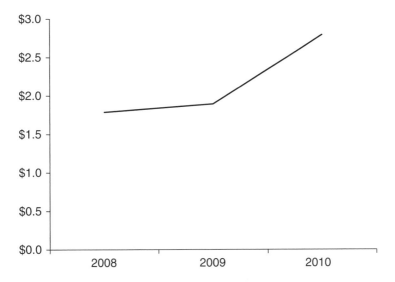

Source: John W. Parker, "Russia and the Iranian Nuclear Program: Replay or Breakthrough?," *Strategic Perspectives*, No. 9, March 2012, Institute for National Strategic Studies, http://www.ndu.edu/press/lib/pdf/strategic-perspectives/Strategic-9.pdf, p. 19.

Russia was willing to sell equipment to Iran, but only up to a point: Anything that would provoke a strong negative reaction from the United States was off the agenda.[169]

The Iranian vector is promoted primarily by a handful of powerful state companies in the defense and atomic energy sectors, but these industries have shown that their support for Iran is conditional; if better opportunities arise elsewhere, they have acquiesced to stronger pressure on Tehran. Starting in 2009, the Medvedev administration, in particular, believed that the prospect for enhanced nuclear cooperation with the United States as well as the possibility of new lucrative arms deals with Iran's Arab opponents would make up any shortfalls that might come from adopting a more confrontational posture with Iran. A harsher Iran policy was also seen as an important step to improve Russia's relations with Israel and the United States. Russia backed a harsh new sanctions resolution against Iran at the United Nations in June 2010 that, among other things, struck hard at Iran's financial institutions. In September 2010, Medvedev issued a decree banning the sale of a wide variety of military equipment to Iran, including tanks and helicopters, effectively terminating what had been a lucrative $5 billion business.[170] At the Caspian Summit in Baku in November 2010, Medvedev bluntly told Ahmadinejad that the burden of proof was now on Iran to show that its nuclear program was for peaceful, civilian purposes only.[171]

After the decision to cancel the sale of the S-300s, Ahmadinejad lashed out at the Russian government, saying it had "sold out" Iran to the United States. Criticizing the pro-American faction within the Russian government, and implicitly Medvedev himself, the Iranian president said,

> Some people who are under the influence of Satan [the United States] thought that if they unilaterally and illegally cancel some defence agreements that they have with us, it will hurt the Iranian nation. They went and sold us out to our enemies by unilaterally cancelling the agreement for which they have been paid.[172]

In fall 2011, Iran filed suit with the International Court of Justice, accusing Russia of a breach in its contractual obligations to supply the system to Iran.

Nevertheless, there remains a good deal of support for the Iranian vector in Russian foreign policy, which raises the question of whether the limits have been reached as to how far Russia might side with the United States against Iran. On February 15, 2011, Foreign Minister Lavrov ruled out Russian support for any further sanctions and criticized the efforts of the United States and the European Union to tighten economic pressure on Iran. "Further sanctions will exacerbate the Iranian economic status. We cannot support that." He also reiterated that the goal, from Russia's perspective, was to ensure that Iran's nuclear program had no military component, not that it should be terminated altogether.[173] In January 2012, Lavrov reiterated the Russian position in arguing against either further sanctions or military action—and Putin, after returning to the presidency, has shown no interest in changing this approach.

For some in the Russian foreign policy establishment, Iran remains a useful hedge against the United States. Despite the dressing down in Baku, Ahmadinejad was invited to and attended the Shanghai Cooperation Organization summit in Astana in June 2011. As the United States has proceeded with its plans for a missile defense system in Europe, Iran's ambassador to Russia, Ali Akbar Salehi, argued the case for closer Russian–Iranian relations to offset the United States.[174]

However, some decisions will not be reversed. There was speculation at the beginning of 2012 that, due to worsening U.S.–Russia relations, Moscow might revisit the sale of the S-300 air defense system to Iran. However, Deputy Defense Minister Anatoly Antonov made it clear in March 2012: "All restrictions imposed by the UN Security Council will be observed. I assure you that [the restrictions] are strictly observed and Russia is not acting in breach of sanctions."[175] But because of Iran's importance as a regional power, Russia will always have a relationship with Tehran. In January 2012, Iranian Interior Minister Mostafa Mohammad Najjar and the head of Russia's federal drug control service, Viktor Ivanov, an important aide to Putin, signed agreements on combating drugs and policing the Caspian Sea.[176]

After Putin was re-elected, the Iranian government, sensing that with Medvedev out of the Kremlin, it might be possible to restart better relations with Russia, again reached out to Moscow to discuss expanding economic cooperation. All of this indicates that Russia will continue to try and balance an Iranian vector with other foreign policy interests.[177]

OVERALL CONCLUSION

The Arab Spring of 2011 significantly altered the trajectory of Russian foreign policy in the Middle East. In 2010, Russia appeared to have been able to balance its traditional relationships with states like Iran, Syria, and Libya with pursuing new openings with Turkey, Israel, and Saudi Arabia, in part by offering Moscow as an alternative to continued unilateral dependence on the United States. But maintaining this balance has proven to be difficult, as Russia has found itself becoming more isolated in the region. This has led experts to conclude that "Russian activity in the Middle East is being impacted by the new and unpredictable realities in the area as well. Russia finds itself with dramatically reduced regional influence, forcing it to alter attitudes and tactics and seek new opportunities."[178] It remains an open question whether Russia can succeed in keeping on the same balance sheet both old clients and new customers that, in some cases, view each other as deadly enemies.

NOTES

1. James E. Montgomery, "Ibn Fadlan and the Rusiyyah," *Journal of Arabic and Islamic Studies* 3 (2000): 1–25.

2. C. Raymond Beazley, "The Oldest Monument of Russian Travel," *Transactions of the Royal Historical Society, New Series* 14 (1900): 175–185.

3. Paul Meyendorff, *Russia: Ritual and Reform* (Crestwood, NY: St. Vladimir's Seminary Press, 1991), esp. 47–52, 60–61, 66, 103–104.

4. And, it might be added, attracted the interest of foreign merchants as well. See the account of Anthony Jenkinson, the factor of the English Muscovy Company, for his travels, as recorded in Richard Hakluyt's *The Principal Navigations, Voyages, Traffiques and Discoveries of the English Nation*, volume II (Glasgow, 1903–1905), 449–479.

5. Janet Martin, *Medieval Russia 980–1584* (Cambridge, UK: Cambridge University Press, 1993), 322.

6. Rudi Matthee, "Anti-Ottoman Politics and Transit Rights: The Seventeenth-Century Trade in Silk between Safavid Iran and Muscovy," *Cahiers du Monde Russe* 35, no. 4 (October/December 1994): 739–761.

7. Nikolas K. Gvosdev, *Imperial Policies and Perspectives Towards Georgia, 1760–1819* (Houndmills, Basingstoke: Macmillan Press Ltd, 2000), 48–51.

8. Alexander Onou, "The Memoirs of Count N. Ignatyev," *The Slavonic and East European Review* 10, no. 29 (December 1931): 389.

9. This is covered in Theofanis George Stavrou, *Russian Interests in Palestine, 1882–1914* (Thessaloniki: Institute for Balkan Studies, 1963); see also Serge A. Zenkovsky's review of Stavrou's book in *Russian Review* 24, no. 2 (April 1965): 198.

10. Firuz Kazemzadeh, *Russia and Britain in Persia, 1864–1914: A Study in Imperialism* (New Haven, CT: Yale University Press, 1968), 499–501.

11. The decree is cited in Victor S. Mamatey, *Soviet Russian Imperialism* (New York: Van Nostrand Reinhold Company, 1964), 119.

12. Jon Jacobson, *When the Soviet Union Entered World Politics* (Berkeley, CA: University of California Press, 1994), 178.

13. Soviet leaders, however, were initially divided on how to respond to revolutions that brought Arab nationalists (not Communists) to power and the risks of supporting them, particularly if it worsened relations with the United States. See Vitaly Naumkin, "Moving From the Bottom Up and Back Down Again," *Russia in Global Affairs*, September 24, 2011, at http://eng.globalaffairs.ru/number/Moving-From-the-Bottom-Up-and-Back-Down-Again-15327.

14. Christopher Andrew and Vasili Mitrokhin, *The World Was Going Our Way: The KGB and the Battle for the Third World* (New York: Basic Books, 2005), 141.

15. Sebastien Peyrouse, "The Relationship Between Church and State in the Post-Soviet World: The Case of Christianity in Central Asia," *Perspectives on Church–State Relations in Russia,* eds. Wallace L. Daniel, Peter L. Berger, and Christopher Marsh (Waco, TX: Institute of Church-State Studies, 2008), 174.

16. Andrew and Mitrokhin, 142.

17. Quoted in James W. Warhola, "Religion and Politics under the Putin Administration: Accommodation and Confrontation within 'Managed Pluralism,'" in *Church-State Relations in Russia,* 121.

18. "Pravoslavie blizhe k islamu chem. Katolitsism," *BaltInfo,* December 16, 2010, at http://www.baltinfo.ru/2010/12/16/Pravoslavie-blizhe-k-islamu-chem-katolitcizm—Putin-177816.

19. Sergei Luzyanin, "Russia Looks to the Orient," *Russia in Global Affairs* 2 (April–June 2007), at http://eng.globalaffairs.ru/number/n_8541.

20. Ellen Barry, "As Nations Line Up Against Syrian Government, Russia Sides Firmly With Assad," *New York Times,* January 28, 2012, A8, at http://www.nytimes.com/2012/01/28/world/europe/russia-sides-firmly-with-assad-government-in-syria.html?_r=2&ref=world.

21. For instance, the Soviet Union provided aid in the industrialization of the Turkish textile industry. A. I. Gadzhaev, "Investitsionnoe Sotrudnichestvo Rossii I Turtsii," *Rossiia I Islamskii Mir,* ed. M.S. Grikurov (Moscow: Kraft Plus, 2009), 202.

22. I. Nazarov, "The Soviet Union and Turkey Can Live in Friendship," *Pravda,* June 3, 1960, 5; in *Current Digest of the Soviet Press* 12, no. 22 (June 29, 1960): 32.

23. Ihsan Bal, "The Distance Between Ankara and Moscow is Disappearing," *Turkish Weekly,* May 27, 2010, at http://www.turkishweekly.net/print.asp?type=4&id=3339.

24. Comments of Jenia Ustinova in "Global Insider: Russia-Turkey Relations," *World Politics Review,* February 9, 2011, at http://www.worldpoliticsreview.com/trend-lines/7834/global-insider-russia-turkey-relations.

25. Brian Glyn Williams, "Turkish Volunteers in Chechnya," *Terrorism Monitor* 3, no. 7 (May 5, 2005), at http://www.jamestown.org/single/?no_cache=1&tx_ttnews[tt_news]=300.

26. Orkhan Gafarli, "Russian Foreign Policy in Light of Changing Balances in the Middle East," *Turkish Policy Quarterly* 10, no. 4 (2011): 147.

27. Gadzhaev, 203.

28. E. I. Urazova, "Aktual'nye Voprosy Rossiisko-Turetskogo Regional'nogo Ekonomicheskogo Sotrudnichestvo v Evrazii," *Rossiia I Islamskii Mir,* 194.

29. N. Iu. Ul'chenko, "Rossiia I Turtsii: Osnovnye Etapy Sotsial'no-Politicheskogo Razvitiia I Dvukhstoronnnego Ekonomicheskogo Sotrudnichestvo," *Rossiia I Islamskii Mir,* 24.

30. Morton Abramowitz and Henri J. Barkey, "Turkey's Transformers," *Foreign Affairs,* November/December 2009, 125.

31. Luzyanin, op. cit.

32. Ul'chenko, 27.

33. Vladimir Soldatkin, "Russia Tatneft says re-routed Druzhba oil to Turkey," *Reuters,* July 15, 2008, at http://uk.reuters.com/article/2008/07/15/czech-russia-oil-idUKL1562819220080715.

34. Gadzhaev, 204–206.

35. Dince Gokce, "Russia, Turkey may jointly operate Kavkaz Port," *Hurriyet,* July 9, 2010, at http://www.hurriyetdailynews.com/n.php?n=russia-turkey-may-jointly-operate-kavkaz-port-2010-07-09.

36. Faruk Akkan, "Visa-free regime with Russia officially begins today," *Today's Zaman,* April 16, 2011, at http://www.todayszaman.com/newsDetail_getNewsById.action?newsId=241173.

37. Hakan Tasci, "Anatolian business clusters: the new center of gravity in Turkey," *Today's Zaman,* December 7, 2010. A copy is available at http://www.tuskonus.org/tuskon.php?c=22&s=&e=186.

38. Gadzhaev, 203.

39. Vladimir Socor, "Gazprom, Turkey Resolve and Reconfigure Blue Stream II," *Eurasia Daily Monitor* 6, no. 154 (August 11, 2009), at http://www.jamestown.org/single/?no_cache=1&tx_ttnews%5Btt_news%5D=35394.

40. Bal, op. cit.

41. "Russia no longer 'security threat' to Turkey," *RIA Novosti,* August 23, 2010, at http://en.rian.ru/russia/20100823/160305808.html.

42. Yigal Schleifer, "A Thinker in the Halls of Power," *World Politics Review,* February 2, 2010, 1–2.

43. "Turkey to alter national security strategy," *United Press International,* August 25, 2010, at http://www.upi.com/Top_News/Special/2010/08/25/Turkey-to-alter-national-security-strategy/UPI-58161282750850/.

44. Urazova, 198.

45. Abramowitz and Barkey, 125.

46. "Turkey-Abkhazia relations may harm Turkish-Georgian friendship," *Azerbaijan Today,* September 6, 2009, at http://www.azerbaijantoday.com/index.php?mod=article&cat=InternationalTrade&article=318.

47. Justin Lyle, "Turkey's Caucasus Conundrum," *Russia Profile,* February 24, 2011, at http://russiaprofile.org/international/32901.html.

48. Urazova, 200.

49. "Russia, Turkey becoming strategic partners—Medvedev," *RIA Novosti,* May 10, 2010, at http://en.rian.ru/world/20100510/158954539.html.

50. John Helmer, "Sechin Divides the Black Sea," *Asia Times,* November 3, 2009, at http://www.atimes.com/atimes/Central_Asia/KK03Ag01.html.

51. Orhan Coskun and Gleb Bryanski, "Turkey, Russia Reach South Stream Gas Deal," *Reuters,* December 28, 2011, at http://www.reuters.com/article/2011/12/28/turkey-russia-southstream-idUSL6E7NS0LU20111228.

52. Saban Kardas, "Turkey Strengthens Nuclear Cooperation with Russia," *Eurasia Daily Monitor* 7, no. 213 (November 30, 2010), at http://www.jamestown.org/single/?no_cache=1&tx_ttnews%5Btt_news%5D=37219&tx_ttnews%5BbackPid%5D=7&cHash=0ac627c5a7.

53. "Giant partnership formed between Çalik Enerji and Rosneft," *Sabah,* December 17, 2010, at http://www.sabahenglish.com/Economy/2010/12/17/giant_partnership_formed_between_calik_enerji_and_rosneft.

54. "In talks with Russia, Turkey urges Iran for nuke assurances," *Today's Zaman*, January 21, 2011, at http://www.todayszaman.com/news-233082-in-talks-with-russia-tur key-urges-iran-for-nuke-assurances.html.

55. Bal, op. cit.

56. Williams, "Turkish Volunteers," op. cit.

57. Irina Kobrinskaya, "The Black Sea Region in Russia's Current Foreign Policy Paradigm," *PONARS Eurasia Policy Memo #41*, December 2008, 3.

58. Dimitar Bechev, "Putin's visit rekindles the Russia-Turkey affair," *CNN*, December 4, 2012, at http://globalpublicsquare.blogs.cnn.com/2012/12/04/putins-visit-rekindles-the-russia-turkey-affair/.

59. "Dozens protest killing of Chechens in Turkey," *Today's Zaman*, September 25, 2011, at http://www.todayszaman.com/newsDetail_getNewsById.action?load=detay&new sId=257856&link=257856. Some have alleged that Turkish authorities have turned a blind eye to these acts, allowing the pro–Moscow government in Chechnya headed by Ramazan Kadyrov to take action against the separatists living in exile in Turkey. See "Kadyrov says Turkey helps to kill Chechens in Istanbul. Turkish authorities are silent," *Kavkaz Center*, December 2, 2011, at http://kavkazcenter.com/eng/content/2011/12/02/15456.shtml.

60. Gadzhaev, 207–208.

61. Bal, op. cit.

62. "Turkey's Erdogan Pays Visit To Tatarstan," *Radio Free Europe/Radio Liberty*, March 17, 2011, at http://www.rferl.org/content/erdogan_turkey_tatarstan/2340790.html.

63. "Giant partnership formed between Çalik Enerji and Rosneft," op. cit.

64. Wojciech Konończuk, Sławomir Matuszak, and Ewa Paszyc, "Russian-Turkish agreement on the South Stream pipeline—an instrument of pressure on Ukraine," *East Week* 1, no. 277 (January 4, 2012), at http://www.osw.waw.pl/en/publikacje/east week/2012-01-04/russianturkish-agreement-south-stream-pipeline-instrument-pres sure-uk.

65. Jean Christou, "Greece and Russia Rally Behind Cyprus," *Cyprus Mail*, October 2, 2011, at http://www.cyprus-mail.com/cyprus/greece-and-russia-rally-behind-cyprus/20111002; "Turkey, Israel, Greece and Russia Mobilizing over Cyprus," *AsiaNews.it*, October 5, 2011.

66. Younkyoo Kim and Stephen Blank, *Russo-Turkish Divergence (Part I): The Security Dimension* (Tel Aviv: The GLORIA Center, April 23, 2012), at http://www.gloria-center .org/2012/04/russo-turkish-divergence-part-i-the-security-dimension/.

67. Gafarli, 149.

68. "Ahmet Davutoglu: NATO threatens neither Iran nor Russia," *Interfax*, January 26, 2012, at http://www.interfax.com/interview.asp?id=304568.

69. Nader Habibi, "Ties With Russia, China Constrain Turkey's Options on Syria," *World Politics Review*, March 5, 2012, at http://www.worldpoliticsreview.com/articles/11667/ ties-with-russia-china-constrain-turkeys-options-on-syria.

70. Nikolas K. Gvosdev, "The Realist Prism: Selective Partnerships the Norm in New Middle East," *World Politics Review*, October 12, 2012, at http://www.worldpoliticsreview .com/articles/12414/the-realist-prism-selective-partnerships-the-norm-in-new-middle-east.

71. Abdullah Buzkurt, "De-coupling fears for Turkey-Russia ties over Syria," *Al-Arabiya News,* October 19, 2012, at http://english.alarabiya.net/en/News/2012/10/19/De-coupling-fears-for-Turkey-Russia-ties-over-Syria.html.

72. Bechev, op. cit.

73. "PM Netanyahu meets with Russian PM Putin in Moscow," Israel Ministry of Foreign Affairs, February 16, 2010, at http://www.mfa.gov.il/MFA/Government/Speeches+by+Israeli+leaders/2010/PM_Netanyahu_meets_Russian_PM_Putin_16-Feb-2010.htm.

74. Shlomo Avineri, *Israel-Russia Relations* (Carnegie Endowment Report), April 2001, at http://www.carnegieendowment.org/2001/04/02/israel-russia-relations/4gl.

75. See his statement in *Nezavisimaya Gazeta,* November 17, 2000.

76. Katz, "Putin's Pro-Israel," 56.

77. Malkah Fleischer, "Russia Scuttles Anti-Israel Resolutions at UNESCO," *Jewish Press,* October 18, 2012, at http://www.jewishpress.com/news/russia-scuttles-anti-israel-resolutions-at-unesco/2012/10/18/.

78. Mark Katz, "Putin's Pro-Israel Policy," *Middle East Quarterly* XII, no. 1 (Winter 2005): 55.

79. Contacts are maintained with key Kremlin officials via the prime minister's office in Israel. See Elad Benari, "Russia's Putin to Visit Israel Next Month," *Arutz Sheva,* May 25, 2012, at http://www.israelnationalnews.com/News/News.aspx/156231.

80. Charles Ganske, "Russia and Israel: Public Hints of a Discreet Partnership," *World Politics Review,* September 13, 2010, at http://www.worldpoliticsreview.com/articles/6385/russia-and-israel-public-hints-of-a-discreet-partnership.

81. Oganesyan, 5–6.

82. "PM Netanyahu meets," op. cit.

83. "Israel sets sights on Russian gas," *Upstreamonline.com,* February 8, 2007, at http://www.upstreamonline.com/live/article127529.ece.

84. "Gazprom in LNG purchase deal with Israel," *New Europe,* March 2, 2013, at http://www.neurope.eu/article/gazprom-lng-purchase-deal-israel.

85. Arye Egozi, "Russia Builds Intelligence Base in Syria," *Kefar Sava,* October 9, 2011.

86. Michael Cecire, "Georgia-Israel Love Affair Now a Messy Divorce," *World Politics Review,* May 10, 2012, at http://www.worldpoliticsreview.com/articles/11939/georgia-israel-love-affair-now-a-messy-divorce.

87. "Israeli defense minister heads to Russia for military talks," *RIA Novosti,* September 6, 2010, at http://en.rian.ru/russia/20100906/160478297.html.

88. Cem Barber, "Russian Navy Nears Cyprus Drilling Zone," *Famagusta Gazette,* November 24, 2011, at http://famagusta-gazette.com/russian-navy-nears-cyprus-drilling-zone-p13594-69.htm.

89. Merav Yudilovitch, "Peres pushes Putin on Iran nuclear issue," *Ynet.news,* November 8, 2012, at http://www.ynetnews.com/articles/0,7340,L-4303115,00.html.

90. William B. Quandt, *Saudi Arabia in the 1980s: Foreign Policy, Security and Oil* (Washington, DC: The Brookings Institution, 1981), 64.

91. Ibid., 64–68.

92. Ibid., 166.

93. Dick Combs, *Inside the Soviet Alternative Universe: The Cold War's End and the Soviet Union's Fall Reappraised* (University Park: Pennsylvania State University Press, 2008), 231.

94. E. S. Melkumyan, "Rossiia I Arabskie Gosudarstva Zaliva: Vozmozhnosti Vzaimodeitstviia," *Rossiia I Islamskii Mir,* 144–145.

95. Robert Baer, *Sleeping with the Devil* (New York: Crown Publishers, 2003), 162–163, 184.

96. Subhash Kapila, "Middle East Changing Dynamics: Strategic Perspectives on Power Play of US, Russia and China," *Eurasia Review,* February 15, 2011, at http://www.eurasiareview.com/analysis/middle-east-changing-dynamics-strategic-perspectives-on-power-play-of-us-russia-and-china-15022011/.

97. "Russia looking for scapegoat for 'failure' in Chechnya: Saudi paper," *Agence France Presse,* July 3, 2000.

98. Kapila, op. cit.

99. Mark N. Katz, "The Emerging Saudi-Russian Partnership," *Mideast Monitor* 3, no. 1 (January–March 2008), at http://digilib.gmu.edu/dspace/bitstream/1920/3015/1/The%20Emerging%20Saudi-Russian%20Partnership.pdf.

100. Murad B. Al-Shishani, "Ahmad Kadyrov's Visit to Saudi Arabia," *CACI Analyst,* January 28, 2004, at http://www.cacianalyst.org/?q=node/1808.

101. Luzyanin, op. cit.

102. "Russia, Saudi Arabia energy partners, not rivals—Putin," *RIA Novosti,* February 12, 2007, at http://en.rian.ru/russia/20070212/60580105.html.

103. John C. K. Daily, "Saudi-Russian Military Cooperation," *Eurasia Daily Monitor* 5, no. 137 (July 18, 2008), at http://www.jamestown.org/programs/edm/single/?tx_ttnews%5Btt_news%5D=33812&tx_ttnews%5BbackPid%5D=166&no_cache=1.

104. Comments of Giacomo Luciani, director of the Gulf Research Center Foundation, in "Global Insider: Saudi Arabia's Nuclear Energy Plans," *World Politics Review,* February 15, 2011, at http://www.worldpoliticsreview.com/trend-lines/7892/global-insider-saudi-arabias-nuclear-energy-plans; Acil Tabbara, "Oil giant Saudi Arabia looks to alternative energy," *Agence France Press,* January 24, 2011, at http://www.google.com/hostednews/afp/article/ALeqM5itqKHsX-s5XsPJDuP8YE04GxPV2w?docId=CNG.8c338e3b1bec49650ef90f296bedf8dc.121; Saurav Jha, "Saudi Arabia's Nuclear Ambitions Part of Broader Strategy," *World Politics Review,* June 16, 2011, at http://www.worldpoliticsreview.com/articles/9186/saudi-arabias-nuclear-ambitions-part-of-broader-strategy.

105. "Russia, Saudi Arabia in talks on major arms deal," *RIA Novosti,* February 15, 2010, at http://en.rian.ru/russia/20100215/157892206.html.

106. "U.S. backs Yemen, Russia arms it," *United Press International,* January 11, 2010, at http://www.upi.com/Business_News/Security-Industry/2010/01/11/US-backs-Yemen-Russia-arms-it/UPI-60911263241218/; David Rosenberg, "For Russia, new Middle East will be a tough arms market," *Jerusalem Post,* September 5, 2011, at http://www.jpost.com/MiddleEast/Article.aspx?id=236713.

107. Armen Ognanesyan, "Russia and the Middle East," *International Affairs* 1 (2010): 4–5.

108. Richard Galpin, "Russian arms shipments bolster embattled Assad," *BBC World News,* January 30, 2012, at http://www.bbc.co.uk/news/mobile/world-middle-east-16797818.

109. "Saudi King tells Medvedev 'No Point in Syria Talks,'" *Day Press,* February 23, 2012, at http://www.dp-news.com/en/detail.aspx?articleid=112696.

110. Asma Alsharif, "Russia's Lavrov in Saudi Seeking Progress on Syria," *Reuters,* November 14, 2012, at http://www.reuters.com/article/2012/11/14/russia-saudi-idUSL5E 8MEEBZ20121114.

111. Mark N. Katz, "Russia and Algeria: Partners or Competitors?" *Middle East Policy* 14, no. 4 (Winter 2007): 152.

112. *Soviet Military Power 1987* (Washington, DC: U.S. Government Printing Office, 1987), 139, 140.

113. Katz, "Russia and Algeria," 152.

114. "Russia pursues new Algeria deals with Medvedev visit," *BBC News,* October 6, 2010, at http://www.bbc.co.uk/news/world-africa-11484201.

115. Quoted in *Il Sole 24 Ore,* February 24, 2006.

116. "Russia pursues new Algeria deals with Medvedev visit," op cit.

117. Eldar Kasayev, "Algeria: An Oil and Gas Partnership with Russia and the Investment Climate," *New Eastern Outlook,* October 10, 2010, at http://journal-neo .com/?q=node/2188.

118. "Algeria Gives Russian Shipyard Contract to Modernize Warships," *Marine Link,* April 6, 2012, at http://www.marinelink.com/news/modernize-shipyard343649.aspx; "Algeria Orders Two MEKO 200 Class Frigates: TKMS to supply 2 MEKO frigates and six Super Lynx helicopters in €2.5bn deal," *Defence Professionals,* April 5, 2012, at http://www .w54.biz/showthread.php?1372-Warship-Design/page2.

119. Mark Katz, "The Russian-Libyan Rapprochement: What Has Moscow Gained," *Middle East Policy,* Fall 2007, at http://www.mepc.org/journal/middle-east-policy-archives/ russian-libyan-rapprochement-what-has-moscow-gained.

120. Nikolas K. Gvosdev, "Libya Could Shift NATO Focus Southward," *World Politics Review,* April 1, 2011, at http://www.worldpoliticsreview.com/articles/8371/the-realist- prism-libya-could-shift-nato-focus-southward.

121. "Libya to honor Russian contracts—PM," *RIA Novosti,* November 1, 2011, at http://en.rian.ru/world/20111101/168325302.html.

122. "Russian envoy arrives in Libya for talks with leadership," *RIA Novosti,* December 21, 2011.

123. Dmitri Trenin, "Russia and Egypt: An Old Relationship," *Aspenia Online,* February 11, 2011, archived at http://carnegieendowment.org/2011/02/11/russia-and- egypt-old-relationship/81h.

124. "Russian-Egyptian relations are strategic partnership—Lavrov," *Voice of Russia,* December 28, 2011, at http://english.ruvr.ru/2011/12/28/63043944.html.

125. Kazem Sajjadpour: "Neutral Statements, Committed Practice: The USSR and the War," *Iranian Perspectives on the Iran–Iraq War,* ed. Farhang Rajaee (Gainesville, FL: University Press of Florida, 1997), 34.

126. "Global Insider: Russia-Iraq Relations," *World Politics Review,* June 14, 2011, at http://www.worldpoliticsreview.com/trend-lines/9141/global-insider-russia-iraq-relations; for more on the Oil-for-Food program, see Sharon Otterman, "Iraq: Oil for Food Scandal,"

Council on Foreign Relations Backgrounder, October 28, 2005, at http://www.cfr.org/un/iraq-oil-food-scandal/p7631.

127. Habibe Özdal, "A Russian Plan for Iraq or the Same Old Story?" *Hurriyet Daily News,* March 14, 2012. An English translation is available at http://www.usak.org.tr/EN/makale.asp?id=2598.

128. Aleks Grigoriyev, "Rossiiskoe oruzhie dlia Iraka: simvol peremen," *Golos Ameriky,* October 9, 2012, at http://www.golos-ameriki.ru/content/iraq-russia-guns/1523610.html.

129. Statistics cited in James Denselow, "Russia shows US how to deal with Syria," *Guardian,* May 10, 2010, at http://www.guardian.co.uk/commentisfree/2010/may/19/syria-russia-arms-middle-east.

130. Bonnie F. Saunders, *The United States and Arab Nationalism: The Syrian Case, 1953–1960* (Westport, CT: Praeger Publishers, 1996), 33–34.

131. "Russia set to build up its naval facilities in Syria," *RIA Novosti,* July 20, 2009.

132. Vladimir Dunayev, "Hafez Assad Comes to Moscow with 'Cold Cash,'" *Izvestia,* July 7, 1999, 1 cited in *Current Digest of the Post-Soviet Press,* August 4, 1999, 19.

133. Mark N. Katz, "Putin's Foreign Policy Towards Syria," *Middle East Review of International Affairs* 10, no. 1 (March 2006), at http://digilib.gmu.edu/dspace/bitstream/1920/3024/1/Putin%20Syria%20MERIA.pdf.

134. Kobrinskaya, 2–3.

135. Frida Ghitis, "World Citizen: Arab States Building Arsenal for War with Iran," *World Politics Review,* October 14, 2010, at http://www.worldpoliticsreview.com/articles/6701/world-citizen-arabs-states-building-arsenal-for-war-with-iran.

136. Holly Yan, "Why China, Russia won't condemn Syrian regime," *CNN,* February 5, 2012, at http://articles.cnn.com/2012-02-05/middleast/world_meast_syria-china-russia-relations_1_syrian-president-bashar-al-assad-syrian-government-syrian-regime?_s=PM:MIDDLEEAST.

137. Barry, op. cit.

138. Garfarli, 146.

139. "Squad of Russian Warships Leaves Syrian Territorial Waters—Ministry," *Interfax,* January 10, 2012, at http://www.interfax.co.uk/russia-cis-general-news-bulletins-in-english/squad-of-russian-warships-leaves-syrian-territorial-waters-%E2%80%93-ministry-2/.

140. Comments of Nikolas K. Gvosdev, "A Closer Look at the Assad Regime," *The Takeaway,* February 9, 2012, at http://www.thetakeaway.org/2012/feb/09/russias-ties-assad-regime/.

141. Maksim Iusin, "Strana Pretknoveniia," *Kommersant,* February 1, 2012, at http://kommersant.ru/doc/1862721.

142. Alessandra Prentice, "Russia accuses U.S. of double standards over Syria," *Reuters,* February 22, 2013, at http://www.reuters.com/article/2013/02/22/us-syria-crisis-russia-idUSBRE91L0BH20130222.

143. Baqer Moin, *Khomeini: Life of the Ayatollah* (New York: St Martin's Press, 1999), 274–275.

144. Ray Takeyh, *Guardians of the Revolution: Iran and the World in the Age of the Ayatollahs* (New York: Oxford University Press, 2009), 150.

145. Ali A. Jalali, "The Strategic Partnership of Russia and Iran," *Parameters*, Winter 2001/02, at http://www.carlisle.army.mil/usawc/parameters/Articles/01winter/jalali.htm.

146. Melkumyan, 146.

147. Robert H. Donaldson and Joseph L. Nogee, *The Foreign Policy of Russia: Changing Systems, Enduring Interests*, 4th edition (Armonk, NY: M.E. Sharpe, 2009), 225.

148. Jalali, op. cit.

149. Ray Takeyh, *Guardians of the Revolution: Iran and the World in the Age of the Ayatollahs* (Oxford: Oxford University Press, 2009), 150, 151–52.

150. See, for instance, Hanna Yousif Freij, "State Interests vs. the Umma: Iranian Policy in Central Asia," *Middle East Journal* (Winter 1996): 71–83.

151. Takeyh, 150.

152. *Kayhan*, March 9, 1996, cited in Takeyh, 151.

153. Michael Eisenstadt, "Russian Arms and Technology Transfers to Iran: Policy Challenges for the United States," *Arms Control Today*, March 2001, at http://www.armscontrol.org/act/2001_03/eisenstadt.

154. From a report cited by Interfax, March 15, 2001.

155. Gafarli, 144.

156. Jalili, op. cit.

157. Nikolas K. Gvosdev, *Parting with Illusions* (Washington, DC: Cato Institute Policy Brief 611, February 29, 2008), 11.

158. Statement on Moscow Channel One TV news, November 10, 2003.

159. Andrey Reznichenko, "Russia, Iran set up joint venture to operate Bushehr power station," *RIA Novosti*, August 21, 2010, at http://en.rian.ru/world/20100821/160285719.html.

160. John W. Parker, *Persian Dreams: Moscow and Tehran Since the Fall of the Shah* (Washington, DC: Potomac Books, 2009), 33.

161. Gafarli, 145.

162. "Security Council Demands Iran Suspend Uranium Enrichment by 31 July, Or Face Possible Economic, Diplomatic Sanctions," Department of Public Information, UN Security Council press release SC 8792, July 31, 2006, at http://www.un.org/News/Press/docs/2006/sc8792.doc.htm.

163. Parker, 33.

164. Gafarli, 145.

165. Interview with Hassan Beheshtipour. "Iran Viewpoint: Iran-Russia-China Relations: Challenges And Interests—OpEd," *Iran Review*, January 15, 2012, at http://www.eurasiareview.com/15012012-iran-viewpoint-iran-russia-china-relations-challenges-and-interests-oped/.

166. Parker, 19.

167. Andrei Terekhov, "Iranian Bargaining of Moscow and Washington," *Nezavisimaia Gazeta* (September 29, 2010): 8.

168. Luzyanin, op. cit.

169. Parker, 23.

170. "Medvedev bans sale of S-300 missiles, other weapons to Iran," *RIA Novosti*, September 22, 2010, at http://en.rian.ru/mlitary_news/20100922/160688354.html.

171. Parker, 24.

172. "For annulling the S-300 missiles deal, Ahmadinejad slams Russia for 'selling out to Satan,'" *Al-Arabiya,* November 3, 2010, at http://www.spacewar.com/reports/Ahmadinejad_slams_Russia_for_selling_out_to_Satan_999.html.

173. "Russia can no longer support future sanctions on Iran—Lavrov," *RIA Novosti,* February 15, 2011, at http://en.rian.ru/russia/20110215/162616657.html.

174. Konstantin Volkov, "Iran Offers Russia Friendship Against Turkey, Both Sides Are Interested in Cooperation, but Moscow Prefers Caspian Alliance to Anti-Turkish One," *Izvestiya,* October 18, 2011.

175. "Russia: No Plans to Resume S-300 Sales to Iran," *RIA Novosti,* March 13, 2012 , at http://en.ria.ru/mlitary_news/20120313/172133153.html.

176. "Iran, Russia Ink Security Agreement," *Fars News Agency,* January 25, 2012, at http://english.farsnews.com/newstext.php?nn=9010172449.

177. "Ahmadinejad, Putin Discuss Upcoming Talks between Iran, World Powers," *Fars News Agency,* May 12, 2012, at http://english.farsnews.com/newstext.php?nn=9102111752.

178. Zvi Magen, "Russia in the Post Arab Spring Middle East," *Valdai Discussion Club,* March 11, 2012, at http://valdaiclub.com/middle_east/39740.html.

CHAPTER 9

Call Across the Himalayas

The South Asia Vector

South Asia has long been linked to the Russian lands through trade and commerce. Coins from the Indian subcontinent have been discovered in archeological excavations, and it is likely that merchants from India and Rus' interacted in the bazaars of the cities along the Caspian Sea.

In the 15th century, Afanasy Nikitin, a merchant of the Russian city of Tver,' attempted to develop a north–south trading route that would link Russia to South Asia. Nikitin's journey, however, undertaken between 1466 and 1472, was not successful as a commercial enterprise.[1] In turn, an Indian merchant named Husein arrived in Moscow in 1532 as the envoy of Babur, the founder of the Moghul Empire, to discuss trading relations.[2] During this time, Paolo Centurione, a merchant of Venice, proposed to Grand Duke Vasily of Moscow the opening of a trade route from India and Iran to Russia via the Caspian Sea and from Russia to Western Europe via the Baltic ports—one of the first iterations of what has been rechristened in modern times as the north–south corridor.[3]

Throughout the centuries, indirect contacts continued, usually through the intermediation of Armenian merchants based in the Persian Empire, and the occasional Russian merchant sometimes arrived in India (for instance, Simeon Malinkov, who arrived in Delhi in 1696). Peter the Great also hoped to initiate commerce by sea with India, with an expedition sent from the Baltic Sea to travel around Africa to India, which ultimately proved to be unsuccessful. Nevertheless, by the end of the 18th century, Russia was engaged in a lively trade with South Asia through Persia, obtaining silks, cotton, sugar, and coffee and exporting furs, iron, linens, and copper products. In 1798, a Russian diplomat stationed in Persia, Mikhail Skibinevskii, penned a report, "A Short Description of Russian Trade with Persia," highlighting the importance of these commercial contacts. Indeed, securing Russia's trade routes with South Asia was part of the rationale for the annexation of Georgia (the other being the defense of Christian Georgia against the Muslim encroachment of Persia and the Ottoman Empire). A report prepared by Count Apollon A. Musin-Pushkin argued that a permanent Russian presence south of the Caucasus Mountains was important to secure the Caspian basin and thus Russia's ability to trade with the East, especially with India.[4]

The commercial interests supporting a Russian vector toward India were soon joined by strategic considerations. As Britain acquired a larger colonial establishment in South Asia, Russian military planners considered the option of an attack on England's possessions in India. In 1800, Count Fedor Rostopchin outlined to Emperor Paul a plan for the dispatch of Cossack troops across Central Asia to attack India. In 1801, Paul authorized this mission, ordering General Vassilii Orlov, commander of the Don Cossack host, to begin moving forces. In a series of orders, Orlov was directed to make common cause with Indian princes and rulers against the British and to ensure that conditions favorable for Russian trade and industry were created.[5] After Paul's assassination that same year, the expedition was recalled by his successor, Emperor Alexander, but the stage was set for a century of the Great Game between Britain and Russia, in which India became a strategic target as part of Russia's plans for containing British power.[6]

Imperial Russia's interest in India as the soft underbelly of the British Empire was transferred to its Soviet successor. In September 1920, at the famous Congress of the Peoples of the East, delegates from all across the Near East and South Asia were summoned to a *jihad* against British imperialism. The Soviet regime, however, did not initially see the Indian National Congress as a revolutionary force; Mahatma Gandhi was denounced as an advocate for "class peace" and the Congress viewed as an agent of the Indian bourgeoisie rather than the representative of India's working masses.[7] After both India and Pakistan received their independence in 1947, neither government was seen as particularly pro-Soviet. Given the importance of Islam in shaping Pakistani identity, the atheism of the Soviet Union was particularly abhorrent. India under its first prime minister, Jawaharlal Nehru, was also initially suspicious of Soviet intentions, particularly Moscow's sponsorship of the Indian Communist Party.[8] Nehru, therefore, preferred to pursue a policy of nonalignment rather than moving too close to either global superpower.

After an initial embrace of nonalignment by the first Pakistani government, however, Pakistan took the opportunity to forge closer ties with Washington and assist in America's containment strategy against the Soviet Union, in order to receive aid and assistance that would enable Islamabad to hold its own with India, with whom it had already fought a war over the disputed province of Kashmir. In 1954, Pakistan acceded to the South-East Asia Treaty Organization and in 1955 joined the Central Treaty Organization, a U.S.-led security alliance for the Middle East.[9]

The post–Stalin Soviet leadership, notably Prime Minister Nikolai Bulganin and General Secretary Nikita Khrushchev (who both made visits to India), shifted Soviet policy regarding India away from enticing India to join the Soviet bloc to working to prevent New Delhi from forging closer ties with the United States—a stance assisted by Washington's own perceived tilt toward Pakistan. In turn, while India was a recipient of U.S. economic aid, the United States declined to support large, state-owned industrial projects, also providing an opening for the Soviet Union.

The Soviet Union began to assist India's industrialization, starting with the massive Bhilai steel works. Because India remained a nonaligned power, it could not buy the American weaponry that Pakistan, as an allied state, was eligible to purchase, so India turned to the Soviet Union. In 1960, a contract was signed not simply for the sale of MiG fighters but also for the construction in India of a plant to manufacture them under license, initiating an enduring relationship between the defense industries of the two countries. In the end, Soviet economic aid fostered the construction of enterprises responsible for 60% of India's oil production, 20% of its electrical power generation, 80% of its capacity for manufacturing heavy metallurgical equipment, and 60% of its manufacturing capacity for electric equipment, while more than 60% of India's military materiel was imported from the USSR.[10] Indeed, Khrushchev advised the Indians to "shout across the Himalayas" if they needed assistance from the Soviet Union.

The Soviet Union attempted to reach out to Pakistan after the United States cut off military aid to Pakistan in the aftermath of the 1965 India–Pakistan clash over Kashmir, in an effort to encourage Islamabad also to move toward a more nonaligned position and so reduce U.S. and Western influence in South Asia. Under the leadership of Premier Aleksei Kosygin, the USSR brokered a series of talks between Indian and Pakistani leaders in Tashkent in 1966 that helped to reduce tensions between both sides and increased Soviet visibility in the region.[11] The Soviet Union concluded an agreement with Pakistan on economic cooperation that same year, and Kosygin visited Pakistan in 1968.[12]

Moscow, however, was only willing to supply a limited quantity of weapons to Pakistan.[13] Under the leadership of General Yahya Khan, Pakistan returned to the U.S. orbit and also cultivated closer ties with the People's Republic of China, which now had increasingly tense relations with Moscow as well. In turn, India, feeling the effects of isolation both from the United States and from having fought a short, undeclared war with China in 1962, worked to cement a closer relationship with the Soviet Union. In 1971, New Delhi and Moscow concluded a treaty of "peace, friendship and cooperation" that, while falling short of an alliance, committed both sides to a strategic partnership.[14] Significantly, Article 9 committed both sides "to abstain from providing any assistance to any third country that engages in armed conflict with the other Party"; moreover, while neither side pledged to automatically come to the defense of the other in the event of war, both the Soviet Union and India agreed that "in the event of either being subjected to an attack or a threat thereof, the High Contracting Parties shall immediately enter into mutual consultations in order to remove such threat and to take appropriate effective measures to ensure peace and the security of their countries."

Soviet–Pakistan relations, on the other hand, sharply deteriorated after the 1979 invasion of Afghanistan, when the USSR intervened to prop up an Afghan Communist government. Pakistan under President Muhammed Zia-ul-Haq became a main sponsor of the anti-Soviet *mujahideen* fighters and also served as the conduit for dispersing millions of dollars in American and Saudi aid.[15] Indeed, the Soviet Union and Pakistan at times engaged in a covert proxy war— and not only on the territory of Afghanistan. While the Soviets attempted to exploit ethnic tensions in Pakistan itself, the Pakistani intelligence agencies were also engaged in operations inside the Soviet Union.[16]

When Mikhail Gorbachev took office, the USSR was engaged in counterinsurgency operations in Afghanistan and faced off against Pakistan, China, and the United States in South Asia. The entente with India was critical to Moscow's efforts to maintain its position in the region and served to bolster India against its historic rivals Pakistan and China.[17] Commenting on Indo-Soviet ties, Ronald H. Donaldson summed them up as follows: "Moscow's relationship with New Delhi has been built primarily on a mutual sense of need—a shared perception in which each states that the friendship of the other is essential to the preservation of its own security."[18]

THE IMMEDIATE POST–SOVIET POLICY

Mikhail Gorbachev's "new thinking" had a major impact on Soviet (and then Russian) relations with South Asia. Gorbachev's commitment to withdrawing from Afghanistan (the last Soviet troops left in February 1989) removed a major irritant in relations with the United States and Pakistan. His attempts to repair the frayed Sino-Soviet relationship and his vision for Moscow's role in Asia, as outlined in his 1986 Vladivostok address, constituted a strategic shift that in turn challenged the assumptions on which the Soviet-Indian partnership had been built for the previous two decades—and laid the groundwork for downgrading the importance of New Delhi.[19]

The collapse of the Soviet Union led to a temporary Russian withdrawal from South Asian affairs. And the tilt in Russian foreign policy during the early 1990s toward the Euro-Atlantic world downgraded relations in general with South Asia, which ranked seventh out of a list of 10 Russian foreign policy priorities as listed in the 1993 Foreign Policy Concept.[20]

The Soviet Union had withdrawn its combat forces from Afghanistan in 1989, but the new post–Soviet Russian government ceased all aid and assistance to the pro–Soviet government of Mohammed Najibullah, which hastened its collapse in the spring of 1992 and so removed what had been the critical point of friction with Pakistan. Improved relations with China and efforts to forge a post-Cold War relationship with the United States decreased India's strategic importance, and the severely weakened Russian economy did not have the resources to sustain Soviet-era aid and assistance programs to New Delhi. In particular, the collapse of Russian industry deprived India, particularly its armed forces, of military equipment and spare parts, in some cases dropping operational readiness of the Indian military's tanks and aircraft to an alarmingly low level of 25%.[21]

Moreover, in seeking an accommodation with the United States in the immediate post-Cold War period, the Russian government drastically reduced its scientific-military cooperation with India. Washington objected to the sale of cryogenic engines and other missile technologies for use in India's space program, arguing that this would violate the Missile Technology Control Regime. The United States wanted Russia's active assistance in preventing India from becoming a full-fledged nuclear power, as this would further destabilize the fragile India–Pakistan relationship.[22] Post-Soviet Russia also moved, in the negotiations to replace the original 1971 Peace and Friendship Treaty, not to commit to renewing the terms of Article 9.[23]

Relations between Moscow and New Delhi also suffered as Russia started a new diplomatic outreach to Pakistan. Initially, this opening was designed to ensure Pakistani support in getting back all remaining prisoners of war from the Afghan War who were still being held by Pakistani-backed *mujahideen* factions. The Russian vice president, Aleksandr Rutskoi, visited Pakistan in December 1991 and announced the effective abandonment of the Najibullah government and signed a joint communiqué with the Pakistanis calling for an "independent, non-aligned and Islamic Afghanistan."[24] Rutskoi's visit reflected the ascendancy of the anti–Soviet reaction in immediate post-Soviet Russian foreign policy. Since Pakistan had been a close ally of the United States, an effort was made to improve a newly democratic Russia's own ties to Islamabad. In addition, a number of the experts in the Russian Foreign Ministry argued that Pakistan "had a vital role in fulfilling Russia's immediate concerns of foreign policy and security, and that Islamic fundamentalism, boiling over in Russia's southern flank, would be best tackled by working closely with Pakistan . . ."[25] Moscow even endorsed a Pakistani proposal at the United Nations calling for a nuclear-free zone in South Asia—an approach that was directed against a nascent Indian nuclear capability. Moreover, Rutskoi's statement on Kashmir indicated a departure from earlier support for the Indian position on this disputed territory.

In the aftermath of the Afghan war, moreover, Pakistan's own usefulness to Washington was now at an end. As sanctions began to be imposed by the United

States on Pakistan for its nuclear program, Islamabad began to consider whether Russia might become an alternate supplier of arms and technologies. Two high-level Pakistani delegations, one led by Foreign Minister Akram Zaki, the other by Minister of State for Economic Affairs Sardar Assef Ahmad Ali, visited Russia in 1992.[26] Russia, for its part, adopted a policy of equidistance toward both Pakistan and India.[27]

But efforts to rebalance Russia's relations with the two South Asian powers failed. Unlike the major improvement in relations between Russia and Saudi Arabia that occurred once Moscow was no longer actively promoting an atheistic ideology that threatened the core interests of that key Islamic power, relations between Moscow and Islamabad continued to be strained throughout the 1990s. The fact that Islamist groups in Pakistan—some with ties to the state—continued to call for the further breakup of the Russian Federation, through the formation of Islamic federations in the Caucasus and in the Muslim areas of the Volga-Ural region, and evidence that suggested these groups were actively supporting separatists, notably in Chechnya, made it difficult to sustain a pro-Pakistani tilt in Russian foreign policy.[28] In contrast, India—itself concerned about the specter of separatism as it relates to Kashmir—extended full support to the Russian position on Chechnya. Moreover, the sense of shared danger from extremism emanating from Pakistan also led to cooperation in Afghanistan, supporting the Northern Alliance against the Pakistani-backed Taliban.[29]

As the initial enthusiasm for the Euro-Atlantic vector cooled in Moscow, restoring Soviet-era friendships became a higher priority for the Kremlin. Moreover, the "red directors"[30]—the CEOs of the state enterprises—were interested in restoring economic ties with India, particularly in the defense field. Boris Yeltsin visited India in January 1993 and signed a number of economic cooperation agreements; Indian Prime Minister P. V. Narasimha Rao paid a return visit to Russia in 1994 and completed the process of "untying the knots" that had crippled relations between Moscow and New Delhi.[31] When Prime Minister Viktor Chernomyrdin visited the country in November 1994, Russian–Indian ties were on the mend, and the appointment of Yevgeny Primakov as foreign minister in 1996 "rekindled the desire to work out a strategic partnership."[32] By choosing to make India his first foreign visit after assuming the ministry, Primakov signaled the renewed importance of India in his thinking about foreign policy after the years of neglect in the first part of the Yeltsin administration. The steel frame of the Russian–Indian relationship—a series of regular meetings between presidents and prime ministers, annual summits in one or the other country, and a plethora of working groups and intergovernmental commissions—was restored and in some cases upgraded. As a result, observers noted that within a span of 9 years after the collapse of the USSR, a new basis for a renewed strategic partnership between India and Russia had emerged.[33] Moreover, after Putin succeeded to the presidency, his insistence on having a more substantial "eastern policy" to balance the overemphasis on the Euro-Atlantic world during the Yeltsin years meant that there would be a push to rebuild Russia–India ties.[34] At the same time, the outbreak of the second Chechen war (in 1999) and Russian efforts to prevent the Taliban from completely taking over in Afghanistan complicated relations with Pakistan.[35]

THE FAILED RAPPROCHEMENT WITH PAKISTAN?

In the aftermath of 9/11, there were efforts in both Moscow and Islamabad to improve ties. General Pervez Musharraf "proposed burying all past misunderstandings between the two countries and focusing on their potential for building new relations"[36] and promised to share all the information about Chechen separatists and other Islamic militants involved in activities in Russia that Pakistan had collected.[37] When he conferred with Putin in Moscow in February 2003, Musharraf became the first Pakistani leader to visit Russia in more than three decades. He hoped to start a new dialogue that might lead to improved relations.[38] There were also pragmatic considerations; Musharraf was looking to diversify Pakistan's relationships and possibly obtain high-technology goods not available from the United States. Meanwhile, as India moved to improve its own relations with Washington, Russia's rapprochement with Islamabad was meant to send a signal to New Delhi that if India were to end "or significantly cut back on arms purchases from Russia, Moscow can readily sell weapons to Pakistan."[39] Finally, the personal chemistry between the two presidents was an important factor in helping to improve Russia–Pakistan relations.[40]

To try and better institutionalize the relationship, Putin and Musharraf agreed to create a Pakistan–Russia Consultative Group on Strategic Stability to provide a format for both sides to address concerns about regional security. Putin and Musharraf also carried out a diplomatic quid pro quo. Russia dropped any objections to Pakistan being given observer status in the Shanghai Cooperation Organization (SCO), while Pakistan helped Russia obtain observer status at the Organization of the Islamic Conference. Putin and Musharraf met again on the sidelines of the SCO summit in Shanghai in June 2006.[41] High-level contacts between Russian and Pakistani leaders now occur on a regular basis at SCO meetings.

As some disagreements have entered into the U.S.–Pakistan relationship over how to stabilize the situation in Afghanistan, this has created an opportunity for Russia to reach out to Islamabad. At the 2009 SCO summit in Yekaterinburg, Pakistan's President Asif Ali Zardari met with Russian President Medvedev and Afghanistan's President Hamid Karzai; at the end of July, these three leaders along with Tajikistan's President Emomali Rakhmon convened a quadrilateral regional security summit in Dushanbe. A second session was held in Sochi in August 2010.[42]

The thaw in Russia–Pakistan relations has led to some equities taking shape. In 2009, Russia lifted its objections to Pakistan's purchase of Chinese JF-17 fighter jets, powered by Russian RD-93 engines.[43] With the Russian defense industry always looking for new contracts, Russia is in no position to turn down potential sales of equipment and components to Pakistan.[44] Likewise, Russian firms have taken a greater interest in using Pakistan as a hub to distribute Russian energy in South Asia, connecting to proposed pipelines running through Central Asia[45] and Iran.[46] In October 2005, Gazprom's chairman Aleksei Miller visited Islamabad to discuss energy cooperation and signed a memorandum of understanding outlining areas for joint action.[47]

But when compared against the immense web of interests that undergird the Russia–India relationship, Russian ties to Pakistan are paltry, and the lack of specific, concrete Russo–Pakistani projects makes statements about improving relations very general and abstract.[48] Pakistan's Prime Minister Shaukat Aziz in 2007 lamented that his government's lack of military-technical cooperation with Russia was a manifestation of "old thinking" that precluded an improved relationship with Russia.[49] The departure of Pervez Musharraf in 2008 and the return to power of civilian leaders interested in restoring closer ties to the United States ended what might be termed Pakistan's Eurasian phase, signaled by moves to enter the Shanghai Cooperation Organization. The chemistry between Putin and Musharraf was never formalized into stronger government-to-government relations,[50] however, meaning that in the absence of a strong institutional framework, it has been extremely hard to generate the interest groups needed to sustain a Pakistani vector in Russian foreign policy. Most energy projects remain unrealized because of the war in Afghanistan. Smaller Russian firms have expressed interest in developing projects in Pakistan, but not much has been done to advance these proposals.[51] Should an Iran–Pakistan natural gas pipeline be constructed, Russia would be involved indirectly, because the Iranian gas that would be supplied would come from the South Pars field, in which Gazprom is an investor, and the Russians might assist in the construction of the line. However, at present, Russia does not have much of an energy partnership with Pakistan that could transform the bilateral relationship in the way that the gas trade has fundamentally altered the Russia–Turkey relationship. Indeed, much of the trade between Pakistan and Russia is indirect, conducted via intermediaries in Central Asia,[52] so no business lobby has emerged in either capital to push for improved relations.

Old issues also remain unresolved. Russia continues to adhere strongly to the Indian position on Kashmir, a stance reaffirmed in 2002 by Foreign Minister Igor

Ivanov.[53] Continued Pakistani support for the Taliban in Afghanistan and other militant groups means that the "perceptional gap" between Moscow and Islamabad endures; Russia still considers Pakistan to be sympathetic to groups that are destabilizing the North Caucasus and Central Asia[54] and who have managed to strike even in Moscow itself, especially after the January 2011 bombing at Domodedevo airport carried out by the Caucasus Emirate. Finally and most importantly, Russia is not willing to downgrade its relationship with India to improve ties with Pakistan. In March 2010, then–Prime Minister Putin emphasized that there would be no attempt to develop a strategic partnership with Pakistan, taking "into account the concerns of [our] Indian partners."[55]

Pakistan and Russia are no longer engaged in a cold war in Central Asia, and the foundations for an improved relationship have been laid: "Pakistan-Russia relations are undergoing a process of normalization, which presently is moving at a slow pace."[56] Yet even this slow pace could be jeopardized as the two states pursue different objectives in Afghanistan. Given continued Russian support to the Uzbeks and Tajiks who formerly constituted the Northern Alliance and Pakistan's preference for the Pashtuns who have made up the core of the Taliban and comprise a significant minority in their own country, there is a strong possibility that "the Russian-Pakistani relationship would most likely return to its accustomed mutual antagonism."[57] While Pakistan has supported efforts to bring the Taliban into the government of Afghanistan, Russian Deputy Foreign Minister Sergei Ryabkov reiterated that Russia "would definitely not accept what is being called re-Talibanization."[58]

In an effort to use shared economic interests as a way to mitigate differences between Moscow and Islamabad over Afghanistan and reflecting the influence of the energy companies in Russian foreign policy, the visit of Afghan President Karzai to Russia in January 2011 (the first visit of an Afghan leader to Moscow since 1991) saw several proposals advanced that would more closely tie Russia, Pakistan, and Afghanistan. Gazprom signaled interest in joining the Trans-Afghanistan Pipeline project, which would ship natural gas from Central Asia to Afghanistan and Pakistan (and possibly even India); the power utility Inter RAO presented plans for developing the infrastructure that would transmit excess electrical power from Central Asia to Afghanistan and Pakistan. On the other hand, possible deals to supply Russian military equipment to Afghanistan (despite the NATO mission, Afghan government forces still rely heavily on Soviet-derived equipment, which is plentiful in the country) could complicate matters if the strengthening of central government capacity undermined Pakistani interests.[59]

Growing tensions in the U.S.–Pakistan relationship in 2011, especially over the killing of Osama bin Laden on Pakistani soil by a U.S. Navy SEAL team and the

November deaths of Pakistani soldiers killed by American artillery strikes on the Pakistan-Afghanistan border, however, have kept the Pakistani vector on the table. In May 2011, Pakistani President Zardari traveled to Russia to try and build the frameworks for mutual cooperation in trade and energy projects. A working group to pursue energy cooperation met in October 2011, while the commander of Russia's ground forces, General Aleksandr Postnikov, has proposed to Pakistan's army chief of staff Afshaq Parvez Kayani closer military–military relations. And in February 2012, Pakistan's Foreign Minister Hina Rabbani Khar went to Moscow in an effort to further boost bilateral relations—and some in Pakistan are hoping that energy cooperation may be the way forward, as it proved to be in Turkey, for changing the dynamics of the Russia-Pakistan relationship.[60] Whether this amounts to a revival of Pakistan's Eurasian orientation, however, remains to be seen. Lavrov declared that improving Russia's relations with Pakistan would be a "foreign policy priority" in 2012—and Russian defense and energy firms believe that Pakistan represents a vast untapped market and have made some progress in getting new contracts signed.[61] But it is not clear that the modest improvement in Pakistani-Russian relations can impact the long-standing Indo-Russian partnership. As Dimitri Trenin concludes, "Moscow has yet to figure out how to deal with Pakistan without spoiling the relationship with New Delhi," and as long as this cipher remains unsolved, there can be no major improvements in Russia's relationship with Pakistan.[62]

THE MODEL PARTNERSHIP: INDIA

Post-Soviet Russia has a highly institutionalized partnership with India in place, one that stretches across the entire spectrum of the Russian foreign policy establishment. This means that no agency or ministry in Russia has a proprietary lock on the relationship with India, and it also signifies that there is broad support for good relations with New Delhi. Indian analysts themselves conclude: "The distinctive feature of the Russia–India relations nowadays is the exceptional intensity of political contacts with summits every year or even more often, meetings of bilateral intergovernmental commissions on cooperation, expanding ties between the regions of the two countries."[63] India is a regular destination for top-level delegations of the Russian government, and India, no less than the United States or European countries, is regularly visited by the president himself. In recent years, President Putin made a state visit to India in January 2007, and President Medvedev traveled to New Delhi in December 2008 and again in December 2010. Putin himself, in both his capacity as president and then as prime minister, made five summit-level visits to India between 2000 and 2010.[64]

Beyond the top-level contacts between presidents and prime ministers, the backbone of the India–Russia relationship is a series of commissions that ties together the relevant bureaucracies of the two governments. One of the most important is the India-Russia Inter-Governmental Commission on Military-Technical Cooperation (IRIGC-MTC), which handles all aspects of defense cooperation, planning, and development.[65] When Indian Defense Minister A. K. Antony met his Russian counterpart Anatoly Serdyukov in 2009 for the ninth session of the MTC, they were supervising some 200 joint defense projects—including the development of a new fifth-generation fighter.[66] India is extremely critical to the health of the Russian defense industry, as orders have supported Russia's research and development efforts into new weapons systems.[67] Indian financial support was vital in the development of the new SU-30 MK aircraft,[68] and India is expected to be the main purchaser of Russian-produced combat aircraft through 2025.[69] All in all, some 800 Russian defense firms depend on contracts with India.[70] Military analyst Ilya Kramnik pointed out, "The Indian leadership has decided that joint development is the most promising form of military-technical cooperation because it enables India to develop its scientific and technical expertise while obtaining the results guaranteed by its partner's more significant advancement."[71] In addition to a fifth-generation fighter, based on the recently unveiled Russian T-50, Russian design bureaus are helping India design new destroyers, frigates, and nuclear submarines, while India also continues to buy Russian vessels, such as frigates and submarines. Despite delays and setbacks, Russia is also retrofitting a former Soviet aircraft carrier (the *Admiral Gorshkov*) for Indian use as the *INS Vikramaditya*. Joint India–Russia cooperation has resulted in new weapons systems, such as an improved T-90 tank and the BrahMos supersonic cruise missile. In turn, through military cooperation with India in improving Russian designs, the prospect of selling weaponry to other markets has increased. Kramnik notes:

> In terms of the prospects for military-technical cooperation with India, it should be noted that Russia will likely continue to supply the bulk of aircraft and warships . . . the Indian Air Force and Navy are among the strongest in the world and require large supplies of modern technology to maintain their current force and underwrite their future development. Moreover, it is possible that in the future Russia and India will align to fill orders from third-party nations through joint production and export.[72]

And while India has broadened its defense cooperation in recent years with other states, notably Israel and the United States, "Nevertheless, Russia remains the only state willing to share defense technology of a strategic nature with

India."[73] The military cooperation agreement remains in force until 2020, and, as Anatoly Isaikin, the head of Rosoboronexport, observed, India remains Russia's largest strategic partner in military-technical cooperation.[74]

These defense projects are particularly important to Russian regions that depend on military contracts. Indian purchases of ships have enabled key regional employers, such as the Yantar shipyards in Kaliningrad, to remain in business.[75] Throughout the archipelago of the Russian defense industry, there is broad support for the India vector, given the importance of these contracts to the future of the military-industrial complex.

In addition to joint research-and-development projects, the Russian and Indian militaries undertake joint training exercises. In October 2010, both nations participated in the INDRA-2010 drill, a counterterrorism simulation in the Himalayan foothills. Since 2003, the Indian and Russian militaries have held regular joint training exercises, including biannual peacekeeping drills. INDRA-2005 (held in Agra) and INDRA-2007 (held in Pskov) were land-based operations; INDRA-2009 had six Russian ships, including the *Peter the Great,* the nuclear-powered missile cruiser, undertake live-fire drills with their Indian counterparts in the Arabian Sea.[76] Additional joint exercises are scheduled for 2013 and beyond.[77] Such exercises have built up the professional contacts between the two country's military establishments, which helps to reinforce the bilateral relationship.

The India-Russia Inter-Governmental Commission on Trade, Economic, Scientific, Technological and Cultural Cooperation (IRIGC) is cochaired by the external affairs minister from the Indian side and a deputy prime minister from the Russian side. In the Medvedev administration, this portfolio has been assigned both to Deputy Prime Minister Alexander Zhukov and the former defense minister, Sergei Ivanov. After his return to the presidency in 2012, Putin selected Deputy Prime Minister Dmitry Rogozin to represent the Russian side. The commission held its first meeting in 1994 and has 10 working groups combining officials from ministries and agencies in both countries.[78] The Integrated Long-Term Programme of Cooperation (ILTP) oversees joint research-and-development projects and is run jointly by India's Department of Science and Technology and by Russia's Academy of Sciences and the Ministry of Industry. To stimulate trade and investment, Russia's Ministry of Economic Development and India's Commerce and Industry Ministry facilitate business dialogues and have set up a joint study group to oversee the increasing levels of trade between the two countries. In their 2010 meeting, Elvira Nabiullina and Anand Sharma also inaugurated the Indian–Russian Investment and Technology Forum to further expand commercial ties between the two countries.[79] All of this has led to a robust revival of commerce between India and Russia (see Figure 9.1).

FIGURE 9.1

The Growth in Russian–Indian Trade, 2000–2011 (in billions of U.S. dollars)

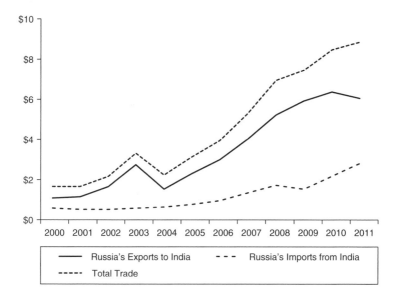

Source: State Customs Committee of the Russian Federation.

Since 2005, bilateral trade has grown at the rate of about 30% a year, and despite the economic downturn of 2008 to 2009, which depressed global trade overall, Indo-Russian trade during the worst months of the crisis actually increased by 17%. Deputy Prime Minister Alexander Zhukov, in his capacity as the cochair of the IRIGC, observed, "India is one of the very few countries with whom Russian trade is growing, rather than declining [in 2009]."[80]

Foreign and defense policy is also coordinated between the two governments. There is a Russian-Indian Joint Working Group on Combating International Terrorism and a joint group to confer about and coordinate policy on Afghanistan.[81] The Russian Foreign Ministry and the Indian External Affairs Ministry, every 2 years, lay out a common agenda of items to be discussed and maintain a regular system of consultations between a Russian deputy foreign minister designated to oversee the dialogue and the Indian foreign secretary. There is also a system for regular meetings between the Russian Security Council and the Indian National Security Council, with a "joint coordination group" functioning at the deputy level.[82] And, as we will discuss below, Russia also coordinates with India in international assemblies such as the Russia-India-China trilateral forum (RIC) and the BRIC (Brazil-Russia-India-China) forum.

The India–Russia partnership has also shown it can withstand the test of time as well as significant political changes in India. Partnership with Russia has been embraced by both conservative and left-leaning governments in India. The restoration of India's ties with Russia that had begun between Boris Yeltsin and Prime Minister P. V. Narasimha Rao continued when the National Democratic Alliance, headed by Atal Bihari Vajpayee, took power in 1998. Even though Vajpayee helped to initiate a warming of relations with the United States, Vajpayee did not neglect the Indo-Russian connection and during his November 2003 visit to Moscow signed a raft of new agreements with Russia, expanding military and technological cooperation.[83] Since 2004, although power shifted to the United Progressive Alliance, installing Manmohan Singh as prime minister, there has been no interruption of the partnership with Russia.

Part of the reason for the strong support for the partnership with Russia across the political spectrum in India has been Moscow's continued endorsement of India's aspirations to play a greater role in international affairs. In keeping with the Primakovian vision of a multipolar world, Russia has helped India in its efforts to be recognized as a global power. Russia invited India to be present at the G-8 summit in St. Petersburg in 2006.[84] Moscow has long backed New Delhi's aspiration to be granted a permanent position on the United Nations Security Council.[85] Russia has also backed India's aspirations to be recognized as a full member of the global nuclear club by promoting its full membership in the Missile Technology Control Regime and the Wassenaar Arrangement (another multilateral organization that supervises the spread of dual-use technologies).[86] Finally, in helping to create the BRIC, Russia endorsed the demands of the rising powers for changing the balance of power in international institutions; the BRIC has, in turn, emerged as a counterweight to the Euro-Atlantic bloc in world affairs.[87] (The BRIC will be discussed in greater detail in Chapter 10.) India backs many of Russia's proposals in international meetings because both parties are interested in a "profound rearrangement of the global financial and economic framework," to quote from a joint Indian–Russian communiqué issued in December 2008.[88] India also finds itself in some agreement with the Russian position on sovereignty—that decisions taken by a government internally should not be subject to review by other countries.[89]

While government-to-government ties are highly institutionalized, the links between the countries' two business communities have lagged. Both sides have set a target to increase trade between India and Russia to $20 billion by 2015. This led to the creation, in 2008, of the India-Russia Chamber of Commerce to facilitate ties between the Russian and Indian business communities.[90] The Russian-based Business Council on Cooperation with India, chaired by Sergei Cheremin, the vice president of Sistema (a Moscow-based conglomerate with approximately

$18 billion in annual revenue that focuses on telecommunications, real estate, banking, and technology), works to identify promising projects in coordination with the Confederation of Indian Industry (CII). The Chamber also sponsors a regular series of meetings under the aegis of the India-Russia Business Dialogue.[91] In advance of the 2010 India-Russia Summit, the business dialogue was issuing proposals for the creation of free economic zones and encouraging Russian and Indian conglomerates to set up joint ventures following the model trailblazed by Sistema and India's Shyam Group in the sphere of telecommunications.[92]

India is actively soliciting Russian investment, and Russian companies, who are looking for alternatives to overdependence on European markets, find the subcontinent to be a promising field for expansion.[93] Sistema, via its Sistema Shyam Teleservices venture, makes the Russian company the largest foreign investor in India.[94] In a sign, however, that Russian businesses do not enjoy a privileged position in India, this joint venture was stripped by the Supreme Court of telecom licenses it had received because of charges of corruption in how they were allotted.[95] While this case works its way through the Indian judicial system, it has put a damper on other Russian investment activities in India.

There is a desire to expand the relationship to cover areas such as biotechnology and alternative energy, fusing India's technology sector and Russia's research and industrial base. When Commerce and Industry Minister Anand Sharma traveled to Russia in June 2010, then–Prime Minister Putin stressed to him that Indian firms, in turn, would be welcomed in Russia's energy, pharmaceutical, and information technology sectors. Putin also indicated that the government would support a bid by India for inclusion in the Sakhalin-3 oil and gas project, and India's energy firm ONGC and Gazprom are investigating the possibility of developing a Liquefied Natural Gas (LNG) plant in the Yamal peninsula in Siberia that would ship energy directly to a growing Indian market.[96]

The energy partnership between the two countries serves a number of key strategic interests. By inviting Indian participation in the Sakhalin-1 oil and gas complex in 2001 (OGNC Videsh invested some $1.7 billion to obtain a 20% stake), the Russian government found a non–Western partner prepared to invest in a major energy venture, and the start of energy shipments from Sakhalin to India provides Russia with an alternate customer to China so as not to become dependent on Chinese demand. East Siberian oil allows India to diversify its oil imports, reducing dependence on the volatile Persian Gulf. Indian investors, led by the Gujarat State Petroleum Corporation, are investing in Russia's capacity to liquefy natural gas and to ship it by tanker from Russia's Far East to India—again an important step in New Delhi's efforts to secure energy supplies and an important hedge for Gazprom in order to give it alternatives to the European market.[97] Russia's Far East could end up becoming a new source of supply for India's vastly growing energy demands.[98]

Finally, Russia and India are cooperating in Central Asia. In keeping with the historic Russian interest in the north-south corridor, efforts are being made to develop a 21st-century version that would link St. Petersburg with Mumbai through a combination of rail, sea, and road routes via the Caspian Sea through Iran. In turn, India sees Russia as supporting its economic expansion into Central Asia (and serving as a counterweight to China's expanding influence in the region). But there have also been some important limitations. India's efforts to use Ayni airbase in Tajikistan to permanently deploy fighters and helicopters in Central Asia came to a close in early 2011, in part due to Russian opposition.[99] Developing a north-south energy corridor is also proceeding apace. Should a pipeline be built that connects Central Asia with India (the Trans-Afghanistan Pipeline Initiative, or TAPI, could be in place after 2014), it would be possible, using the existing network of lines that tie the Russian and Central Asian networks together, to ultimately send natural gas and oil from West Siberia to India, further assisting India's desire to secure energy supplies from areas other than the Persian Gulf and giving Russia an alternative to overdependence on European markets.[100] Gazprom has also been interested in building a pipeline that would connect Iran to Pakistan and India.[101] While it might seem counterintuitive for Russian companies to support a project that would increase Iran's market share in India, it actually serves key Russian interests. Gazprom is a shareholder in Iran's giant South Pars natural gas field and, more importantly, linking Iran's tremendous natural gas reserves to supply a growing South Asia market—which Russia could not by itself hope to dominate—removes Iranian gas as a threatening competitor for Russia's market access in Europe.

2010 saw two major Russian visits to India: that of Prime Minister Putin in March and President Medvedev in December. Putin arrived in New Delhi to sign new contracts worth up to $10 billion—including those for the purchase of Russian weapons and nuclear technology.[102] In addition, Putin worked to promote commercial ties designed to increase the volume of Indo-Russian trade, including new contracts for the leading firm Uralkali to ship fertilizer and the diamond concern ALROSA to supply diamonds directly to Indian firms, rather than selling them indirectly via De Beers. India looks to increase its 4% share of the Russian pharmaceutical market by becoming a larger supplier of medical goods to Russia. Building on pre-existing nuclear cooperation (Russia is helping to construct two nuclear reactors at Kundankulam), Putin agreed to a roadmap for cooperation that calls for the construction of an additional 12 reactors and the creation of a joint Russian-Indian venture to mine uranium in Sakha.[103]

President Medvedev's December 2010 visit to India resulted in a new package of agreements being signed across the entire spectrum, setting the parameters for Russia-India cooperation for the foreseeable future and again demonstrating the broad foundations for the Indian relationship in the Russian foreign policy establishment. At the Russia–India summit, both countries agreed to elevate their relationship to that of a Special and Privileged Strategic Partnership—although falling just short of a formal alliance. Significantly, the ILTP was extended and plans for joint military and counterterrorism exercises were discussed. And even a quick and partial perusal of the documents signed testifies not only to the breadth of the relationship but also to the various stakeholders who accompanied Medvedev on his trip:

- A preliminary design contract for the fifth-generation fighter aircraft between Hindustan Aeronautics Limited and Russia's Sukhoi Design Bureau and Rosoboronexport was signed.

- Alexander Leonov, Director-General of Machinostroyenie Production Association, and Sivathanu Pillai, Managing Director of BrahMos Aerospace, signed an agreement on expediting the deliveries of the jointly produced BrahMos cruise missiles for use in the Indian military.

- Russian Minister of Energy Sergei Shmatko and Indian Union Minister of Petroleum and Natural Gas Murli Deora signed an agreement on the development of cooperation in the oil and gas sphere.

- Russian Minister of Education Andrei Fursenko and Indian Union Minister of Science and Technology Kapil Sibal inked a program to promote cooperation to enhance technological innovation in Russian and Indian industry, including the creation of a joint center to be run by both ministries.

- Sergei Kiriyenko, Director-General of Rosatom Corporation, and Shrikumar Banergi, head of the Indian Commission for Atomic Energy, signed a memorandum of understanding on the expansion of scientific and technological cooperation in the peaceful use of the atomic energy.

- The Deputy Minister of Industry and Trade Denis Manturov and the head of the Indian Department of Pharmaceuticals Mukul Joshi signed a memorandum of understanding on cooperative projects in the fields of biotechnology and pharmaceuticals.

In addition, Russia's state investment bank Vneshekonombank reached agreements with the Bank of India and India's Export-Import Bank; Russian oil and petrochemical firm Sibur agreed to set up a joint venture; and Sistema signed a framework agreement with India's OHGC Oil and Gas corporation on producing hydrocarbons together.[104]

The degree of investment in the Indian economy across the sectors was clearly on display at the 4th Indian-Russian Forum on Trade and Investments, held to coincide with Medvedev's visit in December 2010. The forum, which started with the official opening of the Gazprombank office in New Delhi, testified to the growing financial linkages between the two countries and featured a series of Russian federal, regional, and business leaders. This included the deputy prime minister, Sergei Ivanov; Stanislav Voskresensky, the deputy minister for economic development; Denis Manturov, the deputy minister of trade; representatives from the regional governments including those of Kaluga, Volgograd, and Sakha; the presidents of major corporations such as Mikhail Shamolin of MTS, one of Russia's largest telecoms, and Aleksei Fedorov, the head of United Aircraft Corporation, and Sergei Kogogin, the general director of KAMAZ, the largest truck manufacturer in Russia, and senior representatives from Stroitransgaz, which builds energy pipelines, Atomenergomash, the nuclear power components manufacturer, and the major financial institutions Sberbank and Vneshekonombank.[105] The 2011 India-Russia summit, held in Moscow in December 2011 when Prime Minister Manmohan Singh traveled to Russia, reviewed the progress that has been made and reaffirmed the partnership between both countries.

But there have been difficulties in the bilateral relationship. In October 2012, Rogozin complained about Indian regulations and government actions that were delaying or negatively affecting Russian projects in India, including conflicts between the Russian firm Severstal and its Indian partner, delays in getting the Sistema telecom project up and running, and liability issues for nuclear projects. In turn, the Indian side complained about delays in receiving promised assets from Russia, including the refitting of the aircraft carrier *Admiral Gorshkov* and Indian access to oil and natural gas assets in Russia.[106] These tensions have led some Indians to advocate decreasing their reliance on Russia and turning to other countries, most notably the United States.

When India began to seek improved relations with the United States, there were concerns in Moscow that this would negatively impact the Indo–Russian partnership. Certainly India has benefited from closer ties with Washington, securing a landmark civil nuclear agreement and being granted permission to purchase high-technology U.S. goods and weaponry. India has chosen some U.S. products over Russian ones, most notably choosing to purchase Boeing Chinook helicopters instead of the Russian Mi-26s. However, despite all the rhetoric about a closer partnership between the world's "oldest and largest democracies," India and the United States still do not see eye to eye on a number of issues. America's interests in East Asia and South Asia—especially vis-à-vis China, Pakistan, and Afghanistan— do not necessarily converge with India's. A perceived willingness of the United States to seek a compromise between India and Pakistan on the status of Kashmir and Pakistan's status as a non–NATO ally of the United States also complicate matters. Finally, the United States has also not fully opened up its storehouse of technology for Indian use. This means that, as Neeta Lal concluded, "Moscow has deftly exploited this gap to bolster cooperation with New Delhi in sensitive areas such as reprocessing technology, as well as joint projects on the thorium-based fuel cycle and fast neutron reactors."[107] For its part, Russia is supplying India with its first nuclear-powered submarine. The Indian navy took delivery of a K-152 Nerpa nuclear-powered attack submarine, which left Russian waters in January 2012 with an Indian crew and took up service in the Indian navy in March as the *INS Chakra*.[108] India is also engaged[109] in discussions to lease a second submarine, which would enable the Amur Shipyard to finish work on a existing hull that was never completed due to lack of funds. Russia is also supplying technology to India so it can produce its own intercontinental ballistic missiles—aid that Indian officials acknowledged was absolutely essential: "Given [the] discriminatory attitude against India by some advanced countries, including the U.S. vis-à-vis sharing advanced technology over the last two decades, it was tough going for the missile project . . . till Russia agreed to come to India's rescue."[110]

Indeed, the 12th session of the IRIGC-MTC in October 2012 reconfirmed Russia's position as India's largest supplier of military technology and India as a main source of funding for Russia's own research-and-development programs. Indian Defense Minister Antony described Russia as India's "time-tested and reliable friend" and noted that with the various contracts now in the pipeline, India will spend some $50 billion over the next two decades to purchase Russian equipment. Even setbacks, such as the delay in providing India with the refurbished *Admiral Gorshkov* aircraft carrier (the *INS Vikramaditya*) to the end of 2013, have not dampened the pace of India–Russia cooperation.[111] Putin's visit to India in December 2012 for the yearly India–Russia summit saw both sides reaffirming their special relationship.

India cannot abandon Russia and is not prepared to sacrifice its existing relationship with Moscow in the hopes of better ties to Washington. As Vladimir Baranovsky, the deputy director of the Institute of World Economy and International Relations, concluded: "In an era of massive realignment, Russia appreciates India's continuing insistence with nonaligned status and its caution and restraint in development of ties with the United States of America."[112] India will continue to balance between Russia and the United States because, as Lal notes,

> India needs both Moscow and Washington in order to advance its strategic interests. The U.S. holds the key to an international legal architecture that enables India's pursuit of high technology programs, while Russia is a valued partner for strategic transfers. As a result, India is likely to continue pursuing a policy of vigorous engagement with America, even as it adds ballast to its old ties with Russia.[113]

THE RUSSIA–INDIA–CHINA TROIKA

When then–Foreign Minister Evgeny Primakov visited India in 1998, he proposed a trilateral framework among India, Russia, and China, in order to promote stability in Asia and to counteract the predominance of the United States in world affairs.[114] But while many in the United States interpreted this project as an anti–American gesture, there were other compelling reasons for Russia to try and bring China and India together. The pre-eminent challenge in Russian foreign affairs today is how to minimize the possibility of a major disruption in relations between Beijing and New Delhi—two historic rivals who see themselves as vying for predominance in Asia. Both India and China are key partners for Russia, and Moscow wants to avoid having to choose sides in the event of a clash between the two. The Russian Foreign Ministry thus has put a great deal of effort into creating the trilateral Russia-India-China (RIC) forum.[115] The defense industry has been a major supporter of the RIC approach, because, at the beginning of the millennium, Indian and Chinese purchases together represented some 80% of the value of Russian arms exports.[116]

Harnessing Russia to the two rising superpowers of the 21st century is also a way for Russia to regain some of its relevance in the global arena. Indian analysts, for instance, see in the RIC an attempt by

> Russia to check NATO's eastward expansion. It would pose as an alternative power bloc to the US and boost Russia's role in world politics. Some analysts say that Russia's aim is to solidify Moscow's place between East and the West, Atlantic and the Pacific, NATO and China.[117]

The RIC forum began informally in 2002, with meetings organized on the margins of major multilateral conferences, and the three heads of state met on the sidelines of the United Nations General Assembly in September 2003.[118] The first stand-alone meeting of the RIC occurred in June 2005, when the foreign ministers of China, India, and Russia assembled in Vladivostok to discuss issues of mutual concern to the three states. After Prime Minister Manmohan Singh, President Vladimir Putin, and President Hu Jintao met in St. Petersburg in July 2006 (during the G-8 summit), the foreign ministers again convened as the RIC in New Delhi in February 2007, inaugurating a regular set of RIC summits.[119] (Since the 2008 Yekaterinburg summit, where the foreign ministers of Russia, India, China, and Brazil met together [followed up by the summit of leaders in 2009, also in Yekaterinburg], the RIC has often met simultaneously during meetings of the BRIC, although there are also sometimes stand-alone meetings of the RIC.) The ninth RIC meeting was held at the end of October

2009 in Bangalore, when Russian Foreign Minister Sergei Lavrov, Chinese Foreign Minister Yang Jiechi, and India's External Affairs Minister S. M. Krishna met to discuss Afghanistan, regional security, and trade and investment opportunities. What also made this meeting significant is that the RIC meeting followed up on items discussed at the 15th session of the Indian–Russian intergovernmental commission meetings in Moscow and the sideline summit between Indian Prime Minister Manmohan Singh and Chinese Premier Wen Jiabao during the India–ASEAN meeting in Thailand.[120] Because the RIC also is folded into the larger BRIC process, it means that senior officials from all three states are having regular meetings and exchanges. As former Indian diplomat M. K. Bhadrakumar has noted, the RIC allows the "three big countries with common concerns in the Asian continent [to] come together within an exclusive format to discuss shared interests on the core issues of regional security . . . and coordinate their policies."[121]

RIC is not an alliance, nor does it presume that all three states must come to agreement on all policy issues. Instead, RIC is a platform to iron out differences and keep lines of communication between the parties open. There is also a belief that greater coordination between Russia, China, and India can help the three states gain leverage in international forums. Manish Chand argues that the greatest benefit of the RIC is that it has given the three countries "greater leverage on international issues where the West tends to impose its views through the West-controlled multilateral institutions."[122] Russia, India, and China share similar positions when it comes to matters such as the supremacy of state sovereignty, the overriding importance of territorial integrity (which led all three to oppose U.S. plans to recognize the independence of Kosovo), and a distrust of the concept of humanitarian intervention.[123] In addition to coordinating their positions in international organizations, the RIC also sponsors trilateral groups of experts on issues such as agriculture and health in an effort to promote greater ties between the three states.[124]

Building on the institutional framework of the RIC, Russia has been trying to encourage Sino–Indian rapport and to encourage India to play a greater role in the work of the Shanghai Cooperation Organization in the hopes of further decreasing tensions between Beijing and New Delhi.[125] Russia continues to push for Indian membership in the SCO and sponsored India to become an observer in 2005.[126] More recently, Russia has voiced some support for the idea of making both Pakistan and India full members—a position reiterated at the SCO foreign ministerial meeting in Beijing in May 2012.[127] Some Russian policy observers have wondered whether the SCO, if it expanded to encompass both India and Pakistan, could promote a degree of reconciliation not dissimilar to Franco–German rapprochement within NATO after World War II. So Russia will continue to use the

RIC and SCO formats to continue to balance its relations with Asia's two giants. Stanislav Secrieru, a European observer of Russia's Eastern policies, concluded:

> Relations with China are more intensive because of the frontier and the Central Asian neighborhood Russia shares with it but Moscow has strived to maintain the equilibrium and ease any suspicions on the Indian side. The economic crisis and strong performance of China and India only reconfirmed for Moscow that it needs to foster a balanced relationship.[128]

DRIVERS OF THE INDO–RUSSIAN ENTENTE

A number of factors drive Russian interest in India, which makes this relationship one of Russia's most important but also makes it difficult for Russia to alter its foreign policy trajectory in the South Asian vector. India remains one of Russia's largest customers for arms, but this relationship is being transformed from a simple buyer–seller relationship into projects for joint research and production of fourth- and fifth-generation systems, along with increased military cooperation. The Indian economic and strategic interest in Central Asia allows Russia to offset the increased presence of China; both countries also have similar interests in Afghanistan: preventing the marginalization of the Northern Alliance in favor of bringing the Taliban back into the government.

Russia's desire to promote its own alternate north–south trade and transport routes—linking Russia to the Persian Gulf and Indian Ocean—is designed to reduce the attractiveness of U.S.-sponsored projects along the Silk Road westward, especially to the states of Central Asia. The concept for the Socio-Economic Development of Russia sees increased business with South Asia—both in sales of commodities and in advanced technologies—as vital to the economic revitalization of Russia. In turn, trade ties with Russia help India avoid dependence on any one source, particularly in sensitive areas such as nuclear technology.

Russia's articulation of sovereign democracy resonates with the Indian political elite, who are also strong proponents of state sovereignty. As the weakest of the great powers, India and Russia also mutually reinforce each other's position in international institutions, seeking to prevent the marginalization of both Moscow and New Delhi in favor of the Big Three of the United States, Europe, and China. India and Russia share a common interest to avoid any division of the greater Eurasian continent into two spheres, one defined by the EU, the other by China. At the same time, the promotion of both the RIC and BRIC meetings offers both countries a way to hedge against the Euro-Atlantic community by including China (and Brazil) to forge a loose coalition of the rising South and

East to balance the Brussels-Washington axis. For all of these reasons, continuing the Indo-Russian entente serves the interests of both nations—even as they seek to improve or strengthen ties with other major powers.

NOTES

1. Nikitin wrote up his travels as the "Khozhdenie za tri moria" ("A Journey Across Three Seas"). Serge A. Zenkovsy has prepared an excerpted English translation, see his *Medieval Russia's Epics, Chronicles and Tales,* revised and expanded edition (New York: E. P. Dutton, 1963, 1974), 333–353.

2. Harold T. Cheshire, "The Expansion of Imperial Russia to the Indian Border," *Slavonic and East European Review* 13:37 (July 1934), 86.

3. Ibid., 86.

4. Skibinevskii's report can be found in the Arkhiv Gosudarstvennogo Soveta, Volume II: *Sovet v' Tsarstvovannie Imp. Pavla I (1796–1801)* (St. Petersburg: State Publishing House, 1888), 687–726; see also Nikolas K. Gvosdev, *Imperial Policies and Perspectives Toward Georgia, 1760–1819* (New York: St. Martin's Press, 2000), 79–81.

5. Alex Zotov has collected materials related to the Franco-Russian expedition to India at http://history-gatchina.ru/paul/india/india7.htm. Emperor Paul's directives are available letters to general Orlov RFO Archives f. 409, 8–12.

6. An overview of the "Great Game" is provided by Karl E. Meyer and Shareen Blair Brysac, *Tournament of Shadows: The Great Game and the Race for Empire in Central Asia* (Washington, DC: Counterpoint, 1999).

7. Aswini K. Ray, "Pakistan as a Factor in Indo-Soviet Relations," *Economic and Political Weekly* 1, no. 12 (November 5, 1966): 503.

8. For a discussion of Nehru's evolution in attitude toward the Soviet Union, see Sankar Ghose, *Jawaharlal Nehru: A Biography* (Bombay, India: Allied Publishing, Ltd., 1993), 272–275.

9. Azmat Kayat Khan, "Pakistan-Russia Relations: Pre- and Post-9/11 Perspective," *Rossiia I Islamskii Mir,* ed. M.S. Grikurov (Moscow: Kraft Plus, 2009), 42.

10. Jyotsna Bakshi, "Russian Policy towards South Asia," *Strategic Analysis* 23, no. 8 (November 1999): 1371.

11. Ray, 503.

12. Bakshi, 1370.

13. Khan, 43–44.

14. For India's perspective, see Robert L. Hardgrave Jr. and Stanley A. Kochanek, *India: Government and Politics in a Developing Nation,* 4th ed. (San Diego: Harcourt Brace Jovanovich, 1970, 1986), 356–358.

15. Khan, 44.

16. Milt Bearden and James Risen, *The Main Enemy: The Inside Story of the CIA's Final Showdown with the KGB* (New York: Random House, 2003), 290–296.

17. Narayan Menon, "India-Russia: Strategic Relations," *Indian Defence Review* 23, no. 1 (January–March 2008), at http://www.indiandefencereview.com/news/india-russia-strategic-relations/.

18. Ronald H. Donaldson, "Soviet Security Interests in South Asia," *The Subcontinent in World Politics: India, its Neighbors and the Great Powers,* ed. Lawrence Ziring (New York: Praeger, 1982), 184.

19. Subhash Kapila, "India-Russia Strategic Cooperation: Time to Move Away," *South Asia Analysis Group Paper no. 144,* September 7, 2000, at http://www.southasiaanalysis.org/paper144.

20. Bakshi, 1374.

21. Menon, op. cit. (http://www.indiandefencereview.com/news/india-russia-strategic-relations/).

22. Bakshi, 1380.

23. Kapila, op. cit.

24. Bakshi, 1373.

25. Menon, op. cit. (http://www.indiandefencereview.com/news/india-russia-strategic-relations/).

26. Khan, 45–46; Baskhi, 1377.

27. Nirmala Joshi, "India-Russia Relations and the Strategic Environment in Eurasia," *Eager Eyes Fixed on Eurasia, volume I, Russia and Its Neighbors in Crisis* (Sapporo: Slavic Research Center Hokkaido University, 2007), 204.

28. Bakshi, 1377–78.

29. Joshi, 204.

30. Anders Aslund, "Why Has Russia's Economic Transformation Been So Arduous?" Paper delivered at the World Bank Conference on Developmental Economics, April 28–30, 1999, at http://www.carnegieendowment.org/publications/index.cfm?fa=view&id=201.

31. Pavel Shinkarenko, "Trade with India will Double," *Current Digest of the Post–Soviet Press* 46, no. 26 (July 27, 1994): 23.

32. Ranjana Mishra, "Russia and India: BrahMos Reaffirms Faith," *Significance of Indo–Russian Relations in the 21st Century,* ed. V. D. Chopra (Delhi: Kalpaz Publications, 2008), 164.

33. Joshi, 195.

34. Felix N. Yuralov, "Russia: Problems of Security in Post Cold War World," *World Affairs* 4, no. 2 (April–June 2000): 55.

35. V. P. Dutt, "India-Russia Relations: Regional and Global Significance," *Significance of Indo-Russian Relations,* 24.

36. From a statement issued by ITAR-TASS, February 6, 2003.

37. Mark N. Katz, "Exploiting Rivalries for Prestige and Profit: An Assessment of Putin's Foreign Policy Approach," *Problems of Post-Communism* 52, no. 3 (May/June 2005): 32.

38. Fazal-ur-Rahman, "Pakistan's Evolving Relations with China, Russia and Central Asia," *Eager Eyes Fixed on Eurasia,* 223.

39. Katz, 33.

40. Rizwan Zeb, "Pakistan and the Shanghai Cooperation Organization," *China and Eurasia Forum Quarterly* 4, no. 4 (2006): 57.

41. Rahman, 223.

42. "Medvedev, Karzai, Zardari pledge united front on terror," *Agence France Press,* June 15, 2009; "Tajikistan: Russian President Medvedev Arrives in Dushanbe for Talks," *Eurasianet.org,* July 29, 2009, at http://www.eurasianet.org/departments/insightb/articles/ eav073009b.shtml; Stan Rogers, "Medvedev, Karzai, Rahmon, Zardari convene in Sochi," *Central Asia Online,* August 18, 2010, at http://centralasiaonline.com/cocoon/caii/xhtml/ en_GB/newsbriefs/caii/newsbriefs/2010/08/18/newsbrief-03.

43. Rupakjyoti Borah, "The Russia-India Partnership Loses Its Luster," *World Politics Review,* December 23, 2010, at http://www.worldpoliticsreview.com/articles/7421/the-russia-india-partnership-loses-its-luster.

44. Boris Volkhonsky, "Looking Back at New Delhi," *Vremya Novostei,* August 19, 2010, 2.

45. "Gazprom may take part in TAPI pipeline," *The Nation,* October 23, 2010, at http://www.nation.com.pk/pakistan-news-newspaper-daily-english-online/Business/23-Oct-2010/Gazprom-may-take-part-in-TAPI-pipeline.

46. "Iran, Pakistan, Russia to talk Gazprom's entry to IPI," *Tehran Times,* January 7, 2010, at http://www.tehrantimes.com/index_View.asp?code=211581.

47. Rahman, 224.

48. See the conclusion of Russian and Pakistani experts, in Zahid Anwar, "Pakistan-Russia Relations in a Regional and Global Context," *Central Asia-Caucasus Institute Analyst,* June 30, 2004, at http://www.cacianalyst.org/?q=node/2237.

49. V. N. Moskalenko, "Rossiisko-Pakistanskie Otnosheniia I Islam: Problemy I Perspektivy," *Rossiia I Islamskii Mir,* 77.

50. Zeb, 60.

51. "Russians interested in investing in oil, gas sector," *Daily Times,* April 13, 2006, at http://www.dailytimes.com.pk/default.asp?page=2006\04\13\story_13-4-2006_pg5_2.

52. Rahman, 224.

53. Joshi, 209.

54. Rahman, 222.

55. "Russia Against Developing Military Ties with Pakistan," *RIA Novosti,* March 12, 2010, at http://en.rian.ru/mlitary_news/20100312/158177001.html.

56. Rahman, 220.

57. Mark N. Katz, "Understanding Russia's Approach on Afghanistan, Pakistan," *EurasiaNet.org,* June 25, 2010, at http://www.eurasianet.org/node/61407.

58. Walter Pincus, "Russia's Ryabkov on U.S.-Russia relations: 'We can offer tangible results, and we will do more in the future,'" *Washington Post,* January 31, 2011, at http://www.washingtonpost.com/wp-dyn/content/article/2011/01/31/AR2011013105212.html.

59. Richard Weitz, "Russia's 'Return' to Afghanistan," *World Politics Review,* January 25, 2011, at http://www.worldpoliticsreview.com/articles/7653/global-insights-russias-return-to-afghanistan.

60. The hope that Russia would take part in the TAPI project is the basis for such assessments. See, for instance, the comments of Massood Khan, Pakistan's ambassador to

China: Andrey Evkin, "Russia seems to be getting more interested in the TAPI project," *ITAR-TASS,* August 23, 2011, at http://www.itar-tass.com/en/c38/209808.html.

61. Ali Ashraf Khan, "Happy New Year, Pakistan!" *Pakistan Observer,* January 7, 2012, at http://pakobserver.net/201201/07/detailnews.asp?id=134231. See also Saurav Jha, "Russia Looks to Build Strategic Leverage in Pakistan," *World Politics Review,* August 10, 2012, at http://www.worldpoliticsreview.com/articles/12252/russia-looks-to-build-strate gic-leverage-in-pakistan.

62. "Global Insider: Russia-Pakistan Relations," *World Politics Review,* February 18, 2011, at http://www.worldpoliticsreview.com/trend-lines/7933/global-insider-russia-pakistan-relations.

63. "A friendship between Russia and India never governed by transient political factors," *Daily News and Analysis,* December 22, 2010, at http://www.dnaindia.com/world/report_a-friendship-between-russia-and-india-never-governed-by-transient-political-factors_1484750.

64. Neeta Lal, "India, Russia and the U.S.: Three's a Crowd?" *World Politics Review,* April 6, 2010, at http://www.worldpoliticsreview.com/article.aspx?id=5378. Putin visited India in 2000, 2002, 2004, 2007, and 2010.

65. Dmitry Ermolayev, "2008—a landmark year in Russia-India relations," *Russia Beyond the Headlines,* June 7, 2008, at http://rbth.ru/articles/2008/06/07/india1.html.

66. Robert Bridge, "India and Russia's 'time-tested' military relationship rolls on," *Russia Today,* October 21, 2009, at http://rt.com/politics/india-russia-military-rolls/.

67. Alexander Rybas, "Breakthrough into the Global Arms Market," *Russia in Global Affairs* 2 (April–June 2008), at http://eng.globalaffairs.ru/numbers/23/1198.html.

68. Kapila, op. cit.

69. "Russia signs a $1.5-bln fighter jet contract with India," *RIA Novosti,* March 3, 2010, at http://en.rian.ru/mlitary_news/20100312/158174946.html.

70. Kapila, op. cit.

71. Ilya Kramnik, "From the Admiral Gorshkov to the T-50," *RIA Novosti,* December 22, 2010, at http://en.rian.ru/analysis/20101222/161887184.html.

72. Ibid.

73. Harsh V. Pant, "India, Russia Revive a Time-Tested Partnership," *World Politics Review,* October 15, 2010, at http://www.worldpoliticsreview.com/articles/6720/india-russia-revive-a-time-tested-partnership.

74. "India, Russia to Review Defence Ties," *Zee News,* October 4, 2011, at http://zeenews.india.com/news/nation/india-russia-to-review-defence-ties_734934.html.

75. "Yantar Shipyard to Transfer Tarkash Frigate to Indian Navy in Early Nov," *Interfax-AVN,* October 17, 2012, at http://www.interfax.co.uk/russia-military-news/yantar-shipyard-to-transfer-tarkash-frigate-to-indian-navy-in-early-nov/.

76. "Russian-Indian Indra 2010 military exercises ends," *Frontier India,* October 25, 2010, at http://frontierindia.net/russian-indian-indra-2010-military-exercises-ends; "Russian, Indian troops complete military exercises in Himalayas," *RIA Novosti,* October 23, 2010, at http://en.rian.ru/mlitary_news/20101023/161062082.html; "Russia, India to hold joint naval exercise in January," *Thaindian,* January 11, 2009, at http://www.thain

dian.com/newsportal/politics/russia-india-to-hold-joint-naval-exercise-in-january_1001 41117.html.

77. "Russian-Indian Anti-Piracy Drills to Take Place in India in Late 2012-Early 2013," *Interfax,* October 11, 2012.

78. Manohar Singh Batra, "Sixty Years of India-Russia Cooperation," *Significance of Indo-Russian Relations,* 90.

79. Sergei Borovkov, "Russia-India: Cooperation levels below potential?" *Russia and India report,* June 30, 2010, at http://in.rbth.ru/articles/2010/06/30/300610_spbforum .html.

80. Vladimir Radyuhin, "India-Russia trade target set at $20 b," *The Hindu,* September 30, 2009, at http://www.hindu.com/2009/09/30/stories/2009093055791400.htm.

81. Dutt, 24.

82. Based on materials obtained from India's External Affairs Ministry.

83. Batra, 92.

84. Tatiana Zakaurtseva, "The Current Foreign Policy of Russia," *Eager Eyes Fixed on Eurasia,* 111.

85. "Russia supports India UN seat quest, clinches deals," *Kuwait Times,* December 22, 2010, at http://www.europenews.net/story.php?rid=41449642.

86. "Russia, India sign package of 30 documents," *Russia and India Report,* December 21, 2010, at http://indrus.in/articles/2010/12/21/russia_india_sign_package_of_30_docu ments05000.html.

87. Lal, op. cit.

88. From the December 2008 joint Indian–Russian declaration, quoted in Sergei Vladimirov, "Russia and India: Bilateral Cooperation Elevated to Strategic Level," *Rossiiskie Vesti* 43 (December 11–17, 2008): 5.

89. See, for instance, Leonid Polyakov, "Sovereign Democracy as a Concept for Russia," *Russia Beyond the Headlines,* October 25, 2007, at http://rbth.ru/articles/2007/10/25/ sovereign_democracy_as_a_concept_for_russia.html.

90. Ermolayev, op. cit.

91. Vinay Shkula, "CII seeks acceleration in Russia-India trade," *Press Trust of India,* June 18, 2010, at http://business.rediff.com/report/2010/jun/18/cii-seeks-acceleration-in-rus-ind-trade.htm.

92. "Russia intends to create $3 billion free economic zone in India," *RIA Novosti,* March 12, 2010, at http://en.rian.ru/russia/20100312/158172157.html.

93. Nick Amies, "Putin's India visit part of Russia's balancing act with Asia's rising powers," *Deutsche Welle,* March 10, 2010, at http://www.dw-world.de/dw/article/0,,5334 948,00.html.

94. Vladimr Radyuhin, "Russia Invites Indian Investment," *The Hindu,* June 19, 2010, at http://beta.thehindu.com/business/Economy/article474492.ece.

95. Olga Razumovskaya, "Sistema Shyam not to participate in India spectrum auction," *Dow Jones Newswire,* October 19, 2012, at http://www.totaltele.com/view.aspx? ID=477188.

96. Radyuhin, op. cit.

97. Sanjay Dutta, "Sakhalin route to energy security," *Times of India,* December 8, 2006, at http://articles.timesofindia.indiatimes.com/2006-12-08/india-business/27801781_1_sakhalin-3-gas-field-ongc-videsh; Venera Reztsova, "Asia-Pacific energy race hots up," *Russia and India Report,* February 4, 2011, at http://indrus.in/articles/2011/02/04/asia-pacific_energy_race_hots_up_12129.html.

98. Joshi, 208.

99. Martin Sieff, "Indian-Tajik air base negotiations expose India's limited regional influence," *Central Asia Newswire,* January 3, 2011, at http://centralasianewswire.com/Security/Indian-Tajik-air-base-negotiations-demonstrate-Indiarsquos-limited-influence/viewstory.aspx?id=2820.

100. Reztsvoa, op. cit.

101. Robert M. Cutler, "India Seeks To Re-enter Iran-Pakistan Gas Deal," *CACI Analyst,* April 28, 2010, at http://www.cacianalyst.org/?q=node/5314.

102. "Putin Begins Working Visit to India," *RIA Novosti,* March 12, 2010, at http://en.rian.ru/world/20100312/158167637.html.

103. Gleb Ivashentsov, "India and Russia: Longstanding and Good Partners," *International Affairs* 4 (2010): 62-63.

104. "Russia, India sign package of 30 documents," *Russia and India Report,* December 21, 2010, at http://indrus.in/articles/2010/12/21/russia_india_sign_package_of_30_documents05000.html.

105. A full list of the speakers at this event is archived at http://en.restec-international.com/projects/india/programme/.

106. "Russia unhappy with delays in joint projects," *The Hindu,* October 15, 2012, at http://www.thehindu.com/news/national/russia-unhappy-with-delays-in-joint-projects/article3999928.ece.

107. Lal, op. cit.

108. "Russian Nuclear Submarine to Reach Indian Shores in Mid-March," *Indo-Asian News Service,* February 28, 2012, at http://www.ndtv.com/article/india/russian-submarine-to-reach-indian-shores-mid-march-180705.

109. Vladimir Radyuhin, "India in talks with Russia on lease of second nuclear submarine," *The Hindu,* March 13, 2013, at http://www.thehindu.com/news/international/india-in-talks-with-russia-on-lease-of-second-nuclear-submarine/article4505333.ece.

110. Rahul Datta, "With Russian Help, India To Join ICBM Big League," *The Pioneer,* October 8, 2011, at http://www.defence.pk/forums/indian-defence/133548-russian-help-india-join-icbm-big-league-soon.html.

111. "India, Russia Line Up Mega Defence Deals," *Times of India,* October 11, 2012, at http://timesofindia.indiatimes.com/india/India-Russia-line-up-mega-defence-deals/articleshow/16759670.cms.

112. Vladimir Baranovsky, "Challenges and Opportunities for National and International Security," *Russia and Asia: The Emerging Security Agenda,* ed. Gennady Chufrin (Oxford: Oxford University Press, 1999), 25-26.

113. Lal, op. cit.

114. Pant, op. cit.

115. M. K. Bhadrakumar, "Russia, India and China go their ways," *Asia Times,* November 5, 2009, at http://www.atimes.com/atimes/Central_Asia/KK05Ag01.html.

116. Rybas, op. cit.

117. Abanti Bhattacharya, "The Fallacy in the Russia-India-China Triangle," *Strategic Analysis* 28, no. 2 (April–June 2004): 260.

118. Suvorkarnal Dutta, "The India-China-Russia Troika: Is it Possible?" *Merinews,* October 26, 2007, at http://www.merinews.com/article/the-india-china-russia-troika-is-it-possible/127244.shtml.

119. Rajiv Sikri, "India-China-Russia: Alliance in the making?" *South Asia Analysis Group* paper no. 2152 (February 26, 2007), at http://www.rediff.com/news/2007/feb/22 guest.htm.

120. "Russia, India, China trilateral meet starts in Bangalore," *Thaindian News,* October 29, 2009, at http://www.thaindian.com/newsportal/business/russia-india-china-trilateral-meet-starts-in-bangalore_100266096.html.

121. Bhadrakumar, "Russia, India and China," op. cit.

122. Manish Chand, "Russia-India-China triangle: Promise and reality," *Russia and India Report,* June 30, 2010, at http://in.rbth.ru/articles/2010/06/30/300610_ric.html.

123. Nikolas K. Gvosdev, "Kagan's Dreaming," *National Interest,* May 8, 2008, at http://nationalinterest.org/article/kagans-dreaming-2086.

124. Chand, op. cit.

125. M. K. Bhadrakumar, "India, Russia Regain Elan of Friendship," *Asia Times,* December 9, 2008, 1, at http://www.atimes.com/atimes/South_Asia/JL09Df02.html.

126. Siddharth Varadarajan, "Russia, India, China won't cross U.S. on AfPak," *The Hindu,* November 16, 2010, at http://www.hindu.com/2010/11/16/stories/2010111655781 200.htm.

127. "Russia calls to speed up India and Pakistan joining SCO," *Russia Today,* May 12, 2012, at http://rt.com/politics/russia-sco-pakistan-india-lavrov-076/.

128. Amies, op. cit.

CHAPTER 10

Africa and Latin America

The Southern Vector

T he southern vector is the least developed of Russia's foreign policy orienta-
tions, in part because Africa and Latin America have historically had few
connections to Russia. It is true that there were some contacts with Africa (via
the Orthodox Patriarchate of Alexandria) in the days of Kievan Rus,' and the
merchant Afanasy Nikitin, in attempting to open a trading route between Russia
and India, both met with Ethiopians in India and, on his return to Russia,
stopped in Ethiopia for "five days."[1] In 1723, Peter the Great sent an expedition
to open relations with the island of Madagascar (and to explore the possibility of
planting a Russian colony there) in order to create a base for trade with Africa
and India. Peter also explored the possibility of forging closer ties with the
Ethiopian state.[2] By the 19th century, there was in fact a small but growing commercial and diplomatic connection between the Russian Empire and Ethiopia,
forged in part on the basis of similarities between the Russian and Ethiopian
Orthodox Churches. Tsar Nicholas II extended some support—including military
supplies—to Emperor Menelik II, which helped the Ethiopians to resist Italian
encroachments and prevent Ethiopia's colonization.[3] But much of Africa was of
little interest to the Russian state, and Russia was the only European power not
to engage in the "scramble for Africa."

Latin America was similarly a region beyond the pale for Russian interests in
tsarist times. While there was some intermittent contact between the Russian
and Spanish colonies in the Americas, Latin America was not a particular priority
or interest to the Russian Empire. For instance, diplomatic relations between
Russia and Argentina were not started until 1885 and those with Mexico were not
established until 1890.[4]

After the 1917 October Revolution, the Communists who took power, in looking for allies in spreading the world revolution, began to look further afield than
the traditional regions of interest to tsarist foreign policy. After the failure of
revolutionary movements to take power in Western Europe in the aftermath of
World War I, Vladimir Lenin concluded that the new Soviet state might have to
turn to the less-developed world, including Africa and Latin America, noting:

> . . . in the coming decisive battles of the world revolution, this movement of
> the majority of the world's population, originally aimed at national liberation,

will turn against capitalism and imperialism and will, perhaps, play a much more revolutionary role than we have been led to expect.[5]

Josef Stalin's preoccupation with "building socialism in one country" in the 1930s and in obtaining control over the Soviet bloc in Europe and East Asia after World War II meant that the southern vector was less important during this time. However, Nikita Khrushchev saw new openings for advancing the Soviet Union's global position by positioning the USSR as a more attractive alternative to developing countries to obtain economic assistance for modernization, declaring: "Today, they need not go begging for up-to-date equipment to their former oppressors. They can get it in the socialist countries, without assuming any political or military commitments."[6] In addition, the Soviet Union offered large numbers of scholarships to students from developing countries.[7]

Beginning in the mid-1950s, the Soviet Union set up industrial plants, offered advantageous terms of trade for both raw materials like oil and developed goods (such as weaponry and machinery), and provided educational opportunities for thousands of students from Africa, Asia, and Latin America. It also backed revolutionary movements that either sought to throw off colonial rule or to overthrow pro-Western governments.[8] In some cases, Moscow sought to create Communist governments; in other cases, it backed non-Communist but left-wing and anti-Western nationalist movements. There were also strategic considerations at play: The development of ties between Latin American and African states and the USSR allowed Moscow to break the "encirclement" of the Eurasian landmass by the United States and its allies and, significantly, gave the Soviets access to naval and air facilities to greatly expand their global reach.

The successful rebellion of Fidel Castro in Cuba (1959) and the advent of decolonization in Africa laid the basis for the emergence of a Soviet bloc in Africa and Latin America, in parts of the world where there had been no previous, tsarist Russian influence. By 1980, the Soviet Union could count as it allies Cuba, Nicaragua, and Grenada in the Western Hemisphere (with pro-Soviet rebels in El Salvador gaining in strength and influence); in Africa, countries like Angola, Ethiopia, Somalia, Congo, Mozambique, Zambia, Guinea Bissau, and Benin were firmly in the Soviet camp. Revolutionary movements such as the African National Congress (in South Africa), the South-West African People's Organization (in Namibia), and the Zimbabwe African People's Union were backed by Moscow. Other Latin American and African states (such as Peru or Nigeria), which remained generally pro-Western in orientation, nevertheless accepted aid from the Soviet Union and helped to extend Moscow's global reach. In particular, the Soviet outreach to these parts of the world enabled these countries to turn to Moscow for aid, arms and support if Washington was not forthcoming. For instance, when the United States refused to sell weaponry to Nigeria during the Biafran rebellion (1967–1970), the Soviet Union attempted to gain greater influence by becoming an alternate supplier of military equipment.

The Soviet presence in areas of the world far removed from its Eurasian core helped to validate Moscow's self-image as a global superpower. Yuri Andropov, the chairman of the KGB (who subsequently became General Secretary of the Communist Party from 1982 to his death in 1984), argued that the rise of Soviet influence in the Third World was shifting the global balance of power in Moscow's favor.[9]

However, support for the southern vector—or, as it was termed in Soviet times, a "forward policy"—in the countries of the Third World was not evenly distributed among all sectors of the Soviet foreign policy apparatus. In particular, a noticeable divide opened up between the Foreign Ministry on the one hand and the International Department of the Central Committee of the Communist Party on the other. The Foreign Ministry tended to focus on Moscow's relations with the great powers, especially the United States, and to be concerned with the key developments in Europe and Asia. In particular, Andrei Gromyko, the long-serving Soviet foreign minister, saw Soviet adventures in the Third World as a distraction and an unnecessarily complicating factor in Soviet relations with the United States. Senior Soviet leaders also did not travel to Africa or Latin America; one exception was Leonid Brezhnev's decision, in 1975, to attend a Communist Party congress in Cuba. As a result, the International Department of the Communist Party and the intelligence services, including the KGB, tended to take the lead in handling relations with Latin America and Africa.[10]

Moreover, Soviet assistance to Africa and Latin America was extremely costly. In addition to the outright expenditures on aid and assistance, lopsided terms of trade—with the Soviet Union purchasing goods from client states as a way to support their economies or supplying oil or machinery at lower-than-market prices—negatively impacted the Soviet economy. A Soviet foreign trade minister, Boris Aristov, complained, "We import large amounts of various primary goods and materials whose purchases can be cut considerably provided they can be produced at home. . . . It is unjustifiable to import . . . goods which can and should be produced at home."[11]

It was inevitable that during the tenure of Mikhail S. Gorbachev, there would be a significant re-evaluation of Soviet foreign policy priorities in Africa and Latin America. Indeed,

> The Gorbachev era was marked by a growing sense that involvement in sub-Saharan Africa represented an unacceptable drain on Soviet resources, by deepening pessimism about the region's revolutionary potential, and by an increasing conviction that its manifold problems were peripheral to Soviet interests.[12]

In 1990, he notified Soviet aid recipients in the developing world that the assistance they received from Moscow would be reviewed to take into account the "real capabilities of our country."[13]

Gorbachev also worked to terminate proxy wars and struggles with the United States in the Third World. As the ex–Soviet president noted in 2000,

> joint actions by the two governments began, coordinated with other interested countries, aimed at resolving conflicts in Africa (Namibia, Angola, Mozambique), Asia (above all, in Cambodia) and Central America. These joint efforts produced quite satisfactory results in Namibia and Central America.[14]

While Moscow hoped that pro–Soviet regimes might yet survive in place—or that Soviet influence could still be maintained with neutral regimes—the reality is that many of Moscow's Third World allies either collapsed or were overthrown. In the space of a few short years, major Soviet partners like the Sandinistas in Nicaragua or the Dergue in Ethiopia were swept away. Gorbachev also began to pull back the Soviet presence, for instance, withdrawing the Soviet military brigade that had been stationed in Cuba.[15]

When the Soviet Union itself collapsed, the Yeltsin administration moved quickly to terminate what it saw as Soviet liabilities draining a post–Soviet Russia. Moscow was no longer committed to a struggle for influence in the Third World with the United States. The Yeltsin government terminated Soviet foreign aid programs for African and Latin American states, began to demand that previous loans be repaid promptly to a cash-strapped Russia, and closed embassies and consulates in order to save money. Trade relations plummeted. If Soviet trade with African countries had been valued at $2.7 billion in 1990, it fell to only $740 million by 1994.[16] Russian trade with Cuba also collapsed; the 1992 level of trade between Moscow and Havana was a scant 7% of the activity in 1991.[17]

For the Atlanticists who dominated foreign-policy decision making in the Russian Federation during the first term of the Yeltsin administration, Russia's future was best secured by pursuing integration with the Euro-Atlantic region, and so relations with the countries of the southern vector were deemed of low importance by the government.[18] Indeed, some within the foreign policy establishment blamed "Russia's economic woes partly on its inherited Third World debt" and wanted to end Russian involvement in this part of the world.[19] Given the lack of state interest, it was acknowledged that the motor powering Russian interest in this part of the world would "have to be private enterprise."[20] However, given its own economic difficulties during this period, the face of this effort was often that of shadowy arms dealers (like Viktor Bout), brokering sales of surplus Soviet military equipment in shady deals throughout Africa and Latin America (and captured in a 2005 film, *The Lord of War,* based largely on Bout's own career).[21]

During his tenure as foreign minister, Yevgeny Primakov began to refocus Russian interest in Latin America and Africa, arguing that "Russia naturally should have multilateral ties with all continents."[22] Putin's election as president in 2000 and his reliance on former and current members of the security services to staff his presidential administration also meant that there were a number of veterans with African and Latin American experience, among them Igor Sechin and Viktor Ivanov, both of whom served as aides to the president.

THE RETURN TO AFRICA

When asked to assess the state of Russian relations with the countries of sub–Saharan Africa, Oleg Muradyan, a vice president with the state-owned investment bank VTB, commented that the decade-long pause in Moscow's involvement in the continent "was caused by the demise of the Soviet Union and the chaotic period of meltdown and rebound in the Russian economy."[23] The recovery of the Russian economy and the search by Russian companies for new sources of oil, gas, and raw materials to augment Russia's own natural resource base helped to propel the return to Africa. Mikhail Margelov, the chairman of the Foreign Affairs Committee of the Federation Council (and often used as a special envoy for African affairs), concluded:

> After the break in the 1990s, Russia is making a comeback to the African continent. Russian oil companies and mining companies are already operating in African countries; they have announced investment plans totaling up to $10 billion for those countries.[24]

Russia's ability to forge new connections in Africa is based in part on the 50,000 or so African alumni of Soviet universities and other training programs, many of whom have moved into key political and business positions. By 2002, these included three heads of state—Thabo Mbeki of South Africa, José Eduardo dos Santos of Angola, and Amadou Toumani Touré of Mali.[25] Such "personal links developed during the time of the Soviet Union" were invaluable in helping to set up new business opportunities.[26] For instance, Muradyan argued that VTB was able to find a positive climate for its operations in Namibia because of the "Soviet support for the South West African People's Organization which fought against apartheid for the country's independence" from South Africa.[27] African leaders, for their part, were interested in better and expanded ties with Moscow as a way to counterbalance Western and Chinese interests in the continent.[28] To capitalize on this trend, Putin also appointed (in 2006) Alexei M. Vasiliev, director of the Institute for African Studies, as his Special Envoy for Liaison with African leaders.[29] Moreover, some of those close to Putin in the presidential administration were former special services personnel who had Africa experience, among them Igor Sechin, who ended up becoming a deputy prime minister and has also been involved in overseeing several state companies.[30] These influences led Putin to undertake visits to Africa, a region that had been completely ignored by his predecessor.

Putin moved to cancel some of the debt owed by African countries for developmental projects and military supplies incurred during the Cold War (approximately $20 billion was forgiven by 2007). Russian personnel were also dispatched to eight UN peacekeeping operations on the continent.[31] African leaders began to include Moscow as a stop, with Putin welcoming the leaders of Gabon, Guinea, Nigeria, and Ethiopia during his first term of office. Foreign Minister Sergei Lavrov also made the case that Russia was prepared to act as a representative for the interests of African states in multilateral fora such as the Group of Eight, noting that "Russia continues to be an influential player in the system of global ties" and would "seek to use the authority and weight of our country on the international scene in the course of the solution of the tasks of development, particularly those directly affecting the interests of the African continent."[32]

One of the things that is most striking about Russia's Africa policy, however, is the extent to which it is *not* driven by the Foreign Ministry or the traditional foreign policy bureaucracy. Nor, other than the antipiracy mission off the waters of Somalia, is there much interest in Africa from the military establishment.[33] Vasiliev, the first special envoy for Africa, was an academic; his successor, Margelov, is a member of the upper house of the legislature. In addition, Africa is one of the areas in which "business diplomacy" is very much in evidence and where Russian firms—both private and state-owned companies like Norilsk Nickel, RUSAL, Renova, ALROSA, LUKoil, Rosneft, and Stroitransgaz—are advancing Russian interests.[34] If, during the Cold War, Soviet diplomats focused on gaining control of strategic territories, the emphasis today is on defending and expanding Russian business opportunities throughout the region.[35] The key government figure on Africa, especially during the second part of the first Putin administration and in the Medvedev administration, was not a foreign policy functionary but the Minister of Natural Resources, Yuri Trutnev, who chaired the intergovernmental commissions dealing with relations with South Africa, Guinea, Angola, and Namibia.

This highlights the importance that Russia puts on economic projects for building stronger ties to Africa. In Angola, South Africa, and Namibia, Trutnev's interlocutors were not government ministers in charge of the economy but the foreign ministers, acknowledging his wide brief in handling Russia's bilateral relations beyond a narrow economic portfolio.[36] And when Medvedev made a presidential visit to Africa in 2009, he was accompanied not by his "hard power" ministers (defense or foreign affairs) but by Trutnev, as well as leading Russian business figures.[37] Since 2012, another key figure in Russia's Africa diplomacy has been Industry and Trade Minister Denis Manturov, again highlighting how economics plays the key role in determining Russian policy toward this region.

Throughout the continent, Russia is offering itself as a business partner. In southern Africa, the focus is on offering Russia as an alternative to Western or Chinese firms in resource extraction efforts and helping build up the industrial and technological base, particularly in South Africa. An energy strategy for West Africa seeks to develop a trans-Sahara pipeline that would transport West African sources of energy to European markets, augmented with natural gas from Algeria. Here, relations with Nigeria play a critical role.[38] Finally, in North Africa, Moscow wants new energy contracts for its companies and also to expand military-technical cooperation as these states seek to use oil and gas revenue to update their armed forces.[39] Russia also hopes to leverage its own technical assistance as a basis for gaining footholds throughout the continent; during Dmitry Medvedev's 2009 tour of Africa, he inked deals providing for a variety of new economic ventures, including "the establishment of a joint venture between Gazprom and the Nigerian National Petroleum Corporation and on the establishment, with Russian assistance, of the Angolan national satellite communication and broadcasting system Angosat."[40]

The Russian business community plays a major role in keeping Africa on the foreign policy agenda. Four leading Russian conglomerates—RUSAL, Norilsk Nickel, ALROSA, and Renova—have investments in sub-Saharan Africa totaling more than $5 billion.[41] It is also important to note that of these four, only one—ALROSA—is a state company; the others are private. Private firms like oil major LUKoil are the ones spearheading new development projects in West Africa, not the Russian state.[42] The most effective lobbyist for southern Africa in Moscow is not a government figure but Viktor Vekselberg, the president of the Renova Group, the cochairman of the Russia-South Africa Business Council, set up when Vladimir Putin visited South Africa in 2006.[43] In contrast to the Soviet pattern, where the state sponsored major developmental projects in an effort to project Moscow's influence, Russian businesses today are engaged in smaller-scale activities. Igor Yurgens, in his capacity as the chairman of the board of directors of Renaissance Capital, had this to say about Russia's economic strategy for Africa:

> When the energy situation stabilises, other projects will follow, such as telecoms and mining. Russia is unlikely to undertake megaprojects, such as the Aswan Dam, but its nuclear energy expertise could prove useful. By helping Africa, we are also helping ourselves.[44]

The importance of Russian business in driving Africa policy was again reinforced during Manturov's October 2012 visit to southern Africa; accompanying the minister in his meetings in Mozambique and Zimbabwe were representatives of a number of major Russian firms, including Russian Helicopter, the oil firm Rosneft, and Norilsk Nickel.[45]

The active involvement of the business community in Africa policy is seen via its role in helping to set up government-to-government contacts. In 2009, the Russian Chamber of Industry and Commerce elected Vladimir Vasiliev, the chairman of the state-controlled investment bank Vnesheconombank, as chairman of the Coordinating Committee on Economic Cooperation with African Countries to the South of the Sahara, a group that enjoys the support of Vasiliev, the presidential envoy to Africa.[46] The 2010 International Parliamentary Assembly Conference Russia-Africa, which brought the legislators of various African states to Moscow, was organized by the State Duma with support from both the Foreign Ministry and the Chamber of Commerce and Industry. Addressing the participants, UNIDO (United Nations Industrial Development Organization) Director General Kandeh K. Yumkella endorsed the "business diplomacy" model pursued by Russia, in particular focusing on technology transfer as opposed to developmental aid as a key factor, while also noting this would benefit Russian companies.[47] Russian efforts to forgive African debt were also predicated on the countries using the savings to purchase Russian goods and services, a point stressed in 2006 by Deputy Finance Minister Sergei Storchak.[48]

Whether business diplomacy can succeed in upgrading low-key diplomatic relations is being tested in Nigeria. By 2010, the value of Russian–Nigerian direct and indirect trade was estimated to have reached $1.5 billion (Nigeria is Russia's second-largest sub-Saharan trading partner), and the first stages of a more comprehensive Russian–Nigerian relationship were being established, particularly after Medvedev's visit in 2009. To discuss the implementation of accords signed at that time, the foreign minister, Ojo Maduekwe, the minister of justice, Michael Aondoakaa, and the minister of science and technology, Al Hassan Zaku, visited Moscow. The economic focus reflects the fact that the main framework for Russo–Nigerian relations is the Intergovernmental Commission on Economic and Scientific-Technical Cooperation (ICESTC), established in 1998. Moving beyond the investments made by RUSAL in the aluminum sector, Russia's ambassador to Nigeria, Aleksandr Polyakov, outlined a $1 billion investment plan through 2015 to concentrate on upgrading the country's natural gas infrastructure and power grid.[49] Nigeria is hoping to utilize the expertise of Gazprom as well as other Russian oil and gas firms to further the development of its own energy sector and to strengthen the bilateral relationship.[50]

Given the preoccupation of the central foreign policy apparatus with the more traditional vectors for Russian foreign policy, and in order to link some of Russia's industrial regions with emerging markets in Africa, Trutnev, himself a former governor of the Perm region, also sought to increase the involvement of Russia's regions in strengthening Moscow's business diplomacy in Africa. For instance, in February 2010, a SADC-(the countries of the SADC include the Democratic Republic of the Congo, South Africa, Zambia, Tanzania, Madagascar, and Namibia) Russia forum was held in the Urals region, with contacts being made by the Governor of Sverdlovsk oblast,' A. S. Misharin, and the heads of the region's leading companies in aircraft building, machine building, and mining. Reflecting also the important role that is played by Russia's academic community in fostering ties with Africa, this forum was co-organized by the Foreign Ministry and the Institute for African Studies of the Academy of Sciences.[51]

Over the last decade, there has been a measurable resurgence of Russian influence in Africa. Russian trade with Africa has recovered from the doldrums of the early 1990s and now stands at a value of more than $6 billion. Yet despite all these measures, Russian engagement with Africa still lags behind not only the developed Western countries and China (China's trade with Africa is estimated at $70 billion), but also other rising powers like India and Brazil. On paper, Russian declarations sound quite impressive; when Medvedev visited Angola in 2009, for instance, he signed a number of agreements with Angolan President Jose Eduardo dos Santos pledging joint cooperation to boost the bilateral relationship.[52] But Russia accounts for 0.1% of Angola's trade. In contrast, China, the European Union, and the United States each account for nearly a quarter of Angola's trade (for a grand total of 77.5% in 2009).[53] This is why African diplomats stationed in Moscow have called for the Russian government to do more to enhance its "economic partnerships and cooperation with Africa" in ways similar to those undertaken by China, India, and Japan.[54] Margelov agrees, citing the need for an "integrated approach" that will strengthen the Russian position.[55] And the perception that Africa is still relegated to the sidelines has hurt the Russian effort to rebuild Moscow's influence on the continent.[56]

Russia has especially courted South Africa since the 1990s, especially once black-majority rule was established in 1994 and Nelson Mandela ascended to the presidency, given historic Soviet support for the African National Congress.[57] Presidential advisor Vasiliev has influenced both Putin and Medvedev in pursuing a closer relationship with South Africa, and Putin became the first Russian leader ever to visit South Africa, in September 2006. Vasiliev has noted that South Africa represents some 30% of Africa's entire gross domestic product and, as a result, is the linchpin state for the continent.[58] Both state and private companies have expressed keen interest in South Africa's nuclear power, aluminum, and diamond industries. After Putin's 2006 visit, joint projects were set up for cooperation in nuclear and space technology, mining, and energy.[59] In all of these areas, there was a strong expectation that closer Russian–South African ties would generate jobs and contracts for Russian companies. Putin also tended to tilt in favor of cultivating South Africa as opposed to Africa's other major power, Nigeria, because of commercial disputes and because the Nigerian decision to award lucrative defense contracts to China instead of Russia seemed to contradict earlier agreements reached when Nigerian President Olusegun Obasanjo had visited Russia in 2001.[60]

Russo–South African trade is now almost as large as Russia's 1992 overall trade with the continent as a whole—reaching some $690 million in 2009—but this is still dwarfed by South Africa's trade relations with China ($16 billion). With South Africa responsible for 0.1% of all Russian trade, the economic relationship is simply not yet generating large-scale equities to impact foreign policy. In addition, Egypt still retained its position as Russia's leading trading partner on the continent.[61] Moreover, Russia is a far more important market for South Africa than vice versa, leading to an imbalance in trading relations (see Figure 10.1).

But while the overall figures are low, Russia is seen as critical to South Africa's own plans for becoming a major global power in its own right. Both Thabo Mbeki (in office 1999–2008) and his successor as president of South Africa, Jacob Zuma, have turned to Russia to provide access to high technology in order to help develop the country's nuclear and aerospace industries. In 2009, South Africa joined the ranks of spacefaring nations when Russia launched the country's first satellite.[62] In 2010, Russia agreed to set up a scientific station in South Africa that could receive data from Russian remote-sensing satellites in orbit around Earth to process and analyze data as it related to Africa.[63]

Russia has also cultivated South Africa's sense of itself as a rising global power. During the Putin administration, the Russian government advanced a proposal for expanding the G-8 group of nations to include new powers including South Africa (a proposal that was overtaken by events once the G-8 agreed to be superseded by the G-20 in 2009).[64] Moscow has not thrown cold water on Pretoria's bid for a permanent UN Security Council seat and agreed that Africa needs greater representation in global institutions.[65] In recognition of South Africa's

FIGURE 10.1

The Growth in Russian–South African Trade, 2002–2008 (in millions of U.S. dollars)

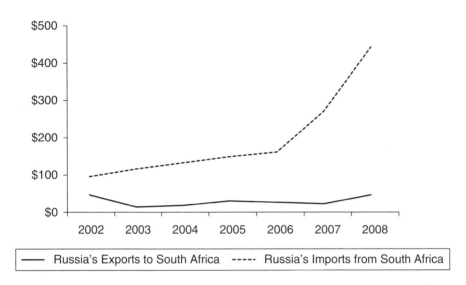

Russia's Exports to South Africa   - - - - - Russia's Imports from South Africa

Source: State Customs Committee of the Russian Federation.

growing pre-eminence, Russia welcomed South Africa to join the BRIC grouping in 2011, and South Africa hosted the BRICS leaders in Durban in March 2013, signaling Pretoria's arrival as an emerging power.[66] The Russian Foreign Ministry released a statement observing that South Africa, as a "leading African country . . . will not only increase the total economic weight of our association but also will help build up opportunities for mutually beneficial practical cooperation within BRIC."[67] These diplomatic gestures, while not requiring any great outlay of resources on Russia's part, nonetheless have allowed Russia to reap extensive goodwill in South Africa.

Zuma made a state visit to Russia in 2010; to underscore the seriousness with which his government approaches relations with Russia, the South African president was accompanied by 11 cabinet ministers and more than 100 South African business figures. Both Zuma and Medvedev indicated that they want to "take this relationship to the level of strategic partnership."[68] Zuma returned to Russia for a repeat visit in 2011 and also held a bilateral summit with Medvedev on the sideline of the BRICS summit. But while relations between South Africa and Russia are quite warm, the relationship for both sides is not a fundamental national priority. While the foundations have been laid for an Indian-style partnership—the

Inter-Governmental Committee on Trade and Economic Cooperation (ITEC) had convened 10 times by 2011, and there is an intergovernmental commission for military cooperation and a Russia-South Africa Business Council—the equities are not yet in place to shift the relationship into higher gear. In part, the relationship is still handled at the level of deputies rather than principals at both the foreign and defense ministries. In turn, South Africa's ambassador in Russia, Bheki Langa, lamented in 2010 that there were still too few business and commercial exchanges in place that could help cement stronger ties.[69] Some progress was made in 2013. Defense Minister Nosiviwe Mapisa-Nqakula traveled to Moscow in January to accelerate plans for further military cooperation, and Lavrov visited South Africa in February to discuss with Minister of International Relations Maite Nkoana-Mashabane the "operationalisation of the High Level Bilateral Mechanism" that would regulate Russia–South Africa relations. In addition, Lavrov set the agenda for Putin's own visit to South Africa in March, both to attend the BRICS summit in Durban and to conduct direct talks with Zuma.[70]

However, the African continent as a whole will never be a core area of interest for Russian foreign policy.[71] Nevertheless, Russia has demonstrated its ability to sustain a modest level of engagement, one that brings benefits to some economic sectors in Russia and also allows contemporary Russia to conceive of itself as a global rather than merely a regional actor in international affairs. But precisely because the Russian presence is modest, it does not lead to serious tensions with the major players competing for influence in Africa: the United States, China, Europe, Brazil, and India.

LATIN AMERICA BECKONS

After the collapse of the Soviet Union, Russia no longer had the inclination to sustain engagement in Latin America, both because of the economic crisis at home and also out of a sense that pursuing a geopolitical rivalry with the United States in its geographic backyard no longer made sense, in keeping with the foreign policy line of the first post–Soviet Russian Foreign Minister, Andrei Kozyrev.[72]

But in keeping with Yevgeny Primakov's multipolar approach, Russian interest and influence in Latin America began to revive in the late 1990s. In pursuit of a more multipolar world, Primakov raised the profile of the region in Russian diplomacy, making visits to Argentina, Brazil, Costa Rica, Colombia, Cuba, Mexico, and Venezuela during 1996 and 1997. In turn, Latin American leaders traveled to Moscow—notably the presidents of Argentina (1998) and Venezuela (2001).[73] Primakov identified Latin America as "a promising commercial and economic partner of Russia,"[74] but just as important, a Russian return to Latin America was predicated on responding to U.S. support for the eastward expansion of NATO into the former Soviet bloc.[75] Finally, Vladimir Putin became the first post–Soviet Russian leader to visit Latin America, starting with a trip to Cuba in December 2000.[76] This has inaugurated a regular series of visits by both Russian presidents and prime ministers to the region; both Prime Minister Putin and President Medvedev made visits to Latin America in 2010. In 2003, Foreign Minister Igor Ivanov invited a delegation of the Rio Group (a multilateral forum comprised of most of the states of Latin America and the Caribbean) to hold discussions in Moscow on reshaping the global order; Peru's Foreign Minister Allan Wagner, Costa Rica's Foreign Minister Roberto Tovar, and Brazilian Foreign Minister Celso Amorim held talks with both Ivanov and President Putin. This also initiated a regular dialogue between the Rio Group and Russia, reflecting Moscow's renewed interest in Latin America.[77]

Russia has pursued a two-track approach in the region, not dissimilar to its efforts in the Middle East, reviving former Soviet-era ties with countries in Latin America and the Caribbean (such as Cuba and Nicaragua), as well as establishing new relationships with countries that were in the American camp during the Cold War, like Venezuela, Brazil, and Argentina.[78] And, as with Africa, the impetus for a more active Russian foreign policy in Latin America was driven less by the Foreign Ministry and more by those in the government with ties to the special services as well as Russian commercial interests. During the Medvedev years, Deputy Prime Minister Igor Sechin served as the head of the government commission for cooperation with Cuba and the troubleshooter for the Russian–Venezuelan relationship.[79] He combined both aspects of this new style of diplomacy, negotiating contracts for the sale of Russian weaponry and for the expansion of the activities of Russian energy and mining companies in the region. Another key interlocutor in the Russian government with Latin America has been the head of the Security Council, Nikolai Patrushev.

Sechin and Patrushev put together a coalition of different interests and sectors to support a more robust Russian presence in the region. In particular, business and security interests—including those of the Russian Navy and Air Force—that have been threatened by the gains made by the Euro-Atlantic community at Russia's expense in Eastern Europe and Eurasia have supported a return to Latin America as a way to put pressure on the United States by operating in Washington's "back yard," particularly after the 2008 Russian–Georgian conflict. This Latin vector has, at times, conducted policy initiatives that have been at odds with the diplomatic efforts of the Foreign Ministry and the presidential staff to improve Russia's relations with the United States, highlighting "the rivalry that opens up areas for well-connected political entrepreneurs like Igor Sechin . . . to launch defense and foreign policy initiatives" that appear to bypass the established chain of command.[80]

Cuba was once Moscow's closest partner in the Western Hemisphere. After early expectations that the government of Fidel Castro would collapse once Russian support for his regime dried up after the Soviet collapse in 1991, the Russians began to re-explore the possibility of what was termed a "constructive partnership" after Primakov's visit to the island in 1996.[81] But debt owed by Havana—both for Soviet-era deliveries as well as arrears on a line of credit opened in 1993—complicated ties. (At the close of 2010, Cuba continued to owe some $27 billion to Russia—more than 40% of the total of all the external debt held by Russia.[82]) An upswing in Russian–Cuban relations began in 1999—coincidentally during a period when Russian–American relations were at a low point following the NATO intervention against Serbia over Kosovo. Building on that momentum, Cuban Foreign Minister Felipe Perez Roque traveled to Moscow in January 2000 to meet with Putin, who had just assumed the presidency after the resignation of Boris Yeltsin; Putin would travel to Cuba at the end of the year. But there were limits to any renewal in ties, given Cuba's debt to Russia and Moscow's desire not to complicate relations with the United States. Indeed, Castro would be highly disillusioned by Putin's decision, in October 2001, to close down the Soviet-era intelligence facility at Lourdes, justified as both a cost-saving measure and a gesture of goodwill to the United States.[83] Putin himself characterized the visit as "cleaning up the mess" left by the collapse of the Soviet Union and that in the future Russia would focus on "choosing priorities of cooperation between the two states in the economic sphere."[84] While not closing down the relationship, Putin was prepared to downgrade Cuba because it "did not present the potential for profitability" and because Putin was displeased with Castro's efforts to evade repayment of the debt.[85]

There does exist, however, a Cuba lobby within the Russian foreign policy establishment. There remains significant support for Cuba within the ex-Communist and nationalist wings of the political spectrum, who argue that as long as the United States continues to expand its sphere of influence in eastern Europe and the Eurasian space, Russia ought to maintain its ties to Cuba.[86] The Russian Orthodox Church has also weighed in on support for Cuba after it was given permission to build a church on the island, which was consecrated in 2008.[87] The presidential transition from Fidel Castro to his brother Raul (who became acting president in 2006 and was inaugurated as the 23rd president of Cuba in 2008) has also changed the dynamic because of Raul's focus on economic modernization.[88] To encourage Cuban purchases of Russian industrial goods and benefit Russian companies, the government extended a new $355 million credit line in 2006. And once the United States committed itself to building an antiballistic missile defense system in Europe, which the Russian military viewed as a threat to Russia's own nuclear deterrent, Cuba regained some of its strategic importance given its location off the southern U.S. coast. In August 2007, President Putin announced the resumption of Russian strategic flights that had been suspended for 15 years.[89] Following President Medvedev's 2008 visit to Cuba, a Russian naval detachment led by the *Admiral Chabanenko* visited Cuba, the first Russian ships to visit since the end of the Cold War.[90] Oil company Zarubezhneft has signed contracts to explore for oil off the Cuban coast, and during his 2009 visit, Deputy Prime Minister Igor Sechin signed other contracts expanding Russia's economic presence, following up on agreements reached when President Raul Castro had visited Moscow. Foreign Minister Sergei Lavrov characterized the Russian–Cuban relationship as a "strategic association" during a visit in February 2010, signing agreements to help modernize the Cuban military and to continue with economic cooperation.[91] Yet when Russian–Cuban trade peaked in 2007, the total value was still only reckoned at $285 million, and Cuba accounts for a tiny 0.05% of Russia's total trade.[92] The main driver for the Cuba vector, therefore, remains a desire on the part of Moscow to have a strategic presence close to the United States to offset America's presence in the former Soviet space.[93]

During the 1980s, the Sandinista government in Nicaragua had sought close ties with Moscow; indeed, Nicaragua only opened diplomatic relations with the Soviet Union after the 1979 revolution. The Soviet withdrawal from Central America and the agreement to permit free elections led to a non–Communist government taking power in 1990, which re-established much closer relations with the United States. Russia forgave the bulk of the Soviet-era debt owed by Nicaragua in 1996. After Daniel Ortega and the Sandinistas returned to power in 2006, the new government turned again to Russia to provide alternative economic and military arrangements, fearing the possible interruption of assistance from the United States.[94]

Nicaragua was the first country (after Russia) to extend diplomatic recognition to the breakaway Georgian republics of Abkhazia and South Ossetia in an attempt to help Russia legitimate its stance (and enabling Moscow to argue in favor of applying a Kosovo precedent to these regions).[95] Nicaragua also welcomed a visit of a Russian naval detachment in December 2008. Following Medvedev's 2008 visit to Nicaragua, Ortega traveled to Moscow (for the first time since the 1980s) and pledged to restart Russian–Nicaraguan relations on a new economic basis. He signed agreements with Sechin on joint cooperation in oil, gas, hydroelectric, and geothermal projects.[96] The Russian deputy prime minister has become the point person for pursuing Russia ties with Nicaragua (and, by extension, with the rest of Latin America), with regular visits to Managua. While handling the military account, Sechin was accompanied on his July 2009 tour by Energy Minister Sergei Shmatko—reflecting Russian interest in helping to develop the country's offshore oil and gas reserves—and Andrei Krainy, a key figure in Russia's fishing industry, reflecting efforts to increase the export of Nicaraguan seafood to Russian markets.[97]

In June 2010, the Russian-Nicaraguan intergovernmental commission met in Managua for the first time, picking up from an earlier Soviet-Nicaraguan body that had existed during the 1980s.[98] In 2012, new agreements were signed for Nicaragua to obtain military and police equipment from Russia, in part because of strained relations between Nicaragua and the United States.[99]

Russia has sought to move beyond its old Soviet-era partners. Taking advantage of a growing wave of anti–Americanism in the region, the Russian government, in the conclusion of U.S. analyst Stephen Blank, has increased its "efforts to penetrate Latin America using its favorite means of expanding its influence abroad, supporting anti-American regimes with energy deals and arms sales."[100] Just like African countries, Latin American states look to Russia to offset the United States—particularly to obtain advanced technology—and to counterbalance a growing Chinese presence. When Argentina's President Cristina Fernandez de Kirchner visited Moscow in December 2008, her agenda included exploring purchases of Russian arms; securing Russian involvement in Argentina's growing energy sector; and obtaining Russian cooperation in modernizing the country's transportation infrastructure.[101] Growing economic ties, in turn, are expected to lead to closer political ties. In advance of Medvedev's April 2010 visit to Argentina, Argentine Foreign Minister Jorge Taina, emerging from talks with Russian Deputy Foreign Minister Sergei Riabkov, declared, "There is much interest in going further to strengthen coordination in political and economic issues at the international level."[102] Ecuadorian President Rafael Correa visited Russia in October 2009, wanting to purchase Russian weaponry to "increase the country's defensive capabilities" and to sign deals for technical cooperation in the fields of nuclear and hydroelectric power generation.[103] Bolivia's President Evo Morales has solicited Russian participation in his energy sector and also sought to purchase Russian weaponry for his country's armed forces. Latin America is a growing and important market for Rosobornexport; the growing interest in nuclear power opens new prospects for Russia's atomic energy industry; and Russia may become a growing player in the region's energy infrastructure. Gazprom, for instance, is reviewing "possible participation in Bolivian gas and oil projects" as well as a "pipeline project to link Bolivia with Argentina"—proposals under review by Gazprom's Deputy CEO Alexander Medvedev, who has traveled to the region to assess conditions for further Russian commercial expansion.[104]

But with some Latin American countries, relationships are quite underdeveloped, and they are not a particular priority for the Russian foreign policy establishment. Because Mexico, for instance, is part of a number of multilateral organizations of which Russia is also a member, particularly the Group of 20 (G-20) and the Asia Pacific Economic Cooperation (APEC) forum, there are regular consultations between Mexico's Foreign Minister Patricia Espinosa and Russian Foreign Minister Sergei Lavrov on political matters, but the intergovernmental commission on economic and commercial matters, while it is headed up by the Mexican secretary of energy (Georgina Kessel Martinez in 2010), her counterpart on the Russian side is the minister of education, Andrei Fursenko.[105]

It is Russia's relations with Venezuela that most clearly demonstrate the post-Soviet Russian approach to the region and Moscow's ability to offer itself as an alternative. In order to pursue his Bolivarian Revolution following his inauguration as president in 1999, Hugo Chavez began to look for alternatives—in Russia and in China—to replace Venezuela's traditional source of economic and military support, the United States.[106] Trade between Russia and Venezuela increased by more than 350% in 2000, and both countries, dependent on energy exports for budget revenue, found it useful to coordinate their plans and work to keep world prices stable. Chavez visited Moscow in May 2001 and, after his meetings with Putin, declared "a strategic alliance has begun, a joint path."[107] But the relationship foundered over differences in oil policy, because Russia's expansion of production contradicted Venezuela's efforts in OPEC to cut production to raise oil prices.[108]

Following an attempted coup attempt against Chavez in 2002, which he alleged the United States backed, Chavez radically increased his purchases of weaponry from Russia to better protect his administration, including high-technology arms that the United States refused to sell. Venezuela was also unable to purchase spare parts for its American-made aircraft. With the rise in world oil prices, Venezuela now had additional income with which to pay for Russian weapons.[109] When Chavez traveled to Moscow in November 2004 for his third meeting with President Putin, definitive agreements were reached for Russia to supply advanced weaponry to Venezuela. Venezuela has bought rifles, short-range missiles, helicopters, and fighter jets and has discussed the purchase of T-90 tanks, submarines, and the advanced S-300 air defense system; indeed, Venezuela considered purchasing the missiles that were originally intended to have been sold to Iran.[110] Since 2005, Venezuela has purchased some $4.4 billion in Russian arms, helping to diversify Russia's traditional dependence on clients like India and China.[111] Venezuela is responsible for 80% of all Russian weapons sales in Latin America.[112]

Finally, Venezuela has hosted Russian military forces for joint exercises, notably at the end of 2008 (VenRus 2008). This deployment took on added significance for the Russian military, because having ships and planes present in the Caribbean Basin was meant to signal to Washington Russia's unease and displeasure with the U.S. naval presence in the Black Sea region following the

Russo–Georgian conflict. The four-vessel task force of the Northern Fleet, led by the missile cruiser *Peter the Great*, was the largest Russian naval presence in the Caribbean since the Cold War, and President Medvedev, who was in Venezuela on a state visit when the ships arrived, visited the detachment with Chavez.[113]

As with other countries in the developing world, Russia has offered opportunities to develop Venezuela's high-technology sector, including joint projects in atomic energy and space exploration. But energy and raw materials are also a powerful economic bond. All the major Russian energy companies—Rosneft, LUKoil, Gazprom, TNK-BP, and Surgutneftegaz—are present in Venezuela, helping Chavez to displace Western firms. The Russian–Venezuelan relationship is beginning to take on a much more institutionalized character. Sechin inaugurated an intergovernmental commission in 2008 to oversee relations, and during this visit was accompanied by the deputy CEO of Gazprom, Medvedev.[114] During his April 2010 visit to Caracas—Putin's first trip to Venezuela—the prime minister presided over the signing of some 31 agreements designed to facilitate greater trade and cooperation in the oil and nuclear industries.[115] Venezuela is now Russia's number-two trading partner in Latin America, with trade turnover, for 2011, at $1.5 billion. Russia is Venezuela's number-three partner in terms of imports (particularly weaponry and equipment) and Venezuela's number-four destination in terms of its exports; Russia is Venezuela's number-three trading partner, after the United States and China.[116] But Venezuela's ability to sustain this business relationship with Russia depends on the global oil price, and, as Mark Katz concluded, "Lower oil prices would mean that Venezuela would have less money for Russian arms, and Russian petroleum companies would have less money—and less incentive—to invest in Venezuela."[117]

Just as important is the extent to which Russia wants to spend money on developing Venezuela as a base for extending Russian influence in the Western Hemisphere, especially for further military activity. Military expert Viktor Litovkin notes that Russia would need to "set up military and naval bases and construct the corresponding infrastructure . . . in a word, to do this work would require spending a serious amount of money"[118]—expenditures the Kremlin may not want to make, particularly if there is lasting improvement in the relationship with the United States.[119] Chavez's disputes with his neighbors also created difficult balancing acts for the Russians, who want to continue a lucrative stream of contracts with Venezuela but not to foreclose opportunities in other Latin American states.

Chavez visited Russia nearly every year and continued to receive high-ranking Russian visitors, including both President Medvedev (in 2008) and Prime Minister Putin (2010); Deputy Prime Minister Sechin, in his capacity as head of the intergovernmental commission, makes regular trips to Venezuela and is considered to be the manager of the Russian side of the bilateral relationship. Even after leaving the cabinet, Sechin, in his capacity as chairman of Rosneft, has continued to oversee the bilateral relationship. Sechin's visit in late 2011 saw new agreements signed that would expand Russian energy investment in Venezuela; Putin and Chavez reconfirmed these understandings in January 2012. Sechin returned to Venezuela in September 2012, prior to the elections that returned Chavez to office for another term, to assess progress in Russia's investments.[120] Chavez's death in March 2013 highlighted how "Chavez was personally behind all the major projects with Russia."[121] In addition to Lavrov and the speaker of the Federation Council, Valentina Matviyenko, the Russian delegation to the funeral included both Sechin and the head of Russian Technologies (the holding company that controls much of the defense-industrial complex), Sergei Chemezov, representing the two main areas of Russian economic interest in Venezuela. Their meetings with the government danced around the unspoken question of whether the Russo–Venezuelan relationship is built on truly enduring foundations of national interest; as Russian experts worry, "how long the friendship with the Chavez regime will last."[122] Chavez's preference for Russian involvement in his country's economy and security posture faced opposition within Venezuela,[123] raising the possibility that a post-Chavez Venezuela might distance itself from Moscow. If Russo–Venezuela relations were based largely on the dynamism of Hugo Chavez, Russia has tried to build a relationship with Brazil that appeals to the national interests of both countries. Moreover, given Brazil's status as an emerging global power, the relationship between Moscow and Brasilia is undertaken at the highest levels of government. Traditionally, Russia had lackluster relations with Brazil; diplomatic relations were not established between the USSR and Brazil until 1945. Brazilian leaders, particularly its military (who took power in 1964 and did not relinquish control to an elected civilian government until 1985), were suspicious of the Soviet Union and its efforts to spread its ideology in Latin America, although they were prepared to enter into some commercial agreements, particularly concerning scientific and technical matters.[124] The end of the Cold War, however, changed the perception of Russia in Brazilian governmental circles. President Fernando Henrique Cardoso (1995–2003) sought to expand and develop ties with post-Soviet Russia, realizing that Brazil's own rise to be a regional power and emerging global actor required diversifying the country's relationships and finding new business opportunities to avoid dependence on the United States. Cardoso reached a series of agreements with the Yeltsin administration in 1997 that laid the basis for a new Russian–Brazilian relationship. Primakov arrived in Brasilia in November of that year to initial a Declaration of Principles of Russian–Brazilian Cooperation Oriented Toward the 21st Century; in keeping with the pattern observed in Russian relations with India and South Africa, Moscow offered its assistance in developing Brazil's nuclear power and aerospace industries.[125] Highlighting the importance that the Putin administration placed on jump-starting relations with Brazil, Prime Minister Mikhail Kasyanov headed the inter-governmental Brazil–Russia commission, set up in 2001, along with Brazilian Vice President Marco Maciel.[126]

Under Cardoso's successor, Luiz Inácio Lula da Silva (2003–2011), ties expanded rapidly. Lula's Workers' Party (PT) had had extensive contacts with Castro's Cuba, which in turn engendered some ties with the Soviet Union, which carried over into a more sympathetic approach to Russia.[127] Russian–Brazilian trade expanded rapidly, and Brazil became Russia's number-one trading partner in Latin America.[128] Maciel's successor as vice president of Brazil during the Lula administration, José Alencar, traveled to Moscow in September 2003 to sign an agreement on military cooperation and the transfer of technology with Russia. Putin visited Brazil in November 2004, and during this meeting, the seeds of what was to become the BRIC forum were planted (this will be discussed in greater detail later in this chapter), and both sides pledged to increase bilateral trade. Putin in particular discussed aerospace and nuclear deals with his Brazilian counterpart.[129]

Despite the growth in Brazilian–Russian commercial ties, as with South Africa, the rhetoric can overshadow the reality. About 1% of Russia's foreign trade is generated by ties with Brazil. But continuing the comparison with South Africa, Brazil has also sought to further its ties with Russia as part of Lula's Foreign Minister Celso Amorim's strategy of redefining global institutions and getting Brazil on the international stage.[130] Lula's own predisposition for an "antihegemonic" approach to foreign affairs—and unease with American pre-dominance in both the hemisphere and the global arena—furthered his interest in reaching out to Moscow as well as to other rising powers.[131] Moreover, while Deputy Prime Minister Sechin has usually been the main figure in charge of Latin American relations, the tie with Brazil is managed at the very top. Lula visited Moscow in October 2005 to proclaim a strategic partnership with Russia and, significantly, received Russia's public endorsement of its aspirations to obtain a permanent seat on the UN Security Council.[132] Foreign Minister Sergei Lavrov traveled to Brazil in December 2006, and Medvedev made a state visit in November 2008. Russia sees Brazil as a linchpin state and as its stepping stone to Latin America as a whole and so has devoted a great deal of attention to building up the relationship.[133] Just as important, the desire to cultivate Brazil has acted as a brake on the Russian–Venezuelan relationship. While oil-rich Venezuela has had ready cash to purchase Russian weapons and equipment, Brazil is the long-term prize. The Venezuela vector that has been promoted, particularly by Igor Sechin, is seen as a short-term interest and is balanced by those in the Russian

FIGURE 10.2
The Growth in Russian–Brazilian Trade, 2002–2008 (in billions of U.S. dollars)

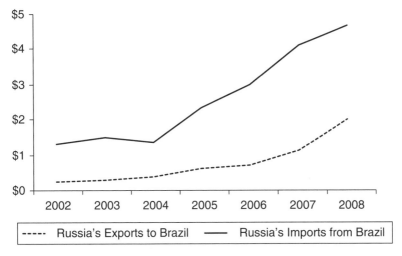

----- Russia's Exports to Brazil ——— Russia's Imports from Brazil

Source: State Customs Committee of the Russian Federation.

government who see Brazil as the priority and who do not wish to alienate it by too close an embrace of Venezuela.[134]

One way that Russia has gained inroads in Brazil has been to play upon Brasilia's disappointments with the United States. After NASA was unable to come to an agreement with the Brazilian Space Agency (Agencia Espacial Brasileiria) to send the first Brazilian astronaut to the International Space Station, Russia signed an agreement with Brazil during Lula's 2005 Moscow summit that sent Marcus Ponte into space in 2006 and also committed the two countries' space agencies to work on joint development of rockets and satellites.[135] Brazil's efforts to purchase American aircraft foundered on the unwillingness of U.S. firms to allow Brazil to manufacture some of the planes under license at Brazilian facilities. In contrast, Russia has shown a willingness to explore developing a military partnership with Brazil along the lines of the relationship it has with India, especially in the design and manufacture of aircraft. This would be attractive to Brazil because instead of simply purchasing "off-the-shelf" products from U.S. and European firms, it wants to be able to develop its own domestic defense industry; Russia would benefit from the contracts and Brazil's willingness to invest in research and design.[136] Another symbolic step was the introduction of visa-free travel between the two countries in 2010, the fulfillment of an agreement initialed between Lula and Medvedev during the latter's 2008 visit.

The energy sector in Russia is also a major backer of the Brazil vector. Rosatom, the nuclear power conglomerate, has an agreement with Brazil's National Nuclear Energy Commission for joint activities in mining uranium and developing new reactors.[137] Gazprom is cooperating with Brazil's Petrobras on a number of energy projects, including development of liquefied natural gas (LNG) capacity and exploration of promising offshore fields; Gazprom is also promoting the development of pan-South America pipelines that would link all of the countries of the region in a shared energy network. Significantly, Gazprom's office in Rio de Janeiro is set to coordinate its Latin America operation.[138]

Russian-Brazilian relations could be on the cusp of developing into a strong, multisector partnership on the Indo-Russian model. During his last visit to Moscow in May 2010, Lula noted the rapid progress—with bilateral trade having grown five times—but also bluntly concluded, "But that is not enough. We need to make a quantitative new leap and define new areas for partnership in areas like energy, infrastructure and space exploration."[139] Additional agreements were signed to augment the strategic partnership, and both sides set up a joint working group to explore trading directly using Russian rubles and Brazilian reals rather than converting to dollars, which would boost both countries' currencies.[140] Lula handed to his successor as president, Dilma Rousseff, a foundation on which a vastly expanded Russian-Brazilian relationship can be constructed. Medvedev visited Brazil in February 2013 and signed several new agreements for bilateral cooperation; he and Rousseff also pledged to raise the value of bilateral trade to $10 billion by 2015.[141]

BUILDING THE BRICS

When economist Jim O'Neill coined the term *BRIC* and described the economic potential of Brazil, Russia, India, and China in a 2001 Goldman Sachs Economic Paper (*Building Better Global Economic BRICS*), he did not foresee that he might be serving as godfather to a new international alignment.[142] O'Neill's term—rapidly adopted by financial and emerging-market analysts all around the world—happened to be released at an opportune time. Having been influenced by Yevgeny Primakov's vision of a multipolar world and Primakov's counsel that Russia needed to find partners among the emerging and rising powers,[143] Putin was interested in augmenting Russia's cooperation with Brazil, India, and China and in leveraging their growing economic and political clout in world affairs.

The RIC (Russia-India-China) trilateral forum was already being constructed (as discussed in Chapter 9), and once that format was underway in 2003, broadening it to include Brazil did not present insurmountable challenges.[144] Russia either had or was in the process of concluding strategic partnership agreements with the other three states.[145] (It also helped that Brazil was partnered with India in the India-Brazil-South Africa forum and also concluded a strategic partnership with China.) The Russian foreign policy establishment saw the BRIC process as putting Russia in the "uniquely advantageous position of coordinator and mediator between Western and non–Western centers of a multipolar world,"[146] thus preserving a global role for a Russia that by itself may no longer wield enough clout in global affairs. Thus, there was a clear desire on the part of Moscow to transform BRIC into a "genuine center of power"[147] to offset the traditional predominance of the Euro-Atlantic world in international organizations such as the International Monetary Fund.

After the RIC process began in 2003, the next step was to expand it to encompass Brazil, which would give the forum more of a global reach. Putin discussed a proposed BRIC format with Lula during his November 2004 visit to Brazil and found that "Brazil is very open to the coalition concept where these large countries support each other in terms of trade, economics, international politics and defense."[148] The BRIC is usually understood to have been inaugurated in September 2006, when the foreign ministers of Brazil, Russia, India, and China met at the UN General Assembly in New York, starting the first of a series of regular meetings. In 2008, the first stand-alone summit of the BRIC took place in Yekaterinburg, Russia, immediately after the Shanghai Cooperation Organization meeting, and the first summit of the four BRIC heads of state met the following summer, again in Yekaterinburg. At that summit, the leaders decided to further institutionalize the forum, setting procedures for the foreign ministers, finance ministers, and heads of the central banks of the members to meet on a regular basis, culminating in an annual yearly summit of the heads of state.[149] After the 2009 BRIC summit in Russia, the 2010 meeting was held in Brazil. The 2011 session, held in China, also marked the accession of South Africa to the bloc, with President Jacob Zuma traveling to the island of Hainan to meet with Dmitry Medvedev, Dilma Rousseff, Manmohan Singh, and Hu Jintao. India hosted the next leaders' summit in March 2012, and with that meeting, BRICS showed that it had achieved a certain degree of permanence. Of particular importance was the decision taken for the BRICS nations to sponsor their own development bank and reserve currency system as an alternative to the Western-dominated International Monetary Fund (IMF) and World Bank.[150] The five executives also met on the sidelines of the G-20 summit in Cabo San Lucas, Mexico, in June 2012. South Africa hosted the BRICS leaders in Durban in March 2013, an important meeting because it featured the new Chinese leader Xi Jingping at his first BRICS summit, as well as the first time Putin has taken part in a BRICS meeting as president. The Durban meeting focused on efforts to further solidify economic and financial links among the BRICS states (building on the decisions taken in Delhi), in part to decrease reliance upon Western-led institutions, as well as the setting up of a permanent secretariat.[151]

The BRICS encompasses five major states across four continents and provides a framework for projecting global influence. However, the BRICS grouping, at present, is more a dream than a reality. Russia's overall trade with the other members of the BRICS combined only comes to about 10% of its total foreign trade; contrast this with the EU, which accounts for nearly half of Russia's trade. Yet the BRICS process is a start; Timofei Bordachev, director of the Center for European Studies, concludes: "This is genuine diversification of Russia's foreign economic policy."[152] Over time, the proportion of the BRICS countries as a share of Russia's foreign economic relations is slated to rise. The Russians are especially hopeful about possible joint projects for cooperation in energy, telecommunications, and pharmaceuticals—and what this might do for further renovating the Russian economy. As an economic bloc, the BRICS is in its infancy, but by 2005, intra-BRIC trade totaled some $127.4 billion, and trade among the BRICS members was growing at a much faster rate than their economic relations with other states and blocs.[153] Given that intra-BRICS trade was valued at around $15 billion only 5 years before, this was an impressive rate of growth. Russian experts predict that by 2030, intra-BRICS trade could reach $1 trillion in value.[154]

Bringing Brazil into an existing Russia-India-China group was also been an important part of the Russian strategy of reaching out to Brasilia. This enabled Lula to put forth his vision of a reformed global order and to proclaim that "the BRICs have become essential players in major international decision-making."[155] President Medvedev, in turn, paid tribute to Lula's stewardship as the chair of the BRIC in 2009 to 2010:

> We appreciate the active and creative efforts of the Brazilian Chairmanship that brought BRIC cooperation to a qualitatively new level. BRIC has recently held a number of very useful meetings of finance ministers, senior representatives on security issues and development banks' officials. What is especially important is that our cooperation is expanding due to the involvement of the business community and civil society.... Since the first full-scale BRIC summit in Yekaterinburg (June 16, 2009), we have managed to make a good start in many areas of work that we have identified. Our states actively participate in the Group of Twenty that has become the key mechanism for coordination of international efforts ... Thanks to a common approach, we were able to successfully redistribute five percent of voting shares in the IMF and three percent in the World Bank ..."[156]

In turn, the decision to include South Africa in the forum helped to cement President Zuma's emergence as a global leader and recognition of South

Africa's position as Africa's dominant state. Now, proposals have emerged for Indonesia to join the bloc, with the country's ambassador to Russia, Djauhari Oratmangun, expressing Jakarta's interest. If Indonesia were to join, it would continue to enhance the forum as the leading representative of the major non-Western powers.[157]

Despite these grandiose visions of the future, however, there is also realism in Russian policy circles about what the BRICS can achieve. The spring 2012 New Delhi summit, in particular, showed the difficulties in shifting the forum from simply opposing Euro-American dominance in global institutions to actually constructing alternatives to the IMF and World Bank. While the BRICS countries have shown they can "loosely harmonize" some of their policies, the "relative political disunity" of the five prevents closer integration.[158] Russian political analysts noted that groups like the BRICS "are more communications platforms than decision-making centers," but maintain that they do enable the five leaders—and more importantly, their staffs and political establishments—to exchange opinions and information.[159] Moreover, "The Russian approach is based on the understanding that cooperation in the framework of BRIC[S] will develop gradually as mutual trust accumulates, as does the experience in coordinated efforts in those areas where our interests coincide."[160] Under the BRICS rubric, the first efforts to bring together the nongovernmental sector of the four countries is also starting, beginning with a BRICS sister universities project (St. Petersburg, Rio de Janeiro, Mumbai, Shanghai, and Qingdao) and contacts between municipalities and public organizations.[161]

At the same time, the Russians have blocked one initiative supported by other BRICS members: their desire to become observers of the Arctic Council and to have access to the resources of the north. In particular, both India and China have pushed to be included in Arctic arrangements—yet Russia "is among the loudest protesters against expanding the Arctic Council to include fellow BRICS members."[162]

What sustains the BRICS process is that all five states are interested in revising the terms of the existing international order, "looking for a new weight in global decision making bodies."[163] By working together and presenting consensus positions, the BRIC did manage to alter in its favor the distribution of votes within the International Monetary Fund and, after the start of the global financial crisis in 2008, helped to set the rules for how the Group of 20 (G-20) was to operate, preventing the United States and other developed Western economies from controlling the agenda.[164] With the possible exception of China, it would be very difficult for Russia, Brazil, or India to have as much impact; this is why Lula proclaimed that "Brazil, Russia, India and China have a fundamental role in creating a new international order."[165] The BRICS format also means that government officials in all five countries are becoming habituated to working with each other; in particular, relationships are forming between the staffs of the relevant chief executives, including their national security advisors.[166]

The BRICS process also interconnects with Russia's ambitions within the Group of Twenty (G-20)—the forum that brings together the rising powers with the established industrial nations of the West to discuss global issues. On its own, Russia is not a significant member of the G-20; however, Russia's ability to leverage the endorsement of the other BRICS members gives any Russian proposal "a higher chance of being approved by the G-20, both because of the joint economic weight of the BRICS countries and the higher probability of getting support from other developing countries in the G-20."[167] Russia, which assumed the presidency of the G-20 for 2013, has made correcting the pro–Western tilt in international institutions like the World Bank and the International Monetary Fund part of its agenda for the year.[168] The BRICS leaders planned to meet in that format simultaneously during the September 2013 G-20 summit in St. Petersburg, following up on their conclave on the sidelines of the G-20 summit in Cabo San Lucas in 2012. By combining the BRICS and G-20 meetings,

> Russia would try to articulate her vision of the global economy with the support of BRICS partners. And this is the reason why BRICS summit in St-Petersburg is to be held on the sidelines of G20 forum. Russia needs BRICS to fully throw its weight behind her, so that her G20 presidency would be a success. On the other hand, BRICS partners would also try to capitalize on Russia's G20 chairmanship to articulate their own agendas.[169]

Like the Shanghai Cooperation Organization, the BRICS forum, which did not exist 20 years ago, reflects a new, flexible, and dynamic approach on the part of Russian foreign policy, seeking to maximize Russia's influence on the world stage, while acknowledging that Russia cannot bear the burden of playing at the role of a global superpower. Thus, the effort is underway to hitch Russia's chariot to the energy and dynamism of the rising powers as a way of retaining Russia's relevance as a global player.

NOTES

1. See the version of Nikitin's "Journey Across Three Seas" as prepared by Serge A. Zenkovsy, in *Medieval Russia's Epics, Chronicles and Tales,* revised and expanded edition (New York: E. P. Dutton, 1963, 1974), 351–352.

2. Sergius Yakobson, "Russia and Africa," *Slavonic and East European Review* 17, no. 51 (April 1939): 628–630.

3. Negussey Ayele, "Adwa 1896: Who Was Civilized and Who Was Savage," *The Battle of Adwa,* eds. Paulos Milkias and Gatechew Mateferi (New York: Algora Publishing, 2005), 152.

4. Igor S. Ivanov, *The New Russian Diplomacy* (Washington, DC: Brookings Institution Press, 2002), 133.

5. Quoted in Christopher Andrew and Vasili Mitrokhin, *The World Was Going Our Way: The KGB and the Battle for the Third World* (New York: Basic Books, 2005), 1.

6. Andrew and Mitrokhin, 5.

7. In 1981, the United States offered 8,772 scholarships for students from developing countries; the Soviet Union and the Soviet bloc countries offered 72,092. See Colin W. Lawson, "Soviet Economic Aid to Africa," *African Affairs* 87, no. 349 (October 1988): 513.

8. See the discussion in John Gunther, *Inside Russia Today,* revised edition (New York: Harper and Row, 1957, 1962), esp. 518–524.

9. Andrew and Mitrokhin, 471.

10. See, for instance, the recollections of long-serving Soviet diplomat Anatoly Dobrynin, *In Confidence* (New York: Times Books, 1995), 404–405; KGB general Nikolai Leonov, *Likholet'e* (Moscow: Mezhdunarodnye Otnosheniia, 1995), 141; or the diplomat and defector Arkady Shevchenko, *Breaking with Moscow* (New York: Alfred A. Knopf, 1985), 152.

11. Lawson, 517.

12. Andrew and Mitrokhin, 469.

13. Quoted in "Soviet Charity Will Begin At Home," *Chicago Tribune,* July 28, 1990, at http://articles.chicagotribune.com/1990-07-28/news/9003030467_1_president-mikhail-gorbachev-soviet-union-socialism-or-death.

14. Mikhail Gorbachev, *On My Country and the World* (New York: Columbia University Press, 2000), 199.

15. Robert H. Donaldson and Joseph L. Nogee, *The Foreign Policy of Russia: Changing Systems, Enduring Interests,* 4th edition (Armonk, NY: M.E. Sharpe, 2009), 334.

16. Ivanov, 140.

17. Donaldson and Nogee, 334.

18. Jyotsna Bakshi, "Russian Policy towards South Asia," *Strategic Analysis* 23, no. 8 (November 1999): 1374.

19. Pamela A. Jordan, "A Bridge Between the Global North and Africa? Putin's Russia and G8 Development Commitments," *African Studies Quarterly* 11, no. 4 (Summer 2010): 87.

20. Ivanov, 140.

21. Seth Mydans, "Russian Arrives in U.S. to Face Arms Charges," *New York Times,* November 16, 2010, at http://www.nytimes.com/2010/11/17/world/asia/17thai.html?src=mv.

22. Quoted in Donaldson and Nogee, 332.

23. See his interview with Aleksandr Shaverdov, in *Voennyi Diplomat* 4 (2006): 33.

24. Mikhail Margelov, "Advancing into Africa," *Rossiiskaia Gazeta,* December 10, 2008, 1.

25. J. Peter Pham, "The Russian Bear Returns to Africa," *World Defense Review,* August 21, 2008, at http://worlddefensereview.com/pham082108.shtml.

26. Kalman Kalotay, "How to explain the foreign expansion of Russian firms," *Journal of Financial Transformation* 24 (2008): 59.

27. Shaverdov, 33.

28. Irina Abramova and Leonid Fituni, "Competing for Africa's Natural Resources," *International Affairs* 3 (2009): 49.

29. Vladimir Fedotov and Galina Sidorova, "Africa and Russia: Prospects for Cooperation," *International Affairs* 4 (2010): 71.

30. Yekaterina Grishkovets, "Igor Sechin Shows His Energy Cards," *Kommersant,* October 24, 2008, 17, in *Current Digest of the Post–Soviet Press* 60, no. 42, (November 11, 2008): 10, 11.

31. Jordan, 87, 88.

32. "Russian Relations with Sub-Saharan African Countries," fact sheet released by the Russian Ministry of Foreign Affairs, December 20, 2006, at http://www.mid.ru/brp_4 .nsf/itogi06/DEF4B16F1CA22378C325725100416ACD.

33. "Russian Navy to Preventing Pirate Attacks Northern Africa Areas," *Interfax,* October 17, 2012, at http://rbth.ru/articles/2012/10/17/russian_navy_to_preventing_ pirate_attacks_northern_africa_areas_19175.html.

34. Abramova and Fituni, 56–57. At the end of 2006, the Russian Ministry highlighted the following companies and projects: "Active on the continent are such large companies as Alrosa in Angola (the Catoca and Luo diamond projects) and the Democratic Republic of the Congo (diamond deposit development); FGUP VO Tekhnopromexport in Angola (the Capanda and Chicapa hydro-electric schemes); Rusal in Guinea (bauxite and alumina deposit development), in Nigeria (participation in the privatization and modernization of the aluminum smelter company ALSCON), in Ghana (plans for bauxite deposit development and the purchase of an aluminum plant), in the DRC and the Republic of the Congo (a project for an energy pool to provide a bauxite processing plant with electricity); Renova in Gabon (plans for joint exploitation of manganese ore deposits) and in South Africa (development of manganese ore deposits); Klyuchevsky Ferroalloy Works in the DRC (joint rare earth metals development); Zarubezhneft in Nigeria (acquisition of a right to participate in exploration and development of two oil areas); Stroitransgaz, Rosneft, and Zarubezhvodstroi in Algeria (construction of the Souguer-Hadjret En Nouss oil pipeline, oil and gas prospecting and production in the southeast of the country, irrigation and hydraulic structures); Tekhnopromexport and Tatneft in Libya (implementation of the contract for the expansion of Tripoli West power-and-heating generation station and development of an oil block respectively), and Tyazhpromexport and Siloviye Mashiny in Egypt (reconstruction of the Helwan iron and steel works and by-product coke plant and modernization of the generators of the Aswan hydropower plant)." "Russian Relations with Sub-Saharan African Countries," fact sheet released by the Russian Ministry of Foreign Affairs, December 20, 2006, at http://www.mid.ru/brp_4.nsf/itogi06/DEF4B16F1CA22378C325725100416ACD.

35. Yevgeny Shestakov, "Battle for Africa," *Rossiiskaia Gazeta,* December 25, 2007, 8; in *Current Digest of the Post–Soviet Press* 59, no. 51 (January 6, 2008): 22.

36. "Russian natural resources minister to head to Angola, Namibia," *RIA Novosti,* October 13, 2010, at http://en.rian.ru/world/20101013/160933225.html; "Zuma visit

strengthens SA, Russia ties," *SouthAfrica.info,* August 6, 2010, at http://www.southafrica
.info/news/international/russia-060810.htm.

37. "Medvedev vows 'pragmatic' relations with Africa," *RIA Novosti,* June 25, 2009, at
http://en.rian.ru/russia/20090625/155352473.html.

38. Abramova and Fituni, 53.

39. Shestakov, 22–23.

40. Fedotov and Sidorov, 70–71.

41. Alexander Koliandre, "Russia revives links with Africa," *BBC News,* July 16, 2007,
at http://news.bbc.co.uk/2/hi/business/6897865.stm.

42. For more on the LUKoil presence in western Africa, see Howard Amos, "LUKoil
Mulls More Investments in Africa," *Moscow Times,* 4551 (December 29, 2010), at http://
www.themoscowtimes.com/business/article/lukoil-mulls-more-investments-in-africa/
427965.html.

43. More information on the Council is available at the website of the Russian
Embassy in South Africa at http://www.russianembassy.org.za/economic/links.html.

44. Koliandre, op. cit.

45. Anatoly Medetsky, "Rosneft Nears African Pipeline Deal," *Moscow Times,* October
14, 2012, at http://www.themoscowtimes.com/business/article/russia-abroad-rosneft-
nears-african-pipeline-deal/469716.html.

46. "On Electing Vladimir Dmitriev as Chairman of the Coordinating Committee on
Economic Cooperation with African Countries to the South of the Sahara," *Russian
Banking News,* June 20, 2009, at http://www.russiabankingnews.com/ceo/4599.html.

47. "Yumkella calls on Russian business to invest in Africa, commends UNIDO-
Russia cooperation," *UNIDO* press release, June 15, 2010, at http://www.unido.org/index
.php?id=7881&tx_ttnews%5Btt_news%5D=483&cHash=3bcb3e51ca2d89c0ebb13b4a4277
dbf5.

48. Cited in Jordan, 93.

49. "Russia Hinges $1B Investment Plan on Free, Fair Polls," *NBF News,* December
28, 2010, at http://www.nigerianbestforum.com/blog/?p=71850; "Russian envoy seeks
stronger ties with Nigeria," *Blueprint,* June 14, 2012, at http://blueprintng.com/2012/06/
russian-envoy-seeks-stronger-ties-with-nigeria/.

50. "Trade deficit with Russia worries Nigeria," *Xinhua,* November 11, 2012, at http://
news.xinhuanet.com/english/business/2012–11/11/c_131966431.htm.

51. Fedotov and Sidorova, 78.

52. "Russia to increase investment in large projects in Angola," *RIA Novosti,* June 26,
2009, at http://en.rian.ru/world/20090626/155364462.html.

53. Based on statistics provided by EUROSTAT at http://trade.ec.europa.eu/doclib/
docs/2006/september/tradoc_122456.pdf.

54. Kester Kenn Klomegahm, "Russia lags behind in building African relations," *Mail
and Guardian,* July 15, 2008, at http://www.mg.co.za/article/2008-07-15-russia-lags-
behind-in-building-african-relations.

55. Margelov, op. cit.

56. Jordan, 94.

57. Mariette Le Roux, "Putin in talks with President Mbeki," *The Namibian,* September 6, 2006, at http://www.namibian.com.na/index.php?id=28&tx_ttnews%5Btt_news%5D=30706&no_cache=1.

58. Henry Meyer, Ilya Khrennikov and Loyiso Langeni, "Russia backs SA to join BRIC next year," *Business Day,* December 23, 2010, at http://www.businessday.co.za/articles/Content.aspx?id=130144.

59. Jordan, 89.

60. Sergei Blagov, "Russia, Nigeria trade agreement follows arms pledge," *Asia Times,* March 9, 2001, at http://atimes.com/c-asia/CC09Ag01.html; John Helmer, "Russia Builds Resource Alliances with Africa," *Mineweb,* April 26, 2006, archived at http://en.civilg8.ru/1487.php.

61. Kari Lipschitz, "Global Insider: Russia's Stake in Africa," *World Politics Review,* June 1, 2010, at http://www.worldpoliticsreview.com/trend-lines/5660/global-insider-russias-stake-in-africa.

62. "Zuma arrives in Russia for trade talks with Medvedev," Deutsche Presse-Agentur, August 5, 2010, at http://www.monstersandcritics.com/news/europe/news/article_1575645.php/Zuma-arrives-in-Russia-for-trade-talks-with-Medvedev.

63. "Russia to provide South Africa access to surface sensing satellites—Roscosmos," *RIA Novosti,* August 5, 2010, at http://en.rian.ru/world/20100805/160083368.html.

64. Jordan, 89.

65. Le Roux, op. cit.

66. "South Africa: BRICs Summit Preparations Under Way," *All Africa,* October 9, 2012, at http://allafrica.com/stories/201210091099.html.

67. "Russia hails South Africa's accession to BRIC," *Xinhua,* December 30, 2010, at http://news.xinhuanet.com/english2010/world/2010–12/30/c_13669841.htm.

68. Mzukisi Qobo, "Zuma's State Visit and the Challenges of Doing Business in Russia," *South African Institute for International Affairs,* August 12, 2010, at http://www.saiia.org.za/great-powers-africa-opinion/zuma-s-state-visit-and-the-challenges-of-doing-business-in-russia.html.

69. "Interview with Bheki Langa, Ambassador of the South Africa to Russia," *Africa-Russia P&S,* April 26, 2010, at http://rusafr.com/index.php?option=com_content&view=article&id=175&catid=49&Itemid=75.

70. "Remarks by the Minister of International Relations and Cooperation, H. E. Ms Maite Nkoana-Mashabane, on the occasion of the Joint Press Conference following the conclusion of the Bilateral Meeting with the Minister of Foreign Affairs of the Russian Federation, H.E. Minister Sergey Lavrov, Pretoria," February 12, 2013. Archived at the ministry site at http://www.dfa.gov.za/docs/speeches/2013/mash0212.html.

71. For instance, in February 2012, the main achievement of the Russia-Angola bilateral commission was to increase the number of Angolan students going for higher education in Russia. "Russia, Angola step up ties," *Voice of Russia,* February 15, 2012, at http://english.ruvr.ru/2012/02/15/66085523.html.

72. Karen Khachaturov, "Russian Breakthrough in Latin America," *Nezavisimaia Gazeta,* May 29, 1996, 4; Alex Sánchez, "Russia Returns to Latin America," *Council on*

Hemispheric Affairs Report, February 14, 2007, at http://www.coha.org/russia-returns-to-latin-america/.

73. Ivanov, 134–135.

74. "Russian Foreign Minister Launches Latin America Trip," *Monitor* 2, no. 99 (May 22, 1996), at http://www.jamestown.org/single/?no_cache=1&tx_ttnews%5Btt_news%5D=15261&tx_ttnews%5BbackPid%5D=210.

75. Khachaturov, 4.

76. Ivanov, 135.

77. "The Rio Group is Pleased with its Moscow Dialogue," *Diplomat* 6, no. 110 (2003). A copy is archived on the website of the Russian Embassy in Chile at http://www.chile.mid.ru/01d/ros_alat/ros_alat_01.html.

78. Sanchez, op. cit.; Richard Weitz, "Russia-Venezuela Ties Driven by Energy, Not Arms," *World Politics Review*, April 6, 2010, at http://www.worldpoliticsreview.com/articles/5377/global-insights-russia-venezuela-ties-driven-by-energy-not-arms.

79. Alexander Gabuyev, Alexandra Gritskova, and Denis Rebrov, "Igor Sechin Discovered Friendly America," *Kommersant*, September 18, 2008, 9.

80. Stephen J. Blank, "Civil–Military Relations and Russian Security," in *Civil–Military Relations in Medvedev's Russia* (Carlisle, PA: Strategic Studies Institute, 2011), 47.

81. Khachaturov, 4.

82. "Cuba, N. Korea Owe $37 Bln," *Moscow Times*, December 1, 2010, at http://www.themoscowtimes.com/business/article/cuba-n-korea-owe-37bln/425372.html.

83. J. L. Black, *Vladimir Putin and the New World Order: Looking East, Looking West?* (Lanham, MD: Rowman and Littlefield, 2004), 342.

84. Quoted in Patrick E. Tyler, "Putin, in Cuba, Signals Priority of Ties to U.S.," *New York Times*, December 16, 2000, at http://query.nytimes.com/gst/fullpage.html?res=9E00E3DE1739F935A25751C1A9669C8B63&pagewanted=1.

85. Mark N. Katz, "The Putin-Chavez Relationship," *Problems of Post–Communism* 53, no. 4 (July–August 2006): 4.

86. Black, 343.

87. Mark Frank, "Raul Castro attends Cuba opening of Russian church," *Reuters*, October 19, 2008, at http://www.reuters.com/article/2008/10/19/us-cuba-russia-idUSTRE49I20H20081019.

88. Donald K. Hansen and Alan M. Marblestone, "Cuba After the Castros: What Next?" *Case Studies in Policy Making*, 12th edition, eds. Hayat Alvi and Nikolas K. Gvosdev (Newport, RI: Naval War College, 2010), 45, 56.

89. Adrian Blomfield, "Russia to resume Cold War bomber flights," *The Telegraph*, August 17, 2007, at http://www.telegraph.co.uk/news/worldnews/1560606/Russia-to-resume-Cold-War-bomber-flights.html.

90. "Russian Navy sails for Cuba," *Russia Today*, December 16, 2008, at http://rt.com/news/russian-navy-sails-for-cuba/.

91. Rosa Tania Valdes, "Russian says Cuba relations now 'truly strategic,'" *Reuters*, February 11, 2010, at http://uk.reuters.com/article/2010/02/11/cuba-russia-idUKN1111891820100211?pageNumber=1.

92. Evgenij Haperskij, "Cuba—Russia Now and Then," *Caribbean Analysis,* February 24, 2010, at http://www.caribbeananalysis.com/cuba-%E2%80%93-russia-now-and-then/.

93. See the comments of Nikolas K. Gvosdev and Marek Jan Chodakiewicz, in "A New Cold War? Western-Hemispheric Maneuvers," *National Review Online,* December 8, 2008, at http://www.nationalreview.com/articles/226481/new-cold-war/nro-symposium.

94. Alex Leff, "For Nicaragua, a Russian Relations Revival," *Americas Quarterly,* August 7, 2009, at http://www.americasquarterly.org/node/824.

95. "Nicaragua to recognize South Ossetia and Abkhazia independence," *Russia-Information Centre,* September 4, 2008, at http://www.russia-ic.com/news/show/7008/.

96. "Ortega, Medvedev renew Soviet-era ties," *New Europe,* 813 (December 19, 2008), at http://www.neurope.eu/node/17423.

97. "Sechin visits Nicaragua for energy, trade talks after Venezuela," *RIA Novosti,* July 28, 2009, at http://en.rian.ru/russia/20090728/155650439.html.

98. "Russian-Nicaraguan commission to meet in Managua," *RIA Novosti,* June 1, 2010, at http://en.rian.ru/world/20100601/159242040.html.

99. "Russia to arm Nicaragua's war on drugs," *Russia Today,* October 1, 2012, at http://rt.com/politics/russia-nicaragua-drugs-war-423/.

100. Stephen Blank, "Putin Makes Energy and Arms Deals with Potential Latin American Allies: Part One," *Eurasia Daily Monitor* 7, no. 92 (May 12, 2010), at http://www.jamestown.org/single/?no_cache=1&tx_ttnews%5Btt_news%5D=36366&tx_ttnews%5BbackPid%5D=13&cHash=d2f3128584.

101. Alexander Gabuyev and Vyacheslav Leonov, "President of Argentina Visits Russia," *Kommersant,* December 10, 2008, 9.

102. "First Russian head of state visit to Argentina next month," *MercoPress,* March 17, 2010, at http://en.mercopress.com/2010/03/17/first-russian-head-of-state-visit-to-argentina-next-month.

103. Natalya Portyakova and Aleksei Nikolskii, "Following in Chavez's Footsteps," *Vedomosti,* October 27, 2009, 1.

104. Blank, op. cit.

105. Lourdes Aranda Bezury, "The Potential of Our Relations Is Very Big," *International Affairs* 2 (2010): 193, 194.

106. Emil Dabagyan, "Latin America's Leftist March," *Current Digest of the Post–Soviet Press* 58, no. 20 (June 14, 2006): 16.

107. "Putin, Venezuela's Chavez Plan Anti-U.S. Alliance," *United Press International,* May 15, 2001.

108. Katz, 5.

109. Artur Blinov, "Ugo Chaves, 'Venseremos!'"*Nezavisimaia Gazeta,* November 29, 2004, 3.

110. "Russia may sell S-300 missiles to Venezuela, instead of Iran—analyst," *RIA Novosti,* October 15, 2010, at http://en.rian.ru/mlitary_news/20101015/160963585.html; Sara Miller Llana and Fred Weir, "Russia's new presence in Latin America," *Christian Science Monitor,* November 25, 2008, at http://www.csmonitor.com/World/Americas/2008/1125/p01s01-woam.html.

111. Statistic cited in Benedict Mander, "Venezuela heats up Russian affair," *Financial Times*, October 15, 2010, at http://blogs.ft.com/beyond-brics/2010/10/15/venezuela-heats-up-russian-affair/.

112. Stephen J. Flanagan and Johanna Mendelson Forman, "Russia's Reengagement in the Western Hemisphere: Just Business or a Geopolitical Gambit?" *CSIS Critical Questions*, November 25, 2008, at http://csis.org/files/media/csis/pubs/081125_cq_mendelson_flanagan_russia.pdf.

113. Viktor Litovkin, "Sindrom Karibskogo Krizica 1962 goda," *Nezavisimoye Voennoe Obozrenie*, September 12, 2008, 3.

114. Humberto Márquez, "Business Deals Consolidate Alliance," *Inter Press Service*, November 13, 2008, at http://ipsnews.net/news.asp?idnews=44687; see also "Russia, Venezuela agree to TNK-BP purchase of BP's assets," *RIA Novosti*, October 15, 2010, at http://en.rian.ru/business/20101015/160967013.html.

115. Alex Anishyuk, "Putin, Chavez Boost Ties in Oil, Nuclear Power," *Moscow Times*, April 5, 2010, at http://www.themoscowtimes.com/business/article/putin-chavez-boost-ties-in-oil-nuclear-power/403210.html.

116. "Putin and Chavez discuss bilateral cooperation," *The Voice of Russia*, January 18, 2012, at http://english.ruvr.ru/2012/01/18/64054948.html. See also information provided by Eurostat, at http://trade.ec.europa.eu/doclib/docs/2006/september/tradoc_113462.pdf.

117. Katz, 7.

118. Litvokin, op. cit.

119. Katz, 8.

120. "Rosneft President Igor Sechin Visits Venezuela," *Eurasia Review*, September 27, 2012, at http://www.eurasiareview.com/27092012-rosneft-president-igor-sechin-visits-venezuela/.

121. Georgy Bovt, "Russia Put All of Its Eggs in Chavez's Basket," *Moscow Times*, 5085 (March 11, 2013), at http://www.themoscowtimes.com/opinion/article/russia-put-all-of-its-eggs-in-chavezs-basket/476737.html.

122. Litovkin, op. cit.

123. Llana and Weir, op. cit.

124. Nicola Miller, *Soviet Relations with Latin America, 1959–1987* (Cambridge, UK: Cambridge University Press, 1989), 172–180.

125. Ivan Andreyev, "Primakov Visits Latin America," *Kommersant*, November 26, 1997, 5.

126. "On the Stay of Chairman of the Russian Government Mikhail Kasyanov in Brazil," press release of the Russian Ministry of Foreign Affairs, December 14, 2001, at http://www.ln.mid.ru/bl.nsf/5d5fc0348b8b2d26c3256def0051fa20/5061b24025fd1b8043256b2200550ac9?OpenDocument.

127. On the foreign policy background of the PT, see Paulo Robert de Almeida, "Never Before Seen in Brazil: Luis Inacio Lula da Silva's Grand Diplomacy," *Revista Brasileira de Politica Internacional* 53, no. 2 (2010): 162–163.

128. Alexander Gabuyev, "Strengthening Ties," *Kommersant*, May 14, 2010, 8.

129. "Putin in Brazil for space talks," *BBC News*, November 22, 2004, at http://news.bbc.co.uk/2/hi/americas/4032715.stm.

130. Leticia Pinheiro, "Celso Amorim: Right Man, Right Place, Right Time," *World Politics Review,* February 2, 2010, 10–12.

131. Paulo Roberto de Almeida, "Lula's Foreign Policy: Regional and Global Strategies," in *Brazil under Lula: Economy, Politics and Society under the Worker-President,* eds. Joseph L. Love and Werner Baer (New York: Palgrave Macmillan, 2009), 171.

132. "Vladimir Putin met with the President of Brazil, Luiz Inacio Lula da Silva, Moscow, the Kremlin, October 18, 2005," press release of the Russian Ministry of Foreign Affairs, at http://www.ln.mid.ru/brp_4.nsf/sps/E16B85059BF20711C325709F00469AE7.

133. Sudhir Chadda, "Russia and China become part of strategic alliance—Putin now looks at BRICS alliance," *India Daily,* February 16, 2005, at http://www.indiadaily.com/editorial/1627.asp.

134. "Friends of opportunity," *The Economist,* November 27, 2008, at http://www.economist.com/node/12684849.

135. Tariq Malik, "Russia Agrees to Launch Brazil's First Astronaut to ISS," *Space.com,* October 18,2005, at http://www.space.com/1688-russia-agrees-launch-brazil-astronaut-iss.html.

136. Ilya Kramnik, "Russia to offer fifth-generation prototype fighter to Brazil?" *RIA Novosti,* January 28, 2011, at http://en.rian.ru/analysis/20110128/162357069.html; "Brazil may produce Russian fighters under license," *Asian Defence News,* June 25, 2010, at http://www.asian-defence.blogspot.com/2010/06/brazil-may-produce-russian-fighter-jets.html.

137. "Rosatom and National Nuclear Energy Commission of Brazil sign a memorandum of mutual understanding for cooperation in the field of peaceful uses of nuclear energy," *Russia Energy,* July 21, 2009, at http://www.russiaenergy.com/index.php#state=NewsDetail&id=1843.

138. Bruno de Nicola, "Russia's Gazprom to Open Brazilian Office," *Rio Times,* October 20, 2009, at http://riotimesonline.com/brazil-news/rio-business/gazprom-to-open-brazilian-office/; John C. K. Daly, "Analysis: Gazprom Enters Brazil," *United Press International,* December 4, 2008.

139. Michael Stott and Fernando Exman, "Brazil, Russia plan to boost trade, investment," *Reuters,* May 14, 2010, at http://www.reuters.com/article/2010/05/14/russia-brazil-idUSLDE64D00G20100514.

140. "Strategic partnership measured in roubles and reais," *Russia Today,* May 154, 2010, at http://rt.com/news/brazilian-president-silva-visit/.

141. "Brazil/Russia agree to increase trade and cooperation in agriculture and defense," *MercoPress,* February 22, 2013, at http://en.mercopress.com/2013/02/22/brazil-russia-agree-to-increase-trade-and-cooperation-in-agriculture-and-defense.

142. O'Neill's own perspective on the evolution of the BRIC is contained in this interview, Beth Kowitt, "For Mr. BRIC, nations meeting a milestone," *Fortune,* June 17, 2009, at http://money.cnn.com/2009/06/17/news/economy/goldman_sachs_jim_oneill_interview.fortune/index.htm. The original Goldman Sachs Economic Paper no. 66, released on November 30, 2001, is available at http://www.goldmansachs.com/our-thinking/archive/archive-pdfs/build-better-brics.pdf.

143. Lena Jonson, *Vladimir Putin and Central Asia: The Shaping of Russian Foreign Policy* (London: I. B. Tauris, 2004), 134.

144. Chadda, op. cit.

145. See that comment of P. Kuprikov, the deputy head of the department of foreign economic and international relations of the Moscow city government, in the roundtable, "BRIC as a New Form of Multilateral Diplomacy," *International Affairs* 2 (2010): 107.

146. Alexander Lukin, "Russia to Reinforce the Asian Vector," *Russia in Global Affairs* 2 (April–June 2009), at http://eng.globalaffairs.ru/number/n_13030.

147. Alexander Gabuyev, "Strengthening Ties," *Kommersant,* May 14, 2010, 8.

148. Chadda, op. cit.

149. Comment of L. Kadyshev, deputy director of the foreign policy planning department of the Ministry of Foreign Affairs, in "BRIC as a New Form," 100.

150. Jeremy Warren, "Why a BRICs-built bank to rival the IMF is doomed to fail," *Daily Telegraph,* March 29, 2012, at http://www.telegraph.co.uk/finance/financial crisis/9173668/Why-a-Brics-built-bank-to-rival-the-IMF-is-doomed-to-fail.html.

151. Jagannath P. Panda, "BRICS Development Bank: Figuring out the Durban Bid," *IDSA Comment,* March 8, 2013, at http://www.idsa.in/idsacomments/BRICSDevelopment Bank_jppanda_080313.

152. Quoted in Elina Bilevskaya, "Moscow is Dragging BRIC into G-8," *Nezavisimaia Gazeta,* June 17, 2009, 1.

153. Manab Majumbar, "Trade links on a new high," *Financial Express,* July 25, 2007, at http://www.financialexpress.com/news/trade-links-on-a-new-high/206620/0.

154. "The New Geography of International Trade: How the Emerging Markets are Rapidly Changing Global Trade," *Skolkovo Institute for Emerging Market Studies Monthly Bulletin,* March 2010, 8.

155. Luiz Inacio Lula Da Sliva, "The BRICs Come of Global Age," *New Perspectives Quarterly* 27, no. 3 (Summer 2010): 21.

156. Dmitry Medvedev, "Strany BRIK: Obshchie tseli—Obshchie deistviia," *Vedomosti* 65, no. 2583 (April 13, 2010), at http://www.vedomosti.ru/newspaper/article/2010/04/13/231127.

157. "Indonesia considers joining BRICS," *ITAR-TASS,* March 7, 2012, at http://www .itar-tass.com/en/c154/361586.html.

158. Kedar Pavgi, "BRICS Not Ready for Joint Development Bank," *World Politics Review,* April 10, 2012, at http://www.worldpoliticsreview.com/articles/11825/brics-not-ready-for-joint-development-bank.

159. Bilevskaya, 1.

160. Comment of L. Kadyshev, "BRIC as a New Form," 100.

161. Comments of A. Orlov, director of the Institute of International Studies, Moscow State Institute of International Relations, ibid., 98.

162. Raja Murthy, "China, India enter heating-up Arctic race," *Asia Times,* January 25, 2012, at http://www.atimes.com/atimes/South_Asia/NA25Df01.html.

163. Comments of A. Shchetinini, the deputy director of the Latin American department of the Ministry of Foreign Affairs, ibid., 101.

164. Sanjay Suri, "Moving Up BRIC by BRIC," *Inter Press Service,* September 4, 2009, at http://ipsnews.net/news.asp?idnews=48339.

165. Gideon Rachman, "The realities and myths of Brazilian life under Lula," *Business Day,* September 29, 2010, at http://www.businessday.co.za/articles/Content.aspx?id=122233.

166. Nikolas K. Gvosdev, "An Iran BRIC-bat for Obama," *World Politics Review,* April 23, 2010, at http://www.worldpoliticsreview.com/articles/5455/the-realist-prism-an-iran-bric-bat-for-obama.

167. Natalya Volchkova and Maria Ryabtseva, *Russia–South Africa Relations: Collaboration in BRICS and the G-20,* South African Institute of International Affairs Occasional Paper no. 135 (February 2013), 11, at http://www.polity.org.za/article/russiasouth-africa-rela tions-collaboration-in-brics-and-the-g-20-march-2013-2013-03-11.

168. Kseniya Yudayeva, the G-20 "Sherpa" for Putin, has talked about "developing a new system of global institutions." "Kseniya Yudayeva: dlia G-20 nastupil kriticheskii moment," *Vesti Ekonomiki,* January 3, 2013, at http://www.vestifinance.ru/articles/21588.

169. Sergey Strokan, "Uphill Battle: Russia at the helm of G20," *Russia Today,* December 10, 2012, at http://rt.com/op-edge/russia-g20-uphill-battle/.

CHAPTER 11

Epilogue

On February 12, 2013, Russian president Vladimir Putin signed the fourth iteration of the Foreign Policy Concept of the Russian Federation.[1] After the initial draft was presented to him in November 2012, it underwent a review process within the presidential administration, with Putin and his staff making comments on the draft document. In addition, the document was revised to take into account changes in the world situation, particularly in the U.S.–Russia relationship, before a final version was presented for his signature.[2]

This strategic framework for guiding how Russia conducts its foreign relations continues the evolution of Russian policy away from coping with the aftermath of the Soviet collapse more than two decades ago toward a more forward-looking agenda for the country in the global environment of the 21st century. In contrast to previous versions, the 2013 concept makes no mention of the Cold War or the Soviet period as a point of reference for contemporary Russian foreign policy. It complements Putin's assertion that the post–Soviet period in Russian history has come to an end. Fyodor Lukyanov, the editor of *Russia in Global Affairs,* noted:

> For the first time ever, the concept does not mention the Cold War. All past incarnations invariably blamed the country's current problems on the legacy of the Soviet Union. While justified at first, this gradually came to sound like an excuse—an attempt to offer a simple explanation that would be acceptable to all. Today, 20 years after the end of the Cold War, it is clear that Russia's problems are rooted in contradictions that have little connection to that time.[3]

Reinforcing earlier versions, the newest Russian Foreign Policy Concept reiterates that one of the goals of Russian foreign policy should be "the development of the country [to] guarantee its competitiveness in a globalized world," while a related goal is preserving Russian influence in global affairs, starting with the main international organizations such as the United Nations but also highlighting the importance of newer constructions like the BRICS and the G-20. Russia continues to embrace its view of itself as one of the agenda-setting powers of the world in noting that Russia will "recognize its responsibility for the maintenance of security in the world at both the global, as well as the regional, level." These aspirations, however, are tempered by Russia's unwillingness to assume new burdens for helping to bankroll the international system, as its reaction to the spring 2013 financial crisis in Cyprus demonstrated.[4]

In setting priorities, the concept stresses the importance of connections with three main regions of the world: the Euro-Atlantic, the Eurasian, and the Asia-Pacific. The 2013 revision gives primacy of place to the Eurasian vector, followed by relations with the West—including both Europe and the United States—and then to a rising Asia. The European Union is still described as Russia's "most important" external partner, but the "most important vector for Russian foreign policy is the development of friendly relations with China and India." Interestingly, the document both highlights the importance of a close partnership with China but then name-checks a number of smaller Asia-Pacific countries, ranging from Mongolia[5] to Australia,[6] with whom Russia ought to strengthen relations. After these three regions, the priorities are listed as the Middle East, Latin America, and Africa, in that order. Both the Arctic and Antarctica are also highlighted as regions of concern.

The new concept places emphasis on prioritizing those relationships that will facilitate the country's development and maintenance of its great power status. It commits Russia to a strategy of pursuing a multivector approach to Russian foreign policy and does not presuppose a particular outcome (e.g., full Russian membership in Euro-Atlantic organizations or a binding entente with China). Indeed, the 2013 version drops the reference from the 2008 concept of securing a "strategic partnership" with the United States. In contrast to the 1990s, when there was a clear and unequivocal tilt westward, Moscow's emphasis today is on balance. While Russia's ties to the European Union and the United States are important and vital, there is no longer a willingness to undercut Russia's potential and future interests in the Eurasian space and in the larger non–Western world simply to guarantee good relations with Washington and Brussels. Harnessing the dynamism of the rising powers of the global South and East in order to help revitalize Russia is just as important as cultivating Russia's traditional European partners and searching for a strategic relationship with the United States. Putin began his presidency in 2000 "with a sincere and genuine attempt at cooperation"[7] with the European Union and the United States, but by 2013, given his own assessment of the growing importance of the overall eastern vector for Russia's own future as a great power,[8] the traditional tilt in Russian foreign policy toward the countries of the developed West is being replaced by a much more even-handed approach. At the same time, however, Russia is not prepared to turn its back on the West. While new infrastructure projects that would more closely link Russia with Asia are being discussed, progress has also been made in overcoming some of the obstacles that in the past have prevented closer integration between Russia and the European Union.[9]

The shift toward balance is also being reflected in the stance taken by major sectors within Russia; the state oil company Rosneft, for instance, is simultaneously looking to the East and West for partners to further develop the Russian Arctic—with firms from the United States, Britain, Norway, Italy, China, South Korea, and Japan all being approached—as well as looking at new projects in the Gulf of Mexico, Vietnam, Brazil, and Venezuela.[10]

The document also reflects on paper the reality of the Russian foreign policy-making process: It is a balance of forces between different factions with different visions for Russia's future. While diminished, there are still key constituencies that adhere to the notion of what has been termed a "modernization alliance" with the West, particularly with Europe but also, ultimately, with the United States, that would see the Russian state and economy ultimately patterned on Western models. Those who support a more eastern orientation, while now in the ascendancy, must nonetheless contend with the arguments of those who maintain that overdependence on China will result in Russia becoming a satellite of Beijing, if not an outright target. Finally, while the proponents of the Eurasian Union cite the importance of regional consolidation as the first step to dealing with an increasingly unstable world—and argue against Russia becoming subordinated to either the West or a rising China—they also must acknowledge that focusing on the Eurasian space is not the most economically profitable approach to ensuring Russia's own development.[11] These various inconsistencies, as reflected in the concept, all provide "insight into how Russia's leadership sees the world" in 2013.[12] Indeed, the newest iteration "adequately reflects the main vectors of Moscow's foreign policy" without necessarily prejudging which ones will be predominant.[13]

But the future course of Russian foreign policy will also depend on the calculations of the other major powers as to how relations with Russia fit in with their own interests. To the extent that the international environment of the early 21st century is defined by the policies undertaken by China and the United States, how both of these states relate with Russia becomes quite important.

Xi Jinping's decision to make Russia his first major overseas trip after becoming president of China (coincidentally arriving in Moscow on March 22, the day that talks between Russia and the European Commission wrapped up[14]) suggests that Beijing still places great importance on its close relations with Moscow, especially when faced with the prospect of an American "pivot" to the Asia-Pacific region.[15] Closer coordination with China has helped Russia withstand some of the pressures from the West for change in Moscow's policy, but whether Beijing will be as supportive of Russia's efforts to consolidate the Eurasian space remains to be seen. But in the short term, both sides are committed to what Prime Ministers Dmitry Medvedev and Li Keqiang have described as the "high level of the comprehensive strategic partnership of coordination between Russia and China."[16]

At the same time, relations with the government of the United States continue to be strained, in part because of a so-called "values gap" but also because Russia's desire for regional hegemony in the Eurasian space clashes with U.S. interests, while American policies (such as aiding the anti-Assad opposition in Syria) contradict Russia's own preferences.[17] The Edward Snowden affair also complicated matters.

The announcement in March 2013, however, that the focus of U.S. missile defense efforts would shift from Europe to Northeast Asia—and that, due to budgetary restrictions, the final stage of the proposed American development and deployment of interceptors for the European theater would be scrapped—raised the possibility that one of the major irritants in the U.S.-Russia relationship could be addressed. It remains to be seen whether Moscow and Washington can cement a pragmatic approach to their bilateral relationship that will enable productive cooperation to move forward while fencing off the unresolved issues that have stymied partnership in the past.[18] This development holds out the possibility that U.S.-Russia relations could stabilize, even in the absence of any particularly strong personal relationship between Presidents Obama and Putin.

What we hope that readers of this volume will take away from this survey of contemporary Russian foreign policy is that there is no clear or predetermined outcome. Integration with the West, closer ties with Asia, consolidation of the Eurasian space, a policy of equidistance between Europe and China, the embrace of rising powers like Brazil, South Africa, and India—all of these are plausible futures for Russia, each with its proponents in the Kremlin and other centers of power in Russia. But final decisions will arise from how different vectors and sectors in the Russian establishment articulate how their foreign policy preferences align with Russia's core national interests. Russia no longer has a preset ideological blueprint for how it approaches the world. Instead, it will aim in all directions in support of its efforts to remain one of the world's great powers, pursuing any and all vectors that promise to aid in this task.[19]

NOTES

1. A copy of the text has been archived on the website of the Russian Foreign Ministry at http://www.mid.ru/bdomp/ns-osndoc.nsf/e2f289bea62097f9c325787a003 4c255/c32577ca0017434944257b160051bf7f!OpenDocument.

2. Sergei Strokan, Elena Chernenko, and Ivan Safronov, "Putin delays signing Russia's foreign policy draft," *Russia Beyond the Headlines,* February 2, 2013, at http://rbth .ru/politics/2013/02/01/putin_delays_signing_russias_foreign_policy_draft_22425.html.

3. Fyodor Lukyanov, "Uncertain World: Russian Diplomats Move in to the Real World," *RIA Novosti*, February 28, 2013, at http://en.ria.ru/columnists/20130228/179741025/ Uncertain-World-Russian-Diplomats-Move-in-to-the-Real-World.html.

4. Olga Tanas and Ilya Arkhipov, "Russia Rejects Cyprus Financial Rescue Bid as Deadline Looms," *Bloomberg*, March 22, 2013, at http://www.bloomberg.com/news/2013 -03-22/cyprus-s-sarris-to-leave-moscow-without-russian-financial-help.html.

5. Mongolia celebrated the 100th anniversary of its recognition by Russia as a state separate from the Chinese Empire in 2012 despite some friction with China, which contests this interpretation, and despite its new relationship with the United States. Mongolia has been working to restore closer economic and security ties with Russia. Alicia J. Campi, "Mongolia and Russia Re-Invigorate Mutual Ties," *Eurasia Daily Monitor*, 9, no. 207 (November 12, 2012), at http://www.jamestown.org/programs/edm/single/?tx_ttnews %5Btt_news%5D=40096&cHash=dbfb61fec4f65458bec5ede28263296c.

6. Russia, for instance, has an annual trade turnover of some $1 billion with Australia, but getting "Australian companies to become more actively engaged in our investment projects, including in modernization projects in the Far East and Siberia" is now becoming more of a priority. Ekaterina Zabrovskaya, "Russia and Australia need to fill information gap," *Russia Beyond the Headlines*, October 19, 2012, at http://rbth.ru/arti cles/2012/10/19/russian_and_australia_need_to_fill_information_vacuum_19265 .html.

7. Mark Sleboda, "Russia has always been regarded as 'barbarian' and 'the other' on the periphery by the West," *Voice of Russia*, March 11, 2013, at http://english.ruvr .ru/2013_03_11/Russia-has-always-been-regarded-as-barbarian-and-the-other-on-the -periphery-by-the-West/.

8. "Rosneft's Sechin to discuss offshore projects in Japan visit," *Reuters*, February 19, 2013, at http://uk.reuters.com/article/2013/02/19/rosneft-japan-idUKL6N0BJ0YL2013 0219.

9. "Russia welcomes progress in visa talks with EU—Russia's EU Ambassador," *Interfax*, March 18, 2013, archived at http://rbth.ru/news/2013/03/18/russia_welcomes _progress_in_visa_talks_with_eu_-_russias_eu_ambassador_23960.html.

10. Isabel Gorst, "TNK-BP and Rosneft: global ambitions," *Financial Times*, February 21, 2013, at http://blogs.ft.com/beyond-brics/2013/02/21/tnk-bp-and-rosneft-global- ambitions/#axzz2Nuf3hCPG; Isabel Gorst, "Rosneft looks east for new partners," *Financial Times*, February 19, 2013, at http://blogs.ft.com/beyond-brics/2013/02/19/rosneft-looks -east-for-new-partners/#axzz2Nuf3hCPG; Isabel Gorst, "China-Russia: a whole lot of energy deals," *Financial Times*, March 22, 2013, at http://blogs.ft.com/beyond-brics/2013/ 03/22/china-russia-a-whole-lot-of-energy-deals/#axzz20NOV6tSE.

11. Maxim Makarychev and Kira Latukhina, "Russia updates its foreign policy concept," *Russia Beyond the Headlines*, February 25, 2013, at http://rbth.ru/interna tional/2013/02/25/russia_updates_its_foreign_policy_concept_23211.html; Sleboda, op. cit.

12. Lukyanov, op. cit.

13. Irina Bubnova, "Russia' foreign policy concept: constructive dialogue with the West in new, multi-polar environment," *Voice of Russia*, March 11, 2013, at http://english

.ruvr.ru/2013_03_11/Russia-foreign-policy-concept-constructive-dialogue-with-the-West-in-new-multi-polar-environment/.

14. At this meeting, Prime Minister Medvedev and European Commission President Jose Manuel Barroso signed a "roadmap" for Russia–EU energy cooperation through to 2050. "Russia, EU Sign Energy Cooperation Roadmap," *RIA Novosti*, March 22, 2013, at http://en.ria.ru/russia/20130322/180194423.html.

15. John Garnaut, "Xi Pivots to Moscow," *Foreign Policy*, March 13, 2013, at http://www.foreignpolicy.com/articles/2013/03/14/xi_pivots_to_moscow.

16. "Chinese, Russian PMs Agree to Promote Cooperation," *Xinhua*, March 19, 2013, archived at http://english.cri.cn/6909/2013/03/19/2361s754494.htm.

17. Mark Adomanis, "The 'Putin Doctrine' and the Real Reason for Russian-American Conflict," *Forbes*, March 13, 2013, at http://www.forbes.com/sites/markadomanis/2013/03/13/the-putin-doctrine-and-the-real-reason-for-russian-american-conflict/; Colum Lynch, "Rice, Churkin Trade Blows in Security Council," *Foreign Policy*, March 13, 2013, at http://turtlebay.foreignpolicy.com/posts/2013/03/13/cold_war_un_rice_churkin?wp_login_redirect=0.

18. Gabriela Baczynska, "Russian lawmaker not reassured by U.S. missile defense plan," *Reuters*, March 18, 2013, at http://www.reuters.com/article/2013/03/17/us-russia-usa-defence-idUSBRE92G0CU20130317.

19. See, for instance, Leon Aron, "The Putin Doctrine," *Foreign Affairs*, March 8, 2013, at http://www.foreignaffairs.com/articles/139049/leon-aron/the-putin-doctrine.

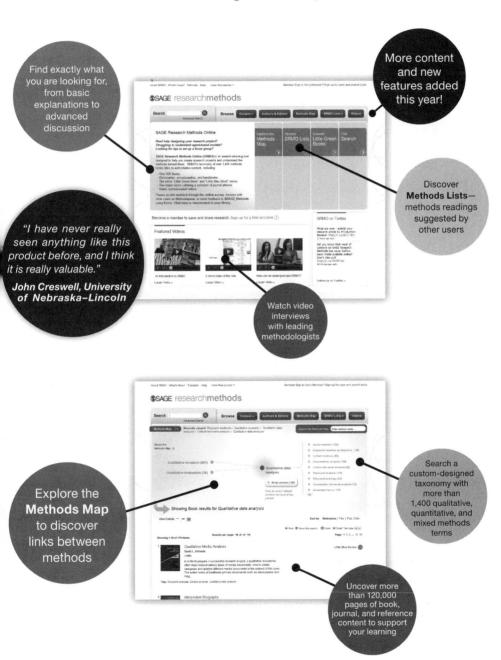